From
Kay [illegible]

The Worship of the Church

The Paschal Mystery
(Crucifix in Church of San Damiano, Assisi)

The Worship of the Church

A Companion to Liturgical Studies

by William J. O'Shea, S. S., D. D.

THE NEWMAN PRESS
WESTMINSTER, MARYLAND
1957

Nihil obstat: EDWARD A. CERNY, S.S., D.D.
Censor Librorum

Imprimatur: FRANCIS P. KEOUGH, D.D.
Archbishop of Baltimore

March 19, 1957

The *nihil obstat* and *imprimatur* are official declarations that a book or pamphlet is free of doctrinal and moral error. No implication is contained therein that those who have granted the *nihil obstat* and *imprimatur* agree with the opinions expressed.

Library of Congress Catalog Card Number: 56–8428
Printed in the United States of America

TO MY FATHER

AND MOTHER

Contents

Illustrations

Introduction

During the first half of the twentieth century a movement arose in the Catholic Church, and particularly in the Western patriarchate, which many students and thinkers call the most significant and most important of the last three or four hundred years. It is a current of thought and action which aims at vitalizing the liturgy of the Church and making it in the true sense a *living* liturgy—a worship that is alive and which is engaged in by people who are alive, alert, and intensely interested. During the past fifty years, by every means of scholarship and research at their command, by study and prayer, by conferences, conventions, retreats and missions, men and women have tried to make the members of the Church liturgy-conscious—aware of what the liturgy really is, of its power to enlighten, enrich and sanctify. They have gone back to the sources of the liturgy—the Bible and the teaching of the Church in both its solemn and ordinary magisterium (the biblical and theological revivals are closely related to the liturgical revival), there to gain insight into the great themes and an understanding of the great ideas that lie behind the liturgy itself. Side by side with the biblical and liturgical revival has gone the patristic revival, because men came to see more and more that the world of the liturgy and the Bible is a world in which the Church Fathers were thoroughly at home. The key ideas that dominate Scripture also dominate the liturgy and the writings of the Fathers; they are intimately related, and understanding of the one leads to an understanding of the others as well.

All this recent study and activity has resulted in a better understanding of what the liturgy really is, and a corresponding correction of the false and misleading ideas about its nature and purpose that have prevailed for so many centuries. The impetus to the liturgical revival was given by the Holy See, particularly in the writings of Saint Pius X; each of the latter pontiff's successors has in one way or another contributed to keeping the revival alive, to strengthening and guiding it, to preserving it from aberrations and errors. The Benedictine Order, always conscious of the pre-eminence of the liturgical life, has provided the current revival with some of its greatest inspiration and leaders, but activity has not been confined to the Benedictines alone. The liturgical movement has not remained academic; increasing numbers of bishops and priests have come to realize that the liturgy—the public worship of the Church—must of its nature be essentially a *pastoral* activity, the concern not only of scholars and savants, but of everyone in the Church and of pastors especially. For the liturgical movement is more than a movement—it is an apostolate. By and through the liturgy, as Christ intended, the spiritual welfare of the Church is served and secured.

Before all else the liturgical movement is a going back to the sources of the Christian life itself. Only those—and their number is still too great—who persist in misunderstanding what the liturgy is and who consequently never adequately comprehend what the liturgy does and is divinely intended to do, fail to grasp the spiritual and pastoral implications of the Church's worship. That is why it is so necessary to know what the liturgy is and what it is not before we can hope to understand that it has a great work to do: nothing less than the Christianization of society and the redemption of the world. As long as we persist in regarding the liturgy as merely a code of laws and rules regulating public worship, or as a kind of fad for dilettantes, or at best as the special activity of an elite, or as fostering a romantic, detached outlook upon the world and life, a kind of spiritual luxury for those with a bent for that sort of thing, or in any one of a thousand incomplete, one-sided ways, we shall never enter with enthusiasm and joy into the liturgical life, nor shall we see the spiritual implications without which the liturgy would be as dull, formless, meaningless and irrelevant as too many are inclined to think it is.

We must, then, examine the notion of liturgy itself, look into it and assimilate it. We must courageously rid ourselves of any or all prejudices that spring from misunderstanding and ignorance. It is not too much to say that we must give the liturgy a chance to show its real face to us, and we must be willing to embrace the idea and live with it. If we are unwilling to do this we cannot complain later on that we do not understand it, that it does nothing for us, that it is all right only for some, and so on. We are in no position to evaluate—much less to criticize—what we do not know, what has never been shown to us or what we have deliberately refused to dwell upon and to consider. On the other hand, those who have looked into the liturgy and assimilated it are in a position to understand it and to live it. They have looked upon what some one has with happy inspiration called "the true face of the liturgy," and it has not disappointed them. Like the seeker for wisdom in the Scriptures they have found her and all riches together with her, indeed the greatest treasure of all. They have found that herein is contained the fountain springing up unto eternal life.

This book developed from mimeographed notes which the author has used for some years at St. Mary's Seminary of Theology in Roland Park, Baltimore. The writer freely admits his indebtedness to the distinguished scholars whose works he consulted—indeed one reason for publishing the present work was to make available to readers the results of the careful scholarship with which such men as Jungmann, Righietti, Bayart, Eisenhöfer and many others have enriched the Church during recent decades.

The sub-title, "A Companion to Liturgical Studies," was chosen because the author does not believe that it is possible to write a textbook in the conventional sense for a liturgy course, and because the true textbook must always be the very text of the liturgy itself—the Missal, Breviary, Pontifical and Ritual. More can be gained from direct contact with these sources than from all the so-called textbooks written. What is needed is a book to supplement the indispensable study of these sources, one that will supply the student with up-to-date information as well as guidance and direction.

There are, of course, a number of manuals of liturgy in English, but some of these are inadequate and most are now out of date. Again, there are a number of excellent books dealing with one aspect or other of the liturgy, but none of them is comprehensive enough to serve the purpose which this author had in mind when he began to give a course in liturgy some thirteen years ago. Thus, Louis Bouyer's *Liturgical Piety* treats the theological background of the liturgy but does not (and cannot) go into detail about such matters as the history of the Mass or the vestments or church furnishings; J. B. O'Connell has written an excellent book on church building and furnishings but even in that limited field he does not discuss the vestments or the sacred vessels; Dom E. A. Roulin's classic work on the vestments treats of nothing else; Josef Jungmann's monumental *Mass of the Roman Rite*, a mine of information on the Mass and all that is related to it, is confined to the Mass alone. Even in the excellent manuals written in German and Italian one looks in vain for direction and guidance in the matter of liturgical art. It seems to the present writer, at any rate, that a book intended for use by seminarians and priests should make some attempt at providing direction in these and related matters, along with giving information. Whether the advice is accepted or not, readers are entitled to find it in a work of this kind.

The Worship of the Church

CHAPTER 1

Liturgy As a Sacred Science

History

Explanations and descriptions of the worship of the Church of varying degrees of value were produced as early as the fourth century. However, the beginnings of a solid, scientific treatment of the subject, based upon a careful study of the sources, go back only to the sixteenth or, more exactly, the seventeenth century. This new science, for such we must call it, was one of the results of the rise of critical history. The true father of liturgical studies was the learned and holy Cardinal John Bona, the first writer to attempt a complete treatise on the liturgy of the Church with his *De Divina Psalmodia,* on the Divine Office, and his *Rerum Liturgicarum libri duo,* on the Mass; both these works were published in the last half of the seventeenth century.

In the patristic period we find scattered references to the different rites of the first three centuries along with longer accounts of what was done or on the manner in which the liturgy should be carried out, works like the *Didache,* the *Apologies* of Justin, the works of Tertullian, or the *Apostolic Tradition* of

Hippolytus. Not until the fourth century was there anything like a systematic explanation of the sacred rites; these are the instructions given to the catechumens by St. Ambrose in his *De Sacramentis* and his *De Mysteriis*, and by St. Cyril in his *Catechetical Lectures*. St. Augustine gives many valuable explanations of the liturgy in his sermons and in other works. From the fifth century we have the invaluable diary of her pilgrimage to Jerusalem written by Etheria Sylvia, the Spanish nun, so important for the history of the liturgy of Jerusalem.

The early Middle Ages and the Carolingian period saw the rise and the spread of the detailed allegorical expositions of the liturgy, which, while undeniably devotional, were lacking in any solid and scientific basis. The leading exponents of this school of liturgical thought were Alcuin and Amalarius of Metz. These allegorical writers exercised a very great influence throughout the Middle Ages, but they did not have it all their own way; their explanations were contested and opposed by other writers, among whom the most prominent was St. Albert the Great. Valuable treatises on various aspects of the liturgy that steered away from excessive allegory were written by Innocent III and Denis the Carthusian (1471). But the most influential and popular work on the liturgy during the Middle Ages was thoroughly in the allegorical tradition: *Rationale Divinorum Officiorum* of Durandus of Mende (1296).

The necessity of answering the attacks of the reformers upon the whole body of Catholic worship, and the need of explaining the sacred rites to the people, itself a kind of by-product of the intellectual quickening of the time, caused a revival of liturgical studies after a long period of decadence. From that time to the present the science of liturgy, or liturgics, has grown and developed enormously and a vast literature has appeared on the subject. The seventeenth and eighteenth centuries were the golden age of this new science; they produced a multitude of great liturgists whose works have never been surpassed and hardly equalled since. Besides Bona, whom we have already mentioned, there were Blessed Joseph Tomassi (1713), Dom Mabillon (1707), Dom Martène (1739), Muratori (1750), P. Lebrun (1729), the Assemani family in the eighteenth century, Renaudot (1720) and many others. They edited the ancient liturgical books of East and West, or wrote treatises on the Missal, the Breviary, the Ritual and the Pontifical. Nor was all this work done by Catholics alone; one of the greatest contributions was made by Jeremy Bingham, whose *Antiquities of the Christian Church,* though marred by prejudice against the Catholic Church, nevertheless remains a classic in its field.

The French Revolution and the accompanying upheaval of society caused a long decline in liturgical studies during the first half of the nineteenth century, as well as in Catholic cultural life in general. Consequently, the first stirrings of a new awakening came only in 1840 with the publication of Guéranger's *L'Année liturgique* which went far towards creating a deeper appreciation for the beauty of the liturgy. It was translated into many languages and widely read. Then towards the end of the century there began to appear the first of those scientific works which have done so much to revive liturgical studies: the editing of the Gelasian and Leonine Sacramentaries by Wilson and Feltoe, the great work of Msgr. Duchesne, *Origines du Culte Chrétien,* and his classic edition of the *Liber Pontificalis,* Baumer's massive *Geschichte des Breviers* and the many writings of Probst in Germany. All through the last half of the same century we have the many editions of liturgical texts by the Henry Surtees Society of London.

It was reserved to the twentieth century to be the most productive of all. Merely to catalogue what has been done would run into many pages. During the past fifty-six years liturgical studies have been solidly established and placed upon a firm, scientific basis. The history of the sacred rites has been thoroughly investigated, and with increased knowledge has come a deeper understanding and greater love, not only of these rites themselves but of the Church and of the Church's teaching. At the beginning of the century the liturgical scholarship of the Benedictines of Solesmes and Farnborough gave us the *Monumenta Ecclesiae Liturgicae* and especially the great masterpiece that is the *Dictionnaire d'archéologie et liturgie*. From then until now the number of books and of authors increases and with them increases our debt to Bishop, Callewaert, Frere, Thurston, Dix, Fortescue, Thalhofer, Eisenhöfer, Cabrol, Morin, Leclercq, Kellner, Baumstark, Drews, Klauser, Righietti, Schuster, Jungmann, Beauduin and Cappelle. Besides these individual works there are the many periodicals published particularly in France and Germany during the past half century.

Nor must we forget the incalculable good work that has been done by the *Centre Pastorale et Liturgique* of Paris through their books and periodicals, amounting in itself to a renaissance, not only liturgical but biblical and theological as well.

While they are not in a class with the more scientific work of a Duchesne or a Leclercq, the writings of Pius Parsch, particularly his *Das Jahr des Heiles*, have done much to popularize liturgical studies. The same must be said of the many editions of the Missal, particularly those of Dom Gaspar Lefebvre and many others that have appeared in the past thirty years. Any attempt to discuss or even mention the many other centers and institutions for studying the liturgy and awakening interest in it would take us too far away from our purpose—to outline the growth and development of the science of liturgy itself, which must be based solidly on the careful study of the texts.

Nature of the Liturgy

Looked at from the outside it is easy enough to say what liturgy is—it goes on every day, it can be seen and heard on every side. All that goes on, all that is done in the churches of Christendom or in the homes of the faithful or in the streets of cities and towns as an expression of the corporate external worship of the Church is liturgy. Seen from this point of view, and defining it as one would define the word in a dictionary, the liturgy *is the celebration of the solemn corporate worship of God by that priestly society which is the Church.* It is the worship that is officially organized and directed by the Church and is offered by the members of the Church either by themselves or in their name. The term "liturgy" or "the liturgy" is applied particularly to the doing of the rite which was instituted by Christ Himself to be the peculiar and distinctive rite of His followers—and which has been since His time the center and the heart of all Christian life as well as worship—the Holy Eucharist or the Holy Sacrifice of the Mass. But if the word is particularly (and by the Eastern Churches exclusively) applied to the Holy Sacrifice it also includes those other rites and prayers which have a bearing upon the Mass and are related to it, the sacraments, the sacramentals and blessings, and the Divine Office, which is the perpetual round of worship continued through the day. All these are included in the study of liturgy; since all of them are expressions of the corporate worship of the church, they are part of the liturgy.

Viewed as a subject of special study, "liturgy" encompasses the *history* of the liturgy; liturgical *theology* (liturgy and liturgical prayer are the expression of a theology); liturgical *law* which emphasizes rubrics and ceremonies; the liturgical *books* which set forth the content of the rites and prayers; and lastly those *arts* which form the setting in which and by which the liturgy is accomplished: architecture, painting, sculpture, metal-crafts, chant, Church music and ecclesiastical costume. These arts are regulated and governed by the valid, objective principles of aesthetics.

But while any one or all of these may be included in the term "liturgy" they are not to be identified with it. The notes that are written in a musical score and the instruments that perform it are indeed inseparably associated with the art of music, but they do not of themselves *constitute* music. You do not have music until someone takes up an instrument and, using the notes before him, plays a musical piece. So it is with the liturgy: none of these things taken singly nor all of them taken together are the liturgy, though they may be liturgical. Liturgy is essentially something *done;* it is above all else an *action,* an action which the Church believes is done in obedience to the command and by the will of Christ. "Do this for a commemoration of Me." It would be taking the part for the whole to identify rubrics, or chant, or vestments, or even theology or the prayers in which theology is expressed, with the liturgy, as though they were one and the same thing. For what we have here is the material out of which the liturgy is constructed, or the forms in which it is clothed. We do not have the liturgy itself until we *do* something, because essentially the liturgy is an action or an act.

Even when we understand this we have only partially grasped what the liturgy is. It is an action indeed, but whose action? The outsider sees it as something done, but sees it only as something done by churchmen; it is a religious service indeed; God is worshipped and glorified by it—all its forms and the whole tenor of its actions proclaim this—yet one remains an outsider until it is seen *whose* action it is. Here we come closest to the heart of the matter, and until we can see who is the real actor in the liturgical act we remain apart from it, we cannot enter into it nor comprehend it. It was largely because people lost sight of this that so many erroneous ideas about the liturgy grew up and flourished. They lost sight of the principal actor in the liturgical act and with that lost the key to the act itself. What they should have been vitally interested in and should have taken part in became a frozen code of etiquette, a formal way of worshipping God that had to be *performed* by those competent to do it, but in which they (the people) felt they had no part. And even when there was a movement towards more correct and stately worship as in the past century it was still looked upon as something that should be beautifully and even prayerfully done, a kind of performance by specialists and a spectacle to behold and admire, rather than an action in which all should take part. It would perhaps be unkind and supercilious on our part to say that they missed the whole point; let us say rather that the point had been so long obscured that it took many more years and many more efforts before the complete idea caught on.

It was reserved to the twentieth century and particularly to the school of Maria Laach in Germany to come much closer to a true understanding of what is done in the public worship of the Church, to see what the liturgy really is. This understanding was the result of a deep study of the Fathers of the Church and their doctrine, which had of course never been lost in the Church, but had definitely become obscured. The core of this doctrine is that the liturgy is a re-enactment of the redeeming work of Christ, of the act of our Lord that accomplished our salvation. This act of Christ is re-enacted by the Church. It is the continuation of the priesthood of Christ in, by, and for the Church. The liturgy is the action of the Church, and the Church is the Body of Christ, His fullness and mysterious prolongation on earth. By this action the saving activity of Christ is extended through time. We can see now more clearly how misleading many so-called definitions of the liturgy are, precisely because they remain outside the very center of the whole matter. It is not the official regulation of external worship that we are dealing with here, nor a way of worshipping God that we are free to cultivate or ignore, but it is *itself* the worship of God offered by the Church. Pius XII in the encyclical *Mediator Dei* has expressly shown how false and incomplete is the idea that the liturgy is but "the official regulation of external worship" and has carefully and thoroughly unfolded the true idea of Christian worship itself. After showing that it is Christ's worship of the Father, begun on earth, continuing now forever in Heaven, carried on and developed by the Church, the sovereign pontiff gives what must be regarded as the best and most satisfactory definition of liturgy when he says:

The holy liturgy, therefore, is the public worship which is offered to the Father by our Redeemer as Head of the Church; it is also the worship offered by the society of faithful to its Head, and through Him to the eternal Father. In a word it is the whole worship of the Mystical Body of Jesus Christ, that is, of the Head and of its members.*

By providing us with what may be called an official definition of the liturgy, a definition that, let it be remembered, is the product of many decades of study and research that preceded it and consequently is the expression of the traditional teaching of the Church, the pope has made it unnecessary to seek (as writers on the liturgy had to seek in years gone by) for a definition of the liturgy that would satisfy everyone. It remains for us now only to analyze this definition and to bring out the riches it contains. In times past authors examined in great detail the meaning of the word itself and then its use in the Scriptures and in patristic literature, and tried to come to a definition that was acceptable and which would contribute to our understanding of the liturgy itself. This procedure is still not without value —at least insofar as looking into the meaning of the word and its use in Scripture and the Fathers is concerned. It sheds light on the idea and that in itself justifies the study, but it is no longer necessary to seek for a definition in that way.

The word "liturgy" is very ancient and goes back to pagan times when the Greeks used it to mean a work done in the public interest by the citizens of the state (*leitos:* belonging to or pertaining to the people; and *ergon*—a work, an action, a service). Liturgy meant some action that was a contribution to the public welfare, a service to the people done either by the people themselves or by someone acting in their name and for their interest. From the word "liturgy" comes the term that describes the one who fulfills it, the liturgist: one who does a service for the public and in their name.

* Encyclical *Mediator Dei,* No. 20.

While this word primarily designated civil, political or military public service, it had acquired a religious sense even among the pagans, so that when the Jews translated the Bible into Greek they used the Greek word *leitourgia* to describe the priestly service of divine worship. The word does retain, both in the Old and New Testaments, the wider sense of a public service, but even that public service has a kind of religious association. In the New Testament the word is used as a synonym for "ministry," whether that ministry is civil or, as referring to Christ and to the priesthood, religious. More and more (though not exclusively) we find the word used in the early Church as referring primarily to the worship of God or to the public ministry rendered to God and to the Lord. The ministry is the *liturgy* and those who perform it are *liturgists*. The work of Christ—His eternal priesthood and ministry—is described as His "liturgy" in the classic treatment of that priesthood, the Epistle to the Hebrews, where He is called "the liturgist of the Holy of Holies" (Heb. 7:25).

From all this we can see that the root idea of the liturgy is contained in the word itself (a public work, a common act, an official service done in the public interest) and in the religious associations joined to the word by Jews and Christians from the beginning. And while it is undoubtedly true that the idea itself has received development and enlargement in subsequent centuries, so that it is not enough to have recourse to the etymology of the word to understand it, the root meaning throws much light on the essential nature of the thing the word now designates. For the liturgy is essentially something *done* and done by the people in the public interest, to which Jews and Christians have added the idea of something done by the people about and for God. In the next chapter we shall return to the definition of liturgy which was formulated by Pius XII in order to examine it in greater detail, but the first step towards understanding the liturgy is to see that it is not primarily the work of men, however holy or learned they may be; it is the work of

God, the *Opus Dei.* God gathers His people together, speaks to them and acts in them; He regulates their prayer and inspires it. He forms them into a royal nation, a kingly priesthood and a priestly people. The whole direction of the Old Testament is towards the choosing and forming of a holy people, a people that would worship God according to the pattern He Himself gave them. The way was prepared for the fullness of time when God sent His Son in whom His people are gathered anew. But now this people of God is no longer coterminous with the Jewish people. All men are gathered together and built into a dwelling place of God in the Spirit. Through Christ and with Him and in Him they are built into the temple not made of hands, and a new race is formed with the aim that they should offer acceptable sacrifice to God. The Church is above all a worshiping community, an assembly, a gathering, an *ecclesia,* formed by God Himself and committed to "announce His virtues who hath called them out of darkness into His marvelous light." The first and greatest activity of that Church is worship, an activity that is regulated and governed by God, an activity that *is* God's. God speaks in the assembly and His word is worship; He acts in and through the sacraments and all the sacred rites, and His action is worship. If the community He has gathered together sings a hymn it is inspired to do this by Him and His Holy Spirit: "No one can say the Lord Jesus except by the Holy Spirit."

If the Church prays, it prays as He taught His disciples to pray; if it offers sacrifice, it is doing what He commanded to be done "in memory of me"; if it blesses, it is His blessing that is invoked. When the Church seeks to praise and glorify Him, it is to the psalter that she turns, there to find God's own expression of adoration, praise and thanksgiving. From beginning to end, from first to last, it is God who guides and directs the liturgy and forms a worshiping community that offers this service to God. It is never man who takes the initiative, nor man's own praise and prayer that is offered to God; it is God who calls, who inspires and who orders all things according to His good pleasure.

This is the inward way of regarding the liturgy and the only way that we can be safeguarded from misunderstanding it altogether.

CHAPTER 2

The Church Worships God in Christ

The liturgy is the public worship that the Church, in union with Christ, renders to God. The idea of worship is closely and inseparably associated with liturgy, for liturgy *is* worship and worship is nothing else than the response of the creature to the Creator, the acknowledgment of God's transcendent excellence made by man, who alone of all creatures can recognize and admire it. This is but another way of saying that worship is man's response to reality, the recognition of the purpose of his being, which is to praise and glorify God. By it we acknowledge God's claim over us; we are moved by awe and reverence to fall down before Him, to "come into His presence with thanksgiving," to "make a joyful sound before Him." His *is;* and His very being calls for a response from us. Awareness that He made us and not we ourselves, that we depend upon Him, makes us *adore* Him. The consciousness of what He has done for us by creating us and marvellously endowing us makes us *give thanks.*

Because we see that He is all holy and that we are prone to evil in so many ways, we ask pardon for our offenses and sins, whereby His majesty and holiness were set at nought and outraged. When we reflect on our weakness and our need of His help, we ask for aid and assistance. Hence we have the various acts of worship: adoration, thanksgiving, penitence and petition. They are the response to God awakened in every human heart that is in any way religious.

Worship begins within. It springs from the intellect and the will, the spiritual part of man (insofar as man can really be divided in this way, since he is not so much "made up of body and soul" as he is embodied spirit). It must, however, at the same time express itself externally in that body which is the inseparable companion of the soul. A worship which remains within is unnatural and incomplete: unnatural because it is man's nature to join the body to the soul's activity, incomplete because a whole area of man's being finds no expression. To pray, to sing God's praises, to cry aloud to Him, to kneel, to strike the breast in contrition, or any of the acts of external worship, are not optional activities but the natural, spontaneous, and complete outward expression of what lies within. With them and by them the whole man takes part. The nature of man conditions the nature of his worship, so that while it must be spiritual it must also be corporal and external. Either one alone would be a maimed and deformed worship, and would not represent the complete response to God that true worship involves. There is always, of course, the risk that external worship may become externalism and ritualism, but it is a risk we must take; the answer to the danger is not to abolish or minimize external worship, but rather it is to intensify the spiritual, and to make external religion truly express what is within. In other words, we must not divorce the two but rather intensify the bond that unites them.

External worship, far from competing against internal worship, rather strengthens and intensifies it. A mother's caress does not indicate that she loves her child less because she shows her love in an outward way; rather the caress is at one and the same time a sign of the inward love and a means of increasing it. So external worship is not in opposition to internal worship but rather complements and completes it. Strictly speaking, it is a mistake to divide them. Worship is *one* response to God, a single reality with its internal and external phases; that is all. Furthermore, all things being equal, a worship expressed outwardly is superior to one that is merely interior. External acts and formulae should be considered as intimately linked to internal worship which they awaken, stir up and call forth, to which they give direction, and which they insure. All human worship must, then, be given external expression.

Now man is a social being and, as we have seen, worship must be according to his nature. This is but another way of saying that all human worship is ultimately, to be complete, a social worship. Man does not exist alone; he belongs to a society which is the human race. Just as man himself must worship, so must society as a body acknowledge God's excellence and pay Him the tribute of devotion and sacrifice. The same motives that move man as an individual can move society itself, conceived as a whole and as a body, to offer worship to God. In whatever manner man may worship as an individual, he cannot worship in society or in community without external corporate actions. That much should be obvious. When men worship in a group they must know what is being thought, which involves speaking; they must act together, which involves external actions. This corporate worship cannot, of course, be without the inner spiritual element that informs it, but the latter must be outwardly expressed. Otherwise it would not be the worship of body, and society is a body.

Thus far we have been considering man's worship from the standpoint of philosophy, that is, in the light of natural reason, and what we have said about it would certainly apply even if we had no further light upon man and his destiny. But as Christians we have to consider the whole question of worship in the light of Christian revelation. Man is not only a rational spiritual animal; he is redeemed and raised to a supernatural level. Humanity is a redeemed humanity and man belongs (or is called to belong) not only to the society of his fellow men but to the fellowship of the Son of God. The worship that he offers to God he offers as the member of a society that transcends human society, and it is the worship of one who is not only God's creature, but God's son, a sharer in the divine nature, a member of a chosen people, a holy nation, a kingly priesthood. When we speak of public worship we mean only that which is exercised in the name of a public society by its members (or their representatives) under the direction of the heads of that society and in the forms prescribed by them. It is not necessarily materially collective, but it is always formally so; that is, it is always done by the whole body, even if the whole body is not gathered together at the time.

The Church

Fundamental to the whole idea of liturgy is an understanding of the Church. It is highly significant that the renewed interest in "the public worship of the Church" has gone hand in hand with an awakening of interest in the Church itself, what it is and what it does. This is no accident, because just as no one can adequately understand what the Church is except by a deeper understanding of the Church's greatest activity, which is precisely the liturgy, so no one can understand the liturgy without understanding the Church. For the Church is above all a priestly society and its work is to continue the priestly work of Christ. The only adequate concept of the Church is that which keeps it united to Christ, which sees it not merely as an organization or an institution, or even as a supernatural society (all of which it is of course), but primarily as a living organism, His Body, and His Bride. It is the "family of God," "the people of God," "the Kingdom," "the assembly (*ecclesia*) of the redeemed," not an accidental association, but a true organic society, living a life that is nothing less than the life of Christ Himself. Its members adhere to one another and to Christ as branches to the vine. It is God's dwelling place with men; He lives and acts in and through His Church, which is the "great mystery" wherein God is joined to men and communicates Himself to them and works in them. Indeed, the favorite biblical image of the Church is that of the Spouse or Wife of God; the most tender and intimate of human unions is used more than once in both Old and New Testaments to show the union between mankind and God, culminating in the glorious passage of St. Paul's Epistle to the Ephesians. It would be hard to express the idea of God's union with mankind more realistically than this, and let us remember it is God's own way of expressing it:

> Husbands, love your wives, just as Christ also loved the Church, and delivered himself up for her, that he might sanctify her, cleansing her in the bath of water by means of the word; in order that he might present to himself the Church in all her glory, not having spot or wrinkle or any such thing, but that she might be holy and without blemish. . . . He who loves his own wife, loves himself. For no one ever hated his own flesh; on the contrary he nourishes and cherishes it, as Christ also does the Church (because we are members of his body, made from his flesh and from his bones) (Eph. 5:25–30).

This bridal imagery is used also by St. John in several places in the Apocalypse, and is borrowed by the Church for the Mass of the *Dedicatio Ecclesiae:* "I saw the holy city, the new Jerusalem, coming down from heaven prepared as a bride adorned for her husband"; again as the "marriage feast of the Lamb," for which the Spouse prepares herself: "Come, I will show you the bride, the Spouse of the Lamb." The nuptial and bridal imagery set forth in the Bible captivated the Fathers who delighted in developing and expanding it. This Bride of Christ was for them born from the pierced side of Christ, and nourished as well as represented by the water and the blood.

Closely related to the bridal imagery, but much more developed in our own times, is the imagery of the Body, which we owe particularly to St. Paul: "You are the body of Christ and members of his members"; "Though many we are one Body." Many members form one body and live a common life, whose source is Christ. They are incorporated into Christ by Baptism: "For in one Spirit we are all baptized into one body" and kept together and nourished by the Eucharist, the source and symbol of unity: "Because the head is one, we though many, are one body, all of us who partake of the one bread." It is not just any body or any society, even any *religious* society, but "the Body of Christ," "his own body." The Church is so indissolubly, so naturally and essentially united to Christ, that He lives and works in the Church and through the Church; the Church lives with His life and possesses His power and strength. Whatever one's body does is attributed to the person who lives in it; whatever the Church does (in a supernatural way) is attributed to Christ. "He is the head of the Body the Church"; "God has subjected all things under his feet, and Him he has given head over the whole church, which is his body, the completion of him who fills all with all"; and the faithful are ". . . the members of his body, of his flesh and bones."

Between the members of the Body and the Head there is the closest possible union, a union that is real, a union that is supernatural, so that each member of the Mystical Body can say what St. Paul said so confidently: "I live now not I but Christ lives in me." But the union is not only between the Head and the members; the members are joined together so closely that St. Paul could say: "You are all *one* in Christ Jesus." This union is brought about by the Holy Spirit who dwells in His Church ("You are the temple of the Holy Spirit") through the sacraments of Baptism and the Eucharist.

It is true that the image of the Mystical Body is only an analogy and falls short of the reality; yet it conveys ideas to us that we could not otherwise grasp. Because the Church is the Body of Christ and Christ is the Head of that Body, we can say that just as the body cannot act without the head, nor the head except in relation to the body and for its benefit, so with Christ. The Head and the Body are inseparably joined together and form one Christ—Head and Body. It is this Body that worships, that gives expression to its adoration, praise, thanksgiving, contrition and petition. The Church does this not on her own, as it were, but always and of necessity in union with Christ. His adoration, praise, petition and thanksgiving become hers. What He did, the Church, "His fullness," "His body," does now. She acts, offers, prays, in a word—*worships,* as a unit, joined to Him. That is why liturgical worship is superior to any other worship, why the public prayer of the Church enjoys pre-eminence. It is because liturgical worship is the prayer of Christ. Every time the Church, as the Church, goes into action, it is Christ who is acting. "Peter baptizes, it is Christ who baptizes," says St. Augustine, the great doctor of the Mystical Body.

The Church is primarily the assembly of all those who are reborn with water and the Holy Ghost. It is not too much to say that it is Christ passing through the centuries and in some way multiplying Himself. To look at it in this way is not to consider the Church according to its external appearance alone. More than that, such a view of the Church helps us understand what the liturgy is: not the cold, formal, exterior, official worship of an institution, but the prayer of a living body, in fact, the prayer of a person. The Church is not an abstraction; it is men and women; it is you and I, who belong to Christ and who are joined to Him, His people. When we say "the liturgy of the Church," we are saying the "prayer of the people of God."

The Priesthood of Christ

"The liturgy is the public worship which the Church, in union with her Divine Founder, offers to God." In these words we have the very essence of the liturgy, which is that it is the worship offered by Christ. He is the first, greatest and principal liturgist or worshipper, and the liturgy is the priesthood of Christ in action. His priesthood is the center and the soul of the liturgy. Christ is the greatest, and more than that, the only Priest, because only Christ can do what a priest by the very definition of the word must do: *Sacer-dos*—one who offers sacrifice. Only Christ can offer adequate sacrifice: "Offerings and sacrifices pleased Thee not. . . . I said, behold I come. To do thy will O God is my pleasure." Only Christ is God and Man. To be a priest He must be a man, because a priest is one who offers holy things to God and who brings holy things from God to man. But a priest who is only a man cannot really mediate between God and man, since the mediator must have a certain equality between himself and those for whom he mediates. Hence Christ, though He was God, took on a human nature and became man, that He might act in and with a human nature, and at the same time might give His human acts a divine value. "The Lord anointed him with the Holy Spirit and power"; "The spirit of the Lord is upon me, whereby he hath anointed me," to be "a priest forever according to the order of Melchisedech." By the grace of the hypostatic union He was made a priest, "holy, innocent, higher than the heavens." From the moment of the Incarnation He was a priest because He alone fulfilled the requirements. All the actions of His life were priestly actions, dedicated to God, to Whom He offered Himself from His "coming into the world," climaxed by the supreme sacrifice and the great offering of His Passion and Death, for which His whole life was the preparation. "By one offering he completed forever," and became "the cause of eternal salvation to all those who received him."

His priesthood did not cease with His death; rather it was fixed forever. His sacrificial death was accepted by God who raised Him up and made Him sit down with Him in the heavenly places, where He ever lives to make intercession for us.

There He prays for us and offers praise and satisfaction in the name of sinners. "He appears now in the sight of God on our behalf," pleading His wounds. He is ever the "lamb standing as though slain" and thus continues the one offering of His unique priesthood. Indeed it is only since His Resurrection and His heavenly session that He attains the consummation of His priesthood and His "liturgy." For it is only then that His humanity is freed from the bondage that sin lays upon the human race, and is made altogether spiritual. Now it can give God in Heaven a heavenly and eternal worship. "A sacrifice is all that which we do to come near to God and to unite ourselves to Him." * Since Christ in Heaven continues to draw all things to God and to unite them to Him, He is continually offering sacrifice; He remains the Liturgist of the Heavenly Sanctuary. The Redemption has brought men to God, opened the way to Him for them, but it also inaugurated a new and eternal Covenant. Once redeemed, all men and the whole world are thereby associated with Christ in an eternal liturgy. His sacrifice is permanent; offered once in a bloody manner, it persists in the form of a spiritual and heavenly worship. Just as death fixes all men in a state of good or evil, so the death of Christ has fixed His Sacred Humanity in a state of perfect and eternal oblation. Through that sacred humanity the Word of God is joined to mankind. By His Incarnation the Word of God becomes one with humanity, and because of that solidarity the Priesthood of Christ becomes the priesthood of His Mystical Body; His sacrifice becomes the sacrifice of the Church.

The only way that the Church can offer a worship to God that is agreeable to Him is by uniting herself to the only worship that is perfectly acceptable. That worship is going on in Heaven because the Priest is there. The worship of the Church, then, must be joined to the worship in Heaven; it must reflect it on earth. The true sanctuary of the Church's worship is the

* St. Augustine, *De Civitate Dei,* 10, 6.

heavenly sanctuary. Her worship is in the literal sense a divine and heavenly worship. Christ has accomplished the great liturgy of the new and eternal Covenant; the Church, which is His Body and the new people of God, is intimately associated with this liturgy. Through the Mass and the sacraments the priesthood of Christ is made active upon earth; Heaven and earth are joined together; mankind is drawn to God and adheres to Him; the work of the Redemption in all its amplitude and in all its phases is continually being accomplished. The Church is continually in the process of being formed; "all things are being brought to a head in Christ." All the liturgical acts of the Church are related to Heaven and have their terminus there as well as their source. The Mass is the Sacrifice of the eternal High Priest; Holy Communion is the heavenly banquet which joins us to Christ and gives us a foretaste of Heaven, sows in us the seeds of immortality; the liturgical assembly of the faithful on earth reflects and points towards the eternal assembly of Heaven; the chant of the Church assembled on earth is an imitation, a faint echo of the never-ending *sanctus*; the psalms of the Office are only an image and a foreshadowing of the eternal occupation of the heavenly Jerusalem.

But you have come to Mount Sion, and to the city of the living God, the heavenly Jerusalem, and to the company of many thousands of angels, and to the church of the firstborn who are enrolled in the heavens, and to God, the judge of all, and to the spirits of the just made perfect, and to Jesus, mediator of a new covenant, and to a sprinkling of blood which speaks better than Abel (Heb. 12: 22–24).

In this magnificent passage the author of the Epistle to the Hebrews sets forth the great theme that we have tried to unfold in the last few pages. Better than anything else it shows us what is involved. The great imagery of the passage is at the same time the expression of a profound reality and speaks powerfully to our hearts. The sphere of the liturgy of the Church is altogether heavenly; the Priesthood of Christ is its mainspring and source. Its aim is to bring all men together in a holy and heavenly society to praise and glorify God forever.

The Church is, then, a priestly society. The whole Church is engaged in worship. "Faithful to the teaching of her founder," she "continues the priestly office of Jesus Christ and does this primarily through the sacred liturgy." *

"Christ is present in every liturgical action." These words of Pius XII are but an echo of our Lord's own words: "Where two or three are gathered together for my sake, there am I in the midst of them" (Matt. 18:20), and "Behold, I am with you all days even to the consummation of the world" (Matt. 28:20). It is this presence of Christ that establishes worship and makes it possible. For it is only in Christ, who is God and man, that man and God can meet together; He is the link that joins them, the sacred meeting place where God and man are reunited. "Destroy this temple and in three days I will raise it up" (John 2:19). It is not so much that "he comes down in our midst" as that He lifts us up with Him and in Him to that heavenly sanctuary where He is "ever living to make intercession for us." We who are the Church are made "partakers of Christ and His Kingdom" (Heb. 3:14).

The Church bears witness to the presence of Christ and manifests His presence by fulfilling in each age His own threefold ministry. To express it more correctly and more in accord with tradition, Christ manifests Himself in the worship of the Church in His threefold office of Prophet, Priest and King.

He was and He remains "the great prophet." The prophet's role was to bring the word of God to the people—to announce the coming of the Kingdom of God, to be the mediator between God and His people. Christ fulfilled that prophetic office more than all the prophets who had gone before Him. He is not only the bearer of the word of God but is Himself that living Word,

* *Mediator Dei,* Introduction, No. 2.

the very Word Incarnate who not only announced and proclaimed the Kingdom of God to be near at hand but who expressed it by His life. His actions, no less than the words of His mouth, are prophetic—not in the narrow sense that they foretell the future, but that they are the voice of God speaking to His people.

The Church continues His prophetic ministry first of all by reading His own words in the Gospel, and then by reading all the other Scripture lessons which are the word of God; the Church sings the psalms and canticles which announce and describe His Kingdom in advance. These lessons and chants are a continued proclamation of the Word of God. They are the voice of God speaking to us through His Son. We are made present at the Sermon on the Mount, by the well of Sichar, in the temple on the festival day, in Rome, Corinth, Ephesus, Thessalonica, in Judea and Galilee, wherever His voice has been heard in the past. We become contemporaries of the events that are recalled for us.

This prophetic ministry is not confined to the reading of the Scripture, but is also exercised through the sermon, which is in the highest and truest sense, liturgical—an act of worship—the explanation of the word of God and its application to the here and now. God speaks through the voice of the preacher and inspires the members of the Church to hear His voice.

Christ was also and above all else a priest—one who offers sacrifice, one who dedicates and consecrates to God. His whole life was an offering to God and dedicated to His service: "Behold I come to do thy will, O God." He offered His life upon the cross and He continues to offer for all eternity in the holy of holies of the heavenly tabernacle the blood which was poured out on Calvary. "We have in Jesus the Son of God a High Priest who has penetrated the heavens. . . . He possesses a priesthood which is not changed. . . . He is a priest forever" (Heb. 4:14; 7:17, 24).

The Church in turn reflects the priesthood of her Lord. She

is the "royal priesthood, the holy nation, the spiritual house to offer spiritual sacrifices agreeable to God by Jesus Christ" (1 Peter 2:5). Her worship is as priestly as it is prophetic; united to the community as the head of the body, Christ continues His priestly prayer and sacrifice in her and through her; the offering of all that she is and has is His offering, and through her hands He offers again His redeeming death. Christ prolongs in space and time His priestly prayer through the prayer of the Church. All the prayers of the Church are presented to God "through Christ our Lord." The prayer of every Christian is a prayer of Christ, but it is as a people and a nation that the Church offers His own prayer expressed either in His own words or in the way He taught us to pray—in the spirit and with that tone of adoration and praise that marked His prayer.

Last of all, Christ is a King—"King of Kings and Lord of Lords" (Apoc. 19:6); "All power is given to me in heaven and upon earth" (Matt. 28:18); "Thou sayest, I am a king" (John 18:37); "God has placed all things under his feet" (Eph. 1:22); He gained a kingdom by his precious blood making us "a kingdom unto God and priests" (Apoc. 5:10). The Church is the sign and the witness of that Kingdom. She is indeed the Kingdom of God upon earth, the Holy City, the new Jerusalem coming down from Heaven, adorned as a bride for her husband. Therefore she reflects something of the majesty and power and beauty of that Kingdom. Her worship proclaims in word and deed, in songs, hymns, in the beauty of stone and wood and precious metal that she is conscious of the presence in her midst of Him who was dead and is now alive forever and ever, of Him who is in every sense the Victor King. Something of the majesty of the risen King of Glory must fill His temple. If it did not, the Church would be unfaithful to her mission to be a prophetic sign to the world of the Kingdom that is to come.

Few conceptions of the liturgy are as illuminating and all embracing as this, that it must be the reflection on earth of the eternal liturgy in Heaven, described for us in the Apocalypse. In every place and at all times that liturgy must be the pattern and exemplar of our own. Nor is this in any way incompatible with true simplicity, or with worship in spirit and in truth. There is the story of the Russian envoys who after a visit to Constantinople were so impressed with the liturgy there that they returned to Russia proclaiming that they had been in Heaven. The story may or may not be historically true, but it does express a great truth nevertheless. Authentic Christian worship must always convey something of that impression—a reflection of the glory of the *Christos Kyrios*—the majesty of the King of Glory. For it is the glorified Christ who stands in the midst of His disciples and brings them His message of heavenly peace. His presence in our worship means that the world to come, the *vitam venturi saeculi,* breaks in upon this world, and Heaven comes down to earth. During the days of our life here on earth we already partake of the Kingdom that is to come. We enter into the new order of things inaugurated by Christ on the day of His Ascension. The divine service of the Church is at the same time the worship of pilgrims and travellers on this earth and the worship of citizens of the heavenly city who have already come to the end of their pilgrimage. For "we have not here a lasting city" and "our manner of living is in the heavens."

CHAPTER 3

The Purpose of the Liturgy

The Glory of God

It is a commonplace to say that the purpose of the liturgy is to give glory to God. However, we do not always see what this implies. For "glory" is not altogether a self-evident concept; it demands examination and explanation. We take for granted that we know what it is, but it is not by any means a familiar idea, especially to modern man. St. Thomas defines it as the "knowledge and acclaim of the excellence of someone." First of all, then, it involves a knowledge of the excellence, then a proclamation (acclaim) of the excellence known. We praise and glorify God when we make His goodness and perfections known, when we tell what He is and what He has done. We give God *glory* when we make known His perfections, His goodness, power, holiness, wisdom, justice, and all His many claims to our appreciation.

God has created all things precisely for His glory. They are to proclaim the excellence of Him who made them, and they do that just by being. "The heavens proclaim the glory of God, and the whole round world tells of the work of His hands." Merely by *being* and following His infinitely wise laws, all things tell us about God and give abundant knowledge of what He is.

But for man merely to *be* is not enough (although he gives glory to God that way to a certain extent); he must give *intelligent* praise. For man to give glory according to his nature involves of necessity a rational praise, a praise which he expresses with mind, voice, body, will. By all these he serves the Lord and shows the proper honor and reverence due Him.

This rational praise and glorification is expressed by adoration, thanksgiving, penance and even petition, although the last is perhaps not as obvious as the others. Adoration proclaims the transcendent greatness of God, thanksgiving His omnipotence and goodness, penance bears witness to His holiness and justice and mercy, petition acknowledges His power, supremacy and providence.

Thus in every form of human worship we find acts and words that express the glory of God. Men are ultimately impelled to worship by this motive: that thereby they may praise and glorify God and give Him thanks for benefits received.

Both the Old and the New Testaments call for and proclaim this glory that is due to God. The Psalms in particular are preoccupied with singing about God as the creator, of His greatness, perfections and "wondrous deeds" in the visible and invisible world alike.

Christ's whole life was directed to the honor and glory of God: "I do always the things that please Him"; "that they may know Thee and him whom Thou hast sent, Jesus Christ"; "Behold I come . . . to do Thy will, O God." All His life and work are summed up in these phrases. This same duty and life work is carried on by the Church, the Body and the Spouse of Christ, through her public worship, which is ordered and directed to glorifying God through Jesus Christ. It is this preoccupation with God's glory that is the mainspring of all the Church's worshipping activity; it inspires her prayers, the reading of the Scriptures (which deal with God's great actions "among the children of men"), the composition of hymns, the offering of sacrifice, the whole ordering of divine service. "In hymns and psalms and spiritual canticles" the Church speaks of God, proclaims aloud all that He is and does. How often the words "glory," "praise," "thanksgiving," are upon her lips! We need only recall the orations, the prefaces, the doxologies. Almost any oration, even when asking for blessings or graces for us, begins by telling of God, in other words by "glorifying Him," proclaiming His omnipotence, His clemency, His wisdom, His mercy; the orations describe Him and by doing so magnify and glorify Him. The *Gloria Patri* resounds at the end of each psalm, echoing and crystallizing the thoughts expressed in the psalm itself. In greater detail and with more direct intent, the *Te Deum* and the *Gloria in Excelsis* develop the theme of God's glory, call it to mind, and express it in words.

In the course of the liturgy we very often hear the *Alleluia, Benedicamus Domino, Deo Gratias, Laus tibi Christe, Laus tibi Rex aeternae gloriae*—ideas that receive more developed treatment in the larger doxologies from St. Paul and the Apocalypse: "*Regi saeculorum immortali et invisibili, soli Deo honor et gloria in saecula saeculorum*"; "*Benedictio et claritas et gratiarum actio, honor et gloria Deo nostro in saecula saeculorum.*" The daily canticles of praise, such as the *Magnificat, Benedictus, Nunc Dimittis,* and the *Sanctus,* are each dedicated to that selfless worshipping praise which God deserves, and they daily keep alive among men His holy and worshipful name.

Even in the cult of our Lady and the saints, when it might seem that to honor them is the primary concern of the liturgy of the day, we are struck by the same preoccupation with God's glory. "Celebrating the festivals of the saints we are thereby proclaiming thy own glory," one of the orations in the Leonine Sacramentary says, and thereby expresses with great conciseness the idea that underlies the whole cult of the saints and of their relics. It is God whom we honor in the saints when we extol them in hymns, antiphons, responsories; in the prayers and lessons of the Missal, we are in reality bearing witness to the whole marvelous new creation that God has established by the Death and Resurrection of His Son.

It is in the Holy Sacrifice of the Mass in particular that the greatest and most complete honor and glory is given to God by Christ Himself, the God-Man. "By him and with him and in him is to thee God the Father, in union with the Holy Spirit, all honor and glory." It is more than a form of words; it is an action whereby man adores (*adoramus te*), praises (*nos tibi semper et ubique gratias agere*), gives thanks, and asks graces and blessings (*omni benedictione caelesti et gratia repleamur*) of the triune God.

Just as Christ could say of Himself that He came into the world to glorify His Father, we can say that He left to His Church, through and by means of the liturgy, the power to glorify God by Him and with Him and through Him, with greater ease and in a more effective way.

The Sanctification of Man

The liturgy is indeed directed to God; however, its purpose is not only to give glory to God, but to bring men to holiness. That is readily seen when we think of the Mass, "in which Thou hast placed the fountain of all holiness," (Secret Prayer, Mass of St. Ignatius Loyola) and the sacraments, which bring the divine life to men, sustain it, or restore it when it is lost. We may sometimes lose sight of the fact that the whole body of prayers and rites comprising the liturgy—not only the Mass and the sacraments, but the lessons, chants, hymns, prayers, psalms, antiphons, the rites and ceremonies, and even the church building, all of which form the setting for the Mass and the sacraments—make up a powerful instrument or means of drawing men to God and bringing God to men, of enlightening their faith and stirring up their love, of forming in them that mind which is in Christ Jesus, of instructing, edifying, and inspiring us. To be holy means above all to put on Christ, to have the mind of Christ, and to allow Christ to live in us. The formulae and prayers of the liturgy are a vast storehouse of religion, of right ideas about God, of instruction in goodness and holiness. To take part in the liturgy is a kind of discipline which affords light to the mind and brings warmth to the heart. It shows men how to pray by praying, how to act by doing. In addition, the prayers of the liturgy ask for the graces we need to live holy lives, while at the same time showing us what a holy life is. Through the liturgy the Church teaches us true faith and inculcates Christian virtues. "That they may see what things are to be done, and that they may be able to fulfill these things," says the prayer on the second Sunday after the Epiphany; and again on the fourth Sunday after Easter, in the Secret Prayer, the Church prays "that as we know thy truth we may live accordingly." By the soundness of their lives and virtues the faithful become worthy to take part in the sacred mysteries, and by taking part in them, they acquire virtue and grace and show the effect of this participation in their daily lives. A true and fruitful celebration of the liturgy at once demands and secures a truly Christian life.

The whole nature and arrangement of the liturgy, by making us praise, adore, and worship God, tends to school us in prayer and worship, making us like to Christ, the perfect adorer of His Father. We come to see everything from His point of view: "Let that mind be in you which was also in Christ Jesus"; day by day "Christ is formed in us," and because our attitudes and our outlooks have been formed in this way, we will do the deeds that Christ did—"the things that are pleasing to Him I do always." Thus we are made outwardly conformable to Him whom inwardly we are refashioned to resemble. Because in the liturgy our whole lives move in an atmosphere that is saturated with the supernatural—in the atmosphere of the Old and New Testaments—because we live with and contemplate all the wonderful realities which faith unfolds before us, we truly live lives that are "hidden with Christ in God" and "seek the things that are above, where Christ sits at the right hand of God the Father, not the things that are upon the earth." As a result we "so pass through the joys of this life as not to miss the joys that never end."

In the liturgy taken as a whole, we find authentic Christianity at its source, Christianity whole and entire. Whatever can be proposed to our minds and to our wills of Christian life and virtue anywhere else, we find it here in its fullness. On Christmas day, for example, through the orations, chants, lessons, preface, antiphons, hymns and psalms, we contemplate the *whole* mystery of the Nativity, not just a part of it, not a one-sided view of it, not some individual writer's conception of it, but the whole mystery in itself and in its implications for us. We are thoroughly indoctrinated with it and we see all that it means for God and for us. We see it all in its proper perspective and in all its fullness.

The ultimate reason why the liturgy sanctifies men is that it is a "mystery," a ". . . sacred and worshipping action in which the redemptive work of the past is made present in a determined rite: the congregation, when accomplishing this sacred rite, enters into participation with the redemptive fact thus evoked and so acquires its own salvation." * Through the liturgy one enters into contact with the mystery of salvation, which is the mystery of Christ. For to be saved and to be redeemed is nothing less than to be established "in Christ." We share and take part in His redeeming work; we go through the same process He did: "If any man will be my disciple let him take up his cross and follow me"; "Christ also suffered for us, leaving you an example that you should follow in his steps." The act whereby He redeemed the world, His paschal mystery—His Passion, Death, Resurrection and Ascension—is made present and

* Dom Odo Casel, O.S.B., *Le mystère du culte* (Paris: Les Editions du Cerf, 1947).

operative in the sacred mysteries of the liturgy, which is nothing else than the priesthood of Christ in action. All the various parts of the liturgy go together to achieve that end; the prayers, lessons, chants, hymns, and psalms are designed to awaken our faith, to nourish and sustain it. They express the meaning of what is being done; they show us what we must do and be. "In every liturgical action Christ is present." † If He is present, Christ is *acting*, drawing us into the mystery, making us live it with understanding and love, imprinting its meaning on our minds and stirring our wills to admire and to follow what is done. The ultimate aim of the whole liturgical action is to make us one with Christ, so that as a holy people who have entered into an alliance and a covenant with God, we may offer spiritual sacrifices acceptable to God, through Christ. "To bring all things to a head in Christ," was St. Paul's way of putting it.

In effect, the liturgy, as an act and as a proclamation of the truth in word and deed, is nothing less than a great school of Christian life, a teacher of piety, charity, zeal. We are brought closer to God and united to Him by the deeds and the words of the liturgy; through the prayers, lessons, and chants we are instructed and edified and inspired; by the words of the liturgy our faith is strengthened, nourished, and enriched. Through the liturgical year we live over in our lives the life and mysteries of Christ.

Rightly understood as the priesthood of Christ in action, the liturgy is a powerful means of growth and progress in the spiritual life, and a safe and healthy guide to rich Christian living. It awakens the community spirit, makes us aware of our privileges and our duties as members of the Body of Christ, gives support and depth to our prayers, even those which we say or make privately and apart from the community. The spirituality engendered and fostered by the liturgy, a spirituality that has its roots in Scripture and which centers around the Mass and the

† *Mediator Dei*, 20.

sacraments, is everyman's spirituality. It cannot fail to form the "true Christian spirit."

The Liturgy Is a School of Christian Life

The full implications of this statement can only be appreciated in practice. Nevertheless, a theoretical consideration is not only of great value but even necessary. It is precisely because we have tended to lose sight of the great truth that the liturgy is the primary and indispensable source of the true Christian spirit, that it has not been given full scope to accomplish what it can certainly do, namely, the Christianization and sanctification of society in general and of individuals in particular. In our own day men are beginning to see more clearly that, whatever other methods and devices may be used, here we have the oldest, most objective, and most persuasive method of all to educate and refine the Christian mind, heart and spirit.

Liturgy as the Source and Teacher of Holiness. That the Mass and the sacraments are the great sources of Christian life and holiness hardly needs to be demonstrated. By them the Incarnation is prolonged and the fruits of the Redemption communicated to men; they are the "fountains of the Savior" and carry with them all grace, all life, the very substance of Christianity, because they are the chosen means whereby we grow in the Christ-life, or, better still, whereby He lives and grows in us. The Christian life is in itself a sacramental life. It is true that the sacraments will not be *for us* the source of holiness unless we receive them and take part in them in the right spirit; but that is not the point we are making at present. Taken objectively, the Mass, the sacraments and *all that surrounds them and forms their setting*, the sacramentals and the Divine Office included, proclaim, make present and available, set forth and express in one way or another the whole redeeming work of Christ. They thus, in themselves, contain and embody the whole supernatural world.

It is precisely in the way the great truths of religion are set forth that they contribute powerfully to instruct, edify and nourish the Christian spirit. The lessons, prayers, chants, hymns—the whole vast body of sacred rites—show us how we are to think, to believe, to hope and to act. It might be said that they are the Church's reaction to the great message of salvation. They teach us how we are to respond, not in a formal way, but by the way of example. More than that, they contain the graces we need to bring our minds into conformity with the mind of Christ; they show us how we are to live when confronted with the tremendous fact that they embody and show forth, and they ask for the graces which will make us conform to what we believe. There are degrees in holiness, and every man must measure up to the graces that are given him. It still remains true that we find out how to pray as we ought, not in books of devotion or manuals of ascetical theology, however good they may be, but in the pages of the Missal, Breviary and Ritual. They contain the full Christian teaching and present it in all its aspects and with all its implications.

The Liturgy and Ascetics. The liturgy is an act. It is the Church engaged in her most important action, the worship of God. The liturgy is not, then, primarily a system, in the sense that it is a calculated effort to draw up rules and principles. Rather, it proceeds from principles and translates them into action. Still less is it a system of ascetics. Yet it is true to say that, without intending to be, it actually does constitute a method, if not indeed a system of ascetics. It is an ascetical discipline in the true sense of the word, because it produces in him who submits himself to it all the effects of any ascetical system. Some go so far as to claim that it is the greatest, the best, the most authoritative, the safest of all ascetical systems. We need not enter into a discussion of that idea at present; but we must consider the method pursued by the liturgy in sanctifying men and educating them in the Christian spirit.

Once we embark upon this, we shall see more and more clearly that there is an intimate link between ascetics and liturgy, and that in many ways the liturgy will be seen as a true school of spirituality for everyone. No matter what school of spirituality one may follow, he will find that the liturgy abundantly supplements and reinforces all that any ascetical system may teach him.

All ascetical systems aim at subduing the flesh and lower nature to the spirit, at "forming Christ in us." By prayer and by good works, by fasting, mortification and almsgiving, we die to self, to sin and to our lower nature, "putting off the old man with his vices and ungodly desires and putting on the new man who is created according to justice and true holiness." We do this, not on our own nor by our own efforts, but by sharing in the Death and Resurrection of Christ, knowing that if we suffer with Him we shall be glorified with Him. This dying and rising with Christ is at the bottom of all ascetical activity, and here precisely we see the first link between the liturgy and the ascetical life, because the mystery of the Death and Resurrection of Christ is the central fact of the liturgy as well as of the ascetical life. Whenever the sacrifice of the Mass is offered we "show forth the death of the Lord until he comes again." In this august mystery (an action in the present that contains what was done in the past) Christ, the High Priest and the holy and undefiled Victim, offers Himself and is offered by us "for the remission of sins," "for our salvation and that of all." He gives Himself that we might "have life and have it more abundantly." He associates us with Him, making His offering ours, so that we die with Him and rise with Him. "That mind which is in Christ Jesus" is formed in us. Our lowly bodies are transformed into His glorious body; we are inwardly conformed to Him whom we outwardly resemble; we become a royal nation and a kingly priesthood, who offer spiritual sacrifices and become "ourselves a gift pleasing to him." This paschal mystery is at the heart of Christianity, and it is made available and accessible to us in the

Holy Sacrifice. The Mass is, then, the center of Christian life as it is the center of Christian worship. We are drawn into this mystery; we live it, and by living it we live the Christian life. We draw from this Sacrifice-banquet the graces and the strength we need to make our lives the very life of Christ in us. For to all of us, whether priest or layman, the words of the ordaining prelate may be applied: "Realize what you are doing [when you offer the Holy Sacrifice] and imitate the mystery which you celebrate."

History shows us that the connection between the ascetical life and the Holy Sacrifice is very close, because wherever and whenever the people have lost their understanding of the Sacrifice *and of their part in it,* there has been a corresponding decline in Christian fervor and spiritual life. When St. Pius X wanted to restore the spirit of religion, which he felt had lost ground among the people, it was precisely to a more active part in the Sacrifice that he directed them.

This ascetical or spiritual life is conceived in a positive and objective way: as a grace given by God, sanctifying and refining the human spirit. The emphasis is placed upon God's activity in us, rather than upon our own activity, although that is necessary and not to be neglected. True Christian asceticism is neither Pelagian nor Quietistic, but may be summed up in the formula "*Gratia Dei mecum,*" which asserts the primacy of God's grace and the necessity of our co-operation. Yet the long history of Christian spirituality shows that it is quite possible to exaggerate the one or the other: the subjective or the objective. For the most part, the tendency has been to exaggerate the subjective, to insist overmuch upon ascetical exercises and human methods rather than upon God's action in us. Whatever faults we may attribute to the liturgy, we cannot say that it insists overmuch on man's activity; rather the liturgy is so theocentric as to leave some with the feeling that it plays down human activity. This feeling is not supported by the facts, but its very existence is demonstration enough that the liturgy does not neglect nor play down God's part in the sanctification of men. The prayers of the Missal in particular afford us an admirable example of this God-centered, objective presentation of the Christian life, and at the same time they show how man's co-operation with God's grace is demanded and expected of us. The total effect of these prayers is to unfold for us a very thorough and complete system of ascetics, while never consciously setting out to do so.

The liturgy as an ascetical system or as a spirituality must be considered as the spirituality of the Church. Whatever other ascetical system or spirituality we may follow (and we are at liberty to follow any one of many), we must always, to a certain extent at least, draw upon this spirituality under pain of cutting ourselves off from the current of thought and ideas that has flowed through the Church from the beginning. We must at the different seasons of the Church year, for example, join with other Christians in the ascetical practices that the Church has fostered and encouraged; we must pray and fast in Lent, rejoice and aspire towards heavenly things in Eastertide; be filled with yearning for the coming of God's kingdom in Advent. Whatever other society we belong to, or whatever "school" of spirituality we follow, we are first of all members of the Church and must *sentire cum Ecclesia* in thought and feeling and action. And that thought and feeling and action is and always has been guided and inspired by the Church *through her public worship.* The liturgy, then, is the ordinary way of piety and spirituality open to everyone and directed to everyone, and the celebration of the liturgical rites is itself a school of spirituality for everyone —layman, religious or priest. There is no conflict between the ascetical and the liturgical life, as some seem to imagine; rather there is the greatest concord and harmony. They are but the working out of the one Christian life. The liturgy is not a kind of distraction from the ascetical life, but a means to foster and nourish it. No one can celebrate the liturgy properly who does not lead the ascetical life; nor, on the other hand, can any one lead the ascetical life without drawing the strength, enlightenment and power that he needs from the liturgy.

To center our life in the Mass, to live by the sacraments of Baptism and the Eucharist, to be virtuous, in other words, to develop in us the awareness of our belonging to the Church by praying in union with the Church—what is all this except to live the liturgical life? And is it not at the same time to live the ascetical life in a way that is most accessible to all and most certain to bring about the Christianization of the individual and of society?

In the texts and the sacred rites the liturgy continually *teaches* those principles and rules that go to make up a full Christian life; it quickens the minds of the faithful to contemplate the highest truths. By presenting to them the example of Christ and the saints it moves their wills to practice virtue and all good works; and all of this is conducive to form the Christian in the true Christian spirit.

The faith and doctrine of the Church is set forth in a variety of ways, easy to understand and to grasp; every one of the human senses is used to convey the teaching. By repeating these truths and ideas the liturgy does not allow us to forget them, and thus keeps them ever before the mind. This is in itself a powerful method of teaching. What is often repeated is better understood, is held more firmly in the mind, and passes into action. The worship of the Church is a vast repository of truth, of ideas, of knowledge, a kind of compendium of religion which is made accessible to all. What is more, side by side with the theoretical instruction, so abundantly given, is a whole body of practical wisdom, advice, warning, encouragement, moral guidance, tending to stimulate good will. Consider the lessons, psalms, antiphons, responsories, graduals, communion chants, hymns, orations, postcommunions, the wealth of knowledge and instruction contained in even one day's liturgy—to say nothing of what is unfolded in the Ritual or Pontifical for special occasions. Considered objectively (prescinding from the language question), the impact of what it has to offer must be great. The leaders of a mob get their ideas across simply by repeating slogans and by unwearying propaganda; all this is effective because it takes into account a fundamental law of human nature: we absorb what we hear and see often enough. We know that in Christian antiquity the only instruction the people received came from the liturgy; yet it was effective in forming a Christian outlook and mentality. It was and can be effective again because its power is intrinsic to the very nature of the liturgy, which presents truths to us in the most natural and effective way. Doctrinal and moral instruction go hand in hand, and the speculative truths which are set forth in the lessons and other texts of the liturgy are proposed as the motive for every-day living, for which they provide the driving force.

St. Leo shows how this is done in his famous passage in the Christmas Office when he says, speaking of the Incarnation, "Recognize the dignity to which you are raised, O Christian man, and since you are made a partaker and sharer in the divine nature, do not return to your former unredeemed state by leading a wicked life." Or again the relation between believing and living—doctrine and morals—is shown when we hear or read at Eastertime: "If you be risen with Christ, then seek the things that are above"; or at Ascension time: ". . . that we who believe that thy Son on this day did ascend to heaven, may ourselves continually dwell therein in affection and desire."

The fact that the liturgy is prayer in common demands that it be based upon dogma and be the expression of objective truth. It must have content and ideas in order to be universal and make a universal appeal; it cannot be merely emotional, nor sentimental, nor subjective.

Even a very rapid examination of the liturgical books will demonstrate abundantly that the liturgy is based upon dogma and that it contains in one way or another all the truths of our faith. In fact, the liturgical year is very largely a dramatization or a celebration of all the articles of the Apostles' Creed which are recalled, relived and prayed over in many different ways during the course of the year. That is especially true of the "idea feasts" which have been added in the past few centuries. One reason for their institution was precisely to instruct the people in doctrine. For example, in the incomparable Office and Mass of the Feast of Corpus Christi the Church unfolds for our contemplation the Eucharist, Sacrifice and sacrament; the Feast of Christ the King describes the Kingdom of Christ; the Feast of the Sacred Heart teaches the theology of the love of Christ; the Immaculate Conception the doctrine of Mary's sinlessness, or the rôle of Mary as Mother of God.

It has been well said that the liturgy is dogma expressed in prayer. The famous theological axiom "*lex orandi, lex credendi,*" or more correctly "*legem credendi statuit lex supplicandi,*" expresses the intimate relation between the two and at the same time brings out that prayer rests upon dogma; otherwise it could not serve as a norm of faith nor as an indication of what is to be believed.

It is no exaggeration to say that we can find the whole content of our faith in the liturgical books, nor would it be difficult to draw up a rather complete summa of doctrine from the pages of the Missal, Breviary and Ritual. For example, we find a full treatise on the sacrament of Baptism in the liturgy of Easter and Pentecost: washing with water, cleansing from sin, new birth in the spirit, new life, adoption of sons, clothing with Christ, and so on. Or we can find a most illuminating discussion of the nature and mission of the Church in the Office and Mass of the Dedication: it is the House of God, the Gate of Heaven, the Spouse of Christ, built of living stones, new Jerusalem. The nature and object of prayer can be seen in many places, particularly in the fifth Sunday after Easter, the Rogation days and in the Litany of the Saints. How much the postcommunions tell us of the effects of Holy Communion!

By dividing the content of the teaching of the liturgy into the chief subject headings—God, man, and Christ—we can draw up an imposing body of teaching almost exclusively from the orations alone, to say nothing of the hymns, lessons, antiphons, and responsories:

God is omnipotent, and eternal, the light of all lights, the source of all good, without whom nothing is healthy, nothing holy, from whom all good things proceed, to whom every good and perfect work belongs, who has wonderfully created us and still more wonderfully refashioned us. He is almighty, but He shows His omnipotence chiefly by sparing us and having mercy upon us: it is His special characteristic to show mercy and to spare; His mercy is boundless and His treasure of goodness inexhaustible. He wishes the salvation of all and the loss of no one; He is the author and lover of peace, and to serve Him is to reign. (Every one of these phrases, a small selection of the many that could be quoted, is from one or another oration in the Missal.)

Then man, created by God, raised to an incomparable dignity which was lost by our first parents, falls into misery and wretchedness; he is rescued, redeemed, sanctified, purchased at a great price, made the child of God, the brother of Christ, the temple of the spirit, a member of the flock of the elect. Yet at the same time he is not confirmed in grace, he can sin and lose all he has gained; his life on earth is a warfare against the malice and snares of the demon; he needs the continual help of grace. That grace comes to us abundantly in Christ who is our hope.

Christ is the center of the liturgy and its teaching about Him is inexhaustible: the great aim of God is to bring all things to a head in Christ. He is the image of the invisible God; by the mystery of the Word made flesh we contemplate God visible in human form and thereby are drawn to the love of the invisible God. Through Him we become partakers of the divine nature. This process of deification is emphasized especially at Christmas time: twice on Christmas day the liturgy affirms that God became man that man might become God-like; we become inwardly like Him who shares outward likeness with us. The whole life of a Christian becomes a participation in the mystery of Christ. This is done particularly through the Holy Eucharist, the "mystery of Faith" where every day we come into contact with His redeeming death on the cross and are nourished with the Bread of Life and the chalice of eternal salvation. All through the year we contemplate Christ in His mysteries through the prayers, lessons, chants, hymns, antiphons, and responsories of the various seasons and feasts. The events of His life are unfolded before us and their inner significance is shown to us. Through the liturgy we profess our faith in Christ; we rejoice in it and express our joy; in countless ways we find that it tells us about Christ with a completeness and a thoroughness that we find nowhere else. Our prayer is really based upon Truth, the Incarnate Truth, and, as a result, it becomes the source of life: "For this is eternal life: to know thee the one true God and him whom thou hast sent, Jesus Christ." The life and virtues of Christ are not just narrated but are presented to us in such a way that we may *savor* them. This is done by the dramatic and even lyrical setting of many of the antiphons, responsories, and hymns: the *O Admirabile Commercium* of New Year's Day, the *Ante luciferum genitus* of the Epiphany, the *O Sacrum Convivium* of Corpus Christi, the *Vexilla Regis* of Passiontide, the invitatories of the various feasts and seasons, which, as it were, make us present and attentive to what is going on. What a wealth of doctrine about Christ, His person, mission, message, is to be found in the antiphons and responsories of even one Sunday in Advent!

The liturgy not only teaches and instructs us by words, it does it by actions. For our purposes, a few examples will suffice: the blessing and procession of the palms on Palm Sunday, which dramatizes for us the triumphal entry of Christ as Messiah and King into Jerusalem; the blessing of candles and the procession on Candlemas Day, which is a dramatization of the meeting of Israel with its God, the Light of the World; all the impressive rites of the restored Easter Vigil, which dramatize Christ's victory over darkness and the grave, or any of the multitudinous rites which the Church performs every day as part of the setting for the sacraments. Consider only the wealth of dogmatic teaching that is crystallized in the Sign of the Cross!

For all these reasons the liturgy is an important *locus theologicus;* it demonstrates and shows what the Faith is. It does not create either doctrine or dogma, but it necessarily presupposes the one and the other, and by its very nature has to be the expression of the Faith. It is not indeed the official expression of the Faith of the Church—that is done by the creeds, the decrees of the councils and the *ex cathedra* teaching of the popes. The liturgy is an organ or instrument of tradition; it reflects the belief of the Church and bears witness to that belief. This enables us to tell by the liturgy what the people believe about this or that doctrine, and what they have always believed. The Council of Trent found support for the doctrine that faith, hope, and charity could increase or decrease in the just by referring to the collect of the thirteenth Sunday after Pentecost: "*Da nobis fidei, spei, et caritatis augmentum.*" As a *locus theologicus* the liturgy takes its place immediately after the solemn documents of the infallible magisterium and before any or all of the Fathers or theologians. Naturally it must be used with care and due regard made to the geographical extent and the historical time of the witness in question; purely local festivals, for example, or prayers that were in use only for a short time and only in some places, can hardly express the Faith and belief of the entire Christian people at all times. But once due caution and circumspection has been observed, the value of the liturgy as affording arguments for a doctrine or showing its range and its implications, in short for enlightenment, must be apparent to everyone. The growth and development of a real "liturgical theology" in recent decades abundantly testifies that the liturgy has much to offer in the way of enlightenment and our understanding of the Faith.

The Liturgy as a School of Doctrine

The liturgy has one great task which it is continually performing; but because this is done indirectly rather than directly, the extent of its accomplishment is not readily appreciated. What that task is was well described by Pius XI when he said that the liturgy is the "*didascalia*" of the Church, the pedagogue or the school which teaches the Church about God and about the life and the activity of God. It is not in itself theology but it teaches theology; not in itself the Faith but it presents the Faith for our learning, understanding and enlightenment. The Pope developed that theme at greater length in the encyclical *Quas Primas* establishing the Feast of Christ the King. The fact is, as he tells his readers, that other kinds of instruction (writing, catechetical instruction, sermons and conferences) reach only certain people at certain times. They can soon forget what they have read or heard. But the great ideas and themes of the liturgy reach everyone. They hear them not once or twice but over and over again; they are continually under their influence, and they hear them not only in part but in their entirety. What the liturgy amounts to, then, is a vast system of education, an admirably organized school which imparts a complete course of instruction from which everyone can learn something, and which provides in reality the *only* religious instruction that the great majority of Christians ever get—at least from the day they leave school or college.*

* Inevitably the reader will wonder whether the liturgy as it is now arranged can achieve its great purpose. It is difficult not to bring up the question of the use of the vernacular, but to do so here would only confuse the issue. The subject under discussion is the educative value of the liturgy itself, of its content and method, and the point we wish to make at present is that it has a content that is instructive and a method that is soundly pedagogical. Besides, the life-giving texts are accessible even now in the language of the people; they can follow what is going on and thus can absorb more than a little of the content. The liturgy is an instrument of learning and instruction in the Faith; that it would be more so if it were in the language of the people it is hard to deny, but the fact remains that in itself and objectively it presents ideas in a language which is intel-

The liturgy first of all presents the Faith to us; it deals with God, with the Creation, Incarnation, Redemption, with the whole body of Catholic doctrine, and, without deliberately setting out to do so, gives us an immense amount of enlightenment about them. That is theology, but not theology in the specialized sense in which we usually think of the word. There is unfolded before our eyes and held up for our contemplation the whole wide world that is Christianity, the fullness of Christian life and thought. And it is done not in a dry or too systematic a fashion, such as we might (rightly or wrongly) associate with the lectures of professors, or with scientific treatises written by specialists, but in a living and dynamic fashion. The liturgy dramatizes theology for us, or, better still, we live it while we celebrate it.

In imbuing the faithful with those things which belong to the Faith and in awakening them to the inner joys of life, the *celebration* throughout the year of the sacred mysteries has much more effect than even the most important documents of the teaching authority of the Church; for these reach only a few of the more learned and instructed men, while the celebrations affect all the faithful and teach them; the documents only once, the celebrations year after year, and as we might say, perpetually, speak to them; documents affect the mind principally while the celebrations affect in a most salutary way not only the mind but the spirit and the soul, in fact the whole man. Certainly since man is made up of body and spirit he must be moved and stimulated by the outward solemnities or festival days, that he may take in divine teaching more abundantly through the variety and beauty of the sacred rites, and the heavenly doctrine will penetrate so deeply into him as to become like the living sap and life-blood whose energies he will make use of to make progress in the spiritual life.*

ligible; it communicates. Whether it could communicate better and more directly in the language that people use in daily life is an interesting and important question, but not the question immediately at hand.

* Pope Pius XI, Encyclical *Quas Primas.*

The liturgy expresses what the Faith is, what the Church believes and how she wishes God to be honored, and it does so by the manner in which it praises God and prays to Him. Nothing can conceivably be found in the liturgy which is in any way at variance with sound doctrine. That is why we can expect to find the Faith expressed accurately and in its entirety in the formulae the Church uses in her worship. The Church has the duty of proclaiming the truth, and the liturgy is one of the ways, one of the most ordinary ways, in which she proclaims it. Here is another reason why the liturgy is a *locus theologicus:* if a doctrine is found in an authorized liturgy, it is there because the *consensus fidelium* has always maintained that particular truth. The liturgy does not create the teaching of the Church; it reflects it and is based upon it. There are many points of doctrine that have never been formally defined by the Church; yet no one would dare call them into question, precisely because the Church has always proclaimed them in her public worship. They may not be expressed in the language of conciliar decrees; they are nevertheless true because the Church has always believed them and acted upon them. For it is the Church which through the liturgy proposes its faith and its teaching and imposes it upon the faithful. She approves and imposes the liturgical books which contain her doctrine adapted to the nature as well as the ends of worship. She it is who institutes the feasts of the Church year and expresses in the Masses and Offices of those feasts their meaning and doctrinal content.

CHAPTER 4

The Regulation of the Liturgy

The Liturgical Books

The liturgy of the Church is contained in the books which set down the prayers and rites, together with the directions for carrying them out. Only what is contained in the approved liturgical books is the official worship of the Church; any other service, even though made up of liturgical texts, is extra-liturgical: it is not according to what is set down in the approved books. The liturgical books comprise: the Roman Missal (Editio typica 1920), the Roman Breviary (1949), the Martyrology (1913), the Roman Ritual (1952) (for the United States the *Collectio Rituum* [1954] is one of the approved books), the Roman Pontifical (1888), the *Caeremoniale Episcoporum* (1886), and for small churches the *Memoriale Rituum* (1920). The Clementine Instruction (for the "Forty Hours") (1705) is usually included in the list, which might also, to be complete, include the Roman or Vatican Graduale (1907), the Kyriale (1905), and the Antiphonale (1912).

The oldest book used in the liturgy is, of course, the Bible and particularly the psalter. The prayers used by the celebrant, at first improvised, were finally written down in the fourth century and are contained in a book called the Sacramentary (*Euchologion* among the Greeks). The other texts used at Mass were contained in different books: the Evangelarium, the Graduale (for the chants), and so forth. A small library was needed for the Mass, made up of the books used by the different ministers and by the choir.

Our modern "*Missale plenum*" owes its origin to the increase in the number of private Masses said at the side altars in monasteries, or the Masses said in public, without solemnity, in the smaller churches where there was only one priest, no clerics and little or no choir. The priest in these situations had to say or sing all the parts of the Mass. About the eighth or ninth centuries little missals began to appear which contained the full text of the Masses more commonly said, that is, the requiems and votive Masses. As these missals were copied out by hand, they tended to contain only a small number of such Masses. More and more Masses were added as time went on, so that the Sacramentary of the priest would also contain the texts (in whole or in part) of the other parts of the Mass. By the thirteenth century the process had reached full maturity. During the following centuries, abuses crept in, unauthorized texts were used, and the demand for a correct text became louder. The Council of Trent undertook a revision, and a revised Missal, based upon one that had been used at the Roman Court since the thirteenth century, was imposed upon the churches of the Roman Rite in 1570, to be used by all those who did not have a rite that was at least two hundred years old. This was the Missal of St. Pius V, which, with some changes and modifications, such as the addition of new Masses and four Prefaces (during the last forty years), is still used today. The Missal has been affected much less than the Breviary by the changes of 1955; in neither one have any texts been changed or altered in themselves.

Sources of the Missal

The first sources of the Missal are the Sacramentaries. Three of these have come down to us: the Leonianum, Gelasianum, and Gregorianum.

The Leonine Sacramentary. There is general agreement among scholars that the Sacramentary of Verona, better known as the Leonine Sacramentary, is in its present form a seventh century manuscript, but that it represents a copy or an editing of an earlier collection. Several distinct problems connected with it claim attention: the source and the date of the present manuscript, the source and date of the collection itself, the author of this original collection. These questions have to be kept separate.

First of all, the manuscript was found at Verona, but it is felt that it most likely came from somewhere else in Italy. As we have said, the date is usually given as the seventh century.

The real problems about the Leonine Sacramentary are those which concern the collection itself. At one time it was considered to be an original document, but now it appears that it is but a copy of an earlier collection, and the problem arises as to the date and the source of that earlier work. Closer examination of the text shows that it is undoubtedly Roman for the most part in style, in phrasing, in diction, and in the abundance of references to the local church of Rome and its customs. Yet there are some indications that the collection may have been made in another place, by one who made use of a basic Roman text. If this is true, other questions arise. Who was the editor of this compilation and, still more important, who was the author of the great bulk of the prayers?

The general opinion among those who have studied it leans to the late fifth or early sixth century for the compilation of this book, but the compiler is unknown. (It might be said here that most scholars are certain that, as it stands, the Sacramentary was not used for church services; rather, it seems to have been intended for private use, *i.e.*, the *prayers* were used in church, the *collection* was not.) That the greater part of the prayers were composed by one person is an opinion that recommends itself very strongly when we examine their style and phrasing, but who that author could have been is something which we can only guess at in the present state of liturgical science. When Joseph Biancini found this Sacramentary in the eighteenth century, he attributed it to St. Leo the Great, and while there is at present no way of knowing definitely whether Biancini was altogether right in doing so, there seems to be no one else who would be more likely to have composed them. In style and diction they resemble very much the authentic writings of this great pope. Beyond that we cannot go.

The Masses in the Leonianum are divided according to the months of the year; the collection begins with the month of April. There are two or three collects, a Secret prayer, a Preface and a Postcommunion for each day; some days have as many as fifteen distinct and different Mass-formularies. There is no complete text of the Canon, but some of the Masses have a variable *Hanc Igitur* and *Communicantes*. Besides the Masses there are other rites, such as Baptism and Ordination (episcopate, priesthood, diaconate).

The collection is exceedingly rich and varied and the style of the orations particularly is stamped with the true Roman flavor. A rather large number of these prayers have fortunately passed into the modern Missal; a good example of their form and spirit is the Collect used at the blessing of the water in the Offertory rite of the present Roman Mass. Originally a Collect for Christmas time, it has been adapted to its present purpose by inserting the words "through this mystery of the water and wine."

The Gelasian Sacramentary. The work attributed to Gelasius is now seen to be neither Gelasian nor purely Roman, but is a collection made after his time when the influence of the Gallican church had already begun to be felt. The time of its composition is usually given as the seventh century and it seems to have been written in France, probably for use at the Abbey of St. Denis. It does not bear the name of Gelasius at all, and was attributed to him because he was supposed, according to the *Liber Pontificalis,* to have composed some prayers. Even if he had composed prayers, this would not mean that he was the author of a whole collection.

The book differs from the Leonianum in that the Masses are not arranged according to the months of the year but according to the season or saints' feasts. It is divided into three books, of which the first contains the *proprium de tempore:* Masses for the seasons and feasts, along with much that would in our day be found in the Pontifical (the forms for ordinations, the reconciliation of penitents, and for the consecration of the oils). The second book contains the *proprium sanctorum:* Masses for the saints' feasts, but also Masses that would belong rather to the first book, like the Masses for the Sundays of Advent. In the third book are a series of Masses which correspond to the present Masses after Pentecost in the Roman Missal, along with the Canon, a collection of Masses for special purposes, and the rites for marriage and the burial of the dead. As we can see, the arrangement of this Sacramentary corresponds roughly to the arrangement of the present Missal with its propers of the season and of the saints and its votive Masses. There are many indications that the work is later than Gelasius, the most prominent being the "*diesque nostros in tua pace disponas,*" which was added by St. Gregory, and the Masses for Wednesdays, Fridays and Saturdays in Lent, established as stations by the same pope. On the other hand, there are no Masses for Thursdays in Lent, which shows that the work was compiled before the eighth century, when they were added to the Sacramentary.

The document as it stands is fundamentaly Roman, but that Roman foundation had undergone many changes, modifications and additions from Gallican sources.

The Gregorian Sacramentary. Like the preceding Sacramentary, the Gregorian has undergone many interpolations and additions. St. Gregory did indeed *edit* the Gelasian Sacramentary, shortening it and dropping certain things out. It was this book that Hadrian I sent to Gaul in the eighth century with what results we know. A Gallican liturgist, most likely Alcuin, touched it up and added to it. At first these additions were placed in a supplement, but gradually the two parts were fused together. Alcuin, if it was he, borrowed from the Gelasian Sacramentary as well as from Gallican and Ambrosian books for his "supplement" to the pure Gregorian book that the Roman Pontiff had sent. The result of all this was a liturgical book of great variety and richness; the Sacramentary of Gregory had acquired many new treasures, particularly an abundance of Mass texts for the different seasons of the year, formularies that were varied and developed, but it retained its own fundamental characteristics, a spirit of measure, balance, and a fine selection of saints' Masses. This was the Sacramentary, still called Gregorian but no longer purely so, that returned to Rome in the Middle Ages. It was from this Sacramentary, no longer Roman but Romano-Gallican, that our present Missal was finally derived.

Other Sources of the Missal: Lectionaries, Evangeliaries, Antiphonaries

The early Christians continued the Jewish practice of reading the Scriptures in the liturgical assembly, but added their own sacred writings, the New Testament, to those books already read in the synagogue. For a long time this reading was done from the very Scriptures themselves; the most ancient manuscripts of the Bible that we have are those that were used for the liturgical service. The passages to be read in each service were selected by the one who presided over the assembly and he it was who gave the signal to stop. As time went on these sections (*pericopes*) were marked off in the manuscript and certain passages were selected for each Sunday and each feast. Thus it was determined in advance what should be read, instead of at the time of the service, as was the rule at first. The passages marked off were either indicated in the margin of the manuscript or in a special table placed at the beginning of the book.

The first stage in the development of the Lectionary was to put the beginning and end of each passage to be read in a separate book called the *liber comicus*. The next step was to remove these marked passages and put them in a separate book. Thus we have Evangeliaries containing the Gospels to be read and Lectionaries or Epistolaries for the lessons. Later on these passages were all put in the one Lectionary. The Lectionary for the Church at Rome in the sixth century has come down to us; many of the lessons are the same as those read today.

Just as Alcuin revised or at least retouched the Sacramentary, he also added to the Lectionary, and our present Lectionary is derived from the Romano-Gallican work that came from his hand. The Lectionary now used in the Missal and in the Office dates substantially from the ninth century; additions were made in the course of time as new feasts were added, but the greater part of it is as it was then.

The Antiphonary. That the Roman Antiphonary, from which the bulk of the proper chants of the Missal are taken, is very ancient is shown by the fact that the text of the scriptural chants is drawn from the old Itala version of the Bible. St. Gregory edited and compiled it, but that he is not the author of the whole Antiphonary is quite clear to all historians of the chant and of the liturgy. Apparently he went to work on a previous collection, revised, retouched and, when necessary, augmented it by putting in new texts and composing the music for them.

Like the Sacramentary and the Lectionary, this work of St. Gregory traveled forth to the Frankish domains, and like them it was revised and re-edited, sometimes considerably, by the Gallican liturgists, particularly by Amalarius. This revision or augmentation brought many riches into the Antiphonary and again, as with the Sacramentary and the Lectionary, it was this Romano-Gallican document that entered into our modern Roman Missal.

The Ritual. About the seventh or eighth century a little collection of prayers and formulae for the use of priests in conferring the sacraments and performing certain other rites was made by taking them from the Sacramentary, where they had been first written down. Larger Rituals were a development of the Middle Ages. As with the Missal, there was no official edition of the Ritual for the whole Church until after the Council of Trent, when the *Rituale Romanum* was adopted in 1614. This gradually helped to eliminate the anarchy that reigned in the field of ritual in some parts of the Church. The latest revision was in 1925, with the publication of the Editio Typica by Pius XI. This latter was enriched with new blessings and brought into conformity with the new Code of Canon Law.

The Pontifical. As its name indicates, this book contains those rites which are reserved to a bishop. In its present form it comes not from Rome but from France. The bishops in Italy had used the Sacramentary, which contained their rites as well as those used by all priests; the ceremonies accompanying the rites were contained in the *Ordines Romani.* It was in the Frankish lands that the idea first came of putting all these episcopal rites and ceremonies in one book (Confirmation, Ordination, consecration of churches, *etc.*). The new book thus created contained a mingling of Roman and Gallican elements, and when it entered Italy in the eleventh century it was no longer Roman, but Romano-Gallican, with many of the rites augmented and elaborated in the Gallican style. Then this *Pontificale Romano-Germanicum* (as it was styled) underwent new modifications. The other bishops adopted the Pontifical used at Rome for their own use. One of them, Durandus of Mende in France, rearranged it and made it strictly a bishop's book. It was his revision that became the official Pontifical when in the fifteenth century Innocent VIII adopted it for the use of all the bishops of the Latin Church, and when, finally, Clement VIII gave it formal approval in 1596.

The Caeremoniale Episcoporum. The ceremonies which regulated the manner of celebrating the liturgy were set down in special books called *Ordines* (beginning in the sixth century), then in the *Caeremoniale* (beginning in the fourteenth). Before the sixth century they were scattered through the different liturgical books then in use, such as the "Apostolic Constitutions" and the "Testament of the Lord." The *Ordines* represent the first attempt to gather them together with some kind of system, whence the name "ordo" (regulation).

For over a thousand years the ceremonies of the Church of Rome were kept in the collection of *Ordines Romani,* making up fifteen books. They were later published by Mabillon, then reprinted by Migne as a supplement to the works of St. Gregory, and are usually divided into two groups, one of nine, the other of six. The first group records for our information the ceremonial of the papal Mass, particularly the stational Mass celebrated by the Pope in one of the designated churches throughout the city of Rome, as well as the other ceremonies during the year—those of Easter and the ordinations. The second group, from Book ten through fifteen, takes in the various ceremonies throughout the Church year—the papal ceremonies, such as canonizations, consistories, councils, and many other functions. The last Roman Ordo, called the sixteenth, is largely concerned with the ceremonies accompanying the sickness, death and burial of the popes, and the conclave for the election of a successor.

All these details were gathered together in one work which was first called the official Ceremonial of the Roman Church, then in 1600 renamed the *Caeremoniale Episcoporum,* containing the rules for the celebration of all episcopal liturgical functions. To a great extent it determines the rules for the setting of divine worship in general.

The Memoriale Rituum is a little book that adapts the rites of Holy Week and other rites during the year to small churches. Originally used by Cardinal Orsini in his diocese of Benevento, it was extended to the whole Church when he became pope, but became an official liturgical book only with St. Pius X. Pope Benedict XV published the first "*editio typica.*"

The Clementine Instruction was drawn up to provide for the ceremonial of the Forty Hours devotion by Clement XI in 1705.

The Martyrology contains the list of saints venerated throughout the Church in the course of the year. It is arranged according to the days of the month with each saint listed on the day of his death (*dies natalis*), or his burial (*depositio*), or the moving of his remains from one church to another (*translatio*). It began with the local list preserved in each church, called at first the Calendar. The first Martyrology was the so-called *Martyrologium Hieronymianum*, which dates from the second half of the sixth century. Others followed in the ninth century, the most famous of these being the Martyrologies of Bede and Usuard. The Martyrologies added many details not found in the Calendars. They were read in the public recitation of the Office from the eighth century, but were never required in the private recitation. Worked over in the sixteenth century, particularly by Baronius, the Martyrology was given its present form by Benedict XIV in the eighteenth century.

The Congregation of Sacred Rites

For some centuries there was little or no regulation of the liturgical rites such as we know today. A fixed pattern was more-or-less followed, but within the limits of this latter a wide latitude in observing details was allowed. Even when the various liturgies began to crystallize and were written down, the regulations were of the most general kind. A whole body of practices grew up in connection with the services of the Church during the fourth century and after, and a certain uniformity was sought at least within each diocese. Some of the great Fathers, particularly St. Basil, John Chrysostom, and Ambrose, concerned themselves with regulating the liturgical services. But this was still along broad general lines and was chiefly concerned with simplifying, selecting, arranging and enriching the entire service. Most of the regulating was in the hands of the bishops who enjoyed great authority in these matters.

The Carolingian reform which was imposed upon the Frankish domains by Pepin and Charlemagne went far towards bringing about liturgical uniformity in the West. The Gallican Rite gave place to the Roman, although much of the former continued to influence the latter. The popes in time followed up this lead and tended to influence the development of liturgical practice, but still left much latitude to the bishops. By the end of the Middle Ages, though the Roman Rite was nearly everywhere in use throughout the West, there were many local variants, along with what can only be called many abuses. Finally, in response to powerful pressures, a strong reform movement was inaugurated by the Council of Trent. For the first time in history the regulation of the liturgy became the exclusive prerogative of the Holy See. This included the correction and revision of the liturgical books and the establishment of the Congregation of Sacred Rites. The rubrics were codified, the books and their contents examined, and the entire structure and content of the liturgy—feasts, offices, Masses, sacred rites and ceremonies—were organized and put into order. The most complete uniformity was thus secured throughout the Western patriarchate. Only those rites or variants of the Roman Rite that could claim a tradition of two hundred years' standing were exempted. The missions which were embarked upon at the time on so great a scale extended the newly revised liturgy to Asia, Africa and America, and attempts to adapt it to those peoples who were newly evangelized were not allowed to continue.

Present Law. In this modern period the Code of Canon Law reaffirms the exclusive right of the Holy See to regulate the liturgy and to approve liturgical books (Can. 1257), and at the same time directs that everything in the liturgical books remains in force. This means that the present liturgical law takes in all that is in the liturgical books and all the directions pertaining to the liturgy which proceed from the Holy See, directly or indirectly, as well as any reasonable and laudable custom that supplements or complements what is in the law.

The interpretation of liturgical law is very largely in the hands of the Congregation of Rites, and even when questions are asked the Congregation by individuals or local groups, their answers, when they interpret general laws, are regarded as decrees binding on all. Their decrees are collected in the *Decreta Authentica* of the Congregation of Rites which was published in 1898 and continued until 1926. After that they appear in the *Acta Apostolicae Sedis.*

The role of the bishops is largely that of watching over the performing of the liturgy in their dioceses, approving certain prayers and devotions that are extra-liturgical, such as Benediction of the Blessed Sacrament, of prescribing under certain conditions the *oratio imperata*, and of preventing abuses. A bishop in whose diocese *editiones typicae* of the liturgical books are published has the right to issue the *imprimatur.* The bishop may also make more specific regulations in matters that the law has left open.

The liturgical laws are binding in conscience as are all the laws of the Church; nothing is left to the judgment, still less to the vagaries, of individual celebrants. This is, of course, as it should be, since the liturgy is by definition something official and must be regulated by authority. On the other hand, a too rigid interpretation of the text of the rubrics, particularly those parts that regulate certain actions, does not seem to be imposed as much as many appear to think. They are supposed to be interpreted intelligently. It should be remembered that many of these laws were framed for a certain purpose, and if that purpose is no longer achieved by them, they can hardly be said to apply. Or they are intended to indicate a norm, or a minimum, or simply the best and most natural way to do something. Too literal an interpretation sometimes defeats their purpose and violates the spirit that prompted them. Nor should they all be regarded as of equal importance; there is certainly a vast difference, for example, between *what* is commanded and the way we are directed to do it. Sometimes, too, it is not a question of rubrics, but of the conclusions drawn by rubricists, which is not the same thing.

By this we do not mean that every man should be his own Congregation of Rites, but we do mean that the Church has no obvious intention of binding us with the rigidity of a strait jacket nor certainly of turning the worship of the living God into a fussy ritualism. Rubrics are means, not ends in themselves, but it is easy to understand how we can forget that at times. It was undoubtedly to safeguard the liturgy of the Church from fossilization and to make sure that we do not ignore realities that Pius XI instituted a historical section for the Congregation of Rites. A knowledge of the history behind our worship is essential to an understanding of the worship itself; knowing why and under what circumstances this or that grew up often goes a long way towards helping us to put it all in the proper perspective.

Custom. In liturgical law as well as with any laws of the Church the principle holds good that "custom is the best interpreter of law." This is particularly true of those customs which are "*praeter legem*"—in tune with or in harmony with the law. They grew up as extensions, clarifications, or applications of the laws. Customs of that kind can be introduced and maintained when they have the approval of authority.

When customs are contrary to the law, yet are introduced with at least the tacit consent or even only the toleration of authority, they may be maintained if they are of long standing, which, according to the Code, means they have been in vogue for forty years (always with the consent or toleration of authority).

The Church law on customs is complicated and not easy to interpret, but there is definitely room for the introduction and maintaining of customs which themselves acquire the force of law.

CHAPTER 5

The Words and Actions of the Liturgy

The Language of the Liturgy

There is no question that the language of the liturgy was originally the language of the people who used it. The Gospel was preached in the tongue understood by the people in Apostolic times, which was usually Greek, the great common language of the Roman Empire, and the liturgy was celebrated in the same tongue—though not exclusively, as other languages were used as well. There was never any deliberate plan to use an unknown tongue in Christian worship; *every single language used today in the East and West made its way into the liturgy as a living language.* Only with the passage of time did it cease to be understood by the people. It was never regarded as desirable in itself that the people should not understand the language in which they worshipped God. This is in keeping with the very nature of liturgy, which though directed to God is the expression of the worship of the people; which aims not only at praising God, but at awakening as well the sentiments of adoration, praise, and thanksgiving in those who take part in it. Liturgy is of its very nature a proclamation, a heralding of the Gospel. And this is done most effectively when people understand it.

The use of the language of the people in the liturgy has always been a principle in the East much more than in the West, and a great variety of languages are used to this day in the Eastern Rites. The same principle was observed in the West at first, for we know that the Latin peoples in the rural areas who knew no Greek changed the liturgy into Latin before the Christian community at Rome did so. Greek continued to be spoken and understood in the cities for some time, but even at Rome the liturgy was changed into Latin by the fourth century, precisely because that had become the language of the people. Latin was also the vernacular in Spain, Gaul and parts of Britain. This proved to be the last time that the liturgy was changed into the vernacular on any great scale in the West. The missionaries who went into the Teutonic regions, or into Ireland, Scotland, Britain and Scandinavia, made no effort to translate the liturgy into the language of these peoples either because they did not have the necessary knowledge of the languages, or because by the time they reached some of these countries Latin was already regarded as the liturgical language and no one seriously thought of using any other. The difficulty of translating it only increased in time with the fuller development of a specifically Christian Latin which contained so many terms that expressed the ideas and the doctrine of the Christian religion. The fathers of the Council of Trent refused to consider seriously any change in this respect, in spite of the strong inducement there must have been to counteract the efforts of the reformers. Precisely because a language understood by the people was insisted upon so much by the reformers, the Catholics reacted against the use of the vernacular in the liturgy to the point of making the use of Latin seem synonymous with orthodoxy. This

Catholic reaction retained its full vigor and power almost into our own time.

With the coming of the liturgical revival there has been a renewed interest in the question of the possibility of a vernacular liturgy. The whole question is being re-examined again and is much discussed in our time. For it seems inevitable that those who take an active interest in the liturgy must come to the growing realization that, in the words of Pius XII, "there may be advantages to the use of the vernacular." Certainly many of the old arguments—or rather *post-factum* justifications—in favor of the *exclusive* use of Latin do not sound as convincing as they once did. With a growth in understanding of the true meaning of liturgy must come also the strong conviction that there is something anomalous about not having a "service for and of the people" ("liturgy") in a language that these same people cannot understand. If our forefathers in the Faith did as the Eastern Rite missionaries had done and translated the liturgy into the language and the dialects of those to whom they were sent, the problem would be greatly simplified. They did not do so and it is left to us and to those who will come after us to try to adjust to it. It is true that we would lose much by such a translation. The question is, would we gain more than we lost? We already have a precedent set by the Holy See for the United States, France, Germany and India, where Rome has conceded the abundant use of the vernacular in the Ritual. The Germans have the further privilege of using some German in their High Masses. This means that to a certain extent the Holy See has abandoned the exclusive use of Latin as the liturgical language of the West, and made English, German and the Hindu language liturgical languages too. If this can be done with the Ritual, why not with the Missal and Breviary as well? Some kind of compromise—such as permission to have the Epistle and Gospel sung or said in the vernacular—would seem to be in order. All this is, of course, subject to the decisions of the Holy See, which has been well disposed in this matter for some time now. One thing is certain: we are not indefinitely committed to the use of Latin as a principle, and the increased interest in the liturgy makes the present time ideal for introducing those lawful changes which would be of immense benefit to all. Many earnest and zealous pastors have led the way in asking that the whole problem at least be studied, whatever ultimate solution may be reached in the matter, which is as delicate as it is important.*

At the present time much of this discussion is only theoretical because the liturgical language of the Roman Rite, with a few exceptions (some parts of Jugoslavia were allowed to use the Roman Missal in the vernacular—the Germans and Austrians are permitted to sing some of the people's chants of the Mass in the German language), is of course the Latin tongue.

The greater part of the liturgy as we know it today, as expressed in the liturgical books, has developed in this language and the doctrines enshrined in the liturgy have found noble expression in the stately words of the language once spoken throughout the Roman Empire. As a result, a special kind of Latin has grown up, which we call ecclesiastical Latin, with its own special vocabulary. A full and complete appreciation of the Roman Rite demands a thorough knowledge of the Latin of the Church and a feeling for the way that words are used by

* The idea of communication is bound up with the very idea of liturgy itself, and communication in our own day suffers to a certain degree even when we have a translation of what is being said. A translation will suffice for certain short formulae, but what of the longer hymns, antiphons, responsories and prayers that are intended to reach not the eye but the ear? Besides, to follow the service in translation does not secure participation, and participation is the crux of the whole problem. Effective participation cannot be secured by using Latin alone, and you cannot have a really living liturgy without full participation. We might have the essentials, but there is still no vital contact and hence no direct formation through the liturgy. It is true that we can and should for the time being teach the responses to the people, but that can only go so far. We pray awkwardly in any tongue other than our own. That is true of all of us but particularly of the laity who are by education and circumstance cut off from the use of Latin.

the Church in her prayers. The Latin tongue has shown itself marvellously adapted to the concise and felicitous expression of liturgical thought. It sets forth the doctrine of the Church in singularly appropriate words and formulae which often defy translation altogether or at least lose much when they are put into other languages. For that reason the priest and the future priest will never feel that he knows enough Latin; he will try as much as possible to think in Latin and to savor to the utmost the words and forms of the liturgy. Enthusiasm for the vernacular should never lead us to neglect the language in which the liturgy is actually celebrated. Those parts of the liturgy which are to be read aloud should receive special attention; we must read them intelligently and correctly so that even those who know no Latin will see that the words mean something.

The Scriptures in the Liturgy

The reading of the Scriptures and the singing of the psalms and other biblical canticles has always had a prominent place in the worship of the Church, because the Bible is the word of God and the Church is committed to proclaim the word of God. As we have seen, the worship of the Church cannot be anything else except the proclaiming of Christ who is Himself the Incarnate Word, the center and the key of the Scriptures.

This proclamation of the Word must first of all be a communication of the literal sense of the Bible, because the Bible is above all else the history of salvation and that is made known to us in and by the literal sense. To do otherwise would be to falsify the message of God and to misuse the Scriptures.

Through the medium of the word, read or sung, the Eternal Word of God is present in His Church and speaks to us; we are listening to His voice when we listen to the reading of the Scriptures.

It must be admitted that the Church in her worship feels free to give a special meaning to the Scriptures besides the literal or the spiritual sense—a meaning that we may call the liturgical sense. The worship of the Church uses the Scriptures not only to awaken and quicken our faith or to praise God in a becoming manner, but also to present doctrine in an appealing way. The truths of the Christian religion are expressed, illumined, explained, or at least recalled and suggested by these texts or by the way in which they are used. They are given a context and a setting certainly not intended by the original writer, but when they are used in that setting these texts are most effective. When on the first Sunday of Lent the words of St. Paul, "Now is the acceptable time, now is the day of salvation," are applied to Lent, they take on a new meaning in the context of this first Sunday that they did not have when St. Paul wrote them. He certainly was not speaking of Lent when he used these words. Yet how well they sum up the situation—Lent is indeed for us the "acceptable time" and the "day of salvation." Or, we may take as an example the use of the phrase, "The Lord is near at hand," which is used in the Advent liturgy; originally it was used by St. Paul to mean that the Lord is near to us—present in our midst and therefore our manner of living should reflect our consciousness of that presence. In the liturgy it is rather a reference to the Parousia, the Second Coming, and also in a lesser degree is an allusion to the nearness of Christmas. Again the words are given a meaning over and above what the writer intended. There is no intention of affirming that this is the literal meaning of these words or phrases, but that they do in fact express spiritual realities in a much better way than we of ourselves could. They sum up a situation or describe persons or things so well and so beautifully that they cannot be improved upon. The lessons used in so many feasts of our Lady, taken from the Canticle of Canticles or the Wisdom literature, are another example of this use. No one pretends that they are intended even indirectly as prophecies of our Lady. But they describe her so well and convey in poetic language something of her inexpressible beauty and spiritual riches.

The Masses in Passiontide use passages from the psalms

which in their setting are the voice of Christ in His Passion. Some of them may actually be at least indirect prophecies of Christ, but they do not all belong to that class. Yet in their setting they at least make us think of Christ and they become descriptions of Him and reflections of the state of His mind. The use of these psalms and other Scripture texts in the liturgy gives greater fullness, richness and resonance to the presentation of the event or person that the liturgy is commemorating or recalling. That is the purpose they are intended to achieve and they do it admirably.

Liturgical Formulae

The liturgy abounds in brief and simple formulae of prayer, in acclamations which give expression to the faith of the people or the praise of God or to petitions of one kind or another. Most of these come down from the Jewish liturgy, or at least go back to apostolic times. The simple concepts they embody have won them popularity in all liturgies and make them beautiful and moving expressions of the unanimous sentiments of the faithful. The principal ones are the following:

Amen—This is a Hebrew word which was used in the Temple services, signifying consent, approbation, approval, augury for the future, or affirmation. In the last sense we often find it used by Christ in His discourses: "Amen, Amen I say unto you." St. John in his Apocalypse, St. Peter in his letters, and the ancient Christian writers use it as an affirmative conclusion in doxologies and in deprecatory formulae: "To him be glory and power unto ages of ages, Amen" (Tit. 3:15).

Amen was used in the primitive liturgical service in response to the forms of blessing and prayer, which usage the Church has retained for all time at the conclusion of the priest's prayer and in general after all important formulae used in worship.

The most striking use of the word, dating from the sub-Apostolic era, is as a response to the great Eucharistic prayer (the Canon or Anaphora) where it is an act of faith in the efficacy of the sacramental words and in the real presence of Christ on the altar. According to St. Augustine it means that thereby the people *subscribe* to what has been said.

Alleluia—This is another Hebrew liturgical formula passed over into the Church which can be translated as "Praise to God." By Christians and Jews alike the *Alleluia* was ever considered as an acclamation of triumph. St. John tells us of hearing it in Heaven—a sound like the rolling of thunder. The Church began to use it very early as a kind of responsory for the so-called *Alleluia* psalms and particularly for the chants of Easter time.

During the fourth and fifth centuries the *Alleluia* was extremely popular among the ordinary Christians. It was sung by sailors at sea, by workers in the fields, and by soldiers in battle. It was used even at funerals where it was associated with the joys of Heaven to which the departed soul had gone.

In the liturgy there grew up a musical setting for the *Alleluia* which was one of the most beautiful and artistic in the chant. The Middle Ages developed the *Alleluia* into the Sequences which derived their name precisely from the fact that they were continuations (*sequentia*) of the *Alleluia* chant.

Deo Gratias—Like the Amen and *Alleluia, Deo Gratias* is a biblical formula often used in the Gospel and in St. Paul. It has passed into liturgical and extra-liturgical use as an expression of thanksgiving and, in general, of appreciation to God for all He has done. We meet it in the Acts of the Martyrs as a cry of greeting by the martyrs in the face of death. The African Christians made use of it as a war cry, and St. Augustine exhorts them not to abandon it. With the monks and ordinary Christians as well it was a greeting to one another within the house, and a normal response to something that was told them, signifying that they had heard. That is the best explanation of its use in the liturgy.

Kyrie Eleison—(Lord have mercy). We frequently find this simple invocation in the Old as well as in the New Testament, and even in pagan writings. As a liturgical formula it was first used in the East, where it is recorded in the Apostolic Constitutions. Etheria Sylvia found it in use in Jerusalem, but remarks that in her country the Latin form was used, not the Greek. By the fifth century it had been introduced into Rome from where it passed into Gaul.

The variant form *Christe Eleison* was added by St. Gregory. It had already been prescribed for the Office by the Benedictine Rule where it was followed by the *Pater Noster*. From this it passed into the Roman Office where it begins the *Preces* and into the Ritual, leading to the various litanies that we find there. The *Christe Eleison* was also very popular as an ejaculatory prayer in some parts of Europe during the Middle Ages.

The *Hail Mary*—The "angelic salutation," as it is called in many modern languages, is known to us under the simpler form of the Hail Mary. It is a prayer that has developed considerably from the first words spoken by the angel. The words of Elizabeth, "blessed art thou among women and blessed is the fruit of thy womb," were added at an early date to the actual greeting used by the angel, and that is the part that we usually find in the antiphons of the Breviary and Missal. The holy name of Jesus was added in the fourteenth century and the entire last part, "Holy Mary Mother of God," only in the sixteenth century. It is interesting to note that the first part differs widely in content and expression from the second: whereas the first is an objective contemplation of Mary as she is, her dignity and her holiness, the second part is almost exclusively a prayer for ourselves, with little more than a passing reference to the Blessed Virgin. Thus we can see preserved for us in this one prayer the difference in outlook between the first centuries and the late Middle Ages. The Hail Mary did not come into general use until the twelfth or thirteenth century. With the new revision of the rubrics it will as such disappear altogether from the Office, though a portion of it is used as an antiphon.

The *Gloria Patri*—At first this was a simple development of the baptismal formula, made into a doxology with the addition of the Hebrew expression "*in saecula saeculorum.*" It is perhaps very ancient, but it comes into prominence with the Arian controversy, when it was often used as a profession of faith in the equality of the persons: "*Gloria Patri et Filio et Spiritui Sancto et nunc et in saecula saeculorum. Amen.*" In that form it has continued to be used in the East, but the churches of the West adopted the "*sicut erat*" about the fifth or sixth century. Pope Damasus is usually credited with introducing it into the Office as a conclusion to each of the Psalms (fifth century).

Outside of the liturgy it enjoyed great popularity among the people, particularly during the Middle Ages—a fact that explains its use in the rosary and, to a certain extent, in other devotions. It serves the twofold purpose of being a doxology and a profession of faith.

The Apostles' Creed—The Apostles' Creed, while very ancient, does not go back to Apostolic times in its present form. It was drawn up to serve as a résumé and a profession of the faith for those about to be baptized. That is why it is in the singular; each candidate, speaking for himself, recited it before his baptism. The Baptismal Creed was thus part of the liturgy: the candidate had to recite it aloud in the presence of the congregation as an integral part of the rite of baptism. Though containing the teaching of the apostles, it was not composed directly by them nor in their lifetime. Originally known as *regula fidei* (or *veritatis*), *tessera*, or *sacramentum*, it was called *symbolum* by the third century.

The Apostles' Creed is the product of a rather long development and apparently it is the result of a combination of two formulae: the Christological, starting from Jesus Christ, the Son of God; and the Trinitarian formula, starting with the Lord's command to baptize. Such a creed was in use at Rome during the second century, with the Christological part much more developed than the rest, possibly in opposition to the gnostic heretics who denied the reality of the Incarnation, the suffering and death of Christ. It was this Creed, slightly more expanded, that finally prevailed throughout the West. The present text appears as such for the first time in the sixth century in Gaul, from where it returned to Rome in the ninth century.

Throughout the Christian centuries the Creed has retained its place in the rite of Baptism and in the life of the Church. It has been at once the great formula of faith and the ground plan of systematic instruction in the main truths of religion. Recited first of all at Baptism, it is frequently recited during life by Christians as a kind of watchword; during the Middle Ages it served as a weapon against the demons, and still forms part of the rite of exorcism. Admitted into the Office only in the eighth or ninth century, the Creed will now disappear from it entirely with the new changes.

Liturgical Gesture

Language is not confined to words; we express ourselves by actions, not only of the hands but by the entire body. Words reach the ear primarily, whereas actions of the body reach the eye first of all, but have great effect upon the whole man—often they are more effective than any words. Normally, however, they both work together to express the full range of thought and sentiment. It would be surprising then if both forms did not find a place in the liturgy of the Church, and if the Church were not to have added to the formulae the expressive and rich symbolism of the actions of the human body. All such movements are included and comprised under the name of liturgical gesture—a term which sounds clumsy in English, but unless we use the more correct term, ceremonial (which is confusing), we must be satisfied with it.

There are an extraordinary number of such gestures. Some are more-or-less the imitative and natural expression in act of the ideas contained in the words accompanying them: hands are extended to protect and bless, the knee bends in adoration, and so forth. Or words will have existed long before the action that now accompanies them. In the latter case the gesture serves to underline the importance of the words and to bring them into greater prominence. The word has suggested the act. If we examine the ceremonial of the Mass we see that the lifting of the chalice at "*accipiens et hunc praeclarem calicem*," the signs of the cross during the Canon, and many other such actions were not originally part of the rite but were a later comment-in-act upon the texts.

On the other hand, there are many gestures which once stood by themselves but with the passing of time have been fitted with formulae which express in words the ideas which the action was originally left to convey by itself. During the Middle Ages and particularly in Frankish lands it became almost a principle to have every action accompanied by a formula. Twice in the Mass the priest now says prayers to accompany the kissing of the altar, but for many centuries he kissed it without saying anything. Again, when the priest washes his hands he says the *Lavabo*; originally and for many centuries he said nothing, as the bishop still does when he washes his hands at the throne. These are cases where we may say that the act suggested the formula that goes with it.

The actions and positions of the body during prayer are so many and diverse that for the sake of convenience it will be best to give some kind of unity to their treatment here by grouping them according to the characteristics that they may possess in common with others related to them.

(1) *Sacramental actions*, which would include the imposition of hands and the sign of the cross.

(2) *Gestures and actions used during prayer*, such as standing at prayer with hands extended or joined together, kneeling and genuflection, turning towards the east, prayer with raised eyes.

(3) *Penitential gestures:* kneeling, prostrations, bows, striking of the breast.

(4) *Actions of offering:* the elevation at the end of the Canon.

(5) *Actions indicating reverence or brotherly love:* the liturgical kiss, incensing, bows and genuflections.

(6) *Actions done for convenience sake:* the sitting position, washing the hands, presenting and receiving liturgical objects.

(7) *Processions.*

The Imposition of Hands. The first and most important of all the liturgical gestures is also the most ancient, going back even beyond apostolic times to the Jewish Church. The "laying-on of hands" (*cheirotomia*) was regarded by the Jews as a symbol of the transmission of power, strength, authority, and blessing. Numerous passages in the Old Testament show us this. The hand is a symbol of man's activity, the means by which help is given; for these reasons it becomes a natural symbol of blessing and of priestly activity in general. It was natural for the Apostles to use it in their turn, and the "Acts of the Apostles" speaks of the imposition of hands as the means of ordaining the ministers of the New Testament and of imparting the power of the Holy Spirit in Confirmation. But it was not confined to these sacraments alone: in the early Church hands were laid upon the catechumens as part of their preparation for Baptism, during the administration of the Last Anointing and the sacrament of Penance, as a part of the Eucharistic rite. (The hands were held over the *oblata* during the consecration prayer in the Mass of a newly consecrated bishop.)

Besides what we might call the exclusively sacramental use of this gesture, we see it used extensively in many other rites that were not sacraments. With the development of these other rites we find the laying on of hands used in the consecration of virgins, in the blessing of abbots and later on of abbesses, in exorcisms, in the Canon of the Mass, in many blessings. Indeed the very term "*benedicere*" in ancient and mediaeval writings is a synonym for imposition of the hands. When we say imposition of hands we do not mean necessarily that both hands were used or that the hands were necessarily laid upon the person or object concerned. They might be extended over or pointed towards these persons or objects, instead of being laid upon them.

The meaning of this gesture varied according to the rite—sometimes it showed that a person was chosen or designated for a certain office and endowed with the power or authority that went with the office—or it symbolized and conferred the blessing of God, showing that the person was consecrated to Him. It might even be a kind of symbol of heavenly blessing to come, or the sign of purification from sin and deliverance from demoniacal possession. The gesture at the *Hanc Igitur* would seem to be unique in indicating that the *oblata* is to become the victim of expiation for the sins of the world. While it is often made in silence, the imposition of hands could be just as frequently accompanied by a formula of prayer indicating its meaning. It is interesting to note that from the beginning it was an action reserved to ecclesiastics—to bishops above all, and later to priests, deacons, and exorcists, but never to laymen.

In modern times it survives in the sacrament of Penance in the form of the raising of the hand in absolution, which is a modification of the ancient laying on of hands. The anointing in Confirmation and Extreme Unction is a form of "laying on of hands" quite different from the ancient. In Confirmation we see still another way of laying on hands: the bishop stretches them out towards those to be confirmed.

The Sign of the Cross. The sign of the cross is closely associated with the administration of the sacraments and to a much greater extent with all the other sacred rites. It is certainly the most characteristic and familiar gesture employed in the entire liturgy. A perpetual reminder to the Christian of the source of his redemption, it is the sign of his deliverance and the symbol of his hope. Its use is as ancient as it is widespread. The earliest references to the sign of the cross indicate that by the third century it was already long associated with the Christian name and profession. Tertullian's classic passage on the sign of the cross shows that it was the great "popular devotion" of the third century Christian, an instructive gesture that had its roots in Apostolic times. No action, no matter how important or how trivial, whether it was setting out on a journey or putting on one's clothes, coming in or going out, sitting down to table or lying down to rest, was begun or completed without making the sign of the cross on the forehead. (*De Corona Militis,* III.) In another less well-known passage from St. Cyril of Jerusalem we encounter the same testimony to the ever-present sign which sanctified all the Christian's actions, the least as well as the greatest. (Catech. XIII, 36.)

The sign of the cross that is spoken of in these passages and in others of the patristic period is not the large sign now familiar to us, but the little sign made on the forehead or the breast or other parts of the body with the thumb or index finger. It survives now, if we except the sacraments, only in the sign made at the beginning of the Gospel or the opening words of Matins. But for many centuries it was the only way of making the sign of the cross and it was usually made upon the forehead. The Greeks called this signing of the forehead the *sphragis* or seal, and the *symbolum.* The Latin referred to it as *signum, signa-*

culum or *trophaeum*—all expressive of its role as a mark or seal, or a sign of victory.

About a century later we read of the signing of the breast along with the forehead. This additional rite seems to have begun in the East from where it passed on into Gaul and then into the Roman ritual of Baptism where it still remains.

The large sign of the cross which is so familiar to us was rather late in coming. No one is certain how old it really is, but its first definite appearance in history was in the tenth century when it appears as a monastic practice. By the thirteenth century it was the accepted way of blessing oneself. For a long time it was made with the three middle fingers—with the thumb and little finger joined together—from the forehead to the breast, then from the right to the left shoulder. With the passing of time the extended hand replaced the three joined fingers and instead of going from right to left the hand went from the left to the right shoulder. It was only with the reform of St. Pius V that the present practice was officially introduced into the liturgy.

The custom among the Orientals of making the sign of the cross with two fingers (thumb and index finger joined together) had its origin in the sixth century as a protest against the Monophysite heresy. Others began to use the three first fingers joined together as a symbol of the Holy Trinity or of the Holy Name (IXC—*Jesus Xpistos Soter*—each finger representing one of the letters). This custom passed into the liturgy in some parts of the West and for a time it was the usual manner of making the sign of the cross among the people. But it did not last; we find the Easterners in the eleventh century reproaching the Latins for using the open hand for blessing themselves instead of using the three joined fingers. In the West the Pope alone to this day uses the three joined fingers in giving his blessing.

The words which accompany the sign of the cross are the most ancient, as we might imagine. But other formulae were used in the past and some still survive in the liturgy. The forms

"Adjutorium nostrum in nomine Domini," "Deus in adjutorium," "Dominus nos benedicat," and others are accompanied by the sign of the cross. One formula very often used in the Middle Ages, *"Ecce Crucem Domini—fugite partes adversae, vicit leo de tribu Juda, Radix David, Amen,"* a kind of exorcism or a prayer to ward off evil spirits, is still retained in one present-day Ritual.

An ancient rubric directed that whenever the word "bless" was found in the text in any form, the sign of the cross should be made.

There is an exceedingly rich variety of meanings in the sign of the cross as it appears in the liturgy. In Baptism it is the mark of Christ, a sign that the baptized belongs to Him entirely; hence we find it not only on the forehead but on the breast and the shoulders. And in the last anointing each one of the senses receives the mark of the cross which acts as a seal securing the whole man for Christ and marking him as His property. Whether made upon the forehead with the thumb or upon the whole body with the open hand it becomes a profession of faith, a proclamation in act of the belief that "Jesus is Lord." "Already [the catechumen] bears the Cross of Christ upon his forehead and does not blush at the cross of his Lord." (St. Augustin, *Tract in Joannem,* XI, 3.) As the above quoted prayer of the Ritual indicates, it is also *an affirmation of the power of Christ over evil spirits*—"Behold the Cross of Christ—flee ye enemy spirits, *etc.*" For that reason it finds a place in exorcisms. It frequently acts as *an invocation of God's grace,* grace that is asked to good effect through the infinite merits of Christ's passion and death represented by the cross. Hence its frequent use in the administration of the sacraments and other rites. (The custom of making the sign of the cross in the pouring of the baptismal water which is accompanied with the Trinitarian formula "In the name of the Father and of the Son and of the Holy Ghost" may explain the reason why the sign of the cross is made at the end of the other longer Trinitarian formulae used in the Mass: the Gloria and the Credo.)

Because the cross is the source of all blessing the sign of the cross becomes itself a *blessing for persons and objects*. It is a tangible way of indicating that the person or object signed with the cross is made holy, set aside for God, consecrated to His service. Whenever the words, "*benedicere, sanctificare, consecrare*" appear in the liturgy, the concept they represent is, as it were, translated into deed by the sign of the cross.

The principle contained in this practice was not always applied as it should have been; forgetting that "*benedicere*" also had the meaning of giving glory and praise to God, men began to bless themselves whenever the word appeared without stopping to ask whether it was appropriate or not. So at "*Sit nomen Domini benedictum,*" at "*Benedictus qui venit in nomine domini,*" and at "*Benedictus Dominus Deus Israel*" the rubrics prescribed and continue to prescribe the sign of the cross. (The sign of the cross at the beginning of the *Nunc Dimittis* and the *Magnificat* are an extension of the sign made at the beginning of the *Benedictus*. It is not there because they are gospel canticles, as some have attempted to explain it.)

Postures for Prayer. The posture taken for prayer is always of considerable importance. In line with what has been said about the part that the body plays in worship, it has ever been regarded as the outward expression of the inner sentiment of man towards God. So much is this true and so closely is the posture of the body related to the disposition of the soul that it directly affects the prayer itself and is almost inseparable from it. Men naturally and instinctively fall into certain attitudes and postures when they call upon God.

Prayer said standing and with arms outstretched. We associate kneeling so much with prayer that we find it strange to think of prayer said standing. Yet that was the most common posture for prayer in antiquity and even to this day it is regarded as the most solemn manner of praying known to the liturgy, which reserves prayer on the knees for penitential seasons and for those parts of the service which call for humble adoration. Even in the latter case kneeling was introduced very late under the influence of changed attitudes in such matters. The classical position for the priest, and very often for the people, is standing. It expresses the idea of attention, watchfulness, and respect. Standing brings home to us an awareness of our dignity as Christian men, ennobled with the liberty with which Christ has set us free, that we are the children of the Resurrection. It was this last consideration which prompted the legislation that there was to be no kneeling (in public prayer) during the entire Easter season nor on any Sunday, and which survives to this day in the custom of standing during the *Angelus* on Saturday and Sunday afternoons, and during the *Regina Coeli* every day during the Easter season.

The first Christians continued the Jewish custom of standing at prayer, a custom which is frequently referred to in the Gospels. (Matt. 6:5; Mark 11:25; Luke 18:11.) Like the Jews they stood with uncovered heads and extended arms. With the coming of Christianity the ancient posture took on new meaning; for them it symbolized their new dignity, that of God's children, set free from sin and its slavery who could now stand before God and lift their eyes and arms to Him who was revealed to them in Christ as their Father. The characteristic picture of the early Christian is the *orante* found in such profusion on the walls of the catacombs; it represents him standing erect with eyes and arms raised up to heaven. That this was the ordinary posture of all the faithful at prayer during the first centuries is witnessed by many of the contemporary writers. By the twentieth Canon of the Council of Nicaea the already ancient custom became a law. The liturgy has preserved this position for us in somewhat modified form in the posture assumed by the priest during those parts of the Mass when he stands at prayer. And while they no longer extend the arms in the form of a cross, the people too stand during the orations at solemn Mass, during the singing of the Gospel, and again at solemn Mass during the Canon, kneeling only during the Consecration. Outside of Mass both priest and people stand during the more solemn parts of other services. At one time they stood even during the singing of the psalms. To this day pews are unknown in the older churches of Europe and even chairs are rare. The ancient monastic rules ordered that the monks stand during the singing of the psalms. In later centuries a ledge, appropriately called *misericordia*, or misericord, was placed on the under side of the choir stalls so that the monks, while not exactly sitting, could nevertheless have some relief from standing during the long offices. The canons in the cathedrals sat down for the psalms, and the *Ceremoniale* made this the rule. But the older compromise between sitting and standing is still retained in many monasteries and convents.

There was a further reason why the priest should stand at prayer and that was his office of mediator or spokesman for the people before God. It was always considered proper that a mediator should stand; St. John Chrysostom says that standing is a sign that one is doing a liturgical action (act of worship). The priest does not sit, but stands, for standing is a sign of liturgical action. The earliest representation of the Mass that we have, in the cemetery of St. Calixtus, shows the priest standing with hands outstretched over the table of sacrifice, which indicates the antiquity of the present discipline in this matter. The only priestly act performed while sitting is the sacrament of Penance, and (by bishops) the sacrament of Confirmation. The standing position is the normal one for all priestly acts. (Priests also sit during the reading of the psalms when they recite the Office in common, which has become regrettably rare in the West.)

If the standing position has survived to a great extent, the same cannot be said of the gesture which so often accompanied it in Christian antiquity, the extending of the arms in the form of a cross. It was precisely this resemblance to the crucified which made this gesture so popular among the Christians; lifting up the arms was known to the Jews and pagans, it is true, but when Christians used it they thought of Another who stretched out His arms on the cross for the world's redemption. "We do not only lift up our arms but we stretch out our hands, and in the likeness of the Lord's passion, praying, we praise the Lord Christ" (Tertullian, *De Oratione*, 14). St. Ambrose says, "You should represent the cross of the Lord when you pray" (*De Sacramentis*, VI, 4). In this he gave a touching example himself; his biographer tells us that on his deathbed the saint prayed with arms extended in the form of a cross. And his contemporary, St. Maximus of Turin, ever a precious source of knowledge about Christian antiquities, explains to his people that they are urged to pray with arms extended because by doing so they "proclaim the passion of the Lord" (Hom. II, *De Cruce Domini*, PL, LVII, 342).

The custom fell into disuse in popular practice, perhaps because of the spread of the later custom of praying with joined hands. But it survives in the Mass where it is associated with the most solemn and more ancient parts: the orations, the Canon, and the *Pater Noster*. It survives, too, outside the liturgy in the ascetic practices of certain religious communities where curiously it is often joined with the kneeling position, instead of the standing position observed in Christian antiquity. (In the rite of some religious orders the celebrant extends his arms wide in the form of a cross after the Consecration. This was a widespread custom in the Middle Ages adopted deliberately to call into remembrance the thought of Christ on the Cross.)

Another primitive observance was that of turning towards the East when praying, whence Christ, the Morning Star, "*Oriens ex alto*," was expected to come. It was always more an Oriental than a Western custom, although for a time it gained force in the West through the Byzantine influence, especially in the seventh and eighth centuries. For a time the churches were deliberately designed so that the congregation faced the East, and the celebrant when he prayed often turned in that direction. Later on, when the consciousness of the immanence of the Second Coming very largely had died out, this custom fell into almost complete disuse at least officially, although it was a practice of private devotion during the Middle Ages.

The practice of raising the eyes to heaven, inherited from the Jews, was common among the early Christians. Tertullian alludes to it and it seems that the *Sursum Corda* was for a long time a command to raise the eyes as well as the heart. It was a natural gesture in any case and its survival outside the liturgy as well as in it was to be expected. Actually it is prescribed at various points in the Mass; most often it is no more than a glance, but at two places a longer look is prescribed. It expresses the sentiments of adoration of God and filial confidence in His loving care for us.

Prayer upon the knees. If the preferred attitude for prayer in the liturgy is standing, kneeling is not thereby excluded. In fact it is prescribed at certain times, where it is always a sign of penance or of profoundest adoration. In private prayer it is of course the normal attitude, going back very likely to Apostolic times. It, too, is a natural expression of man's attitude towards God and is associated with times of crisis and deepest feeling in the spiritual life. We read of Christ praying on His knees during His agony, of St. Stephen on his knees when suffering martyrdom, of St. Ignatius of Antioch kneeling in the same circumstance.

In the liturgy the deacon echoes the ancient invitation to kneel before prayer on penitential days. The people kneel during the oration, during the entire Canon after the Consecration and even during the *Pater* of the requiem Mass; they kneel also at the Consecration in a solemn Mass and when they receive Communion, as well as during Benediction and at the singing of certain invocations and certain verses of some of the hymns—the "*Veni Sancte Spiritus*" in the gradual for Pentecost Sunday, the verse "*O Crux Ave, Spes Unica*" in the hymn "*Vexilla Regis.*" The reason for kneeling varies: sometimes it is a sign of penance, at other times a sign of mourning. Or it may be a mark of adoration and extraordinary reverence, as when we kneel before the Blessed Sacrament when it is borne in procession, or during the verse "*O Crux Ave, Spes Unica.*" Often it is a sign not only of penance but of the intensity of our supplication, as, for example, kneeling during the Litany of the Saints.

For a long time it has been the custom for the faithful to kneel during the greater part of the low Mass, but that is not prescribed nor would it even seem desirable. The more important parts of the Mass should be marked by a significant change in position, e.g., standing during the Preface and *Pater Noster*, kneeling during the Consecration and Communion.

The Hands Joined in Prayer. The hands joined in prayer is a gesture that we associate so much with prayer that we are likely to be surprised to find that it came into usage at a late date. It is an interesting example of the way that actions which have their source and their symbolic meaning in civil life may become associated with the sanctuary and with religion. The joined hands expressed originally submission and loyalty to a feudal chief; vassals placed their joined hands in the hands of their lords on the day they swore allegiance to him. (Newly ordained priests still do this before their bishop when making the promise of reverence and obedience.) By the twelfth century it had become the usual way of holding the hands at prayer.

Striking the Breast. Striking the breast as a sign of sorrow and contrition seems to have been an ancient practice among pagans as well as Jews. The heart was regarded as the seat of affection and feeling and consequently of guilt. To beat the breast was a way of striking at the source of the guilt. It appears to have been carried over quite naturally into Christian practice and was associated in due time with the *Confiteor* said before the confession of sins. Now it finds a place in many rites where allusion is made to sin—in the *Confiteor*, during the *Agnus Dei* and so on.

Genuflection. Bending the knee is a gesture that in itself goes back to pre-Christian times. It was an expression of the sense of guilt and the position taken when making a petition, but above all it was an attitude of adoration and worship. As such it was used as a salutation to the statues of the gods and also to "divine" rulers and even to representations or portraits of rulers. For this reason the early Christians avoided this attitude and certainly did not genuflect to any human being or to his picture or statue. As time went on the gesture lost its religious associations and became a mark of courtesy to the ruler—much as it is today in England, where for certain ceremonial occasions it is the custom to drop on one knee to kiss the sovereign's hand. In time this was not only permitted by the Christians but even adopted into their own lives—as a mark of respect to the altar, to relics, and to images of our Lord and the saints. It was even adopted as a sign of respect to the bishop. Much later the genuflection became again what it had started out to be in pagan times: an act of worship and adoration. In the eleventh century it became the custom to genuflect to the Blessed Eucharist in the tabernacle. As it is now, the genuflection is used sometimes as a mark of honor and reverence when made to the bishop, the altar, and the crucifix; but it is mainly thought of by us as an act of adoration—so much so that although genuflecting to the bishop, altar and cross is more ancient than genuflecting to the Blessed Sacrament, the former now seems out of place to us (and actually in this country the genuflection to the bishop at Mass has largely disappeared—a good example of interpretation and adaptation of rubrics) and we tend to associate it exclusively with the divinity. Genuflecting at Mass is a late mediaeval addition, introduced about the fifteenth century.

Bows. The bow or inclination of head and shoulders is a rather natural sign of submission, veneration, and respect when directed to men or to objects; towards God it is a mark of adoration and of humble supplication. This form of showing respect and reverence is very ancient in the Church, and for a long time supplied the place now held by the genuflection in our own day. (To this day the genuflection is unknown in the Eastern Rites; its place is taken by the profound bow.) Yet the bow is still prescribed at many places in the liturgy where it not only expresses the sentiment of adoration or reverence but, like so many other actions, intensifies it.

The Liturgical Kiss. As a sign of brotherhood and as a mark of reverence and respect, the use of the kiss is very ancient, as the letters of St. Paul and the writing of the early Fathers testify: "Greet the brethren with a holy kiss" (Rom. 7:16). That it was a liturgical rite in the time of St. Paul we cannot be sure, but it certainly had become so by the time of St. Justin. At first it was a real kiss, bestowed upon the lips; it remained so until the thirteenth century, and at Mass the kiss of peace was given not only among the clergy but among the laity as well—men to men and women to women. In the thirteenth century, under the influence of the Franciscans, it became an embrace and that embrace in time became stylized and finally confined to the clergy. Before the last stage in its development was reached, the kiss was transmitted among the people by means of an "*instrumentum pacis*" or "*pax brede*" (a paten, a book, or a tablet). Even that led to abuses and was finally confined to the clergy.

The kiss of peace was also given to any one who became a member of the Christian family. It was bestowed upon the newly-baptized as a sign of admission to the brotherhood. It was also given by the bishops to newly-consecrated bishops, to the newly-ordained clergy, to the newly-confirmed (very likely the origin of the *alapa* still given at Confirmation), to the newly-professed monks by the community, to the penitents reconciled to the Church and so forth. This mark of welcome to the ranks of the clergy is still bestowed at consecrations and ordinations.

As a mark of reverence and respect, the Christian clergy and people from very early times kissed the altar and the book of the Gospels. Later on they kissed the holy oils, the paten at Mass, the sacred vestments and, in general, anything given or received in the liturgical rites.

The kissing of the hand is a very ancient mark of respect to bishops and, later on, to priests. It survives to this day in the kissing of the bishop's ring (it is really to his hand that the kiss is directed, whether he wears his ring or not). As late as the eleventh century people kissed the hand of the priest at Communion. The kissing of the bishop's ring (when it is done at all) at Communion is a survival of that.

Another mark of respect to bishops and priests was the kissing of the feet. That, in time, was restricted to the pope, and has largely died out.

Processions. The practice itself is a very natural and universal one, known to all religions, pagan as well as Christian. It has about it the spontaneous character of a triumph, and for Christians the symbolic association of the march to the Promised Land.

Processions have entered greatly into the liturgy and are associated with many of its rites. Some of them have been curtailed considerably from what they once were, and in general we do not have as many as they once had, nor do we hold them as often. Still, in recent decades we may say that they have been coming back into prominence, at least in certain places.

The best-known processions and those still most widely practiced are, of course, the Eucharistic processions: Forty Hours, Corpus Christi, Holy Thursday. Then there is the procession of the Holy Oils (in cathedrals) on Holy Thursday; the funeral procession, the *Asperges* on Sunday before high Mass, the procession of the palms and, naturally, the procession (very much restricted indeed) of the celebrant and sacred ministers to the altar for high Mass. Less well-known and practiced, unhappily, are the Rogation procession and the procession on Candlemas Day. Outside the liturgy there is the practice, much observed in many places, of the May procession.

Of the Eucharistic processions, the oldest is that of Holy Week. Corpus Christi comes next, having become general in the Church during the fourteenth century. This is the most popular of the processions—a community affair in Europe, at least until very recent times. Most unhappily, it has been allowed to lose much of its splendor and impressiveness among us. The procession of the Forty Hours came in with the devotion itself in the sixteenth century.

The procession of the Holy Oils came in during the tenth century; it is Gallican in origin and in turn was borrowed from the Byzantine Rite.

Some authors maintain that the oldest procession known to us is the funeral procession, which survives, in part at least, into our own day.* It began with the carrying of the body to the cemetery and, from the fourth century on, to the church. The clergy and people accompanied the body, singing psalms and carrying lights. For many centuries it was more like a triumphal procession than one of mourning. The lights have survived in the form of the candles now placed around the coffin. Originally serving a practical purpose (funerals were held at night), the lights soon took on a symbolic meaning—representing the light of faith or the divine Light. In our own day this procession usually takes place by motor car and the clergy accompany the body only from the church door to the altar, and after Mass back to the door again. The funeral procession has thus been considerably reduced.

The procession at the *Asperges* was at one time a most solemn affair; it was intended to commemorate Baptism, and the sprinkling of the holy water was a reminder of the sacrament which for a long time was received only at Easter. Easter itself was recalled on Sunday; hence the practice of commemorating Bap-

* Righietti, *Storia Liturgica*, IV.

tism on Sunday. It originated in France during the eighth century and spread from there throughout the Western Church.

Outside of Paschal time the antiphon *Asperges me*, which has given its name to the ceremony, is sung with the first verse only of Psalm 50. While the psalm itself is penitential, it has of course been selected for the sake of the antiphon which refers to the purity of heart with which we should approach the sacred mysteries about to be offered in our midst. During Paschal time the *Asperges me* gives place to a most appropriate antiphon taken from Ezechiel, the *Vidi aquam*. It refers directly to the water pouring from the side of Christ which is the great symbol of Baptism. With it goes one of the chief Easter psalms, *Confitemini Domino quoniam bonus*. This antiphon more directly reminds us of the baptismal associations of this ceremony.

The entrance of the clergy for high Mass should be rather solemn, as far as circumstances permit, especially for the pontifical Mass in a cathedral on great feasts. Even such an entrance falls far short of the splendor of the papal entrance of bygone days, from which the present procession is descended. An imposing cortege, made up of priests, seven deacons, seven acolytes, servers with lights and incense, accompanied the pontiff to the altar. This custom was maintained not only by the pope, but by the greater bishops of the Latin Church until the Middle Ages, and still survives on one day of the year, Holy Thursday, when in all cathedrals the bishop goes to the altar surrounded by a slight modification of the same elaborate escort.

The procession of the palms on Palm Sunday is also very ancient, going back to fourth century Jerusalem and spreading from there through the West (again by way of the Frankish domains). It commemorates the triumphal entry of Christ into Jerusalem and is altogether a joyful affair. Revised in the new Ordo for Holy Week, it is treated in detail in a later chapter.

Rogation days are days of special prayer and penance, to ask God's blessing upon the fields and upon the fruits of the earth. The procession for the occasion is penitential, and the prayer that goes with the procession is the Litany of the Saints. It originated in Gaul in the fifth century, going from there to Italy and on throughout the West. This should be a very popular procession in rural areas and an excellent way of Christianizing the daily life and labors of those who till the soil, and of calling God's blessing upon them.

The Candlemas Day procession is treated elsewhere.

Processions are traditionally associated with song; it is part of the movement essential to a procession. "To take part in a procession" means singing while walking, and not to sing is being half-hearted about it all.

CHAPTER 6

Liturgical Music

The musical setting of the liturgy should not be regarded as something more-or-less accidental or optional, as though the liturgy could get along without it. The full and complete liturgical action demands a musical setting because it is essentially a celebration, and a celebration is inconceivable without song. Furthermore, the words of the liturgy and the musical setting in which these words are presented are so closely bound up together that the liturgy depends upon the music to give it proper expression without which it falls short of its purpose. It is possible to have the liturgy without a musical setting, but the texts are not seen in their full meaning without the melodies that clothe and interpret them.

Sacred music, being a complementary part of the solemn liturgy, participates in the general scope of the liturgy, which is the glory of God and the sanctification and edification of the faithful. It contributes to the decorum and splendor of the ecclesiastical ceremonies, and since its principal office is to clothe with suitable melody the liturgical text proposed for the understanding of the faithful, its proper aim is to add greater efficacy to the text in order that through it the faithful may be the more easily moved to devotion and better disposed for the reception of the fruits of grace belonging to the celebration of the most holy mysteries.*

From the above it is clear enough that Church music is not a matter of indifference, or a matter of taste, still less a kind of preoccupation of a group of aesthetes. Indeed, it is apparent that in the mind of the Church *the music as such is secondary*, that it has no other aim except "to clothe with suitable melody the liturgical text proposed for the understanding of the faithful." This means that the text is what counts, and the whole aim is to get the text across to the people.

The ideal church music must always be that which in no way draws attention to itself; like a handsome dish on which a delicious food is placed, its only purpose is to serve up the meat upon which we are to feed our minds and hearts. Having done that it retires without ever trying to make us—even for a moment—forget what it presents to us. We are not in church to listen to a concert, even a sacred one, but to penetrate the meaning of the texts and draw from them light, understanding, and grace. We may wish it were otherwise perhaps, but our wishes are not the norm of what should be done in the public worship of the Church. The music is not supposed to act upon us directly; we are not to expect that it will entertain us or thrill us, or even that we will find it, in itself, to our liking. It is concerned only with one thing: the restrained, disciplined, orderly and effective presentation of the words of the liturgy. We must not expect from it or ask from it more than that. On the other hand, we do have the right to demand that it does not distract us from our high purpose, that it does not in any way obscure the sacred text, that it be not cheap or trivial or theatrical, eccentric or sensational. That it had become all these things by

* *Motu Proprio* of St. Pius X (1902).

1902 no one would dare to deny. And there is an everpresent danger that it can become so again, whenever we forget the great principle enunciated by the same Pius X: "In general it must be considered a very grave abuse when the liturgy is made to appear secondary to and in a manner at the service of, the music, for the music is merely a part of the liturgy and its humble handmaid." *

The music, then, must be conceived as adding something to the words and actions: by lending greater emphasis to them, or by giving fuller expression to the prayers and praise contained in them. A psalm that is sung will be more effective than a psalm that is only recited, even to the point of sanctifying and edifying more than mere recitation, because the minds of the faithful are "more easily moved to devotion and better disposed for the reception of the fruits of grace." The pope himself has reminded us of this, but many are unwilling (unconsciously perhaps) to follow him and to assert confidently that the music of the Church has a sanctifying power. We are willing to ascribe that power to the liturgy in general or to the moving words of human speakers, but we stop short at ascribing it to any one of the arts, even the most spiritual of all. Yet we have the sure teaching of the Church that Church music *can* sanctify us by lifting up our minds and hearts to heavenly things, by removing what is distracting and worldly, by enabling us to participate more intensely and earnestly in the sanctifying actions and holy, life-giving rites. For example, Vespers that are well sung—sung, that is, with prayerful understanding and devotion—will definitely and infallibly sanctify us, and will do it far better and more effectively than many other things that we would perhaps more naturally expect to edify and sanctify. The Christian cannot engage in the worship of the Church without being a better man for it: his spirit of prayer is intensified; his mind and heart are raised to God; his will is stimulated to good; his faith and understanding are enlightened. In all of that music plays its

* *Ibid.*

part, especially when it is made to serve its great end: to clothe the sacred texts with suitable melody.

The same is true of the Mass: the singing of the texts adds something to them and to our understanding of them. It is an aid to contemplation and fosters the spirit of recollection and prayer. We need not be afraid to admit this view and follow it to its logical conclusion. The same Pius X said that "the active participation of the people in the solemn and public prayer of the Church is the primary and indispensable source of the true Christian spirit." This is but another way of saying that the music of the Church contributes to edify and to sanctify. This is not the teaching of some extremist or the view of a theorist, but part of the ordinary teaching of the Church.

The great role of Church music in general is, then, to serve the ends of the liturgy. Of all forms of music that which does this best is the Gregorian chant. The repeated statements of the popes on this point have certainly removed the matter from any or all controversy. After saying that sacred music should possess in the highest degree the qualities proper to the liturgy, especially sanctity, beauty of form and universality, St. Pius X in the *Motu Proprio* on Church music says that these qualities are found to an eminent degree in Gregorian chant. It is preeminently *the* sacred music, and all other music is good only insofar as it approaches the Gregorian. The official liturgical chant of the Roman Church is Gregorian chant. Needless to say other music is not excluded: polyphonic and modern music are even encouraged, but only on condition that they conform to the rules which the Gregorian exemplifies so well.

This is not to say that all chant, every single piece of it, is perfect—as music. Some pieces are naturally better than others. Nor does it mean that we have to *like* chant. As a matter of fact that consideration does not enter into the picture at all, although from the musical standpoint chant is regarded by those who are competent to judge as music of a very high order. It does mean that chant as a whole best serves the ends of the liturgy; consequently, the Church's official music is chant, and, all things being equal, it is the music that should be used the most. For one thing it must be admitted that in most instances it expresses what we want it to express better than any other music written for liturgical texts. If we want any proof for this we need only examine some of the compositions of well-meaning but really inferior craftsmen and compare them with the chant written for the same text. The great test of liturgical music is that it be fitting for its purpose, that it be fit to sing in church, that it be dignified and prayerful enough. That test has long been passed by chant and in most instances all that we need do is concentrate on doing the chant well. For it is unhappily true that the chant *can* be poorly done, run off mechanically, without heart or spirit, without understanding or love, just because it is required or because some bishop demands that the laws of Church music giving pre-eminence to chant be respected. That is not fair to the chant; we are not giving it a chance. Rather we must accept what the Church teaches about it and expend just as much time, care, and energy on it as we do upon the ceremonies, church furnishings, decorations, or the vestments. Nor need we feel that *only* chant should be used (although that would not be the great affliction that some imagine it would be). But if we keep in mind the first principle that the music is altogether ancillary to the liturgy, and if we overcome the idea that we are supposed to be entertained in church, or to entertain there, we shall not find it too hard to achieve the ideal; indeed we shall be anxious to have Church music that is above the criticism that it draws attention to itself.

It is precisely here that the chant excels—in its indifference to applause, to praise or blame from men. All that it is concerned with is praising God. It does not aim at arousing the emotions or reaching the mind or heart directly; it is altogether pre-occupied with God and with worshipping Him in a lowly and humble spirit. Penetrated with the thought of the majesty of God, it tries to set forth His praise in a manner worthy of

Him. So we may say that chant is *theocentric* rather than anthropocentric, that it is objective rather than subjective. Nevertheless, without aiming at it, chant does reach the minds and hearts of men, fills them with reverent, adoring awe and love, and does this far more effectively and permanently than any mere appeal to the emotions can ever hope to effect.

The great principle that must always guide us in dealing with the music of the Church is that it is above all else prayer sung and never music rendered. This will keep us from ever overemphasizing the music or concentrating on it for its own sake. For Church music is pre-eminently contemplative and it must foster and encourage the spirit of recollection, inspiring us to pray. There must always be an atmosphere of repose about it—a tranquility which is not of earth but of Heaven. This can be achieved only by a certain austerity, what may very well amount to a rigorous self-denial, a refusal to gratify our own tastes, to luxuriate in what we like or what appeals to us. The danger is that what we like or what appeals to us may be a distraction, leading us to forget the words altogether or to think that as long as we sing the proper texts we have done all that is expected of us—when in reality our duty is above all to interpret the texts. We are not merely to run through the texts but to linger upon them.

History of Sacred Music

From the beginning the Church has associated music with her worship. In doing so she was only carrying on a long tradition among Jews and Gentiles alike. The first Christians, coming from Judaism, brought with them the musical forms used in Jewish worship and adapted them to their own use. At the same time they were influenced by the music of the world in which the Church grew and developed, particularly the music of the Greeks, more varied and harmonious than the music used in Jewish worship. It is very probable that the chant used for the orations, the lessons, the psalms, the vocalization of the *Alleluia*, all came from the synagogue service, while the melodies for other chants were drawn in one way or another from the Greeks.

The favorite method of singing the psalms in the Eucharistic service was the responsorial: a cantor would sing a verse of the psalm and the people would sing the refrain. This process was repeated until the psalm was finished. The Canticle of the Three Youths in the fiery furnace, which is in our Missal to this day for the Ember Saturdays, with its refrain "*et laudabilis et gloriosus in saecula*," gives us an idea of how this was done. The people all joined in this response, making it with one voice.

This responsorial psalmody was the first to undergo considerable melodic development during the fourth century; borrowing their vocalizations from the Greek melodies, the soloists made their singing a real art. No part of this liturgical chant was as varied and rich as the chant of the *Alleluia*.

During the same century the antiphonal chant of the psalms was brought in from the East. This differed from responsorial singing in that the verses were sung one right after the other by alternate choirs. Or one choir (or group of people) would sing the verse while the other sang what we would today call an antiphon: a verse between each verse of the psalm.

During the fifth and sixth centuries this flowering of liturgical music continued in the Church. St. Gregory the Great is credited with gathering all this musical work together and putting it into order, to such an extent that the chant which existed before his time was nevertheless given his name and associated with him. The full extent of his work is not clearly known, but it is generally agreed that it was in the direction of organization rather than creation. A further great contribution of his was the establishment or reorganization of the Roman "*schola cantorum*" with a view to ensuring the worthy performance of the chant.

St. Gregory was primarily interested in the singing in Rome and more particularly of the papal liturgy, but his influence spread through Europe and the Gregorian chant was adopted by churches other than Rome. That was particularly true of the Frankish domains in the eighth and ninth centuries.

During the Middle Ages chant became more and more elaborate and artistic, less simple and more complicated than it had been at first. New forms of liturgical chant developed through the sequences, tropes and verses, which delighted the men of the mediaeval period. While many lovely melodies were composed during that time, it becomes increasingly clear that the decline of the Middle Ages brought with it a decline in the artistic power of the chant; the period of decadence set in. Many new ways of singing broke up the old unity and simplicity of the chant and the original rhythm was gradually lost and abandoned.

The growth and development of polyphonic music, in itself so beautiful and rich, helped to bring about the further decline of the chant, so that by the sixteenth century the Gregorian tradition was lost. One of the causes that contributed to this was the way the manuscripts were copied: the copyists abandoned the rhythmic signs in the texts and later on gave an arbitrary meaning to the duration of the different forms of the notes. The execution of the chant became intolerably heavy and ugly; all the grace and beauty went out of it. An attempt was made in the seventeenth century to rectify this by dropping notes which resulted in a general disfiguration. The only way to rectify the situation was to get back to the right text, which meant re-editing the chant on the basis of the oldest manuscripts. Only in that way could an unmutilated and undisfigured text be obtained. This was actually what the Benedictines of Solesmes did, and when they finished with their work, they offered it to the pope and gave up all rights to it. Pius X gratefully accepted their offer and this restored chant became the official chant of the Roman Rite.

By his *Motu Proprio* of 1903 the same pope outlawed all music that was too secular or unsuited for church use, and without imposing the chant exclusively, nevertheless set it up as the norm. Other music, whether polyphony or strictly modern, was to be admitted only when it partook of the spirit of the chant. By this action of the pope a tremendous amount of music, much of it good and even great *as music*, was declared unsuitable for church use. The real significance of this document, considered unbearably reactionary in many quarters, was that it reaffirmed something that had been forgotten and that badly needed restatement: that music is ancillary to the liturgy and that it must be kept in its place, a place which even if honorable is nevertheless subordinate.

CHAPTER 7

The History of the Liturgy

Apostolic Times

The word *Eucharist* by which the central part of the liturgy is known originated in the *blessing* pronounced over the bread and wine by our Lord at the Last Supper. The action which goes by that name is essentially the same which He did. Our purpose in the following pages is to show how the Eucharist as we know it developed from that rite which our Lord left to the Church to be done in memory of Him. The student will find it profitable to examine the early history of the liturgy for the light that it throws on the later development of the Eucharist.

The Mass grew within and out of the framework of a Jewish ritual meal which was in itself a "thanksgiving," an offering to God of what was about to be eaten. In that sense it was a sacrifice—*sacrum facere*. The Christian Sacrifice remains essentially a ritual sacrificial meal; one of its oldest and most beloved names is precisely *Coena Domini*—the "Supper of the Lord."

Our Lord took bread and blessed it—made thanksgiving, eucharist, over it—and followed that by doing the same thing over the wine. The word eucharist meant an act of praise or thanksgiving addressed to God for the food about to be eaten, and the blessing was at the same time an offering. Then our Lord broke the bread and gave it to eat, saying the words which identified the bread with His Body. The same was done with the wine. By the expression, "Blood of the New Testament" (or Covenant), He was in reality giving a new meaning to what the apostles and disciples as devout Jews would do in any case. The ritual supper now became the Lord's supper. By His words, "This is my blood of the covenant, which is shed for many for the remission of sins," He at once connects this meal with His passion and interprets the full meaning of that passion. His death and the blood that is to be shed are to be a sacrifice by which the new covenant of the Kingdom will be inaugurated. By giving them this bread (which is His body, about to be sacrificed for them) and this wine (which is His blood about to be shed for them) to eat and to drink, He thus associates them with Him in His passion and death and therefore in the covenant inaugurated by this passion; they are made thereby inheritors of the messianic Kingdom that is to come. This sacrifice-banquet is an anticipation of that Kingdom.

That is made more clear by the whole context of the Last Supper as it appears in St. Luke's narrative, where the references to the kingdom and the covenant are striking: "As my father has allotted a kingdom to me, so I allot a place to eat and drink at my table in my Kingdom" (22:29). (Allotted here means "devise by covenant.") And again, "I have longed and longed to share this paschal meal with you before my passion; I tell you I shall not eat it again until it finds its fulfillment in the kingdom of God" (22:15–16); or, "I shall not drink of the fruit of the vine again until the kingdom come" (22:18–19).

The words, "do this for a commemoration of me," indicate that this meal or supper will henceforth be a recalling or *anamnesis,* a commemoration of Jesus. As St. Paul so beautifully and meaningfully expressed it all, it was to be "a proclamation of the death of the Lord until he comes."

The intimate connection between this Supper and the Kingdom it prepares for and inaugurates is shown by the whole tenor of St. John's Gospel, although he gives no specific account of the institution of the Eucharist. "He that eats my flesh and drinks my blood *has* eternal life. *And I shall raise him up on the last day*" (6:54).

We have, then, at the Last Supper all the elements of a liturgy, and we can see the direct descent of the present day Mass from what He *did* and commanded His disciples *to do in memory of Him.*

There is the setting aside of the bread and wine, the Offertory: He took bread; He took the chalice.

There is the prayer said over the bread and the wine, the Blessing or Consecration: He blessed it (using the Jewish table blessing from which our Canon [*Anaphora,* Great Prayer] comes).

Then there is the Fraction: "He broke it,"

Finally there is the Communion: He gave it to His disciples saying, "take ye and eat."

These actions formed the nucleus and the core of all the Christian eucharistic liturgies from the beginning. Wherever we find accounts of the Eucharist in the first centuries as well as in the centuries that follow, this (with very few changes) is what His followers were always doing. They did it on the morrow of His Ascension; they did it three centuries afterward, and they continue to do it today. They did it at Jerusalem, at Antioch, at Rome; in Gaul, and in Ireland; and later on in Mexico and Canada. It is essential that we understand these features of the Last Supper, as they explain the subsequent development of the Eucharist within the Church: first of all the offering; then the great prayer of blessing and thanksgiving (always with the words that He used—the words of consecration); then the bread is broken and distributed and the wine is passed around. They are the symbol and the pledge of the union and fellowship of the faithful with Christ and with one another. From this many-sided action come the names by which the rite was known—the Eucharist, the Breaking of the Bread, the Communion.

The next mention that we find of the rite in the New Testament occurs in the early chapters of Acts. Appropriately and significantly we find it in the account of the primitive Christian community at Jerusalem. Worship was the center of their lives and the mainspring of their actions. They were a holy and consecrated people and among the features which marked their daily, wholly consecrated lives was their persevering "with one heart and mind" in the "teaching of the Apostles, the breaking of the bread, and the prayers" (Act 2:42). Later on in the same chapter we see that they were strong in the religious habits of devout Jews and continued to attend the Temple services; but when they met as the new *ecclesia*, as a Church, they gathered in the homes of their fellow Christians to do what Christ had done. Their ritual meal was now charged with associations coming from the Last Supper; what they did was truly "in memory of Him."

Further on in Acts we have an account of St. Paul's visit to Troas. Some years had passed by since the earlier community met at Jerusalem. Now, in a Greek city in Asia Minor, we find a gathering "on the first day of the week"; the purpose of this gathering is again "to break the bread." There is a festive character about the occasion, and on the whole there is more formality: there are "many lights"; it takes place on a definite day; St. Paul discoursed at great length and then broke bread in the middle of the night. There is little doubt that this is the same "supper of the Lord" done "in memory of Him."

These fragmentary and passing references in Acts are supplemented by the more complete and detailed account of St. Paul in his first Epistle to the Corinthians, which is very probably the oldest of the New Testament accounts of the Last Supper. St. Paul speaks of a meal which he calls "the supper of the

Lord" that proclaims the death of Christ until He comes again. There is no question here of introducing or promulgating something new; St. Paul merely reaffirms the meaning of the rite and recalls its origin and source. This indicates that the Church at Corinth is already doing what Christ did. For St. Paul this supper is done, in our Lord's own words, "in memory of Me," and it is a proclamation or setting forth of the death of the Lord until He comes again. It is not a proclamation made with words alone but a real, objective recalling and representation of the sacrifice of Calvary in the sight of God and man, and at the same time it involves a sharing in that sacrifice. St. Paul speaks of the blessing over the cup and the breaking of the bread and of the Communion in the Body and Blood of Christ that is involved in eating this bread and drinking this cup: "The cup of blessing that we bless, is it not the sharing of the blood of Christ? And the bread that we break, is it not the partaking of the body of the Lord?" (I Cor., 10:16).

The Supper of the Lord is, then, a sacrifice-banquet, and one of its effects is to unite the faithful not only to Christ, but to one another: a unity that is not only effected but symbolized in the one loaf which is a type of the one body.

There is evidence in both Acts and the Epistles of St. Paul that the Eucharist was preceded and accompanied by other acts which derived ultimately from the Jewish synagogue service. There were prayers, hymns, psalms, reading from the Scriptures, preaching—all intended to furnish the faithful with instruction and edification. There was also the kiss of peace. In the second century these preliminaries emerged as the "service of the Word" and in due time became the invariable introduction to the Eucharist proper.

Two other books of the New Testament besides Acts and the Epistle to the Corinthians influenced the theology and the vocabulary of later liturgical writing. They are the Epistle to the Hebrews, with its concept of the heavenly and eternal priesthood of Christ; and the Apocalypse, with its "heavenly altar" and the "Lamb standing as though slain." Both these works contain many references and phrases which in one way or another passed over into the liturgical language of later times and left their impress upon it, forming the background of the eucharistic language and greatly influencing the whole range of liturgical thought.

The Eucharist in the Second Century

The "riddle of the *Didache*" seems no nearer an ultimate solution now than it ever did. Its date of course greatly affects its value as a witness to Church life and liturgical practice in the sub-apostolic period. The first part of the second century is a likely date.

The later portion of this enigmatic work contains many liturgical directions: first about Baptism and fasting, then in greater detail about the Eucharist.

Whether all the prayers quoted are truly liturgical prayers or not they do appear to have eucharistic associations. In any case we see from chapter fourteen of the *Didache* that the weekly gathering for public worship on the Lord's Day has taken on the more formal character of an act of worship. The purpose of this gathering is to break bread and give thanks; it is preceded by a confession of sin "that your sacrifice may be pure," and that sacrifice is identified with the pure offering of which Malachy, the prophet, spoke. The offering is apparently in charge of bishops and deacons.

The prayers in chapters nine and ten are ancient and deeply mystical. There is a prayer for the cup and one for the broken bread—the first is closely related to the Jewish prayer over the cup but is given a Christian turn by allusion to Christ. The prayer over the bread contains the beautiful petition for the gathering of the Church from the ends of the earth into God's Kingdom, itself reminiscent of the language of St. John, and still touched upon in our modern Canon. Then follow short fragments, echoes no doubt of the prayers that accompanied the

Eucharist and marked by the strong eschatological flavor we associate with the very early Church. There is indication that the prayers used in the Eucharist are not stereotyped or set down; considerable latitude is allowed to the celebrant.

St. Clement's Letter to the Corinthians contains allusions to the Eucharist as the public service of all the members of the Church in which each has his part according to his rank. In many places the letter is colored by liturgical language and contains phraseology which has become familiar in the liturgies since his time. He seems to allude to the Preface and the Sanctus, and in the long prayer of chapters fifty-nine to sixty-one we hear echoes of the phrases used in Christian worship, or at least we can see a kinship between this prayer and the type of prayer which we find later on when the actual liturgical texts are set down.

St. Ignatius of Antioch refers to the Eucharist and its place in public worship. The "one Eucharist" is the sign of unity, and is not to be celebrated apart from the bishop. Scattered through his letters are references to the Eucharist: it is the common thanksgiving and prayer of the Church; it may or may not be separated from the *agape;* he speaks of the Eucharist as a communion feast upon the flesh and blood of Christ.

The *Apology* of St. Justin furnishes us with the first full account of the pre-Nicene Eucharist and is a most precious document. Indeed there are two accounts which, when we put them together, give us the scheme of the entire service:

1. Lessons: "memoirs of the Apostles" and "writings of the prophets."
2. Sermon by the "President."
3. Intercessions for all men, said standing.
4. "The kiss of peace."
5. The bringing to the "President" of bread and a cup of wine mixed with water.
6. Praise, prayer, and thanksgiving offered to the Father

through the Son and Holy Spirit. This is one prayer offered by the "President" and is extempore. The congregation answers it with an Amen.

7. The administration of the bread and cup to those present and the reservation for the absent.

The sketch which St. Justin gives us shows the Sunday Eucharist as separated from the *agape* and as preceded by the "service of the Word," which was known as the "*Missa Catechumenorum*" in later times. We see the beginning of the Offertory and the prominence of that prayer which we know now as the Canon. It is still extempore (in words) but follows a fixed theme: the commemoration of God's work in the creation and redemption of man.

The last writer of the second century to refer to the Eucharist is Irenaeus whose *Adversus Haereses* has several references to the Eucharist. He calls it "the oblation of the Church," "the new oblation of the new covenant," "the pure sacrifice." It is an offering of the first fruits of the earth as an expression of gratitude to God, and as sanctifying the creature. It was Christ who taught us this rite which the "Church receiving from the Apostles offers throughout the whole world to God." That rite included:

1. Offering of first fruits (bread and wine).
2. A Thanksgiving said over them.
3. The Invocation—(*Epiclesis*).

He refers to the benefits of Communion and is the first of the Fathers to refer to the "altar in heaven" to which the prayers and oblations are directed.

By the end of the second century we can say that the Eucharist has been separated from the common meal and has become a more formal act of worship: a Sacrifice. Already there is considerable theological development on the meaning of that Sacrifice, which is offered by the whole Church and expresses the unity of the Church.

The Eucharist in the Third Century

There is a great wealth of information in the third century about the Eucharist in the years preceding the Council of Nicaea. We cannot hope to dwell upon it all, but only to select certain parts of that information which can fill in the outline we are attempting to draw up.

In the East we have the testimony of Clement of Alexandria and Origen who tell us about that which was to develop into the Alexandrian Rite. Clement speaks in surpassingly beautiful language of the "mysteries of the Logos." The Eucharist is a Sacrifice, celebrated by Christ the High Priest, in which we are taught by Him and in which He prays for us. Clement alludes to chants, to hymns, to lessons, to the prayers of the catechumens and those of the faithful, to the sermon, to lights carried in the service, the Kiss of Peace, and, less clearly, to the Sanctus.

Origen, too, often refers to the Eucharist and makes a distinction between the liturgy of the catechumens and that of the faithful. He alludes to the psalms, insists on public prayer in church, quotes liturgical prayers, including the Our Father, and speaks of the attitudes assumed in praying. He alludes to the Sanctus, describes the Consecration, speaks of "the food sanctified by a word of God and prayer," and gives the outline of the *Anaphora* (Canon) which we find later, but more substantially, in the liturgy of St. Mark. He mentions a Communion antiphon, the sign of the cross, special vestments, possibly incense; the rite is altogether more ornate than any we have seen hitherto.

Dionysius of Alexandria gives some information about the way Communion was received and reserved, and he includes other details already mentioned by Origen.

Another source on Eastern liturgies is the second book of the Apostolic Constitutions, which gives a fairly complete outline of the liturgy of Antioch.

In the West, most of the information we have about the liturgy at Rome is given us by St. Hippolytus in his *Apostolic Tradition*. It contains a very ancient *Anaphora*, the only pre-

Nicene text of an unrevised eucharistic prayer that we have. He tells us that the Christian Eucharist is a Sacrifice that renews the Last Supper and the Passion of Christ. The offering of the bread and wine is united with that of the Last Supper. The prayer is an uninterrupted one; there is no Sanctus. It is not a fixed prayer, but an improvised one that follows a general theme and contains formulae which were later to become crystallized.

St. Hippolytus does not give us the whole Mass, but only the prayer recited by the celebrant. We can find traces of the later liturgical development of the Roman Canon in this primitive prayer.

Tertullian and Cyprian give us very detailed information about the liturgy of the Church of Africa, which some think may have been the parent rite of the later Gallican Rite that prevailed in certain parts of the West. There is the same division between the Mass of the Catechumens and the Mass of the Faithful we have noticed in other places and the same general outline of each which we find in Alexandria and Antioch.

We may sum up the information which we have about the first three centuries by saying that there was in those times a liturgy which was more-or-less uniform in outline, but fluid and elastic in its details. There was a fixed order for the Eucharist, and the ancient *Synaxis* or service of the catechumens had been attached permanently to the Eucharist proper. There was considerable liberty in making up the prayers, but they tended to a certain pattern with the passage of time. There were no liturgical books as we have today and certainly little or no formal ritual; nevertheless there was a tendency towards fixing the manner of doing and saying these things, so that from a certain uniformity there developed diversity and the great rites began to evolve.

The Eucharist in the Fourth Century

The fourth and fifth centuries have been called the golden age of liturgy. They are the years in which the great historic Rites assume the form in which they are preserved to our day.

The vast changes introduced by the coming of toleration under Constantine had effects beyond any man's power to foresee. These results stamped themselves upon the liturgy, expanding and developing and profoundly altering it. The growth of the Christian population brought about a corresponding growth and development in liturgical life and worship.

The first three centuries saw the fixing of the outline of the Eucharist; the pattern was established at that time. The following centuries saw enrichments of that pattern; the traditional worship was given scope for development while its core or center remained the same. Not only the rites themselves, but the doctrine which underlay these rites received a profound development. The point of view of the pre-Nicene Church was considerably modified and that modification found new expression.

The first change we may speak of is that of the fusion of the *Synaxis* (*Missa Catechumenorum*) and the Eucharist (*Missa Fidelium*) into one service. This took place gradually during the fourth century. The growth in the number of Christians brought this about because with the conversion of the Empire, there ceased to be any division between the faithful and the catechumens. All were now entitled to be present at the second part of the Mass as well as at the first. Other causes operated to produce this effect, but this was the most prominent.

We have an abundance of material about the liturgy of the fourth century. The Fathers, and particularly St. Cyril of Jerusalem, give us very detailed descriptions of the liturgy which they celebrated in Jerusalem, Antioch and Alexandria. (Unfortunately, we know less about the Roman Rite of this time than we do about any other.) From the fourth and fifth centuries we have not merely fragmentary allusions and incomplete references but whole liturgical texts. This age brought about the first sacramentaries and *euchologia*; the old rite had crystallized into different liturgies in different places.

This general crystallization of rites may be said to have begun with the writing down in a book of the prayers which until that time had been extempore. The great centers of Christendom influenced the bishops of adjoining dioceses and brought about different types of liturgy. Even then there was considerable latitude, because the types of liturgy emanating from these centers were fluid and not fixed. So we have, first of all, the Antiochene Rite, then the Alexandrine Rite, then the Roman Rite, and lastly the Gallican Rite. These are the four main rites (some would reduce the four parent rites to two), but many others developed from them which we call derived liturgies. The general rule is that rite follows patriarchate, but there are exceptions to this even in the patriarchate of Rome itself, where the old Gallican liturgy survives in a modified form.

The oldest of the rites is the Antiochene Rite, which in reality comes from Jerusalem and which is the parent rite of (a) the great Byzantine Rite, by far the most widespread of the Eastern rites; (b) the Chaldean Rite used in Persia and India; (c) the Armenian Rite; (d) the Syrian Rite. Our sources of information about the Antiochene Rite are the eighth book of the *Apostolic Constitutions*, and the writings of St. Cyril of Jerusalem, particularly his *Catechetical Lectures* and the *Pilgrimage of Etheria Sylvia.*

The Syrian Rite

The main source of information about the Syrian Rite or Antiochene Rite is the so-called Clementine Liturgy, which is preserved for us in the eighth book of the *Apostolic Constitutions.* It is not itself a service book but a private compilation; yet it appears to be based upon a rite in use at the time in the Syrian Church and at Antioch during the last half of the fourth century. Whatever may be said about some of the details it is generally conceded that we have here the parent rite of all the Eastern rites. It has further value in that it claims to be the first complete liturgy that has been preserved into our own day. The following outline will help us to see its essential features:

The Liturgy of the Word

Prayers, litanies.
Readings from the Old and New Testaments, each followed by psalms sung by cantors, except the Gospel.
Sermon.
Dismissal of each class of catechumens (four classes) with deacon's litany and bishop's blessing for each class.

The Liturgy of the Upper Room

Deacon's litany and bishop's prayer for the faithful.
Greeting of assembly and response.
Kiss of Peace with words and response.
Offertory: Washing of Hands; Presentation of bread and wine by deacons.
Fencing of Table by Deacon.
Greeting.
"Lift Up Your Hearts."
The Great Prayer of Blessing: Preface—Thanksgiving for creation and Providence; *Trisagion;* Thanksgiving for Redemption; *Anamnesis*—words of Consecration, Memorial and Offering.
Epiclesis.
Great Intercession (Our Father?).
Deacon's litany and bishop's prayer.
Elevation of the elements: "Holy things to the holy"; response, "Glory to God in the highest" (one verse only); "Blessed is He who comes" (Matt. 11), with the addition of the words, "God is the Lord and has appeared to us."
Communion, during which Psalm 33 is sung: words of administration, "The Body of Christ; the Blood of Christ, the cup of Life."
Deacon's exhortation and invitation to prayer.
Bishop's prayer after Communion, thanksgiving and intercession.

Bishop's prayer of blessing.
Dismissal by deacon.

This service took place in a basilica with an apse in which the bishop's throne stood; the building was pointed towards the East. The priests were seated around the bishop; the deacons stood by; the men in the congregation were on one side, the women on the other. What is described for us in the *Apostolic Constitutions* is the foundation upon which all the Eastern rites of the Syrian or Antiochene family were built; they all resemble it and, so far as we know, derive from it.

In the writings of St. John Chrysostom we can see that the liturgy he knew at Antioch and later at Constantinople is substantially the one described in the *Apostolic Constitutions* with a few changes and elaborations. Chrysostom himself is credited with shortening and re-arranging this rite which existed before his time; and it is this derived rite that is used in the Greek churches and which, translated into old Slavonic, was brought into Russia and the other Slav nations.

The many rites derived from the Antiochene liturgy did not all develop in the fourth century. They are very ancient, nevertheless, and are spread throughout the East except in Egypt, where the second great parent rite of Christendom had its origin.

The Alexandrine Rite

The Alexandrine Rite appears as early as the writings of Clement of Alexandria and Origen, but its source is the "Liturgy of St. Mark," who was considered to be the Apostle of Alexandria. The oldest text of this rite that we have is the *Prayerbook of Serapion*. This little document was discovered in 1897 and is an immensely valuable source of knowledge about the early liturgy.

The *Prayerbook of Serapion* is a collection of prayers for the use of a bishop and appears to have been compiled by or for Serapion, Bishop of Thmunis, friend of St. Athanasius. This prayerbook is the first to set down the text for those prayers said in the first part of the Mass. It provides us with a Sunday prayer which asks the help of God's grace for the faithful and that He send His Holy Spirit to enlighten them. Next is a prayer after the Homily, probably for the catechumens; then another, definitely for the catechumens; also a blessing for the catechumens who were undoubtedly dismissed at this point. The latter blessing is followed by the prayers of the faithful, intercessions for the sick, for the Church, for the fruits of the earth, for the bishop, priests, deacons, for all classes of people, *etc.* Each one of these prayers is concluded with a doxology: "Through Thy only begotten Son Jesus Christ in the Holy Spirit by whom is to Thee glory and power now and unto ages of ages. Amen."

The *Anaphora*, or Consecration prayer, opens in the usual manner with the words, "It is truly fitting and proper . . ." It is a true hymn of praise to God the Creator who sends His Son by whom we know Him and through whom, with the Holy Spirit, we come to the praise of God. Unlike Hippolytus, who leads directly up to the words of Consecration, Serapion first introduces the myriads of angels praising God and singing the Sanctus (which is in the form that we associate later with the Egyptian Rites). Taking up the cue from the word "full," the prayer resumes: "Full are the heavens and the earth, O Master, fill also this sacrifice . . ."; and thus it leads up to the words of institution which differ somewhat from that in the present Roman Rite, yet approach those reproduced in the *De Sacramentis* of St. Ambrose. Like all the later Eastern Rites it begins with St. Paul's expression, "Who on the *night* before He suffered" instead of "the day," and it uses the terms "likeness of the body" and "likeness of the blood," which expressions have here a technical sense and certainly do not mean what they would mean to us. The prayer for the gathering together of the Church that follows, with its comparison of the bread scattered on the mountain in the form of wheat and now gathered together, closely follows a similar prayer in the *Didache*. It also shows the influence of Syrian thought and that certain concepts were general and widespread, forming everywhere a universal pattern. The *Anamnesis* is not as developed as that of the Roman Rite; it too corresponds closely with the later Egyptian form. Serapion's Epiclesis is an invocation of the *Logos* rather than of the Holy Spirit, and this is another Alexandrine characteristic. For the first time in the history of the liturgy there is an intercession for the dead which takes place after the Consecration, as in the modern Roman Rite. The intercession for the living and the usual doxology close the prayer.

The *Anaphora* is followed by a prayer for the breaking of the bread, for the communion of the clergy, a blessing of the people, then the Communion of the laity and a Postcommunion.

The importance of the *Anaphora* of Serapion lies in the fact that it presents us with the text of a prayer that comes down from the earlier period before the liturgy became crystallized into different rites. Yet it already has certain characteristics of the later Alexandrine Rite and shows the direction that the liturgy was to take in Egypt.

Fragments discovered in upper Egypt in 1928 carry us a little further upon the way of the development of the Egyptian liturgy and bring us a little closer to the liturgy of St. Mark. The Der-Balyzeh-Papyrus, as these fragments are called, contain:

1. Common prayer of the Church (what we call prayers of the faithful).
2. *Anaphora* with *Trisagion*, Invocation, Words of Institution, *Anamnesis*.
3. Prayers for fruitful Communion.
4. A short Creed.

The most important part is the *Anaphora*, which resembles that of Serapion and yet comes closer to the liturgy of St. Mark. It represents in places an advance upon the language and thought of Serapion and moves nearer to the later Alexandrine form.

Other ancient texts have been discovered which add to our information. Various allusions in the writings of the Egyptian fathers of the fourth and fifth century show that during this time much development took place in the furnishing and equipment of the churches: the altar, sometimes of wood and sometimes of stone, the seat of the bishop and the clergy around the altar, the sanctuary, the vestments, particularly the *pallium* or *omophorion*, and the deacon's stole and the albs, are all mentioned. SS. Athanasius and Makarius both refer to the reading of the lessons, the responsorial singing of the psalms, the Gospel usually read by the archdeacon but occasionally by the bishop. The catechumens are dismissed before the Eucharist proper begins; the deacons direct the prayer of the people, which is made for various intentions; the offerings are presented and offered and what is left over is distributed among the clergy and the faithful; the Sanctus has a permanent place in the liturgy. There is an Invocation (*Epiclesis*) not only of the Holy Spirit, but of the *Logos* as well. The bread is broken before Communion; the Our Father gradually found a place in the liturgy; the formula, "Holy things to the holy," was used from the fifth century, and there is a ritual dismissal. In our own day the Alexandrine liturgy is used by the Copts and the Ethiopians.

The most striking characteristics of all Eastern liturgies, as we find them in their most primitive form, are: the Invocation of the Holy Spirit to consecrate the bread and wine; the Litanies of Intercession by the deacon; the variable *Anaphora*, and the position of the Kiss of Peace. The Eastern rites are also distinguished for their "corporateness"; there is much greater participation. The litanies and the chants are answered by the people and the deacon continually stimulates active participation, acting as a link between priest and people and as a guide and director.

The Liturgies of the West

By the sixth and seventh centuries there were two liturgies in the West, derived ultimately from the synagogue services and the action of the Upper Room. Like the other rites of Christendom, they took a form peculiar to the section of the ancient empire in which they grew and developed.

Contrasted with the liturgies of the East, those of the West, and especially the Roman Rite, were marked by brevity, sobriety of expression and terseness. The Eastern rites were more diffuse and flamboyant. Besides these distinguishing marks, the Western rites were remarkable for the many variable parts which were called the Propers; this was in contrast to the more fixed liturgy of the East.

The Gallican Rite. Until a few years ago the Gallican Rite was thought by some to have been Oriental in origin; others thought that it was the natural development of the old original fluid rite among the barbarian peoples. Now the opinion is gaining ground that it was originally the old Roman Rite modified in the regions to the north and west and affected to a certain extent by Oriental influences.

The Gallican Mass began with a chant composed of antiphon and psalm which corresponded to that which became the Introit of the Roman Rite. The greeting to the people was "*Dominus sit semper vobiscum*" (as it is in the Mozarabic Rite); this was followed by the *Kyrie* and the *Benedictus* or the *Gloria:* only then was the Collect sung. There were three lessons, one from the Old Testament, two from the New Testament, the Epistle and the Gospel, the last followed by a chant, the Epistle by the canticle *Benedictus es*, the Gospel by a psalm. The reading of the Gospel itself was accompanied by great solemnity. Then came the Deacon's Litany to which the people answered.

The offering of the bread and wine was made by the people during which a chant was sung. At this time the names were read and the Kiss of Peace given; there were two orations, one for the Kiss of Peace and one after the reading of the names. All this corresponds to the usages of the Ambrosian and Mozarabic Rites and this leads scholars to the view that it was done in the earlier Roman Rite as well.

The Preface, called *contestatio* or *immolatio*, followed; it was very long and wordy and there were a great many of them. As in the Roman Rite it ended with the *Sanctus*. A prayer beginning Vere *Sanctus* made the transition to the Consecration, which followed nearly the same form as the Roman. There was no *Anamnesis*, but a prayer "*post mysteria*," which looks very much like an *Epiclesis* in the Oriental style. The Fraction and Immixtion took place immediately, accompanied by a chant called the *confractorium*.

As in the Roman Rite before St. Gregory, the *Pater* with its prelude and conclusion was recited after the Fraction. Communion was preceded by a blessing and here again we have a usage which at one time seems to have taken place in the Roman Rite as well. The Communion itself had no special rite, except that the Communion antiphon was nearly always taken from Psalm 33, another ancient and, it would seem, universal usage. There was a Postcommunion and then with the words, "*Missa acta est*," or "*In Pace*," the service was concluded.

This rite in one form or another was spread all over western Europe (Spain, France, England, Ireland, Scotland, the Rhineland). It was displaced by the Roman Rite largely through the activity of Pepin and Charlemagne who insisted that the Roman Rite should be observed throughout their domains and who sent to Rome for a sacramentary that would be used as a norm. They did succeed in imposing the Roman Rite upon the Franks and before very long the old Gallican Rite died out. But not completely. Those who were charged with copying the Roman service books managed to incorporate many Gallican elements, so that the rite that they created and which spread through Europe and returned to Rome was neither Roman nor Gallican, but Romano-Gallican, a combination rite rather than a pure one.

The Gallican Rite differed considerably from the Roman Rite in many ways. There was a barbaric splendor about it foreign to the more austere Rite of Rome and central Italy. The ceremonial was more solemn and elaborate; the prayers longer, more diffuse, more ornate and more varied; there was a larger place given to the dramatic, the symbolic and the sensible. Some of these were no doubt the effects of Oriental influences, which appear to have been considerable, but at the same time they seem to have been congenial to the temper of these people in whom so many different elements were mixed. We note in this rite and its observances the strong subjective strain so characteristic of the Germanic people in later times.

The Milanese or Ambrosian Rite, used today chiefly in the Archdiocese of Milan, was once regarded as a survival of the Gallican Rite. It now appears to be a sister rite of the Roman, many of the usages of which it has retained even though they are no longer in the Roman Rite itself. Although it was to a certain extent subjected to Oriental influences, it remained substantially not an Oriental or a Gallican, but a rite of the Roman or Italian type.

The rite is marked by the reading of three lessons at Mass, which seems to have been the primitive Roman custom, by the Litany of the Deacon to which the people respond (on certain days), by the ancient formula used in the Kiss of Peace, by the Offering of the bread and wine made by the people (at least in the Cathedral), by the many variable Prefaces, by traces of a variable *Anaphora* instead of a fixed one, by a longer Doxology at the end of the Canon. The Fraction comes before the *Pater Noster* and there is no *Agnus Dei* except at requiem Masses; a "*confractorium*," or fraction chant, is sung instead. Baptism is by immersion; the Divine Office and the liturgical year differ considerably from those of the Roman Rite.

The Mozarabic Rite. Now confined to one chapel of the Cathedral of Toledo in Spain, the Mozarabic Rite is all that is left of the ancient Visigothic liturgy that once spread all over Spain. Its main interest for us lies in the fact that it is at least related to the Gallican Rite, if it is not indeed the last survival of this once so widespread liturgy. All evidence points to a common origin.

Like the Ambrosian Rite it has three lessons in every Mass, but it has the further peculiarity of a chant psalm with *Alleluia* after the Gospel. The ancient Litany of the Deacon and the people survives in this Mass, the *Pater* follows the Fraction and the people answer Amen to every phrase. There are many Prefaces, called *illatio* in the books of this rite, very long in comparison with ours, but all leading to the *Sanctus.* The Consecration comes sooner after this Preface than ours and the *Anaphora* or Canon is in the Gallican style, that is, made up of different prayers. The ancient formula, "Holy things to the Holy," is still said just before Communion, and the Communion chant is the one once used by everyone, "Taste and see" (Ps. 33:8).

The Office is remarkable in that it still preserves the ancient distinction between the Office recited in a monastery and the Office recited in a secular church. There is no Prime and Compline in the Office said in the cathedral, for example, and most of the time the Office consists only of Matins (morning prayers) and Vespers (evening prayers), as it was everywhere at one time. Terce, Sext and None are said only in Lent. Furthermore, the Office is not said every day but only on days when Mass is said, and there are many more a-liturgical days in the Mozarabic Rite than in the Roman Rite.

The Roman Rite. The earliest official Roman service book that we have is the Gelasian Sacramentary (sixth and seventh centuries). This means that we are at a great disadvantage in dealing with the early Roman liturgy, particularly in its formative years when it began to emerge from the original universal fluid rite used throughout Christendom. There is a wide gap between the prayer of St. Hippolytus and the Roman Canon as it is found in the Gelasian, many centuries about which we know tantalizingly little. Yet we are not altogether in the dark, at least not as much as we were some decades ago. The close agreement between the *Anaphora* in the *De Sacramentis* of Saint Ambrose and the Canon in the Gelasian permit us to see the former as an earlier stage in the development of the latter, which brings us back to the fourth century. And there are other pieces of information, fragmentary indeed, that throw a little more light on the whole rite.

The first Christian community at Rome was Greek and Greek-speaking, as the list of bishops, the letter of Clement, the Shepherd of Hermes and other documents show us. Justin's description of the Mass in the second century, already discussed in these pages, is at the same time a description of the Mass as it was celebrated at Rome where it was written. The next source of information that we have is the *Apostolic Tradition* of Hippolytus, which can be taken to represent in its general outline and structure the practice in Rome at his time. Though this prayer exercised no direct influence on the later Roman Canon, it follows in the second part the sequence of ideas which is familiar later on: the narrative of the institution of the Eucharist, the *anamnesis* of the offering of the gifts, the prayer for fruitful Communion. The opening greeting of our present Canon, "*Dominus Vobiscum*" and the "*Sursum corda*" with its answer, are found here for the first time.

Among the fragments of information between the time of Hippolytus and the time of Ambrose we find that the communicant answered "Amen" to the formula used by the priest in giving the sacred bread, that the Gospel is read by the deacon, and that he also reads publicly the names of the contributors of the bread and wine at the Offertory, that the *Sanctus* is sung, that the Body and blood of Christ is consecrated by the prayer of the priest, that the bishops baptize and pray at the Eucharist for the coming of the Lord, that the Lord's Prayer is used and most probably introduced by the formula familiar to us, that the Kiss of Peace occupied its present place (immediately before Holy Communion), and that the communicant answered "Amen" to the formula used by the priest in giving Communion. All this information we owe to St. Jerome. Another ancient writer commenting on the psalms uses words that closely parallel some of the phrases of the modern *Nobis quoque*. Still another alludes to the phrase *Summus sacerdos* in the liturgy when speaking of Melchisedech.

The fourth century *De Sacramentis* of St. Ambrose corresponds so closely with the first text of the Roman Canon that there we are justified in arguing that it represents substantially the *Anaphora* used in the Church at Rome in his day, the more so when we recall that Ambrose came from Rome and is supposed to have introduced Roman practices in Milan. The Canon of St. Ambrose is very likely the Roman Canon in an earlier stage of development. There are striking divergencies and the contents of some parts are arranged differently. All in all it represents a less developed eucharistic terminology than the Gelasian Canon. The divergencies show the influence of Eastern ideas; they may have been current in Rome but more likely they were current in Milan when Ambrose went there, and he did not disturb them. The parallels suggest that the present Roman Canon goes back substantially to the fourth century and earlier.

One more document adds to the incomplete information left us about the development of the Roman Rite before the sixth century, and that is the letter of St. Innocent I to Decentius, Bishop of Gubbio, A.D. 416. The purpose of the letter is to urge this Umbrian bishop to hold fast to the liturgical traditions of the Roman Church. From Innocent we learn that the Kiss of Peace should take place after the Canon, that there is a prayer corresponding to our Secret Prayer in which the offerings are commended to God, that the names of those who have offered are announced during the Canon and that the consecrated Eucharist, called *fermentum,* is sent from the bishop's Mass to the priests throughout the city.

From the *Liber Pontificalis* we learn that St. Leo the Great added "*sanctum sacrificium, immaculatam hostiam*" to the Canon, and that St. Gregory in the sixth century added "*diesque nostros in tua pace disponas*" to the *Hanc Igitur.* St. Gregory himself tells us that he placed the Lord's Prayer in its present position.

These facts are all that we know about the Roman Rite prior to its emergence in the first official service book. We do have information contained in the Leonine Sacramentary, but that does not contain the Canon, and it is with the Canon and its development that we are most concerned.

As we had occasion to say before, the Roman Rite encroached more and more upon the territory of the Gallican Rites, although it was in turn considerably modified by them, until by the late Middle Ages, in spite of survivals here and there, the Roman Rite was the most widespread in the West.

The Roman Rite at the time of St. Gregory the Great. By the time of St. Gregory we may say that except for some accidental modifications, the Roman Rite was substantially the same as it is today. It had undergone development and taken on the characteristics which give it individuality and distinctness: simplicity, terseness, austerity; economy of words, structure and ceremonies.

First Part: Mass of the Catechumens

The Introit (sung by two choirs as the clergy enter).
The Kissing of the Altar.
The *Kyries.*
(The *Gloria in Excelsis*).
The *Dominus Vobiscum.*
The Collects.

(The Prophecy: an Old Testament Lesson).
The Epistle.
The Gradual or Tract.
The *Alleluia*.
The Gospel (with procession, lights, incense).
The Dismissal.

Mass of the Faithful

The Offertory (collection of bread and wine; spreading of corporal; preparation of elements; offering of gifts; singing of psalm).
The Secret Prayer.
The Dialogue.
The Preface (variable).
The *Sanctus*.
The *Canon Actionis*.
The Lord's Prayer (with introduction and conclusion).
The Fraction (Immixtion, Kiss of Peace).
(The *Agnus Dei*).
The Communion (singing of Communion psalm).
The Postcommunion.
The Dismissal by Deacon.

The rite that is described here is that of the high Mass or more precisely the bishop's Mass, celebrated in the traditional setting—upon an altar facing the congregation with the chair or *cathedra* of the bishop placed in the semicircular apse behind the altar and surrounded by the seats of the priests. The deacons stood during the service, as did the people who filled the nave, with the women on the left and the men on the right. We see in this rite the greatest expression of community solidarity and harmony—true corporate worship, the clergy and people gathered around their bishop and joining with him in a united offering of praise and sacrifice. From every point of view this was ideal—the expression of the Church's unity and solidarity.

For a long time this form persisted in the West and is still used to this day in the Eastern rites. Each had his part to play—the bishop, the priests who surrounded him and concelebrated with him,* the deacons who regulated the service, the choir which sang the more difficult chants, and the people who followed the action and responded to the prayers.

The outline of the service was simple, clear-cut and even austere, at least by comparison with the Oriental rites. The presence of the papal court contributed to making the worship of the Church at Rome more splendid, and many ceremonial details were added during the seventh and eighth centuries; however, we do not get the impression of elaborateness so much as one of ordered splendor. The rite retains much of the sobriety and restraint which we associate with the austere Roman genius.

This was the liturgy of Rome and the surrounding towns, hardly known elsewhere until a great event of the eighth century took place that was to spread it through Western Europe, and at the same time to transform it greatly in the process. That decisive action, which has influenced the entire subsequent history of the Roman liturgy, was the request of the king of the Franks that a copy of the Roman Sacramentary be sent to Aix la Chapelle to serve as the basis for the liturgical reforms which he intended to impose upon his domain. As a result of Pepin's rather high-handed action, the Roman Rite acquired a new sphere of activity, but at the same time it was to be greatly influenced by its new environment. The old Gallican Rite affected the rite which replaced it (not by papal command but by royal fiat, it should be noted). Those who copied the Roman Sacramentary, which was sent to them as a model, did so most faithfully: they included many things which were really proper and peculiar to Rome, such as the reference to stational

* Concelebration did not mean saying the words of the prayers as newly ordained priests do at their ordination nowadays. Rather, the priests merely stood around the altar; the bishop said the prayers and the priests received Communion from his hand.

churches; but at the same time the copyists added many of their own prayers and ceremonies. The result was to be a profound alteration of the Roman Rite—so much so that we can no longer in strict accuracy speak of a Roman Rite, but of a Romano-Gallican Rite. The ceremonial was elaborated, as we can see for example in the development and multiplication of incensations, much restricted in the pure Roman Rite. Prayers were multiplied throughout, and the original clear-cut structure of the Mass became overlaid with a multiplicity of details which have persisted to this day: the prayers at the foot of the altar, extra collects, prayers during the Offertory, during incensation and before Communion. Not only were these prayers additions to the old Roman Mass, but they differed vastly in tone and spirit as well as in style and expression from the Roman formularies. The new prayers were often intensely individualistic and subjective, wordy and verbose, mostly concerned with the dispositions of the celebrant rather than with an objective statement of doctrine. This was the time that saw a great increase of those peculiarly Gallican prayer-forms called "*apologia sacerdotis,*" long avowals of sin and guilt to be used as private devotions by the priest. They reflect that almost unhealthy preoccupation with the condition of the soul which was a characteristic of Frankish piety. The struggles with the later Arian heretics had their repercussions in the Gallican prayers; in a desire to stress the equality of the persons in the Trinity, the Gallican prayers tended to be addressed to the Trinity itself or to the Son, in contrast to the Roman prayers which were almost always addressed to the Father.

These changes and additions by no means exhaust the Gallican contribution to the formation of the rite that we call the Romano-Gallican. There were also many changes in emphasis and outlook that vastly affected the whole mediaeval way of looking at the liturgy and nearly all of these had their beginning in the Frankish territory. The tendency to look upon the liturgy as the special preserve of the clergy—something which they did for the faithful while the laity looked on; the emphasis on the juridical concept of the Church as an institution governed by the clergy rather than as a community of the redeemed; the accent upon the mysterious in worship which led to saying silently words and prayers that were once said aloud, itself a by-product of the concept that the Mass was an epiphany where God manifested Himself to men rather than an offering by the Church of a sacrifice of praise to God—all these ideas were imported into the Roman Rite from Gaul and the northern lands and found a resting place there. In general, it must be said that an all-embracing subjectivism invaded the liturgy at almost every point.

Even the architecture and arrangement of the churches, which in the Roman Rite had contributed so much to emphasize the community aspect of worship, were now modified under the influence of practices that had found a ready field for development in the lands beyond the Alps. The altar became quite often a shrine for relics or the bodies of saints and this had led to pushing it back against the wall; in cathedral churches it became necessary to take the bishop's throne out of the apse and place it to one side, a most unhappy disarrangement which threw everything off balance and out of focus. The seats of the clergy were brought out in front of the altar and placed in rows along the sanctuary wall facing one another. As a consequence of all this the sanctuary became deeper and the altar farther away from the people. The practice of the priest facing away from the people was another development largely unknown to the Roman Rite of the eighth century; it also developed in Frankish lands.

Another change introduced into the Roman Rite in France and Germany at that time was the use of unleavened bread and of thin white wafers or hosts instead of the loaves of leavened bread used hitherto. All the expressive symbolism of breaking the bread, of sharing the loaf, disappeared with the use of leavened bread. Communion was no longer given into the hands of those receiving—that became difficult to manage with small hosts; it was now placed on the tongue and that in turn brought about kneeling to receive it instead of the old standing position.

Along with all these changes, and often closely related to some of them, came the new way of explaining the Mass to the people, called the allegorical method. Begun by Alcuin and developed into a fine art by Amalarius, this approach to the Mass was to see the sacred action not so much as the offering of Christ's sacrifice made by the Church to God, but as a kind of sacred drama—a religious mystery play which portrayed the life and particularly the passion of our Lord. The actors in this play were the clergy; and the people were the spectators. This allegorical explanation of the Mass underwent greater development later on during the Middle Ages, but it had its beginning at this period.

Thus the transplanting of the Roman Rite into the Frankish domain had effects that no man could have foreseen, and when in the tenth and eleventh centuries the rite returned to the place from which it had originally come, so much had been added and changed that, while the main outline was still recognizable, it was overlaid with so many encrustations that it was in reality a new thing. Even in the center of Christendom the old primitive Roman Rite disappeared and the new Romano-Gallican took its place. The city of Rome had ceased to produce copies of the liturgical books and the clergy welcomed the Missals, Sacramentaries, Pontificals and Rituals which came from the North. By the thirteenth century the official Missal of the Papal Court, as well as the Breviary, was one based upon those books which came from beyond the Alps. Largely through the influence of the Franciscans these were the books that in turn went out of Rome into the West.

By the end of the Middle Ages Latin had ceased to be the language of the people, and knowledge of it was restricted to the clergy and the educated laity. As a result the people were no longer able to follow the service, not even by reading a Missal as they can do today, since printing was not invented until the late fifteenth century. Inevitably they were cut off by this from active participation in the prayer of the Church. Nor was participation in the sacrifice by going to Communion very common. The reception of the Eucharist had declined lamentably—so much so that the fourth Lateran Council had to make it an *obligation* to go to Communion once a year. That such a law was necessary tells us much about mediaeval religious practice, even if we had no other evidence. Then, too, the singing of the chants of the Mass exclusively by the choir, a practice that was made necessary by the difficulty of the music, deprived them of another means of participation, even supposing that they could read the words and the music, which most of them could not. The decline of the sung Mass, brought about largely by the popularity of the low Mass, was a further cause of the loss of the sense of corporate worship. More and more as the Middle Ages drew to a close, the people had become spectators, looking on at a service that they could not comprehend, or engaging in their own private devotions. The ancient concept of the Mass as an activity of the whole Church was certainly obscured when it was not lost altogether. Men had very largely lost sight of the idea that the Mass is the Supper of the Lord and regarded it almost exclusively as a propitiatory sacrifice—something which they need not even attend, though indeed they were not lacking in devotion to assistance at Mass. And here we have another characteristic of the mediaeval devotion to the Mass—the faithful thought of it as something at which they were *to assist* rather than something in which they were *to participate*.

Another cause which contributed to this one-sided view of the Mass as a drama to be looked at, was the widespread diffusion of allegorical explanations which did duty for sound theological expositions of the true meaning of the Mass. The Mass was regarded as a kind of play depicting the life of Christ and especially the events of His Passion. Everything in the Mass

Sacrifice of Abel and Melchisedech
(Mosaic in the Sanctuary of San Vitale, Ravenna)

Abraham's Sacrifice
(Mosaic in the Sanctuary of San Vitale, Ravenna)

Christus Pantocrator
(Mosaic in the Apse of the Cathedral of Cefalú, Sicily)

Glorious, Ever Virgin, Mother of God
(Altar Retable by Giovanni Cimabue, Florence)

was interpreted in that light and, what is more disquieting, ceremonies and rites were added to bear out that interpretation. For example, the signs of the cross in the Canon were deliberately multiplied (we must remember that the rite was very loosely regulated before the Council of Trent and consequently it was an easy matter to add to it) and in many places the hands extended in prayer was transformed into an imitation of the extended arms of Christ upon the cross. (This latter practice survives in some of the mediaeval uses derived from the Roman Rite.)

The Eucharist was viewed almost entirely from the viewpoint of the Real Presence; the focal point and center of the Mass was not the Consecration but the Elevation. Even the theologians concentrated more and more upon the questions of the manner of the presence and the way it was achieved. The Mass was looked upon as primarily a manifestation of God's presence rather than as the offering of the whole Church, the Sacrifice and Sacrificial Meal. Eucharistic devotion was not thought of as primarily devotion to sharing in the Mass through Communion, but as devotion to the Real Presence. It must be emphasized again and again that there can be no criticism of this devotion to the Real Presence in itself; and it is certainly true that the Mass is an epiphany—a manifestation of Emmanuel—God with us. But the over-emphasis of any aspect of devotional life is bound to result in a one-sided presentation of the truth and a corresponding failure to achieve an integral grasp of the whole doctrine involved. When that over-emphasized aspect is itself something secondary and when primary aspects consequently fall into second place or are obscured altogether, the damage is much greater.

One other mediaeval development remains to be considered, since it has had far-reaching influence upon the worship of the Church and upon the whole concept of corporate worship. This is the rise and spread of the low Mass, which was non-existent in the West as a public service before the Middle Ages and has ended by becoming in practice the usual way of celebrating the Mass rite.

From the time of the apostles until the Middle Ages, even in times of great stress and persecution, the Mass was, even in its external expression, altogether a corporate affair in which each and all had a part to play. As became such a corporate celebration, the Mass was *sung*—some parts more elaborately than others, it is true, but sung nevertheless. That in itself would always secure a certain corporateness—a choir and sacred ministers would be necessary for a sung Mass, even without any other congregation. Actually, there would always be a congregation, great or small, because no one thought of offering what was essentially a community service without a community being present at it. But as time went on the idea of the Mass as a source of graces and blessings led to the multiplication of celebrations—people more and more asked that this Mass or that be offered for special intentions and particularly for the souls of the faithful departed. Endowments for Mass foundations increased enormously during the mediaeval period and made inevitable the corresponding increase in Masses and in clergy to offer them. It requires no great effort of the imagination to see what this would lead to in time—a Mass rite that could be performed without the numerous people necessary for a high Mass. Another cause which contributed to the multiplication of private or low Masses was undoubtedly the devotion of individual celebrants, especially in the monasteries. Priests wanted to say Mass more often than they could by celebrating the public Mass in their turn; so they often celebrated Mass privately, and in the course of time this became a daily occurrence. The private or low Mass did not originate in the Middle Ages, but it certainly became a common practice during that time. What is more to the point is that it became a normal way of celebrating *public* Mass only during the later Middle Ages. The parts of the Mass intended to be sung by the ministers, the choir or the congregation would in a private Mass be said by the celebrant. What began as an exception ended by becoming the normal way of celebrating the Mass. The old idea that the community Mass should be a true communal celebration broke down towards the end of the mediaeval period and the Masses which had once been celebrated privately became public—with the server, who once took the place of the absent congregation, continuing to take their place even when they were present.

So it was that the great development of the private celebration contributed to diminish still more the participation of the congregation. The old idea that the Mass was a corporate celebration gave place to the subjective and individualistic view that it was essentially an act of devotion on the part of the priest and that all the people had to do, or indeed were expected to do, was to assist at it. As a consequence the content of the readings, lessons, prayers and chants became of less importance. They were retained in the books, it is true, but people rather generally forgot their original purpose, which was precisely to awaken faith and devotion. In the minds of most they became something quite accidental and unnecessary—something to be gone through before the main part of the Mass.

It was left to the counter-reformation period to carry this emphasis on the low Mass as the normal celebration of the Eucharist still further by treating the high Mass as a kind of *occasional solemnity* for great days or big feasts, when something special was called for in the way of a celebration. The elaborate music which had come to be the rule for such occasions helped to further this notion. As a result it was all viewed as external pomp and festivity; by contrast, the low Mass was the more devotional celebration—not so much a distraction as the high Mass tended to be. Theoretically, the high Mass remained the approved way of celebrating the Supper of the Lord, but in practice men preferred the more tranquil, less complicated, and what they really believed in their hearts to be the more spiritual (because less external), low Mass. This was the attitude that had to be overcome with such great difficulty when the modern liturgical revival tried to revive the true concept of the Mass as a corporate action. It is an attitude that has by no means died out but rather continues to be held by many in our own day in spite of all that has been done to correct it.

The Period of Liturgical Uniformity

At the close of the Middle Ages the liturgy had developed as we have described it. The main outlines of the Romano-Gallican Rite as we have it today had long since taken shape and had been fixed into the forms that were set down in the liturgical books. Yet within that framework the greatest freedom, not to say anarchy, reigned from diocese to diocese and from religious order to religious order. The Missal itself needed to be revised and some sort of standard set that would be binding upon all. Many of the Mass texts needed to be gone over and their errors and blemishes pruned away. Uniformity in the Mass-rite itself had to be insisted upon and abuses done away with. It was a stupendous task and the Council of Trent could do little more than set up a commission and recommend the reform to the Holy See. With this action of the council the period of liturgical uniformity, so necessary if the liturgy was to be preserved at all, began. The Missal According to the Usage of the Roman Curia was used as the basis for the revision. It was provided with a set of directions called the "*Rubricae Generales Missalis*" and the "*Ritus Servandus in Celebratione Missae*" and published in 1570 as the *Missale Romanum,* binding upon the whole Western Church, except those churches and orders which could show that they possessed a rite of their own that was at least two hundred years old. The guiding idea behind the whole reform was a return to the liturgy of the Church of Rome. By publishing this Missal in 1570 and the Breviary in 1568, and by affirming the exclusive right of the Holy See to regulate and order the liturgy, liturgical uniformity was secured to an extent and to a degree never before achieved. This liturgical uniformity was further attained by establishing the Congregation of Sacred Rites in 1588 which was entrusted with seeing to it that the prescribed manner of celebrating the Holy Sacrifice of the Mass and of carrying out the other liturgical rites was followed everywhere. This congregation was not to preside over any development; its task was to preserve the newly established uniformity, to interpret the newly regulated rubrics and in general to maintain order and discipline in the performance of the liturgy. Development was in fact arrested: the liturgy became fixed for centuries, and the wide latitude of former days in these matters was rigorously curtailed. Not only was the *Ordo Missae* permanently fixed and no divergencies or developments tolerated, but the whole body of liturgical law was fixed as well, with all the rites prescribed down to the smallest detail. This condition has prevailed into our own days with the rubrics and rubricists playing a far more important part than they had in the past. Nor can there be any doubt that under the circumstances there was little else that could be done: unquestionably this uniformity saved from destruction much that would have been lost or badly damaged if it had not thus been made secure from tampering. At the same time it is equally true that it resulted in a certain rigidity and an over-systematization which left little provision for later necessary adaptation and development. The end necessary at the time was secured, but at the cost of future advantages. By fixing the worship of the Church in this inalterable pattern, the concept of the liturgy as almost altogether the affair of the clergy, which had been growing and spreading during the late Middle Ages, was strengthened. The devotional life of the people had not been fed by the liturgy for a long time and this situation was now to continue. Preoccupied as they were with safeguarding the worship of the Church from abuses, and with answering the charges and complaints of the reformers, those entrusted with reforming the liturgy could not be expected to do all that and still give new life and meaning to the whole body of liturgical worship. The rift between the liturgy and the life of the people was not closed at this time; if anything, it was merely widened. During the sixteenth century and those that followed it little was done to improve this situation.

In the eighteenth century there was a liturgical revival in France which at another time and under different circumstances might have accomplished much. Unfortunately, those who were active along these lines were associated rightly or wrongly with Gallicanism and Jansenism and were looked upon with suspicion. Besides, while many of the ideas held by these men were right and good, they lessened their influence and spoiled the good they might have done by excessive devotion to ancient practices and by their general spirit of independence. It was not from such men that a true and solid liturgical reform could come, although some of their ideas were taken up and espoused even by the Holy See more than a century later. In any case, the time had not come; a solid foundation had to be laid before a lasting structure could be built. And much groundwork had to be done before even the foundation could be laid.

The nineteenth century was to provide the period of this groundwork, which came about in several ways. The revival of theological and historical studies—particularly the production of new editions of the Fathers and the opening of the catacombs—contributed to bring about a new interest in the early Church and in the ideals and the spirit which animated it. The writings of Dom Guéranger awakened widespread enthusiasm for the liturgy of the Church. More scholarly and scientific work was done by those that came after him, it is true, but his *Liturgical Year*, with all its defects, must always be regarded as the starting point of the modern liturgical revival. He was also a pioneer in the restoration of Gregorian chant to its true place.

The awakening liturgical revival received its real impetus from St. Pius X: first of all, by his *Motu Proprio* on church music in 1903, and even more so—although it was not obvious at the time—by his decree (1905) on frequent and daily Communion. From frequent Communion to an appreciation of its place in the Mass, then to a deepened understanding and appreciation of the Mass itself were steps that were rapidly made during the next two decades. The liturgical movement or revival was on its way. The use of the Missal spread through all the countries of the West and before long people saw that following the Mass with the eyes was not enough; they wanted to participate vocally. The way was opened to the singing of the Mass texts by the people or to the reciting of these texts in the Dialogue Mass. Progress in this closer participation has varied in different lands but the trend in that direction has continued with very little or no set-back to the present. It has borne fruit and gained the support of the Holy See in the recent restored Order for Holy Week, where for the first time in centuries participation in liturgical rites is not only recommended but insisted upon.

The Period of Change and Restoration

As recently as the present decade of this century it was perfectly correct for historians to refer to the time since the Council of Trent as the era of the fixed and unchanging in liturgical matters. Beyond the few additions indicated above not a single change in the structure of the Mass-rite had taken place in nearly four hundred years. The Mass was said and the services conducted down to the least detail as they had been for centuries. No concessions were made to the conditions of the time —nothing done to alter in any way what had been handed down, if not from the beginning, at least for many centuries. The Divine Office had been rather thoroughly revised by St. Pius X, but this revision was almost exclusively a re-distribution of the psalter; the substance of the Office and even most of the accidents, the calendar, the classification of feasts, and the octaves remained untouched. Nothing was done to alter the Mass-rite in any way.

During the decades that have elapsed since 1911 the ever-deepening appreciation of the true nature of the liturgy and of its purpose brought about a re-examination of its whole structure and inspired a series of requests, timid and infrequent at first, but more courageous and more frequent as time went on, that something be done to make the liturgy what it had been in the past, and what of its very nature it is intended to be at all times, a real influence on the lives of priests and people. Those who were skilled in liturgical studies, grasping more and more the pastoral import of the sacred rites, made suggestions from time to time that were ultimately received and accepted by the Holy See itself. After the second World War these suggestions towards a general restoration of the liturgy began to bear fruit in the concession of a greater use of vernacular in the Rituals used in France, Germany and India, in the relaxation of the Eucharistic fast, in the permission for evening Masses, and finally in the restoration of the Easter celebration, when the ordinary permitted it, to its proper place during the night between Holy Saturday and Easter Sunday. In this last change the rubrics of the Missal, untouched for centuries, were altered in many important respects. The rubrics of the Breviary and Missal were further affected by the decree of 1955, when customs and practices that stretched back to mediaeval times were swept away, the Office freed of many accretions and the entire burden considerably lightened. The greatest changes of all, of course, have been in the revised ordo for Holy Week, when once again, and even more thoroughly than by the decree of 1951, the structure of the Mass-rite itself has been affected in many ways. The accent upon participation by the people (which is no longer, if it ever was, at the option of the clergy), the restoration of the pauses for prayer, the elimination of the superfluous and whatever obscured the main lines of these rites, the insistence upon the singing of the chants of the Mass at the proper times, all this and much more not only achieve a true restoration of the liturgy of Holy Week to its proper place in the life of the people, but definitely indicate that the way is now open to a restoration of the entire liturgical year. Even if we had no other evidence than this, it alone would be enough to justify our calling this century the age of change and restoration. Already we have witnessed changes that would have been simply out of the question twenty-five years ago, and there is every reason to believe that before twenty-five years more have passed there will be a complete restoration of the entire liturgy along the lines and in the direction in which we have been travelling during the past two decades.

CHAPTER 8

The Setting of the Liturgy

The Church Building

The liturgy does not remain imprisoned in the liturgical books. Of its very nature it must find expression, and expression through the various material media by which it is celebrated Being something in time, it must also be in place, and though carrying the seeds of eternal and spiritual life it must reveal itself to men in an external form. The singing of the texts gives us liturgical music; the acting out of the liturgical drama gives us rites and ceremonies; the proper vesting of its ministers gives us liturgical vesture; the worthy reservation of the Body and Blood of Christ gives us liturgical craftsmanship in metals; liturgical ideas expressed in paint, in stone, in wood, and in glass give us liturgical painting and sculpture and stained glass. All these arts form the setting of the liturgy.

But there is one art which in a sense embraces them all, and that is architecture. The church building in a special way forms the background of the liturgy and is its chief setting. Indeed the first purpose of a church is to be a place set aside for the proper and entire performance of the liturgy.* Here as everywhere else it is very important to know just what something is intended to be and do before we can form an idea of how it is to be made. The church is not supposed to be a show-piece, or even primarily a thing of beauty; it has a work to do and a task to perform. Insofar as it falls short of that it falls short of its purpose, of its reason for being.

The liturgy is more than worship expressed in external forms; it is a way of life: "The primary and indispensable source of the true Christian spirit," the embodiment of the divine in sacramental form. The church building must be, as it were, the "sacrament of the liturgy"; it must reflect the liturgy and transmit this idea to the people. It must be a real aid in lifting the mind and heart to God; it must be what the liturgy itself calls it: the "House of God and the Gate of Heaven." Consequently the church building must be in harmony with the nature and purpose of the liturgy. It should speak of God, not as remote and far off in Heaven, but as present—present above all in the mysteries of the altar and also working through the rites and gestures and formulae of the sacred liturgy, the Priesthood of Christ in action.

The church must be the physical embodiment of the spiritual

* The church is the house of God and "the place where his glory dwells" by the very fact that it is set aside for divine worship and that the church (the assembly) meets there for worship. For that reason we should be careful to avoid the exaggerated language of those who speak and write about the church building as though it had no other reason for existing than to be a "home for our Eucharistic Lord"—and consequently as though it were "desolate," "empty," "dismal," "lonely," and even "not a church at all" without the Blessed Sacrament. This is very dubious theology to say the least. Certainly it finds no support in the Church's own view of what a church is, expressed in the rite of Dedication and in the Office and Mass of the Dedication, both of which were written long before the Blessed Sacrament was reserved in the churches in the manner that it is today. The plain truth is that the church building does not exist primarily to hold the reserved Sacrament. From the very nature of things that is a secondary purpose of the church building.

edifice which is the Mystical Body of Christ. It expresses in wood or stone the faith (which here includes hope and love) of those who belong to the Body of Christ and who built it. It must, then, be the "tabernacle of God with men," His dwelling place, the shining forth as well as the receptacle of His presence. The true Christian church, however small or unpretentious it may be, will convey an atmosphere of awe and majesty which we associate with God Himself. "This is an awe-inspiring place; it is the house of God and the Gate of Heaven and shall be called the palace of God" (Introit of the Mass of Dedication).

A church that is built in harmony with the nature and purpose of the liturgy will be a constant invitation to *participate* in the sacred mysteries; it will inspire people to pray and worship and make it easy for them to take part actively and intelligently. The very atmosphere of the church and *all that is in it* must be redolent of the Christ-life that is lived in it and that is active within its walls. The church building must not be a barrier but a help to liturgical worship. The church building is not an end in itself; it exists to further the interests of the liturgy. While all this may appear to be insisting on the obvious, it is necessary to restate these principles continually. Almost everyone can recall many instances in which these fundamental ideas have been ignored or neglected.

The first function of a church, then, is to provide a place for the offering of the Sacrifice of the Mass. There must, consequently, be *room* in the sanctuary and at the altar for the adequate performance of the ceremonies of the Mass—the High Mass, which is the normal worship of the Mystical Body. The altar must first of all be *seen* so that people may follow the rite from beginning to end. The church must be well-lighted that all may see what is going on. The acoustics must be perfect so that everyone may *hear* the priest, not only when he preaches but whenever he reads or sings.

The procession is a part of the liturgy and there has been a revival of interest in it in our time; hence space should be provided for dignified processions. Space must also be provided for the free and unhampered movement of the congregation inside the church (going to and from the altar rail and so forth).

Great care should be taken to provide a place for the *schola* in accord with sound principles and with consideration for the purpose of the choir, which is to *guide* and *lead* the congregation in worship.

There should be an adequate sacristy, so located that a processional approach from it to the altar is possible.

The baptistery should be carefully designed, made large enough for its function, and located near the door. The altar and the baptismal font should be the two foci of church architecture, just as the sacraments of Baptism and the Eucharist are the two centers of liturgical life. By placing them architecturally in relation to one another we show the relationship between these two sacraments: Baptism leads to the Eucharist. The font at one end of the church points to the altar at the other end. If the church is built around this idea, will not the architecture be more expressive of its primary aim than if we were to build according to some pre-conceived notion of what a church "should look like"? The plan of the church should be organic, should grow from within outward. That is only logical.

The whole church should be becomingly decorated with appropriate symbolism and furnished with due regard for the purpose of the building—it is the house of God!

Even externally the church building should proclaim its purpose; not only must it *be* a church; it should *look* like one. There should be nothing bizarre or eccentric about its appearance; on the other hand, it should not be a slavish copy of any past architectural style. Still less should it be of inferior, unbecoming and poor construction. "To look like a church" does not mean that it must be according to the popular concept of what a church looks like. It is imperative that it be a noble and beautiful building that looks (and is) at home in contemporary surroundings; yet it must not be worldly nor secular.

The Laws of Church Building

The general law governing church building and furnishing is expressed in the Code of Canon Law which states that the bishops are to see to it that "in the building or repair of churches the forms received from Christian tradition are preserved" and the "laws of sacred art" are observed (Canon 1164, no. 1); and again, "regarding the matter and form of sacred furnishings, liturgical law, ecclesiastical tradition, and also as far as possible, the laws of sacred art, are to be observed" (Canon 1296, no. 3). From this it is clear that liturgical law comes first, then ecclesiastical tradition, and finally the laws of sacred art. The law is set down in the liturgical books and in the decrees of the Congregation of Sacred Rites. Of the three the liturgical laws are the easiest to find, but the traditions are deduced from the history and practice of the Church, the laws of sacred art from the nature of the Church and the directions which are given from time to time by ecclesiastical authority, and in many individual cases by consulting the experts in the matter. The general idea is that there is a way of building and furnishing the church which is becoming and fitting for its purpose and that is in accord with the Christian spirit, and there is a way of doing it that is not becoming and fitting, and that is foreign to the Christian spirit. Within those rather broad limits everyone enjoys the greatest latitude. No one is held to reproduce slavishly the past just because it is the past. Quite the contrary: we are encouraged to find new ways of expressing the eternal and imperishable truths which were expressed in other ways in the past. Not copying or reproduction, but a kind of creativity seems to be the ideal. Naturally in a book of this kind we must confine ourselves more or less to general norms which will serve to guide in a general way; in individual cases more particular study would be required. It would be an excellent idea to have a commission in each diocese which, without tying the hands of pastor and architect, would nevertheless pass upon the fitness of what is being done and thus preserve some kind of equilibrium.

Sacred art is art used for a religious, or here more precisely, a liturgical purpose: to serve the ends of the liturgy, to contribute to the glory of God and sanctification of men by setting forth religious ideas and concepts in material and beautiful forms. The Church has always made it a point to use beauty in its approach to the God who is as beautiful as He is holy; she cannot be indifferent to so powerful a means of expressing and enhancing the worship of Him of whom the Psalmist sings, "The Lord reigns, he is clothed in beauty." Because beauty has often been confused with the merely sensual, people have made the mistake of distrusting it. But true beauty is a spiritual thing and is inseparable from the spirit, which it refines, ennobles and uplifts. This is indeed the purpose of sacred art: to raise our minds and hearts to heavenly things, to present the sacred and the divine in a setting which befits them, to be the outward embodiment of inner beauty and harmony. We cannot, then, regard sacred art as something optional, something helpful to a few but a matter of indifference to others—or worse still, as something that is vaguely not quite right, or even harmful. "It is the function and duty of sacred art, by reason of its very definition, to enhance the beauty of the house of God, *and to foster the faith and piety of those who gather in a church* to *assist at the divine offices and to implore heavenly favors.*" * We must cultivate sacred art, not for its own sake, but as inseparably connected with and related to the service of God. Any other attitude—consciously or unconsciously assumed—is certainly not the Catholic attitude, nor will it find any support in the tradition of the Church. It is true that some monastic re-

* Instruction of the Holy Office on Sacred Art—June 30, 1952, no. 1.

formers have at times crusaded for greater simplicity in their churches and in church furnishings; however, their action did not proceed from any lack of appreciation for beauty itself, but was a protest against what they regarded in their day and in their conditions as a departure from monastic austerity. It was a question of *applying* principles; the principles themselves were not denied. And it is always possible, of course, for worldliness to creep into the sanctuary under the guise of beauty. Sacred art should have a certain austerity about it, and the worldly or merely expensive is not by any means to be confused with the beautiful. On the other hand we must remember that protests which begin legitimately sometimes have a way of swinging to the opposite extreme: they become extremes themselves.

Sacred art, rightly conceived, is supposed to help religion and to be at the service of worship. It can and must do this by raising men's minds to holy thoughts and stirring their wills to good deeds, by aiding and fostering recollection and devotion. This it does by helping to present religion in an attractive and appealing way. A noble hymn, written in becoming and beautiful language, set to music that is dignified and inspiring, and sung with fervor and religious intensity, must do much for those who hear it and take part in it. A Mass that is celebrated well, sung with feeling and devotion, offered in surroundings which speak of God and of His majesty, with the altar and the sacred ministers becomingly vested and celebrating the sacred rites with reverence, is in itself, along with the sacred mystery it makes present again, a true reflection of the never-ending liturgy that goes on in Heaven, and is consequently a most powerful incentive to prayer, worship, adoration and praise. It truly "fosters the faith and piety" of those who gather at it; indeed we can be assured that it cannot fail to do so. A slovenly and disorganized celebration, with music that is poor or cheap and unworthy of its purpose, offered in surroundings that are an affront to the Christian sense—such a service dishonors religion, shows that it is held in light esteem, and thereby contributes to weaken faith and destroy piety. This is not something that is open to discussion; we may take it as axiomatic that whatever fosters devotion, recollection and piety, or on the other hand destroys and diminishes them, is not a matter of indifference. Sacred art in all its phases is, then, a great and indispensable handmaid of true worship because it helps to create, to arouse, to intensify and to keep alive those religious sentiments which true worship is ever concerned with. "The function of every art consists in breaking through the narrow and sad enclosure of the finite, in which man is immersed while he is living here below, and opening a window to his spirit aspiring to the infinite." *

When the Church speaks of the "laws of sacred art" she does not mean that these are laws set down in the same way as the liturgical laws; rather she means laws in the sense of *norms* which almost instinctively reject whatever is out of place, whatever can offend or shock Christian sensibilities, and which welcome whatever can minister to the decorous and worthy performance of worship, and the fitting adornment of the house of God.

When she says that the church building and furnishings are to be in conformity with ecclesiastical tradition she means only that there is a traditional appearance a church is supposed to have, and that there are certain things that must be provided for in Christian worship, and that this principle must be taken into account and followed when a church is being built or repaired. The simplest way of putting it is that the building must look like a church interiorly and exteriorly, and that it must be planned like a church, having all that it needs to fulfill its purpose adequately. "Sacred architecture, although it may adopt new styles, must not in any way be equated with profane building." † "All styles are admissible, provided they are con-

* Pius XII.

† Instruction of the Holy Office, no. 11.

formable to this fundamental principle that a church must be and must appear to be, the house of God and the forecourt of Heaven, the dwelling place of God and the ladder of Heaven . . ." * "The salvation of sacred architecture will be secured by turning to tradition, not to copy forms that have passed away, but only to recover the elements that have always persevered through all the styles and make them flourish again and be clothed with new life, life that beats in unison with the life of today. Not copies of old buildings but old elements that are the very stuff of architecture, reinvigorated with new life." † Ecclesiastical tradition shows us what has been accepted in the past as becoming and befitting sacred art; it provides us with a body of thought and a certain Catholic sense which guides us and prevents us from encouraging what is merely sensational or bizarre, or which caters to a love of novelty. Traditions are conservative of what is the best; ecclesiastical traditions pass on to us that attitude and outlook which we call "the mind of the Church."

The Decoration of the Church

The purpose of church decorating is shown in the very word itself which means to make beautiful, to embellish and to adorn. By means of painting, sculpture, stained-glass, metalwork and textiles it creates the atmosphere of a church and cries out aloud that the building is what it professes to be: the house of God and the place where His glory dwells. Hence, the decorations will be beautiful—dignified, restrained, becoming, fostering recollection and awakening devotion. They will afford instruction, too, according to their power and thus contribute to a better understanding of the mysteries of religion. By thus providing a proper setting for the performance of the liturgy, decoration will play a part in the sanctifying mission of the liturgy. At all times the decoration of the church remains as a

* *Ibid.* "*Fede et Arte*," II, 34.

† Cardinal Constantini in *Osservatore Romano*, July 30, 1952.

perpetual sermon, calling attention to the nature of the sacred place, emphasizing its purpose, speaking to the people of God and heavenly things: "*ut ipsi quoque in coelestibus habitemus.*" Understood in this sense decoration is seen to be a part of the liturgy itself, an expression in stone, wood, marble or metal of the public worship of the Church. We think of the mosaics above the side aisles of St. Apollinaris in Ravenna, which are an eloquent acting out of the Offertory procession that existed in the liturgy of the time; or of the Lamb-standing-as-though-slain in so many ancient churches, an ever-present reminder of the unceasing liturgy of Heaven and the eternal Priesthood of Christ.

Decorations should not be haphazard but planned, and planned carefully, with a good combination of theological learning and artistic sense. Theological learning will show what should be depicted and what should be emphasized; artistic sense will show how the things to be depicted should be made: with what order, harmony, and proportion. Theology will guide the selection of the motifs to adorn the sanctuary, or the baptistery, or the body of the church, assigning to each what is proper to it according to the purpose of that particular part of the church. It will preside over the decorations on the confessional, for example, which will proclaim what sacrament is administered and received there by appropriate symbols or texts; it will see that the sanctuary is most impressively marked off and attention focused upon the altar, and will by symbol and painting tell what is done there. Artistic sense and skill will see that the right colors are selected, that the decoration does not pass the bounds of restraint and dignity, that lines and surfaces are not too broken up, that the general effect is restful rather than agitating or tiresome, that the decoration is subordinate to the architectural lines of the building and does not conflict with it.

In general, decoration should be dignified and restrained; all that is worldly, theatrical, cheap, tawdry, ugly, and inadequate should be kept out, and every encouragement given to what is noble, inspiring, rich and finished, large and handsome. Here is the last place where we should economize with that "penny-wise, pound-foolish" approach which comes from a want of magnanimity and generosity. The decoration of the church must be sincere and true as well as dignified; all sham and imitation should be excluded as a matter of principle. You cannot paint wood to resemble marble and there is no use trying. Pretentious ostentation is out of place in the house of God. Yet good decoration need not be expensive if we decorate according to our means. When funds are limited we should be satisfied with what is simple, quiet, and dignified; in this way we shall achieve far more than a tasteless extravagance can ever attain.

It is better that the decoration, particularly of the sanctuary, be liturgical rather than historical. That is, the pictures and symbols should represent ideas and motifs that illustrate what is going on *here and now* rather than what is past. The apses of the early basilicas represented Christ in majesty and glory as the *Kyrios Pantocrator*, or the cross glowing with gems and color to bring out the triumph of the Redeemer, or the Lamb standing as though slain; our Lady was depicted as the *Theotokos* holding her divine child and surrounded by angels and saints. The effect of such a universal treatment, transcending time and space, must have been and still is tremendous, as well as indescribably majestic, and it certainly must have lifted up the minds and hearts of the worshippers to heavenly things. Within the limits imposed upon us we should do the same in our churches. Very appropriate to the sanctuary are scenes taken from the Canon of the Mass: Abraham's sacrifice; Melchisedech's offering; the saints of the Canon of the Mass; the heavenly altar; the Paschal Lamb; or eucharistic symbols drawn from the traditional art of the Church's past. The merely historical, incidental, or psychological should be avoided. (DaVinci's *Last Supper* is a great picture, but it does not belong in the sanctuary, still less on the altar, because it does not depict the Supper itself nor the institution of the Eucharist, but is a psychological study of the reaction of the apostles to "One of you is about to betray me.") The *Te Deum* or some of the redemptive events in the life of Christ can furnish us with a variety of themes. The idea is that the decoration of the church and particularly the sanctuary should have some bearing on what goes on there.

Special parts of the church, such as chapels, if there are any, dedicated to our Lady and the saints, or the baptistery, can receive appropriate treatment inspired by the purpose which they serve.

There is a vast array of symbols which can be used in decorating the church, but we must remember that many of them are not easily understood nor appreciated in this modern world. On the other hand (and this was not true during the time when many symbols grew up and developed), everyone today can read, and a judicious selection of texts, attractively and artistically painted on walls and windows, can be most effective. (Needless to say if one uses texts they should be in English!)

A final word might be said in this section about the great decorative possibilities of light: glass blocks, glass walls, large windows; colors bright, cheerful, and restful. Together these two elements bring to the church that atmosphere of brightness and joy that is singularly befitting to the house of God. There is no excuse for the dingy, dim, colorless, drab interiors which too often are associated with the church—and with religion!

Architectural Styles

The Earliest Churches. The early Christian converts from Judaism continued for a time to go to the temple or the synagogue for prayer, but they also gathered in one or other of their homes to celebrate the Eucharist. It was natural that the best room (or the most spacious) in the house should be used: a room ordinarily reserved for the great family feasts. When the Church spread through the cities of the empire and more and more Gentiles became converts to the Faith, the original custom of holding the Christian reunions in private homes was continued for some decades. These places of reunion for the sacred mysteries were consequently known as house-churches (*domus ecclesiae*). Later on, even during the period of persecution, buildings specifically intended for worship were built, but as nearly all were destroyed, particularly during the persecution of Diocletian, we know very little about them.

At one time it was thought that Christian architecture evolved from the house-churches used in the first three centuries. But this theory always presented many difficulties and is now almost completely discredited. Christian architecture as we know it today appears almost certainly to have developed in the West from the civil basilica, or the Roman law court; and in the East from the plan of the family tomb. In spite of this there still seems to be room for the theory that the name of the church-building came from the circumstance that the first churches were family houses: the "House of God," the "House of the Church" (*Kuriakon:* Greek for Lord's house, whence our word *Church*).

The Basilica Type: After the conversion of Constantine when the Christians had secured tolerance and were free to grow and develop in an unrestricted way, Christian architecture properly so-called began. In the West the new church buildings that rose on every side, particularly in Italy, took the form of the civil basilica or law court. These were great halls divided by columns into a nave and side aisles leading to a semi-circular apse (called *Exedra*), which became the presbytery or sanctuary when the building was adapted for Church use. There was a place for the throne of the bishop with seats for the clergy to each side. In the front, standing free and facing both the clergy and the people, stood the altar, a block or cube of wood or marble, over which stood a canopy (*ciborium*) resting on four or more posts. The people stood in the nave facing the apse, women on one side, men on the other. The basilica was built of brick with a slanting roof (wood on the inside; tile on the outside). The light came in through the windows in the walls above the columns. Sometimes there was a transept crossing between the apse and the nave, giving the whole building the rough outline of a cross. Usually there was a court or *atrium* in front of the building which contained trees and flowers and usually a small pool of water (*cantharus*) in the center.

Though the walls of the basilica were of the simplest, the interior (and sometimes the exterior façade) was often sumptuously decorated, and the finest colored marble and gold gave it a splendor that was restrained but nevertheless singularly impressive. Particularly was this true of the mosaics, especially the large one over the apse, which depicted Christ Himself, or the cross, or the Lamb "standing as though slain."

This type of architecture was altogether well adapted for the celebration of the Christian liturgy. The forecourt separated the building from the noise of the street and helped to secure that atmosphere of quiet and recollection so fitting for the religious rites celebrated within. On entering the church the attention is at once drawn to the sanctuary and by the parallel row of columns focused upon the altar in the apse. The great mosaic, usually representing Christ as the *Kyrios Pantocrator*, dominates the sanctuary and the whole building. The altar is set off by the *ciborium*, the canopy on four posts that stands above and around it. The clergy are gathered around the altar and the bishop from his throne in the apse has the entire congregation before him; he truly presides over the assembly, which in turn has an unobstructed view of him, the clergy and the altar especially. How clearly this impressed the assembly with the idea that the whole Church was gathered around the altar, a priestly society engaged in worshipping God!

The Centralized Plan: side by side with the rectangular type of basilica, but more commonly in the East, there developed the centralized plan of church building. Instead of a rectangle it formed a square or a circle, and in many instances a polygon. This type of architectural plan arose in all likelihood from the separate tombs built in the East for the martyrs. Buildings of this type were at first mortuary chapels only, but they were adapted for use as churches. The altar usually stood in an apse added to one side of the centralized building, but it sometimes stood in the center. The circular church is encountered in Italy and in other parts of the West, but it never enjoyed the popularity it has had in the East.

Strangely enough this centralized plan has been revived in modern times, but with the altar in the center. This latter arrangement is not the happiest one, but it has the one great advantage of bringing the people closer to the altar.

The Byzantine Style. Churches built in the eastern part of the empire were usually concentric in plan and covered with one or more domes. Indeed it was the development of the dome that determined the Byzantine style. The outside walls were brick, often covered with a sheath of marble (not always, however). The interior was covered with colored marble and mosaics with backgrounds of gold. Byzantine architecture is easily the most elaborate and sumptuous of architectures. Ivory and gold, silver and precious stones are seen everywhere. Even the pavement was made with marbles and mosaics carried out in a great variety of patterns. The walls and arches were adorned with elaborate iconography, which crept up to the dome or domes. The general gold background gives unity to the whole surface. Capitals on pillars have their own peculiar form and are elaborately carved, each with its own design. These formed a perfect setting for the opulent Eastern Rites which reached the summit of ritual splendor.

Romanesque. This is a blend of Roman, barbarian and Oriental architecture, heavy and massive, with thick stone walls and characterized by round arches. It sprang up in Europe between the eighth and eleventh centuries. The ruins of older Roman buildings supplied the material and the arches gave it its form; hence the name Romanesque (related to Roman). This architecture followed the traditional basilica plan, but departed from the latter in the use of materials and the vaulted roof instead of a flat or sloping roof. This new departure became the master idea from which all mediaeval architecture in the West developed. The windows were placed in both nave and aisles, small at first but larger as time went on, and were filled with jewelled glass, an art that was just beginning. The walls, on which all the weight of the vaulted roof rested, were supported at intervals by buttresses. Sculpture was rude and rough. A horizontal rather than a vertical architecture, Romanesque continued to focus attention on the altar or at least on the sanctuary.

The Gothic Style. Gothic owes its name, originally intended to be disparaging, to the men of the Renaissance who considered it as a debased and barbarian architecture. It was the result of a gradual development from Romanesque, a development which had been going on for some time before the actual flowering of Gothic architecture. Gothic was a style which lent itself to great architectural triumphs and has for a long time, at least in the popular mind, been identified with church architecture almost to the exclusion of any other.

This style is characterized by the pointed cross-vaults which developed from the round vaults of the Romanesque, and which form an organic skeletal structure in stone analogous to our structure of steel girders; by the "flying buttress" which like gigantic arms hold up the walls; by the comparative thinness of these walls and by the great area covered by the glass windows. The walls were no longer needed to support the roof; the latter rested on the vaults which carried the weight down through the many pillars to the ground. Thus more space was liberated for the windows in which the art of stained glass now reached its full development, particularly during the thirteenth century. Gothic architecture permits a very high structure supported by a bewildering complexity of columns and arches. It is perhaps the most organic of architectures, a real symphony in stone. Later architects have tried to capture its form without realizing that the form is a result of its structure; mere pointed arches do not make Gothic architecture. The complexity of the building was intensified by the marvellous carvings and sculpture that adorned it both within and without.

The great difficulty with Gothic architecture is that it is an architecture of detail, enormously difficult and expensive to reproduce, even if one would wish to reproduce it. Besides, it is not an architecture that lends itself to corporate worship; more vertical than horizontal, it carries the eye upward rather than drawing it to the altar. Furthermore, its enormous size makes participation difficult; it tends to scatter rather than to unite. In its own setting, which is Europe, a true Gothic cathedral is enormously impressive; as a reproduction in other lands and in modern times, it always seems to be no more than a reproduction and an anachronism.

The Renaissance. With the revival of learning and of classical studies there came a new architecture which turned away completely from the Gothic and sought inspiration in the classical forms of the Graeco-Roman past. Pillars with their various orders, pilasters, arches and domes, vast expanses of space and great floods of light characterize this architecture. The dome and the lantern replaced the towers and steeples of the mediaeval period, and classic moulding was substituted for the carvings of the Gothic arches. A perfection of form and an orderly symmetrical arrangement of detail dominated these buildings, of which St. Peter's in Rome gives the best example. It received its inspiration from the past but was truly a new creation.

For all of its perfection Renaissance or neo-classic architecture was a bit too cold and formal, at least for churches. It was more an architecture for civic buildings and royal palaces. From it evolved a later form: the Baroque, which was in part a reaction against the too formal rules of later Renaissance architects, and which has been called "at least an assertion of freedom and at worst a lapse into license." In general we must say that Baroque architecture with its lavish painting and decoration was much too theatrical and worldly an architecture for churches; it was little suited to provide that atmosphere of repose that should mark the "house of God and the gate of heaven."

Modern. During the nineteenth century there was little original architecture; artists by and large imitated, when they did not slavishly copy, the past. Only in the twentieth century has an architecture developed that we can call truly original, an architecture which belongs to the times in which we live, which aims at being functional first, then beautiful. Perhaps some of these forms are a little extreme, but they have the merit of a certain sincerity. They make use of modern materials, particularly steel, stone, bricks, and glass, to very good effect. There is a danger that churches built in modern styles may sometimes look like theatres or shops; but this is something architects must see to. In any case we can truly speak of a revival of church architecture in our own day, and of building that is dominated by the idea of erecting churches that are primarily intended for use.

The Rite of the Dedication of Churches

The dedication of a church has its remote beginnings in the blessing and placing of the first stone. Thus its sacredness is proclaimed and emphasized from the very start. This prelude to the dedication proper is made up of two distinct rites: the blessing and the setting up of the cornerstone, and the blessing of the site of the new church and of the foundations, if they exist at that time. It centers around the cornerstone, emblem and symbol of Christ, the true Cornerstone. Like the more elaborate consecration, this service is marked by the use of the litany and of appropriate psalms, antiphons and orations. The same familiar themes that we meet later in the actual dedication and in the Mass and Office of the Dedication are here too: Jacob and the stone he anointed with oil; "Unless the Lord build the house he labors in vain who builds it"; "how awesome is this place, the house of God and the gate of heaven"; "How lovely are Thy tabernacles, O Lord of Hosts."

When a church is to be blessed, which is the usual situation, there is a much shorter rite modelled upon the dedication itself which is used instead. It may be done by a priest, although the bishop usually officiates himself. The blessing consists of going around the outer walls of the church, sprinkling the upper and lower parts with holy water, then entering the church during the Litany of the Saints, which has appropriate invocations at the end: "*Ut hanc ecclesiam benedicere et purificare digneris.*" This is followed by a kind of brief Office, with three of the usual dedication psalms (119, 120, 121) and orations. The inner walls are then blessed and the Mass of the day or the titular is said.

The true dedication of the church is the consecration, whereby the building is irrevocably set aside for God's service. The concept underlying this rite is very ancient and was known both to pagans and Jews. From the latter particularly much of the imagery and symbolism is borrowed, but it has been added to and perfected by the Christian symbolism in rites which have largely been borrowed from the Gallican Rite. There is, however, at the same time a strong Roman influence underlying the whole ceremony. For the Romans, the church (or more precisely the altar) was conceived as a tomb. It was built over the tombs of the martyrs and the essence of the dedication rite was the placing of the body or the relics of the martyr in the tomb and sealing it. That is why even today the procession of the relics and the placing of them in the altar occupies so prominent a place in the rite of dedication: in reality it is a burial rite. The Gallican idea was, perhaps, more dynamic. The church was looked upon almost as a living thing and it was set aside for God's service by rites analogous to those that accompanied Christian initiation: the washing of the walls and particularly the anointing. By these actions the building was made sacred: a holy place, belonging to God. Both these concepts enter into our present rite, but it is the anointing that is regarded as essential.

The service is extremely long, perhaps too much so for our modern taste; but that is a result of a fusion of two rites. Besides, it comes down to us from a more leisurely age than our own, and a large part of it from a people who revelled in ritual splendor. It begins the night before, with the watch or vigil of the relics; the clergy attached to the church recite Matins and Lauds from the Common of Martyrs.

The first part of the actual ceremony parallels the exorcisms used in Baptism: purifying the building, driving the evil spirits and their influence from it, then taking possession of it for God. The second part consists in the anointing of the altar and the attendant rites, and then the anointing of the twelve crosses on the walls.

On the morning of the consecration the bishop, the clergy and people come to a church that is or should be completely empty. The first rite is a purification. The bishop goes around the outside of the church three times, sprinkling it with holy water. This is followed by the knocking upon the doors of the church, with the request that they be opened to let the King of Glory come in. This impressive rite symbolizes the idea of God's taking possession of His house. An exorcism is then performed with the bishop making a sign of the cross on the threshold, saying as he does so the ancient formula, "*Ecce crucem domini: fugite partes adversi.*" The bishop and his attendants now enter and begin the curious rite of tracing the Latin and Greek alphabets with the foot of the crozier upon a large St.

Andrew's cross in ashes which covers the floor of the church. This rite is borrowed from the ancient Roman surveyors, who took possession of the land in this fashion. Before he begins, the bishop intones the *Veni Creator;* during the rite the Litany of the Saints with its appropriate invocations is sung; as is also the *Benedictus,* with its antiphon which might be called the *leit-motiv* of the entire ceremony, and of the Mass and Office of the Dedication as well: "*O quam metuendus est locus iste, vere non est hic aliud nisi domus dei et porta coeli.*"

The purification is carried on by the long ceremony of the washing with Gregorian water (a mixture of salt, water, ashes and wine) of the altar, the walls and the floor of the church. The altar is anointed with the mixture, the five crosses inscribed on its surface, then sprinkled with the water as the bishop goes around the altar seven times. Meanwhile the choir sings the antiphon *Introibo,* the Psalm *Judica,* and the Psalm *Miserere.* After that the bishop goes around the church three times, sprinkling the walls and floor with the Gregorian water. During this time appropriate psalms and antiphons are sung.

The great consecratory preface is then sung, a magnificent prayer in the tradition of the Eucharistic prayers of the early Church:

Be pleased to bless, purify and consecrate this church by the eternal abundance of Thy hallowing, in honor of Thy holy and victorious cross. . . . May the priests offer to Thee here the sacrifice of praise; may the faithful people pay their vows here. Here may the debt of sinners be cancelled, and may those of the faithful who have fallen here be raised up again. In this house, which is Thine, O Lord, may the sick be healed, the lepers purified, the blind receive their sight, the demons be put to flight. By Thy coming in may the weaknesses of all the weak be cast out and the bonds of all sinners be broken. May all those who enter this temple to ask for true blessings from Thee rejoice at obtaining all they ask; may the mercy which they seek become, by the gift of Thy bounty, their eternal glory.

Now the church has become the house of God, purified, made holy and consecrated. Nevertheless, still more needs to be done; the church exists for the altar and the altar must be consecrated, too.

Since the ancient Roman Rite of Consecration consisted exclusively in bringing the relics in, sealing them into the altar and then saying Mass upon it, the first part of the modern Rite of Consecration begins with a solemn procession of the relics. It is in reality a funeral procession, but a triumphant one after the manner of the early Christians. The bishop and the clergy go to the chapel where the relics are kept and carry them in triumph around the church, singing psalms and antiphons with a deeply mystical flavor. They stop at the door of the church, which the bishop anoints with holy chrism, saying the words "In the name of the Father," *etc.*, and then, "Be blessed, sanctified, consecrated, marked and entrusted to the Lord God, door of this church; be the entrance of salvation and peace; be a peaceful door. Through Him Who called Himself the Door, Jesus Christ our Lord, *etc.*" To the accompaniment of the singing of antiphons in honor of the saints, all now enter the church. The casket of relics is carried to the altar and placed on the gospel side, and, after the sepulcher prepared for them in the altar is anointed, they are placed inside.

The incensing and anointing of the altar completes the Rite of Dedication. First the bishop incenses the altar at the five crosses, then goes around it three times with incense. His place is then taken by a priest, who goes around the altar all during the anointing. The anointing is done three times, the first two times with the oil of catechumens, the last time with chrism, in the same five places marked with the cross. Meanwhile appropriate psalms and antiphons are sung, and once more the bishop incenses the altar. He then spreads a mixture of all three oils over the front of the altar.

The anointing with chrism means nothing less than making the stone, hitherto like any other stone, represent Christ, the "anointed One" above all others, "Who is our Altar, Victim and Priest."

The anointing of the crosses on the walls with chrism is the essential part of the Rite of Consecration. These material walls become for us a symbol and a sacrament of the walls of the new Jerusalem, and a beautiful responsory sung at this point makes that clear to us, together with Psalm 147, "*Lauda Jerusalem Domino*." The bishop anoints each of the twelve crosses with holy chrism, saying, "May this temple be sanctified and consecrated. In the Name of the Father, *etc.*," and incenses each cross three times. Under the anointing hand of the bishop the stone of the altar became a living stone. Under the same consecrating unction the walls of the church likewise undergo a transformation. In the exquisite language of the antiphons of the Pontifical, sung during this part of the rite, the material walls glow with the brightness of eternal light; it is no longer the church edifice made by hands that we contemplate, but the heavenly Jerusalem: "All thy walls are precious stones, and the towers of Jerusalem are built with gems. Thy streets, O Jerusalem, are paved with pure gold, and the song of joy will be sung within thy gates. . . . Thou shalt glow with shining light and all the ends of the earth shall venerate thee."

The crosses all anointed (a candle burns before each), the bishop returns to the altar and completes its dedication. Incense is burned in the five crosses, and among the prayers that are said the Preface is especially noteworthy: it recalls before God what part this newly-consecrated stone will play in the new church; asks Him to bless it and to be pleased to receive the offerings that are going to be presented to Him upon it. The altar is now wiped clean and vested, and the Mass of Dedication is said. The candles glow before the newly-consecrated crosses. The sacrifice that unites the Church and renews daily the covenant with God is offered on the new altar. God has taken possession of His holy temple: "Behold the dwelling-place of God with men"; "This day salvation has come to this house."

It is a strange and not-too-familiar world into which we are plunged when we celebrate the dedication of a church. Rich in imagery and beautiful symbols, it is at the same time a rite unfolded in an atmosphere that is of the past: Jacob and the stone that he set up for a monument in Bethel; the tabernacle and the altar consecrated by Moses; the rites accompanying the dedication of Solomon's temple and its restoration after the captivity; the new temple envisioned by the prophets. None of these things form any part of the equipment of modern men's minds, cut off as they are from that familiar communing with the Old Testament which was one of the normal disciplines of the age that saw this rite grow up and develop. Yet it would be a mistake to dismiss it all as meaningless or as a tedious archaeological survival. There is a whole theology here, a long, leisurely commentary on the inner nature and meaning of the altar and the church, the place where the Incarnation is continued and the Priesthood of Christ is working for the salvation of the nations. By a sympathetic accord of mind and heart with this living theology, we gain insight into the entire mystery of the Church herself. This church, which we have dedicated with solemn rites, is but the symbol and the sacrament of the eternal city, "the new Jerusalem coming down from heaven adorned as a bride for her husband." This church is the antechamber of Heaven, God's dwelling-place with men, where the great mystery of the Redemption is accomplished and our citizenship in the new and heavenly Jerusalem assured. Here the Bride of Christ is augmented and takes on new increase. By the sacraments, which are, as it were, deposited within its walls as a precious treasure, the gates of the heavenly Jerusalem are opened and the members of the Church, by entering into the consecrated church, enter Heaven in advance and catch a glimpse of its happiness. The Church on earth becomes the heavenly Jerusalem for them. That is why the Christian who sees the church building can cry out with St. John: "I saw the holy city, the new Jerusalem, coming down from heaven adorned as a Bride for her husband." That is why in the Mass of the Dedication, which completes the rite, the Church sings the gradual chant: "This place has been made by God; it is a *Sacrament* of incalculable worth; it is above reproach"; "This is an awe-inspiring place indeed; it is the House of God and the Gate of Heaven and shall be called the court of God."

CHAPTER *9*

The Altar and Its Adornment

The general idea to be borne in mind is that the altar represents Christ "who is Altar, Priest and Victim" (Roman Breviary); "the altar is Christ Himself" (Pontifical—Ordination of Subdeacons). Liturgy translates dogma into the concrete, and the altar is the material expression of the dogma of sacrifice. Hence the respect that surrounds it; hence also its importance. It is the focal point of the liturgy: everything should be ordered towards it. It is the most important object of furniture in the church and should be made to appear that way.

History and Development of the Altar

The word altar is taken from the Latin *alta are*, high altar. The Greek word is *thusiasterion*. (The word *ara*, the most common pagan word for altar, was avoided religiously by the early Christians.) It has also been known as the *trapeza kuriou*, "the Lord's table."

There were no altars properly so-called in the very early Christian centuries (the Apostolic and sub-Apostolic periods); the same tables utilized for ordinary meals were used during the

Eucharist and returned to their customary use when it was over. Hence the Christians were accused of atheism; they had no altars in the pagan or Jewish sense of objects set aside exclusively for sacrifice. Before long, however, as the understanding of the eucharistic mysteries deepened, and the *agape* was separated from the Lord's Supper, a special table (still a *table*, however) was set aside for the exclusive use of the liturgical sacrifice and called "the Lord's table" (*mensa dominica, trapeza kuriou*). These first altars were most likely three-legged tables of a type quite common in the houses of the well-to-do (where the eucharistic assembly most often was held). The deacons had charge of these altars, bringing them out for the service and returning them to the place where they were kept when it was over. Indeed the oldest picture of an altar which we possess in the cemetery of St. Calixtus shows just such an altar: the priest is standing with outstretched arms near a tripod on which bread and a fish are placed. The very use of this table for the sacrifice helped to give it a special prestige as having been "consecrated by the blood of Christ" (Origen), and for a long time the consecration of an altar consisted in offering the sacrifice on it. No other rite was considered necessary.

The altars continued to be movable for a long time, but the shape varied, sometimes circular, sometimes square or rectangular. As might be expected from its origin, it was made of wood and was large enough to hold the bread and wine used for the sacrifice. During the service it was usually covered with a white cloth, most likely going down to the floor on all sides. By the fourth century stone altars began to replace the wooden ones, but there was no legislation proscribing wood until the sixth century. There is no real proof that the sacrifice was offered on the slabs which covered the martyrs' tombs. When it was offered at the tomb, a wooden altar (or a marble slab reserved for the purpose) was used.

The Introduction of Fixed Stone Altars Associated with the

Relics of the Martyrs. With the peace of Constantine the development of the altar entered a new phase: wood was gradually abandoned as a material and replaced by stone, marble, or precious metals. The altar became fixed to one spot and was regularly associated with the relics of the martyrs.

While the persecutions were going on the altar could be secured from profanation by being easily moved; once these were over and the Church had attained its freedom, such a precaution was no longer necessary, and it was more natural (especially when regular churches were built) that the altar should remain in a fixed position. The same circumstance helped to bring about the use of stone altars; they were more solid, fitted more easily into the setting of the new churches, and were more dignified than wood. Perhaps the fact that pagan altars were made of stone may have helped. Certainly these altars were at times transformed into Christian altars and thus contributed to the idea that all altars should be of stone.

Mystical considerations too influenced the idea that the altar should be of stone. Christ was Himself regarded as the altar of His own sacrifice; He was in His own words the Cornerstone upon which the holy temple of the faithful (the "living stones") should be built up. Naturally this symbolism was brought out more clearly by a stone altar.

To the idea that the altar should be fixed and made of stone was added another which completed the table-tomb association evoked by the very word itself. It was the bringing of the martyrs into relation with the altar, a practice which became general with the development of the cult of the martyrs. Christ was symbolized by the altar, but He was not complete without His members. Of these members the martyrs were regarded as the most illustrious, and indeed as the most closely united to Him. For they had "washed their robes in the blood of the Lamb" (Apoc. 6:9) and are pictured as being "beneath the altar of God." This symbolic language of the Apocalypse was given real expression by the actual placing of the relics of the martyrs in the altar itself. St. Ambrose says that Christ is *on* the altar because He is the victim who suffers for all; the martyrs are *underneath* the altar because they have been redeemed by His passion and death. St. Paul's words about completing what was wanting to the sufferings of Christ had their influence here also. Since the sufferings of the members were in a sense necessary to complete the sacrifice of the Head, the tombs of the martyrs were considered as the complement and the most worthy support of the table upon which this sacrifice was offered.

Then, too, the desire of remaining in communion with the dead led to the placing of relics of the martyrs near or under the altar, so that the bond of union might be made and retained with them through the sacrifice of Christ. All these considerations helped shape a practice which in so many ways corresponded to their most cherished desires.

This arrangement of the altar was secured in many different ways: the relics might be placed in a depression in the table itself, or, if the altar were in the form of a cube, the relics might be deposited inside (as in a box) usually with some kind of opening in front (*cancellae*) through which cloths might be thrust to touch the relics. The most elaborate arrangement was a little room built under the altar which could be reached from the floor above by stairs. The body of the saint was placed in this room (called *confessio*) and the altar built directly above it. In any case the remains of the martyrs were definitely associated with the altar; if martyrs' relics could not be obtained, the relics of confessors or virgins would suffice. In many places, until the practice was forbidden by law, even the Eucharist was placed in the altars.

This ancient discipline (of the Latin church) has been retained to the present day: there must be relics of martyrs or other saints in every altar.

For centuries the altar kept the modest dimensions of the earlier period. It was usually a cube, with a square (or slightly rectangular) top, standing free on all sides. Its position varied:

sometimes it stood in the apse, in front of the bishop's throne, sometimes in the middle of the nave (St. Peter's in Rome), sometimes at the head of the nave (St. Paul Outside the Walls, St. John Lateran). No steps led up to it (they were a later addition); the altar stood directly on the pavement, which might itself be elevated, however. There was neither back nor front to it; the celebrant faced the congregation and they in turn faced the east where the celebrant stood.

About the sixth or seventh century came the first of the changes which were to lead to a profound modification of the altar and even of the whole liturgy. The celebrant, who hitherto always faced the people at prayer, began to turn to the east, which involved turning his back to the altar and the people. This was not done everywhere, nor all at once, but in time it became the general practice not only during the orations but during the Canon as well. Beyond doubt this change must be regarded as contributing greatly to cutting off the faithful from direct participation in the liturgy and perhaps ultimately to the silent recitation of the Canon, which up until the eighth or ninth centuries was proclaimed aloud as a matter of course.

The Altar Acquires a Front and Back: Reliquaries, Retables, Reredos. Until the ninth century a most rigid rule, which permitted of no exceptions, kept everything off the altar except the *oblata*, the sacramentary and the Gospel-book. Towards the end of that century came the first departure from this rule. The results of the change no one could have foreseen, but they were to be very great; certainly they affected the construction of the altar for over a thousand years, and made it what it most often is today. The old free-standing altar, small in proportions, gave place to a structure which very often was but the base of a great shrine; the modest cubes which had hitherto served as altars were now made into elongated tables or blocks which would harmonize better with the large coffers that contained the relics, or often the whole bodies of the saints. This relaxation of primitive discipline came just at the time when there was a great flowering of the cultus of the saints. Their bodies were taken from the crypts or from under the altars and placed above them or behind them, with the foot of the reliquary resting on the altar or on a structure built upon the altar. Naturally this involved a certain number of additions to the structure of the altar which were intended to enhance the dignity of the relics. The baldachin over the altar gave place to a smaller canopy immediately over the reliquary of the saint.

Another custom with far-reaching results grew up at the same time—one that some say was intended to compensate for the absence of reliquaries when they could not be obtained. This was the placing on the altar of long, low ornamental tablets of wood or stone or metal, on which would be painted images of Christ, our Lady, or the saints, or scenes from their lives. We call them retables or altar pieces, and though they were at first low in height and temporary, in time they were built higher and became permanent. From a small tablet they grew into enormous structures called the reredos. The reredos are undoubtedly among the finest pieces of Christian art, but they went a long way towards depriving the altar itself of the prominence and the autonomy it once possessed. The retable began as an accessory to the altar; when the development was finished the *altar* had become accessory to the *retable*, which now made up the great part of the entire structure. This tendency reached its full development in the Renaissance and Baroque eras when the altar, now placed against the wall, seemed to be but a base or foundation for the monumental apotheosis of the saint or mystery to which the church was dedicated.

The sixteenth century saw the addition of two more features which only complicated the structure of the altar more than ever. Gradines or steps were introduced upon the altar table to provide more space for flower pots, extra candlesticks, and other objects. The second addition was the tabernacle which hitherto had either hung over the altar or had its special place in the sanctuary. These tabernacles were often enormous and dwarfed everything around them; they contributed their share to draw attention away from the altar.

The eighteenth and nineteenth centuries and the early twentieth continued this tendency to such a degree that the original idea of an altar was almost completely lost. What had been accidental became normal. It must be said too that while the altar-piece or reredos could be—and was for centuries—in itself a work of art, those made in great numbers in the last century and early in this century did not even possess that merit. Most often they were dreary affairs, incredibly ugly, dull and uninspiring imitations which at best make us shudder when we come upon them now in all their vulgarity and sham splendor.

The addition of the tabernacle brought about another change in the attitude of people towards the altar. Its original purpose as the table of sacrifice receded into the background and it became usual to regard the altar almost exclusively as the place where the Blessed Sacrament was reserved. The tabernacle became the important part of the altar, and it was often so large and so ornamented and so placed that it was impossible to cover it with the veil that is prescribed. During the nineteenth century in particular the popularity of Exposition and Benediction caused the wholesale introduction of niches or canopies over the tabernacle, where the Blessed Sacrament could be exposed. The altar thus became a kind of permanent throne of Exposition, almost as if it had been built primarily for that purpose instead of for the Mass. Furthermore, the altar cross often had to be placed in the throne, a practice that is actually forbidden, and which also meant that the cross had to be made much smaller than it should be. The tabernacle thus had a canopy which the law ordered to be reserved for the altar itself, or, what was much worse, the canopy was nearly everywhere abandoned altogether. Here as in earlier additions, popular piety brought about the exaltation of what is secondary and occasional at the expense of the liturgical laws and of the respect that is due to the altar itself.

The altar thus gradually lost in the eyes of the faithful its uniqueness and autonomy and even much of the reverence formerly associated with it; these were now transferred to the relics of the saint or to the pictures or statues in the reredos or to the tabernacle and exposition throne. What is significant is that with the decline in respect for the altar went a decline in appreciation for the Sacrifice itself which the altar symbolized and which it should have kept before the eyes and minds of the faithful.

The shape of the altar itself was also affected. From a cube, which had been eminently satisfactory while it stood under its ciborium or canopy, it was elongated into a rectangle so that it would harmonize with the long coffer containing the body of the saint which now stood above it, or with the retable and reredos which were becoming more monumental all the time. Its position was changed: once it had stood out, now it was placed against the wall. Naturally with all these changes it was impossible for the celebrant to keep even for a short time the ancient position *facing* the people. He had to turn his back to them permanently.

Only in recent years has there been a trend towards altars of greater simplicity and consequently of greater beauty. The growing appreciation of the position the altar holds in the liturgy has inspired many to bring it into greater prominence. We are happy to be able to say that this reawakened awareness of what the altar is has led priests and architects to emphasize and to bring out the essential elements of the altar, to restore its dignity and consequently the understanding of what it represents. This means that whatever is accidental or secondary must be kept in its proper place—subordinated to the altar itself. The revival of the long-neglected ciborium has contributed to this, although we should not make the mistake of thinking that there is only one form of altar. Here as elsewhere, there is wide latitude for designs which are noble and effective. If the altar itself stands out by the richness of its material and decoration it really does not matter what kind of setting is used (ciborium or reredos), provided that the setting fits in with the altar and church. Side altars, incidentally, call for different treatment than that given to main altars.

Position of the Altar

For nearly a thousand years the altar stood out from the wall in such a way that Mass was said facing the people. But by the year 1000 the position that we are familiar with obtained nearly everywhere: the front of the altar faced the congregation. Nevertheless, the ancient position had not completely died out, and in modern times, with the growth in the understanding of the Mass and the meaning of the altar itself, there have been many attempts to place it so that people may gather around it in one way or another. Thus some altars stand in the center of the church; some are placed farther out in the sanctuary; some are built so that Mass can be said facing the congregation. The ideal arrangement would be to build the altar so that either position might be taken. For Mass facing the people has definite advantages and should contribute greatly to that more active participation which is always the ideal. At the same time the other position has its defenders, and too radical a change in this important matter might be unwise. Gradual changes are always safest and best. A hanging crucifix, candles placed near the ends of the altar on both sides, a low tabernacle, and smaller altar cards would obviate some of the difficulties urged against the "*versus populum*" celebration, for which the permission of the ordinary is required.

The Construction of the Altar and Its Adornment

Altars are of two kinds: fixed and portable. The *fixed* type is a permanent stone altar with table and support consecrated together. It cannot be separated and consists of four parts: the *mensa, stipites, sepulcrum,* and *substructure*. The *mensa* is made of natural stone which cannot easily be broken. The *stipites* is also of natural stone which need not be a solid piece but usually is. The *sepulcrum* or cavity for relics opens on the *mensa,* has a stone cover, and may be located in several places. It is, in other words, a reliquary containing the relics of two saints (authentic parts of saints' bodies), three grains of incense, and a parchment certificate. The relics should be those of martyrs, but may be those of a confessor or a virgin. The *substructure* is a permanent stone pavement standing free on all sides upon which the altar rests; it must be consecrated by a bishop. The *portable* type altar is simply a small, consecrated stone, large enough for its purpose and set in a frame of wood or metal. It too contains relics and should also have a title. When the portable type is used as part of a larger altar the former is known as a quasi-fixed altar.

The Furnishings of the Altar

According to the rubrics of the missal, the altar is to be furnished with a crucifix, candlesticks and candles, antependium, and altar cloths. The tabernacle is required for altars of the Blessed Sacrament. When Mass is said the Missal and altar cards are added. These may be called the essential furnishings of the altar, but we might add that a canopy is also required by law for at least the main altar.

The Altar Canopy. Although it has fallen into disuse in so many places, the canopy remains a necessary part of the adornment of the altar. Without it the altar is incomplete; with it the altar gains immeasurably in dignity and distinction. This canopy may be placed upon four or more posts, in which case it is called a *ciborium* or *civory;* or it may hang either from the ceiling or the back wall, when it is called a *baldachin* or a *tester*. In either case it must cover both the altar and the foot-pace. Of the two the *ciborium* is the older and, all things considered, the more appropriate form, although all will not agree on that point! It has the advantage of focusing attention upon the altar, of framing it as it were, and giving it a distinction that a *baldachin* does not so readily give.

Some authors claim that the *ciborium* goes back to the fourth century. It is in any case very ancient. The practice seems to have derived at least in part from the imperial or royal throne; it may also have come from the custom in some places of putting a structure of this kind over the images of the gods in pagan temples, and even over tombs. It is evidently an attribute of divinity and majesty, a mark of honor and respect which has the effect of setting a spot aside and proclaiming it as holy and sacred. Its use was widespread in the earlier part of the Middle Ages, but with the introduction of reliquaries on or behind the altar its use began to decline, although it has always been retained in Rome, at least in the older basilicas. In many other places it was either abandoned altogether or replaced by the *baldachin* in one form or another. The *baldachin* is more recent than the *ciborium* from which it most likely developed. The essential difference between them lies in the four posts.

The law prescribes a canopy for all altars where the Blessed Sacrament is reserved, and also for the cathedral altar, whether the Blessed Sacrament is reserved there or not. That canopy of course may take any shape or form, but recently there has been a widespread return to the *ciborium* type. There is little doubt that the latter forms an excellent and impressive setting for the altar, provided that it is not too heavy or ponderous. The setting must not draw away our attention from the altar itself, nor must it interfere with the ceremonies. A little care in planning the altar and consulting with competent masters of ceremonies should result in the best arrangement.

The Altar Steps. The altar is to be approached by one or more steps and the usual custom has been to have three. Although the first altars were placed on the floor, before too long it became customary to raise them on one step at least, in order to give them greater prominence. The number varied but three became usual almost everywhere by the thirteenth century. Perhaps the Ceremonial directing that the deacon and subdeacon each stand one step below the one higher in rank influenced the fixing of this number, but we do not know for certain.

The steps may be made of any material, but wood is preferred for the top step (foot-pace, *predella*) because stone is not comfortable to stand on, especially during cold weather. The steps should be low and deep with rounded rather than sharp corners, which can be very unpleasant to stumble against. A rug on the foot-pace and on the steps is not only decorative but much easier than stone to kneel or stand upon.

The Cross. For many centuries nothing was allowed on the altar except the altar cloths, the chalice and paten and the book from which Mass was said. Some authors say that the altar cross derives from the processional cross which was at first placed behind the altar after the clergy had reached the sanctuary. But this is not definitely established. There is no explicit reference to a permanent altar cross such as we know it today before the twelfth century; the cross that was used seems to have been removed after Mass. Only by the sixteenth century had the custom spread to the entire Church, and even then there were places where the cross was removed outside of Mass. It is doubtful if the cross bore a figure before the fourteenth century. To this very day the rubrics call for a *cross*, although it is taken for granted that it will be a crucifix.

The history of the cross is a very long and interesting one. We know that the early Christians did not make use of it except in disguised form; its associations were too horrible and painful for them. Even when they showed greater inclination to reproduce it in undisguised form they were content with crosses that were emblems of glory and triumph rather than of death. It was not until the sixth century that Christ was depicted *on* the cross; before that time either there was no figure or the medallion of Christ or the image of the lamb was placed against the background of the cross. Even when the whole figure appeared it was first placed in front of rather than upon the cross.

Once the figure began to be represented it was given a standard treatment from the sixth to the twelfth centuries: Christ was shown as alive, not dead or dying, with eyes wide open, head raised up, clothed in a long robe rather than a loin-cloth, often with a jewelled crown on His head. There were few exceptions to this mystical rather than realistic treatment.

The eleventh to the thirteenth centuries was a transitional period characterized by an approach to a more realistic representation. It is believed that the Crusades and the sojourns of many Europeans in Palestine contributed to the change, as they awakened a more realistic devotion to the Sacred Passion of our Lord. The figure became that of the dead or dying Christ, with thorn-crowned head bent, eyes drooping or closed, body sagging on the nails, sufferings clearly marked on face and body, naked except for the loincloth. This form of the crucifix superseded the earlier form to such an extent that men forgot it was if anything less traditional than its predecessor; they came to believe that it was the only kind of crucifix. The imprudent zeal shown by some in wishing to revive the older crucifix as the *exclusive* way of depicting Christ crucified won rebuke from Pius XII in his *Mediator Dei,* but it should be abundantly clear from history and tradition that the Pope's warning is not to be interpreted as *in any sense* a "condemnation" of the crucifix which represents Christ as "*regnans a ligno.*" Nor is it a condemnation of vested crucifixes, which are in line with the ancient custom in this regard, though we might hesitate to use them exclusively.

Today the cross is the principal and even essential ornament of the altar and should be the most prominent object upon it. Its importance should not be overlooked; it has a definite function to fulfill. Consequently a cross carefully and artistically made, of fine and large proportions (but not monumental), seems to be the ideal. It should be seen easily by all and for that reason should rise above the candlesticks.

As for the material to be used, nothing is prescribed. The form is a matter of taste, but anything savoring of the ultra-theatrical or ultra-realistic is forbidden by the canons of good taste. The crucifix should forcibly remind us, by its magnificent restraint, of the High Priest of our redemption who offered His Sacrifice upon the cross and who re-presents it in the sacred liturgy. It is a reminder of Christ's sufferings, but also of His triumph—indeed, more of His triumph than His sufferings, though the first could not be had without the second. It is the standard of the King, which we solemnly venerate on Good Friday as the "*Lignum Crucis in quo Salus mundi pependit*"; to say the very least, it is an emblem of life as well as of death. For all these reasons it should be rich and splendid and designed to impress.

The position of the crucifix is regulated to the extent that there is a prohibition against placing it before the tabernacle door or on the spot where the Blessed Sacrament is placed at solemn Exposition. It may be placed on the tabernacle, but that is not considered quite proper. It would be best to place it *behind* the tabernacle, rising above the altar, or, if one prefers, to hang it from the canopy or upon the wall behind the altar, but not too high. If there is a permanent exposition throne the cross must not stand in it nor even appear to do so.

The Candlesticks. There seems little doubt that the candlesticks on the altar had their origin in the seven lighted candles carried before the Bishop of Rome in the procession to the altar. When this procession arrived in the sanctuary the acolytes ranged the candlesticks around the altar. The custom spread during the Middle Ages; only in the eleventh century do we find candlesticks *on* the altar instead of around it. The number of candles varied with the feast, but as a rule there seem to have been at least two; sometimes only one was used for Low Mass.

Six candlesticks were prescribed in the fifteenth century. Beyond that there was no exact rule for the number to be used, except at the papal court beginning with the twelfth century, when seven candles were to be lighted at the pope's high Mass.

There should be at least two candlesticks on every altar, but the main altar must have six (seven when bishops pontificate in their own dioceses). No Mass requires more than six candles (although more may be added for Benediction) and the simplicity of the altar should not be spoiled by having more than the required number. Extra candlesticks used for low Mass should be removed afterwards. Branch candlesticks (candelabra) are not allowed for Mass; they are tolerated for Benediction provided the six main candles are also lighted.

No special material is prescribed for candlesticks; anything that is becoming may be used. Naturally the best candlesticks should be used for big feasts. There is no regulation about the form either, except that traditionally they are made up of a foot —a stem and a bowl. We should aim at artistic, well-made candlesticks whatever the material. There is no law against the use of color; it might as a matter of fact be very effective. Harmony should exist between the crucifix and the candlesticks, although that is not commanded. Common sense would tell us there should not be too great a discrepancy in size or material.

Candlesticks should be arranged in a straight line or, if one wishes, sloping upward towards the cross. They may not be arranged in a triangle or semicircle. The best place for them is on the *mensa* or at most on the gradine (step) designed for the purpose. They are not to be put on top of the retable, as is so often done. Since it is forbidden to drape them during Lent and Advent, it may be presumed that it is incorrect to drape them in black for funerals.

Candles. These are the official liturgical lights; any other illumination on the altar is forbidden. The candles are beautiful in themselves and in the symbolism which is attached to them.

They represent Christ, Light of the world. In the production of candles the mediaeval mind saw a parallel between the wax and Christ. The candles represent Christians, too, burning out their lives before Christ with the flame of pure devotion. The law requires that the candles used at Mass and the Paschal Candle be of beeswax (*saltem in maxima parte*). The other candles are also to be made of beeswax, at least for the most part. It belongs to the bishop to specify the beeswax content of the candles made. Candles that contain no beeswax may not be used on the altar for liturgical functions. Unbleached candles are prescribed for requiems, *Tenebrae*, and Good Friday.

Two candles are to be used for a low Mass on ordinary days. On solemn feasts, at the parochial or community Mass, more than two can be used, but not more than six. Six candles are prescribed for solemn Masses, four for a *Missa Cantata*, twelve for Benediction, twenty for Exposition, two for Divine Office without solemnity, four at Vespers with solemnity (although six is the usual custom). There is a prescribed way of lighting and extinguishing candles that must be observed. They need not be blessed, but it is customary to do so.

The Paschal Candlestick. This should be large and impressive, made of gold or silver or other metals, or of polychromed wood, and as rich and as beautiful as possible. Since the fifth century the Paschal candlestick has been a prominent part of the church furnishings and there are some exceedingly handsome examples surviving, particularly in some of the old Roman basilicas, where the candlesticks were attached permanently to the *ambo*. The normal place for them is and has been for centuries in the sanctuary, near the place where the Gospel is sung.

The Paschal candlestick owes its dignity to its function, which is to hold the Paschal Candle, the bright symbol of the risen Christ, recalling the pillar of fire in Exodus. This candle is blessed, according to a form, on Holy Saturday at the opening of the Easter Nightwatch, and remains in the sanctuary until

Ascension Thursday. It should be lighted at solemn Mass and at Vespers on Sundays; it may also be lighted on all solemnities and greater feasts. This candle must *not* be lighted at requiems or at Masses celebrated in purple vestments, nor at Benediction or Exposition of the Blessed Sacrament.

As we have said before, no electric lights are allowed on the altar for any reason whatever. As for the rest of the church, electric lights may be used, but theatrical effects are forbidden. Needless to say, neon lights should never be used in a church.

The Altar Cloths (*mappulae, linteaminae*). The altar cloth originally covered the entire table on all sides, like a modern tablecloth. This linen cloth served as the corporal and perhaps as the pall, and since it covered the front of the altar, it became a frontal as well. In time the one altar cloth developed into the altar cloth proper, the corporal, and (in silk), the frontal. The use of cloths was perhaps practical at first, but they became symbolic of the clothing of Christ and of the wrapping of His sacred body in a linen winding sheet.

This one linen altar cloth was originally put on the altar only during the time of Mass (cf. the liturgy of Good Friday) and was removed when Mass was over. About the year 1000 the altar cloth was left on the altar permanently. The number of cloths varied from one to three, but three became the prescribed number in the seventeenth century.

Three *linen* cloths are required for Mass (hemp is permitted). The top cloth goes down over both sides of the altar and should be of one piece. The two bottom cloths should cover the table only (one linen cloth folded twice may be used here).

The altar cloths should be as simple as possible and had best be made without adornment of any kind; it is a mistake to deform them (and the altar!) with cheap lace, as is often done. It is true that lace is tolerated as an ornament but we can hardly maintain that it is always an improvement. Simplicity is the true handmaid of beauty here as everywhere else. Let the cloths be of plain, white, clean linen, designed to stop at the front edge of the *mensa;* it is much neater if they do not hang over the front. The frontal will provide all the decoration that is necessary for the front of the altar; either lace or the overhanging linen are alike superfluous, particularly when they have scalloped or pointed edges, or hang down in such a way as to hide part of the frontal, which is the true adornment of the altar. The whole effect is fussy and untidy in the extreme; dignified repose and orderliness should mark the altar of God.

The cloths should be only *slightly* starched and are to be blessed according to the form given in the Missal.

The Antependium. This is also called the *pallium* and better still the frontal, and is to be regarded along with the altar cloths as the true ornament of the altar. The *antependium* is prescribed for every altar on which the holy Sacrifice is offered. Some authors maintain that when the front of the altar is ornamented or decorated the frontal need not be used. This of course is a question of opinion. The mind of the Church leans towards the use of the *antependium* if we are to judge by the prescriptions of her liturgical books and her tradition, now very venerable, of employing cloth hangings in front of the altar or all around it if necessary.

The Frontal. The frontal, with the altar cloths, makes up the vesture of the altar. The practice of clothing the altar is very ancient. It probably had its origin in the ordinary tablecloth, but the ritual clothing is mentioned in the fourth century in the East and fifth in the West; very likely the custom is even older. In time silken cloths replaced the original linen and became ornamented with embroidery and adorned with jewels. Sometimes the frontal was even made of precious metals or of painted wood. During the Middle Ages it became customary to have the frontal agree with the color of the vestments; this custom became a law in the seventeenth century. Yet the same seventeenth century saw a widespread discarding of the frontal itself, a tendency which began the century before, and which is to be attributed to the growing inclination to decorate the front of the altar with painting and sculpture.

The clothing of the altar, and especially the frontal, represents the royal vesture of Christ, which royal vesture is the Christian people, as the bishop says in the Ordination of Subdeacons: "The altar cloths and frontal [*pallia et corporalia*] are the members of Christ, the faithful people of God, with whom the Lord, as with costly garments, is clad, in the words of the Psalmist 'The Lord reigns; he is clothed with majesty.' " The vested altar is thus a symbol of the whole Christ, the Mystical Body, Head and members. Indeed it is the only symbol of the Mystical Body that we have.

The frontal is, then, prescribed by liturgical law and it is well that it should be. For it is hard to see what better means could be devised from an artistic and psychological point of view to bring out the altar and give it prominence, variety and beauty, than a tastefully made frontal. It makes for variety and beauty to have the altar hung in the color of the feast or season, gives warmth and life not only to the altar but to the whole sanctuary, and helps to impress the people with the meaning of the feast or season. There is something alive about color and cloth as there is about nothing else. On the other hand, an altar that is not so adorned looks the same on Easter Sunday as on Good Friday and becomes very tiresome as month succeeds month without any striking or arresting change.

The material for the frontal is not prescribed and there is ample scope for artistic talent to choose what is becoming and effective in the way of ornament and design. Panels of velvet or brocade against a plain or figured background can be very elegant, as are symbols when well designed.

The general rule is that the frontal be the color of the day, but there are a few exceptions to that: white is used for the

Blessed Sacrament, the color of the vestments is used for solemn votive Masses, and black or purple for requiems.

The *antependium* will hang best when it is suspended from a rod. A frame is likely to give it too stiff and ugly an appearance.

The Sacred Vessels

The Chalice. As the most important of the sacred vessels the chalice has exacting rules governing its making. The cup must be made of gold or silver and be gold-plated inside. The stem and base may be made of any other decent and durable material. The paten must be gold-plated on the upper side, whatever the material used. Every chalice must have the three parts: cup, node, and base. Whatever style is chosen for the chalice, it should be solid and not easily overturned. It would seem to be more in keeping with the use and character of the vessel that it should not be light and fragile in its construction.

History. The early chalices were made of various materials, glass, wood and stone being the most common; the shape of the original chalice most likely approached that of the Greek drinking-cup (*crater*). Practical considerations as well as reverence prompted gradual legislation against chalices of inferior material. The custom of Communion under both species brought about the using of two chalices, one for the priest, and one (larger, with handles) for the laity.

From the time of the conversion of Constantine the chalices became more precious—often made of gold and adorned with precious stones; the inferior materials of earlier days were abandoned. The barbarian tribes of the north, Goths and Vandals, and later on the Franks, tended to lavish and ostentatious chalices—often enormous in size.

The chalices that were produced from the fourth to the tenth century were of varying shapes and sizes; some of them have been preserved. We know of others through the monuments that have come down to us. Some were cups or goblets, others were more like vases. Most of them follow what was to become the classic pattern: a cup on a raised stem which widens into a base, with a knob or node to grasp it with. Chalices with handles —whether used for Communion under both kinds or not—were very common during the sixth, seventh and eighth centuries. In general, we may say that the chalice was moving during these centuries in the direction of what we know as the Roman style. The cup, node, and base of later times were more in evidence than they had been, but the cup was more egg-shaped than the later Roman cup would be, and the base too was narrower than it would become later on. After the year 1000 the chalices reached the full development of the Roman form: the cup is large in shape, almost a hemisphere, the base round and quite wide, the node large and also round. Many handsome examples of these have been preserved, particularly the chalice of Saint Remi kept at the cathedral of Reims.

The twelfth century saw the introduction of new forms which owe their origin to lengthening the stem, narrowing and lifting the cup, and changing the shape of the base. These new chalices (miscalled Gothic) exemplified a more conscious striving after elegance which easily became ostentatious. The node increased in size, often becoming enormous; decoration became more profuse; the cup rose higher. The Spaniards introduced architectural motifs which made the chalice look more like a building than a sacred vessel.

Whatever changes were introduced in the Middle Ages were merely transitional stages to the finished product of the Renaissance and Baroque eras. The stem became longer; the lips of the cup were curved so that it became tulip-shaped; often a false cup was added. The decorations passed all bounds of restraint and ran riot over the entire chalice; these decorations were in the best Renaissance tradition—cornucopia, angels, dolphins, etc. More often than not they were downright worldly. The chalice was thus completely changed. This was the story of chalices from 1500 to about 1900, except that they kept getting worse! They may have had some artistic merit in the work that was done on them; but certainly they lacked the dignity, restraint, and gravity which should distinguish a church vessel.

Much improvement has been made in recent years. Artists are going back more to the best in the past for inspiration. But it is still too often true that they are designed by men who produce *en masse* chalices of stereotyped, banal, uninteresting design, with a horrifying poverty of ornament and without any originality in design or decoration.

What has been said in this book about sacred art in general holds true of chalices in particular: they should have a certain distinction about them; they should in no way be ordinary or trite, but rather should be decently and becomingly made, pleasing to the eye and certainly as satisfying as the silver and metalware designed for use in homes, which are simple and beautiful objects, often far superior artistically to the much more expensive vessels used in churches. It is becoming more and more rare to encounter secular silver or metalware that is really bad or ordinary. These objects are designed with care and are a delight to the eye. Seldom do they offend against good taste. There is no reason why our chalices cannot attain a like excellence. A long step in that direction would be made if designers of chalices would give up trying to reproduce the past and especially the merely conventional—if they would consider what the chalice is going to be used for and start out with only that in mind. Again it is a matter of creating rather than copying or reproducing.

The Paten. Like the chalice, the paten has a long history. Originally it was much larger than it is today; its very name (*patena*—platter) indicates that. The paten at one time was much larger because it held the large breads offered at Mass. As far as we know, it was used from the earliest times.

The form of the paten has remained much the same through the centuries; it appears to have been round from the beginning.

The greatest change has been in the size and weight: both seem to have diminished with the passing of time. The change in the size of the altar-breads appears to have brought about the use of smaller patens. At certain times in its history the upper surface of the paten was heavily decorated. Practical considerations played no little part in eliminating such adornment.

Today the paten is usually made of the same material as the chalice itself, although that is not prescribed. Of course it must not be of inferior material and it must be gilded on the upper surface. Both chalice and paten must be consecrated. The chalice loses its consecration by notable alteration or deteriorations which change the original form and render it unfit for its purpose, by unbecoming use, or by being exposed for public sale or auction. It must be regilded when necessary.

The Ciborium. This vessel usually follows the same pattern as the chalice, except that it is equipped with a cover. It must be gilded inside, made of solid and decent material, and should be of adequate size but not too heavy or unwieldy. It is to be blessed, not consecrated.

The ciborium seems to have developed from the "*pyx*" which was the ancient name for the round metal box in which the Blessed Sacrament was kept. These round boxes were raised on stands and thus gave the ciborium its present form.

The Monstrance. This is to be made of solid and becoming material; it is recommended that it be at least gilded or silver-plated. The monstrance had its origin in the greatly increased devotion to the Blessed Sacrament which characterized the later Middle Ages. At first reliquaries or pyxes were used for processions and benedictions. The monstrance properly so called was at first a kind of tower; the sunray style so familiar to us is of the Renaissance or Baroque eras in origin.

The monstrance should be surmounted by a cross and in structure should not be so large as to be clumsy and unwieldy.

Strangely enough, while it is permissible to adorn the monstrance with statuettes of angels, this may not be done with images of saints. It need not be blessed, but a blessing is recommended. Before and after use, it should be covered with a veil when it is standing on the altar. If a sermon is preached *coram sanctissimo,* the monstrance is veiled. This veil should not be ornamented; it is better that it be a plain piece of silk.

The Lunette, Custodia, Communion Paten. The real receptacle for the Host in the monstrance is the *lunula* or *lunette,* so-called because of the half-moon shape it originally had. This is to be made of gold, or gold plated, and must be blessed. If glass is used it must not come in contact with the *Sanctissimum.*

The *Custodia* is a receptacle in which to keep the *lunette.* The inside should be gold or silver-plated. It is required only when there is no glass in the *lunette.*

The *Communion Paten* is prescribed and it should be made of silver or at least gold-plated and be provided with a handle. It need not be blessed.

The Altar Cards. Only one (the center card) is required; custom calls for three. They appeared about the sixteenth century; bishops do not use them to this day. The first consideration is that the cards should be legible. It is, therefore, a mistake to lavish attention on borders and frames when the print is too small to be read. Extremes in size should be avoided. The prayers should be arranged with an eye to their use (the *Suscipe* along the top, *etc.*). But above all, altar cards should be *legible.* They should be removed from the altar outside of Mass-time; the altar should not be used as a cupboard, sideboard or table.

The Missal Stand. This is a humble piece of furniture that has its part to play in the Mass. Its first purpose should be to hold the book. If a cushion is used it should not be too large nor too soft. The missal stand is best made of wood; metal is too heavy. It should be artistically made, easy to handle and easy to read from. If possible, it should be covered with a silk cloth the color of the day, but should be uncovered on Good Friday and for requiem Mass.

Flowers are permitted and even encouraged for feast days, but they should be used with restraint. They are accessory, not principal decorations, and should not usurp the place of the *antependium,* which is the true adornment of the altar. Too many flowers cheapen the altar; but a careful, tasteful use of them can make a very effective decoration. They are not to be put before the door of the tabernacle or on it, and they must not be used for requiem Masses or on the Sundays and ferials of Advent and Lent.

Gradines are shelves or steps on each side of the tabernacle to the rear of the altar-table, and are used to hold candles, vases, reliquaries, *etc.* They are useful according to some, a nuisance according to others. They are neither disapproved nor recommended but merely tolerated. An ideal altar will not have them; it is better that it be perfectly flat.

Relics and Statues. In some places it is customary to place reliquaries and small statues between the candlesticks. The rubrics of the Missal do not mention them, but the *Caeremoniale Episcoporum* recommends them for big feasts. The statues referred to are portable metal ones. Some conclude from this that plaster statues should not be used, and that those which are used should be *portable* (*i.e.*, not too large). Statues may not be placed on the tabernacle; they may be placed above the altar, provided they be the patrons of that altar.*

* Canonical legislation about statues in general is to be found in Canons 1278–1280.

The Tabernacle occupies a central position on the altar. It is the focal point of popular devotion and great care is taken by the law that the tabernacle be safeguarded and that its position in the church be emphasized. Thus the law says it must be fixed permanently on the altar and enclosed solidly on all sides; it must stand on the main altar in parish churches (in cathedral churches it may occupy a becomingly adorned side altar). Further prominence is secured by the tabernacle veil, which is *obligatory* and which is to cover the structure *on all sides.*

The minute care which the Church now bestows on the custody of the Eucharist is of relatively modern origin. For many centuries, piety did not express itself in visits to the Blessed Sacrament. The Eucharist was reserved for the sick and was kept in a cupboard or, later on, in a special cabinet in the sanctuary or, particularly in northern France and in Great Britain, in a silver dove which hung over the altar and which was called the *aumbry* or *pyx.* During the sixteenth century it became customary on the European continent to transfer the cabinet of reservation to the altar. The hanging *pyx* was discarded with the overthrowing of the altars in England, but it survived in some parts of France as late as 1939. The place on the altar that the tabernacle had attained by gradual evolution became its place by law. It is noteworthy that the Blessed Sacrament was kept in the tabernacle during the Middle Ages and into modern times *only* for Viaticum and for Benediction, not for Communion during Mass.

The tabernacle should stand on the altar, directly in the center, and should stand free in order that no obstruction prevent the hanging of the *canopaeum* (veil). There is no prescribed shape. A permanent exposition throne is not to be placed over it, as is so often done. The tabernacle has no prescribed dimensions, but it should not be so large as to be monumental, nor so small as to be impractical. The outside should be becomingly decorated in metal or carved wood, but not so elaborately as to provide a temptation to omit the required veil. The inside must be covered with metal or gilded wood or else with white silk, and a corporal placed on its floor. There is a strict law against an electric light inside, and no law prescribing the *inner* veil which is more apt to be a nuisance than a decoration. *Only* the *Blessed Sacrament* may be kept in the tabernacle. The key, ornamented with a gold tassel, should be carefully guarded. The tabernacle should be blessed.

As we have said before, a veil is strictly required. It is suggested that this veil be made of rich material; the ideal is a soft, pliable cloth which will hang all around in graceful folds. It is the true decoration of the tabernacle; its color may be either that of the day (that is ideal) or white; purple is to be used for requiems; black must never be used.

The Additional Parts of the Altar

These are: the *reredos* or, in its place, the *dossal;* on some altars, the *riddels* or side curtains; the canopy (which may either be hung or supported on four or more posts); and the Exposition throne. Of these, the canopy or *baldachin* is the only one prescribed; the others are extras which may or may not be used according to the style of the altar. From an artistic point of view, not to mention its adaptability to the purpose of making the altar stand out, it is hard to improve on the *ciborium* altar (a canopy resting on four or more posts). But this is only one type of altar; it is a question of preference, if not of taste. The permanent Exposition throne is a structure which if used is to be placed either in the *reredos* or in the wall behind the altar. This is recommended for churches or chapels where there is permanent Exposition, but frowned upon by liturgical authors for churches where there is no such Exposition.

CHAPTER 10

The Sanctuary and Its Furnishings

The sanctuary was forbidden to the laity from earliest times, and specific legislation against entry goes back to the fourth century. This law has been preserved in the Church into our own times and the sanctuary is regarded as the special domain of the clergy, except for certain rare occasions. This does not mean that the people are excluded from what goes on in the sanctuary; indeed, they are supposed to have an active part in what goes on there and nothing should be permitted to cut them off from the part they are called on to play. The elaborate choir screens of the Middle Ages, the deep sanctuary which persists into our own day in so many places, may be cited as examples of this unfortunate tendency. The liturgy is a community act, as we are coming to see more and more, and we must not let the proper insistence upon the place of the priest in that action make us forget or minimize the place of the community.

We should not need to be told that the sanctuary is the most important part of the church. It should, first of all, be the focus of attention and be made prominent by being raised above the floor of the church, but not too much so. It is conceivable that if the seats in a church converge downward towards the sanctuary, as they do in some places, the sanctuary can nevertheless be made central and therefore prominent by the right amount of emphasis. Let us agree at the outset that it should be wide and roomy, but not immense, giving ample space for passing to and fro which is demanded by a smoothly functioning ceremony. Nothing takes away so much from the dignity of divine worship as a crowded, small and wretched sanctuary. Even in small parish churches there should be space enough for solemn Mass, so that the ceremonial may be performed becomingly; needless to say, ample space should be a paramount consideration in a cathedral. Too many of our cathedrals are by far inadequate in this respect. Even in a parish church it should be possible to put up a throne for the bishop on his visit without crowding things unduly.

The effect of spaciousness is enhanced if we do not clutter the sanctuary with needless and distracting furniture. Some pieces are of course prescribed; they should be made with taste, with an eye to their usefulness and, let it be said, with an eye to their surroundings. We should never add furnishings merely to fill up space. Anything that is too large or too small, anything that is worldly, or garish, or cheap, does not belong in the house of God. Everything should reflect the dignity of the worship it is intended to enrich and assist: a worship, let it never be forgotten, which is itself a reflection of the never-ending liturgy of Heaven.

In most sanctuaries the necessary furniture will be: the lamps, the credence table, the seats for the clergy, the ambry for the Holy Oils, the ambo or pulpit, the communion rail, the throne for the bishop, and the carpet or rugs on the stairs of the altar and on the floor of the sanctuary.

The Lamps. One lamp must burn before the altar of the Blessed Sacrament at all times, but it is an ancient custom to burn many lamps before the altar. In fact the *Caeremoniale Episcoporum* prescribes this, calling for an uneven number of lamps: three, seven, or nine. Three lamps are to burn before the altar of the Blessed Sacrament, but it is safe to say that this prescription has fallen into disuse, although there is no reason why the custom should not be revived. These lamps are truly *sanctuary* lamps; that is, they are supposed to burn in the sanctuary and before the altar whether the Blessed Sacrament is reserved there or not.

With the coming of peace under Constantine in the fourth century lamps were burned in the churches, not only for the practical purpose of giving light, but for decorative and symbolic reasons. A little later on in the same century lamps were burned *before* altars, tombs of the martyrs, and images—as a mark of honor. Those burning before the altar were often hung from rods between the posts of the altar-ciborium or placed in the round chandeliers or *coronae*. Lamps used in church were fed with olive oil or wax, materials that were often presented with the bread and wine at Mass.

The lamps of the sanctuary may be made of any suitable material, but silver has a special fitness and elegance for this purpose. They should not be too large nor heavy because they are accessory and should not attract undue attention to themselves. They may be of any design, but simplicity is ever to be preferred to elaborateness. Besides, it will be easier to clean lamps of simple design. A clear glass is to be preferred to colored because the flame can be seen better and that is part of the symbolism of the lamp. They may hang on chains or pulleys or from brackets placed on the side walls. It is a mistake to hang lamps directly over the altar because the oil or wax may spill over on the altar cloths. The placing of lamps on stands is a dangerous practice if they can be easily overturned.

Hitherto we have been writing about *lamps* burning before

the altar, but in most places the only lamp is the one which burns before the Blessed Sacrament, as this is the one lamp for which the law clearly provides. Since the second half of the twelfth century there has been a custom, which in time became a law, of burning a lamp before the tabernacle. This lamp must now be placed before the tabernacle, not behind nor above it, nor upon the altar itself. It should burn olive oil or a mixture of olive oil and wax. White or clear glass is to be preferred to colored, although that is tolerated. Other oils may be used with the bishop's permission but he is not to authorize an electric light except when it is very difficult or impossible to obtain oil.

The Credence Table. This stands at the Epistle side of the altar and should be large enough to hold what is needed for Mass or other services. If we remember that a credence table must hold the chalice and paten covered with the humeral veil, the acolytes' candles, the water and wine cruets and dish, the communion plate as well as the Gospel book, we can see that it should be large. Most credence tables now in use are altogether inadequate.

Originally a niche in the wall served the purpose of the credence table, but during the later Middle Ages a table was used and in time this became the accepted practice. It should be made of becoming material and should harmonize with its surroundings, not clash with them. Too often these tables are out of keeping with their purpose and the holy place in which they stand, and are tricked out in unbecoming and untidy coverings. The law provides that they be covered with a white linen cloth reaching to the floor on all sides—like a table cloth. On Good Friday, only the top of the table is covered. If the table were covered completely as it should be, the danger of taking off the cover when the humeral veil is removed would be avoided.

In cathedral churches a second credence table is usually

necessary because of the many extra objects that must be kept on it. This table should stand away from the wall.

The Communion Rail. This is not required by rubrical laws, but must nevertheless be regarded as a practical necessity. It should not attract undue attention to itself by being too highly ornamented or decorated, since it is at most a secondary piece of furniture, and if it is too elaborate will act as a barrier to the altar. When people receive Communion they are in reality receiving it from the altar, and the communion rail becomes as it were an extension of the altar. This idea is brought out better and enhanced by covering the communion rail (which should be *wider* than a mere railing, incidentally) with the communion cloth which is required by law. Sometimes in fact it is called the *altar-rail,* a reminder of the relation between the two.

It is obvious that the communion rail should be high enough in itself to provide support for grown people. There should be a step to kneel on, but no more than one, for the sake of old or infirm people who should not have to climb up steps to receive Communion. It is a good idea to have leather cushions on the step to kneel upon.

For many centuries people received Communion standing, the ancient position of prayer and the position symbolic of the Resurrection. It was only in the late Middle Ages that the kneeling position became universal. Communion rails as such go back to the fifteenth or sixteenth centuries; before that, if they existed at all, they were merely a fence setting off the sanctuary from those who were not clerics.

The Sedilia or Scamnum is the special bench of the celebrant and the sacred ministers. There is scarcely another article of furniture in the church that is as persistently misconstructed and misadorned as this one. Very often it is not a bench at all, which it *must* be by law; instead it is usually an armchair or even a kind of throne (something that is specifically forbidden).

First of all, it should be a simple bench: it may have a back but it is not to have arm-rests, nor is it to be divided in any way whatever. The seats are not to be on different levels; there is simply to be one bench, with room for three persons to sit in comfort. It is not to be raised on steps nor is it to resemble, even faintly, a throne. There is specific legislation against the all-too-familiar armchairs, and in fact against chairs of any sort.

The *sedilia* should be covered with a cloth the color of the day or in green (purple for penitential seasons). An undraped bench is a sign of mourning and is reserved for funerals and for Good Friday. This law has fallen into disuse, but it is one that could be revived to good effect.

The bench is to stand at the Epistle side of the altar, preferably facing the side steps of the latter. It is most often made of wood and this is the preferred material, but it may also be of stone.

Choir stalls, Stools, Benches, and not chairs, are to be used for the other clergy who are present at services. This rule is almost universally disregarded with the result that our sanctuaries are cluttered with most unseemly folding chairs, dining-room chairs and even kitchen chairs, none of which objects contributes anything to the dignity of divine worship. Choir stalls are appropriate in cathedrals where the Divine Office is chanted, at least on the last days of Holy Week, and in monastic churches and in seminary chapels, where the Office is more common. They might be used in parish churches, but since they are associated with the Office it seems better to use benches or stools.

When the bishop confirms or ordains or celebrates Mass befor a greater prelate than himself, he should use the faldstool, which is a folding chair with arm-rests and without a back. He should not use an ordinary chair.

The Ambry for the Holy Oils. The three holy oils used in the administration of the sacraments are to be kept in three distinct metal containers, preferably of silver or pewter, with the name of each oil clearly marked on them. These containers are in turn to be kept in a cabinet which should be on the wall of the sanctuary or in a niche in the wall. At least the sanctuary is the proper place for this cabinet, although the law is fulfilled if it is in the church or, according to some authors, even in the sacristy. The ambry is usually made of wood, but it may be of stone or metal as well; it is lined with white silk and is provided with a lock. A veil of white and purple may be hung before it and there must be a sign on or near it reading "*olea sacra.*"

The Pulpit and Ambo. The modern pulpit is a successor to the earlier *ambo*, which was lower and more simple. In recent years there has been a tendency to return to the form and the position of the *ambo*. This was a low reading desk that stood at the Gospel side in the sanctuary; from it the deacon sang the Gospel and later on the sermon was often given from it. During the later Middle Ages and particularly at the period of the Renaissance and the Reformation, when sermons tended to be detached from the Mass and to acquire a kind of independent existence, the *ambo* was replaced by a larger and more elaborate structure which was often placed outside the sanctuary and even a good distance from it. The Gospel had long since ceased to be sung from the *ambo*; hence it disappeared from use except in some of the old basilicas of Italy.

The pulpit very often stands in the sanctuary. In recent years that is becoming more common; it is an excellent place for it, if for no other reason than it helps us to remember the close connection between the altar and the pulpit from which the word of God is proclaimed to the people. Nothing is said in the liturgical books nor in the decrees of the sacred congregations about its position or its construction, but it is customary that it be on the Gospel side (except in cathedrals) and it should not be too far off to one side. A certain prominence is becoming, but on the other hand a too-elaborate or large structure is out of place on the principle that nothing in the church should ever draw attention from the altar. It may be made of any material: wood, stone, metal, even brick, and it may be adorned with appropriate pictures, symbols or texts. The pulpit should not be too high; it is sufficient that it be raised slightly above the congregation. From a practical point of view, there should be an adequate reading desk at the front with a light that makes reading easy, and it is sincerely hoped that a public speaking system will be attached. We should not hesitate to make use of all modern helps in preaching the word of God.

If the pastor wishes, he may observe the ancient custom of having the Gospel and Epistle sung facing the people. It will certainly contribute to making them realize that these are readings directed to the congregation. If he does this, he may provide another simpler lectern for the Epistle side and use the pulpit for the Gospel. Better still, the Gospel might be read in English immediately after it has been sung in Latin.

On great feasts the pulpit may be adorned with silk hangings of the color of the day and at requiems it may be draped in black, but it is to be left undraped on Holy Thursday and Good Friday.

Rugs and Carpets. According to the *Caeremoniale Episcoporum* the sanctuary is to be covered from end to end with a carpet which may be of any color, although green is the most preferable. The altar steps and the foot-pace, according to the same authority, are to be covered with a rug or carpet on great feast days. Rugs and carpets add a touch of distinction to the altar and the sanctuary and are at least favored if not commanded by the liturgical laws. A fine rug or carpet, especially with an Oriental design, gives color and warmth to the sanctuary and is worth the expenditure involved.

The Bishop's Throne. Only the cathedral may have a *permanent* throne for the bishop. Even when the throne is temporary, however, it is to be set up properly. Originally it was an ornamented chair, usually made of stone and set up in the center of the apse behind the altar, facing out over the latter towards the people. The bishop was thus able to see the entire community: the clergy sat to his side, the ministers stood around the altar, the people filled in the space before him. Many of these fine old episcopal thrones are still standing in the churches of Italy and particularly in Rome. Such thrones are relatively simple chairs raised on a few steps. Later on the canopy and draperies were added. During the Carolingian epoch the throne of the bishop was moved, most likely because of the changes in the structure of the altar, to the Gospel side of the sanctuary.

The modern throne consists of three elements: the *cathedra*, the *platform*, and the *canopy*. The *cathedra* should be an imposing chair. It is to have arm-rests and must rise high in the back, above the bishop's mitre. The platform is to be three steps high and wide enough to hold the seats of the deacons of honor (which seats should not be chairs but stools). The canopy should cover the entire platform (not just the bishop's place). It is to be hung in *silk* either the color of the day or, if preferred, in green; it is draped in purple for funerals. The use of velvet is reserved for the pope and cloth of gold for cardinals. The steps are covered with rugs but cushions are to be used only by the bishop. The *cathedra* itself should be covered in silk.

The ideal place for the throne is, of course, in the apse, as in former times, but the arrangement of most of our cathedrals will not permit it.

The Mass-Bell. The rubrics of the Missal prescribe that a small hand-bell should be used for church services. It was first prescribed only in 1604, and then only for the *Sanctus* and the Elevation. Before that time bells were rung not in the church but from a tower outside it. Only later on was the bell rung at Communion time and at the *Hanc Igitur*.

The bell should be small, preferably single-tongued, made of silver or bronze, with a good clear tone. Chimes are not well-suited for the purpose. Gongs of any kind are specifically forbidden.

Cruets. They are better made of glass so that the contents may be seen, and should preferably be without handles or covers. Originally, when Communion was given under both species, the cruets were necessarily large and often made of precious metals: gold and silver, sometimes jeweled and enameled—very handsome vessels indeed. The small twin cruets (usually made of glass) came into widespread use after Communion was given in the form of bread only (from about the thirteenth century onward).

The Organ. For many centuries after it was first used in churches (eighth or ninth century) the pipe organ was small and was designed to accompany the singing only. The greatest development in organ music occurred during the sixteenth century and after; it was only then that organs began to be used more widely, and instead of merely accompanying the singing, the organ became an instrument of church music in its own right, a fact that was symbolized by placing it in a special large gallery, usually in the rear of the church.

The organ is the only instrument permitted by law for liturgical use. Its primary purpose is still to accompany the singing, but it can be used to great effect for preludes, interludes, and postludes. In some churches there are two organs: a smaller type near or in the sanctuary accompanies the choir, while the large organ is used for organ music independent of the signing. The organ should be selected with care. It is most desirable that it should have a fine tone and more than a little distinction. The electronic organ is permitted when a pipe organ cannot be had, but it should be regarded as a substitute, and not a very good one, for the pipe organ. It can never reproduce the clear and brilliant tone of a good pipe organ.

The Choir. The liturgical choir which sings the proper texts of the Mass and Office (and often the music of the Ordinary as well when the people are unable to do it) is most intimately connected with the liturgy and indeed comes next to the sacred ministers in importance. It is a most necessary part of the worshipping assembly: it is intended to lead and guide the singing, to sing the more difficult pieces, and to provide the commentary on what is going on at the altar. From this it appears that the normal and natural position for the choir is in front of the congregation and near the altar.* The singers may be screened off from the congregation if there is any fear that they may be a distraction, but they should really be no more of a distraction than the sacred ministers. Because the law proscribes women singing in church, the choir should be made up of boys and men who may be vested (they should be vested if they are in the sanctuary). If it is impossible to have men, the women singers might sit outside the sanctuary rails, at the front of the church. Another possible arrangement, though less desirable, would be to have a low gallery in or near the sanctuary.

The details of arranging the position of the organ and choir should be worked out by the priest, choir director, and the architect.

Images and Statues. Christian art was born in the catacombs where the walls were adorned with pictures and images intended to instruct and edify the faithful. When the era of persecutions was over this art flowed into the churches that were built on every side, and ever since the Church has been the mother of the arts. Her doctrines afford unfailing inspiration to artists,

* The sanctuary was the traditional place for the choir until modern times; after the sixteenth century the use of mixed choirs and the distance of the organ, which had become enormous, from the altar, contributed to the modern choir-loft arrangement. Women were not allowed in the sanctuary and the singers had to be near the organ. Also, the idea had already begun to develop that church music was to be listened to and consequently performed. This idea contributed to the new arrangement and in turn it was fostered by the situation it had helped to create.

and the depicting of those persons and events associated with religion, particularly our Lord and our Lady and the Saints, has been a powerful means of decorating the churches and lifting the minds and hearts of the people to heavenly and spiritual things. In many different forms—paintings, mosaics, sculpture, wood carving and stained glass—the whole vast universe of Christian doctrine has been presented to countless thousands through the long centuries.

Laws have been framed by the Church regulating the making of images, but not in detail because that is as impossible as it is undesirable. The laws set down certain general principles as a guide to avoiding whatever is out of keeping with the dignity of the church as the house of God, whatever is doctrinally unsound, or whatever is unworthy of the subject depicted or represented. A wide latitude is left to the artist by such legislation, and a corresponding burden and responsibility are placed upon those who select such work for Church use. The great governing principle is that pictures and statues displayed in the church for public veneration should be dignified and becoming. They need not be great artistic productions but they must be made with a certain skill and fulfill the aim of all art, which is to present the ideal and the spiritual in material forms. We have a right to ask that the pictures and statues in our churches be adequate embodiments of the divine, the spiritual and the supraterrestrial. They cannot *portray* these things but they must suggest them. Otherwise, regardless of how technically skillful they may be, they are flat, lifeless and, oddly enough, unreal. The norm of the excellence or suitability of a picture, statue, or crucifix is not the utterly subjective approach expressed in the words "I can [or 'I can't'] pray in front of that" or, "It arouses no devotion." The fact is that sentimentality and purely natural feeling is too often mistaken for "devotion." The purpose of a sacred picture or statue is not to arouse feelings, but to stimulate devotion, which is another thing altogether. They do that by recalling holy things to our minds: what they are and what they stand for and represent. A picture of our Lady with the Child on her knee can be only the picture of a beautiful and gracious lady; to be really an object of sacred art it must somehow go beyond that and convey Mary's dignity as the *Theotokos*—the Mother of God. It must first do that in itself before it can arouse the proper devotion in the worshiper. The real purpose of sacred art is to give outward expression to the soul of the person depicted and thus to educate the soul of the beholder. It is intended to be *contemplated* and consequently must have depth. It must not be superficial; each time we look at it the painting or statue must convey something to us. A religious painting or statue is a window opening into the world of the spirit or it is nothing.

Statues and pictures of different saints should be different from one another. A statue of St. John the Baptist is bad artistically if the conventional symbols of St. John are merely added to a figure that could just as well represent any other male saint. The representation of John the Baptist should convey something of the Voice crying in the wilderness, something of his fire, his fierce zeal, his great austerity, his vocation as a prophet. A good portrait catches the spirit of the man or woman portrayed, and the same rule holds good for the representations of the saints.

Statues should be made of becoming material, that is to say, of stone or wood; plaster statues had better be avoided. There should not be too many of them; it is better to have a few that are well made and pleasing than a host of inferior, if not unworthy and insipid, images. Statues should also conform to their surroundings in size, material and workmanship. Needless to say, statues or pictures are to be kept subordinate to the altar; they occupy a secondary place and should not attract attention out of all proportion to their importance.

For all these reasons we should think twice about the statues and pictures that we place in our churches. It would be a pity to spoil an otherwise beautiful church by an ill-advised selection of statues or pictures.

Statues or pictures of the patron saint of the church may be placed above the altar, but not upon the tabernacle. The laws of the Church do not permit any unusual picture or image to be placed in a church, nor any that does not conform with the approved usage of the Church, nor finally any representations that are not dogmatically correct or which may lead people into error. In these matters the ordinary is to be the judge. Certainly the intention of the Church is not to stifle nor to discourage artistic talent. What is intended is to keep out anything that is bizarre or outrageously unusual. The word "unusual" should not be too strictly interpreted, since excellence is unhappily unusual in one sense. Nor should we too easily criticize the idea of distortion, because a certain amount of "distortion" is necessary in any great work of art insofar as departure from mere photographic realism is distortion. The idea of art is not to present things as they are externally but as they are inwardly. A good portrait painter must "distort" to a certain extent in order to bring out the inner character of his subject. That is one reason why even the best photographs cannot be good portraits; the camera cannot capture anything but the physical and material. There are certainly extremes in modern art; when portraits and statues are manifestly so they should be avoided. The church should not be treated as a museum of modern art nor a place for experimentation in it. However, it must be said that the danger here at least is from the opposite direction; we are more inclined to be unduly conservative in these matters and too often encourage an art that is lifeless and dull when it is not sentimental and banal.

Other Places Associated with Worship

The Baptistery. The Baptistery contains the font (*piscina, natatorium*). The older baptismal fonts are reminiscent of the original method of Baptism by immersion (although infusion seems to be of equal antiquity). They are low pools into which one might step down. The change of customs, the practice of infant Baptism, the cold climate of the north, all contributed to give the font its present shape. The baptistery should be, if possible, separate from the church. If that is not possible it should at least be railed off from the rest of the church. There should be a picture or statue of the baptism of Christ. It is recommended that the baptistery be adorned with fitting texts and symbols—"*ad instruendam.*" Provision should be made for keeping the oils there, for a *sacrarium,* and for a cabinet or closet to take care of the vestments and instruments needed.

The Font should be solid in construction (wood, if used, must be lined with metal), high enough, wide enough and covered with a lid. It is most convenient to have two compartments in the font. Near the font must be kept the sacred oils, the salt, the baptismal shell, cotton, stole and surplice, white linen garment, candle, Ritual, register.

The Sacristy is a place where those things necessary for church functions are kept and where the clergy and assistants prepare for those functions. It should be large, well-lighted, well-appointed. Two sacristies are used in many places. The sacristy contains a vestment case, crucifix, prayers for vesting, title card, cabinets, safe, sacrarium, wash basin, prie-dieu, and the books needed.

There should be a room for the accessories that are not in constant use where they may be stored during the year. It is a good idea to have an altar in the sacristy too, where infirm or blind priests may celebrate Mass, and a confessional for the deaf, etc. Great care should be taken to have a clean and *orderly* sacristy.

Confessionals should be conspicuous and easily accessible, made with due regard for comfort and convenience, soundproof, ventilated. There should be a surplice and stole for confession, electric light, and a crucifix in the penitent's compartment. The confessional is perhaps best located near the door of the church with ample space around it.

Church Bells. Although it seems that they have largely gone out of fashion in our modern churches, bells are an altogether desirable addition to the furnishing of a church. The laws of the Church recommend their use and prescribe that they be consecrated or blessed, and provide that the ringing of them be absolutely under the control of the church. There is no law governing the number or form of these bells. Most of the details regulating their use are in the *Caeremoniale Episcoporum.* According to these rules, the bell plays a great part in the life of the parish and the faithful: it rings joyously to call them to church services on feast days; to announce the coming of the bishop or a greater prelate; during the Mass at the Elevation; while the procession of the Blessed Sacrament is in progress; at Benediction and the Communion of the sick; during the *Gloria in Excelsis* on Maundy Thursday and other days determined by the Ceremonial; and for the Angelus. It is tolled when some one is dying; to announce a death, and for funerals. The bell may not be rung on the last three days of Holy Week.

Ringing the bell is the privilege of the porter, as the Rite of Ordination to the *ostariate* shows, but this duty has fallen in practice upon the sacristan or sexton.

The use of bells is very ancient, as they are the most universal of musical instruments and they appear fairly early in the history of the Church. Some churches seem to have had them in the fifth century. They were small at first, but from the eighth century onward grew in size and importance; it was about the same time that the Rite of Consecration of Church Bells arose. Like most of the elaborate rites of the Pontifical, this rite owes its present form to the enrichment brought by the Gallican Rite: the bell is anointed with chrism and the oil of the sick, sprinkled with holy water and sweet-smelling perfumes.

The Cemetery. Among the places which the Church sets off with a special blessing is the cemetery, the last resting place of those who "are marked with the sign of faith" and whose bodies await the glorious resurrection. As everyone knows, cemeteries are closely associated with the beginnings of the Church in the catacombs of Rome. Christian art was born in the catacombs and certain permanent features of our liturgy had their origin in the honors paid to the bodies of the martyrs. The walls of these early Christian cemeteries reflected in their pictures and inscriptions many of the exalted truths by which those buried there and those who buried them lived lives so full of the authentic Christian spirit. Almost from the beginning the Christian cemetery has been a sacred place, a place where even in the surroundings of death the hope of a glorious resurrection shone forth, a place where those who rest in Christ proclaim even in death that they await "a place of refreshment, light, and peace."

Because they believed in the resurrection of the body and its sacredness, Christians refused to countenance the cremation so widely practiced by the Romans, and insisted upon a decent burial. The first cemeteries began as family burial grounds when well-to-do Christians permitted the burying of their brethren in the Faith as well as their own relatives. Later on, the pious desire to be buried near the tombs of the martyrs led to burial in or near the churches where their bodies lay. The clergy were buried in the churches as a matter of course, but the privilege was also accorded to some of the laity. Obviously it was not possible for all to be buried in the church; so in the Middle Ages burials were made in the church yard, which was for the purpose regarded as a kind of extension of the church itself. This practice of having the cemetery near the church became widespread and is maintained in many places today. The general custom in this country is to have the cemetery away from the church and usually on the outside of the city or town. Nevertheless, the cemetery remains technically an extension of the church; it is consecrated and dedicated to God; it is a holy place, and may not be alienated from its sacred purpose.

The monuments in a Catholic cemetery should be simple in construction, avoiding all extravagant display as befits the tombs of men and women "who have not here a lasting city." The inscriptions and the decorations on these tombs could express the Christian hope and belief in the glorious resurrection. A large crucifix should dominate the burial ground, reminding us of the ground of our hope, the redeeming death of Christ.

Since the cemetery is church property and a holy place, it would seem more fitting that funerals should be conducted with the full ritual of the Church, with vestments, candles, incense, and processional cross. There really seems to be no good reason why the contrary custom of not wearing all the vestments should be continued. It is a relic of other days when external religious ceremony was kept to a minimum. A small store-house or chapel could be built in the cemetery if need be where these things could be kept ready for use.

The blessing of a cemetery is reserved to bishops and is found in the Pontifical. Five large wooden crosses are placed in the cemetery—one in the center and one in each corner, each with three candles burning before it. The rite itself consists in the singing of the Litany of the Saints with appropriate invocations at the end; reciting the seven penitential psalms and six prayers and in sprinkling the crosses with holy water. The final prayer is a preface in the traditional Eucharistic form, of surpassing beauty. The entire rite develops the themes of light and life, of the resurrection and the life to come, of the promised land, the judgment, of rest and eternal glory. All in all, it is one of the most beautiful, consoling and doctrinal rites that the Church possesses. It goes back in its present form to the ninth century.

CHAPTER 11

Sacred Vestments and Insignia

The Sacred Vestments

By way of introduction, let us say that the vestments worn at the altar were originally the everyday garments of the ordinary Roman citizen and, though they have acquired symbolic meaning with the passing of time, they remain essentially *clothes*, archaic survivals of the vesture of bygone days.

The Roman citizen, whatever his rank, wore as a rule two garments: one an inner robe, long and white, reaching to the feet and kept in place by a cincture; the other an outer garment which was a long, sombre-colored cloak covering the whole body on all sides and provided with a hood. The cloak was worn when the weather was inclement; hence it was called a *pluviale* (raincoat), a name that has adhered to the *cope* which has descended from it.

These clothes eventually became *vestments* in a quite natural manner. Everyone wore them (the wealthy classes used the toga over the tunic instead of the cloak, at least for formal occasions, but few of the early Christians belonged to that class) including the clergy, who of course wore them at the altar and in the liturgical assemblies. They might wear better and cleaner clothes for divine worship, but the form of these was the same as the clothes they wore in daily life. So they first became associated with the liturgy, as "Sunday best," but not as vestments properly so-called.

The coming of the barbarians in the fifth and sixth centuries made changes in the secular costume of the period. Men in general began to wear clothes that were shorter and abandoned the old long garments, but the clergy did not. On the contrary, they continued to wear the more dignified robes which were already associated in a special way with the altar: the long tunic (*alba*) and over-garment called *planeta* or *penula*, usually of a dark shade, brown or purple. Bishops wore a kind of scarf over the chasuble which later developed into the *pallium*, and all the clergy carried long handkerchiefs which later became *maniples*. But the main parts of the costume were the tunic and the full cloak, and they remained so for hundreds of years.

Principles of Church Vestments. What we have just seen will guide us in our approach to the subject of church vestments. We must remember first of all that they are *clothes* and, consequently, that they must do what clothes are intended to do: cover and clothe the body. But they are not *merely* clothes, though they remain essentially so; they are clothes used for divine worship. They should, then, not only cover and clothe the sacred ministers but they should do so elegantly, handsomely and beautifully.

The first general rule is that we should aim at what is noble, dignified and fitting. Anything that is mean, poor, skimpy, incomplete, inadequate; anything that is ridiculous, worldly, or in any way overdone, does not belong in the sanctuary. The liturgy on earth is a reflection of the liturgy that goes on in Heaven. We should not have to make superhuman efforts to remember that; everything about the worship of the Church should help us to remember it. This outlook on the liturgy will inspire us to choose that which will best give expression to this idea. So let us have the best: not the most expensive, nor the showiest, but the best, the best made, best cut, best fitted. Vestments, then, must be long rather than short, not stiff and ugly but falling in soft folds, becomingly and fittingly adorned. Anything that savors of the gaudy or the theatrical, anything that is trite or commonplace, should be avoided. We should get away from the idea that anything we buy in a religious goods store is *ipso facto* fit for divine service. Very often it is anything but fit, and rather perpetuates what is poor and mean and cheap.

The material and the ornament for the vestments should be carefully chosen, avoiding anything that is too stiff or too heavy, and rejecting whatever looks cheap or tawdry, too flashy or too effeminate. The material should be given to someone who is competent to make vestments, and cut according to a good pattern. If ready-made vestments that correspond to these standards can be bought, well and good, but the point is that we do not have to depend upon them. Very handsome vestments can be obtained by having them made to order.

Vestments, as we have said, are clothes—clothes made to be worn by men. They must, then, be *manly* and will be if they are full and noble, if they fit well and hang properly, if they are put on properly and are worn properly. They should *dress* the priest, not merely *adorn* him. The best vestments will not be conspicuous, but will give the definite impression of *belonging*. They will not distract from the liturgy but will contribute to enhance it. And that is all we can reasonably require of them. Vestments show that the priest is an official personage acting *in persona Christi* and in the name of the Church.

The vestments should contribute to the atmosphere of recollection which is rightly associated with the courts of the Lord. They are not only clothes—they are sacred vestments and should contribute to the edification and even the sanctification of the people. This is not a matter of indifference, but rather of the greatest importance. Vestments must promote in the minds of men a sense of the sacred. They will do this if by their sobriety, restraint and simplicity, they proclaim to us that the priest is engaged in a sacred action, that he is doing a great and holy work. They must, then, have about them that seriousness and that respect for truth which we expect to find in whatever is being used for worship. They must not—by their frivolity or ostentatiousness, their want of dignity in other words—distract us from what is being done.

The Amice is a square or rectangular piece of linen or hemp with two strings or ribbons sewn to the upper part of the rectangle to tie it on. It was not intended as a vestment at first, but was worn by monks as a sort of shoulder cape to protect the neck and throat and to provide a kind of cincture worn at work; hence the strings. The *amice* became a vestment in the Middle Ages when it was worn on the head by all priests going to and coming from the altar. The biretta, originally another hood, supplanted it among the secular clergy beginning with the Renaissance. The *amice* represents the "helmet of salvation" (still placed on the head but removed immediately at Mass) and the "*castigatio vocis*." * It may be ornamented with a small cross at the upper edge and may be adorned with embroidery, lace or apparels; but it is perhaps best to have it as simple as possible.

The Alb is a long-sleeved tunic which reaches to the floor. It may be tied at the neck with strings, but a button, or a zipper, or just the opening alone are neater. The greater part of the *alb*, and preferably the whole of it, must be made of linen or hemp. It may be adorned with embroidery, lace, or apparels, but we should remember that these are always accessory. Lace in particular should be used with restraint; most lace *albs* are a dis-

* From the Rite of the Ordination of Subdeacons, a survival of a time when it was used to protect the throat.

grace. Really good lace, heavy and rich, can be quite beautiful, but it is very expensive; consequently, what we see so often in its place has to be not only ordinary but cheap and ugly. There is no law saying that lace must be used at all, although one would think so judging by the widespread idea that *albs* cannot be made of anything else. On the contrary, there is a law that says the lace is not to go above the knees! Only great prelates are permitted the use of full lace *albs* (lace from the waist down) and even they are not obliged to wear them.

The *alb* should be cut according to a good pattern and should be rather full, especially in the lower part, to permit freedom of movement. The most practical thing would be for each to have his own *alb* (two would be better). This vestment should be put on with care, not gathered in the back or bunched up. The best results are obtained when the alb is allowed to hang evenly on all sides and the cincture is tightened just enough to hold it in place.

The *alb* represents purity, innocence, divine grace. This symbolism will help us to remember that it should be a *white* garment. "Clothe me in a white robe, O Lord," the priest says when he is putting on the *alb;* "Linen shining and white," says the Apocalypse, describing the garments worn by the just in Heaven. A white linen *alb* makes the best background for the vestments which appear above it, particularly the stole. Most lace *albs* fade into a grey (or a pink) when they are worn over a black (or purple) cassock. The *alb* thus loses the strength and vigor of linen and becomes vague and weak.

The *alb* may be worn by everyone ministering at the altar, and this includes the altar boys and Mass servers—a practice which should be encouraged for many reasons. Perhaps we would then see an end to all the unathorized frippery in which altar boys are so often decked out in unconscious (let us hope) defiance of the decrees of the Congregation of Rites! A simple white linen alb, well-fitted and properly worn—could anything look better?

The Surplice and the rochet are shortened and ungirded *albs.* They originated in the Middle Ages and were used as a substitute for the *alb.* The large sleeves of the *surplice* owe their fullness to the fact that this garment had to be worn over the fur-lined robes which were used to warm the clergy in choir before the days of central heating. They were deliberately enlarged and beautified in the later Middle Ages. The *rochet,* on the other hand, is the *alb* that was worn in daily life by the mediaeval clergy. It came to be associated with the more prominent clergy and by the end of the Middle Ages was prescribed for prelates. Only in the seventeenth century did it become as short and as adorned with lace as it is today.

The *surplice* can be a very handsome garment if it is long enough and cut properly. It should be made of linen. Other materials may be used because there is no legislation against them, but here again it can be confidently asserted that a great advance would be made towards securing the decency of divine worship by avoiding the use of lace, silk, nylon and other flimsy and frivolous materials. Pleating the *surplice* is an abomination that happily is disappearing. Here as elsewhere natural folds make the best adornment. The surplice should reach at least to the knees. Round necks are more pleasing than square.

The *rochet,* which is not really a vestment, should be as long as the *surplice,* and the more linen it has the better it will look. Fine lace gives it a certain distinction and is apparently called for by the laws regulating the costume of prelates. It is better to comply with the law by having a few inches of really fine lace than to ruin the garment with yards of inferior material. The lace cuffs of the *rochet* are to be lined with red or purple but, contrary to a widespread misapprehension, there is no law prescribing lace cuffs with lining on the alb of a prelate.

Since the *rochet* is not a *surplice* a prelate should never administer the sacraments without wearing a *surplice* over it.

The Cincture is a long cord of linen or silk used to hold up the *alb*. It should not be too bulky nor too long. It now symbolizes chastity ("girding of the loins"), but was purely practical in its origin. It may be of the color of the day, unlike the *alb* or the *amice*.

The outer vestments must be made of silk (natural or artificial) in some one of its forms: plain silk, velvet, damask, or a fabric mixed with silk, but not of linen, cotton or wool. Besides silk, cloth of silver may be used instead of white, and cloth of gold instead of white, red or green. But in these latter cases, the vestments must be made of real gold or silver thread. Cloth of gold or silver is *permitted;* it is not required, and from an aesthetic point of view it is not at all desirable because it is too stiff to hang in the soft graceful folds which make up the essential beauty of a really fine vestment.

The *maniple* (*manipulus, mappula, brachiale*) was perhaps originally a napkin used for practical purposes, but the earliest references to it in Christian times show it as a ceremonial decoration, a mark of honor modelled on a similar ceremonial napkin worn by Roman dignitaries. At first it was peculiar to the clergy of Rome, who carried it in the left hand during the celebration of the liturgy. Later its use was extended to the clergy of other churches, who also carried it in the hand, a custom that lasted until the twelfth century. This in fact explains the rather puzzling name "*maniple*" which means something gathered in the hand. Gradually, after it had begun to be worn upon the arm, it took the form of a band of cloth, became adorned with fringes at both ends and, finally, before the end of the Middle Ages, became the vestment we know today, made of the same material and color as the *chasuble,* and matching the *stole*.

The *maniple* may be fastened to the arm by an elastic loop or by a pin. The first way is preferable for many reasons: it is much neater and is easier on the vestments. There must be a cross in the center, but no other ornament is prescribed. The *maniple* should be long and graceful, neither too narrow nor too wide; if it is made properly, it will not sweep the altar. It need not have a fringe, but if there is one it will look better if it too is long. Short and stubby fringes add nothing to a vestment. And this is a good place to say that fringes are best made of silk—we have had enough gold fringes to last a long time! The long *straight* design is the most pleasing; the day of shovel *maniples* and *stoles* is past. The latter grew out of the unfortunate tendency to splay out the ends.

The symbolic meaning of the *maniple* is that it represents the sheaf (*manipulum*) borne home by the reapers as the "reward of work well done." The *maniple* remains an insignia of rank and a mark of honor reserved for those in major orders, and is to be used only at Mass.

The Stole is a long narrow scarf falling in two equal strips of cloth over the front. It is a liturgical insignia common to deacons, priests and bishops. Originally called the *orarium*, which means a towel or a napkin, it was like the *maniple* a piece of cloth that had a practical purpose at first and then became a sign of distinction and honor and even a mark of office. Though they now look alike it appears that the deacon's *stole* had a different origin from that of the priest's; the deacon's was a true napkin worn outside the *dalmatic* and used for ministering at the liturgical services and at the *agape*. That is why they wore it on the shoulder. On the other hand, the priest's *stole* was a piece of cloth, a scarf worn around the neck to protect him from cold in winter and to absorb the sweat in summer. That is why the priest wore it under the *chasuble*. Very early, however, these practical uses gave way to the ceremonial; *stoles* became vestments in the strict sense but retained traces of their origin in that the deacon still wore his on the shoulder (and for a long time outside the *dalmatic*) and the priest wore his *stole* around the neck. The *stole* became a vestment in its present form before the eighth century. Centuries after it had become a vestment, properly so-called, it retained its beautiful and dignified appearance: long and narrow, reaching almost to the feet; but in the later centuries it became like the *chasuble:* sadly deformed, too short, too wide, with ends splayed out to ridiculous proportions, over-ornamented, and otherwise depressing.

The *stole* should be long enough to reach beyond the *chasuble,* even when it is crossed on the breast; it should be soft and pliable like the *maniple,* with long fringes and becoming adornment (strips of velvet, brocade, colored silk, or symbols at the ends are all very effective).

The name *stole* is really a misnomer because the *stola* was a robe, not a strip of cloth. Nevertheless, it was given its present name in the Middle Ages and from that name derived the symbolic meaning that goes with it: it represents the robe of immortality lost by our first parents, restored in and by Christ. We think of the *stole* above all as the badge and symbol of priestly authority and dignity. Crossing the stole on the breast was first prescribed by the Missal of St. Pius V.

The Chasuble (*planeta, casula, amphibolus*). The law prescribes no definite kind of *chasuble,* though the rubrics presuppose the ample style. Descended from the majestic *paenula nobilis* worn in daily life by the Romans during the earlier centuries of Christianity, it retained its ample lines well into the late Middle Ages, although the shortening and cutting away had begun to a certain extent even then. But the *chasubles* were still ample enough when the rubrics of the Missal and Pontifical were drawn up and edited during the sixteenth century. The "modern" *chasuble* as we know it, in a sadly cut away shape, really goes back only to the eighteenth century, when the shortening and cutting away was done in earnest. The use of heavy brocades and damasks, velvets, and cloth of gold at the time of the Renaissance is usually assigned as the reason for cutting down the fullness of the vestment to make more room for the arms so that they would not be encumbered. Undoubtedly economic considerations played their part too. In any case, we find that by the end of the sixteenth century the cutting away proceeded to the point where St. Charles Borromeo legislated that *chasubles* were not to go above the elbow as a minimum. As we have said before, the real damage was done in the eighteenth century: the vestments were not only cut away and shortened until they could only with difficulty be recognized as descending from the old *planeta,* they were as well made still more hideous by being stiffened with buckram, and the old form was completely mutilated.

The older *chasuble* never really died out but it became so rare that when some zealous lovers of Christian art tried to revive them in 1863, they were not encouraged. But as interest in the liturgy grew, interest in the beauty and dignity of worship grew with it, and more and more men came to see that Church vesture was as decadent and deformed as Church music had become; that the restoration of the true, the sincere, the simple and the dignified was as much in place here as in other departments of the liturgy. As the decades of this century went by, men could rejoice to see the old forms appearing more and more.

Unfortunately, some did not see that it is impossible to restore any one definite period in the past and that the Church is not wedded to the Middle Ages nor to the earlier centuries either. The mistake was made of *copying* the past, and while this resulted in an improvement, it was only a copy after all. The ample *chasuble* was worn in the early days of the Church and worn in the Middle Ages; it can also be worn in modern times, because it is in itself timeless and universal. Because it has a long history it speaks to us of the past; it is traditional in the best sense. But it must not be made to appear as a mere "restoration" of the past.

About 1925 a few bishops asked the Sacred Congregation of Rites if vestments might be made which departed from the use (custom) of the Roman Church, even though they were according to ancient models. The answer was that the Holy See must be consulted before such vestments could be introduced anywhere. The ample vestments were not "condemned" either then or any other time, but the Holy See wished to be consulted about them and invited the bishops to give their reasons for favoring this revival. Since that time ample vestments have spread more and more and are being worn everywhere, and it is safe to say that even the benign answer of the Sacred Congregation of Rites is out of date in the matter by this time. No one seriously believes that the Holy See now expects to be consulted about the use of ample vestments, and the almost universal custom of wearing them amounts to an official approval, if any were needed. Here again we must remember the general principle that the church furnishings and decorations are supposed to be in accord with the norms of sacred art and the tradition of the Church; it is never the intention of the Church to discourage what is good, much less what is the best, in these matters. There was a time when the introduction of what appeared to be new forms might have caused "*admiratio*," and that is one reason why the authorities counseled moderation in the matter; but that danger is past.

The *chasuble*, then, should be ample enough to fall in full, natural folds. The best results are achieved by cutting the cloth so that the vestment reaches to the wrists and beyond the knees of the average wearer.* The opening for the neck should be wide enough for its purpose but not so wide as to be unsightly.

There is no law prescribing the ornamented bands or orphreys, although they are customary in one form or another. They may be of any color. A surprising inventiveness has been shown in this matter in recent years, enough to demonstrate that here as elsewhere there is room for creative activity and

* Most chasubles, even those that are called ample, are not cut properly, and as a result they are not full enough. Perhaps the best results are obtained by cutting them on a semi-circular pattern.

that we get our best effects when we put an end to a mere copying of the past. There is a prohibition against putting the skull and crossbones, images of the dead, or white crosses on black vestments; the greatest latitude is otherwise allowed in the matter of ornament and lining. If lining is used (it need not be) it may be of any color, whether it is a "liturgical color" or not.

Chasubles were once used not only by the celebrant but by all the sacred ministers including the acolytes. A survival of this is the use of "folded *chasubles*" in Advent and Lent. The so-called "broad *stole*" is in reality not a *stole* at all but a *chasuble* folded in "military style" to allow greater freedom of movement to the deacon.

The Dalmatic is the distinctive garb of the deacon and in slightly modified form as the *tunic* it is worn by the subdeacon as well. They both have the same origin: the tunic was worn by peasants in Dalmatia and was wider and fuller than the Roman *tunic*. As a liturgical vestment it was at first peculiar to Rome, where it was worn by the pope under his *chasuble* and by the deacons to whom he gave the privilege of wearing it in the fourth century. Its use was later conceded to bishops and deacons outside of Rome and finally, by the eighth or ninth century, bishops and deacons (and sometimes priests) were wearing it everywhere, with or without authorization.

Originally made of white linen with parallel red or purple bands called *claves*, it later became a silken garment. The white color was retained until after the eleventh century when the *dalmatic* began to match the *chasuble* in this regard.

Because of the fact that the primitive *dalmatic* was white, the *dalmatic* and the *tunic* were considered as festive garments to be worn on joyous occasions; that is why it is not worn in Lent nor Advent nor in penitential times. Oddly enough, it is worn in black at requiems.

The *dalmatic* is essentially a sleeved *tunic* and for centuries was made of ample and dignified proportions. The same sad story of curtailing and stiffening and cutting away (beginning in the Middle Ages) was repeated here again, until the modern *dalmatic* is more often an ornament than a vestment. Fortunately, there is an increasing tendency to make *dalmatics* which are noble and dignified and full. They must be made that way if they are to look proper. *Dalmatics* are best closed on the sides; openings are not needed, as they can be put on just as well without them.

The Cope. Whether this is a doublet of the *chasuble* developing in a different direction, and retaining the hood that the *chasuble* no longer has, or whether it has an independent origin, is not clear. In any case, it was not a liturgical vestment at first, but became one in the ninth century. At that time a cloak with a hood was used by monks (and especially by the cantors) on feast days during the Office. Like the *surplice*, the *cope* was a vestment deliberately introduced to give solemnity to the Offices of the Church, not something carried over from civil life as the Mass vestments were. Because it was used at the Office where incensation and the turning of books demanded freedom for the arms and hands, the cloak was opened in front. By the eleventh century it was used everywhere for the Office and also for processions.

The cope, too, has suffered from the bad taste of vestment makers. It was originally ample and full, falling in soft folds. Later it became stiff, heavy, and skimpy; the hood lost all the appearance of a hood and became a kind of shield, sometimes of tremendous proportions. Fortunately, in recent years the *cope* has been rescued from the decline into which it had fallen. It should be a very graceful garment falling in rich and abundant folds; the hood should not be too large; if the shape and appearance of a real hood is preserved, a handsome effect will have been achieved.

The Humeral Veil. Properly speaking, this is not a vestment at all but a cloth which originally helped the acolyte (later on the subdeacon) to lift heavy altar vessels. At first it was made of linen; in the Middle Ages it became assimilated to the other vestments in material and color.

The *humeral veil* is best left unornamented, as simple and pliable as possible. It is better, too, that the humeral veil be fastened with a clasp rather than ribbons, which are fussy and unhandy.

The *biretta* was originally a large skullcap covering the entire head; in turn this skullcap appears to have evolved from the hood once worn commonly by ecclesiastics and still worn by monks. The purpose of this skullcap was purely utilitarian—to protect the head against the cold. It was equipped with a small top-knot to facilitate taking it off and putting it on. By the end of the Middle Ages it had become a square cap, but the ridges, which derived from folds made by taking it off and putting it on, did not assume their present shape until the late seventeenth or eighteenth centuries. The biretta never became a vestment, nor did it follow the color sequence of the vestments, remaining black for priest, purple for bishops (nineteenth century) and red for cardinals (fifteenth century).

The *biretta* must be worn by the celebrant and the sacred ministers during liturgical services. Contrary to the widespread misapprehension in the matter, there is no law requiring the wearing of the *biretta* in choir or in the sanctuary by those who are not in vestments, and it would be to everyone's advantage if this fact were better known than it is.*

Liturgical colors. The modern sequence of colors is of sur-

* The truth is that the biretta is an altogether secondary affair and its total discontinuance (except for those in sacred vestments) would be no loss to anyone. It is distressing to see people fussing over something that is not nor can ever be of any importance, while far weightier and more important matters are neglected or ignored.

prisingly recent origin in the Church. There was wide variety in this matter in the Middle Ages, and many different local customs. Often the best vestments were used for great feasts regardless of their color. The five modern colors (white, red, purple, green, black) used in the Roman Rite were formally prescribed by St. Pius V. He merely made it obligatory to use the colors which were common in the local Roman Church during the later Middle Ages. The colors now have a symbolic meaning attached to them. Since Pius V's time, rose has been added for use on *Laetare* and *Gaudete* Sundays, and blue is permitted in Spain for certain feasts of our Lady.

Because purple was once used as a substitute for black, the bodies of priests and bishops are usually vested in that color when they are laid out for burial. The pope is vested in red after his death for the same reason: red was once used in the West for funerals as it still is in some Eastern rites.

The Pontifical Insignia

Besides the vestments worn by priests, bishops also wear at a pontifical Mass the *gloves, buskins, sandals, tunic* and *dalmatic*—all in the color of the day. They also wear the *mitre, pectoral cross* and *pontifical ring*. Archbishops use the *pallium* on certain days; both the archbishops and bishops use the *pastoral staff*. Certain lesser prelates have the right to all of the above insignia except the *pallium*.

Bishops once were vested exactly like priests, and it was not until the Middle Ages that they began to wear all the pontifical insignia.

The *Pallium* is the oldest of the pontifical insignia. It has been worn by the popes since the fourth century and was conceded by them to other bishops from the fifth century onward as a sign of papal favor and of ecclesiastical jurisdiction, which of course involved communion with the Roman See. At first the *pallium* was a much longer affair, a kind of woolen scarf adorned with a few red crosses and a red fringe. Later it became stylized and received its present form: the crosses became eight in number and black in color, the fringe became a little piece of lead covered with a black cloth.

The Mitre. There was no liturgical headdress for the first eight or nine centuries; then the mitre made its appearance—not in its present form, but as a low white felt cap derived from the hat worn in civil life. The popes wore it first (ninth-tenth centuries) and then (eleventh century) conceded it to bishops, abbots, and even to priests. By the middle of the twelfth century it had become the distinctive insignia of bishops. At the same time it had begun to be dented down the middle exactly like a modern felt hat and developed so that it looked like the modern mitre worn sideways. Someone evidently felt that this was not very attractive; so it was turned in such a way that the rising sides—now stiffened and adorned—would be worn at the front and back. This latter change probably occurred during the twelfth century.

At first the mitre was low and graceful; when put on, there was a becoming space between the top points of each part filled in with a soft silk. During the Middle Ages the mitre became higher and the points drew closer together. During the eighteenth century it reached its present towering proportions and the becoming space between was closed up so that it appears pointed on all sides. Its adornment changed, too: from the *circulus* that ran around the crown and the *titulus*, which rose at right angles to the *circulus* from the crown to the summit, the decoration developed into a pattern that covered the entire front and back with embroidery, jewels or pearls, and various designs. Thus the mitre too underwent the deformation that had overtaken the other vestments.

Again we see in modern times a tendency to return to more simple and less pretentious mitres. Many exceedingly handsome mitres have been designed and, what is better, are being worn today.

There are three kinds of mitre: the precious mitre, adorned with jewels; the orphreyed mitre, which is decorated only with golden cloth or pearls; the simple linen mitre without any decoration except the red fringes. The two first mitres are made of white silk or cloth of gold and should have the *circulus* and *titulus,* which were mentioned before, either as orphreys or outlined in some way. Although some wore colored mitres in the past, the white mitre has prevailed. A plain white linen mitre is worn for funerals and in penitential seasons.

The Gloves are the full type, covering the wrist as well as the hands. They came into use from the ninth to the twelfth centuries. Later on in the Middle Ages they came to be made exclusively of silk and in the color of the day. Black gloves are not used in the liturgy. The gloves may be adorned with embroidery and even with pearls and precious stones, but a careful and simple design looks best. Too often we see them distorted by stiff cuffs and overrun with meaningless ornament.

Gloves are supposed to symbolize good works.

The Buskins and Shoes. These go together and since the fourteenth century have been the same color as the vestments (none are worn with black). They symbolize the spreading of the Gospel and are inspired by the prophet Isaias. The shoes are very often ornamented—sometimes too much so; restraint and good taste can make them dignified and decorative. There are many mediaeval models extant (at least in paintings) which show how beautiful they can be if they are made properly. They were borrowed by the clergy in the fifth and sixth century from the costume of senators and imperial dignitaries.

The Tunicles have been worn under the *chasuble* by the bishop and other prelates since the twelfth century. This custom had its origin in the fact (already mentioned) that in the fourth century the pope wore a *dalmatic* under his *chasuble* as a mark of rank and dignity; other bishops began to copy this custom. The *tunicles* are supposed to be made of silk and follow the color of the day (even black). Naturally they are made of light silk, but it is better not to have them made of too flimsy material. They look better if they are made longer and fuller than is usually the case.

The Pectoral Cross is strung on a green cord for bishops, a purple cord for other prelates, red for cardinals, black (or any color conceded by indult) for abbots. In reality the pectoral cross is a reliquary, and the law that now requires its use arose from the pious custom of wearing around the neck a reliquary containing a piece of the true cross, a relic of the saints, or a sentence from the Gospel. This custom was widespread in the early centuries, not only among the clergy but among the laity as well. It was not the distinctive insignia of the bishop almost until the Renaissance, and even then it was worn only during Mass.

The Ring is another ornament that was at one time worn by everyone, not only as a kind of modest ornament but also as a signet for sealing documents. Many of these rings have come down to us decorated with Christian symbols: the monogram of Christ for example. Just as with the cross, but many centuries sooner, the ring became the emblem of the episcopal office, symbolizing the bishop's union with his bride, the Church over which he ruled. It was a definite part of the episcopal insignia by the seventh century. The ring is adorned with at least one and often many gems. A special ring is worn at pontifical Mass and all pontifical services.

The Pastoral Staff is quite ancient but, oddly enough, the feature that makes it resemble the shepherd's staff which it is supposed to parallel, the crook or curved head, was unknown until the thirteenth century. The first pastoral staffs or crosiers were just plain sticks with a kind of head shaped like a "tau." This is one reason why they came to be called crosiers: they were in reality a kind of rudimentary cross (*crosse* is still their name in French). While the pastoral staffs seem to have been carried as early as the fifth century, we have no representations of them in art before the eighth century. Their use became general by the ninth century. For some reason the Bishops of Rome have never made use of the crosier. The modern staff is usually made of metal, silver or gold plated, and is surmounted with a crook and equipped with a point at its foot. Many of the mediaeval crosiers were quite handsome, beautifully carved and decorated; during the eighteenth century they too suffered from the over-ornate taste of the time, and some of these types have persisted into our own day. A pastoral staff can be a really fine work of art, like any other church furnishing, as some of the *crosiers* produced in recent years here and abroad can testify.

The pastoral staff symbolizes the duties of the pastor and the pastoral office in general. Bestowed upon a bishop at his consecration since the ninth century, it is also a sign of jurisdiction. It is conceded to abbots and even to abbesses.

The Gremiale. This is a silken ceremonial apron which apparently had a practical origin; it is much like the linen *gremiale* worn nowadays during the anointing of the hands at Ordination to protect the vestments. It became a vestment only in the fifteenth century.

CHAPTER 12

The Liturgical Year

The Meaning, Origin and Development of the Liturgical Year

When we say that in the course of the liturgical year we live over the life of Christ, we do not mean that we merely commemorate past events. Rather, we celebrate these past events; we live them. Through the great sacramental that is the Christian year, Christ is formed in us: we share in the mysteries of His life, death and Resurrection. These events in His life are grace filled and by celebrating them we enter into them. Thus, time itself is drawn into the orbit of Christ's redeeming work and is sanctified by it, becoming an instrument of sanctification for us. The liturgical year is nothing less than the manifestation and the renewing of the mysteries of Christ. More than this it is, as Pius XII says in *Mediator Dei,* "Christ himself" who lives in us, who works in us, who prolongs and continues in us His eternal priesthood and priestly work. "God has predestined us to be conformed to the image of his Son" (Eph. 2:19). By assimilating ourselves to Christ the Son of God and to all His mysteries, we become, by Him and with Him, the children of God.

The ecclesiastical year accomplishes this program in us, first of all, by renewing these mysteries, then by presenting them to us in all their setting, so that our minds are enlightened and our wills are moved to reproduce in us the various states and dispositions of Christ. "Let that mind be in you which was also in Christ Jesus" (Phil. 2:5). We truly follow Christ when in His steps we enter into the society of the Three Divine Persons: "By him we have access in the same holy spirit to the Father" (Eph. 4:18). Just as the Holy Spirit descended upon Christ, so He descended upon the Church to make its members the sons of God; He is the "spirit of adoption of the sons of God" who inspired the Church to organize the worship which sanctifies its members and brings them under the influence of the Priesthood of Christ. This worship, already existing in germ, was developed in the course of the centuries into the liturgical year as the great instrument for making men partakers of the divine nature and sharers in the sonship of the Son of God. It is the manifestation of Christ and His mysteries in the Church and in the souls of the faithful. In it are contained all the works of God: His creation, the Incarnation, the Redemption, the Resurrection and Ascension, the sending of the Holy Spirit and His glorious coming again, the Holy Eucharist, the glories of the Mother of God, the splendor of the angels, the merits and triumphs of the saints. Each year the Church is visited by Christ, her divine Spouse; each year she contemplates Him born in the crib, fasting in the desert, working miracles in Palestine, teaching on the mountainside, dying upon the cross, rising from the tomb, founding His Church, instituting the Eucharist.

The true cell of the liturgical year is the Christian week, a unit of time that is sanctified by various observances. In this the Church continued the practice of the synagogue, with the difference that the center and the head of the week was not Saturday as with the Jews, but the day that recalled the new creation, the day on which the Lord rose from the dead and on which He sent His Holy Spirit upon the Church: the Lord's day, *dies dominica*, or, as we call it following the old pagan terminology, Sunday. The celebration of Sunday, the recalling of all the redemptive work of Christ, is the nucleus and core of the entire rich development which we know as the liturgical year.

Sunday. The origins of the Christian Sunday are not altogether clear. All we know is that it was observed as such certainly in the first century and is alluded to by name in the Apocalypse and the *Didache*, while the Epistles of St. Paul show us that the Christians had already begun the observance of the Sunday assembly for prayer and worship in the first decades of the new era. There was a gradual development here from the observance of the Jewish Sabbath to the specific celebration of the Christian Sunday. It seems that the early Christians, after having gathered in the synagogue for the Saturday evening service, went on to engage in their own proper and peculiar rite of the breaking of bread early Sunday morning. They were apparently moved to select Sunday for their own celebration by the desire to commemorate the day of the Resurrection and the sending of the Spirit. When they finally became separated from the Jewish observances, they parted company with the Sabbath (Saturday) as well, retaining Sunday as their day and the day of the Lord. What we have here is in reality a weekly celebration of Easter, even before there was an annual celebration. "We keep the eighth day with joy," says Pseudo-Barnabas (15:9) "on which also Jesus rose from the dead"; and St. Justin expresses the whole idea of the Christian Sunday most clearly when he says, "We all gather together on Sunday not only because this first day is that on which God . . . created the world but also because Jesus Christ our Savior rose from the dead on the same day" (I *Apology*, 67).

The Resurrection, which put the seal on the divine mission of Christ and which formed the center and heart of the preaching of the apostles, had taken place on this first day of the week; the apparitions of the Risen Savior to the disciples and the sending of the Holy Spirit had happened on the same day. All these associations were attached to this day and it was natural that the first Christians should hold it in special affection and commemorate it with joy and love.

The close connection between Sunday and the day of the Resurrection has been maintained all through the centuries, and explains why even in penitential seasons Sunday has never lost the note of joy and gladness associated with it from the beginning. Neither fasting nor mourning nor any penitential acts have ever been allowed on Sunday. Because it is by Baptism that the Christian shares in the Resurrection which was commemorated on that day, Sunday very early became the weekly reminder of our own Baptism. In fact, what must be called a "Theology of the Sunday" developed in the Church and the day became the symbol of the whole Christian life: to celebrate Sunday was to live the Christian life.

Long before there was any formal legislation on the subject, the celebration of Sunday by taking part in the holy Sacrifice was regarded as a duty by Christians. We have the testimony of Tertullian, St. Justin, and the *Didache* on this, a testimony confirmed by the beautiful response of the Martyrs of Abtina in the persecution of Diocletian: "We observed the assembly with great solemnity, since we cannot be without the Lord's Supper. We could not omit the Lord's Supper." *

Although Sunday obtained and maintained its pre-eminence as *the* liturgical day of the week, it was not provided with the changing propers which now enrich the Missal until some centuries later. The first special propers were for Easter and Pentecost, then for the Sundays of Advent, later the pre-Lenten, the Lenten Sundays, *etc.* It was not until the Middle Ages that they reached their present form. The whole growth was hap-

* Leclercq, *Les Martyrs,* Vol. II (1909), pp. 206–218.

hazard in the extreme and traces of this remain in the Sunday liturgy to this day, particularly in the Sundays after Pentecost when there is no connection between Epistle and Gospel or between the orations in themselves, or between the chants that are used.

Because our Lord was marked for death on a Wednesday and was put to death on Friday, Wednesday and Friday were kept as special days of prayer and fasting, and towards the end of the second century were observed as "station" days on which Christians were to be on guard (literally: *in statione*) against the enemy's assaults. Strictly speaking these observances, while accepted by the Church, were regarded as private and individual devotions. Saturday became a liturgical day in many parts of the Church during the third or fourth century but was observed as a fast day in Rome, along with Wednesday and Friday. In time the Eastern custom prevailed and Saturday ceased to be a fast day anywhere in the Church, except during the Ember weeks, when the old Roman custom survives.

It is not altogether clear why Saturday came in time to be consecrated to the Blessed Virgin, but the custom of honoring her liturgically on that day goes back at least to the eighth century when we find among the votive Masses composed by Alcuin for use on the different days of the week a Mass *De Sancta Maria* apparently intended for Saturday. Latin sacramentaries definitely assigned a Mass *De Sancta Maria* to Saturday. The practice of reciting the Little Office of the Blessed Virgin Mary on Saturday in addition to the Office of the day was practically universal in the Middle Ages; St. Pius V substituted for it the *Officium Sanctae Mariae in Sabbato*, which we now use, and the most recent revision of the Office has increased the number of Saturdays on which that Office is said.

The Ember Days. Four times a year, approximately at the change of the seasons, the Church observes days of special fasting and prayer which we English-speaking people call Ember days. "Ember days" have nothing to do with fires, smouldering or otherwise; the word is a corruption of the Latin *Quatuor Tempora*. The older English term for these days was *Quarter Tense*, which shows a closer relation to the Latin than the present word.

Ember days come to us in the Missal and Breviary with definite characteristics that set them apart from the ordinary run of ferial days. Some of these characteristics they all have in common; others are peculiar to the particular group to which they belong: Advent Ember days and Pentecost Ember days each have their own peculiar flavor, however much they outwardly resemble the others. Each consists of a group of days, Wednesday, Friday, and Saturday; each day has a stational church just like the ferias in Lent and the great feasts, and these stational churches are the same for each season of the year: on Wednesday it is St. Mary Major, Friday the Holy Apostles, and Saturday, St. Peter. The antiquity of the assignment of the last church to Saturday is witnessed by St. Leo the Great in the fifth century when he says, as he does each year in the third Sunday of September, "On Wednesdays and Fridays let us fast; and on Saturday let us keep vigil at the tomb of the Apostle Peter."

Every one of the Ember days has a proper Mass. The Mass of Wednesday always has three lessons and the Mass of Saturday (especially rich) has seven. There is a certain theme associated with each of them, although it is sometimes swallowed up in the thoughts proper to the liturgical season. But Wednesday will allude in the Gospel to our Lady more often than not; Friday usually presents a picture of penance for our contemplation, and Saturday, in two of the four seasons, gives us a gospel of healing.

The origin and purpose of Ember days have been much discussed for a long time, but the hypothesis of the learned Benedictine Dom G. Morin is generally accepted now as being the most satisfactory explanation. Ember days represent the Christian transformation of the pagan seasons of prayers for the fruits of the earth which took place three times a year: once at the beginning of summer (the wheat harvest); one towards the end of summer (the wine harvest); and the most important of all in the week before the winter *solstice*, the *feriae sementinae*, or festival of sowing. It is true that now there are four sets of Ember days, but originally there were but three and these at the approximate time that the pagans celebrated their days. The Lenten Ember days are a late addition.

When we remember that the Ember days in their origin are so closely related to the cycle of the earth's productivity, we can understand better the allusions, direct or indirect, to harvest and to the fruits of the earth that occur even in those Ember days that have been transformed by the influence of the season. Of them all, the September group retains most the influence of this theme. The Advent group, pre-occupied with the coming of the Lord, nevertheless recalls its origin enough to refer to the fruits of the earth, but in such a way as to transform and enrich the original idea, seeing not the material fruit, but the most Blessed Fruit of Mary's womb:

> *Behold a Virgin shall conceive and*
> *bear a Son and His name shall be*
> *called Emmanuel.*

Or,

> *Drop down dew ye heavens from above*
> *and let the clouds rain down the just one . . .*
> *let the earth open up and bud forth a Savior.*

The Pentecost group, dominated by the thought of outpouring of the Spirit, the harvest feast of the Church, has, in the second lesson of Saturday's Mass, a direct allusion taken from Leviticus to offering up the first fruits of the harvest to God.

As they stand now, the Ember days are primarily days of fasting and of more intense and prolonged prayer. The Masses are longer, for one thing, and there are more prayers—some of the most exquisite compositions in the entire missal. The *Flectamus Genua* is at once a vivid and striking reminder of the fact that these are special seasons of prayer and an indication of the quality of the prayer demanded: a humble and penitent prayer. In spite of the gradual encroachment of other themes, these days remain primarily days of prayer for the more abundant fruits of the earth and days of thanksgiving for the harvest.

In the course of time, Ember days have come to be associated with ordinations, and the Ember Saturdays, particularly the Saturday in December, are the most favored for the purpose. This circumstance explains the references to the priesthood in some of the masses. Because of this custom of ordaining on the Saturdays in the *Quatuor Tempora,* the original purpose of the Ember days as days of prayer and fasting for the blessings of an abundant harvest has been widened to include the idea of prayer and fasting for priests, that the Lord may send good laborers into His vineyard and that their ministry may be fruitful.

The Ember days, spaced as they are throughout the year at equal distances, are admirably suited to serve as little seasons of retreat and prayer—times in which we can look back upon the months that are past, awaken the spirit of penance for our wrongdoings, and at the same time look forward to the quarter year that lies ahead, quickening our resolve to lead a better and more intense Christian life during the months to come.

The Christmas Cycle

At the present time the whole question of the origin and development of the two great feasts of the Christmas cycle, the Nativity and the Epiphany, is one of the most difficult in the whole study of liturgy, and a solution of the many problems connected with it is still to be found. That they are both of later origin than Easter or Pentecost is clear enough, but what brought about the creation of these feasts it is not easy to say with certainty. The feasts celebrated in the Church were at one time concerned exclusively with the redeeming work of Christ, rather than with His person. With the passing of time, however, there was considerable theological reflection on the Incarnation as the basis of the Redemption, reflection stimulated by the Gnostic crisis of the second century and intensified in the two centuries which followed, particularly at the time of the great Christological controversies of the fourth century. Whether these controversies brought about the creation of these feasts or merely contributed to their development is not clear. The Philocalian Calendar or Martyrology, dating from the year 354, bears witness to the existence of Christmas (*natus Christus in Bethlehem Judae*) at Rome in the middle of the fourth century, and it is safe to conclude that it was actually established even earlier than that, and that its purpose was to be a commemoration of the Incarnation. As for the Epiphany, all the evidence points to the existence of this feast in the East towards the end of the second century at least, when it was celebrated as a commemoration of the Incarnation and the Baptism of Christ.* In the Roman Rite both feasts came to be celebrated towards the end of the fourth century and with that we have the beginning of a Christmas cycle. The feast of Christmas has its period of preparation: the season of Advent, which arose in the fifth and sixth centuries; and its prolongation, climaxed by the feast of the Presentation of our Lord in the Temple which was added in the sixth century. By that time the two great cycles of the liturgical year—the Easter cycle and the Christmas cycle—had been organized. Christmas and Easter are the two feasts about which the Church's year revolves.

Advent. Originally the beginning of the Church year was counted from March 25, which was believed to be not only the day on which God became man but the day on which the world was created. For that reason March was reckoned as the first

* McArthur, *The Evolution of the Christian Year*, pp. 65–66.

month of the year and the book of Genesis was read in the churches during that time. This last practice survives to this day, when Genesis is read during the pre-Lenten period. With the introduction of the feast of the Nativity, however, a change began to take place and the Christmas season became the beginning of the Church year; the oldest liturgical book in the West, the Gelasian Sacramentary, starts with the Vigil of Christmas. Other Western books followed its example and when Advent became part of the liturgical year (about the eighth century), the beginning of the Church year was fixed at the first Sunday of Advent.

Advent means the Coming of the Lord (*Adventus Domini*) and originally was conceived as a time of preparation for the final coming (the *Parousia*), as the texts in the Breviary and Missal bear abundant witness even to this day. Only later was it widened to include a preparation for Christmas; even now it is only secondarily thought of as a pre-Christmas season. One reason for this change was that the word "Advent" was applied to Christmas, to which it did not refer at first.

The season of Advent seems to have begun about the fourth century in Spain, from where it spread to Gaul. During the sixth century the Church in Gaul observed a kind of second Lent in preparation for the feast of Christmas, lasting from the feast of St. Martin until Christmas time. Some of the Churches of Italy observed the same practice. But Advent as we know it was organized at Rome during the fifth century, although scholars do not agree on the author of that organization. The Roman usage in this matter finally prevailed over the six-week period observed in Gaul, except at Milan where the longer Advent is still observed.

As it now appears in the Missal and Breviary, Advent is a curious blending of sadness and joy—a time of mourning and penance as well as a season of enthusiasm and longing for the coming of the Redeemer and His Kingdom. The purple vestments, the absence of the *Te Deum* and the *Gloria*, give it a character of mourning, but the *Alleluia* is not dropped out and the great majority, if not all the texts, allude only to the coming of Christ. From a lyrical and mystical point of view these texts make Advent one of the richest and most beautiful seasons in the year. The apparent contradictions in the liturgy of this time are explained by the fact that the elements of mourning and sadness are seen upon closer inspection to be external and accidental, and to be additions of the thirteenth and later centuries.

The influence of the concept of the second coming is found in the weeks immediately preceding Advent as well as in Advent itself. During the month of November the writings of the prophets, with their insistence upon the Day of the Lord and the Last Times, are read in the Office, while the same themes are noticeable in the Masses of the last Sundays after Pentecost, not only in the proper chants but to a certain extent in the lessons also.

The chief reason for the extraordinary richness of the Advent season lies in the abundance of the proper texts, particularly in the Office for this season. No other time of the year has so many propers and hardly another season is more beautiful. The Masses—while not so numerous as those of the Lenten season—have their own peculiar power and beauty. A whole book, indeed many volumes, would be needed to do justice to the excellence of this season. Its theme is so universal and the stage on which these themes move is so vast that we would be justified in saying that it is a whole liturgical year in itself. Out of all its abundance certain themes emerge clearly to give unity and coherence to the whole. Advent is a time of waiting—of expectation for the coming of the Redeemer and the triumph of His redeeming work. The center of the whole season is the King who is to come, who is indeed near at hand (Invitatory antiphons, First and Third Sunday). He is the great prophet who will renew Jerusalem (antiphon of Vespers, First Sunday). "Lift up your heads for your redemption is near at hand" (Gospel, First Sunday).

But this kingdom which we await, this day of the Lord which we long for so ardently, borrowing the words of the prophets and particularly those of Isaias to express our longing, has already begun—the day has dawned and we are even now walking in its light. The longing for His coming is balanced by the joyful consciousness that He has already come. The Second Coming "in power and majesty" is closely bound up with the first in lowliness and poverty. But behind so many of the prayers, antiphons, responsories and lessons, there is always the thought that He who was born in Bethlehem will return to accomplish the work of our redemption, to complete what He once began. Even Christmas itself owes all its joy to the fact that we celebrate the beginning of our redemption: "This day has shone upon us the Day of the new Redemption, of the ancient restoration" (Second Responsory, Matins of Christmas). The close relation between the two comings of Christ explains the insistence upon the theme of the Blessed Virgin Mary, never altogether absent and often explicit during these days. For Mary was not only intimately associated with His first coming, whereby joy came into the world, but she is for all time the very personification of our longing for His second coming and final triumph. As no one better prepared for His first coming, no one but she can adequately prepare for His second. She is the model and the pattern of the Church.

Christmas. The exact date of the birth of Christ is not known for certain, nor does there seem to have been any agreement on any particular day in ancient times. When the first evidence of a feast in honor of the Nativity appears in the fourth century, it is kept on December 25th, which was the day celebrated by the pagans as the *Natale Solis Invicti,* the conqueror of darkness. Did the Christians deliberately fix their feast of the birthday of Christ on that day for polemical reasons—to show that Christ is the true Sun, the Sun of Justice and the true Victor over the darkness? That might indeed have been the case, but we have no real proof that it was so. It is possible that the birthday of Christ was determined by working from the traditional date of the Incarnation, March 25th; nine months after that is Christmas. All we can say for certain is that the feast has been celebrated on December 25th at Rome since the fourth century.

From Rome it spread to Milan and gradually to the other dioceses of Italy, and before the end of the fourth century was observed in the Churches of the East, even though these already had a feast that was closely related to it—the Epiphany, celebrated on January 6th. By the beginning of the next century it was observed throughout the Christian world.

Christmas is remarkable for its three proper Masses, and is unique in the Church year for this reason. The custom of saying three Masses on this day is very old; we know that it existed at the time of St. Gregory the Great. The Mass formularies themselves are not equally ancient, however—that used on Christmas day ("*Puer natus est nobis*") is the oldest; the Midnight Mass (a practice borrowed from Jerusalem) is the next, and the Mass at Dawn the latest of the three. In fact, this last named was originally not a Christmas Mass at all but one in honor of St. Anastasia said in her church after the midnight Mass at St. Mary Major, because it was the *dies natalis* of this saint who was held in high honor by the Byzantine court. The pope celebrated this second Mass in her titular church as a mark of honor to the Eastern Roman emperor. In time the Mass of the martyr gave place to a Mass of the Nativity, leaving only the commemoration, which is still found in the Missal. The three Masses (said by three different celebrants) remained a purely local custom of the Church of Rome until the tenth century; the custom of each priest saying three Masses on that day, if he wishes, does not appear until the twelfth. The usual symbolic interpretation of these Masses dates from the Middle Ages and is a little too facile; actually, as an examination of the texts will show, the first deals with the birth of Christ, the second (as befits a Mass said at dawn) emphasizes the idea of Christmas as a feast of light, while the third (and oldest, let us remember) deals with the mystery of the Incarnation in general.

Almost from the time that Christmas began to be celebrated, the Church observed the feasts of certain saints during the days immediately following it. The feast of St. Stephen was observed on December 26th in the East during the fourth century, apparently before even the feast of Christmas was accepted there, which would indicate that at least for St. Stephen's feast this was not done by design. But in any case these saints' feasts are listed not in the *sanctorale* but the *temporale;* they are thus associated more closely to the Redemption than are other saints.

A peculiarity of these feasts—St. Stephen, St. John, Holy Innocents—is that the vespers of the Nativity, up to the *capitulum,* is recited instead of the proper Office we might expect to find. The thought of our Lord's Nativity and what it has brought to the world is thus kept alive and is not permitted to recede into the background.

The great themes of the liturgy at Christmas and the Epiphany are light and life, or light and salvation. "A light shall shine upon us this day" (Introit, Mass at Dawn); "By the mystery of the Word made flesh the light of Thy glory hath shone anew upon the eyes of our minds" (Preface for Christmas); "This day is born to you a Savior, who is Christ the Lord" (Gospel, Midnight Mass); "The Lord hath made known his salvation" (Versicle of the Office for Christmas Day); "Lift up your heads; your redemption is near at hand" (Fifth antiphon, First Vespers of Christmas). These are but different ways of saying the same thing: Christ is our light as well as our salvation and He is the Savior of the world because He is the Light.

In the Gelasian and Gregorian Sacramentaries the eighth day after Christmas is called simply the Octave Day of the Lord; it did not become the independent feast of the Circumcision until the ninth century and is still called the Octave day of

Christmas in the Missal. There is no allusion to the Circumcision outside of the Gospel either in the Mass or the Office.

For a long time, as the seventh century Lectionary of Würzburg informs us, this day was also called the feast day of the Blessed Virgin, and was either a commemoration of her motherhood and her virginity or the anniversary of the dedication of a church in her honor. This feast of the Blessed Virgin had its own Mass texts and it did not allude in any way to the Nativity of our Lord. Even as late as the twelfth century the Mass and Office said at Rome was that of the Blessed Virgin. When the feast of the Circumcision took its place, it retained the oration of the older Marian Mass, "*Deus qui salutis aeternae*," an oration that alludes in no way either to Christmas or the Circumcision. The fact that this was once a Marian feast, at least at Rome, explains the strong Marian flavor of the Office. The antiphons used at Lauds and Vespers are among the finest that we have; they are apparently borrowed from the Byzantine liturgy of the sixth century. As the first antiphon, "*O Admirabile Commercium*," would lead us to think, they were originally used at Christmas (and still are used at Candlemas), but were replaced by the present antiphons in the eleventh century.

The Gallican Rite observed a feast in honor of the Circumcision on this day from the sixth century onward, but Rome continued to celebrate its own Marian feast on that day, accepting the feast of the Circumcision only after the eleventh century.

Devotion to the Holy Name of Jesus, widespread in the late Middle Ages through the preaching of St. Bernardine of Siena, found liturgical expression in the feast of the Holy Name of Jesus, first conceded to the Franciscans in the sixteenth century, then extended to the whole Church in the eighteenth and fixed on January 2nd by St. Pius X.

The Epiphany. As its very name indicates, this feast is Eastern in origin, or, as we shall see, it may have come down to us from the time when Greek was the universal language. It appears to be very ancient and probably goes back to the second century, if not to the first. Originally, it was a unitive feast commemorating both the Incarnation and the Baptism of our Lord. Some Gnostic heretics celebrated it merely as the feast of the Baptism in accord with their belief that it was at His Baptism that Christ became the adopted son of God; they thus considered the Baptism as the divine birthday of Christ, but their feast was a heretical adaptation of the earlier complete feast of the Manifestation of the Incarnate Word. Our Western way of confining the meaning of the Epiphany to the manifestation of our Lord to the Gentiles makes us forget that the original meaning is much wider than that, *i.e.*, signifies the *appearance* of the Son of God in the flesh. The date of the celebration of the feast, January 6th, is of great significance, because long before Christianity there was a pagan festival kept on that day celebrating the birth of light, a day on which, in the popular belief of the pagans, water was changed into wine. In all likelihood, we have in the feast of the Epiphany a very early Christian adaptation of this pagan festival—given new life and meaning in its Christian context, and commemorating the birth of the True Light that shines in the darkness. This helps to explain the circumstance that the Gospel story of the Marriage Feast of Cana has always been associated with the feast of the Epiphany. Everything points to the likelihood that this transformation had taken place even before St. John wrote his Gospel.

The very early association of the Baptism of Jesus with this feast of the Incarnation led to its adoption as a great day for baptisms in the East, a practice that was only intensified when the theme of the Baptism became more prominent and the Epiphany came to mean in the East the manifestation of Christ's divinity made by His Father at His Baptism.

During the fourth century, Christmas, which was actually a doublet of the older feast of the Epiphany, was introduced into the East. As a result of this, the commemoration of the

Incarnation was transferred to that day and the Epiphany became more a commemoration of the Baptism.

In the West the Epiphany was observed in Gaul during the fourth century, and there it appears to have antedated the Roman Christmas. As in the East, it commemorated both the Incarnation and the Baptism. Later on in the West it became almost exclusively a commemoration of the Manifestation of our Lord to the Gentiles, who were represented by the Magi. This narrowing of the scope of the feast is believed to have begun at Rome, which influenced the other Churches of the West in this matter. The ancient feast of the Incarnation became a kind of doublet of Christmas (it is actually called Little Christmas in some places). If the Baptism of Christ and the Theophany receded into the background, they were not forgotten altogether; there are many references to the themes of light and Baptism in the Mass and Office of the feast, and a special commemoration of the Baptism of our Lord is made on the old octave day, now transformed into a new feast on January 13th.

This association of the Baptism with the Epiphany caused the day to be regarded as the great wedding feast of Christ with His Church; the waters of Baptism were looked upon as a nuptial bath in the writings of the fathers. Hence, the introduction of the Marriage Feast of Cana into the Epiphany cycle. The relation of all these events to one another is strikingly brought out in the antiphon for the *Benedictus* on the feast itself: "Today the Church is joined to the Heavenly Spouse, when Christ washed away her sins in the Jordan; the Magi hasten with gifts to the marriage feast and the guests are made glad with water turned into wine." In some churches the Gospels relating these three events (the coming of the Magi, the Baptism of Jesus, and the Marriage Feast of Cana) were read at Matins. The church at Rome introduced the second Gospel into the Mass on the octave day in the eighth century, while the Gospel of the Marriage Feast has been read on the Sunday after the octave for many centuries.

The Masses of the Sundays after Epiphany develop and comment upon the great themes of the feast itself. The Gospels relate some of those miraculous events in the life of our Lord whereby He manifested His divine power and at the same time afforded a demonstration of His redeeming work; the chants are filled with the spirit of adoring awe which the manifestation of God always evokes in men and angels: "Adore God, all his angels, Sion heard and was glad, and the daughters of Juda rejoiced." "The Lord reigns, let the earth rejoice, let many islands be glad."

Candlemas. The celebration of a feast on the fortieth day after the birth of Christ originated in Jerusalem. Its existence there is attested by Etheria Sylvia in the fourth century; it is not likely that it is much older than that. Like other feasts associated with our Lady, it appears to have come to the West in the seventh century. The object of the feast is to commemorate the entrance of Jesus as the Messias into His temple and His meeting there with Simeon who represented Israel. From this the name by which the feast is known in the East is derived: *Hypapante,* the "Meeting," which was translated *Occursus Domini* in the West, and was one of the older names of this feast there. The rite of purification which Mary underwent in obedience to the Law gave this day the name Purification of Mary, but the custom of carrying candles during the procession and at Mass has caused it to be known best of all as Candlemas. The procession appears for the first time in the seventh century, but it is probably much older. Carrying candles was an inevitable dramatization of the words of Simeon in the Gospel used for the feast: "A light to enlighten the Gentiles," signifying our sharing in the Light of Christ which enlightens every man coming into the world, and which dispels the darkness of error and sin.

In spite of its name this feast is in reality a feast of our Lord, closing the Nativity cycle, as the text of the Mass and Office shows. Only the psalms are taken from the common of the Blessed Virgin. The fact, too, that it is a feast of lights shows its affinity with Christmas and the Epiphany.

Easter and Its Cycle

The most ancient as well as the greatest feast of the Christian year is Easter or *Pascha*, which forms the basis and support of the whole edifice of the Church year. We have already seen that each Sunday was not so much a "little Easter" as it was Easter itself celebrated every week. The beginning of what we call the feast of Easter itself goes back so far that it can be said to have hardly *begun;* it was more properly a continuation, with all its associations heightened and given a Christian tone, of the Jewish Passover feast. The Jews kept each year the memory of their deliverance from Egypt and remembered how God had made His destroying angel pass over the homes of the Hebrews because they were adorned with the blood of the lamb; they killed and ate the paschal lamb in commemoration of their deliverance. Christ in His turn delivered His people from bondage; His blood averted God's justice from them; He became our Passover and Paschal Lamb. The parallel was seen and drawn deliberately between the two Passovers, and the first Christian celebration of Easter was intended to be a celebration of our redemption, which the Fathers saw as wrought by the Death, Resurrection and Ascension of our Lord. They saw it as one act and celebrated it accordingly, making no divisions as we are accustomed to do: the Christian *Pascha* included all the acts whereby our deliverance was accomplished and it went to make up one feast with two phases. Ultimately the phase of the Resurrection itself, and of the triumph associated with it, became dominant; but the phase of the Passion and Death has never been separated from it, and the original complete meaning of the day survives in the word *Pascha*, which means Passover, with all its associations of deliverance, the immolation of the Paschal Lamb and the eating of it. All this is clearly expressed in the Preface for Easter, which emphasizes the *Pasch* and the deliverance and the immolation of the Paschal Lamb, rather than the Resurrection as we tend to think of it, isolated from its context. The Church determined very early that the Resurrection of Christ (and our resurrection with Him) should be celebrated on Sunday rather than on the actual calendar day that it had taken place. The symbolism of this we have touched upon in discussing the celebration of Sunday. This day was regarded as the culminating day of the year, as the Resurrection was the greatest event, the crowning event in the life of Christ. Because of the intimate relation between Christ's Resurrection and ours, Easter early became the great baptismal day of the Church: by our baptism we become sharers in the Death and Resurrection of Christ. "If we are planted in the likeness of his death we shall be planted in the likeness of his resurrection" is the doctrine of St. Paul. Easter and Baptism are forever associated. It is the day on which the neophytes begin to walk in the newness of life, to live the risen life; and it is the day when those already baptized renew their baptismal consciousness and make a resolution to walk in the newness of life that came to them at Baptism. The whole Church, then, renews itself at Easter. This is the teaching of the Fathers: to celebrate Easter was for them to rise with Christ again and to live the risen life. At Easter time we all die with Christ, rise again, and lead a life such as He lived: seeking the things that are above. "We cannot ignore the fact," says St. Leo, "that the Paschal mystery is of all Christian solemnities the principal one; all the other periods of the year only dispose us to participate worthily and in a fitting manner in that." *

The Preparation for Easter: Lent. The season of Lent grew out of the very ancient custom, going back apparently almost to

* *Sermo IX de Quadragesimo.*

Apostolic times, of fasting for one or two days before Easter. St. Irenaeus bears witness to the one day fast; according to Tertullian and Hippolytus the custom in the third century was to fast for two days, apparently on the Friday and Saturday before Easter. A little later on in the same century this fast was extended to a whole week.

The first definite reference to a forty-days' fast is to be found in the fifth canon of the council of Nicaea, and it does not appear to be a recent innovation. Somewhere during the last half of the third century the original one week had grown to six weeks or forty days. Fixing this period at forty days was undoubtedly inspired by the forty-days' fast in the desert. Although fasting was not allowed on Sundays, the latter were nevertheless included in the "forty days," and the first Sunday of Lent was the beginning of the Lenten season. By the seventh century men began to feel that there should be forty full fast days, and this led to pushing the beginning of Lent back to Ash Wednesday.

It is not altogether clear that the forty-days' fast was observed at Rome; the historian Socrates in the fourth century says that the custom there was to observe only three weeks of fasting. That is explained by Duchesne and Callewaert to mean that although the Roman Church accepted the forty-day Lenten season, it did not prescribe fasting on all the ferias, but only on those of the first, fourth, and sixth weeks.

The nature and the characteristics of Lent were from the fourth century onward determined by its purpose, which was twofold: the spiritual renewal of the faithful by penance, prayer, fasting and almsgiving; and the preparation of the catechumens for Baptism during the night between Holy Saturday and Easter Sunday. These two purposes are equally reflected to this day in the Masses for the Lenten season. It may be stated as a general rule that the orations and the Preface emphasize the theme of renewal through the disciplines of fasting and prayer, while the lessons are related to Baptism. The many allusions to water, to light (Baptism was the sacrament of enlightenment), and to the raising from the dead show this. There are exceptions to this but it still remains a general rule.

The influence of the catechumenate upon Lent was considerable. Candidates for Baptism were enrolled among the *electi* at the beginning of the season and were instructed in the meaning of the Christian life. They were taught the Apostles' Creed, the four Gospels and the Lord's Prayer. This teaching was called the *traditio* or *redditio* and took place specifically on the third (Apostles' Creed), fourth (Gospels), and fifth (Lord's Prayer) Sundays. Traces of this remain in the Missal today; on these Sundays and on the four chief "liturgical days" (Monday, Wednesday, Friday and Saturday) of the weeks which these Sundays open, the theme of Baptism is most prominent.

A third theme of the Lenten season, which is not as prominent as those of fasting and Baptism, is penance. From the sixth century Holy Thursday was the day for the reconciling of the penitents, and Lent was the time for doing the penances assigned to them. Until the seventh century, penances began on the first Monday in Lent and this explains why there are so many references to doing penance, to binding and loosing, to the judgment, to the cleansing of the temple, and the Canaanite woman in the lessons of the Masses in the first week of Lent.

The penitents (unlike the catechumens) were allowed to remain for the entire Mass, but were, of course, excluded from Communion. Instead, a special prayer was said over them, which remains in our Missal as the *Oratio super populum*. Originally, as its name implies, a prayer or blessing intended for all and said in every Mass, it was confined to weekdays in Lent by Gregory the Great and by association became a special prayer for penitents.

When the beginning of Lent was pushed back to Ash Wednesday (in the seventh century), the penitents were solemnly excluded from the church by a rite which was inspired by the excluding of the first parents from paradise. This ritual exclusion was accompanied by a laying on of hands, later associated with the distribution of ashes. By the eleventh century the rite of distributing ashes was extended to all, and not only to penitents. The idea was that all were enrolled in the penitent class. With the general extension of the penitents came the use of the more specifically penitential chants, particularly the Tract *Domine non secundum* in the Masses of Monday, Wednesday and Friday. The "bending of the knee" associated with this chant is a further indication of its penitential character.

The last of the themes which entered into the building up of the structure of Lent was the Passion of Christ. We think of it as confined to the last two weeks of Lent; actually the theme of the Passion is present from the very beginning of Lent, except that it is viewed on a much wider scale than the actual account of the Passion itself: as a great struggle between Christ and Satan, a conflict between good and evil, light and darkness. As the season goes on, this becomes more pronounced.

Much of what we associate with Passiontide is a later development; the original Passion Sunday was Palm Sunday (it is significant that it is called the *Second Passion* or Palm Sunday in the restored order for Holy Week). What we now call Passion Sunday was called *Dominica in Mediana,* and was thus related to the preceding week, the "middle week" of Lent. There were no allusions to the Passion in the Mass of this Sunday; it was celebrated in the early morning after an all-night vigil at St. Peter's and was an ordination Mass. That explains the Epistle which refers to the Priesthood of Christ.

With the decline of the catechumenate and the spread of the cult of the Holy Cross in the West during the seventh century, the emphasis began to be placed upon the sufferings of Christ, and the texts of Breviary and Missal were affected by this thought. The psalm chants, the hymns and the lessons of the Office all reflected the greater concentration on the theme of the Passion. The Preface of Lent gave way to the Preface of the Cross. However, the older theme of fasting and penance was not altogether abandoned and persists in the prayers of the Masses during this week, and in the first lessons in the invitatory antiphon of Matins.

Lent and Easter are inseparably associated with one another: Lent has no meaning of itself; it must be seen as leading to Easter in order to be understood. It is a most solemn time of prayer and penance and fasting, in preparation for the annual celebration and commemoration of our redemption. As the liturgy of Lent itself tells us, borrowing the words of St. Paul and applying them to the season: "Behold now is the acceptable time, now is the day of salvation." A season of more solemn prayer, Lent is marked by the daily ferial Mass, something unknown at any other season, each with its own proper texts that unfold to us some aspect or other of our redemption, dwelling particularly on the sacrament of Baptism as prefigured and announced in the Old and New Testaments alike; upon the Resurrection, and later on, upon the redemptive Passion of our Savior. The prayers of these Masses dwell upon the instruments of Lenten discipline—prayer, fasting, almsgiving—whereby we are to purify our souls and minds and hearts in order to celebrate more fittingly the great feast of our redemption. Through these great Masses we are schooled in the spirit of Lent and are led to sound the depths of the great Paschal mystery for which it prepares us: "Grant O Lord God that by the annual discipline of the Lenten mystery we may progress in the understanding and knowledge of the mystery of Christ, and that we may by a holy life obtain the effects of that mystery" (Gelasian Sacramentary, 1st Sunday of Lent). The mystery referred to is the mystery of Christ's suffering and redeeming Death. We enter with Christ into the desert during these holy forty days; we stretch ourselves out upon the cross; we die to sin and to our lower nature; we suffer with Him so that we may be glorified with Him; we re-enact in our bodies the mystery of His suffering and dying, so far as we are able. "As dying and behold we live, as sorrowing yet always rejoicing, as having nothing, yet possessing all things." Through the Holy Eucharist which we offer each day we draw the power and strength to live over this phase of Christ's redemptive life; through the readings and prayers we see the dispositions and sentiments we are to have ourselves. Particularly during the last part of Lent we contemplate the mystery of the Passion, not from the outside but from within; we enter the holy sanctuary of Christ's soul, listen to His voice in the Passion as reflected in the psalms and lessons. "We fill up those things that are wanting to the sufferings of Christ" by sharing in His sacrificial dispositions. During all that time the Office supplements what we find in the Mass, maintaining the Lenten mood and later on contemplating in a series of marvelous hymns, responsories, antiphons, lessons and psalms the great High Priest who has redeemed us in His blood and obtained eternal redemption for us.

The hymns of the first part of Lent dwell on the reasons and motives for prayer and penance and give a program of Lenten observance:

Utamur ergo parcius
Verbis cibis et potibus
Somno jocis et arctius
Perstemus in custodia.

Lent is a time of watching—fasting—restraint and self-discipline.

Multum quidem peccavimus
Sed parce confitentibus
Ad nominis laudem tui
Confer medelam languidis.

Concede nostrum conteri
Corpus per abstinentiam
Ut fructuosa sint tuis
Jejuna corda criminum.

This idea of fasting from sin as we fast from food is one of the frequent themes of Lent.

If the hymns of the first part of Lent put the accent on penance and suffering and are moral in tone, the hymns of Passiontide are rather objective and doctrinal, a vast synthesis of the redemption:

Pange lingua gloriosi, lauream certaminis
Et super crucis trophaeam dic triumphum nobilem
Qualiter redemptor orbis immolatus vicerit.

Or,

Vexilla regis prodeunt
Fulget crucis Mysterium
Qua vita mortem pertulit
Et morte vita protulit.

Beata cujus brachiis
Pretium pependit saeculi
Statera facta corporis
Tulitque praedam tartari.

O Crux ave, spes unica
Hoc Passionis tempore
Piis adauge gratiam
Reisque dele crimina.

So important are these Masses and Offices of Lent that St. Pius X gave permission to say the ferial Mass on all doubles not of the first or second class, and more recently Pius XII has extended the privilege to the Office as well. St. Pius X said that henceforth the ancient Sunday and *ferial* Masses would *take their rightful place* in the liturgy. The idea behind these concessions is that we should be able to fix our attention upon the central mystery of the season unimpeded by the feasts of the saints. For a long time the calendar during the Lenten months was kept free of saints' feasts for that very reason.

There is, then, in Lent a special temper and tone which is proper to the time and which the Masses and Offices of the season are calculated to inspire and nourish in us. It calls us to a more sustained practice of the Christian life, to a renewal of the Christian spirit. We should live the Christian life at all times but we are to live it more intensely during Lent. The whole Church joins Christ, our leader and our model, in His "warfare" in the desert. In ancient times Lent was a season during which the catechumens prepared for Baptism and when the penitents prepared for absolution. That is why the present Lenten Masses dwell so much on the two themes of baptism and penance but particularly baptism. Easter was once the great baptismal feast of the Church when the neophytes, instructed all during Lent, went down into the font and received the sacrament of regeneration. Not only the neophytes but all Christians were expected to awaken the spirit of their Baptism so that the whole Church renewed herself at that time.When it was no longer the practice to baptize only at Easter and Pentecost, Lent became instead a call to all Christians to renew their baptismal vows, to reawaken the grace of God that was in them. That is why in the recent revision of the Easter rites so much emphasis is placed upon the renewal of baptismal promises. No one can place himself outside of this unified action of the whole Church.

When have we more cause for recourse to the divine means of salvation than when the very mysteries of the redemption are brought before our minds in the recurrent flow of time? In order that we may celebrate them more worthily, we should prepare for them by the wholesome fast of forty days. Not only those who are to attain the new life through the mystery of Christ's death and resurrection in the rebirth of baptism, but likewise all people who are already reborn will necessarily and with much profit take up the defensive arms of this sanctification: the former in order to receive what they do not yet possess; the latter in order to preserve what has already been received.*

We begin Lent with Ash Wednesday in a spirit of penance, but the true beginning of Lent is the first Sunday of the penitential season, just forty days before Good Friday, the beginning

*St. Leo, Fourth Sermon on Lent.

of the Christian Passover. We are thus prepared and conditioned for the great annual festival of our redemption, which is the climax of Holy Week.

Holy Week

From ancient Christian times until our own day men have agreed to regard the week before Easter as the holiest and greatest time in the Christian year. The number and importance as well as the great and venerable antiquity of its rites and observances work together to give it the first place in the Church's treasury of worship. The singularly great events commemorated, which were the means whereby our redemption was accomplished and which Christ lives over in His Church, make this week of supreme importance in the lives of the faithful. Already in the fourth century it was known by the name it still bears in the Roman Missal and Breviary: *Hebdomada Major*, the Great Week. "Not that the days of that week are longer than other days, for there are days longer still, nor that there are more days in that week than any other, but because extraordinary deeds were done by God during the days of this week." * The name by which we know it, "Holy Week," appears to be equally ancient for it is found in St. Athanasius' letters and in the writings of St. Epiphanius (fourth century).

Originally only Friday and Saturday were observed as holy days, and that apparently from apostolic times; these form the nucleus of the later "Holy Week." By the time of Tertullian they were called days of fasting and mourning. Very early another day was added to these two as a day of mourning; that was Wednesday on which was commemorated "the beginning of the counsel of the Jews to betray the Lord." By the middle of the third century the other days of the week had completed the list of days of mourning and fasting. It was not until later that the week took on the character of a celebration of the great

* St. John Chrysostom, *Hom.* XXX *in Genesis*, no. 1.

events of our redemption. Rather it seems to have been a time of mourning and fasting, with little of the festive about it.

The pre-Nicene Church concentrated upon the celebration of one great feast—the Christian Passover, the *Phase* or *Transitus Domini,* a true festival of the redemption which took place in the night between Saturday and Easter Sunday morning, and which recalled the whole redemptive act of Christ: His Death as well as His Resurrection. It was based upon the Jewish Passover feast (even to the extent that it was celebrated during the night), except that instead of commemorating the deliverance of the Jews from Egypt, it commemorated the Christians' deliverance from sin and from Satan, the "Passover" with Christ into the promised land, "the liberty with which Christ has set us free" and the transference "from the kingdom of darkness into the kingdom of his beloved son."

The ancient concept of redemption itself affected the primitive manner of looking upon it and celebrating it. The redemption was conceived as a new creation—a process of restoration achieved by "putting on the new man who is created according to justice and true holiness." This redemption in the full sense was brought about by the Life, Death, Resurrection and Ascension of our Lord; His Passover, Paschal Sacrifice, the Paschal Mystery. "In Him" the whole Church and every Christian had died upon the cross, risen from the dead and ascended into Heaven. They were partakers of His victory since they were united to Him. These events in the life of Christ whereby the redemption was accomplished were not conceived or held in isolation—it was all part of the one activity—our deliverance and our redemption. There was no concentration on the one to the exclusion of the other. Something of this survives in our own time when on Easter day we refer so often to the immolated Paschal Lamb "who by dying destroyed our death and by rising again restored life to us."

There is evidence that among the lessons read during the original night-long Easter Vigil in the Church at Rome in the third century was the lesson from Exodus about the Paschal Lamb, now read in the synaxis of Good Friday. It is also noteworthy that the *Exultet* or Paschal Proclamation is almost entirely preoccupied with drawing the parallel between the Exodus of the Jews and the New Exodus of the Christians. Easter is the Paschal feast and commemorates and celebrates not the Resurrection alone but the entire mystery of the redemption. That is the reason for the insistence upon baptism during the course of the Great Vigil, because it is through Baptism that the individual is aggregated to the community of the redeemed and the work of the redemption is appropriated to him. The *Transitus Domini*, the Passage from death to life of the Lord, is dramatically re-enacted in the disciple. For we are baptized into His Death and consequently into His Resurrection. Baptism and the accompanying Confirmation were the sacraments of the redemption, which incorporated the individual into Christ. It was highly fitting that this individual redemption should take place at the time when the Church celebrated the mystery whereby our redemption was accomplished. The link between the two events which became one in the Easter celebration was keenly appreciated and felt. And this celebration lasted fifty days, not as a commemoration of the time our Lord spent on earth or of the time between Easter and Pentecost, but as a symbol of the fact that in Christ the Christian Church and its members had entered into the Promised Land, the Kingdom of God.

During the fourth century in Jerusalem this ancient way of looking upon Easter as one united commemoration of the entire Paschal mystery was affected by a new approach: the tendency to commemorate the individual historical events in the history of redemption. It was natural and inevitable that these commemorations should have had their origin in the Holy City where these events had taken place; this served as a stimulus to remember them and, as it turned out, an incentive to re-enact them. The Spanish pilgrim Etheria Sylvia recounts a whole series of such commemorations which she witnessed in the Holy City towards the end of the fourth century (385). Very likely they had begun some time before that, since they appear in her account as of long standing. The influence of the Jerusalem rites was strong and in succeeding centuries these observances penetrated even as far as Gaul and became, with certain modifications, the practice of the entire Church by the seventh century. The ancient unified celebration thus became transformed into a series of historical commemorations of distinct though related events—the betrayal and the institution of the Eucharist on Holy Thursday, the Passion and Death on Good Friday, the Burial of Our Lord on Saturday, the Resurrection on Easter Sunday. When they travelled westward, these observances encountered those already found in the Western Churches and blended with them: the Palm Sunday procession preceding the earlier Mass on the Sunday before Easter, during which the Passion according to St. Matthew was read, the veneration of the cross following the ancient a-liturgical service of Good Friday, etc.

Palm Sunday. In the new rite for Holy Week the procession of the palms has been brought into greater relief by shortening the rite of blessing that preceded it and having the people sing the hymn *Gloria Laus* while the procession is going on. During the distribution of the palms, psalms may be sung. The festive character of the whole rite, which is conceived as the greeting of Israel to her Savior, who comes into her midst to inaugurate the work of His redemption, is emphasized by the wearing of the dalmatic, the sign of joy, instead of the penitential folded chasubles. Moreover, the color is red as befits a triumph in honor of the King of Martyrs. The older *missa sicca* that once took place is dropped out; only the Introit, one collect of blessing, and the Gospel remain. The celebrant no longer stands at the altar but behind the table where the palms are placed and faces the congregation. The palms may be distributed at the door and are blessed while they are held by the faithful. If they are distributed from the sanctuary, antiphons and psalms are sung until everyone has received his palm. The psalms are an addition to the rite, but the antiphons are those used in the older rite. We are reminded of the purpose of the celebration by the psalms that have been selected; they are royal psalms which proclaim the King.

After the Gospel the celebrant invites all to take part in the procession, during which antiphons are sung that recall the *Hosannas* and *Benedictus* of the first Palm Sunday. An innovation introduced into the new rite is the singing of Theodulph of Orleans' famous hymn to Christ the King *during the procession* instead of outside the church doors as in former times. All are encouraged to join in the refrain if possible. A psalm is also sung while the procession is going on. All these—antiphons, hymn, psalm—are intended to emphasize the central importance of the procession itself and to bring out the fact that it is a dramatic representation of the greeting of Israel to her Messias and her king.

The ideal would be to bless the palms in one place and then go in procession to another. If this cannot be done, the clergy and faithful should have the procession out of doors. When they return to the church, they enter it at once and the priest, standing before the altar but facing the people, sings a collect addressed to Christ the Redeemer and King, asking for His blessing and protection.

During the Mass that follows the celebrant and sacred ministers change to purple vestments; deacon and subdeacon wear the dalmatic and tunic. The prayers at the foot of the altar are not said, nor does the celebrant read the lessons to himself as he has done hitherto.

The Mass of Palm Sunday retains much of its primitive character: it is entirely given up to recalling the memory of the Passion of our Lord. To this everything about it contributes—the chants taken in large part from the Twenty-first Psalm which so graphically describes the Passion in advance, the lesson from Philippians, "Christ humbled Himself, becoming obedient unto death, even unto the death of the cross," and particularly the Gospel narrative of the Passion according to St. Matthew. The only change is that this last has been shortened. Originally this Gospel was sung by one deacon who was guided in singing the various parts by three letters: *T* (for the word *tacite* or *trahe*) before the words of Christ, which indicates that they should be drawn out and sung solemnly; *C* (for *celeriter* or *cito*) before the narrative, meaning that these words should be sung briskly; and *S* (*sursum*) before the words of other figures, indicating that they should be sung on a higher note. Later on a cross was substituted for the *T*.

The custom of three deacons singing the Passion was introduced in northern Europe about the year 1000, most likely with a view to making the reading more dramatic and impressive. The kneeling at *emisit spiritum* was a mediaeval innovation adopted at Rome in the fourteenth century.

The entire Passion is sung now in the same tone and the haunting Ambrosian chant of the last part has been discontinued. During all of Holy Week, when solemn Mass is sung, the use of the folded chasubles is abolished, the celebrant does not say the prayers at the foot of the altar nor read the lessons during Mass nor the last Gospel at the end. Whenever the "*Flectamus Genua*" is said, we remain on our knees for a little time, instead of getting up immediately, which was nonsensical from any point of view. Another welcome innovation which is not really an innovation at all is that the names of the Introit, Offertory and Communion chants are changed to *Antiphona ad Introitum, ad Offertorium, ad Communionem*, thereby bringing us back to the original purpose of these chants—to be sung while something is going on, and not after or before.

Wednesday (called Spy Wednesday in former times) is the oldest and most important of the first three days of Holy Week, as the three lessons in the Mass show us. It was one of the first days in this week to be celebrated at Rome and for some time was an a-liturgical day. Later on the Eucharistic Sacrifice was celebrated in the evening. Originally the Passion according to St. Luke was read on this day; in the ninth century the Passion according to St. Mark was assigned. In the new ordo for Holy Week the Passion according to St. Mark has been shortened, as has the Passion according to St. Matthew.

Holy Thursday. Since the fifth century at least this day has been called *Feria Quinta in Coena Domini* (Thursday of the Lord's Supper). In some places it bore the curious name of *Natale Calicis* (Birthday of the Chalice). Both of these names show that it has always commemorated the Last Supper and the Institution of the Eucharist primarily. We say primarily because it was also associated with the sorrowful commemoration of the betrayal of our Lord by Judas and in fact was called in some places *Dies Trahitionis* (day of the betrayal). From very early times the reconciliation of penitents and the consecration of the holy oils also took place on this day. For all these reasons there were three Masses on Holy Thursday in the Church of Rome, the first for the reconciliation of the penitents, the second for the consecration of the oils, the third, held in the evening, to commemorate the institution of the Eucharist. This last practice of an evening celebration was also observed in other parts of the West and in the East. The Gelasian Sacramentary provides formulae for these three Masses, but the Gregorian Sacramentary some centuries later provides only a *Missa Chrismalis,* for the blessing of the oils, celebrated late in the afternoon. This Mass had a festive character about it; white vestments were worn and the Gloria sung for the first time since Lent began. Though the formulae were changed later on, this festive note was retained into modern times. The chrismal Mass was dropped some time after and the Holy Thursday Mass familiar to us until this year, with the accent on the institution of the Eucharist and celebrated in the morning, took its place.

The Introit was taken from the Mass of Tuesday in Holy Week, the collect from Good Friday, and the Gospel was that read formerly on Tuesday before the substitution of the Passion according to St. Mark in the seventh century. The new order for Holy Week provides a morning Mass for cathedral churches with texts referring exclusively to the blessing of the oils and an evening Mass for all other churches with the customary Holy Thursday texts.

The institution of the Eucharist is commemorated in the Epistle, the Secret Prayer, the proper *Hanc Igitur* and *Communicantes*. There was at one time a fine Preface referring to the betrayal by Judas, but later the Preface of the Cross was substituted for it. The Offertory antiphon with its glad cry, "I shall not die but live," and the Gradual "*Christus Factus est*" with its "For which cause God hath exalted Him," are a reminder that the triumph of Christ cannot be disassociated from His sufferings.

A particular feature of this day's Mass is that the "*qui pridie*" retains its earlier and primitive wording "*qui pridie quam pro nostra omniumque salute . . . pateretur.*"

The ancient rite which gave its name to this day in English-speaking lands, the *Mandatum* or Washing of the Feet, has been restored by the new Order for Holy Week. This rite is not obligatory but is highly recommended. It may follow the Gospel or be held at another time. During the *Mandatum* new antiphons, drawn mostly from the Gospel of the day, are sung; near the end of the rite the ancient hymn "*Ubi caritas et amor*" is sung. These chants again underline the meaning of the rite: an act of brotherly love, "He loved them to the uttermost," that love which is nourished and strengthened by the Eucharist instituted on this day.

The hosts consecrated for the Communion service on Good Friday are carried in procession after Mass to the repository which, according to the provisions of the new rite, is to be very simple and austere, a protest against the tendency which had hardened almost into a tradition to overemphasize a secondary feature of the day. After the procession the altar is stripped of its ornaments while Psalm 21 is sung because of its verse, "They parted my garments among them," which forms the antiphon for the service. This stripping of the altar is almost certainly a survival, somewhat developed, of the primitive practice of removing the altar cloths after every Mass.

Good Friday. In the early centuries there was no celebration of Good Friday—certainly no adoration of the cross nor Communion service. It has always, both in the East and West, been an a-liturgical day when the sacred mysteries could not be celebrated. Tertullian gives an interesting reason why this should be so—one that throws a flood of light on the way Christian antiquity viewed the Mass. "It is not fitting that we should celebrate a feast on the day on which the bridegroom is taken from us."

Since the fifth century the station for this day's service was held at the church of the Holy Cross in Jerusalem, a Roman church where the relics of the true Cross were kept and therefore regarded as a part of the Holy Land transported to Rome.

The *synaxis* or reading service, which makes up the first of the three distinct parts of the Good Friday rite, goes back almost without change to the pre-Nicene period, or at least to the fourth century. It represents the a-liturgical services held in Africa and in Italy at this time and in fact reproduces substantially the foremass of the ancient rite, with its three lessons, its responsorial chant and its prayer for the whole Church. This was the only service, besides the Office, that was held in Rome and the surrounding towns until the seventh century. It began in the afternoon—about three or four o'clock—a practice that the new Holy Week order has revived.

There is no entrance chant nor prayer at the foot of the altar; these were introduced into the Mass later on. The celebrant and ministers lie prostrate before the altar, as they did at every

Mass in early times. Nothing is placed upon the altar—neither cloths nor candlesticks. In the new rite the ministers no longer wear chasubles, but they do continue to wear black: stoles for celebrant and deacon, maniples for all.

Formerly the service opened directly with the lesson; now it is begun with a collect which asks that we be made comformable to the Passion which has delivered us from death. The first lesson from the Prophet Osee was substituted some time later for the original lesson from Philippians read at this point. It makes a direct reference to the Resurrection and to the redemption: "He will revive us after two days; on the third day he will raise us up and we shall live in his sight."

The canticle sung after this lesson is from Habacuc: the Lord will avenge the persecution of the Messias. The mistranslation, "in the midst of two creatures," led to the interpretation that this referred to the circumstance that Christ was crucified between two thieves. But this is a sheer accommodation. It is significant that the name of the chant has been changed from tract to responsorial chant, another indication of the stress put upon participation in this new rite.

Time is given to kneel for silent prayer. This was the original meaning of "Let us kneel down," which in the course of time came to be interpreted as a mere genuflection. The collect is then sung with everyone standing. It is the same collect as that of Holy Thursday and asks for the grace of the Resurrection.

The second lesson is the story of the paschal lamb, taken from Exodus. In this sacrifice of the lamb and the sprinkling of the doorposts with its blood, the Church has always seen the figure of the sacrifice of Christ and of the redemption His Blood has brought to us.

After the responsorial singing of Psalm 179, which expresses the frame of mind of Christ in His Passion, His confidence in God, the Passion according to St. John is sung, beginning now with the Agony in the Garden. No comment is necessary on the appropriateness of this selection for Good Friday; St. John was an eyewitness to the Passion and Death of the Savior and we see it through his eyes.

This part of the service concludes with the ancient *orationes fidelium,* the antiquity of which is attested by St. Justin. Once sung at all Masses, they survive only on this day—a beautiful and impressive example of what intercessory prayer should be. A feature of the new rite is the prayer for the civil rulers in place of the long unused prayer for the Roman emperor.

It is in the two latter parts of the Good Friday service that the greatest changes have been made. The Adoration or Veneration of the Cross is transformed into a real triumph, and while the old rite remains in substance the same, it receives almost a new bent and direction by the prominence now given to the cross itself.

The rite originated in Jerusalem in the fourth century as an extra-liturgical veneration of the true cross, a veneration which was very simple and even austere, unaccompanied by any singing and performed in deepest silence. It is most important for a complete understanding of the rite as we have it today to remember that it was thus originally a matter of paying homage to the *true* cross, a circumstance which would give much greater immediacy and pertinence to the whole action. As a matter of fact, we see that when the Jerusalem rite first spread to other places it was only to those churches which had a relic of the true cross. That explains the antiphon sung in unveiling the cross: "*Ecce lignum crucis,*" which we now apply to all crucifixes but which originally could have point only with a real relic of the true cross.

No one knows for certain when the Adoration of the Cross was introduced into Rome, but it seems to have been known there in the seventh century. According to an eighth century ordo the relic of the true cross was brought to the altar in a precious casket and left there during the entire service. In fact, the service began with the pope uncovering the relic and kissing it, the clergy venerating it after him. Then the regular Good

Friday service followed with the relic of the Cross remaining on the altar all this time. After the end of the service the people in their turn venerated the relic. The only elaboration which developed in the native Roman Rite was the singing of the antiphon "*Ecce lignum crucis*" alternating with Psalm 118 in the procession from the Lateran and, later on, while the people venerated the cross.

In Spain and the Frankish domains the practice of adoring the cross was also borrowed from Jerusalem, but in those places it developed characteristically into a most elaborate and dramatic rite, with the uncovering and showing of the cross, the threefold prostration, the singing of the reproaches, the hymn "*Pange Lingua*" and, borrowed from Byzantium, the "*Agios o Theos*" and the "*Crucem tuam.*" All these elaborations found their way into the Roman Rite from the ninth to the eleventh centuries.

In the twelfth century the threefold progressive showing of the cross to the people at the singing of the antiphon "*Ecce Lignum Crucis*" was introduced, but the changing of place and the progressive lifting of the voice and raising of the cross came in only in the fourteenth century. We can see that it is very difficult to follow the stages of the development of this rite from a simple placing of the relic of the true cross upon the altar to our modern showing and veneration of the crucifix; the elaboration of a simple extra-liturgical devotion to a most elaborate rite represents many stages in a long growth.

The new rite changes very little of all this except to bring the cross itself into greater prominence by escorting it from the sacristy to the sanctuary in procession and by having it held up by acolytes during the veneration. Lighted candles on each side, borne by two more acolytes, help to concentrate attention upon it. "For this is the Pasch, the Passover of the Lord"; we are celebrating His victory; this is the triumph of the Crucified.

The Communion Service. From the seventh century until the Middle Ages, Communion was received on this day. After the practice died out in the greater part of the Church (though it still survived here and there into modern times) the many rites which aimed at making the old Communion service resemble a real Mass—incensing, elevation, *orate fratres*, etc.—were added in the late Middle Ages.

The most striking feature of the new ordo for Holy Week is the restoration of the old Communion service. For this the celebrant and sacred ministers change to purple vestments—chasuble, dalmatic and tunic. The deacon goes to the altar of repose and returns with the ciborium containing the hosts and places it on the altar. Then all present join the celebrant in *saying* the Our Father in Latin. He sings the *Libera nos* with hands extended and says one of the three prayers before Communion. After the celebrant's Communion, the Communion of the clergy and people follows in the usual manner. During the distribution Psalm 21, the Passion Psalm, or one of the responses for Matins may be sung. Three new Postcommunions close the whole service.

Holy Saturday—The Easter Vigil. This day was for centuries truly a-liturgical, without Mass or even Communion, and dedicated to commemorating the burial of our Lord and His sojourn in the grave. The celebration of the great night-watch or vigil was held during the night between Saturday and Sunday morning, beginning after dark and with the lessons, prayers and baptisms lasting all night until morning. This great night, most important of the year, was called the "Mother of all holy Vigils" (St. Augustine).

In reality this vigil was the true celebration of Easter itself. It was held during the night for several reasons, and it is necessary to understand these if we are to understand the feast itself and why such a great point was made of restoring the *nocturnal* celebration in the decree of 1951. First of all, the feast of Easter is essentially the Christian Passover, and the Paschal feast of the Jews commemorated an event that had taken place at night—

the deliverance from Egypt. Because of this the Jewish commemoration of that deliverance also took place at night. The early Christians, who saw their own feast as the Christian Passover, naturally celebrated their feast at night also. The fact that Christ rose from the dead during the night and that He will come again during the night (according to the manner in which the Scriptures speak of His coming) all enter into the insistence upon the celebration of Easter at this hour. All the important texts of the Easter Vigil Office and Mass presuppose that the service is taking place during the night. That these texts were at variance with the actual facts for so many centuries worked great detriment to the feast and inevitably gave it an air of unreality, and this was most regrettable because the Vigil still remained, theoretically at least, the true Easter celebration, though it was anticipated by almost a whole day.

Because the sacrament of Baptism is so closely bound up with the Resurrection of our Lord (it is the Resurrection re-enacted in the Christian community and in the individual members), the waters of Baptism were blessed on this night and the sacrament solemnly administered. With the lessons and chants this took all night, and the Holy Eucharist which crowned and completed the service took place, most appropriately, at dawn on Easter Day. The fact that Baptism was administered on this night explains the choice of the lessons (twelve of them until 1951, now reduced to four) which describe the effects of Baptism, and also the chants, particularly Moses' Canticle of Victory after the Jews had crossed safely over the Red Sea, a song which upon the lips of the new Israel becomes a canticle of the redeemed.

With the decline of the catechumenate came the decline of this great vigil. Gradually it was pushed back—first to the evening of Holy Saturday, then to the afternoon and finally, by the end of the Middle Ages, to the morning. Both Easter and Holy Saturday suffered from this arrangement: the one unduly anticipated, the other cut down to a few hours. The aim of the decree of 1951 was to restore the celebration of Easter to its proper place and to re-affirm the ancient idea that Holy Saturday is a day of recollection and of mourning. At first this was optional, but in 1955 it became obligatory upon every one in the Western Church. (It should be mentioned here that the nocturnal celebration of Easter has never died out in the Eastern churches—another instance of the marked tendency of the Eastern rites to preserve the primitive and traditional observances intact.)

The modern Easter night-watch begins either in the early evening or after ten o'clock with the blessing of the new fire in the vestibule or the church yard. This is in all probability a pagan custom from northern lands that was Christianized in Gaul and Germany. It was introduced into the Roman Rite about the eleventh or twelfth century. The new fire is of course a symbol of Christ and His Resurrection.

The celebrant then prepares the paschal candle, marking it with the cross, the A and Ω, and the year; then he places the five grains of incense in the candle. After this he lights it with the new fire. By this rite the paschal candle is made the symbol of the risen Christ, marked with His wounds but shining with light.

The origin of the paschal candle is disputed, but the most satisfactory explanation is that it comes from the service of the *lucernarium:* the light necessary for the evening service was blessed and offered to God. This was once done many times during the year; the blessing and the candle survive only on this one day. That would explain why the deacon has so prominent a role in the service; deacons were in charge of lighting the churches. The deacon was also expected to prepare the formula of blessing—our *exultet.* This rite of blessing the candle (in the ancient sense of dedicating it to God) was not introduced into the Church of Rome until the eighth century.

Now the paschal candle is blessed by the celebrant and carried lighted into the darkened church by the deacon, who announces its coming with the glad cry "*Lumen Christi!*" The symbolism of carrying the candle into the church by the deacon followed by the clergy and people is obvious: Christ, the Light of the world, overcomes the darkness and dispels it with the brightness of His Resurrection, and as once the pillar of fire led the Israelites out of Egypt, now Christ leads His people into the true promised land. When the deacon arrives in the sanctuary, he places the candle in its candlestick. Meanwhile all the clergy and people have had their candles lighted, symbolic of the light of Christ spread abroad and communicated.

The *Praeconium Paschale* or *Exultet* follows, sung by the deacon. Its theme is the victory of Christ over death, sin and darkness on this night, the redemption being prefigured and foretold in the Old Testament deliverance from Egypt. This is the true Passover feast that we are celebrating, when the blood of the Divine Paschal Lamb saved us all and made it possible for us to pass over the Red Sea into the promised land. This is the night on which Christ rose from the tomb and put darkness to flight. The work of our redemption was completed by the Resurrection; that is why so much of this prayer is a hymn of the redemption. In honor of all these events, to commemorate and symbolize Christ's victory and our deliverance, the Church lights this candle and offers it to God. The hymn concludes with intercessions for the Church, clergy and people, and last of all for the civil authorities.

No one knows for certain who composed the *Exultet*. It has been attributed both to St. Ambrose and St. Augustine, but there is no real proof that it was written by either of them. It appears for the first time in the Gelasian Sacramentary (seventh century) but belongs in tone and expression to the golden age of liturgical composition (fifth century). The new order has happily restored the ancient practice of singing it straight through without interruption.

The service of readings and chants follows the proclamation. The new rite has retained four lessons: they describe the first creation (which is the type and pattern of the second creation that is the redemption); the Exodus from Egypt, again the great type and foreshadowing of the redemption; the holy city of Jerusalem which is the city of the saved, and the order to Joshua to lead the people into the promised land. After each lesson there is a collect which sums up its meaning and after three of them a chant which expresses in song some aspect of this night's work.

When the reading service is over, the Litany of the Saints is sung, interrupted half-way through by the blessing of the font and, if possible, by the administration of Baptism. The restored Easter Vigil service calls for doing all this in the sanctuary instead of the sacristy, so that all may see it and profit from it. The rite of blessing the font and of Baptism itself is described elsewhere in this book.

The restored Easter Vigil has added a new rite that is very beautiful and at the same time very significant: the renewal of the baptismal promises, which is preceded by a brief exhortation. The people are to participate actively in this—answering the questions, then reciting the Lord's Prayer with the celebrant. This whole rite is to be conducted in the vernacular to ensure the greatest participation. After the promises have been made, the priest sprinkles the congregation with the newly blessed baptismal water. The idea behind it is to renew in the people the spirit of their Baptism and to recall to them the obligations that it has laid upon them. The sprinkling with baptismal water is a symbolic renewal of Baptism itself. We say it is significant because it is an altogether new rite and therefore shows that the Church does not hesitate to create new rites for new needs, and because it is in the vernacular which means that when the good of souls demands it the Church will not hesitate to employ necessary means.

The crown of the Easter Vigil service is the offering of the Paschal Sacrifice, the true Easter Mass. There is no Introit because the clergy are already in the sanctuary. The *Gloria* is sung with solemnity and the *Alleluia*, the very quintessence of Easter, is sung for the first time since Septuagesima, not only once but three times, not by the choir alone but by the celebrant and the people. The omission of some of the Mass chants, of lights at the Gospel, and of the singing of the Creed is explained by the fact that all these things were introduced into the liturgy long after the time that this Mass was composed. The absence of the Kiss of Peace goes back to the time when this service was advanced to Holy Saturday morning and people ceased to go to Communion, since the Kiss of Peace and Communion were closely related in earlier times. The texts of the Mass allude to the Resurrection, as we might expect, but they have also been heavily influenced by the circumstance that this is the great time for Baptism; the Collect, Epistle, and *Hanc Igitur* all refer to the neophytes either directly or indirectly.

Until the present time Vespers was always sung after Communion; now, since it is after midnight, we sing Lauds—a very short Office which actually grew up quite by accident. It originated in the tenth century as a Communion chant; the *Alleluia*, the *Laudate* and the *Magnificat* were sung during Communion as ideal expressions of joy and thanksgiving. Later on when the whole service had been pushed back into Holy Saturday, this part was reached about sunset, the normal time for Vespers. Consequently, it was either considered as a species of Vespers, or even as a substitute for Vespers, which it was never meant to be. The Communion of the people had long ceased to be a practice and the original purpose of these chants was forgotten.

The new rite has substituted Psalm 150 for Psalm 116, which has already been sung during Mass.

The Office During the Triduum Sacrum. On the last three days of Holy Week the Office retains much of the spirit and the forms of the Roman Office of the sixth and seventh centuries. Until the decree of 1955 Matins and Lauds of each day were anticipated on the day before, and, because they were said in the late afternoon or evening, were called *Tenebrae* (*Matutinae* understood), which literally means Matins said in the dark. Now these hours may not be anticipated in public recitation and must be said in the morning. With the evening recitation there also disappear many of the customs associated with it: the triangular candlestick and the candles, the noise made in choir after Lauds, *etc.*

All those parts left out of the Office itself—the invitatory, hymns, *gloria patri,* blessings before lessons, capitularies—are omitted simply because the Office on these days has kept substantially the form of the primitive Office as it was before all these practices were introduced. The Psalm *Miserere* which came to be recited after all the hours on these days was originally private and from now on will be dropped from the Office; each hour will end with the *Pater* and the oration "*Respice*" (*Concede,*" on Holy Saturday).

The antiphons and responsories of these three days follow rather closely the general theme of each day. They are largely taken from the Scriptures, and all provide a striking example of the sober restraint with which the Bible and the Church approach the events of our redemption.

On Thursday and Friday Vespers are not said by those who take part in the services, because Vespers are *evening* prayers and the evening service of that day takes their place. On the other hand, Holy Saturday has Vespers but not Compline, because Compline is a prayer said before going to bed, and we do not go to bed that night. This is a most happy regulation in every way and points towards the restoring of the Office to its proper place as an *hour* prayer to be said at the proper times of the day, and not merely as an obligation to be discharged at any time with as little inconvenience as possible.

These Offices of the *Triduum Sacrum,* for all their comparative austerity, are very beautiful and impressive, the antiphons and responsories being particularly striking. The psalms used on

Thursday are the usual ferial psalms for that day, but special ones have been chosen for Friday and Saturday.

Easter Day. "The solemnity of solemnities and our Easter" are the words used by the Roman Martyrology to describe this day, words which are but an echo of the superlatives always employed by the Fathers when speaking of this great feast of Christ and of His Church: It is "the great day," "the feast of feasts," "the queen of days," "the happiest day"—all these and many more abound in their writings. It is truly a day of joy and thanksgiving: "This is the day the Lord has made; let us be glad and rejoice therein."

Because the feast was celebrated during the night for so many centuries, a special Mass over and above the Mass which came at dawn after the all-night Vigil was not necessary. Only when that Mass was pushed back into Holy Saturday did a Mass for Easter day make its appearance in the Sacramentaries. The present Mass, "*in die Paschae*," goes back to the seventh century, and the lessons and chants are inspired largely by the event of the Resurrection which it commemorates, although it retains in the Canon the references to Baptism which mark the Mass of the Vigil (*Communicantes, Hanc Igitur,* Preface). The exquisite Sequence was added about the eleventh century. A characteristic of this Mass and all those of Easter week is the Gradual "*Haec Dies,*" taken from Psalm 117. Apparently the entire psalm was sung at this point and this is all that remains of it.

The Octave of Easter. Closely related to Easter and prolonging it is the Octave which, like Easter itself, had a precedent among the Jews. The great themes of Easter—Baptism, the apparitions of the risen Lord, the Resurrection itself—are developed and amplified during these days in the Masses, which themselves go back to the sixth century.

The time after Easter until Pentecost was considered in ancient times as one continual feast and known as the Holy Fifty Days, or simply as the Pentecost. During these days of joy the Eucharist was celebrated every day, kneeling at public prayer and fasting were forbidden, and the glad song of the *Alleluia* marked the liturgical celebration. Just as the Jews celebrated during these days the entrance of the Israelites into the promised land, the Christians rejoiced over possession of the Kingdom of God which they had already entered into by anticipation and of which they were inheritors through the Resurrection. The liturgy has preserved much of this primitive spirit of joy in the Offices and Masses of the Easter season. During the whole time the *Alleluia* resounds in abundance and the texts that are drawn upon for the chants and lessons keep alive the joyful sentiments of the season.

The Sundays after Easter which, though hardly older than the fifth century, are very ancient, reflect in abundance the Christian delight and rejoicing in the Resurrection and in the redemption which it has brought. The Masses are all variations on the theme of Christ's victory; the chants are usually proclamations of the redeeming work; the Epistles show us the manner in which the redeemed should live; the Gospels are all from St. John and bring us his own insight into Christ's personality and work. As the weeks go by, another theme claims our attention with increasing importunity: the thought of Heaven and of the place that He has gone to prepare for us.

During this time the Church continues to contemplate the Resurrection and the glory that it brought to Christ, to the Head and the members. The dominant idea which becomes stronger as the feast of the Ascension approaches is expressed in our Lord's own words, "I go to the Father" (John 14:12). He returns whence He came; He passed through suffering and death to the Resurrection and the Ascension to the right hand of His Father. He goes before us, but it is to prepare a place for us that He goes: our redemption is closely bound up with

His glorification. These are the great themes of the Easter season: the redemption and the glorification. In reality, of course, it is but one theme, that of the return to the Father: His return becomes ours.

There is only one exception to this sustained rejoicing. The penitential atmosphere is evoked in the observance of the Rogation days, a time of special prayer marked by the recitation of the litanies: the major litanies on the feast of St. Mark and the minor litanies with procession and special Mass on the two days immediately preceding the feast of the Ascension. The major litanies are a Christian transformation of the pagan custom in Rome of going in procession through the fields to invoke the blessing of the gods upon the harvest. This observance was called the *Rubigalia* and was deeply entrenched among the people; the Church adopted the custom in the fifth century, giving it a Christian direction. The great prayer of supplication, the litany, was sung during the procession. Because of this the day was known as the Major Litany.

The days of prayer immediately preceding the feast of the Ascension owe their origin to St. Mammertus of Vienne in Gaul, who began the practice of special prayer against the danger of earthquake. This practice was taken up in other places and extended to include prayers against all manner of natural disaster. The litanies were added to these days during the Middle Ages; but the term minor litanies is used to distinguish it from the older and more important "litany" held on April 25. The Mass texts for the Rogation days, which give them their name, were composed before the ninth century and stress the necessity and importance of preserving prayer. From days of prayer for the fruits of the earth the Rogation days have become times of more earnest prayer for all God's gifts.

The Feast of the Ascension. Forty days after Easter the Church celebrates the feast of the Ascension as it has since the fourth century. The Canon of the Mass calls it the *glorious*

Ascension and all the ancient Sacramentaries contain Mass formularies for it. Although it is celebrated now as a separate feast, it appears to have originated as a kind of appendage of Pentecost; the two events are in fact very closely related. The present Mass for the feast is the one found in the Gregorian Sacramentary and represents a re-editing of earlier texts, done in all likelihood by St. Gregory.

The note of joyous longing and homesickness pervades this feast, the significance of which is beautifully expressed by St. Leo in the lessons read on that day: "Christ's ascension is our own advancement," * and in the collect: ". . . that we too may ever dwell in spirit in heaven." The great themes of this feast are the triumph and glorification of Christ, the placing of His human nature at the right hand of God: in Him we too enter into the possession of the Kingdom prepared for us. "He has raised us up with Him and made us sit down together with Him at the right hand of God." These are themes that are given full development in the Mass and Office. The octave of this feast has been abolished. After the singing of the Gospel of this feast the paschal candle is extinguished to symbolize that Christ has ascended to His Father.

Pentecost. With the Jews Pentecost, or the feast of Weeks, held exactly seven weeks after Easter, commemorated the harvest of grain and later on the giving of the Law on Mount Sinai. As they did with the Passover, with which this feast is intimately associated, the Christians seem to have taken this feast over from the Jewish church from the beginning, giving it their own special direction and meaning; they continued to celebrate it as a commemoration of the sending of the Spirit and of the inauguration of the Church's mission to preach the gospel and bear witness to Christ. This Christian meaning is expressed in the antiphon of second Vespers of the feast. In reality Pentecost is the climax as well as the close of the paschal season and seems

* *Sermo* I *In Ascen.*

to have been considered as such during the first centuries. Not until the Middle Ages was there an octave; the feast itself closed the paschal season.

The relation between Easter and Pentecost was brought out by the circumstance that the sacrament of Baptism was bestowed in the night before the feast upon those who for one reason or another had not been baptized at Easter. There was a night vigil as at Easter, but with fewer lessons; and the Mass now said in the vigil was celebrated at dawn on the Sunday. By the eighth or ninth century this service was anticipated in the afternoon of the Saturday and gradually pushed back to the morning.

The present Office of Pentecost was derived from the Gallican Church about the tenth century; the custom of singing the "*Veni Creator*" at Terce originated in the monastery of Cluny. The Mass for the feast is remarkable for the Sequence. "*Veni Sancte Spiritus*" and for the unusual ending of the Preface "Qua propter . . ." which was transferred from the Preface of Easter, where it originally belonged, by St. Gregory. The Octave, with its rich proper Masses for each day, was not everywhere observed until the eleventh century, although it was introduced, in imitation of the Easter Octave, during the sixth. The Masses of this week develop the theme of the sending of the Spirit and, to a certain extent, of Baptism and the Eucharist.

The first Sunday after Pentecost was originally a free Sunday (*Dominica vacat*); the custom grew up in the Frankish lands of using on that day the Mass formulary composed by Alcuin in honor of the Holy Trinity. The Holy See disapproved of the idea, at least for Rome, maintaining that every Sunday and indeed every day honored the Trinity, and there was consequently no need for a special feast.* In spite of papal disapproval the idea continued to spread and in the fourteenth cen-

* Pope Alexander III (☩1181) in a letter to the Bishop of Terdon, quoted by Righietti, *Storia Liturgica*, Vol. II, p. 220.

tury one of the Avignon popes extended the feast to the whole Church.

Time After Pentecost

The Feast of Corpus Christi began at Liége in Belgium just before the middle of the thirteenth century as the result of the visions of Blessed Juliana that pointed out the lack of a feast in honor of the Blessed Sacrament. Her confessor brought the matter to the attention of the bishop who forthwith instituted the feast, fixing it on the Thursday after the Octave of Pentecost. Some years after, Urban IV was urged to extend the feast to the entire Church, and though he hesitated at first, the miracle of Bolsena overcame his hesitation and in 1264 he acceded to the requests made to him. But he died before the decree instituting the feast could go into effect and it was not until 1312 that it was confirmed and extended to the whole Church.

The Office and Mass of Corpus Chrisi, with the exception of the responsories which are from an earlier source, were composed by St. Thomas Aquinas and are a triumph of doctrine and piety as everyone admits. Particularly worthy of comment are the hymns used in the Office and the Sequence used in the Mass. The Collect, Secret and Postcommunion are the expression in prayer of the symbolic meaning of the Eucharist: It recalls the past (*memoria passionis*), expresses the present (*unitatis et pacis quae oblatis muneribus mystice designantur*), and is a pledge and a sign of the future (*Quam temporalis praeceptio praefigurat*). These three meanings are woven together in the matchless antiphon of second Vespers, "*O Sacrum Convivium.*"

The feast of Corpus Christi has a peculiar unction and warmth about it well calculated to arouse a devotion to the Eucharist, sacrifice and sacrament, which recalls that of the primitive Church and which is one of the fairest flowers of Christian piety in any age.

Last in the series of feasts in the temporal cycle is the *feast of the Sacred Heart*, permanently fixed to the Friday after the now-suppressed Octave of Corpus Christi. This feast is a kind of double of Good Friday, a Good Friday celebrated without the mourning associated with Good Friday; we contemplate not so much the Passion of Christ as the love that inspired all His wonderful works, the love that caused Him to create, to become man, to redeem us, to send the Spirit and to institute the Eucharist. This mystery of love is symbolized for us by the pierced heart of the Redeemer. This love, "that creative love" (hymn for Matins), is the central theme of the Mass and Office of this feast. Although the institution of the feast of the Sacred Heart was urged in the seventeenth century, it was not extended to the universal Church until the nineteenth, under Pius IX. The Mass and Office used at first were changed in 1928 to bring them into greater conformity with the object of the feast.

The Sundays after Pentecost. The last part of the Church year to be organized was the group of Sundays from Pentecost to Advent, called now in our Missals the Sundays after Pentecost. There is no such arrangement in the Leonine Sacramentary, oldest of Roman liturgical books; only a series of general Sunday Mass formulae, no organized list as we know it today. The first beginnings of our present series is found in the Gelasian, where there are sixteen Masses that are the same as those from the fifth to the twentieth Sundays after Pentecost in the Roman Missal. These, of course, comprise the orations and prefaces; the lessons appear only later. The oldest lists of such lessons show that these Sundays, which still do not stand apart from the feasts of the saints, are grouped not "after Pentecost" but around the great saints' feasts of the summer: before and after SS. Peter and Paul, or after St. Laurence, or after St. Cyprian or St. Michael. Traces of this earlier arrangement survive, for example, in the Mass of the 4th Sunday after Pentecost, once the first after the "*natale*" of SS. Peter and Paul, which has as a Gospel the story of the miraculous catch of fishes made from Peter's boat. The first liturgical book to use the name "Sundays after Pentecost" is the Gregorian Sacramentary. Of these the first five are related to the Sundays after Easter and the Epistles, like those of these Sundays, are taken not from St. Paul but from the writings of the other Apostles. On the other hand, the Epistles read from the sixth Sunday on are from those of St. Paul in their canonical order, a survival of the old "*lectio continuata.*"

The Chants of the first sixteen of these Masses are taken from the psalter almost exclusively, and there seems to have been some attempt to follow the order of the psalter in selecting them; those of the last group are often from other sources. Given the rather aimless manner in which these Sundays after Pentecost took shape and the fact that the propers have been dislocated (Gospels originally belonging to one Sunday read on the next, *etc.*), it seems a particularly fruitless task to find any unity of themes in these Masses. Taken all together, they are a series of instructions upon the Christian life viewed as a whole, without having that particular flavor which marks the Sundays after Easter. Yet these Sundays often express the theme of the redemption directly in many of the texts. The greatest criticism we might make is that they do not always make it clear enough or particular enough. The original reason for the selection of these texts, particularly the Gospels, has been lost and there is much wisdom in the suggestion, heard often in recent years, of a new selection or a triple series of lessons for these days that would give greater variety to this season. Since the eighteenth century, the Preface of the Trinity is recited on these Sundays; this would seem to be a reflection of the old idea that Sunday is a kind of feast of the Trinity, an idea which was not well received at Rome, we will recall. Since Sunday is primarily a weekly celebration of the Resurrection, a Preface which would bring out that idea would seem to be more in keeping with the object of the Sunday.

There are three feasts of our Lord which are outside the temporal cycle, connected neither with Christmas nor Easter. They are the *feast of the Precious Blood* on July 1st, the *feast of the Transfiguration* on August 6th, and the *feast of Christ the King* on the last Sunday of October. The first was instituted by Pius IX in 1849 to commemorate his successful flight from Rome to Gaeta in 1848. It is a feast of the redemption—"Thou hast redeemed us, O Lord, in thy blood from every tribe and tongue and people and nation, and made us a kingdom unto our God" (Introit of the Feast)—and may be considered another double of Good Friday. The object of the feast is the Precious Blood of the Lamb without spot, by which we were bought at a great price.

Although the feast of the Transfiguration was celebrated in the East since the fifth century, and while the redemptive event that it commemorates is one of the most significant in the life of Christ, it is strange that there was no feast anywhere in the West until the fifteenth century, when Callixtus III instituted it to commemorate the raising of the seige of Belgrade by the Turks in 1457. The feast of the Transfiguration is closely related to Easter, which it foreshadowed, and also to Christmas, because it is a manifestation of the Divinity of Christ, the King of Glory. The Transfiguration has always been held in great veneration by the Eastern Church, which sees it as a great symbol and parable of the consequence, result and effects of our own life in Christ, which will progressively transform us into the likeness of the King of Glory. Much of this idea is expressed in our own Mass and Office for this feast, along with the theme of the Theophany or manifestation of God:

Jesu tibi sit gloria
Qui te revelas parvulis.

The feast of Christ the King is the newest of the feasts of our Lord in time, having been established as late as 1925; yet its themes are among the oldest that we celebrate. It has for its object the Kingship of Christ, which we honor and celebrate throughout the year, but on this day (the last Sunday of October) in a special manner. The feast has close affinity with Easter and the Ascension by which the Kingdom of Christ, His sovereign lordship, His eternal glory and triumph, were assumed; and also with the Epiphany, the oldest Kingship feast. It stands in close relation to the feast of All Saints also, not only in time by immediately preceding it, but in spirit and object. "The Kingdom of justice, holiness and peace" (Preface for the feast of Christ the King), which Christ hands over to His Father, is the "glorious Kingdom" described in the antiphon of the *Magnificat* in the second vespers of the feast of All Saints: "O how glorious is the Kingdom in which all the saints rejoice with Christ! Clad in white robes they follow the Lamb wherever He goes." Coming as they do at the end of the Church year, these two feasts deepen in us the awareness of the final end of all things which is the triumph of God and His Christ.

Special Feasts

Feasts of the Holy Cross. The presence of two feasts of the Holy Cross in our calendar—one in honor of the Finding of the Cross on May 3rd and the other called the Exaltation of the Cross on September 14th—is explained by a confusion which arose about the object of these feasts. Actually, the feast of the Exaltation commemorates the finding of the cross; it began in Jerusalem soon after that event occurred and came to Rome in the seventh century. The Church in Gaul adopted a like feast at the same time, but called it the Finding of the Cross and celebrated it on May 3rd. Later on this feast found its way into the Mass-book which was sent into Gaul from Rome and thus we now have two feasts in reality commemorating the same event! Pope Benedict XIV wished to suppress the later (May 3rd) feast for that reason, but nothing definite was done about it.

Feasts of Saints. Side by side with the Feasts of the temporal cycle is the sanctoral cycle, which commemorates the feasts of the saints. It is very closely bound up with the calendar year because the first and oldest saints' feasts were celebrations held on the anniversary of their *dies natalis,* the day of their entrance into Heaven; and there are many saints' feasts which began as celebrations of a church dedicated in their honor.

The first saints in the calendar were the martyrs, and their feasts form the core of the Sanctoral Cycle. The early Christians celebrated all burials, particularly those of martyrs, who they felt were certainly with God, as feasts, with a complete absence of any mourning of any sort. The anniversary of death was celebrated in the same way: as a feast, with an assembly, with the reading of the account of the martyrdom to inspire and encourage those who were yet alive, and with the offering of the Holy Sacrifice. Of course, the idea of the special power of the martyrs' intercession with God arose very early. For a long time this commemoration, which had arisen in connection with the martyrs' burials, took place only at their tombs, and the day received no liturgical expression anywhere else, even in the city where the martyr (or later, the confessor) was buried. In fact, that is one of the usual explanations of the word "double" in the classification of feasts: a day on which the office of the commemorated martyr or confessor was added to the ferial Office.

It was only in the sixth and seventh centuries, with the spread of the cult of the relics and of altars built in honor of the saints whose relics were kept there, that the custom arose of celebrating the feast day in places other than where the saint was buried. Then the Frankish church borrowed the local calendar of the church of Rome; later on, the mendicant orders spread the use of the Roman calendar everywhere they went, adding saints of their own, until by the end of the Middle Ages the original Roman calendar of saints, considerably augmented (not to say overloaded) with all manner of local saints from other parts of Europe, was everywhere observed throughout the West. The original Roman list was almost exclusively made up of martyrs (male and female); the cultus of confessors, virgins and widows was developed after this calendar was formed. Although this came into use in the fourth and fifth centuries, it received its full development outside of Rome and particularly in the churches of the North. It is significant that the martyrs were so highly honored, and regarded as the perfect type of Christians who most closely resembled Christ in his Passion and Death, that when the other classes of saints began to be venerated too it was because of the idea that their holy life and sufferings made them like the martyrs. Martyrdom was still regarded as the Christian ideal, and the idea persists in the Church which still continues to give the highest place among the saints to those who have shed their blood for Christ. The canonization of saints was reserved to the Holy See by Pope Alexander III in the twelfth century.

The idea of having one feast to commemorate all the saints seems to have come from Ireland about the tenth or eleventh century, but it originated ultimately in the keeping of the anniversary of the dedication of the Church of Sancta Maria ad Martyres (the Pantheon) at Rome. Here, as is so often the case in the calendar, a feast of the dedication of a church became the feast of those in whose honor or under whose invocation the church was dedicated.

From the late Middle Ages to our own time the wholesale introduction of saints' feasts into the calendar of the universal Church has created the problem of maintaining equilibrium between the *Sanctorale* and the *Temporale* (which should strictly speaking be called the *Dominicale* because it belongs to God and to Christ), and of seeing to it that the *Temporale* is not unduly invaded by feasts of saints, with the consequent exaltation of the saints at the expense of the honor due to God and to Christ. Time and time again the popes have unloaded, or tried to unload, the calendar and to prevent the feasts of saints from usurping the Sundays first of all, and then the seasonal days (Lent, Paschal time, Advent). This was the concern of St. Pius X, who did so much to restore the Sunday to its proper place, and in more recent times of Pius XII, whose revision of the rubrics in 1955 provides for the suppression of a number of saints' days and insures a greater observance of the ferial or temporal Office and Mass, especially in Lent, where to the privilege of saying the ferial Mass even on double class feasts is added the optional privilege of saying the ferial Office. There is no question here of diminishing in any way the honor that we should show the saints, but rather of keeping it subordinate to the much greater cultus of God Himself. For while it is undoubtedly true that God is honored when His saints are, it is also true that we can lose sight of this when the cultus of the saints gets out of hand. We tend naturally to concentrate overmuch upon the saint, and that is certainly a reversal of the order of things. There is surely no intrinsic reason why every saint who is canonized should by that very fact have his feast day extended to the universal Church. The principle of honoring the saints can be maintained just as well, and even better perhaps, by restricting the number of days devoted to them, thereby keeping for the direct honoring of God the greater part of the Church year. In any case, that is the tendency which has the upper hand now, as it is the tendency which the popes since the Reformation have encouraged and fostered.

The feasts of the saints are a source of great inspiration; in celebrating them, the Church encourages us to imitate their virtues and to invoke their intercession. These are indeed the two great themes which run through their Offices and Masses during the course of the Church year. They are presented to us as models and as our guides in living the life that Christ said we might have, and have more abundantly. They are a living commentary on the Gospel and an ever-present reminder that what they did we can do, each according to his ability and measure of grace, which by their intercession we can hope to obtain. Through the medium of the texts of the Missal and the

Breviary, the Church contemplates not so much the outward circumstances of the saints' lives, as the inner direction of those lives and the ultimate result of that inner direction.

The Common of Saints as we know it in the Missal reached its present form in the eleventh century. Actually, these Masses were originally in whole or in part proper Masses of different saints: the Mass of the Common of Confessor Bishops, for example, was formed from the proper Masses of SS. Sylvester, Marcellus and Sixtus; that of Virgins, in part from a Mass of Our Lady and in part from the Masses of Virgin Saints. The only new Mass added to the *commune* in nearly a thousand years was that of the *Commune Summorum Pontificum*.

The same procedure was followed in forming the *Commune Sanctorum* in the Office. These texts were used originally for one particular saint or a definite group of saints; they were the proper Offices of that saint or that group of saints, but were applicable to any other saint of the same class and consequently were applied to those saints who were admitted to the calendar at a later date. Like the *commune sanctorum* in the Missal the *commune* in the Office had taken form by the eleventh century. One great drawback of these Commons is that the same texts are read over and over again in the course of a year. This is particularly noticeable in the Missal. Obviously, one way to have greater variety would be to increase the number of Commons.

Feasts of Our Lady. The cycle of feasts of the Blessed Virgin was the last to be added to the calendar. Although the Blessed Virgin was venerated above all the saints and churches were named in her honor and pictures of her abounded in the iconography of the early Church, we know of no feast in her honor until the late fourth century in Syria. And even this was a general commemoration of her rather than a specific feast; there simply were no feasts at all in the West until the sixth or seventh centuries. When the West did adopt feasts of our Lady into the calendar, they were borrowed from the Byzantine Church.

The *Feast of the Assumption* began as a general commemoration of the Blessed Virgin. In the sixth century it became a commemoration of her *dies natalis,* held like the feasts of martyrs on the anniversary of her death, which traditionally was associated with August 15. It was also known as the *Dormition* ("Falling Asleep"), the *Despositio,* or the *Transitus;* all these terms referred to her death. The name Assumption which was to prevail over all the others was given to this feast in the West and already appears in the seventh-century Gelasian Sacramentary. This name carries with it the implication of the glorification of the Blessed Virgin: her taking up into Heaven was a triumph. The object of the feast became more clear in the Middle Ages. Some modern writers have wonderfully expressed the deeper significance of this greatest of our Lady's feasts by calling it "Our Lady's Easter." * When the dogma of the Assumption was defined in 1950, the feast was provided with an entirely new Mass that expresses much more clearly than the old the full meaning of the doctrine.

The *Nativity of the Blessed Virgin* was first celebrated at Jerusalem in the sixth century. Like other feasts of our Lady, it was adopted by the Roman Church in the late seventh century. We are reminded of the Oriental origin of this feast by the exquisite antiphons borrowed from Byzantine liturgical books.

The *Annunciation* is regarded as one of Mary's feasts and in fact has been known in England for many centuries as Lady Day, but it is not easy to see why that should be the case, because the Incarnation of the Son of God would seem to be the dominant theme of the feast, while the honor paid to Mary is subordinated to that great event.

The first certain evidence that we have of the existence of the feast is in the seventh century and that is in the East. In the

* Flicoteaux, *Mystères et Fêtes de la Vierge Marie* (Paris,1956), p. 97.

West it appears a little later in the Gelasian Sacramentary and is referred to in other documents. March 25 is the date assigned for its celebration, largely because of the ancient idea that God became man at the time of the vernal equinox. This meant that the feast would be celebrated in Lent, an inconvenience which was dealt with in different ways by different churches: some, as the church in Spain, transferred it to Advent time, and others, like the churches in the East, which celebrate this feast whenever it falls, even should it coincide with Easter itself. One ritual peculiarity of this feast is that the celebrant and sacred ministers kneel on the altar steps during the "*Et Incarnatus Est*," a rite that is done only on this day and on Christmas.

The *Immaculate Conception* is the only major feast of our Lady added to the calendar in modern times. Like the other Marian feasts it is Eastern in origin, but it began as the *Conception* of Mary by St. Anne. The term *Immaculate* was not applied to it anywhere until 1854. As a matter of fact, the object of the feast was not to honor the Virgin Mary's singular privilege of being preserved from original sin from the first moment of her conception, as it is with us, but the miraculous conception of a child by a mother who had been sterile—the prodigy related by the apocryphal literature. It is still called the Conception of St. Anne in the Eastern Churches.

The feast began in the East in the seventh century; by the ninth it was found in some parts of Italy, from whence it passed into Ireland, where it was called the Conception of Holy Mary. It was observed in England on the eighth of December and held in high honor there as well as in parts of France during the Middle Ages. Along with the spread of its observance went an increasing clarification of the theology of the conception of the Blessed Virgin. There was opposition to the feast and to the doctrine that was emerging more clearly all the time, but both had many friends as well as enemies, and the action of the Franciscans who adopted the feast for the whole order in 1263 gave a tremendous impulse to the cause. The same century saw the brilliant defense of the doctrine itself by the distinguished theologian of the same order, Duns Scotus (1308).

The feast was celebrated by more and more churches during the fourteenth century, only the Dominicans keeping aloof or celebrating it as the "Sanctification" of the Blessed Virgin. It also began to be celebrated by the papal court during this time. A great step forward was taken in the next century when Sixtus IV (himself a Franciscan) instituted the feast for the whole Church with a proper Mass and Office in 1476. He called it the Conception of Mary Immaculate—which was an advance on its earlier title but still did not qualify the Conception itself as Immaculate. Innocent XII made it a double of the second class, and Leo XIII promoted the feast to the rank of double of the first class. The Office and Mass of the feast are very rich and beautiful. This is particularly true of the exquisite Introit, "*Gaudens gaudebo*," which for content and melody must be counted among the best that we have.

These are the three great feasts of the Mother of God; but besides them there are a number of minor feasts which throughout the year commemorate and proclaim the glories of Mary. All but one—that of the Dedication of St. Mary Major, Our Lady of the Snow on August 5—are modern, and they usually commemorate some singular favor obtained through her intercession, some triumphal event associated with her, or some extraordinary manifestation of her power. Thus the feast of Our Lady of the Rosary commemorates the victory over the Turks at Lepanto; the feast of the Apparition of Our Lady at Lourdes recalls that miraculous event, the feast of the Immaculate Heart commemorates Fatima; and the Motherhood recalls the dogmatic definition of her Motherhood at Ephesus. The two feasts of the Seven Sorrows originated in the Middle Ages and reflect the piety of that time towards the Queen of Martyrs.

The feasts of our Blessed Lady make up a cycle in themselves, giving us a complete picture of her life and of her place in the plan of redemption. They honor above all her sublime dignity as the Mother of God and her many other privileges. They also unmistakably present her as the archetype of the Church which to a large extent she personifies. The Offices and Masses of the Blessed Virgin in the course of the year develop this theme in hundreds of ways. She is the Queen of the Saints because she shows us, in all its glowing splendor, what redeemed humanity is called to be; her achievement is a stimulus to our own efforts; she is the living exemplar of all we are called to be. "Blessed are they who hear the word of God and keep it."

The Dedication of Churches. Included among the feasts of our Lord, yet having a complexion of its own, is the feast of the Dedication of Churches. It began as a commemoration of the solemn consecration of the church building to God, and has developed into what is in reality a kind of feast of the Mystical Body. It has one of the richest and most beautiful Offices and Masses of the year.

The practice of dedicating churches to God with solemn rites goes back to the fourth century and seems to have begun in the East. Our modern rite is a combination of the more simple and austere Roman ceremony, which centered about the placing of the relics of the saints (martyrs) in the altar followed by the offering of the Holy Sacrifice, and the very elaborate Gallican Rite, which was characterized by the anointing with oil of the walls of the church. The two rites were fused in the Middle Ages, and the day on which the church was consecrated was celebrated annually. The themes of this feast are: the holiness of the house of God as a place where sacrifice is made to Him, where we pray to Him, where He dwells and works in our midst—"This day is salvation come to this house"; the material church is the symbol and outward sign of the spiritual Church, made up not of stone but of "living stones," the members of the Body of Christ—"O God who of living and chosen stones prepares an eternal dwelling place for yourself"; the material church represents the Heavenly City, the New Jerusalem, the Bride and

Spouse of Christ. Several times during the year, but particularly on the anniversary of the dedication of the cathedral, the chief church of the diocese, we are reminded of these great truths which must continually show us how we are to conduct ourselves in the "Church of the living God, the pillar and ground of truth."

Feasts of Angels. The angels have been honored in the liturgy since the earliest times, but in the West at least some of their feasts are relatively recent. St. Michael's day began as an anniversary of a church dedicated to him, as did the feast of the Apparition of St. Michael on May 8. The feast of the Guardian Angels was introduced only in the seventeenth century, at least for the universal Church, and the feasts of SS. Gabriel and Raphael early in the twentieth.

The cultus of St. Michael enjoyed great popularity during the entire Middle Ages, as the presence of his name in the *Confiteor*, the Litany of the Saints, and in many other places in the liturgy (together with the extraordinary number of churches dedicated to him) bear witness. He was looked upon as the angel specially entrusted with the charge of conducting souls to Heaven, a function alluded to in the Offertory antiphon of the requiem Mass: "*Signifer Sanctus tuus Michael repraesentat eas in lucem sanctam*"; he is represented in the Scriptures as the defender of the Christian people against Satan's power and malice. This latter function is mentioned frequently in the Office and Mass of his feasts and is crystallized into the formula: "Holy Archangel Michael, defend us in battle."

In reality the feast of September 29th is intended to honor not only St. Michael, but all the angels, as the oration and the hymns indicate.

SS. Peter and Paul. The twenty-ninth of June has been observed as the feast of SS. Peter and Paul since the third century, because, as some claim, this was the date of their martyrdom, or more likely because it was the date of the moving of their bodies to the cemetery of St. Sebastian on the Appian Way. The names of the two apostles have always been associated not only in the Church which they founded, but in the Churches in communion with Rome from the fourth century onward. Through the centuries this feast has always been kept as one of the greatest of the Church year, with vigil and octave added by the sixth century. Related to it are the somewhat later feasts of the Chair of Peter and St. Peter in Chains, which originated in Rome—one as a commemoration of St. Peter's establishing his episcopal chair at Rome, the other the anniversary of the dedication of the basilica of St. Peter on the Esquiline Hill. The commemoration of St. Paul began as a visit to his tomb on the day after the feast itself (the distance beween the two tombs made it difficult to go to both on the same day). The Conversion of St. Paul on January 25th began not as a commemoration of that event but rather as a remembrance of a translation of his relics which had taken place on that day.

St. John the Baptist. The part played by St. John the Baptist in the economy of salvation led to the establishment of a feast day in his honor, which was unlike that of any other saint in that it commemorated his birthday into this world instead of into the next. It goes back to the fourth century as St. Augustine testifies and through the centuries has always been considered one of the great feasts of the Church year. At one time there were three Masses celebrated on this day. The commemoration of his beheading (August 20th) is later than the nativity but is still very old and was observed in Gaul as early as the fifth century.

It is a remarkable fact that St. Joseph had to wait until the modern age to receive the honors which we might have expected him to enjoy from early times. Though his name is commemorated in martyrologies of both East and West from the eighth century onward, there is no certain evidence of a feast in his honor until the eleventh or twelfth century, and no proper Office until the thirteenth. A feast of St. Joseph observed on March 19th was kept in various places in Europe during the later Middle Ages, but devotion to St. Joseph did not gain a hold upon the people until the fifteenth century through the preaching of St. Bernardine of Siena and especially through the influence of Gerson.

Sixtus IV admitted the feast into the calendar, but only as a simple; in the seventeenth century Gregory XV made it a holyday of obligation, a distinction it has since lost. Only with Pius IX did it become a double of the first class. The nineteenth century feast of the Patronage of St. Joseph (also called the Solemnity) was suppressed in 1955 and replaced with the feast of St. Joseph the Workman.

Feasts of the Apostles in General. Although all are now observed in the Roman Rite as doubles of the second class at least, the earlier calendars include the feasts of only a few of the apostles. The celebration of these feasts was at first local, like those of the other saints; only in the eighth or ninth century did they become universal feasts. One reason why the anniversary of so few apostles was celebrated in the West is that the apostles did not die in the West but in the East, and some of them even beyond the limits of the Roman Empire. For many centuries the following rule was strictly observed, even when apostles were involved: the *dies natalis* was not celebrated outside of the place where they had died. The date on which their names appear in the calendar is usually that of their death, the *dies natalis*, but this is not always so. It is sometimes the anniversary of the finding or the translation of their relics, or the anniversary of the dedication of a church named after them. Thus, June 29th is in all likelihood the actual anniversary of the martyrdom of St. Peter, while December 27th appears to have been the anniversary of the dedication of a church in honor of St. John. In any case, the oldest feasts seem to be SS. Peter and

Paul and St. Andrew; the others became universal only in the Middle Ages, from the tenth to the thirteenth centuries.

All Souls' Day. A special day for the commemoration of all the faithful departed was kept in different places at different times from the sixth or seventh century onward, but our modern All Souls' Day was established in the late tenth or early eleventh century. Another day was also set aside as a monthly commemoration in all cathedral, monastic, and collegiate churches. With the Mass went the exquisite Office of the Dead consisting of Matins, Lauds, and First Vespers. In both the Mass and the Office the dominant theme was that expressed in the antiphon of the *Benedictus* at Lauds: "*Ego sum resurrectio et vita.*"

The three Masses on All Souls' Day came from Spain where Benedict XV was nuncio before he became pope. He extended this privilege to the whole Church and added the noble Preface of the Dead to the requiem Mass.

Until St. Pius X, the Office of All Souls was added to the Office of the second day in the Octave of All Saints. He equipped this Office of the Dead with the Little Hours and suppressed the additional Office of All Saints on that day.

Liturgy of the Dead

The practice of honoring the dead is ancient and widespread; in continuing it the Christian Church was only obeying one of the most universal of all customs. But the Christian belief in the immortality of the soul, the resurrection of the body, and the life of the world to come was an added reason for the development of funeral rites. The pagans of the Greco-Roman world gathered at the grave to hold a funeral meal called the *refrigerium;* the Christians followed the same practice, but they also held the Supper of the Lord at or near the place of burial. They accompanied the body to the grave as the pagans did, but with songs of rejoicing and hymns rather than with mourning and lamentations. They buried their dead in an honorable grave, but placed a message of hope on it for an epitaph instead of the despairing sentiments expressed in pagan epigraphy.

The modern funeral rite in its complete form consists of escorting the body to the church, the Office of the Dead, the requiem Mass, the absolution, procession to the cemetery, and the burial. Of these the procession to the grave and the Mass (which was originally said at the grave instead of in the church) are the oldest. The Office is a later development of the custom of singing psalms before and during the procession. The body itself was, according to earliest Christian tradition in the matter, treated with the greatest respect—washed, anointed, embalmed, clad in clean grave clothes (a shroud in the past) with a crucifix in the hands, or the hands folded in the form of a cross, and with lighted candles placed near or about the coffin. Nearly every one of these burial customs is pagan in origin, but adopted by the Christians and christianized.

The singing of psalms is supposed to accompany the procession to the church, or, as is the practice in this country, they are sung in the procession from the church door to the sanctuary. The "*De Profundis*" is recited or sung with its antiphon, "*Si Iniquitates,*" then Psalm 50 with the appropriate antiphon, "*Exultabunt Osso Humiliata*" and other psalms taken from the Office of the Dead (if there is time). While the body is carried into the church, the beautiful responsory "*Subvenite Sancti Dei*" is sung, a formulary which appears to belong to very early Christian times; the substance of it is found either in words or in pictures upon some of the earliest epitaphs known to us. The function of the angels as soul-bearers ("*suscipientes animam ejus, offerentes eam in conspectu altissimi*") was much insisted upon in Christian antiquity.

Masses for the Dead. The custom of offering Mass for the dead is itself very ancient in the Church. Although Tertullian is the first to refer clearly to the practice of offering the Sacrifice for the dead, there are earlier indirect allusions which indicate that it is even more ancient.

The Mass offered for the dead was at first apparently the Mass of the day on which the burial took place. Only later on were special formularies used; the oldest proper texts that we have go back to the sixth century. Complete formularies of votive Masses for the dead seem to have appeared only in the eighth or ninth century. The actual texts at present used in the Missal for the funeral Mass belong in part to the seventh century; other parts are more recent. The most ancient chant of this Mass is the Introit, which is taken from the apocryphal book of Esdras; it was used in whole or in part as an epitaph on Christian tombs before it was selected as the Introit. The Chant has about it all the flavor and atmosphere of Christian antiquity and makes an excellent companion-piece to the prayer for the dead in the Canon of the Mass: "*locum refrigerii lucis et pacis ut indulgeas deprecamur.*" We meet the requiem for the first time in the Gregorian Antiphonary. The Gradual with its verse "*In memoria Aeterna*" is of the same age as the Introit. Though the *Alleluia* is excluded from the modern requiem Mass and has been for many centuries, this chant nevertheless accompanied the funerals of Christian antiquity and could be found in the requiem Masses of some churches as late as the eleventh century. In its place there is the Tract "*Absolve Domine*" which accents once again the theme of light: "*et lucis aeternae perfrui.*" The "*Dies Irae*" has been discussed elsewhere. It is the longest text in the requiem Mass and represents a later development in the Christian concept of death, accenting as it does the judgment and the terrors that accompany it. Awe inspiring rather than consoling, it stands in sharp contrast to the other texts of the requiem Mass. Yet it has its tender and touching parts and is not without the note of consolation:

Recordare Jesu pie
Quod sum causa tuae viae
Ne me perdas illa die.

Quaerens me sedisti lassus
Redemisti crucem passus
Tantus labor non sit cassus.

The hymn originally ended with the words "Gere *curam mei finis*"; all that follows was added later to accommodate it to its new purpose as the Sequence of a requiem Mass.

The Offertory antiphon for all requiem Masses is an altogether extraordinary chant for many reasons. Its musical setting alone would mark it as one of the finest in the Missal, but it commands attention also for the ideas it expresses and for the form that it takes. Upon closer examination it will be seen to be an echo of the invocations of the "*Commendatio animae*": "Deliver [in the sense of preserve] the souls of the faithful departed from the pains of hell, from the deep pit, from the lion's mouth. . . . Make them pass from death to life" (the idea of the *transitus*, the exodus, is contained here). Christ is addressed by His most solemn titles: "Lord," "King of Glory," and, implicitly, as Redeemer.

We ask that Michael the standard-bearer fulfill the traditional office of the angels and lead these souls to the eternal light, which God has promised to Abraham and his seed. Here we find one of the favorite themes of the Scriptures and of Christian antiquity: the Promised Land. This last phrase is a refrain repeated twice. We have preserved for us here the ancient responsorial chant. The second part of the antiphon, "*Hostias et preces*," is an expression of the propitiatory character of the Mass: we offer sacrifice and prayer for these souls; that God receive them at our hands and by them make these souls pass from death to life.

In its present form the Offertory antiphon came to us from the Gallican Church in the ninth century; part of it had been borrowed from the Oriental (Egyptian) rites.

The Preface, a composition of singular beauty, rich in scriptural allusions, particularly from St. Paul, was borrowed from the Preface of the dead found in the Missal of Paris, with some modifications which were not altogether happy. It is the newest part of the requiem Mass, added by order of Benedict XV in 1919.

The funeral Mass is festive from beginning to end. That happy effect is achieved by the lessons with their emphasis on Christ's Resurrection and ours, and the chants which develop the theme of light and eternal rest. The whole effect is truly paschal: death is seen in the light of Christian hope as a return to the Father, a transition from death to life, a passover into the promised land: *"Dissoluta hujus incolatus domo, aeternae in coelis habitatio comparatur."* This helps to explain why the funeral Mass is treated as a feast of high liturgical rank to be superseded only by first-class feasts. In this country, by apostolic indult, the funeral Mass may be celebrated even on first-class feasts with few exceptions.

From what has been said about Easter and the time before and after it, we should be able to see more clearly that the liturgical year as a whole is the celebration of the mystery of Christ; that it is, in the words of the present pope, "Christ Himself." * It is Christ who lives and works in us, and no matter what feast we are celebrating, it is His mystery, the Paschal mystery, which is always the object of our worship. Even when we are celebrating Christmas we do not engage in a different celebration from that of Easter: we celebrate the coming of the Savior, but we do not share in His temporal birth in the way that we share in His Death. It is only by sharing in the Death and Resurrection of Christ that we are born again in Baptism to a new life; we cannot be born again by sharing in His temporal birth. Our rebirth to Heaven is not a participation in Christ's birth to this world, but in His Death and Resurrection. Nothing in the liturgical texts for the feasts of the Christmas cycle supports any other view. What *is* dwelt upon at great length, from the first Sunday of Advent to the feast of the Epiphany and

* *Mediator Dei.*

after it, is the Coming of the Redeemer, the coming of His kingdom, and the final triumph of His redeeming work which is accomplished by Him in His Passion, Death, and Resurrection. We, no more than the ancient prophets, are looking for the human birth of our Lord; we are looking rather for the coming of the kingdom of God (of which His birth is the dawn), for the complete destruction of the powers of evil, sin, and death, and for the final manifestation of God to His people. This is what we hope for, and because we know it is going to happen, has already *begun* to happen in fact, we celebrate it. And the great way we have of celebrating it is to offer, even on Christmas day, the Sacrifice which proclaims the Death of the Lord until He *comes* again, and the Paschal mystery which is His own memorial, recalling the past and foreshadowing the future.

Each feast of the liturgical year contains its proper and special grace, a grace of Christ needless to say, which it communicates to us. All graces come to us from the glorified humanity of our Lord; they are stored up in Him and they come to work in us, bringing with them death to sin and a life of grace. All the mysteries of the life of Jesus, which won these graces for us, subsist in Him who is Himself the great Mystery, the great Sacrament. They are the sources of this or that grace which makes us in one way or another conformable to Him. These mysteries operate in us when we are brought into contact with Him, and this contact is established "by faith and the sacrament of faith," as St. Thomas teaches. By this contact Christ dwells in us and we in Him. "I live now not I but Christ lives in me."

This vital contact of faith and love is established by and in the liturgical year, which recalls each one of the mysteries of Christ, particularly the great central mystery of His Passover, and makes them present to us, makes them live again under our eyes. Through the Eucharist (considered as a whole: lessons, chants, prayers, action) the Divine Office, and other rites, the Church awakens our faith and stirs up our love by placing us in an atmosphere where these two great virtues thrive, an atmosphere that is colored by the feast or season we are celebrating, that brings out their hidden meaning and issues a challenge to our love, making us practice virtue. All of this means that we realize (in the true sense) the mystery of Christ's life that we are celebrating. ". . . these things [ceremonies, prayers, the chant] have been so arranged that they are able to make the spirit of the mysteries that we celebrate penetrate profoundly into our spirit, and to carry us to acts and feelings which correspond to them." *

The work of our redemption has been accomplished once and for all, but it must be applied to our souls and bring each one of us into conformity with Christ. That is done by making the mysteries of Christ whereby He accomplished the redemption *our* mysteries, by making us in some way live over these events.

* Catechism of Pius X.

CHAPTER 13

The Holy Sacrifice of the Mass From the Beginning to the Offertory

The Meaning of the Mass

"Do this for a commemoration of me." That is what the Mass is first of all: a rite dedicated to commemorating and recalling Christ. It is essentially the Lord's own Supper, a Supper that is at the same time a Sacrifice. The Mass is not merely a subjective commemoration but an objective one, and it is not only a commemoration of Christ but of His whole redeeming work. "As often as you eat this bread and drink this chalice you proclaim the death of the Lord until he comes again" (1 Cor. 11:26). A commemoration: we mean by that a sacred action which recalls, re-presents the work of salvation as it once took place in the past and brings it into the here and now. It is what we call a mystery. In that mystery Christ is present and operating. The work that He does is His redeeming passion, his *transitus* from this world to the Father, a *transitus* accomplished by His Passion, Death, Resurrection and Ascension. By His suffering and Death "He gave His life as a ransom for many," entered into conflict with the demon and vanquished him, and led a redeemed humanity through suffering and death to victory and glory. With His own blood He sealed the new and eternal Covenant and, passing into the Holy of Holies, obtained eternal redemption for us. (Cf. Heb. 9:11.) He was the true Paschal Lamb whose blood delivered His people from Egypt, who died and lives again and who is the Bridegroom of the eternal wedding feast with the Spouse He has purchased for Himself. In this way He inaugurated the new creation.

On the night before He died, Christ left to His Church as His memorial the Supper that is a Sacrifice. By eating and drinking of this Sacrifice the Church is gathered together into one, eats and drinks of its own redemption, enters into the great redemptive mystery of the Passion, Death and Resurrection of her Lord. By this Memorial that is a Sacrifice, men of all times and all nations are able to take part in that great act of Christ which is His Paschal mystery.

But the Mass is not merely a Supper, nor merely the commemoration of a Sacrifice that has taken place in the past; it is itself a Sacrifice, the Sacrifice that Christ has left to His beloved Bride the Church. His Sacrifice is the Sacrifice of the Church; the Sacrifice of Christ to His heavenly Father is made through the hands of the priest. This much has always been clearly understood and believed, but that the Mass is at the same time the Sacrifice of the Church has been lost sight of to a great extent. Because it was necessary to defend the Sacrifice itself against the reformers, and to emphasize that the Mass was a real Sacrifice, theologians concentrated on that aspect to the exclusion of its corollary: the Sacrifice of Christ is also the Sacrifice of the Church.

In more recent times, and largely as a result of the liturgical movement, attention is being given once again to that complete presentation of the doctrine of the Eucharist which sees the Sacrifice as belonging both to Christ and to the Church. Indeed, as far as the texts of the liturgy go, the Sacrifice of the Church receives the greatest emphasis: the idea presented there is that the Church, the *Plebs Sancta* gathered together here and now, offers Sacrifice to God. That is the clear teaching of the "*Unde et memores*" which of all parts of the Canon most clearly sets forth the meaning of the Mass. That this Sacrifice which the Church offers is the Sacrifice of Christ is, of course, presupposed, but it is never directly called that. This is not only the doctrine of the liturgies, but also of the Fathers, of the Pre-Tridentine theologians and of the Council of Trent itself. The Church offers Sacrifice by joining in the Sacrifice of Christ; His offering becomes her offering; the one eternal Sacrifice is made present by the act of consecration done by the ministry of the priest; the immolated Body of Christ and the blood shed for the remission of sin are presented again to the Father. This is done by an action that is the external sign of Christ's Sacrifice on the cross: it is Christ who performs the action, using the lips of the priest who represents the Church. In the Consecration something is given and dedicated to God, something material is transformed, ceasing to be what it was and becoming "an eternal gift to Thee." By this action the offering of Christ is present upon our altars to give glory to God and to draw the Church and her members into His sacrificial and redemptive action. His *transitus*, His *Pascha*, His Paschal mystery becomes ours; His Sacrifice, the Sacrifice of the Church.

By His death on the cross Christ concluded a covenant between God and His people which bound them to God and God to them: "The chalice of my Blood, of the new and eternal covenant." That covenant must be entered into anew and ratified daily; this is done through the Mass. By it we signify our intention of adhering anew to the covenant and the alliance, of making Christ's Passion our passion and His Sacrifice ours. It is not a mere recalling to mind of something that was done; it is an accepting of it here and now. By accepting this Sacrifice and sharing in it we accept Christ and proclaim our willingness to embrace the cross. This is the very heart of Christianity: "Christ also suffered for us leaving you an example that you should follow his steps"; "Let that mind be in you which was also in Christ Jesus."

We enter into this Sacrifice and make it our own, first of all, by offering for consecration something which represents us in a special way: we offer bread and wine, the products of man's hands and at the same time the great "supports of his weakness," the staple elements of food and nourishment in our Lord's time. In addition, the words which make His sacrificial action present are words spoken by those members of a community who have been set aside to speak them. So in a twofold way the Mass is the offering of the Church: she sets aside the gift which represents her and she offers it to God. Thus the Church is most intimately associated with Christ in offering Sacrifice to God; as He offered Himself, so she offers herself. This means specifically that the faithful, particularly those gathered here and now at this Mass, offer sacrifice to God. The priest is not their *substitute* but their *spokesman,* who acts both in "*persona Christi,*" and in "*persona Ecclesiae*" and who is empowered to present this sacrifice to God as their own Sacrifice.

Nor is this all: the priest offers a Sacrifice which is completed by being eaten; Mass is not offered without someone, at least the priest who represents the *ecclesia,* who eats the bread and drinks the wine. By this sacrificial meal the Church is joined in fellowship with Christ and with the members of Christ. This fellowship involves of necessity a sharing in His Passion, Death and Resurrection. The Mass is thus a Sacrifice-banquet. By eating and drinking of the Sacrifice the Church affirms her intention of joining with Him, of making His Sacrifice her Sacrifice. It is a ratification on her part of the covenant made between God and His people. By the offering she had made and thus ratified the

Church is thereby consecrated and dedicated to God. She not only renews the Sacrifice sacramentally upon the altar but renews it in herself; daily she sacrifices and daily renews her sacrificial frame of mind. That is what we mean when we say that the Mass is the center and source of Christian life, because it is through the Mass that the Church daily chooses to travel the royal road of the cross that leads to victory and ultimately to transfiguration into the likeness of Christ. "For if we suffer with Him we shall be glorified with Him."

Every Mass, then, represents or contains not only the objective representation of Christ's redeeming work—the *opus operatum* as the theologians call it—but also a Godward movement, an offering, an *opus operantis* on the part of the Church. The Mass is, first of all, interior, but it expresses itself in some way outwardly. The more strikingly and emphatically that outward expression is made the better. We can see throughout the history of the Church, and in all the liturgies that have been created to express and contain the worship of the Church, a preoccupation with this external, outward expression. Some liturgies show it more than others, but all of them have worked into the very structure of the worship some declaration in word and act that the Sacrifice which the Church offers daily is the sacrificial return of the whole "*plebs sancta Dei.*"

The Names of the Mass

It is a striking fact that the name by which the Holy Sacrifice is best known in the West is one which in no way expresses what it is, but which has nevertheless gathered about it over the centuries so many associations, that we would never dream of abandoning it. The "Mass" now means to us all that is implied by almost any of the other many names by which the Sacrifice has been and still is called.

Missa is a later Latin word for "dismissal," and because the dismissal of the congregation was so prominent a feature of the service, it became in the popular mind and even to a large extent in the official terminology the all-inclusive term for the Sacrifice.

To give the Mass a name taken from a detail of the service was not a new practice in the Church, but the oldest name of all is "the breaking of the bread," "*Fractio Panis.*" We meet the latter in the Acts of the Apostles and the phrase has decided sacrificial overtones. St. Paul seems to prefer "the Supper of the Lord" and thus brings the banquet or meal aspect to the fore. The name Eucharist is apparently just as old, and has remained closely associated with the rite ever since. This is easy enough to see when we recall that the Mass is above all else the "Sacrifice of thanksgiving" (Eucharist) in all the many rich meanings of the word, involving as it does the reverent praise and recognition by the company of the redeemed of all God's benefits and mercies towards the children of men.

A less common word, yet strongly marking the personal aspect of the Sacrifice, is "*Dominicum*"—that which belongs to the Lord. "Supper" or "Sacrifice" is implied by this expression which was used particularly in Africa in the third and fourth centuries.

The word most widely used for many centuries was the Offering—*Oblatio,* or *offerre,* still used in the Rite of Ordination. Side by side with it we find *Sacrificium,* the preferred word among the African Christians.

Another term which has survived in some modern languages is the "Service," or the "Office" (duty). The Greeks still use this word, *leitourgia,* in their language with almost as much frequency as we say "the Mass."

The Missal preserves here and there traces of the fact that the Mass was also called "*Actio,*" the action *par excellence* of the Church. *Agere* was to offer Mass. "*Agnoscite quod agitis*" in the Rite of Ordination most likely really means "Understand what you are doing when you offer Mass," as the context indicates.

All these terms have yielded in the West to the term we know today. It arose because the "dismissal" was not thought of in antiquity in a negative way; it was associated with the idea of a blessing. Twice in the Service there were such dismissals: one for the catechumens before the Offertory, one for the faithful at the end. The service came to be known as the "*solemnia missarum*" and finally as the "*Missa*," but the word always retained the connotation of "blessing" rather than of an abrupt "dismissal." Later it became a new word altogether, and it is as a new word that we use it today with all the associations that have gathered around it through the centuries.

Preparation for Mass

The priest who is about to say Mass should already have recited Matins and Lauds. There is no real obligation to do so, but it is more fitting. There is no public preparation for the Holy Sacrifice except the rite of the *Asperges* on Sunday. For priests, however, there is a rather elaborate set of prayers to be said every day, taken largely from the psalter with a brief litany and a series of orations. Again, this is not of strict obligation, but priests will find it helpful to stir up devotion before offering the Holy Sacrifice.

Preparatory prayer appeared as a special formula about the eleventh century. During the course of the next few centuries this formula underwent many changes, but substantially it is the "*Preparatio ad Missam*" that we find in our modern Missal. The oldest of the psalms used here are the "*Quam dilecta*" (Ps. 83), which expresses the longing desire of dwelling in the sanctuary; the "*Benedixisti*" (Ps. 84), rich in allusions to the Incarnation and the redemption; and "*Inclina*" (Ps. 85), a prayer for mercy and strength. To them were added "*Credidi.*" (Ps. 115), most appropriate in its reference to taking the saving chalice and calling upon the name of the Lord, and the "*De Profundis*" (Ps. 129), filled with allusions to the redemption and chosen no doubt because it was a penitential psalm. These were in use at the papal court in the thirteenth century as was also the penitential antiphon "*Ne reminiscaris,*" the *Kyrie*,

Pater Noster and seven orations. Six of these ask the help of the Holy Spirit, while the seventh is the only one that prays for purity of heart. The versicles and responses were added later on.

At one time this *preparatio* was a kind of canonical hour, and this is true to this day; where there is a cathedral chapter the canons recite them with the bishop before Mass.

The long and beautiful prayer of St. Ambrose is not from his hand but from an eleventh century writer. It is spread out through the week.

The Missal of St. Pius V recommends these prayers but actually requires only that the priest spend some time in prayer. The modern devotional practice of meditation had already gained considerable popularity by St. Pius V's time and we may see traces of this new influence in the circumstance that these vocal prayers were no longer insisted upon as they had been in the past. The important thing is that a priest awaken in his heart and mind and soul a realization of what he is about to do and of the tremendous mystery he will handle. To achieve this end the slow, devout, prayerful and meditative reading of the *preparatio* with the prayers *pro opportunitate* is admirably suited.

The vesting prayers form a more proximate preparation for Mass and these are obligatory. Like so many other parts of our Ceremonial the solemn vesting originated in the Frankish domains about the ninth century. The Gallican vesting was usually preceded by a washing of the hands and a prayer, but our own modern prayer is of relatively recent date.

The prayers used for vesting varied greatly in different places. They arose from a desire to give a special symbolic meaning to each vestment worn. The symbolic meaning given them has no bearing on the Sacrifice about to be offered; it is based upon an analogy between the vestment worn and the virtue that it suggests, like the prayer said when putting on the *cincture;* or it is inspired by some text of Scripture that the vestment suggests, like the prayer said when putting on the *alb.*

Formerly the *amice* was often put on over the *alb* and worn on the head until the celebrant reached the altar; sometimes it was not lowered until later in the Mass. The *maniple* was often put on last, as it still is by bishops. In some places the vestments or at least part of them were put on at the altar; indeed there was a bewildering variety in all these practices until 1570.

The Mass in Detail

In this study we shall follow the rite of the High Mass which, however rare or unusual it may be in practice, is nevertheless the *normal* celebration of the liturgy. We say normal in the sense of standard; it is the full expression of the social character of the rite, since it involves ideally the active participation of the entire community (parish, religious, monastic, collegiate or seminary), each having his part to play. It is the assembly of the redeemed in action, meeting to worship. The singing is not an accidental embellishment but rather springs from the nature of what is done. It is the sacrifice of praise and thanksgiving, a joyful *celebration* that must break into song, since, as St. Augustine says, "song befits the lover" and it is really unthinkable and inconceivable that so great a matter should be treated without solemnity or the rejoicing that is best expressed in song. In the high Mass we have the worship of the whole man, man as a creature of body and soul, man as a social being, man as a *redeemed* being.

From the first Mass, which was the Last Supper, down to our own times the Church has always maintained the sung Eucharist as the ideal. By it not only has the fitting solemnity and note of rejoicing been retained in Catholic worship, but also that outward participation of the entire congregation which sustains and keeps alive the social and communal aspect of the rite. The private Mass said in public, at which no one answers but the server, was never intended to be the expression of the corporate worship of the community. It fulfills the theological requirements, of course, and assistance at it satisfies the individual's obligation to be present at Mass on Sunday; but this minimum celebration should not be confused or equated with the full, complete and corporate offering that is the solemn Mass. The manner is important as well as the offering.

The high Mass as we have it today is a later simplification of the ancient episcopal or pontifical Mass, celebrated by the bishop as the chief priest (*summus sacerdos*) of his diocese and surrounded by his priests, with the people participating. To this day the Mass offered by the bishop in his cathedral is the most perfect expression of the corporateness and the unity of the Church in that particular locality. When individual priests by delegation from the bishop began in the fourth century to celebrate the holy mysteries by themselves, they gradually simplified the service, conducting at the altar what the bishop had done and still does at the throne. Moreover, during the Middle Ages the low Mass, itself a simplification of the high Mass, began to react upon the ritual of the older, solemn service, until by the sixteenth century the priest read at the altar to himself those parts of the Mass which had been sung by the choir or by the subdeacon and deacon. This anomaly has been more keenly felt in recent years when liturgical studies have increased and deepened, and it is not unlikely that the promised revision of the Mass will eliminate what amounts to a useless duplication, which makes the priest, who should be the leader of the community, withdraw from it to pursue his own devotion. The revised Easter Vigil may be pointing the way in this regard when it directs that the priest "sit and listen" to the lessons and chants, instead of reading them as he had to do in the past.

The Introit. As the sacred ministers approach the altar, the first of the proper chants indicated for each Mass in the Roman Missal is sung by the choir or *schola*. It is a processional hymn and in that respect related to the Offertory and Communion chants, introduced about the fourth century to accompany the procession to the altar. In the basilicas built at the time with the *secretarium* or sacristy located at the entrance, such a procession would be long and rather solemn. We can readily see that a long procession such as this made in silence would be too much to bear: there were no organs and other musical instruments were proscribed; consequently the oldest and the best of musical instruments, the human voice, was used to fill the silence with singing. Naturally the great and treasured hymnbook of the primitive Church, the Book of Psalms, was used, but the psalms were not sung straight through. They were rendered in a special way which is reflected to this day in the musical structure of the Introit. There were two choirs placed on either side of the entrance to the sanctuary; these choirs sang alternately: first a verse that was repeated, and then an entire psalm. We see a survival of this today in our Introit which consists of an antiphon that is sung twice and at least a verse of a psalm with the concluding *Gloria Patri.* The original purpose of the antiphon seems to have been practical: that is, it was a verse pre-intoned to give the singers an idea of the melody of the psalm that followed. Since no musical instruments were used, the pre-intonation was done by singing.

If we consider the history of the Introit it becomes evident that the psalm sung in its entirety was the true entrance chant and that the antiphon was of secondary importance. It may not seem so to us today, as we are more impressed by the antiphon and hardly notice the psalm at all. Only when we read the entire psalm do we see the reason for its selection as the entrance chant for a particular feast. Needless to say, this applies only to the older Masses in the Missal; modern Masses deliberately select psalm verses that are fitting in themselves.

In the third Mass for Christmas day the Introit is taken from Psalm 97 which begins: "*Cantate Domino canticum novum.*" It is only when we read the entire psalm and come to the words, "The Lord has made known his *salvation*" and "all the ends of the earth will see the *salvation* of our God" that we see how appropriate it is. Or, on the feast of the Epiphany we have

"*Deus judicium tuum Regida, et justitiam tuum filio regis,*" which is not altogether inappropriate, but the entire psalm and particularly the verses "*reges tarsis et insulae munera offerent*" show how apposite was its selection for this day. On feasts of confessor-bishops "*Memento David et omnis mansuetudinis ejus*" from Psalm 131 is confusing, but the later verse "*sacerdotes domini induant justitiam*" gives meaning to the choice of this psalm.

The antiphons became longer with the development of music written for them, and this made it more and more difficult to sing the entire psalm before the procession had reached the altar. Also, the fact that the procession no longer came from the entrance brought about the shortening (and in the Ambrosian Rite even the suppression) of the psalm, until in our own times only a verse is sung. The old entrance chant had attained its present truncated form by the ninth century. The processional chant aspect was lost sight of and emphasis thrown upon the antiphon, which became the dominant part—a kind of prelude to the sacred mystery.

It is interesting to note that many of the older Introits are truely processional and entrance chants. Even the words make allusion to *movement;* for example, "Behold the Lord the Ruler *comes*" (Epiphany); "*Come* ye blessed of my father" (Easter Tuesday); "The Lord *led* them into a land flowing with milk and honey" (Easter Monday). Nowadays, as Jungmann observes, if we want to get an idea of the way one of those old entrance chants worked, we may recall the chant accompanying the solemn entrance of a bishop: "*Ecce, Sacerdos Magnus*" which is a true "entrance" and processional song.*

As a general rule the antiphon is taken from the psalm, although the exceptions to that rule are notable and many of the older antiphons are taken from the books of the Old and New Testaments, a fact that has led some historians of the Mass

* *Mass of the Roman Rite,* Vol. I, p. 321.

to maintain that these verses are older than the Introit as we know it and were sung before Mass as a kind of prelude. But of that there is no evidence. When the antiphon is taken from the first verse of the psalm, the psalm is continued in the verse that follows; when it is taken from another verse, the first verse then *follows*. For example: at Midnight Mass of Christmas the antiphon is from the body of the Psalm "*Dominus dixit ad me filius meus es tu, ego hodie genui te*"; then we have as the Psalm "*Quare fremuerunt gentes,*" which is the first verse of Psalm 2. Or, on the twenty-second Sunday after Pentecost when the antiphon is "*Si iniquitates observaveris Domine,*" the Psalm is the first verse of Psalm 129: "*De Profundis clamavi ad te Domine.*" But on the fourth Sunday after Pentecost we have the *first* two verses used as the antiphon: "*Dominus illuminatio mea et salus mea quem timebo? Dominus defensor vitae meae a quo trepidabo?*", and the Psalm is continued: "*Si consistant adversum me castra: non timebit cor meum.*"

Some later Introits, written after men had forgotten the original rules for their composition, have an antiphon from one psalm and a verse from another (e.g., St. Aloysius Gonzaga). Such Introits are termed irregular, which is not necessarily a criticism. The most irregular of all is that of the feast of the Seven Sorrows of our Lady when there is no psalm at all; the historical origin of this Introit seems to have been entirely forgotten: both antiphon and psalm are from the Gospel!

Although most of the antiphons are from the psalms or from other scriptural books, there are some that were composed by churchmen, such as the Introit for the feast of St. Agatha, which was Greek in origin, but later adapted and used for other saints; or the Introit for ordinary feasts of our Lady, written perhaps by Sedulius, an Irish monk. And one at any rate is from the apocryphal books, namely, the Introit for requiems.

As it stands now the Introit is intended to serve as an introduction or prelude to the Mass. Like the overture of an opera it sets the tone, by words and music, for the Mass of the day, suggesting thoughts and to a large extent creating the mood appropriate for the feast or the season. Very often it may be said to strike the keynote of the day's liturgy, giving the theme of the Mass in a few words: "*Viri Galilaei*" at *Ascension; "Spiritus Domini*" at Pentecost; "*Cibavit Eos*" for Corpus Christi, *etc.* Frequently this is done in a very dramatic manner as when we hear our Lord speaking in the Introit for Easter Sunday: "*Resurrexi et adhuc tecum sum,*" or our Lady in the Introit of the feast of the Immaculate Conception: "*Gaudens gaudebo in* Domino," or St. Peter on the feast of SS. Peter and Paul: "*Nunc scio vere quia misit Dominus angelum suum.*" At other times it will be an arresting picture of the saint of the Day: we see the doctor of the Church standing "*In medio ecclesiae*" dressed in his "robe of glory"; or the "just man who flourishes as the palm tree"; or the confessor-bishop adorned with the dignity of the episcopate: "*Statuit ei Dominus testamentum pacis, et principem fuit eum, ut sit illi Sacerdotii dignitas in aeternum.*"

The seasonal Introits reflect the mind of the Church: sorrow and penitence in Lent, the Passion of our Lord in Passion time, joy and gladness at Easter, adoration and praise in the Sundays after Epiphany.

Occasionally the stational church has influenced the selection of the Introit: "Laetare Jerusalem" in the fourth Sunday of Lent when the stational church is Santa Croce in Gerusalemme at Rome, which for the Romans represented Jerusalem.

From a musical point of view we observe that very often the Introit presents the grave and majestic character that we associate with a solemn march. The musical expression varies with the feast or season, sometimes grave and mournful, at other times joyful, almost delirously so—for instance, "*Vocem jecunditatis*" on the Sunday after Easter. So much is this true that the full effect of the Introit cannot be felt or appreciated without hearing the musical setting. The antiphon is the part of the Introit which receives this special musical expression, but even the psalm is sung in a much more elaborate manner than is usually the case in the Church. Even without its appropriate musical setting the Introit remains the prelude or introduction to the Mass and fulfills its essential function of setting the tone for the day.

As early as the seventh century priests began to say the Introit even at low Masses, and by the Middle Ages the rule was that it should be read silently by the priest at high Masses as well. That the Introit is the true beginning of the Mass is shown by the fact that the priest makes the sign of the cross when he says it, a gesture traditionally associated with the beginning of any sacred action.

There is no Introit in the Mass for Holy Saturday nor the Vigil of Pentecost, because in these instances the clergy are in the sanctuary long before the Mass itself begins and because the litany is used as a processional chant when the clergy return to the altar from the Blessing of the Font and Solemn Baptism.

In 1905 the Holy See indicated that the choir should begin the Introit as the clergy approach the altar; in 1947 the singing of more than one verse of the psalm was approved. We can see in these two enactments a tendency to revive the entrance and processional character of this chant.

There is no Introit in the Eastern rites, although there is a solemn "Entrance." In Western rites other than the Roman the Introit is called the *Ingressa, Invitatorium,* or *Officium.*

The Prayers at the Foot of the Altar. As their very name and the place where they are said indicate, these were originally private prayers. They are "prayers *before* Mass" rather than "Mass prayers," preoccupied as they are with preparing the priest to offer the Sacrifice worthily, with cleansed mind and heart. They are an outgrowth of the mediaeval "*apologia sacerdotalis,*" private devotions engaged in by the priest before Mass.

In their present form they have been said publicly only since 1572.

When the celebrant and the sacred ministers reach the altar they genuflect, rise immediately, make the sign of the cross (the celebrant saying the trinitarian formula aloud) and begin the alternate recitation of Psalm 42 with its appropriate antiphon "*Introibo ad altare Dei,*" which together with the *Confiteor* and versicles and orations make up a brief service of prayer.

Standing has been the normal position for public prayer since early Christian times. Kneeling was forbidden in public except during penitential seasons, and even then was done only briefly. Before any prayers were said aloud and publicly at this place in the Mass, the celebrant and sacred ministers knelt or prostrated themselves before the altar for a brief period. This custom survives on Good Friday.

The sign of the cross is the traditional Christian manner of of beginning any action. Indeed, Tertullian tells us that the early Christians accompanied even the most trivial actions of the day with this sacred sign. It is natural, then, to find it at the beginning of the Mass, and we are led to reflect on its appropriateness to inaugurate the sacred mysteries in which the power and virtue of the cross is mediated to men.

We can more readily understand the extraordinary frequency with which the sign of the cross was used in Christian antiquity if we remember that it consisted of a small cross traced across the forehead or breast with the thumb or right forefinger. During the early Middle Ages the monks began and popularized the practice of the great sign drawn from the forehead to the breast and to the left and right shoulders. Gradually this more ample sign supplanted, though not altogether, the smaller sign. By the time the Prayers at the Foot of the Altar were introduced into the Mass, the great sign was the prevailing custom and hence its use at this point in the service.

The sign of the cross is an act of faith and of hope, a compendium of all the mysteries of our religion, recalling as it does the mystery of the Trinity, of the Incarnation and redemption, of the sending of the Holy Spirit.

When we examine the origin of the Prayers at the Foot of the Altar, we find that they had their beginnings in two actions: the approach of the celebrant and ministers to the altar and the prostration. In the Church of Rome and surrounding cities, these actions were accompanied by the chant of the Introit which lasted until the bishop (pope) rose from his knees. In the Frankish churches, however, a more subjective piety was revealed in the regulation that the celebrant was to say the prayers privately as he approached the altar and while he knelt before it. These prayers were called "*apologiae*" and emphasized penance and purification. There was a considerable flowering of this type of prayer in the Gallican and related rites.

A further step towards our present custom was taken when one of the Frankish churches prescribed that Psalm 42 was to be recited by the bishop and clergy with the antiphon "*Introibo ad altare Dei*" and with two orations: one the "*Aufer a nobis,*" the other no longer in use. This prescription was taken up by others so that the custom became widespread though not universal. In the eleventh century the *Confiteor* was inserted before the "*Aufer a nobis,*" even when the psalm was not recited. It is odd that the collect "*Aufer a nobis*" should have been accepted where the psalm and antiphon were not. Even to this day some of the religious orders which have a derived mediaeval rite, the Dominicans and Carthusians, for example, have not admitted the Psalm "*Judica,*" but they do have the *Confiteor* and "*Aufer a nobis.*"

When the psalm was accepted the idea was that it should be recited as the celebrant approached the altar. Sometimes the approach was so small that this recitation was begun in the sacristy or, since the vestments were often put on at the altar, it was said before the altar. The peculiar appropriateness of the psalm, selected of course because of the verse, "I will go in unto the altar of God," was recognized by many and St. Pius V ordered that it be said at the foot of the altar. Naturally the *Confiteor* and "*Aufer a nobis*" would be said there too.

It is interesting to note that the parallel prayers said by the priest after Mass, the *Benedicite* and *Laudate*, never became public prayers. They are still recited between altar and sacristy, just as Psalm 42 was once recited between sacristy and altar.

The second part of the Prayers at the Foot of the Altar consists of the *Confiteor*, which arose from the silent adoration made by the pope (or bishop) before Mass. This kneeling in adoration became a prostration in the seventh century and, again in the Frankish churches, the silent adoration became a prayer for forgiveness for the sins of priests and people. This in turn developed in the early Middle Ages into the *Confiteor*, which is no longer a private prayer for forgiveness but a public avowal of guilt. The *Confiteor* as it developed in the Middle Ages had many forms: the list of saints mentioned was sometimes quite long and eventually had to be limited. Religious orders that had their origin in the Middle Ages still add the name of the founder to the *Confiteor*.

This solemn avowal of sin and guilt leads not only to a prayer for pardon, the *Misereatur*, but also to the *Indulgentiam* which was in fact the older formula of sacramental absolution in the West until it was succeeded by the present form. During the Middle Ages it appears that the *Indulgentiam* was regarded as sacramental, and here is one reason why we make the sign of the cross at this point in the service even today. Only when the Scholastic doctrine of the sacrament of Penance became clarified was it seen that there is no sacrament at this point in the Mass. The priest bows profoundly during this prayer because, as we have seen, it had its origin in the kneeling of the pope at the altar. During the Middle Ages in some places the *Confiteor* was said kneeling.

The *Confiteor* now expresses that sentiment of sorrow and contrition for sin and indirectly that desire for a pure mind and heart which the priest should have when he approaches the Holy of Holies to offer the sacred mysteries.

The series of verses which follow the *Confiteor* serve as a kind of transition to the ancient collect "*Aufer a nobis*," which, in traditional style, concludes the first portion of the service. They are like the *preces* which introduce and accompany the collect in the Office, or like the litany which once preceded the collect in the ancient Roman Mass. They have their counterpart in the series used with the psalms of the Preparation for Mass and they seem to have been borrowed from some such mediaeval formulary as that. Now there are only two of them which express the desire for God's life-giving grace and mercy and ultimately the longing for salvation—all of which we hope for through and in the Holy Sacrifice in which we are about to take part.

The "*Domine exaudi*" is the traditional invocation before prayer and the "*Dominus vobiscum*" the invariable greeting to the community (a very small community here, since originally only the sacred ministers were included in it).

The collect "*Aufer a nobis*" is the oldest part of the Prayers at the Foot of the Altar. Originally it was a prayer said in Lent as a preparation for Easter, which is the "*Sancta Sanctorum*" of the Christian year; we find it in the Leonine Sacramentary for Holy Thursday. Later on, the "*Sancta Sanctorum*" was applied to the sanctuary and finally to the sacred mysteries. In the Middle Ages it was recited in a low voice, a practice influenced by the silence of the Canon.

Looking back upon our sins and forward to the Sacrifice we are about to offer, we ask that we may receive the great grace prayed for throughout this part of the Mass: purity of heart.

The Kissing of the Altar. The priest says the "*Aufer a nobis*" as he mounts the steps of the altar. When he reaches the latter, he kisses it at the words "*quorum reliquiae hic sunt*" of the longer and much inferior prayer that follows. Although the kiss coincides with the reference to the relics and thus seems to be directed to them, actually it is the altar that is being kissed. Long before the prayer "*Oramus te Domine*" was inserted here the altar was kissed as a mark of respect—"For the altar indeed is Christ," as the Roman Pontifical tells us. Besides kissing the altar, bishops also kiss the book of the Gospels, even in a low Mass. Although the priest kisses the altar frequently during the Mass, this first kiss differs from the others in that it is a greeting, just as the last kiss is a leave-taking. That this is so is shown by the fact that as late as the thirteenth century in Rome the altar was kissed only at the beginning and at the end. The modern custom of kissing it each time the celebrant turns to the people was introduced at Rome during the later part of the thirteenth century.

This ceremony seems to have been derived from pagan antiquity, when it was the custom to kiss the doorposts of the temple and the altar. In private life the family table was also saluted in this fashion, because it was regarded as a religious object. Christians kept up the custom in new surroundings. As early as the fourth century kissing the altar by the people outside of Mass appears as a popular devotion which survived into the Middle Ages.

Directed first of all to the altar as the Lord's Table, it became, as it were, intensified by the later development of the concept of the altar as representing Christ. Still later, when relics were inserted into the altar, the kiss was directed to the altar as symbolizing the Mystical Body of Christ. But such an idea represents a much later *interpretation* of a custom long in vogue for other reasons.

The present formula "*Oramus te Domine*" is a private prayer of the celebrant (in contrast to the "*Aufer a nobis*" which is public and social in concept and expression) and made its appearance only in the eleventh century. It is one of the many manifestations of the tendency in our liturgy, originating in the Frankish dominions, to fit words to actions: "no action without its corresponding formula," we might say. Nor was it everywhere used until the close of the Middle Ages.

The Incensing of the Altar. At a solemn Mass the celebrant incenses the altar after he has kissed it. It is clear that its purpose here is to enhance the solemnity of the celebration and make the atmosphere festive. Although incense is a very natural and beautiful symbol of prayer and sacrifice and its use was commanded in the Old Law, the early Christians refused to have anything to do with it because of its pagan associations. For them it had become a symbol of pagan worship and of the denial of the Christian faith.

With the coming of toleration and peace under Constantine, the Christian aversion to incense was diminished—the more so because it was used abundantly in daily life to perfume the homes and public places. It thus came to be regarded as a harmless, if not indeed beneficial, object. We know that before long incense was burned in the churches in stationary incense-burners to purify and sweeten the air, and that in imitation of Roman court etiquette it was carried in procession before the bishop when he entered the churches for the Holy Sacrifice.

Once admitted to the church, incense entered more directly into the liturgy, but sooner in the Eastern and Frankish rites than in the Roman. For a long time the Romans were content to carry the *thurible* in procession and hang it between the posts of the altar canopy during the service without making any direct use of it, except to precede the deacon when he went in procession to sing the Gospel—again as a mark of honor, this time to the book of the Gospels. It was only in the ninth century that the Roman Church, influenced by the Frankish Churches (which in turn had derived the practice from the East) introduced the Rite of Incensation into the Holy Sacrifice, first for the altar, then for the clergy and the *oblata*. The present usage had taken form by the fourteenth century.

The incensation of the altar recalls the ceremony of consecration, wherein it is incensed many times. We may see it as a symbolic renewal of the Consecration of the Altar, a preparing of the altar for the Sacrifice.

The action of incensing the altar not only gives solemnity to the celebration of Mass and intensifies the festive note, but it creates and provides an atmosphere of worship and adoration, in the tradition of the great liturgical scenes of the Book of the Apocalypse.

Incense is more than a symbol; it is a sacramental as well and its use carries a blessing with it: "May this incense blessed by you mount up to you, O God, and thy mercy descend upon us." The symbolic meaning is preserved in the psalm used for incensing at the Offertory: "Let my prayer, O Lord, be directed in thy sight like incense." It also symbolizes sacrifice: the incense is totally dedicated to God and is consumed.

The Kyrie. As it stands now the *Kyrie* is a remnant, a response to the litany which was once recited at this point but which has since been dropped out. It is one of the few parts of the liturgy that is in Greek; yet it is not a survival of the all-Greek liturgy that once obtained in the church at Rome. The *Kyrie* was introduced after the liturgy had become Latin.

This cry for mercy and pardon is one of the shortest and (in one form or another) most used prayers that we have. It runs through the Old and New Testaments alike and wonderfully sums up the fundamental attitude of man conscious of his sin when confronted with his sinless Creator. In its Greek form it is widely known and used even in the non-Greek liturgies of the East and West. One reason for this is that, strictly speaking, the phrase is untranslatable; the name *Kyrios* conveys much more than any other the sovereignty, dominion, power and victory of Christ. The name is rich in associations, secular as well as scriptural. It was the all-embracing title given to the Roman emperor—at least in the East—and all the apostolic *Kerygma* about Christ is caught up in the words "God hath made Him *Kyrios* and Christ." It is this *Kyrios* whom we invoke in the spirit and with the words of the publican: "O God, be merciful to me a sinner." If it is among the shortest it is equally among the most intense of prayers.

Originally it was a response made by the people to a series of invocations recited by the deacon. The Spanish pilgrim Etheria tells of this usage at evening prayer in Jerusalem in the fourth century. The Church of Antioch had a similar litany said after the Gospel in which the celebrant prayed for the Church, for the welfare of different people, for peace, and so forth. This form of prayer was introduced into the West in the fifth century; the response of the people was either retained in Greek or translated into Latin, and sometimes it varied to "*Libera nos domine*" or "*Te rogamus audi nos.*" The survival of the litany in the Ambrosian Rite on certain Sundays gives us an idea of what the ancient Roman litany was like. It too comes after the chant that corresponds to our Introit. Although there is no text for this vanished litany in the older Sacramentaries, we have reason to believe that the so-called *Deprecatio Gelasii* was the one used. Apparently introduced into the Roman Rite by Pope Gelasius in the fifth century, it lasted until the sixth century when it gradually disappeared. Why the response did not disappear also we shall see presently. Gelasius substituted it for the more ancient *Orationes Fidelium.* The text gives us an idea of what it was like:

I. Pro immaculata Dei vivi ecclesia, per totum orbem constituta divinae bonitatis opulentiam deprecamur—Kyrie Eleison.
II. Pro sanctis Dei magni sacerdotibus et ministris sacri altaris cunctisque Deum verum colentibus populis Christum Dominum supplicamus—Kyrie Eleison.
III. Pro universis recte tractantibus verbum veritatis multiformem Verbi Dei sapientiam peculiariter obsecramus—Kyrie Eleison.
IV. Pro his qui se mente et corpore propter coelorum regna castificant, et spiritalium labore desudant, largitorem spiritalium munerum obsecramus—Kyrie Eleison.

V. Pro religiosis principibus omnique militia eorum, qui iustitiam et rectum iudicium diligunt, Domini potentiam obsecramus—Kyrie Eleison.
VI. Pro iocunditate serenitatis et opportunitate pluviae atque aurarum vitalium blandimentis ac diversorum temportum prospero cursu rectorem mundi Dominum deprecamur—Kyrie Eleison.
VII. Pro his quos prima christiani nominis initiavit agnitio, quos iam desiderium gratiae caelestis accendit, omnipotentis Dei misericordiam obsecramus—Kyrie Eleison.
VIII. Pro his quos humanae infirmitatis fragilitas, et quos nequitiae spiritalis invidia, vel varius saeculi error involvit, redemptoris nostri misericordiam imploramus—Kyrie Eleison.
IX. Pro his, quos peregrinationis necessitas, aut iniquae potestatis oppressio vel hostilitatis vexat aerumna, Salvatorem Dominum supplicamus—Kyrie Eleison.
X. Pro iudaica falsitate . . . aut haeretica pravitate deceptis vel gentilium superstitione perfusis veritatis Dominum deprecamus—Kyrie Eleison.
XI. Pro operariis pietatis et his, qui necessitatibus laborantum fraterna caritate subveniunt, misericordiarum Dominum deprecamur—Kyrie Eleison.
XII. Pro omnibus intrantibus in haec sanctae domus Domini atria, qui religioso corde et supplici devotione convenerunt, Dominum gloriae deprecamur—Kyrie Eleison.
XIII. Pro emundatione animarum corporumque nostrorum, et omnium venia peccatorum clementissimum Dominum supplicamus—Kyrie Eleison.
XIV. Pro refrigerio fidelium animarum, praecipue sanctorum Domini sacerdotum, qui huic ecclesiae praefuerunt catholicae, Dominum spirituum et universae carnis iudicem deprecamus—Kyrie Eleison.
XV. Mortificatam vitiis carnem et viventem fide animam—praesta, Domine, praesta.
XVI. Castum timorem et veram dilectionem—praesta, Domine, praesta.
XVII. Gratum vitae ordinem et probabilem exitum—praesta, Domine, praesta.
XVIII. Angelum pacis et solacia sanctorum—praesta, Domine, praesta. Nosmetipsos et omnia nostra, quae orta quae aucta per Dominum ipso auctore suscipimus, ipso custode retinemus,

ipsiusque misericordiae et arbitrio providentiae commendamus—Domine, miserere.

At Rome the *Kyrie* response was varied somewhat by the addition of *Christe Eleison;* St. Gregory is our witness that this was done in his time. He is also witness to the beginning of the disappearance of the litany and the survival of the responses. According to him, the litany was not sung on weekdays but only the responses. The reason he gives for the latter is somewhat surprising: he claimed that this arrangement gave the people more time to ponder the meaning of the response. Surely the heart of a litany is in the invocations, without which the response is almost meaningless. At any rate, after a while the litany was no longer sung even on Sundays.

There had always been a tendency to repeat the *Kyrie,* but this became even more the case after it became a prayer by itself. The earliest Roman *ordos* say that it was repeated until the signal was given to stop; by the eighth or ninth century the present form had become fixed by law: the *Kyrie* three times, the *Christe* three times, followed again by the *Kyrie* three times.

This triple invocation took on a trinitarian significance in the popular mind and there arose the explanation that still persists to our day in popular expositions of the Mass: that the Father is addressed in the first series, the Son in the second, the Holy Spirit in the third. Actually all three (or all nine) invocations are addressed to Christ: He is by tradition the *Kyrios;* we are calling on Him as Lord and Savior.

At first, and certainly as long as there was a litany to which the congregation could respond, the *Kyrie* was the chant of the people. Later on it was taken up by the choir, or rather two choirs who alternated the chant. Even then the people were not excluded; the choir merely *directed* the singing. It was only with the development of more elaborate chant during the Middle Ages that the people were excluded by the simple fact that they could not sing the more difficult music in which the *Kyrie* was now written. The more ancient and more simple melody survives in the chant for the requiem and in a few other Masses. In our own day there has been a movement, more pronounced in other countries than in our own, to restore this chant to the people. But this has also made it necessary to write more simple music! The idea is sound—after all it is the supplication of the *community*, and the danger of leaving such things to the choir, at least as a policy, has been only too evident. The greatest danger is that our worship tends to become a performance at which the people are only spectators, which they only admire or endure, rather than an action in which they take part. Better, then, to have the *Kyrie* sung off key and unartistically than to make people feel they are excluded by entrusting it to those whose only claim to sing it is that they will sing it well. It would be better still to teach the simplest melodies to everyone and see that they do not sing off key!

The *Kyrie* is an invocation that expresses our needy state. We might think of it as an echo of the pleas addressed to Christ by the sick, the crippled and the blind: "Jesus, Master, have mercy on us." Or we might see it as an expression of intense longing; Parsch calls it the "Advent of every Mass," the "*maranatha*" (come, lord Jesus!) of the primitive Church.*

During the Middle Ages the *Kyrie*, like other texts of the Mass, was farced—that is, interpolated with words intended to fill out the long musical neums. These interpolations survive in the names of the Masses in the *Liber Usualis* (*Orbis Factor*, *Lux et Origo*, *Cum Jubilo*, *etc.*), but the practice was outlawed by St. Pius V in 1570.

The Gloria in Excelsis. Doxologies or hymns of glory to God fill the Scriptures; St. Paul's Epistles and St. John's Apocalypse in particular are rich in these cries of praise and homage to God. That is what they are: acclamations rather than hymns as we think of hymns. The early Christians naturally composed hymns of this type based upon the models afforded by the

* *Liturgy of the Mass.*

chants in the sacred books and particularly the psalms. The *Gloria*, although its first words were intoned by the angels, is a developed chant of this kind, admirable for its simplicity and theological richness. Originally written in Greek, it was not composed for use in the Mass but as an expression of popular devotion suitable for any church service. It was first used in the liturgy in the East as a morning prayer, not at Mass but in the Office. The Eastern rites have never admitted it into the Mass. Obviously, the *Gloria* is a very ancient hymn, probably going back to the first century although not used in the liturgy until the third or fourth. No one knows for certain who introduced it into the Mass but the weight of expert opinion indicates the fifth century as the time and Pope Symmachus († 514) as the one who prescribed its use. Initially it was used only by bishops and then only on certain days.

At first the *Gloria* was used only at Christmas time; later it was extended to Sundays and the feasts of martyrs. For a long time priests were not allowed to use this hymn at their Masses; later they were permitted to intone it at Easter and on the day of their first Mass in the church they were to serve. As late as the eleventh century on the one day when it is most appropriate—Christmas day itself—priests were not permitted to sing the *Gloria*. By the end of that same century, however, the restrictions were removed and it became the rule for all to sing the *Gloria* on all feastdays. For a long time after it was introduced into the Mass this hymn continued to be sung in Greek, the language in which it was originally written.

The *Gloria* can truly be said to belong to the Mass by many titles. For the great theme of this hymn is the theme of the Mass itself: glory to God and peace (reconciliation between God and man) towards men whom God has chosen. It sets forth the whole economy of redemption and salvation which is mediated to us in and through the Mass.

The entire hymn, which is not very long when compared with the later rhythmic hymns of the Office, falls into three parts:

the angelic hymn proper, the praise of God, the invocation to Christ. The first is taken directly from the Scriptures and is, one might say, a musical setting of the "good-tidings" proclaimed by the Angel; the end of the Incarnation and the redemption is precisely "Glory to God" and at the same time peace, conceived here as objective reconciliation, between God and men. By men of good will is here meant not the benevolence of men, but that of God who is well-disposed to men. The phrase really means those men whom God chooses out of His loving kindness—in other words, the elect.

The second part of the hymn develops the idea of glory which it ascribes to God in greater detail. It is not a question here of trying to take the individual words apart to arrive at the different shades of meaning between *laudamus* and *glorificamus*; rather the cumulative effect is the important thing. There are different shades of meaning in the terms; yet together they are but an expansion and amplification of the very first word. The "*gratias agimus tibi propter magnam gloriam tuam*" might seem a little strange to us only if we forget that the best translation of "*gratias agere*" is more than "giving thanks" as we usually think of it; it means to proclaim, to exalt, to glorify. God's glory calls for a response on our part and that response is to magnify and proclaim God and all His wondrous works.

The titles that follow in the doxology are the most ancient and becoming to God: "*Domine Deus, Rex Coelestis, Deus Pater Omnipotens.*" The ancients honored God merely by recalling His many titles; they are all in the *Gloria*, expressive of His power, His sovereignty, His excellence, His love. The same may be said of the designations of Christ which begin the third part, what we might call the strictly Christological part of the prayer: "*Domine Fili Unigenite Jesu Christe, Domine Deus Agnus Dei Filius Patris.*" Christ's lordship, His sonship, His redeeming work, are all set forth here.

The strictly christological part of the hymn is a kind of litany addressed to the Lamb of God: "Thou who takest away the sins of the world have mercy upon us. Thou who takest away the sins of the world, receive our prayers. Thou who sittest at the right hand of the Father, have mercy upon us." Christ is seen here under two traditional and ancient images: as the Paschal Lamb ever standing as though slain, and as the risen and ascended Lord sitting at the right hand of God the Father. The Passion, redeeming Death and exaltation of Christ form the themes of the hymn and make it a triumphal chant. Indeed the whole is more like a series of acclamations than a hymn.

This litany passes almost imperceptibly into another and smaller doxology addressed also to Christ: "For thou alone art holy, Thou alone art the Lord, Thou alone art the most high, Jesus Christ, with the Holy Spirit in the glory of God the Father." We have here a reminder of the times in which this hymn was very likely composed, when "there were many gods and many lords" among the pagans. These words express the Christian opposition to the latter state of affairs: Christ alone is the transcendent Lord and God shining in majesty and glory above those poor gods which the human imagination had created for itself. In spite of the reference here to God the Father and to the Holy Spirit, Christ retains the central position; we contemplate Him in His glory, the glory He shares with the Father and the Spirit. The *Gloria* thus begins with glorifying God and finishes by glorifying Christ. The entire piece sets forth the order of the divine economy: God is glorified especially by the Incarnation of His Son and by the redemption He brings to mankind.

The last words of the *Gloria* are found in the ancient Eastern Rite but in the declarative form, and were used as an acclamation by the people at Communion time: "He is holy, he is Lord, he is Jesus Christ in the glory of God the Father." The *Gloria* is above all a song of joy, and at one time was preferred to the *Te Deum* for the expression of public joy and thanksgiving to God. That is why it is excluded from Masses which have a sorrowful or penitential character.

To this day the bishop in a pontifical Mass turns to the people when he intones the *Gloria;* this custom is a vestige of the time when all the people took part in singing, since the *Gloria* was by its nature and by tradition a community chant. The oldest melodies for the *Gloria* that have come down to us show that it was a syllabic recitation, or a declamation on a high note rather than a chant, exactly what we would expect of something that was not intended to be handled by a trained choir but rather by the congregation. Here as elsewhere we find that when a more elaborate chant was developed during the Middle Ages, the people ceased to take part in the singing of something that had become too difficult for them.

The *Gloria* is a hymn of praise and thanksgiving to God, a hymn to Christ, redolent of the faith of the early Church. It is the morning prayer of the Church and has the freshness of that part of the day about it: an assurance of redemption and salvation. Naturally it recalls Christmas since it is the expansion of the angels' hymn. It reminds us that the Church each day encounters the Savior who is Christ the Lord in the Holy Sacrifice. The *Gloria* is a proclamation in prayer of the mystery of salvation which is contained in the Mass.

The simple christology of the *Gloria* is an indication of its antiquity; a post-Nicene chant would insist on greater development and precision.

During the Middle Ages the *Gloria,* like the *Kyrie,* was interpolated or "farced," especially with Marian tropes. All these accretions were abolished by St. Pius V in 1572.

The celebrant originally only intoned the *Gloria.* During the twelfth century the priest-celebrant moved to the center of the altar to intone it, and some time later on in this period he began to recite the remaining words while the choir sang them. The bishop, though remaining at the throne, followed the same custom of reciting it to himself.

The Greeting of the Assembly. Each time in the Mass that

there is to be a new development of the service or when something important is about to happen, the priest greets the congregation with words dating back to biblical times: "The Lord be [is] with you." And the congregation answers with a phrase that owes its origin to the Hebrew tongue: "And with thy spirit," which means "and with thee also." This formula is a greeting indeed, but its position during the Mass shows that it is more than that; it is intended to call the attention of the assembly to what is about to happen: the Collect, the Gospel, the Offertory, the beginning of the Canon, *etc.* Because this greeting calls for a response it also serves to strengthen the sense of community. It is as though the celebrant were to say: here is something that we are doing together; and the answer amounts to a declaration that the people are united with him in sentiment and action. The very gesture that accompanies the "*Dominus Vobiscum*," the stretching out and closing of the hands, is a kind of embrace, a reaching out to draw all present into the action. It signifies the union between priest and people—the *vinculum pacis*, the bond of love in and with Christ.

The greeting that the priest uses goes back to Jewish times; we meet it in the Book of Ruth when Booz goes forth to inspect the work of the harvesters. He says these very words and they answer, "May the Lord bless thee." The response of the congregation at Mass is different from that of the harvesters, but it is the same idea. Originally, of course, the "Lord" mentioned here is God the Father, but on the lips of a Christian the word is the special title of Christ (*Kyrios*). It is not only a wish but a statement of fact: the Lord *is* with us. He is, of course, especially present in and to the liturgical assembly: "Where two or three are gathered together in my name, there am I in the midst of them" (Matt. 18:20). He is the Lord who is with us all days, our Emmanuel.

There is an alternate greeting used by the bishop, who employs the very words of Christ Himself: "Peace be with you." For a time it seemed that it would replace the "*Dominus vobiscum*," but it was finally restricted to the bishop, and then only at the point in the service (after the *Gloria*) where it is particularly appropriate. For a long time, as we have seen, the bishop was the only one who said the *Gloria;* when priests began to say it regularly no one seems to have thought to follow the bishop in using a greeting that would seem more natural.

The full meaning of the "*Dominus Vobiscum*" and its response is somewhat difficult for us to recapture; like other formulae in the liturgy it has become stereotyped: we do not always realize what we are saying. Nevertheless, it is to our interest to re-awaken the sense of community, the consciousness of common action and common prayer which it contains.

The Invitation to Prayer. After greeting the congregation and alerting them to what is to follow, the priest intones an invitation to prayer: "Let us pray." At present, the celebrant uses but one word and the prayer follows immediately, but it is certain that the invitation was at one time longer, that it specified what was to be prayed for, and that time was allowed for silent prayer before the collect was sung. The "*orationes solemniores*" of Good Friday appear to have been the standard usage for every Mass; they have been retained only in the liturgy of that day which has preserved for us the ancient form of the *synaxis* or liturgical assembly held before the Eucharist proper. Vestiges of the pause for silent prayer survive in the "*Flectamus Genua*" and "*Levate*" of certain penitential days, but the pause itself has long since disappeared. The restored Holy Week rite has revived it for the orations following the lessons, and future revisions of the Missal may provide for extending the usage to other days as well.

The practice of kneeling before the collect declined with the development of the idea that no one was to kneel at public prayer during Eastertide or on Sundays. More and more it was regarded as a penitential posture for prayer and consequently out of place on any joyous occasion or on any feast. By the beginning of the Middle Ages this kneeling came to be confined to penitential times and then gradually only to certain days. The practice of kneeling before the prayer was in some instances (requiem Masses) transferred to kneeling during the prayer, which is certainly an anomaly.

The modern practice is to kneel at high Mass during the Introit, the Consecration, and Communion (kneeling during Communion was also a mediaeval practice); but standing is still the *normal* position for prayer even for the congregation. This may seem surprising to us, as we have come to regard kneeling as the *only* posture for prayer.

When the practice of kneeling declined, the "*Flectamus Genua*" was retained only on those days when, technically at least, people were still to kneel. Oddly enough, the pause was eliminated altogether even when the "*Flectamus Genua*" was retained.

The Collect. During the singing of the collect the priest takes the ancient position for prayer which was at one time the position taken by all Christians: standing and with hands extended. This is the posture for prayer familiar to us from the pictures of the *Orantes* on the walls of the catacombs. It was a manner of praying that was particularly attractive and appealing: the standing, erect position symbolizes the new man forever standing erect by the power of Christ's Resurrection from the dead; the extended hands are reminiscent of the outstretched arms of Christ on the cross, reaching out to God on high. The innate conservatism of the Church has retained this beautiful and significant form at least for the official prayers offered in the public assembly of the faithful. It is true that the hands are no longer extended as wide as they once were, nor lifted as high, but the idea is still there and continuity is established between the Church of today and the Church of the first centuries. It is fitting that the priest who is the spokesman of the community should retain this expressive way of praying: standing with hands lifted up to God, whom he addresses in the name of the Church. There is a solemnity about it that fits the occasion.

We should note that the priest prays with hands extended in those parts of the Mass which are the most *ancient* (Collect, Preface, Canon, *Pater, etc.*) and with folded hands in those which were introduced *later on* as private prayers; we can thus see in the structure of the Mass what constitutes the original outline and what has been added to it.

The first public prayer of the Mass is known as the Oration or more often as the Collect. The word oration is a synonym for prayer, but it also means a speech or a discourse and in this we see a description of the special character of this prayer: it has the solemnity and the dignity, the formality that we associate with an "oration" in our own language. The word Collect has caused much discussion among liturgists and historians. It appears now that it owes this name to the fact that it is the prayer which "collects" or gathers up the prayers of the congregation (made silently for a time, as we have said) and presents them to God. The word itself originated in the Gallican Rite; the Romans called it *oratio*. It is clear that the collect or first oration did not form part of the original Roman Rite, at least not at this point in the service; the Mass began with the lessons. Nevertheless it is ancient enough and was introduced according to the most likely guess during the first half of the fifth century.

For the first time in the Mass the priest prays as the leader of the community: the Collect is the celebrant's first independent action as director and spokesman of the Church. There was a time, and it lasted some centuries, when the priest was much more free than he is now in making this prayer; it was left to his discretion to choose the subject and to develop it. He could either compose it himself, or read one of his own choosing that had been composed by another. We still find in the Leonine Sacramentary a choice between two prayers to be said in the Masses. But more and more as time went on a certain framework came into use, together with a special manner of speaking that crystallized eventually into the standard Roman collect which is to be found in the modern Missal. The great majority of these collects came down to us from the period before the Middle Ages. They are perfect expressions of the rather austere Roman genius: brief, concise, close-packed, sometimes rather barren and jejune, let it be said, but for the most part impressive and rich in thought and ideas.

As short lapidary prayers, the Roman collects are without peer, and with their companion pieces, the Secrets and Postcommunions, are among the most priceless treasures of the liturgy. If they appear at first glance to be barren and dull, because too general in tone and phrasing, that is because they are prayers intended for the community, and express what is good for the many instead of what is needed by the few. It has been well said that the collects are not so much prayers as formulae of prayer, showing us what we should ask for, or the way we should ask, or the ground of our asking.* Certainly in most of them the ideas are abundant if close-packed, and material for a whole theology—dogmatic, moral, ascetical and mystical—is contained in a few (surprisingly few) words. It is theology expressing itself in prayer. In them we find luminously exemplified the classic formula "*Legem credendi statuit lex supplicandi.*" Their variety, beauty and richness are inexhaustible. The idea that we come from God and return to Him, that God is all and we are nothing, that we depend on Him and owe everything to Him, what He is and does and has done, His perfections, His beauty, power, majesty, the whole economy of redemption—all these are presented with a wonderful variety of expression.

The collect is essentially a prayer of petition. We ask God for some favor or grace, most often spiritual but not necessarily nor always. Some of the most touching requests are for health of mind and body, for peace, for prosperity, for many other material goods and advantages.

* Zundel, *Splendor of the Liturgy* (New York, 1937).

All the collects have the same pattern. They begin by calling upon God, very often by one of His attributes: *misericors, clemens, bonus,* or by a descriptive dependent clause ("*cui proprium est miserere et parcere*"), or by a dependent clause that sets forth the mystery of the day or the season ("*qui hanc noctem lumine claritatis tuae clarescere voluisti*") or refer to the saint being honored; then comes the request (the heart of the prayer) that is addressed to God in connection with a mystery, a saint, or an attribute; finally there is the conclusion which usually shows the direction of the prayer: "Through Jesus Christ our Lord." In other words, each prayer consists of the *salutation—often* extremely brief and even abrupt, the *dependent clause*—which gives the reason for the *petition,* followed by the *conclusion.* This order is generally followed, except that some collects do not contain any dependent clause at all.

The salutation is directed most often to God the Father and frequently—in collects that are Gallican or modern—to the Son, but never to the Holy Spirit. The reason for this is that the plan of salvation as outlined and indicated by God is demonstrated in this way. The traditional Christian manner of praying in public is to present our prayers to God through Jesus Christ our Lord. A Christian prayer is not necessarily a prayer to Christ—it is above all else a prayer made as He would have it made. "If you ask the Father anything in my name he will give it to you." The role of Christ as the Mediator, the great High Priest of the New Covenant, is set forth by this manner of praying. It is the prayer which wells up from the heart of the Mystical Body and as such it must be directed through Christ to God: "Through him we have access in one spirit to the father." This, at any rate, seems to have been the idea that regulated the arrangement of the ancient Roman collect and the procedure was maintained inviolate until the eleventh century. In the territory where the Gallican Rite was used, the Arian heresy made the authorities sensitive to anything that savored of subordinating Christ, and prayers were directed to Him. This usage has influenced some of the collects of the Roman Rite. In modern times the ancient traditional order was lost sight of and we thus find collects like that for the feasts of St. Thérèse of the Child Jesus and St. Francis Borgia, which begin "*Domine Jesu Christe.*" These latter are theologically correct and doctrinally sound, of course, but they are also departures from the ancient tradition.

The dependent clause which follows the address and contains the reason for the petition about to be made is often a very precise statement of the theology behind the feast, or is a presentation of one of God's attributes; it will dwell on some virtue of a saint or some remarkable incident in his life.

For example, the feast of the Epiphany has ". . . *qui hodierna die unigenitum tuum gentibus stella duce revelasti*"; the collect for the Sunday after Pentecost has ". . . *qui omnipotentiam tuam maxime miserando manifestas*"; the collect for St. John Vianney has ". . . *qui sanctum Joannem Mariam pastorali studio et jugi orationis ac poenitentiae ardore mirabilem effecisti.*" Sometimes there are several dependent clauses and then at other times there will be none at all.

The petition is the heart of the prayer; it contains some of the finest expressions of devotion, and indeed often wondrously sums up the whole meaning of the feast, the mystery, or the season. There may be more than one petition; in fact, some of the older prayers delight in antithetic and parallel petitions: ". . . *ut sic transeamus per bona temporalia ut non ammittamus aeterna,*" or ". . . *ut perficiendo requirant, et quaerendo sine fine percipiant.*" The order of these petitions varies, too: sometimes the request comes before the address. In reality we have two different kinds of petition. One is simple, unadorned, and even abrupt: "*Da Domine*"; the other is more developed and elaborate: "*Deus qui . . . da nobis quaesumus.*" One is more literary, more rhetorical, more formal than the other. Sometimes, too, the petition only seems abrupt. Actually all the elements of protocol are there but the order is reversed; the request is made before God is addressed: "*Gregem tuam, Pastor aeterne, placatus intende.*" It has been remarked that the relative clause is always used on feast days while the "undeveloped" form is usually met only on ferial days. As we might expect, the solemn form is reserved for solemn days.

A remarkable trait of the Roman collects, particularly the older and more simple ones, is manifested in the universality of the petitions. They do not focus upon details, nor become lost in the passing and transitory, but in a way that is difficult to express and to analyze, they go right to the heart of the mystery; they seem to ask not for this or that grace or virtue but for the fullness of the Christian life itself. They try to draw from whatever is being celebrated or commemorated everything it has to offer. That is why we never tire of repeating the collects; there is always more in them than we can carry away. We can always say, for example, ". . . *da nobis in eodem spiritu rectu sapere et de ejus semper consolatione gaudere,*" precisely because we are not asking for something that is passing and transitory nor easily granted nor achieved. In all our life we shall never reach the bottom of this petition, because we are really asking for the fullness of the Christian life.

It is true that these petitions are adapted to the circumstances that inspire them, but it is all the more remarkable that they are in no way impeded or constrained by what might seem to be the limitations thus put upon them. Rather they seem to open out and disclose vast perspectives and inexhaustible depths. This is the Church at prayer, contemplating the mystery and seizing upon it, drawing from it the principles which are to nourish her piety and the piety of her children.

What we have said above applies, of course, particularly to those collects which make up the core of the Roman Missal—collects written in the earlier centuries when the art of composing them was at its best. The modern collects are not always so felicitous and concise. The great reason for this defect is that the collect has been overloaded and has become an unwieldy instrument. This is most apparent on the saints' feasts when the collects are often diffuse and wordy and seem to be the result of an attempt to leave nothing unsaid! The classical example of this is the Collect for St. Jane Frances de Chantal which is more like a second nocturn lesson than a prayer. The collect is ideally a synthesis; it tries to seize on one idea and express it completely and concisely. It is not intended to be a litany nor an analysis of details. Long theological considerations after the manner and style of a meditation may be very edifying, but they are not in the tradition of the Roman collect. There must be, if it is to come off well, a nice balance between prayer and reflection; the material for reflection must be there, but it cannot be drawn-out and set down to the last detail without robbing the collect of its most characteristic beauty, which is to say much in a few words. No clear impression is made when too much is said, and instead of carrying away one idea which will recur again and again to the mind during the day, we are lost in the details.

The majority of the collects are composed according to a definite prose rhythm called the *cursus*; the clauses end in words deliberately arranged in a rhythmical pattern. As a result they have a harmonious sound which gives the whole prayer a dignity and a majesty of utterance that befits the worship of God.

The conclusion of the collect is a stately assemblage of rhythmically arranged words beginning usually with the words, "*Per Dominum Nostrum Jesum Christum.*" This prayer is addressed to God through the mediation of Christ; through the High Priest our prayers are offered to God and become acceptable to Him. The whole Church under the leadership of Christ has made this prayer, and in the conclusion we see the ideas that dominated the Church at the time these prayers and their conclusions were created. It is a magnificent perspective that is presented here, and one that is profoundly doctrinal. We see God the Father in majesty, living and reigning forever and ever.

We see Christ who has won eternal redemption for us and has been established as the Lord of all and our Lord; He is the eternal Son of the Father, alike to Him in majesty and glory; He sits at the right hand of God; He lives and reigns as king in the unity of the Holy Spirit forever and ever. It is He who is ever living to make intercession for us. We lift our eyes to God, certain that He will hear us because our prayers are presented to Him by His son. The response of the people is a simple "Amen"—so simple as to be deceptive. For "Amen" is a most significant word upon the lips of the new Israel. It is no mere formality; by it, the people confirm and approve what has been said by their spokesman. The word itself is, of course, a Hebrew acclamation that has been retained as such in nearly all Christian liturgies; it means consent, approval, asseverance, confirmation. We translate it as "so be it" which it certainly means, but the original word means much more than that. Here it means that the faithful are in accord with the priest and with what he asks for. To appreciate the full meaning of the "Amen" we must try to recapture the spirit of the times in which it arose and see it as a spontaneous, interested cry from the heart of the assembly which speaks with one voice (and in one word!).

When we consider the whole prayer from the "*Dominus Vobiscum*"—which alerted the community—to the "Amen"—which proclaims their adherence—we see that it presents us with the magnificent spectacle of the whole Church gathered together in prayer. We are not dealing here with lifeless formulae nor frozen formality, but with the full assembly of the saints engaged in conversation with God.

For centuries there was only one collect in each Mass as a rule, but when there were more they were separated by the lessons. The idea of stringing prayers together, or making commemorations, came to Rome from the Gallican churches. The original harmony and simplicity has been somewhat injured by the invasion of other collects which took place in the Middle Ages and modern times. The revised rubrics of the Missal call for the elimination of many of these commemorations with the idea of thereby simplifying the rite.

The collect of the Mass is also the prayer used throughout the day's Office; this is one of the places where we see the link between the Mass and the Office, which prolongs the "*sacrificium laudis*" throughout the day. The collect thus plays an important role in expressing the mood and atmosphere of the season or feast and in reflecting the mind of the Church towards what is celebrated on a particular day.

The collect, coming as it does at the end of the *Kyrie* and the *Gloria*, acts as a conclusion to the first part of the Mass, just as the Secret concludes the Offertory and the Postcommunion concludes the Communion. That is not to say this arrangement was deliberately planned. The lessons really constitute a fresh development in the rite, a separate part of the service which we call, somewhat unsatisfactorily, the Mass of the Catechumens, but which could better be known as the Fore-Mass or the Service of the Word.

The Lessons: Epistle and Gospel. The oldest parts of the first section of the Mass are the lessons; we inherited the practice of reading the Scriptures here from the synagogue. To the Jews the Scriptures were the word of God: God speaking to men, enlightening and instructing them. The history of God's mighty acts, of His dealing with His chosen people, the unfolding of His eternal designs, the laws of Moses and the warnings of the prophets, made up the sacred narrative to which they listened Saturday after Saturday. The first Christians were Jews and they continued this "service of the word" as a matter of course, adding to it their own Scripture, the New Testament. By this reading of the Scriptures in our churches we proclaim the good tidings in word just as in the Eucharistic Action we proclaim it in deed. The Scriptures thus become a focus of devotion, the inspired expression of worship, the foundation of solid piety. For the religion of Christ is a biblical religion; it finds its explanation and its very being in the pages which, even more than for the Jews, unfold the history of salvation before us, manifest God's plan in Christ to us, proclaim His glory and His wonderful deeds towards the children of men, particularly the Redemption. The Bible is the Word, the Voice of God, which shows us how we should worship and why; what God is and who He is, what He has done and will continue to do. We cannot dispense ourselves from the Scriptures; they are God's word addressed, first of all, to the assembly which is the Church, then to each member of it. The Scriptures must have a place in Christian worship if for no other reason than that they prepare the way for the Sacrifice that follows; they awaken the proper dispositions which the community should have as they approach the Sacrifice; they arouse our faith, because Christianity is a revealed religion, shown to us by God and grasped by faith; they stir up our devotion and our love; they strengthen our spirit of dedication to God and to His service. Moreover, they as it were make us present at the events they relate: they re-create the past and make it present to us. We see that we are not reading about someone else or about something that happened only in the past; it is our own history that we are listening to and what happened to them is happening to us. They proclaim as present reality the saving mystery of Christ to those who are assembled together in Christ. The lessons are read in the assembly because it is only in the Church that their full meaning is unfolded; we read them in context and see the Bible "from within."

This was much more easy to see in the early centuries when the whole Bible was read through in the Christian liturgical assembly. The continuity and completeness of the history of salvation, the relation between the Old and the New Testaments, the preparation and the fulfillment, were more readily grasped in this way. The reader had no service book that indicated what was to be read; he simply read from the Bible itself until he was told to stop. At the next reading he merely resumed where he had left off. This practice was called "*Lectio continuata*" and there are traces of it yet in the Missal and even more in the Breviary. The length of the lessons was not fixed but the order seems to have been: a lesson from the Old Testament; a lesson from the New other than the Gospel, which was read at the end. After a few centuries the lessons were marked off in the Bible and called *pericopes*. Psalms were sung and prayers said between the lessons. This general plan was followed all through the primitive Church; in greatly shortened form it has been retained to form the main outline of the *Ante-Missa* in the Church to this day.

In the Roman Rite which evolved from the primitive universal rite it was at first the practice to read three lessons, as we do even to this day in certain ferial Masses: one from the Old Testament and two from the New. Gradually the number of lessons was reduced to two; it is likely that this happened very early, certainly by the fifth century. As a rule both lessons were then taken from the New Testament: the Gospel of course, but also the first lesson which came so often from the Epistles of St. Paul or the Epistles of one of the other apostles that it came to be known as the Epistle, even when it happened to be from some other source altogether. The lessons from the Old Testament did not disappear altogether by any means; they survive today for the most part in the ferial Masses of Lent and Advent and in some of the Masses of feasts. The surviving lessons from the Old Testament in the Missal indicate very cleary that they were not read as edifying stories or as impressive accounts of God's dealing with men, but for their bearing on the New Testament and the light that they threw upon it. This relation between the Testaments was much more clearly grasped by the Christians of the first thousand years than it is by us; to them we owe the fact that this relation has been preserved for us to see.

The Epistle. At present the lessons in the feast and ferial

Masses are chosen for their bearing on the feast or season. Very often there is a close relation between the Epistle and the Gospel: what was foretold in the Old Testament is related as happening in the New (e.g., the Epiphany); similarities between the events related are brought out (e.g., Moses striking the rock in the Old Testament, the angel stirring the water in the New). The "just man" or the "valiant woman" of the Old Testament is described in parables by our Lord in the New; Masses of our Lady frequently draw on the Wisdom literature and Mary is compared to "wisdom."

For the Masses of the saints we find passages from either the Old or New Testaments which glorify characteristic virtues of a particular saint, or allude to events in his life. Even though the lesson does not refer primarily to this saint, it is applied and accommodated to him more than once with striking appropriateness. Thus, in the Epistle for the feast of St. Athanasius the words of St. Paul about himself are taken to describe the life and ministry of one who lived long after him.

The Epistles (or lessons) read in the stational churches of St. Peter and St. Paul in the Masses after Easter are invariably selections from the sermons given by them after the event of Pentecost and narrated in the Acts. In these selections the Saint speaks to us now as he once spoke to his ancient hearers.

The Epistles that are read on the Sundays are usually concerned with the moral implications of the Christian life. These are a series of exhortations to live and walk in a manner worthy of our calling. They are selected from the moral part of the Epistles of St. Paul, but they contain doctrine as well. The introductory "*Lectio Epistulae Beati Apostoli Pauli ad Romanos*" or "*Ad Ephesios*" should not make us forget that these readings are addressed to us, that God speaks to us through the words of St. Paul as He once spoke to the Philippians and the Thessalonians.

In ancient times the Epistle was read from the *ambo* by the *lector* without any of the preliminary solemnity which marked the singing of the Gospel. For a long time it was read without any title or response, but these have long since been added to the reading. The actual reading was not a chant but a recitation *recto-tono;* only later on was the solemn tone introduced for Sundays and festivals. In general the tendency has been to keep a certain austerity in the chanting of the Epistle, Gospel, Preface, and orations, all of which have never undergone the musical development associated with the other chants of the Mass. The *lector* faced the congregation: a natural position as the reading was directed to *them.*

Today as for many centuries the Epistle is sung not by the *lector* but by the subdeacon. This change was brought about in part by the mediaeval desire to exalt the subdeacon to a position in the Church analogous to that of the deacon, without being equal to it. The subdeacon no longer faces the people but reads the Epistle facing the back wall of the church. The disappearance of the *ambo* and the influence of the rubrics of the low Mass upon the high Mass appear to be responsible for this change. At a pontifical Mass the subdeacon faces the bishop.

There is an etiquette which governs the introduction of the Epistle: all those lessons taken from the Wisdom literature are called, irrespective of the book they come from, "*Lectio Libri Sapientiae*" (psalms are never used as lessons). The lessons from the prophets, when they give the words of God Himself, always begin "*Haec dicit Dominus*"; otherwise, like the historical lessons, they begin "*In diebus illis.*" In the lessons taken from the New Testament St. Paul always calls his hearers "*Fratres*" while the other apostles say "*Carissimi,*" a term St. Paul also uses in the singular when speaking to SS. Timothy and Titus. Sometimes when an apostrophe is quoted there is no address at all, as on Trinity Sunday.

The "*Deo Gratias*" at the end of the Epistle is an acclamation borrowed from the Office, where it is said after the lessons of Matins. It appears that the "*Deo Gratias*" is not, as it is usually said to be, a thanksgiving to God for the grace of hearing

His word, but a sign that the people have heard and understood it. The phrase "*Deo Gratias*" originated in Africa where it was used as a greeting and a sign of approbation. From there it passed into the West and continued to be used in the same sense: as a greeting or as a sign that one understands or hears what has been said. English-speaking people now say goodbye as a farewell, but they have long since forgotten that it really means "God be with you." The same thing is true of the original sense of "*Deo Gratias*," although there is of course no reason why we cannot mean it as "an act of thanksgiving to God for the grace of hearing His word." The Epistle is a proclamation addressed to everyone; it was inconceivable to those who developed the Roman liturgy that people should be addressed without making some kind of response. Respond they did, with the words which Christians had long since used in private life to show that they heard anything addressed to them: "*Deo Gratias.*"

The Gospel. The Gospel is the climax of the reading service that precedes the Eucharist, and it has always been so. This is natural enough when we consider the importance of the Gospel as the heart of the Scriptures: as the "good news" above all other, as the glad tidings of salvation, ever fresh and new, the very quintessence of Christianity. It is accompanied by great solemnity which is intended to emphasize its importance, a solemnity which has accompanied it almost from the beginning, although naturally the details have been developed. For one thing, the Gospel has been sung by the deacon since at least the fifth century and very likely before that time; indeed in some places, at least on Sundays and feasts, it was sung by the bishop (to whom it would naturally seem to belong before any one else) or by priests; it never seems to have been confined to an ordinary reader or *lector*. The procession which preceded it for over fifteen hundred years was one of the few in the primitive Roman liturgy. It grew out of the action of going to the *ambo* or pulpit to sing the Gospel; we find it in its developed form in the Middle Ages with lights, incense, the book carried from the altar and the deacon blessed by the priest before he began to read. Some of these elements are found in the first Roman ordo (seventh century), but they very likely go back to an earlier time. Gradually, over the centuries, the reading of the Gospel became what it is today: the climax and the closing of the *Ante-Missam* and one of the high points of the entire Mass.

Again as in the collect, but in an infinitely more impressive and striking way, we find the principal thought of the day, the reason for the feast or the season. And it is a remarkable fact that each separate Gospel in the Missal, with few exceptions, contains the whole Gospel of Christ. It announces and proclaims the "good tidings of great joy which shall be to all the people" and manifests Christ to us preaching this fundamental Gospel either by His words or His deeds. By hearing the Gospel the Church can contemplate Christ as though she were present at the scenes that it relates. Better still, the Church *is* present because what Christ did in the pages of the Gospel He continues to do in His Church and in the world: we are not merely witnesses but contemporaries of the Lord.

The relation between the feast and the Gospel read on that feast is best seen on the great days of the Church year when the event we are celebrating is recorded in the section that is read; but we can see it also, at least in type and figure, in the Masses of the Saints when the Gospel passages might deal with the Vigilant Servant, the Five Wise Virgins, the Treasure in the Field, *etc.* Sometimes, as with the Epistle, one phrase, clause or sentence may be enough to cause the passage to be selected as the Gospel for the day. The Church enjoys a certain freedom in this matter and applies verses and passages that originally referred to one thing or person to some other thing or person.

The story of the young man in the Gospel who ultimately rejected Christ's call to follow Him "because he had great riches" is read on the feast of St. Jerome Aemilian; it stops, however, at the words to which the saint responded, if the young man did not: "come follow me." This is the key to St. Jerome's life and is of course addressed no longer to that saint but to all of us. A passage that is selected for a Gospel usually has a certain length which is provided (as in this instance) by telling the story from the beginning or by including more than is strictly needed. In that way abruptness is avoided. The Gospels of the Sundays often deal with the miracles of our Lord which display aspects of His redeeming work. They are parables in action, pointing to Christ as the Savior. The theme of healing and even the word itself occurs in an amazing number of Gospels: "and the boy was healed from that hour"; "Thy faith hath healed thee"; "behold now thou art healed." By phrases such as this Christ points out the meaning behind His miracles: they are signs of the far greater healing He has come to bring to the world.

The solemnity which surrounds the singing of the Gospel: the greeting by the deacon, the acclamations made by the people, the lights and incense, are intended to impress us with the fact that we are in reality listening to Christ. Christ enters the assembly in a triumphant procession; this latter should be richly dramatic, and if well and completely done, it cannot fail to be impressive. This solemnity goes with the singing of the Gospel in all rites, and it is one of the few places in our own rite where there is more ceremonial than is demanded by strictly practical needs.

A good part of this solemnity is directed to the *Evangelarium* or Gospel-book itself. It is a very old Christian idea to honor the book of the Gospels, almost as though it were Christ Himself. Lights and incense were first carried before the bishop as a mark of honor; these marks were extended to the book, as though it were a living creature. The book itself was most handsomely and elegantly bound and decorated; the sacred text was written with the most dignified lettering, often in characters of silver or gold on the best vellum. Later we find bindings of ivory, gold and silver, sometimes adorned with precious stones. A few of these *Evangelaries* still exist today, mute but eloquent witnesses to the faith and the spirit of reverence and worship of those who made them. The book of the Gospels was held in such high esteem that it was kept on the altar, often with lights burning beside it, much like the Holy Eucharist today. It is still kept on the altars in the Eastern churches.

Some of this ancient and ardent devotion to the book of the Gospels survives to this day even outside the liturgy; we still kiss it and treat it with respect and try to have it as beautifully bound and printed as our means will allow. All the more reason, then, why these customs should be preserved in the Church and in everything connected with the Gospel in the liturgy. The very way the book of the Gospels is carried to the pulpit can be a sermon in reverence, and if it is left on the lectern or the pulpit during the week, is there any reason why it cannot rest on a cushion? If lighted candles were to be placed on each side of it, a custom dating back to the first centuries of the Church would be revived. We do, after all, burn candles before an image or a statue; why then should it be regarded as strange to do this with God's own word? Needless to say, the unhappy practice of putting the *Evangelarium* on the *floor* during Mass until such time as the deacon needs it is altogether indefensible. The place for it is on the credence table.

The blessing of the deacon by the celebrant as we know it today is an expanded version of an ancient and more simple form; the "*munda cor meum*," for example, is a later mediaeval addition; the "*Dominus Vobiscum*" and the "*sequentia*" are also ancient. Here they serve to draw attention to the great thing that is about to be done, a solemn introduction for a great action. The phrase "*sequentia*" *etc.* reminds us of the old *lectio continuata* from service to service, once a common practice (of course, the word *Initium* takes its place if needed). The incensing of the text is mediaeval in origin, at once a mark of respect and a symbol of the perfume that fills the word of God.

The sign of the cross on the forehead, the lips, and the breast is made in the ancient manner with the thumb, but the ceremony as such is mediaeval in development. The earliest sign was that made on the forehead, but the custom did not become widespread until the ninth century. By making this sign we profess that we are accepting the Gospel and taking its message into our hearts, but the original idea seems to have been that we are invoking a blessing upon ourselves. The sign of the cross made upon the book by the deacon is a mark of reverence and very likely a way of saying that all blessings and graces come to us from the Gospel of our redemption.

During the singing of the Gospel everyone naturally stands, as they did in the past when a herald was making a proclamation. There was a whole series of gestures of respect made by the people at this point in the service in mediaeval times: kings removed their crowns, knights took out their swords and held them up before them, thus showing their willingness to support the Gospel and to fight for it. To this day the bishop stands with his head uncovered and with both hands on the pastoral staff. At one time the subdeacon carried the book (or the scroll) of the Gospel after it had been sung to all the clerics present in order that they might kiss it; in some places later on even the people were permitted to greet the book in this way. Now it is kissed only by the celebrant or by a greater prelate if one is presiding.

The prayers and actions accompanying the reading of the Gospel (with the necessary adaptations) came into use by the priest at low Mass during the Middle Ages. The deacon turns slightly towards the wall on the Gospel side of the church for a number of reasons that are hard to explain to people today. The practice began in the days when the bishop's throne was in the center of the semi-circular apse of the sanctuary. The deacon stood at his right to sing the Gospel, but he could not turn his back on the bishop. Consequently, he faced across the sanctuary towards the opposite side. That side was either south or north, depending on what end of the church the bishop's throne was found. If it were at the east end, the deacon faced south; if at the west, he faced north. The latter was the more common case and under the influence of the allegorical way of explaining the Mass, the people, particularly in the northern lands, saw it as a symbolic posture, as a reading of the Gospel against the devil who was traditionally supposed to dwell in the north, region of cold and darkness. The present diagonal position of the deacon is, then, the result of two causes: one practical, the other inspired by symbolism. Needless to say this symbolic explanation arose long after people had forgotten the original reason for the position.

The "*Laus tibi Christe*" is another one of those many acclamations which fill the Christian liturgy. It appears to have been adopted at this point in the Low Mass during the Middle Ages.

The whole ceremony of the singing of the Gospel and its place in the *ante-missam* is a vivid reminder that Christ is present and speaking to us, thus giving the words of the Gospel of the day special meaning and emphasis. They are as it were highlighted—placed in a special context, the context of the *Mysterium*. The incidents related are aspects of Christ's redeeming work; the Gospel is seen as the revelation of the mysteries of the Kingdom of God. It is the proclamation of Christ by word as the Eucharist is His proclamation by deed. The Word of Life goes with the Bread of Life: they are related to one another; they complement one another; the meaning of the Eucharist is unfolded in the Gospel. It is more than a simple reading; it is in reality a drama in which we take part. The words of Christ by the seashore or on the mountainside are for us, and we as truly hear His voice as His contemporaries did. The whole Christian life cannot ever be anything other than an acting-out of the Gospel; it is the law and the rule of our lives.

Both the Epistle and the Gospel are our daily nourishment. It is a much richer concept of their role to say with Tertullian that they "*nourish* the faith" rather than just "*instruct.*" The

Epistles are the apostolic and prophetic commentary on the Gospel and on the deposit of faith contained in it. God speaks to us in the Epistle through the writers of the Old Testament and through the apostles; in the Gospel He speaks to us through His Son. They make up what someone has called "two good sermons every day." For these reasons many have proposed the vernacular for the lessons which seems logical in the light of what has been said.

The Interspersed Chants: Gradual, Tract, Alleluia, Sequence. The Jewish practice in the synagogue was to follow the reading of the Scriptures with the singing of psalms, which were a commentary in song upon what had just been read. The Christians took over this practice too, adding the idea that the psalms were prophetic of Christ, the new Moses, and of the Church, the new Israel. Thus, the reading service from the beginning was made up of readings and chants; throughout all the changes that have come to this part of the Mass during the centuries it has kept this fundamental structure.

Singing after the lessons, or between lessons, had a twofold effect: it gave people a chance to react and to participate in one of the oldest and most natural ways of reacting and participating, which is to break into song; and it afforded relief after the rather long lessons. Besides, it gave time for contemplative meditative prayer and the psalms served this purpose admirably.

These interspersed chants are, then, the only chants of the Mass that are sung for their own sake; unlike the Introit, Offertory and Communion, they are not intended to fill in time during a procession or provide a commentary upon it. They are not accidental and, as it were, secondary parts of the Mass; they enter vitally into its very structure; they are the most important as well as the most ancient chants of the Mass.

The Gradual is so named because it was led by a cantor who stood upon the step (*gradus*) of the *ambo*. As the letters V.R. in the Missal indicate, this was at one time a responsorial chant;

that is, it was a psalm equipped with a refrain verse that was sung by the people after each verse of the psalm sung by the cantor. We have one of those refrains in the very text of Psalm 135 itself: "*quoniam in aeternum misericordiam ejus,*" thus showing that the practice was pre-Christian in origin. The cantor intoned the refrain, the people responded; the cantor sang the first verse of the psalm, the people repeated the refrain, and so on to the end. The entire psalm was sung, of course. The development of the elaborate chant brought about the shortening of the psalm until only two verses remain now.

The Gradual is the musical commentary on the Epistle; sometimes it is a direct echo of it (e.g., the feast of the Epiphany). More often it is indirect, reflecting the mood of the season or the feast rather than what is specifically in the lesson itself. Excellent examples of this abound in the Masses of Passiontide when we hear the voice of Christ in His passion as expressed in the messianic psalms selected. The verses that make up the Gradual are selected according to the feast on feastdays, but rather arbitrarily on ordinary Sundays. For the most part the Gradual is from the psalms, but often it is from other books of the Old Testament and sometimes from the New; occasionally it is not from the Scriptures at all.

The Gradual appears to have followed the first lesson while the Tract followed the second. Nowadays the Tract is used only in penitential seasons. It is a less adorned manner of singing the psalm; the word comes from *tractatim*, meaning "sung straight through," that is, without a refrain, or possibly, from the word for a simple melody which was repeated all the way through. Even now the Tract is much less developed musically than the Gradual. What we have here is probably the oldest form of the interspersed chant, which antedates the introduction of the *Alleluia* that has replaced it. It survives now only in penitential Masses, which have never admitted the later *Alleluia*. The Tract shows its antiquity in another way: it is usually longer than the Gradual, sometimes consisting of an entire psalm

(*Laudate* in the Easter Vigil Mass; Psalm 90 in great part on the First Sunday of Lent).

At a rather early period the second psalm was replaced, first at Easter and then in all Masses not of a penitential character, with the *Alleluia,* a Hebrew phrase (*Halleluyah*) meaning "praise God." It was sung twice; the second time the final A was drawn out forming the *jubilus.* The whole chant of the *Alleluia* is supposed to be an expression of joy to which the music contributes. It reaches its high point in the *jubilus* which is, of course, the sound of the name of God Himself, although St. Augustine explains it as "an expression of wordless praise," a joyful sound for the sake of sound. The *Alleluia* very early became the typical Easter song and has remained the one-word hymn *par excellence* of the Christian Church. "We are Easter men, and *Alleluia* is our Song" is no less true of us than it was of the Christians in St. Augustine's day when it was first said.

In time a verse was added to the *Alleluia* chant and the *Alleluia* repeated once more after it. These verses were selected from the psalms, but were very often selected from other sources, sometimes even from the Gospel, which was a departure from the rule that the Gospel reading should be the climax of the Service of the Word. The development of the *Alleluia* chant and the use of Gospel texts worked together to transform this into a kind of prelude to the Gospel rather than a post-lesson chant. It may be interpreted that way now: with the singing of the *Alleluia* the assembly greets Christ who is about to enter the assembly, there to proclaim the Gospel. The chant of the *Alleluia,* as a matter of fact, now accompanies the procession of the deacon as he prepares to sing the Gospel. There is something magnificently appropriate about it at that place.

The *Alleluia* verses as a whole seem to have been selected with an eye to making them suit the joyful and triumphant note associated with the *Alleluia* itself. Here again music expresses the quiet, tranquil and serene joy that lies at the heart of the Christian religion.

Perhaps the *Alleluias* of the Graduals are not always according to modern taste, and certainly some are better than others. One thing is certain, however: they never cause distress nor draw attention to themselves and they generate an atmosphere of calm and peace. If this is done, we have no right to demand more of them. From first to last the liturgy is not, nor ever was intended to be, a concert, even a sacred one.

The Gradual and the *Alleluia* verse, with the Tract in the penitential seasons, contribute to give the Mass the color and tone of the feast or season.

The Roman *Graduale* of 1908 permits the repetition of the refrain, which helps to bring this chant into greater prominence. It is supposed to be a meditation in the ancient style, with emphasis on the repetition of ideas. As the Graduals stand now (excepting the Tract), they are much too short; perhaps a future revision of the Missal will bring about a return to longer Graduals. Meanwhile, the practice of singing the refrain would help. In a dialogue Mass, the Gradual and Tract and *Alleluia* verse could be recited by the congregation or by some of the members. This would bring about greater variety in the celebration of the Mass and make people more conscious that the Mass is truly a community prayer in which each has his part to play. During Eastertide (from Low Sunday to Pentecost) the great *Alleluia* is sung instead of the usual Gradual and *Alleluia*.

The Gradual gives an insight into the thoughts of the psalmist on the feast of the day or on the season. Those of the Sundays after Pentecost are very often a glad song of rejoicing over the redemption of Israel, or they are a shout of confidence in God, or a prayer for help. The Masses of our Lady and of Virgins make use of the nuptial Psalm 44, which so beautifully and lyrically describes the virgin's call: "Hear O daughter and incline thy ear, for the king has greatly desired thy beauty." The Gradual for Confessor Bishops echoes in a prayerful and contemplative mood what has been read in the lesson, and sees the latter in a new and inner light: "Behold a great priest who in his day pleased the Lord." A more thoughtful reading (or hearing) of the Gradual gives us insight into the Scriptures; we see the Bible from within and the concord that exists between all the different parts of the one Revelation of God in Christ. In the psalms we discover the face of Christ and His Church appearing in the faraway past which prepared the way for their coming.

A considerable part of the Gradual's effectiveness comes from the melodies to which it is set. They are among the finest and most moving pieces of chant that we have. Here perhaps more than anywhere else we see that the chant is truly the ideal presentation of the liturgical texts. Consider the "*Christus factus est*" of Holy Thursday, or the "*Justis germinabit*" of the Mass of a confessor, or any one of a hundred examples that will illustrate how they bring out the meaning of the text and surround it with the contemplative atmosphere it demands. This is surely prayer in song.

The *Sequence* is a late mediaeval development of the *Alleluia*. Its proper name is the *prosa* (prose). There are five Sequences in our Missal, after the pruning-away process instituted by Pius V in 1572. During the Middle Ages there were innumerable Sequences of varying degrees of excellence. They are the best examples we have of mediaeval farcing. Originally Sequences were intended as a memory device, in order to remember the *neums* of the *Alleluia;* they were strictly syllabic, having one *punctum* to each syllable. The modern Sequences retain something of the same character in that they are more like prose than poetry. Those which survive in the Missal may be regarded as the best. Five are enough because, beautiful though they may be and are, they are really a foreign growth on the liturgy. Nevertheless, they do contribute to a deeper understanding of the feast or mystery of the day.

The Sequences in the Missal now are:

1. "*Victimae Paschali*" for Easter, written by Wipo in the eleventh century. Its dramatic character made it extremely

popular in the Middle Ages as a mystery play. It is set to a magnificent melody, and is perhaps the finest of all Sequences.

2. "*Veni Sancte Spiritus*" for Pentecost, written by Cardinal Stephen Langton in the thirteenth century. It is a very beautiful meditation on the *Alleluia* verse of the Mass for that day: "*Veni Sancte Spiritus, repletuorum corda fidelium.*"

3. "*Lauda Sion Salvatorem*" for Corpus Christi, composed by St. Thomas in the thirteenth century. It is a compendium of the entire theology of the Eucharist. In contrast to the earlier Sequences its approach is analytical. There are many striking passages.

4. "*Stabat Mater Dolorosa*" was written by Jacopone da Todi, who died in 1306, but it was not intended as a Sequence at first. It is strikingly devotional and reflects the personal piety of the later Middle Ages. It was introduced in the eighteenth century.

5. "*The Dies Irae*" is one of the finest hymns of the Church in the judgment of competent critics. It was supposed to have been written by Thomas of Celano in the thirteenth century but that is now contested. Like the "*Stabat Mater,*" it was a devotional poem at first; it is an anomaly to use it as a Sequence in the requiem Mass since there is no *Alleluia* to introduce it. Daniel hails it as "the highest ornament of sacred poetry and the most precious jewel of the Latin Church."

The Sequence is peculiar to the Roman Rite and the uses derived from it. The older religious orders have many more Sequences in their Missals than we, but most of them are rather second-rate affairs. Even at their best the Sequences must be looked upon as alien to the spirit of the liturgy. A further restriction on their use appears in the new rubrics of the Missal.

The Sermon. After the solemn proclamation of the Word of God by the deacon in the Gospel there comes the homily (from a Greek word which means assembly) or sermon (discourse). Ideally, this should be a further proclamation of the Word, an exposition and explanation of the *ideas* contained in the Gospel, the lessons, or the other parts of the Mass, an announcement of the eternal Word in the language of the modern world and an application of the Gospel to present-day life. The original meaning of the word "preach" is "to herald" or "proclaim." Perhaps that knowledge will help us to keep in mind what preaching is intended to be: the proclamation of the Gospel, *i.e.*, an objective statement of what has happened: "God has visited and redeemed his people," the unfolding and announcing of "the unsearchable mystery of Christ." "We preach Christ crucified."

Conceived as an exposition of the Scriptures read in the Mass, the sermon has been an integral part of the liturgy from the beginning. "The president makes mention of all these things [*i.e.*, the message of the prophets and the memoirs of the apostles] in a speech" says St. Justin, writing in the second century. It was preached by the bishop, who was the liturgical leader of the assembly, from his throne in the apse. The close tie between the two offices—that of breaking the Bread of Life and distributing it and communicating the Word of Life—was shown by this apparently inconsequential fact: the same man did both. Even today the *Caeremoniale Episcoporum* supposes that the bishop will preach when he celebrates pontifical Mass, and it directs that he talk from the throne.

For convenience sake it became the custom to preach from the *ambo* (or Gospel lectern) in the sanctuary, but the modern pulpit as we know it is a late mediaeval development and comes down to us from a time when preaching had become divorced from the Mass, and consequently from the mystery. Late mediaeval preaching wandered far from the original idea and became almost exclusively moral or ethical or preoccupied with edification.

The sermon was originally, at any rate, set in the framework of the Mass and closely related to it, explaining and commenting upon the "mystery." The priest or bishop was the one who initiated into the mystery (*mystagogus*). The sermon was doctrinal rather than moral, a proclamation rather than a lecture in theology, dynamic rather than static, a synthesis rather than an analysis.

This tradition was observed for centuries and the laws of the Church still insist that on Sundays and feast days the pastor must give a homily to the people during Mass. The Council of Trent insisted that at least from time to time the pastor should explain the Mass to the people, but it has taken the modern liturgical and biblical revival to make us see again that the sermon is *part of the liturgy*, that at Mass all sermons are liturgical sermons, that no matter what the particular texts of the day or season may be the sermon is always "on the Gospel" and that "this day the scripture is fulfilled in your ears" is always the text.

The sermon marks the end of the first part of the Mass, the Foremass or "Mass of the Catechumens," which is intimately joined to what follows. The first part paves the way for the second; the readings, prayers and chants set the stage for the second, prepare the assembly for the Eucharist. The faith and piety of the congregation must be nourished first by the word, then by the Incarnate Word Himself, the Bread of Life. The redeeming work of Christ was done by His teaching as well as by His sacrifice; the two were intimately associated and practically inseparable. His Church, which renews, represents and continues His redeeming work, must do as He did. The reading of the Scriptures awakens, stirs up and directs our devotion. It is not by any means a kind of optional appendage to the main thing, but the Church's own preparation for what is to follow, and she would have us share in this preparation. There is a meaning in the word "follow," too: the eucharistic action does not burst abruptly into the assembly; it comes announced and heralded to people who have been prepared and made ready for it: it "follows."

The Creed. Appropriate though it is at this point in the Mass where it serves as a profession of faith in response to the message of the Gospel, the Creed formed no part of the Mass in the beginning. The Church in the Frankish domains, where the remnants of Arianism were still combatted, had added it to the Mass in the sixth or seventh centuries; but St. Henry II, the Holy Roman Emperor, was amazed not to find it at Rome in the eleventh and asked about it. He was told that the Roman Church was never disturbed by heresy and felt no need of a profession of faith in the Mass. Nevertheless, at St. Henry's request the pope admitted the Creed, but stipulated that it was to be sung only on Sundays and those feast days which celebrated events mentioned in it. This has remained the general principle guiding the recitation of the Creed, with the addition of singing it on the feasts of doctors who taught the Church in detail what the Creed affirms and proclaims; and on first-class feasts "*propter solemnitatem.*"

The Creed used in the Mass is called the Creed of Nicaea—Constantinople because it embodies the specific teaching of these Councils against the Arians. This association with the Arians has caused the Creed to be regarded almost exclusively as a profession of faith against heretics and has obscured the fact that the anti-Arian portion of it is by far the smallest. In reality this Creed existed long before the Councils of Nicaea and Constantinople; it is an ancient Creed used in the churches of the East by candidates for Baptism. That is why it is in the singular: each one made his separate profession of faith. In the tradition of Oriental Creeds it is much more developed and detailed (even in the part that was directed against the Arians) than the Creed used in the West, and really amounts to a kind of hymn of the faith. The language is noble and elevated, solemn and impressive, as befits the subject.

The Creed follows the order of the divine economy, beginning with the creation and proceeding to the Incarnation and the redemption (the Passion, Resurrection, Ascension into Heaven, the Heavenly Session and the glorious Coming Again). Then comes the outpouring of the Spirit who is the source of life, who creates the new order and who establishes the Church: one, holy, Catholic and apostolic. Through the Church and particularly through the sacraments (Baptism included them all), the Holy Spirit gives life to the Church and to its members, and plants in them the hope of the resurrection and of the life of the world to come. The change from "*credo*" to "*expecto*" (I await) is most effective and gives dramatic intensity to the final words.

The Creed is, as we have said, the hymn of the faith, a fitting conclusion of the "Mass of the Catechumens" and an appropriate transition to the Mass of the Faithful. The aim of the first is to awaken and nourish the faith; the purpose of the second is to renew in mystery what is proclaimed in the Creed. It is the response of the community to what has been revealed in the lessons which of course set forth the history of salvation.

Because of what it is and what it does the Creed is the longest and in many ways the most solemn of the ordinary chants of the Mass. Its importance has led musicians to try to give it a musical setting worthy of it, but because of the way it is drawn up, it does not lend itself to a musical setting as other parts of the Mass do. It is too long, for one thing. The setting that will best accord with its character is the stately, almost martial, music that we associate with a profession of faith, which is a sober, restrained enumeration of great and sublime facts.

In contrast with these later efforts of musicians, the melodies of the *Graduale* are of the simplest, hardly more than is needed to set forth these facts, just a little beyond a bare recitative. This is explained partly by what we said before about its length being prohibitive of elaboration, about its own sober restrained character, and also partly by the fact that for a long time it was taken for granted that everyone should sing the Creed, or more precisely that they should recite it. One does not sing a profession of faith; one declaims or recites it. It was not until the polyphonic period in music that the Creed began to be really sung, and then by the choir rather than by the people.

The nature of the Creed and its position in the Mass clearly demand that it should be recited by the congregation. The whole community thus joins in professing its faith; like any of the ordinary chants, and even more so, it is not something that we listen to another doing for us.

CHAPTER 14

The Clean Oblation: From the Offertory to the End of the Mass

The Sacrifice—Oblation

During the Creed (or immediately after the sermon if the Creed is not sung) the deacon spreads the *corporal* (which once covered the entire altar) and thus indicates that the Eucharist proper, the Supper of the Lord, is about to begin. In earlier times the *Orationes Fidelium*, the special prayers said by the priest and the faithful for different intentions, were sung at this point (after the Gospel), as they still are on Good Friday. Very likely the form used on that day was the form used in the other days as well. But for some reason the custom fell into disuse. They were called "prayers of the faithful" because they were said only after the catechumens had been dismissed at this point in the Mass.

The Sacrifice proper begins with the *Offertory*. The bread and wine must be placed upon the table and set aside for their sublime purpose before the great prayer of consecration can begin. That is the idea behind the Offertory. Nowadays the bread and wine are prepared beforehand; the chalice and paten are placed on the credence table covered with the *humeral* veil and the *burse*. The wine and water stand in cruets beside the chalice. In the earliest decades of the Christian community's history, it was unnecessary to bring the wine and water to the altar; they were already there during the *agape* which preceded the Eucharist. After the *agape* had fallen into disuse it became necessary to provide bread and wine and bring it to the altar. They were provided by the people who brought them in procession to the altar after the Eucharist proper had begun. That was the reason for the Offertory rite: to present the material for the sacrifice; to offer it to the priest and ultimately to God.

Nowadays the bread is presented to the priest by the deacon after the subdeacon has brought it to the altar. The wine and water are presented by the acolytes. There is no longer any procession except in some places where it has been revived.

The next development in the Mass after the Creed (or the Gospel) is marked by the kissing of the altar and the usual greeting that indicates the beginning of something new and important. The "*Dominus Vobiscum*" once again draws the people's attention and the "*Oremus*" calls the community to prayer. No prayer follows immediately and scholars have tried to explain its absence in many ways. Certainly the invitation does not refer to the Offertory antiphon because "*Oremus*" is an invitation to prayer made to the community. The best explanation would seem to be that the Secret prayer—the most ancient Offertory prayer—is the one that goes with the "*Oremus.*" The pause that once took place after every "*Oremus*" and that has disappeared in other places has been retained here. We are not aware of this now because so many other prayers and actions fill in the space between "*Oremus*" and the Secret prayer.

The Offertory Antiphon. This is sung by the choir when the subdeacon goes to bring the bread and wine for the sacrifice. It is again but a fragment of the longer processional psalm which once accompanied the offering of the bread and wine by the faithful; this took some time and consequently called for a musical interlude, just as the entrance did. The antiphon was the refrain; the psalm the true Offertory chant. Introduced into the Roman Rite during the fourth or fifth century, it had assumed its present form by the twelfth century, largely because the procession had declined. Few losses in the liturgy can be more regretted than the giving up of the active participation of the laity in the Holy Sacrifice which the Offertory procession expressed and dramatized.

The Offertory chant is made up of a single antiphon without refrain, except on the last Sundays after Pentecost, when the "*De Profundis*" is used, and at requiem Masses, when the "*Quam olim Abrahae*" is used as a refrain. These antiphons are taken from the Scriptures for the most part, and very often from the psalms. Occasionally they are from some ecclesiastical composition. They usually contain a note of joy either in the words or the music, or often in both, inspired no doubt by St. Paul's "the Lord loves a cheerful giver." Some of them are prayers (at the requiem Mass and at the Mass of the Holy Cross) rather than antiphons. They usually express some thought connected with the feast or season, very often with an allusion to offering (e.g., "*reges Tharis et insulae munera offerent! Reges Arabae et Sabae dona domino deo adducent*"). Each of the antiphons of the first eighteen Sundays after Pentecost contains some such reference.

The substitution of any other piece for the antiphon proper to the day is an abuse. A supplementary Offertory is allowed, but it should be kept supplementary. The Offertory chants are intended to be sung by a trained choir and are adorned by brilliant melodies (e.g., the "*Jubilate Deo omnis terra*" for the fourth Sunday after Easter) which attain the summit of vocal art.

The Offertory Action. Originally the Offertory was a very solemn part of the Mass, a real action by the people and priest together. The only vestige of this is the Offertory at the Consecration of a Bishop and the collection at Sunday Mass.

The bread used at Mass was ordinarily leavened and consisted of round loaves marked with a cross. (Between the ninth and eleventh centuries azyme bread was adopted.) It was placed on a large platter called the paten. The wine was poured into a large chalice with handles. What was necessary for the Mass was placed upon the altar; the rest was given to the poor.

The whole idea of the Offertory procession was that the faithful gave something to God which symbolized themselves. This bread and wine was transformed into the Body and Blood of Christ. The faithful, like the bread and wine that were their gifts and represented them, were transformed into the likeness of Christ. They received this bread and wine in Holy Communion transformed into the Body and Blood of Christ. That is the essential idea of the Offertory and it is frequently mentioned in the most ancient Offertory prayers, the Secrets. The faithful intended to give themselves to God not in an individual sense, but in a collective sense. It was the oblation of the whole Church; yet it represented the official and personal participation of each *fidelis* in the Sacrifice. It was a corporate act, looking to Communion and in direct rapport with it.

The Offertory procession remained in vigor well into the end of the mediaeval period, at least on certain days during the year and on certain occasions; but the offering of the bread and wine in many places became an offering in kind after the year 1000. The exact causes of the decline of the Offertory of the bread and wine by the people is not known with certainty, but the decrease in Communions and possibly the change from leavened to unleavened bread may have figured in it.

The Prayers Said by the Priest. The old Roman Rite called for no prayers at all during the Offertory action; the bread and wine were placed upon the altar and nothing was said until the entire action was completed. All the prayers which are now said between the Offertory antiphon and the Secret prayer are Gallican or mediaeval in origin, another manifestation of the taste of the Frankish clergy for prayers during all the actions of the Mass. One after another these rites accompanying the offering of the host and of the chalice came to be provided each with its appropriate prayer which in some cases closely parallel our present Offertory prayers. The series of prayers in use today arose in the Frankish domains but was adopted by the Roman Rite and developed during the Middle Ages. They are essentially private prayers, and it is noteworthy that they are expressed in the singular (all except the "*Offerimus*" of the chalice which refers to the joint offering by deacon and priest, and the "*Deus qui humanæ substantiae,*" which is an ancient Christmas collect adapted to the mingling of the water with the wine).

Together this series of prayers makes up what has somewhat infelicitously been called the little Canon. They are not really independent prayers as the Canon is but a kind of running commentary on the various actions of the Offertory rite. These prayer represent a desire to fill in this time of preparing the offerings with the expression of personal sentiments missing from the Canon itself. They are marked with a strong individualistic flavor and give the priest an opportunity to speak for himself such as the Canon itself does not give him. When we analyze them we can see that many are private prayers of the celebrant rather than public prayers. With the exception of the "*Orate Fratres*" and the "*Deus qui humanae substantiae,*" they were never intended to be recited publicly. They are not to be interpreted as in any way an anticipation of the Canon, but they do allude to what is in store for the bread and wine which because of what they are about to become and to do, and because they are already being set aside for that purpose, can be called "*immaculatam hostiam*" and "*calicem salutaris.*"

The mingling of the water with the wine is mentioned by Justin Martyr and Irenaeus in the second century; it is very likely even older than that. Its symbolism is among the most ancient that we have: the union of the divinity with the humanity or the water and blood issuing from the pierced side of Christ.

The Preparation of the Offering. Before the Mass, the bread and wine to be used for the sacrifice have been placed upon the credence table; now they must be brought to the altar and placed upon it. First of all the altar itself is prepared by the deacon who spreads the *corporal.* This is merely the ancient table cloth which with the passing of time has shrunk to its present reduced proportions. (For a solemn papal Mass they still use a *corporal* that is a true table cloth covering the whole altar.) After the singing of "*Oremus*" the subdeacon goes to get the chalice and paten and brings them to the altar. What is done today is the very much reduced survival of the elaborate presentation of the gifts which took place in the early centuries.

Before the Middle Ages the wine was placed in the chalice and mixed with the water before the chalice was brought to the altar; the present arrangement whereby the subdeacon brings an empty chalice to the altar and the wine and water are poured in at the altar itself became general only in 1570. The subdeacon wears the *humeral* veil as a mark of respect for the sacred vessels in accordance with the ancient custom that the sacred vessels should not be touched directly (at least during Mass). For the same reason he wraps the paten in the *humeral* veil during the Canon. The rite of holding the paten goes back to the time when the paten really was what its name means—a large platter. It was used to bring up the loaves of bread which were placed upon the altar. As the paten could not be kept on the altar, it was given to the subdeacon to take care of until it should be needed again. Although the paten has become small and is no longer used for Communion, the subdeacon continues to hold it until after the *Pater Noster*.

The incensing of the *oblata* is, as we said earlier, a mediaeval addition introduced about the twelfth century. The symbolism of this action has already been alluded to. The washing of the hands originally took place before the Offertory (as it still does in the pontifical Mass) and it was done because of the ancient custom of washing the hands before any sacred action. During the Middle Ages this washing was transferred to its present place after the incensation and perhaps because of it. Here again the Frankish custom of having a prayer with each action brought about the recitation first of appropriate verses, then of the whole psalm.

The "*Orate Fratres*" is a final plea for prayers made to those present at Mass. Originally this request seems to have been addressed to the clergy but later it was directed to the congregation, as the "*Orate Fratres et Sorores*" of some places indicates. It is certainly not ancient; it appears for the first time in the eighth century. Now we may see it as an impressive reminder that the sacrifice we are about to offer is the sacrifice of the whole Church. The answer sums up very neatly the chief ends of the Mass and the benefits which come to the Church from it.

The Secret. In the early Roman Rite the celebrant waited until the Offertory procession was over and the gifts placed upon the altar. Only then did he say the prayer which had been preluded by the "*Oremus*," a prayer which dedicated the offering to God. In reality it concludes the Offertory, as the collect concludes the first part of the Mass and the Postcommunion concludes the Communion. Naturally this prayer, like the other orations, was intended to be said aloud, and was sung for many centuries (it still is recited aloud in the Ambrosian Rite). In spite of all the theorizing about it the name apparently comes from the circumstance that by the eleventh century it was recited silently, *secrete*, the *secreta*. Indeed the name comes from the Gallican Rite where the prayer first was said silently. Why it should be said silently when the other two companion prayers are sung aloud is another problem that has not been satisfactorily explained. It may be that during the singing of the Offertory psalm the priest went ahead with the Secret prayer, but the most likely explanation is that it was influenced by the Gallican tendency to say the Offertory prayers silently. In turn that tendency was affected by the Oriental disposition to accompany rites with silent prayers. All the other Offertory prayers were said silently; hence it was thought that the Secret prayer should be said silently too.

The Secret prayer is constructed like the collect except that it is more directly a petition and is preoccupied usually with the thought of the Sacrifice, the theology of which it expresses beautifully. The true meaning and purpose of this prayer is to declare the meaning of the Offertory in the light of what is to follow. The Secrets tell what is the destination of the offering and what it is to accomplish when God has accepted it. There is an infinite variety of formulae in the Secret prayers but one main underlining idea: we present our gifts to God and these material gifts do not make up an offering of themselves but are to be the instruments of the Sacrifice of Christ. Hence the frequent references to these "gifts," these "offerings," these "presents," and at the same time the frequent reference to "victims," to "sacrifices," to "oblations." As a result, the terms often are blended together inextricably. The fruit of the Mass is asked for by way of anticipation even though the Sacrifice has not taken place as yet. We may note another frequent allusion in one form or other to the idea of *exchange:* we give something to God and in exchange He gives us Himself; the Mass itself is a kind of exchange "*sacrosancta commercia,*" "*hujus sacrificii veneranda commercia.*"

Many of the Secrets are adapted to the feast that is being celebrated, and ask that our sacrifice and our prayers may be acceptable to God by the merits of the saint whom we honor, or through the power of the mystery we celebrate. At other times while the prayer asks that the gifts and prayers be acceptable to God there is an exceedingly graceful allusion to the feast without directly basing the request upon the mystery commemorated. Or some incident in the life of a saint prompts an allusion in one way or other to the Mass itself without making it a basis (directly at least) for the request. As a result, the prayers give us a wonderful amount of teaching about the Mass: what it is, what it does, what it signifies—all largely in the way of *obiter dicta*.

We might divide the Secrets into two general categories: those that are adapted directly or indirectly to the feast, the season, or the special occasion; and those that are so general that they could be used for any and all occasions. But every one of them, for whatever occasion or feast, seems to look rather towards the Sacrifice that is to be accomplished than the act of offering, to which they indeed allude. They teach us what the Sacrifice is, what its effects are, what we obtain from it. Like the collects they are filled with the most profound doctrine expressed in concise language with an astonishing economy of words. While they are intensely devotional they are practical too and are directed towards making us realize in our lives the mystery that we celebrate. The general effect of these prayers is to increase and to deepen our understanding of the whole eucharistic mystery.

From the Secret prayers we can make up a whole body of doctrine which amounts to a theology. We learn that the Sacrifice we offer is the Sacrifice of the whole Church ("*munera Ecclesiae tua oblata sanctifica*"); that it is, first of all, a work done by men which God accepts; that it is the giving of external things which signify and effect the gift of ourselves ("*nosmetipsos tibi perfice manus aeternum*"); that in its entirety it is a Sacrifice accomplished by Christ, by the Church and by us; that our Sacrifice is the concern of the whole assembly of Heaven; that the Mass brings glory to God and honor to the saints, while at the same time it cleanses us from sin and works unto an increase of our devotion and for our salvation; that it benefits not only our souls but our bodies and indeed the whole world.

We offer, immolate, and sacrifice, but it is a sacrifice that is sacramental and mystical, though real and complete. We do not make Christ a victim, but we offer Him in His state of victimhood. We are sure that God will accept this sacrifice; yet we ask Him to accept it again, and by our very act of humble prayer strengthen and increase our sacrificial dispositions. "Receive our offerings and prayers" we say, and by these words indicate the whole action of the eucharistic Sacrifice where words and acts, matter and form, go together to form one deed. And the effect of that deed is an exchange between God and us whereby the work of our redemption is accomplished and we become "partakers of the one and sovereign Godhead": we are divinised, become divine.

The effects of Holy Communion are set forth in the Postcommunion, but while it is true that Communion cannot be separated from the Sacrifice, and hence the effects of the one are the effects of the other, it is in the Secret prayers that we see the effects of the Sacrifice itself. The first and the greatest, as far as we are concerned, is the redemption, but often the Secrets speak of the more proximate effects: purification, cleansing, and an increase of devotion. The offering of the Sacrifice is in itself a corrective against sin, repairing and atoning for the honor taken from God and thus making up for what we have done. Thus the Sacrifice purifies and expiates. The devotion referred to so often does not mean religious feeling nor our subjective dispositions, but what it always means in the language of the early Church: consecration, dedication of ourselves to God. The great instrument of that devotion is the Holy Sacrifice in which we join the gift of ourselves, free from sin and obedient to God's will, to the gift of all mankind made once and for all in and by Jesus Christ our Lord. Like the collect the Secret is a community prayer, not only because it is in the plural but because like all true Christian liturgical prayer it is addressed to God through the hands and with the voice of the High Priest Jesus Christ. Unlike the collect which has admitted into its ranks some prayers that are addressed directly to Christ, the Secret has maintained more rigorously the ancient principle: to God through Christ. Like the collect, the Secret prayer is recited with hands extended; there is another survival of the ancient character of the prayer in that the last words, "*Per omnia saecula saeculorum*," are sung aloud and answered by the community.

Saying more than one Secret prayer became the common practice when the collect became multiplied, apparently out of a desire for symmetry, although the result is that very often the same thing is asked for in each Secret, even sometimes in the same words, so that Secrets are repetitions in a way that the collects are not.

The Canon of the Mass

The "*Per omnia saecula saeculorum*" and its "Amen" is, then, not the introduction to the Preface as we might be led to think, but the conclusion of the Secret. The offerings have been set upon the altar, have been set aside for God's use and purpose. The next step is the Sacrifice proper, the consecration of these gifts to God—a consecration which is a blessing expressed in the form of a long and solemn prayer to God. It was in this way that Christ blessed the bread and wine at the Last Supper: by a prayer, a prayer of praise, thanksgiving, and recognition to God.

Although it may not appear to be so, the Canon is one prayer; as a result of that prayer the bread and wine are offered and consecrated and sacrifice is offered to God. It is called the Canon because it is the prayer established by rule (*canonica prex*). Another term for it is the "*Anaphora*," the offering, the word used to describe this prayer in the Oriental rites.

The canon is not only a prayer—although it is *the* prayer (*oratio, prex, canonica prex*)—it is also an action ("*Canon actionis*" means the rules governing the action) by which the Sacrifice, an offering to God filled with all the religion, all the adoration, all the love of the Father of which the priestly soul of Christ was capable, is made present and delivered to us that we might unite ourselves with it and offer it to God. All that Christ did to accomplish our redemption is commemorated here, recalled before God, and pleaded for us.

Since the Canon makes present the sacrifice of the cross, and as it is the memorial of the Lord and of His great victory, it is a liturgy of triumph, a thanksgiving, a "Eucharist" and a eucharistic hymn—"*hymnum gloriae tuae canimus*." Many of its formulae are directly and clearly eucharistic; by them thanksgiving is directed to the Father. Although a large intercessory element has crept into the Canon with the passing of time, and many graces are now asked for us, it retains its dominant note "*hoc sacrificium laudis*."

The Canon grew out of the hymn that was sung at a religious supper held by the Jews, a long prayer in which the head of the family as the spokesman of the gathering and fellowship blessed God and praised Him. The earliest Christian *anaphoras* represent a development from the Jewish prayer; they keep some of the themes and the exalted tone and even the wording in places, but they make additions of their own. As time went on these forms became more and more crystallized and at the same time took on the charactertistics of the local rites. It is clear that the Canon (or *anaphora*) of the primitive Church contained two dominant themes: the one which came directly from the Jewish prayer, theological in content and direction, praising and exalting God the Father for all that He is in Himself and for all that He had done for men and for His chosen people in particular; the other Christological, dwelling with thanksgiving and gratitude upon the Incarnation and the redemption, recalling the mysteries of our Lord's life and especially the redemptive Passion, which led directly to the account of the last Supper and the institution of the Eucharist. This was followed by the *anamnesis*, the offering of the Sacrifice to God and an invocation of the Holy Spirit to impart the fruits of Communion to the faithful. The intercessory prayers that form part of the later Canon were not to be found in any of the early *anaphora;* they were confined to the Offertory (*Preces fidelium*, the Diptychs). A careful examination of the various formulae that have come down to us from the third and fourth century, the oldest *anaphoras* that we have (the Prayer of St. Hippolytus in Rome, the Alexandrine Prayer or Anaphora of Serapion, the Apostolic Constitution of Antioch, the Liturgy of Addai and Marai of Edessa), brings us to certain conclusions about the structure and content of the prayer as it had developed in those various centers of Christian life. Our present Canon, although in itself a later composition, follows the same general lines and can be seen to derive from them in one way or another.

First of all, there is a prologue, introduced by a dialogue between priest and people, during which the eucharistic theme of the prayer is set forth; then a thanksgiving to God for His benefits beginning with creation (the liturgies of Antioch and Jerusalem develop this part more than other liturgies), followed by the theme of the redemptive work accomplished by Christ through His Passion and Death. This latter theme is gloriously developed in the *anaphora* of St. Hippolytus used in Rome during the third century. Even in the distinctly christological part we can see reminiscences of the Jewish prayer in modified and transformed language, leading up to the account of the Last Supper and the institution of the Eucharist. This is the center and the object of the entire rite, the meaning of which is set forth in the *anamnesis*, the recalling and representation of the whole redeeming work of Christ, followed by a twofold *epiclesis* (there is only one in the Prayer of Hippolytus). The first is an invocation of the Holy Spirit to transform the bread and wine into the Body of Christ (sometimes it is after the account of the Institution, sometimes before it); the second a prayer for the fruitful reception of the Body and Blood of Christ. The whole prayer concludes with a doxology, a hymn of praise to God through Christ, and this is answered by all with the final "Amen."

In all these various and varied *anaphoras* we can see that the main outline is the same, that while the form varies, the substance is preserved and that it all points to the apostolic (and therefore divine) origin of the great eucharistic Act itself. We can see a general agreement on what the prayer should contain and what it should do.

Between the first recorded prayer used in the Roman Church, the Prayer of Hippolytus, and the first redaction of our present Roman Canon as it appears in the earliest Sacramentary to contain it, there is a great but not a substantial difference. To begin with, we no longer have a prayer in Greek but in Latin and, next, instead of the smoothly flowing coordinated arrangement of words that distinguishes the lofty prayer of Hippolytus, we have a prayer that is greatly broken up and disjointed. The intrusion of other elements and the consequent breakup of the ordered presentation of the older prayer is very evident. Themes that were highly developed before are only alluded to now, and ideas that had not formed part of the primitive prayer are given full scope. Evidently, then, it had been touched up and added to sometime during the intervening centuries. The presence of large parts of our Canon in the "*De Sacramentis*" of St. Ambrose (396) shows that it was in use in the fourth century and most likely in the second half thereof, at Rome and at Milan. The most striking innovation was the introduction of the intercession (which once took place during or immediately before the offering) into the prayer itself. This brought about a certain readjustment of the prayer resulting in a break in the flow of ideas. Another step in this direction came with the introduction of the *Sanctus* and a consequent rearrangement of the prelude of the prayer. Later on the *Communicantes*, Memento of the Dead, *Nobis quoque*, and *Hanc Igitur* were added and completed the transformation of the original prayer into its present form. The hypothesis of a complete and deliberate rearrangement, once so much in favor, has been almost entirely abandoned. It is a question not of rearrangement but of additions and adjustments. The prayer in its present form was known in the sixth century, and the language in which it is written, the phrases that characterize it, seem to go back to the fifth century or earlier.

The Canon of the Mass was at least edited by one hand if not composed originally by one author. There are stylistic peculiarities which point to this single authorship or editorship. We do not know whose work it is, but the Canon has a distinctive phrasing and a certain rhythm of language which mark it off as unique among the *anaphoras*. There are, for example, the parallel constructions: ". . . *rogamus, ac petimus, uti accepta habeas et benedicas*"; ". . . *catholicae et apostolicae fidei*"; ". . . *fides cognita est, et nota devotio*"; ". . . *sanctas ac venerabiles manus*"; ". . . *de tuis donis, ac datis*"; ". . . *sanctum sacrificium, immaculatam hostiam*"; ". . . *non aestimator meriti, sed veniae largitor*"; "*omnis honor et gloria.*" Then there is the frequent accumulation of terms: ". . . *haec dona, haec munera, haec sancta sacrificia illibata*"; "*Per quem haec omnia, Domine, semper bona creas*"; ". . . *sanctificas, vivificas benedicis et praestas nobis*"; ". . . *quam pacificare, custodire, adunare, et regere digneris*"; ". . . *benedictam, adscriptam, ratam rationabilemque.*" All of these occurring in such abundance give a definite flavor and tone to the prayer and prompt the theory of a single editor. They point also to the likelihood that the prayer is very ancient, going back to the days of the *sermo rhetorica*, to the elevated style of the Roman rhetoricians.

It appears that the author or editor had the texts of the Oriental *anaphoras* (and particularly the Alexandrian) before him as he worked, because there are phrases and concepts borrowed from the Oriental liturgies; in spite of this the prayer has an originality that is its own and the authentic Roman flavor and coloring that we would expect. Since the time of Gregory I, who introduced some changes, it has remained untouched through the centuries.

The dominant theme of the Canon is the idea of offering, expressed very frequently either directly or indirectly throughout this relatively short prayer. Primarily this offering refers to the offering of the Sacrifice by the Church, but also it refers to the offering of the community itself to God.

Silence of the Canon. During the first centuries it was the custom to *sing* the entire eucharistic prayer, during which the Consecration took place out loud; this practice was in keeping with the dominant concept or view of the Mass itself as a "*Eucharistia*," a "*sacrificium laudis*," the Thanksgiving-action of the entire community which welled up from the heart of the Church and found its natural expression in song. The line of movement was upward; the Sacrifice mounted to Heaven. During the seventh and eighth centuries, in some parts of the Church the accent began to be placed not on the idea of something rising to God, but on the idea of the Eucharist as God's gift to men, coming down from Heaven. This idea spread more and more, particularly in the territory of the Gallican and Mozarabic Rites. The eucharist prayer had already been cut into two by the singing of the *Sanctus*. The first part of it came to be considered as an introduction rather than a beginning, while the second part began to be considered as the whole Canon, as the time during which the descent from Heaven took place. This latter part was shrouded in mystery and the sign of this was a reverent silence. It was the sanctuary or holy of holies of the Mass into which the priest alone entered, while the people stayed outside. This concept of the Mass as the descent of God upon the altar, rather than the Sacrifice offered by the community, spread widely through the Church and influenced the Roman Rite as well as the Gallican. With the new view of what went on at the altar came the idea of surrounding the part of the Mass during which it happened with a mysterious silence. Other causes undoubtedly operated to work this change, and one of them is that the musical development of the *Sanctus* and its consequent lengthening led to the practice of the celebrant going on with the Canon silently, as obviously he could not sing it while the choir sang the *Sanctus*. The change from singing the Canon to saying it silently was a gradual one. At first we hear of a recitation in a loud voice, then in a lower tone; but by the ninth or tenth century the present discipline had become the rule.

The Preface. From what has been said so far in these pages we can see that the Preface is not an introduction or a prelude to the Canon but is rather the beginning of the prayer and, far from being distinct from it, forms a most important part of it. We associate the word "Preface" almost exclusively with the idea of a foreword or an introduction, but in the Latin of the time when this part of the Mass developed, "Preface" meant an oration, a solemn address. In the other Latin Rites the Preface was known as the "*contestatio*" (solemn profession of faith), "*immolatio,*" "*illatio,*" (sacrificial prayer), which fact throws considerable light upon the genuine meaning of "*Praefatio*": it is meant to apply to the entire prayer but has become attached only to the beginning of it. In the pre-Carolingian Roman Rite, "*Praefatio*" was indeed the name given to the entire Canon; it was a prayer and solemn oration which set forth the meaning of the entire rite, a sacrifice of thanksgiving by which man responded to what God had done for him. The whole arrangement of the Preface today (solemn introductory dialogue, the impressive chant) shows us that it is not a mere foreword nor an introduction, but the true beginning of the Church's greatest prayer and greatest action.

Introductory Dialogue. The dialogue which introduces the Canon is very ancient and is found in all liturgies; it has a precedent in the Jewish religious supper ritual. The importance of the great prayer of the Church is highlighted, brought forcibly before us, by the solemnity of its introduction. In contrast with other prayers, there is an ascending development, a series of calls to our attention; there is not only a "*Dominus vobiscum*" but a "*Sursum Corda*"; not merely an "*Oremus*" but a "*Gratias agamus Domino Deo nostro.*" The responses of the people are of corresponding solemnity. Something very important is about to take place and we are made to sense it and to understand it. What is more, it is not just a prayer we are entering upon but an *action: "Gratias agamus domino deo nostro"*:—"Let us engage in the eucharistic action"; then the development begins: "*Sursum corda.*" St. Cyprian alludes to this in his treatise on the Lord's Prayer. He sees the dialogue as expressing the fundamental Christian attitude for all prayer. St. Augustine sees it as a response to St. Paul's "*quae sursum sunt sapite.*" The Christian's whole life is lived in Heaven; his heart is fixed where true joys abound; he seeks the things that are above: "*Sursum corda.*" The response is a joyous affirmation that we not only *should* dwell above with Christ but we *do*; by His grace we as a community have entered into the possession of Heaven and we are "ever with the Lord": "*Habemus ad Dominum.*" This should always be true of Christians but it must be true at this point in the service with a greater intensity and concentration upon what the whole Church is doing.

The way has now been prepared for the priest to move on to the action at hand, to invite all to engage together in the Church's act *par excellence: "Gratias agamus Domini Deo nostro.*" No mere formal expression of thanks is involved here; this is a call to do something about all that the Lord God has done for us: "*Quid retribuam Domino, pro omnibus quae retribuit mihi?*" "*Calicem salutaris accipiam.*" What it means is: let us together engage in an action which will show and represent our total response to God, our loving adherence to the whole supernatural order; an action which includes the totality of worship, that embraces adoration, praise, recognition, penitence—all that is caught up and held by the one glad cry "*Gratias agamus Domino Deo Nostro.*" This phrase was already used by the Jews in their ritual, and with it went the response which has also passed into the Christian liturgy: "*Dignum et justum est,*" a phrase that expresses approval and agreement with what is being done. Such acclamations of approval and acquiescence by the people assembled together were much used in antiquity to ratify important decisions taken by the rulers in the public interest. It was a sign that they had a part to play and that it was a community activity, not the action of individuals.

The same idea is behind the responses of the people at this solemn moment. These responses are acclamations which arise from the very nature of the Church and of her worship. The priest, without whom there can be no sacrifice, does not appear before God in his own name, but as a spokesman of the community. So it is that the priest calls upon the faithful to show them what he is about to do, or what all are about to do together under his leadership. And the faithful respond to the call in a way that shows a union of mind and heart, an accord and harmony in all that is being done.

The ideas expressed in the words of the dialogue are expressed also in the actions that accompany it. Here we have another heritage from the early liturgies. When the priest summons the faithful to lift up their hearts, he raises his hands; when he calls on them to give thanks to the Lord, he makes the embracing gesture and the bow. He then opens his hands once again to maintain the posture traditionally associated with public prayer.

Our Lord's prayer of blessing was in the form of a thanksgiving, and this is the form it has taken in all Christian liturgies. The Preface is that part of the Mass which sets forth the reason for giving thanks, and is the only part of the Mass that does so. Of course, in a wide sense, the whole Canon is a thanksgiving; it is a commemoration, a grateful recalling before God of what He has done, a memorial of Christ: "Do this for a commemoration of me." "Thank" and "think of" are related in meaning as well as in their etymology. To thank someone is to think of him with gratitude for something he has done, and when that thoughtful recognition is given external form it is an act of thanksgiving. So it is that a prominent theme of the Preface is the recalling of the various phases of the redeeming work.

In the past, and even today to a certain extent in the Oriental rites, it was the custom to begin the Canon with an enumeration of all God's benefits from the creation to the Redemption and finally to the crowning act of God's condescension: "Who on the day before he suffered, *etc.*" The Consecration thus took place at the end of what we now call the Preface, which was naturally much longer than it is now. At present there is only one clause which assigns some particular reason for being thankful; most often it is a recalling of some phase of the Redemption. During the fifth and sixth centuries the Prefaces were very numerous; many of them departed considerably from the great theme of the Redemption. Those written for the feasts of martyrs, for example, were panegyrics of the saints rather than Prefaces in the strict sense. There are over 250 Prefaces in the Leonine Sacramentary, and even that is incomplete. After the sixth century a reaction set in; the Gregorian Sacramentary contains only fourteen Prefaces and by the Middle Ages (except for proper Prefaces peculiar to certain localities and religious orders), there were only ten. One at least, if not two, were added during the Middle Ages (those of the Blessed Virgin and the Trinity) and four in modern times (Preface of the Dead borrowed from the eighteenth century Paris Missal, Preface of St. Joseph, of the Sacred Heart, and of Christ the King). In some dioceses of France there are special Prefaces for Advent, the Dedication of Churches, and the Saints.

Like the collect and the Gospel, the Preface sets the tone of the feast or season. The individual clauses which do this are sometimes longer and more developed than in the collect, but they are similar in their richness of thought joined with terseness of expression. Some of them (Easter, Sacred Heart, Christ the King) are truly theological discourses, condensing and compressing vast areas of thought into a few well-ordered phrases. The modern tendency to increase their number (three have been added in this century) is extremely gratifying and it is sincerely hoped that their number will be increased still more, thus adding greater variety and emphasis to the liturgical year. There are many splendid Prefaces in the liturgical literature of the Church which were used in the past and which could be drawn upon again to our great profit and delight. The Common Preface which contains no explicit allusion to the redeeming work, and the Preface of the Trinity which is in reality a profession of faith rather than a true Preface, are not as rich nor as satisfying as others would be. A Preface for Sundays dwelling upon the Resurrection, and Prefaces for saints' feasts and the Dedication of Churches are much to be desired.

All the Prefaces take up the words of the response, "*Dignum et justum est*," and echo them: "*Vere dignum et justum est aequum et salutare . . . gratias agere*." The Preface of Easter does not use "*gratias agere*" but an equivalent "*Te quidem, Domine . . . gloriosius praedicare*." "Proclaim" here means to give thanks in the ancient sense of "blessing" and "praising." In the Preface of Our Lady, "*Collaudare, benedicere et praedicare*" are added to "*gratias agere*."

"*Per Christum Dominum nostrum*" in many of the Prefaces recalls the priestly mediation of Christ, but that Priesthood itself is mentioned directly only in one, which is, strangely enough, the most recent of all: the Preface of Christ the King. By that phrase Christ associates us with His redeeming work.

Most of the Prefaces call upon God in the most solemn titles: "*Domine Sancte*," "*Pater Omnipotens*," "*Aeterne Deus*." (The older punctuation was "*Domine, sancte Pater, Omnipotens*.") These titles establish His claim to our worship and praise and at the same time assert the ground of our confidence in Him, particularly the most beautiful title, the most truly Christian of all: "Holy Father." All of them go to make up a contemplation, a dwelling upon God that we are to maintain during the Mass and throughout our lives; they express so well what our attitude towards God should be and how we should think of Him.

"*Per Christum Dominum Nostrum*": These words make our prayer a Christian prayer; they mark it with the sign of the cross and make it truly "*Dignum, justum, aequum et salutare*." They remind us of the priestly mediation of Christ, that we can come to God only through Christ our Lord. They also remind us that this is not merely a prayer, however holy a prayer it may be; it is an *action* in which we are engaging. Christ associates us with His adoration and His sacrifice; our "*gratias agere*" is His; we become "through Him" adorers in spirit and in truth.

There are two usual conclusions to the Preface, "*Per quem majestatem*" and "*Et Ideo*," and one that is unique: "*Qua propter*," used for Pentecost. The first presents Christ not only as priest and Redeemer but as head of all creation; even the angels can offer adoration and praise to God only through Him: "*Per quem majestatem tuam laudant angeli*." The angels are here introduced into the liturgical setting and the way is prepared for the singing of the *Sanctus*.

The last part of the Preface brings before our eyes the majestic vision of the unceasing ("*sine fine*") worship that is going on in Heaven, where the myriad angels cry aloud and join together in festive exultation ("*socia exultatione concelebrant*"). Some Prefaces mention more angels than others but always they make up an imposing array: adoring, praising, trembling with awe before God. In some of the Prefaces we ask that we may join our voices to theirs; in others we declare that we are

San Clemente
(Rome)

Ciborium Altar
(Sant Ambrogio, Milan)

Santa Sabina
(Rome)

Ciborium Altar
(The Cathedral of Parenzo)

"Lumen Christi, Lumen Mundi"
(Gospel Ambo and Paschal Candlestick,
Santa Maria in Cosmedin, Rome)

Offertory Procession
(Mosaic in Sanctuary of San Vitale, Ravenna)

already doing that. The idea is the same: the liturgy of earth joins with the liturgy of Heaven—angels and men with one mind and voice utter the very summit of selfless adoring worship: the angels' hymn, the *Trisagion.*

The Sanctus. This perfect little hymn comes, of course, from the Scriptures (Isai. 6:3) and in its original form it was hardly more than a direct quotation from that source: "Holy, Holy, Holy the Lord God of hosts, the earth is full of His Glory." The allusion in the First Epistle of St. Clement to the singing of this hymn of the angels makes it certain that it was used in the early Church at liturgical assemblies, although not perhaps at this particular point in the service. The Jews had used it in the synagogue and the Christians seem to have borrowed it from them. It appears in all the Christian liturgies and among the ancient prayers is missing only in the Prayer of St. Hippolytus. Probably it was used first in the East and later admitted into the West. When the *Sanctus* was introduced into the liturgy it underwent certain changes. To the "*Pleni est Terra*" of Isaias was added the "*coeli et,*" an apparently slight change which nevertheless adds immeasurably to the hymn: all creation is filled with the glory of God and reflects it. The liturgical text keeps the original Hebrew word "*Sabaoth*" without translating it. Here it means "Lord of all created beings," not just of the hosts of angels. Instead of "*gloria ejus*" the liturgy has "*gloria tua,*" thus making the whole hymn more direct and personal. Altogether the *Sanctus* is transformed from a hymn sung in Heaven by angels into a hymn sung throughout creation by all angels and men who unite together to sing it "*socia exultatione.*" "The glory of the Lord" which once had its dwelling only in Jerusalem now fills the whole earth.

The first petition of the Our Father is "*sanctificetur nomen tuum,*" and this "hallowing" is expressed wonderfully by the threefold *Sanctus* which proclaims that God is above all else holy with a holiness which blinds us by its light and compels our awe-struck worship. In the action which above all others adequately pays the tribute of recognition, praise and thanksgiving to God, nothing is more fitting than this canticle of never-ending praise.

Apparently those who regulated the worship of the Church in the first century felt that the *Sanctus* was, for all its splendor and appropriateness, a little too abrupt taken by itself. In any case, we see that it became the almost universal practice to add some kind of doxology to the *Sanctus* to complete it. That doxology became the *Benedictus*, the words used by the Jewish crowd hailing Christ on His entry into Jerusalem. It was adopted into the Roman Rite again from the Gallican liturgy in the seventh century. Certainly it was a happy inspiration that dictated the selection of this particular chant, for it rounds out the *Sanctus* in a wonderful manner. The connection between the two is evident and at the same time reveals unsuspected depths. It was the ancient messianic cry of the Jews taken from Psalm 117 which is the Paschal Psalm. "Blessed is He who comes in the name of the Lord" describes the work of the Redemption; sung in the Mass at this time it acclaims Christ in the fullness of His mission and work, embracing the past, present and future simultaneously. It joins the Old Testament to the New, for the glory which fills the heavens and the earth was manifested to men in its fullness at the time of the Incarnation of the Son of God. It is a shout of triumph and at the same time a petition and a prophecy.

The refrain, added now to both the *Sanctus* and the *Benedictus* is taken in part also from the account of the entry into Jerusalem, with the addition of "*in excelsis*" to the "*Hosanna.*" The latter originally meant "Save thou!" in Hebrew, but by the time of Christ had become a shout of triumph. Its association with the idea of "save" is nevertheless not without meaning to us. The words "*in excelsis*" appear to have been borrowed from the angels' hymn at the birth of Christ. Thus the entire chant is packed with allusions and rich in associations that range in short compass over many ideas. What we have here is a hymn of praise to God and welcome to Christ.

In reality the *Sanctus* and *Benedictus* go together to form one hymn with its refrain, "*Hosanna in excelsis.*" And for a long time it was sung as one hymn. The oldest musical settings of the *Sanctus* are most simple, continuing the melody of the Preface; the priest and people sang it together as they still do in some Oriental rites. This is in accord with the nature of the hymn and with the words which introduce it: "*Cum quibus et nostras voces ut admitte jubeas, deprecamur.*" The whole assembly of Heaven and the whole assembly on earth cry out with one voice. If ever there was a chant that should be sung by all it is precisely the *Sanctus*, which associates us with the angelic worship in Heaven even while we are yet on earth. Well into the mediaeval period it was taken for granted that it should be sung by the people, or at least by the clergy. However, the development of music, here as elsewhere, made it more difficult to be sung by any but trained singers.

The same cause operated to break up the hymn into two parts, one sung before the Consecration and the second part sung after it. The people and clergy could not finish the entire hymn before the priest, going ahead silently, had reached the Consecration; so the hymn was divided and the second part given a new interpretation in line with the prevailing concept of the Mass at the time: it became a choral accompaniment of the Consecration.

Father Jungmann * makes the very interesting observation that our present arrangement, which prolongs the singing of the *Sanctus–Benedictus* throughout the entire Canon, has in practice done away with the principle of silence accompanying it. The ancient current of praise, adoration and thanksgiving which was once expressed by the priest alone in the great prayer that he recited aloud is now taken up by the choir or the people

* *The Mass of the Roman Rite* (New York, 1951), Vol. II.

instead. The same thing is being done, but in a different way, and by others instead of by the priest.

While the clergy or the people sing the *Sanctus*, the celebrant and the sacred ministers with him recite it, bowing low and rising up at "*Benedictus qui venit.*" In the Roman Rite of the early Middle Ages all those standing near the altar bowed low and remained that way until the Canon was almost concluded; only the celebrant stood erect. This common recitation by the priest and ministers is a survival of the time when all sang the *Sanctus* together.

The Te Igitur. Because of the changes in ceremonial and emphasis, the *Te Igitur* came to be regarded as the beginning of the Canon and was marked as such in many ways. We know now that the Canon begins before this point in the service. Nevertheless, the arrangement of the Missal and the accompanying rites help to perpetuate this misunderstanding. The Preface is still printed as a separate part while the *Te Igitur* is begun on a new page with large print, opposite the large picture of the crucifixion that has found a place here for many centuries.

This picture grew out of an illumination of the large "T" in the *Te Igitur*. In the custom of the early Middle Ages, this capital was adorned and embellished; before long the parallel between the cross and the "T" led the illuminators to adorn the letter with a corpus, transforming it into a crucifix. It required but a step to make it into a full crucifixion scene, so that after a while there was not enough space for it on the same page and it had to be transferred to the opposite one. Naturally the picture lends a greater emphasis to this part of the prayer and contributes to making it seem like a beginning when it is in reality only a continuation.

Other factors that, externally at least, set this part of the prayer off from what preceded it and give the *Te Igitur* the appearance of a new development are the elevating and joining of the hands, the low bow and the kissing of the altar at this point in the service. All these were introduced in the thirteenth century and later; the same idea is behind these gestures that is behind similar actions at the *Gloria* and *Credo:* they are a way of placing oneself in an attitude of prayer at the beginning of an important moment. The gestures are very impressive and, consequently, give emphasis to this part of the prayer.

The section of the Canon from the *Te Igitur* to "*haec sancta sacrificia illibata*" is known as the commendation of the offering (*commendatio oblationis*). The "*igitur*," which once gave so much trouble to interpreters and liturgists, merely indicates that this is a continuation of the idea of "*gratias agere*" in the Preface: It is meet and just to give thanks; therefore we ask that God should accept and bless our offerings whereby our duty of thanksgiving will be fulfilled. We ask humbly and suppliantly that the kindest of Fathers will receive and will bless (consecrate) our gifts and our offerings. The latter are called holy and untouched sacrifices not by way of anticipation nor because they are already consecrated, but because these are the materials out of which our sacrifice is made; they have been set aside for God and are therefore holy and separate from ordinary things.

This first supplication rests solemnly upon the priestly mediation of Christ. The remarkable fact is that this phrase occurs at the beginning of the prayer rather than at the end where we might expect to find it. The question arises, is this an accident or is its position at the beginning intended to emphasize the idea that the oblation is presented to God through Christ? The repetition of synonyms ("*rogamus ac petimus, uti accepta habeas et benedicas*") expresses the intensity and insistency with which the prayer is made. The "*haec dona, haec munera, haec sancta sacrificia illibata*" are synonymous terms which cover the offerings of the faithful, the bread and wine. "*Illibata*" means untouched rather than undefiled or spotless. Like most synonyms the terms used express shades of meaning: "*dona*" is general, any gift; "*munera*," gifts made officially; "*sacrificia*," gifts made to God.

The second part of the *Te Igitur* is the prayer of intercession which indicates the intentions for which the sacrifice is offered: "*In primis, quae tibi offerimus, etc.*" This is the first of the additions to the primitive Canon spoken of above. After recommending the offering to God the Father, the Church develops the intentions for which it is offered. These are in reality the ancient "Prayers of the Faithful" (still used on Good Friday when they are called the *Orationes sollemniores*), much reduced and transferred to this spot. We can see parallels of phrasing and words between this part of the Canon and the *Orationes*.

The sacrifice that we offer to God will be *profitable* to us also; so we ask that the blessings which come from it may reach first of all the Church herself, described here by her two finest titles: Holy and Catholic. The first title is the most ancient descriptive adjective applied to her: she is the holy spouse of Christ, washed clean in the blood of her Spouse; she is the assembly of the saints; she is the mother of saints. The second title is almost as old and almost as perfect a description as the first: she is Catholic, destined for all men and all nations. We ask for this Holy Church the external blessings of peace and protection from enemies, and the more important internal graces of unity ("that they may all be one") and the guidance of God through His Holy Spirit ("*adunare et regere*") wherever the Church may be ("*toto orbe terrarum*").

There is one official who symbolizes and represents the unity of the Church in each diocese, and who has been placed there by the Holy Spirit to rule the Church of God: that is the bishop. Originally only the local bishop was mentioned: *papa* once meant any bishop, but was later restricted to the pope. Outside Rome the words "*et antistite nostro N.*" were added to avoid confusion; our Canon now prays both for the symbol and the center of unity in the Church at large and in each diocese in particular. "*Et omnibus . . . fidei cultoribus*" is an ancient addition which refers not to the faithful but to the other bishops throughout the world, who are the real "*cultores* *fidei": "*maintainers of the catholic, apostolic and orthodox faith." The faith is designated by its ancient titles: it is catholic, for the whole world; apostolic, coming from them and resting upon their teaching; orthodox, the *true* faith.

In bygone days the Catholic sovereigns were mentioned after the bishop: "*rege nostro*" or "*imperatore nostro,*" but this is no longer the case, except in Belgium.

Memento of the Living. This part of the Canon grew out of the practice of mentioning names "*infra mysteria,*" those whose intentions were specially recommended to God at a very sacred moment in the liturgy because they had made offerings for the Mass or for some other reason. The names were once read aloud; this custom was discontinued because it gave rise to pride and vanity, and also no doubt because the rest of the Canon was said in silence, and it was felt that the names should be said in silence too. This was called the "reading of the diptychs"; the names of those to be prayed for were inscribed on folded tablets. After a time the formula was extended so as to cover all those present: "Be mindful, O Lord, of Thy servants and handmaids"; "*famulorum famularumque*": "The members of the household," the "*familia*" of God. The names are recited silently or even only mentally by the celebrant. ". . . *et omnium circumstantium*": "and of all here present"; originally the faithful were gathered in a semi-circle around the altar. ". . . *quorum tibi fides cognita est*": "a tried faith known to Thee"; ". . . *et nota devotio*": "Thou hast experienced their attachment." The latter two phrases treat of the dispositions of those who offer the Sacrifice or for whom the Sacrifice was offered. "*Pro quibus tibi offerimus*" is a more recent addition inserted in the Canon when the people had taken to having the Sacrifice offered rather than assisting at it and "offering" it themselves; *i.e.*, when the idea of the people offering the Sacrifice with the priest had grown dim.

The original or primitive text was a clear affirmation of the part of the faithful in offering the Sacrifice: the "*sacrificium laudis*"—"who offer Thee this Sacrifice of praise." There is no restriction nor qualification here; the faithful do not appear in the Canon as mere passive spectators. It remained for a later age, an age that had grown accustomed to an idea we are familiar with in our time to the effect that "the Canon does not concern the people," to qualify the original statement to a certain extent by inserting "*pro quibus tibi offerimus vel*" before it.

The last part of this section of the Canon deals with what men hope to obtain from the Sacrifice, ". . . *pro se, suisque omnibus*": "for themselves and all belonging to them." ". . . *pro redemptione animarum suarum*": "for the salvation of souls"; the hope of salvation is more solidly established with the phrase, ". . . *pro spe salutis*"; and health of body and mind is granted "*et incolumitatis suae*." These last two are Roman terms; in the terminology of Latin Christianity "*salus*" means health of soul, and "*incolumitatis*" health of body. "*Tibique reddunt vota sua*" is a biblical expression inspired by Psalm 115, meaning that the faithful brought their offerings to the altar and there dedicated them to God in sacrifice. "*Vota*" is, then, a synonym for "sacrifice," or at least for "prayers."

Communicantes is part of the sentence above rather than a new sentence, although it is printed that way in the Missal. The entire paragraph is in reality a development of the *Memento* and the favored reading is: ". . . *tibi reddunt vota sua aeterno Deo, vivo et vero, communicantes et memoriam venerantes*." The underlying idea is to join the Church on earth with the Church in Heaven; we are in communion with the whole vast assembly of the elect in Heaven when we offer this Sacrifice, and we do not forget the honor that is due them. It is not a familiar communion in the sense of over-familiar, but one tinged with becoming veneration: ". . . *et memoriam venerantes*."

Faith and confidence in the communion of saints is expressed throughout the prayer: we are in communion with the saints in offering the sacrifice to God; we venerate them; we have confidence in their merits and prayers; we expect the help that this protection affords us.

The saints mentioned are either those most pleasing to God or the martyrs most honored at Rome. First of all, there is the Blessed Virgin Mary, appearing under her most solemn titles, "*. . . gloriosae semper Virginis Mariae, Genetricis Dei et Domini nostri*"; then the twelve Apostles and twelve martyrs. That the list contains no confessors is an indication of the antiquity of the prayer. It is appropriate that in the great sacrificial prayer there should appear the names of the martyrs who most perfectly shared in the Passion of Christ, headed by the name of her who is the Queen of the Martyrs. The names also remind us that this is a Roman prayer written for use in the Roman Church. New saints have never been permanently added, though the Church has expanded far beyond the limits of the time and place in which the prayer was written, an indication of the conservative tendency of the Roman Rite. "All the saints" are grouped together after those whose names are mentioned specifically.

The list of saints was deliberately arranged in a harmonious and even hierarchical order: first the apostles, then bishops (mostly of Rome with one exception), deacons (e.g., Laurence), clerics (e.g., St. Chrysogonus), and finally laymen (John, Paul, Cosmas, Damian). The list is also arranged in chronological order.

For certain older feasts (Easter, Ascension, *etc.*) the *Communicantes* is expanded by a phrase which alludes to the mystery of the day. This is a later (sixth century?) development and amounts to a special commemoration, or *anamnesis*. In reality it breaks the thread of thought which normally joins the *Communicantes* with the saints. The clauses thus introduced into the Canon contain some very rich theological thought bearing on the great mysteries of the Church's year: ". . . *diem sacratissimum celebrantes, quo Dominus noster unigenitus filius tuus, unitam sibi fragilitatis nostrae substantiam in gloriae tuae dextera collocavit.*" (Ascension.) *

For the first time in the Canon, this part of the prayer concludes with "*Per Christum Dominum Nostrum.*" From the ninth century on "Amen" was added each time this phrase occurs; as a result the oneness and unity of the Canon appears to be broken up and the unique character of the final "Amen" is not as pointed as it once was.

Hanc Igitur. Originally this prayer was intended to recommend intentions of those who made offerings or for whom the offerings were made. It was a more special *Memento*, not just a duplication of the foregoing but a more detailed and specific listing of intentions. That is why it varies (although the variety is not as great as it was at one time!). In form and content it resembles a litany: ". . . *quaesumus, Domine, ut placatus accipias: diesque nostras in tua pace disponas, atquae ab aeterna damnatione nos eripi.*" As we have seen, it was not in the primitive Canon of the Church of Rome but is a later (fifth century?) addition. The *Hanc Igitur* was the last part of the great prayer to be revised or added to; the phrase, "*diesque nostros in tua pace disponas*" was added by St. Gregory I (604) in the days of the Lombard invasions.

"*Servitutis nostrae*" refers to the clergy and means "the offering of thy servants"; ". . . *sed et cunctae familiae tuae*" refers to the laity or the Church as whole, God's family, the community, His household. The offering we are making and the sacrifice we are offering is the Sacrifice of the whole Church;

* "*Infra actionem*" was originally a rubric printed before the variable *Communicantes*, indicating that though printed outside the Canon it was to be said within it. Later both rubric and *Communicantes* were printed inside the Canon.

everyone has an interest and a share in it. " . . . *diesque nostras . . . et in electorum grege admittas*": we ask for peace and blessing in this life and a happy ending of that life, first of all, by a negative request "deliver us from eternal damnation," and then by the positive and touchingly beautiful "*et in electorum tuorum jubeas grege numerari.*" The traditional concept of the sheepfold and of the Eternal Shepherd are implied here. The Good Shepherd gathers all His elect into His flock and leads them to an eternal pasture. Here and there through the Canon exquisite little touches such as this make us sense how deeply mystical this prayer is, how thoroughly saturated with the fragrance of Christian antiquity. The imposition of hands over the chalice is a rite introduced in the fourteenth century to emphasize the idea that this is a sacrifice of propitiation. The high priest in the Old Law laid his hands in this way over the scapegoat which represented the sins of the people.

Quam Oblationem. With this part we rejoin the ancient Canon and resume the line of thought which was to a certain extent interrupted by the intercessory prayers added later. It is a kind of prelude to the words of institution, the *epiclesis* of the Roman Rite. By it God is called upon to take this bread and wine and make it the Body and Blood of Christ, which is the traditional concept of the much discussed and greatly disputed *epiclesis*. The calling down of the Holy Spirit, so emphasized in the Oriental rites, appears to have been unknown in the Roman liturgy.

"*. . . in omnibus, . . . benedictam, . . . facere digneris*": "Deign to bless it in every respect." "To bless" here means to consecrate. "For the service of thy people," says the Roman Pontifical in the Rite of Ordination to the Priesthood, "may they change the bread and wine into the Body and Blood by a spotless blessing."

The other terms are borrowed from Roman law: "*adscriptam*": "registered"; "*ratam*": "ratified, approved"; "*ratio-*

nabilem": spiritual and, consequently, "*acceptabilem*": acceptable to God; that it may become for us the Body and Blood of Christ.

The Consecration. The words of Consecration, as we have them in the Missal, are deliberately arranged in a symmetrical order, as befits something which was intended to be recited or sung aloud, as the Canon once was. What we have now is in reality a hymn, a sacred narrative with the rhythm and flow of a song.

The actions which accompany the words are intended to illustrate very literally the idea that the priest is doing what Christ commanded, that the Priest is in fact letting Christ speak and act through him. So we see that there has always been a tendency to recreate the whole episode, as it were, by a faithful reproduction of what Christ did at the last Supper.

The words of institution are not detached from the context of the Canon; the prayer continues to be addressed to the Eternal Father, and we are recalling before Him the events of the Last Supper. All the liturgies are more or less at one in the form used for the words of institution and in the phrases which introduce them. This indicates a great reluctance to tamper with "what has been handed down." Yet the actual words used are not altogether the same as those used in the Gospel texts. We seem to have here a separate account which, while it parallels those of the Gospels, is independent of them, existing before they were written down, a witness of the oral, liturgical tradition of early times.

The whole rite is invested with great solemnity by the use of such words and phrases as ". . . *in sanctas, ac venerabiles manus suas*"; "*hunc praeclarum Calicem*"; "*novi et aeterni testamenti*"; "*pro vobis et pro multis effundatur*"; "*mysterium fidei.*" This is indeed the heart of the sacred rite and we are made to feel it.

"*Qui pridie*" is peculiar to the Western rites; Eastern rites use "the *night* He was betrayed."

". . . *in sanctas ac venerabiles manus suas*": here the expansion of the phrases used in the Gospels results in a phrase that is majestic and also very ancient; it is found in St. Clement of Rome, and is probably apostolic in origin.

". . . *elevatis oculis in caelum*": a sacrificial action mentioned in the Gospel at the multiplication of the loaves.

". . . *tibi gratias agens, benedixit*": the Eucharist; the idea of consecration is here conveyed: by the great Eucharistic prayer the bread and wine are dedicated to God, blessed and consecrated.

". . . *fregit, deditque discipulis suis*": the priest recalls the entire action, though in re-enacting it he himself does differently. The Sacrifice is a Sacrifice-Banquet; the bread is broken and shared.

"*Simili modo postquam coenatum est*": again the priest recounts the way our Lord did it: "after He had supped." The Church has fused the two separate actions into one, an instance of a legitimate development of the rite.

". . . *hunc praeclarum calicem*": a dramatic identification of the chalice with our Lord's chalice and reminiscent of Psalm 22:5, ". . . how excellent my cup is."

". . . *bibite ex eo omnes*": all who are Christ's are invited to eat and drink of this banquet.

". . . *Calix Sanguinis mei*" points to the Cross; here we have the concept of sacrifice, an offering even unto blood, unto death.

". . . *novi et aeterni testamenti*": this is another scriptural reference: "*mandavit in aeternum testamentum suum*"; by His Blood Christ seals a new alliance, a new covenant with His people, a new and better one, first of all, because of the Sacrifice of Christ, but the accent is not placed upon that fact. Rather we see the Church (". . . *nos servi tui, sed et plebs tua sancta*") gathered together in one assembly, conscious of what she is and what she is doing, speaking and acting, doing without hesitation what she has been commanded to do, and which will always be her first and greatest function: "We, Thy holy people, offer a victim to thy Majesty." The prayer tells more than the meaning of the Sacrifice; it reveals much of the meaning of the Church herself: she is a holy people, a priestly society. The priestly dignity of each one of its members is affirmed concisely and unforgettably in a phrase that recalls in a flash the imposing words of St. Peter in his first Epistle (1 Peter 5).

"*. . . nos servi tui*": the clergy; "*. . . sed et plebs tua sancta*": the people—who are "God's holy people"; "*. . . tam beatae Passionis, etc.*": the Eucharist commemorates and celebrates the whole redeeming work of Christ, sees it as completed. That is why the Second Coming was mentioned here as it is even today in the Oriental liturgies and in the Ambrosian Rite. The Eucharist looks to the future as well as the past.

The Elevation. In the early Middle Ages and up until the thirteenth century the priest held the host up before him while he said the words of Consecration. This meant that the people, whose interest in the Real Presence had grown very much during the preceding century, were in danger of adoring the host *before* it was actually consecrated. To guard against this danger, and to make sure the faithful would know just when to adore, the Bishop of Paris, Eudes de Sully (1208), ordered that his priests were to elevate the host above their heads after they had said the words. This practice spread and finally became the law for all. The genuflections were added later and became of obligation only in 1570.

The mediaeval desire to see the host made the elevation a very popular gesture. People did not feel the same about the chalice; so it was not until the fourteenth century that this was introduced, apparently out of a desire for symmetry.

The raising of the chasuble was necessary when all priests wore the ample chasuble. Now it is only a ritual survival of a once practical action. Incense and the ringing of bells were added out of reverence during the later Middle Ages.

As a result of all this, a result altogether unforeseen, the Elevation and not the Consecration (and certainly not the Great Prayer) has become in practice the high point of the Mass. The idea of the Sacrifice is obscured, and attention directed to adoration of the Blessed Sacrament. In the popular mind and estimation a secondary aspect of the mystery of the Eucharist has became the primary. Devotion to the Real Presence is lawful and demanded by the nature of the case; however, we must make it clear, as the text of the Canon makes it clear, that we do not come to Mass primarily to adore the Blessed Sacrament but to offer sacrifice in and with and through Christ.

Unde et memores. This is the moment when the Church declares what she is doing, comments upon what is being done, interprets its meaning. Moreover, the Church expresses her will to offer the sacrifice to God and tells why she is offering it. This is all done in the form of a prayer, a prayer which takes up the last words of the Rite of Institution: "As often as you do this, you do it in memory of me." The transition is marked by the "*unde*."

The Church, in response to the Lord's command, makes *anamnesis* (a recalling and a memorial) of His redeeming work and she does that by offering a sacrifice to God. The actual offering of the sacrifice is done quickly, but the prayer that explains its meaning must of course take more time.

In this latter prayer we find two elements; the *anamnesis* and the Offering; the Commemoration is alluded to first but the accent is upon the offering whereby the *anamnesis* (commemoration) is made. The recalling or commemorating is very brief: a statement that the act that has been done fulfills the Lord's command; it "proclaims the death of the Lord until He comes again." His death is seen as a triumphant gesture, as the *Transitus Domini,* involving the totality of the Redemption and the redeeming Sacrifice. "Wherefore . . . we Thy servants and Thy holy people also, *recalling* Thy most blessed Passion, but also Thy Resurrection from the dead and Thy glorious Ascension into heaven, offer thee. . . ." We must remember, if we wonder at the brevity of this *anamnesis*, that the recalling in the full sense of the word—the grateful, prayerful, adoring remembrance of Christ and all that He has done for us—has been the theme of the entire Mass up to this point; His memory has been evoked in the lessons, prayers, and chants and our devotion awakened and nourished from the beginning of the Mass. An *objective anamnesis* is the meaning here; the rite that we perform does the recalling.

The second theme of the "*Unde et memores*" is much more developed: the offering of the sacrifice. This is the part of the Canon which more than any other tells what the Mass is and makes clear that it is a memorial Sacrifice. Almost as striking is the fact that this prayer so fully shows what the Mass is and links it up so unmistakably with what He did; the Mass is presented exclusively as the Sacrifice of the Church. We are doing what He did, but it is we who offer the sacrifice. ". . . *offerimus praeclarae majestati tuae, de tuis donis, ac datis*": the Church offers to God from His own gifts the most pleasing victim of all. The transcendent greatness of God is alluded to; we offer in tribute to the Lord of creation that which He Himself has made. ". . . *hostiam puram, hostiam sanctam, hostiam immaculatam*": this is a sacrifice immeasurably superior to all others. Christ is the only victim pleasing to God. ". . . *panem sanctum vitae aeternae*": this Sacrifice is also a banquet leading to eternal life. Christ is Himself the Bread of Life; His Blood is the Chalice of salvation.

"*Supra quae propitio*": this prayer looks to the frame of mind with which we offer the sacrifice; only with the proper dispositions will our sacrifice, insofar as it is ours, be acceptable to God. We offer it, but we ask God to look favorably upon it and to accept it. To ensure His favorable glance we put ourselves in the frame of mind of those who offered perfect sacrifices in the Old Law: Abel, who was a just servant of God, His "child"; Abraham, who was above all else faithful and the father of believers; Melchisedech, who was penetrated with the ideal priestly sentiments, detached from earth and dedicated to God. We associate our sacrifice, the interior frame of mind which is supposed to be behind the external objective sacrifice, with theirs; we choose the best sacrifices of the Old Law because the sacrifice we are offering is the complete and perfect sacrifice that they prefigured, announced and pointed to. Allusions such as these are in line with the viewpoint taken by the early Church that the Old Testament was not superfluous nor outmoded, but always that it led us to the New Testament. The Old Testament belongs to the same history of salvation, is, in fact, the earlier chapter thereof. Thus we see the sacrifice of Abraham as announcing and foretelling the sacrifice of Christ a frequent subject for Christian iconography, particularly in the catacombs. There is a continuity here, realized upon our altars, between these sacrifices and the one perfect offering. "*In figuris praesignatur, dum Isaac immolatur*" (*Lauda Sion*).

"*Sanctum sacrificium immaculatam hostiam*" was introduced into the prayer by St. Leo I as a protest against the Manichees who despised the material creation and particularly looked on wine as evil in itself. Originally the phrase referred only to the bread and wine offered by Melchisedech. The sacrifice offered by Melchisedech prefigured an infinitely more holy offering and victim; it was a holy sacrifice because it was something created by God ("*semper bona creas!*").

"*Supplices te rogamus*": this part is related to the above more than it is an independent prayer by itself. It is not enough to offer sacrifice to God nor to have Him look graciously upon it; He must set His approval upon it; He must accept it and place it among His possessions, just as one who is given something must accept it before one can say it is truly a gift. So this prayer asks for the definite acceptance of the gift by God. It recalls the altar standing in Heaven on which the angel places the sacrifices (perfumes) and prayers of the saints. May our offering be taken up by the angel and placed upon this altar. This is bold and daring language indeed and it is little wonder that some liturgists found this prayer so difficult to understand and comment upon. But it has many parallels in other liturgies, and the idea that the angels play their part in the sacrifice as they played it in the Incarnation and Redemption is an old one in the Church. The "*haec*" in the prayer refers to the *oblata* and then to our sacrificial frame of mind which stands behind the offering and makes it truly ours. The altar of earth gives place in this prayer to the altar that is in heaven which is the true Christian altar.

"*. . . per manus sancti Angeli tui*": the original form was "*sanctorum angelorum*," many angels. "*. . . ut quotquot ex hac altaris participatione*" is a prayer for the fruitful reception of Holy Communion. We receive it from the altar; the Mass is a sacrifice-banquet; the Communion completes it, makes it completely our sacrifice. Consecration and Communion go together. "*. . . omni benedictione caelesti et gratia repleamur*": the Eucharist is the source of all graces and blessings; particularly in this context it is that which makes us live a heavenly life. During this prayer the priest suits the action to the word, bowing low at "*supplices*," kissing the altar when reference is made to the sacrifice, making the signs of the cross upon the *oblata*, and finally blessing himself at "*omni benedictione, etc.*" All these actions, here as elsewhere in the Canon, serve to intensify what is being said, deepening and strengthening the ardor and the spirit of humility which the prayer expresses. The final gesture, as it were, draws the blessing upon the celebrant.

The Memento for the Dead and the *Nobis quoque* are later additions to the Canon. Normally the action of the Mass passes rapidly to the solemn doxology and the showing of the elements to the people as an invitation to Communion.

Memento of the Dead. "Etiam" links the prayer to the last part of the petition just made: "fill us with heavenly blessings and grace; be mindful also of those who have gone before us." The Memento of the Dead did not form part of the Canon of the Mass of Sundays and feasts originally, but was said on week-days and funerals. This restriction, however, was removed in the Middle Ages.

"*. . . qui nos praecesserunt cum signo fidei*": the Lord's servants and handmaids are never called "dead"; they have merely "gone before us." The sign of faith refers to Baptism and indirectly to all the sacraments, particularly Extreme Unction and Viaticum. "*. . . et dormiunt in somno pacis . . . in Christo quiescentibus, locum refrigerii, lucis, et pacis*": all these phrases are reminiscent of the catacombs "penetrated with the perfume of the Church's spring time," as one author beautifully expresses it. The first two phrases allude indirectly to purgatory, but "*locum refrigerii lucis et pacis*" is a brief and exceedingly rich description of heaven.

The inclination of the head at the conclusion of the prayer is explained as having been introduced here during the Middle Ages in line with the tradition of mediaeval allegorism to remind us of the death of Christ upon the cross.

"Nobis quoque peccatoribus." After the prayer for the living in general and the prayer for the dead, the priest would naturally pray for himself and for the whole clerical order. Apparently that is what this prayer was, at least originally, when, like the Memento of the Dead, it was not said in every Mass but only at certain times. The designation "*peccator*" occurs frequently in early mediaeval literature. It may be regarded now as another prayer for all the members of the Church, but originally it was a prayer for the celebrant and the sacred ministers. We have just asked a "place of refreshment, light and peace" for those

who have gone before us; now we ask that we, too, may have some part in that same blessedness, and that we may attain to fellowship with the saints in Heaven. There is an accent of humility about the whole prayer that fits in well with its modest beginning: ". . . *partem aliquam*"; ". . . *non aestimator meriti sed veniae largitor.*" Entry into this company is one of the fruits of the Eucharistic sacrifice. The Roman Rite is unique in that it has two lists of saints in the Canon. The second parallels the first except that it lists several women saints, all of them honored specially at Rome. For some reason St. John the Baptist and St. Stephen were omitted from the first list, but they are now included here, along with SS. Matthias and Barnabas.

The raising of the voice at "*Nobis quoque*" is explained as a signal to the subdeacons, who stood around the altar with heads bowed since the *Sanctus,* to stand erect and prepare for the Rite of Communion. When the Canon was said aloud this signal was unnecessary, but when it became a silent prayer the subdeacons had no other way of knowing that the priest had reached this part of the Mass.

Striking the breast at "*peccatoribus*" is a natural gesture.

"*Per quem haec omnia.*" The last part of the Canon is not a petition in the sense that the main body of the great Prayer is; rather it is a statement of fact ascribing glory and praise to God: it is a doxology. The first words of this doxology have caused much difficulty to scholars and liturgists; these words can be fully understood only when we know that for a long time a blessing of the fruits of the earth was inserted here and the words are all that is left of that blessing. Even today the oil of the sick is blessed at this point in the Mass on Holy Thursday. The words were at one time a kind of little hymn magnifying the creator of "*haec omnia.*" Now the phrase is narrowed down or restricted to the bread and wine which are no less the results of God's creative power and share in a double way the blessing brought to the world by the Incarnation. Behind this prayer is the idea that all created things have been sanctified by the Incarnation, that the material has become the channel of the spiriual. That is true of all created things; how much more true is it of these "*haec omnia*," the bread and wine that now rest on the altar!

"Through whom [Christ] O Lord, Thou dost always create, sanctify, quicken, bless, and bestow upon us all these Thy gifts." This is in reality a hymn in honor of the *Logos*, "by whom all things were made"; "all things were made by Him, and without Him was made nothing that was made" (John 1:3). He is the source of all creation, and at the same time the source of redemption.

In the context of the Mass we may give further and deeper meaning to the prayer by interpreting it thus: "Through whom you always create these good things [the Bread and Wine], you sanctify them [by Consecration], you fill them with life [supernatural and natural life], you bless them [instruments of blessing] and you bestow them upon us [Holy Communion]. In this way they contain a synthesis of the Mass: Offertory, Consecration and Communion. The Eucharist is the compendium of all good things.

"*Per Ipsum*." As we might expect from the nature of the Canon, it closes with a doxology in which the Church glorifies God "by Him": as the Head of the Body and the High Priest; "with him": joined to Him and united with His sacrifice; "*in him*": by virtue of His grace. This is a Christian doxology rooted in the Scriptures, Pauline and Joannine in inspiration. The ancient rule was that public prayers should close with a formula such as this, which would recall that the fundamental purpose of all prayer is to make the creature bow down in adoration before his Creator. This doxology is remarkable for the fact that it not only gives glory to God, which all doxologies do, but it makes that glory pass to God through Jesus Christ.

The phrase "*in unitate Spiritus Sancti*" is, according to some, but another way of referring to the Church, which is gathered into unity by the Spirit "*spiriti sancti congregati.*" All honor and glory goes up to God through Christ from the Church. He does not appear before His Father alone, but as the Head of a praying body, the first-born of many brethren; they, in turn, appear only with Him and make their prayer through Him.

More than any prayer of ours, more than all our prayers taken together, the Eucharistic sacrifice is the real glorification of God. All the meaning of our Christian life is stored up in it, all the final meaning of creation and redemption, all the meaning of Christ and His Church.

It is here, when we see the whole Church gathered around the altar, that we appreciate the full meaning of the words of the prophet Malachias: "From the rising of the sun even until the going down, my name is great among the Gentiles: and in every place there is sacrifice and there is offered to my name a clean oblation" (1:11).

With these final words of the Canon go a series of actions which have to be seen in their historical setting to be properly understood. They culminate in what is called (perhaps not so happily) the Minor Elevation.

In the developed Roman Rite described for us in the *Ordo Romanus Primus*, the archdeacon lifts the chalice and holds it before the pope who then sings the doxology, touching the rim of the chalice with one of the loaves of consecrated bread (his own). This was a very simple rite used at this point in the Mass until the eleventh century; the idea was that the bread and wine went together to make up one mystery.

After the year 1000, instead of merely touching the bread to the chalice, it became customary to make signs of the cross with it. To symbolize the five wounds, five crosses were made. Since this could not be done (at least at low Mass) with the chalice held in the air, the latter was left on the altar until the "*omnis honor et gloria,*" thus diminishing to a large extent the ancient gesture of offering which once took place here. Later, further alterations were introduced—some would say mutilations—by replacing the chalice on the altar and genuflecting before the final words, "*Per Omnia Saecula Saeculorum.*" It was this gravely altered doxology that obtained by the end of the Middle Ages and then passed into the Missal of Pius V. As a consequence, the doxology is split into two and the "*Per Omnia Saecula Saeculorum,*" which really concludes the Canon with its all-important final "Amen," appears to be merely the introduction to the *Pater Noster.*

The "Minor Elevation" is in reality a gesture of offering made to God; unlike the "major elevation" its purpose is not primarily to show the sacred species to the people. Indirectly, however, it indicates that the great prayer is over and the time for Communion is at hand.

The "Amen" made by the people at this point is a sign of approval, sanction, and confirmation of what the priest has done. It is their assent, solemnly given to the corporate action of the whole Church, like a signature on a document. Great importance has always been attached to this sign. Even when the Canon began to be said in silence, those who celebrated the liturgy insisted that at least the last words be sung so that those assisting could sing the "Amen." No one would have dreamt of suppressing it, or of having the priest say it. It is a word that expresses the assent of faith to what has been done at the altar and completes the effective participation of the people in the sacrificial action; it is also an expression of solidarity in a *corporate* action. The many signs of the cross made in the course of the Canon are best explained as a kind of gesture fitting in with the oratorical and rhetorical character of the prayer whereby its meaning is pointed up and emphasized.

The Sacrifice-Banquet

The very nature of the sacrifice that Christ left to His Church demands that it be completed by the eating and drinking of the Body and Blood of the Victim. For it is essentially a supper:

the Supper of the Lord, the great feast which gathers the Church together to enter into most intimate Communion with her Lord and with one another. In fact, the word Communion itself originally referred to the union between the members established by their partaking together of the One Bread. Holy Communion is not a kind of optional adjunct to the Mass, but is so much a part of it that we can scarcely separate the Communion from the Consecration.

At first there were no special rites preparing for Communion, which followed immediately after the great prayer. Gradually, however, beginning in the fourth century, a number of practices and prayers began to surround the last part of the Mass and in time made it stand out more clearly from what preceded it.

Among all these prayers and rites the most venerable and most natural was, as we would expect, the *Pater Noster*. The Lord's Prayer owes its present place in the Mass to St. Gregory the Great, but very likely was used in the liturgy from at least the fourth century. Certainly it is a very natural and fitting introduction to Holy Communion, not only because it asks for our daily bread (which commentators always interpret to mean first of all our Eucharistic food) but also because it is so penetrated with the corporate spirit: a community prayer in the fullest sense. Because of its accents of praise and thanksgiving (in the ancient sense) it is most appropriate for the Mass which is the sacrifice of praise and thanksgiving. Indeed we may say that it parallels the great prayer of Consecration in content and even in expression. Moreover, the Our Father has always been one of the greatest treasures of the Church, long a jealously guarded secret from those outside. Altogether it is inconceivable that it should not find its place, and that an honored one, in the Holy Sacrifice. In most of the Eastern Rites the Our Father is sung by the people; in the West it was sung by the people in the Gallican Rite; in Spain the people took part by saying "Amen" at the end of each clause. Such participation of the people in this greatest prayer of the Mystical Body is eminently appropriate and most meaningful, but the Roman Rite has always reserved it to the priest who is here the spokesman of the assembly. Even in the Roman Rite, however, the people join in the final part.

So holy and sacred a prayer should have some kind of preamble or introduction. At least there is one provided for it in all the ancient Sacramentaries. Ours is unvarying but in other Western Rites different preambles were used according to the feast or the day. We say this truly *daring* prayer, we call God our Father, because Christ taught it to us and the great teaching of the Gospel is precisely this—that by the Holy Spirit we call God our Father.

The *Pater Noster* is a eucharistic prayer because it is directed to God the Father; it glorifies Him, "*sanctificetur nomen tuum*"; it longs for the final coming of His kingdom, "*adveniat regnum tuum*" (every Mass anticipates this and brings it about). It prays for the perfect accomplishment of His will, "*fiat voluntas tua*"—the Mass recalls the perfect obedience of Christ. "*Panem nostram quotidianam*" refers of course to the Eucharist. Then there is the prayer for forgiveness of sins which prepares us for Communion and at the same time is one of the fruits of the Sacrifice. The forgiveness of injuries and the fraternal love that it implies are also fruits of the Eucharist, the "*vinculum charitatis.*" Deliverance from evil and rescue from temptation are accomplished by the Holy Sacrifice of our redemption.

The Libera Nos. The expansion of the last clause of the Lord's Prayer is called the "embolism"; it develops the petition for deliverance from evil and makes a positive plea for peace. This is found in most liturgies: it was once recited aloud in our Rite, as it still is on Good Friday and at all times in the Ambrosian Rite. This is natural enough inasmuch as the prayer is a kind of continuation of the *Pater,* which is sung aloud. It was changed to a silent recitation about the year 1000 for symbolic reasons.

Peace is the theme of the latter part of the *Libera*—"mercifully grant peace in our days"—as it is the dominant theme of this part of the Mass. Peace is one of the great effects of the Eucharist: first of all, peace between man and God, then peace between the members of the Christian family.

The invoking of the saints is natural enough but the mention of St. Andrew almost by himself is surprising. The usual explanation is that his name was added by St. Gregory I who had a special devotion to him, but it may be that it was placed there because of the special veneration in which he was held at Rome. In the past, other saints' names could be added *ad libitum.*

At this point the subdeacon brings the paten to the altar, from which he had carried it at the Offertory. The reason for this is that in earlier times the paten was so large that it had to be removed after the Offertory. As it is needed again for Communion, it is returned. The deacon kisses it respectfully and passes it to the priest who since the twelfth century blesses himself with it and kisses it also. He then slips it under the large host. Formerly other particles were put upon it.

The Fraction. The breaking of the bread, or "*fractio panis,*" has been a characteristic rite from the first, so much so that it gave its name to the Mass itself. This breaking of the bread before Communion is found in all rites and was natural enough in the days when the host was in reality a loaf of bread. The gesture of breaking was both practical and symbolic of sharing in the same bread. This fraction was a very imposing ceremony in the early papal Masses. The pope first broke off a fragment from one of the loaves which he himself had offered and left it on the altar. Then he went to his throne where the clergy gathered around him, and all together broke the bread given to them. It was then distributed to the people and part of it placed in special containers to be carried to other churches as a token of Communion. This piece was known as the "*fermentum*." Then the pope broke off another piece and put it in his chalice, saying as he did so: "*Fiat commixtio et consecratio*." So there were two fractions and one *commixtio*.

Later on the host was broken into three pieces: one for the *commixtion*, one for the Communion of the priest, one for Viaticum or for other communicants. This practice prevailed even after small hosts had been introduced for Viaticum and general Communion.

In our modern Mass the priest breaks the host in three and makes the sign of the cross with one of the particles, saying "*Pax Domini sit semper vobiscum*." Then he drops it into the chalice. According to the best explanation of this exceedingly complicated and obscure part of the Mass, the priest is not continuing the action of the pope mentioned above, but he is performing another rite altogether, the reason for which no longer exists. The priest or bishop in the outlying churches who received the *fermentum* dropped it into the chalice at the words, "*Haec commixtio*." The priest still drops a piece of the host into the chalice, but it is a piece of his own host, not a piece of the pope's or bishop's host, as it once was.

This *fermentum* was an ancient custom springing from the idea, very strong in the early age of the Church, that the Eucharist is the sacrament of unity and the bond of peace, so much so that ideally all should gather around the one altar and receive from the one bishop. That was not always possible, but it was possible to represent the idea symbolically.

When the Roman Rite passed over into the Frankish lands, the Church there knew nothing about the *fermentum* but knew that there were two fractions and *commixtions* in the Roman Mass. The Frankish church at first adopted them both, but after a while abandoned one before Communion and kept only the other at this point, giving it a new symbolic explanation. But the "*Pax Domini*" remains to tell us of the ancient custom; it was an appropriate formula for that action: the Eucharist symbolized unity and peace between the churches which sent and received it.

The purpose of the *commixtion* would seem to have been partly symbolic: to represent the unity of the two species. It was also practiced in the earlier Mass for other reasons which at present are not sufficiently clear. In any case the *commixtion* has been taken out of its proper place which was just before Communion.

The Agnus Dei. This beautiful chant, so appropriate for Communion time with its evocation of the Victim of the sacrifice and of the Paschal Lamb (the Mass is the offering and the consuming of the Paschal Lamb; we partake of His sacrifice and share in it), was introduced about the seventh century to accompany the solemn rite of the *Fractio Panis* described above. It was sung by the clergy and the people. Now it is a kind of Communion chant and lends itself to that interpretation, but it was introduced for other reasons. In the Oriental rites from which it was borrowed, it had long been associated with the suffering and death of our Lord and was addressed to Christ as the Victim of sacrifice in the Eucharist: a kind of hymn or series of acclamations. As it was to be sung by the people, it was written in the simplest music (our modern requiem Mass chant preserves the melody). Later on that music became more elaborate and therefore the hymn ceased to be sung by the people.

When the great fraction disappeared from the Mass (ninth and tenth centuries) the *Agnus Dei* became associated with the ceremony of the *Pax,* and the third "*miserere*" gave place to "*dona nobis pacem.*" When the *Agnus Dei* was still a fraction chant it was sung an indefinite number of times; later the number was fixed at three. "*Dona eis requiem*" was added for requiem Masses in the eleventh century.

This ancient and noble chant opens up to us the magnificent perspective of the Book of the Apocalypse, recalls the Lamb standing as though slain, and the whole Church in Heaven and on earth gathered together for the nuptial feast of the Lamb, whose nuptials were first celebrated in His blood. We think of His suffering and death, of His triumph and of His glory.

The Kiss of Peace. Nowadays the Kiss of Peace is exchanged during the singing of the *Agnus Dei,* which was formerly sung during the Fraction. The "*Pax Domini sit semper vobiscum*" was at one time the signal for this rite which in the Roman Rite took place not at the Offertory as in the other liturgies, but quite *appropriately before Communion.* At first it consisted of turning and kissing one's neighbor; later on the kiss was transmitted from the celebrant throughout the congregation and became a stylized action. In some Oriental rites the kiss is merely a bow, and in our own it is little more than that. The ancient *osculum pacis* has given place to the more reserved gesture with which we are familiar; even that is now confined to the clergy.

Unlike the sign of the cross, or the genuflection, or other signs which have been preserved among the people, the Kiss of Peace has become a purely clerical ceremony. Yet it is the consecrated sign of fellowship and union, the *vinculum pacis,* intimately bound up with the very idea of Communion. The Eucharist should have as one of its chief effects to attach us more closely to the Church and to one another.

The main reason why the kiss is not given in requiem Masses is that they were originally private or votive Masses added to the main Mass; people did not communicate at them. That is also why in these Masses the paten is not taken from the altar and returned to it: there was no need of using it.

The Communion. The three prayers said by the priest after the *Agnus Dei* were private prayers that found their way into the Missal at a late date. The prayers which accompany the reception of Holy Communion by the priest are the result of attempts to fit appropriate words and prayers to the action.

The *Confiteor* and the prayers which go with it were once

said for Communion outside Mass and found their way into the Missal by the thirteenth century. The prayer "*Corpus Domini Nostri*" is an expansion of the original "*Corpus Domini!*" said by the priest before he administered Communion. The answer was "Amen." In the early days of the Church and for several centuries the Eucharist was received into the hand, with the communicant standing. The custom of placing it in the mouth is mentioned in the sixth century, but for a long time the two methods were used. There was a Kiss of Peace given before the Communion, which now survives only in the kissing of the bishop's ring.

Although Communion under both species, with the deacon acting as minister of the chalice, was the normal way of receiving Communion down to about the twelfth century, the Church has never made a principle out of it. Abundant evidence shows that Communion was received under the form of bread alone, or of wine alone, in the early days of the Church. The change to the universality (among Latins) of Communion under one kind was gradual and was brought about by considerations of reverence. No one felt indignant at the "withdrawal of the cup from the laity" until the period immediately preceding the Reformation.

The whole concept of the Mass as a Sacrifice-Banquet makes it not only natural but imperative that Communion should be given from hosts consecrated at that Mass. The modern practice of giving Communion from the tabernacle during Mass goes back only to the seventeenth century, and must when examined appear undesirable because it undoubtedly obscures the connection between the Mass and Holy Communion. That is what is behind Pius XII's earnest recommendation that Communion be given with hosts that have just been consecrated, allowing for reasonable exceptions.

Once the celebrant has consumed the Precious Blood and has given Communion, if there are any other communicants, he goes on to purify his fingers and washes the chalice. This is a natural action but it was many centuries before it became the ceremony we know today. For some time the second ablution was not drunk but poured into the *sacrarium*. Of the two prayers which accompany the rite the first is ancient in origin and the second mediaeval.

Communion Antiphon—Postcommunion

Just as the Introit and Offertory chants were introduced to accompany the procession, so it was with the *Communion* antiphon. Originally a whole psalm was sung during the rather long time during which Communion was administered. The psalm was selected for its appropriateness: e.g., Psalm 33: "Taste and see how sweet the Lord is." By the twelfth century the chant was sung after the Communion and in a shortened form. Unlike the Introit it has retained only the antiphon. Very often the antiphon does not allude directly or obviously to the Holy Eucharist but to the feast that is being celebrated. Nevertheless, it is remarkable how many can be seen to have at least an indirect allusion to the Blessed Sacrament (Mass of St. Thomas, Pentecost, Confessor Pontiff). The more modern Masses and some of the Sunday Masses have direct allusions to the Communion just received.

The source of many of the Antiphons is the psalter, but the Gospels and Epistles contribute their share, and occasionally some other books of the Old Testament. Now and then we have one that is non-scriptural. Sometimes the Introit antiphon reappears as the Communion. Only one preserves the ancient form of antiphon and verse. Psalms are selected which have antiphons that can be used as refrains.

When the Church teaches us she also directs us and forms us; we should, hence, enter into the dispositions and resolutions suggested by the antiphon, as we have here a practical direction for our piety as communicants.

The Gospel antiphons are adapted to Communion in a particular way. They make us contemplate Christ in one of His mysteries. They speak directly of the Eucharist, repeat an order, a promise, a word of encouragement from Christ. Sometimes the Gospel of the day is linked to the eucharistic action.

The Mass comes to an end once the Communion is over. The Prayer of Thanksgiving is said and the Dismissal follows immediately thereafter. The former is called the Postcommunion Prayer. In the Masses of ferias in Lent there is another prayer *Super Populum* which was at one time a blessing given at all Masses, and later restricted to the penitents.

The Postcommunion, though it nearly always at least alludes to the Communion, is not very often a *thanksgiving prayer*. It is usually a petition for some grace called for by the occasion or feast. Structurally, it parallels the collect, and in some of the later Masses has undergone the same loss of simplicity we have noted in the modern collect. Our *first* Communion prayer should be a prayer in union with the Church. Receiving Communion should not separate but unite.

The doctrine and practice of the Eucharist are set forth in the Postcommunion: it satisfies us, fills us, remakes us, recreates us, sustains us; it is our nourishment, our food. "*Actu et fructu*": sign and *effect*. The effects are that it produces or accomplishes what it signifies, that it penetrates us, possesses us, transforms us, lives and perseveres in us, makes us new and sanctifies us, brings knowledge and vigor. "*Beneficia potiora sumamus*": it makes us partakers of divinity; it is the pledge and promise of future glory; it assures us of redemption and salvation. It acts upon our conduct: we are led not by nature but by grace; it purifies, heals and renews, sows seeds of eternal desires; it is a remedy. The Eucharist builds up the Body of Christ that is the Church. It assures the progress of the Christian in faith and growth in the love of Christ.

One idea becomes clear when we examine the pages of the Missal, the writings of the Fathers, the accounts of the Communion service given us by St. Augustine and others, and that is the great change in the way people have come to look upon the Eucharist and specifically upon the act of Holy Communion. To those in the early Church, Communion was the bond that united the faithful together in one body, which bound the community together. While it united the faithful Christian to Christ, through Him Communion united them to one another. For the early Christians, Mass was a community act, a social act, the sacred common action of the Family of God, wherein the needs of individuals gave place to the collective needs of the Church.

The modern concept, which had its inception in the Middle Ages, is much more individualistic. Men tend to look upon Communion as anything but a social act; instead, it is for too many a purely private and personal affair, bound up with the pursuit of one's own perfection. Even when it is accompanied by a desire to share in the passion and death of our Savior, that too is often viewed in an altogether subjective and individualistic way. There is nothing wrong with such a view in itself, but it is incomplete and needs to be corrected and brought into focus by grasping the complete doctrine of the Church as it is presented in the Postcommunions.

Ite Missa est—Benedicamus Domino—Blessing

While nearly all liturgies have some formula for dismissal, the Roman Rite seems to have always had "*Ite, Missa est*" at this point in the service. It means: "Go, it is the dismissal," which is often taken by modern liturgists as a command to bring the Mass into our daily lives. The alternate form, "*Benedicamus Domino,*" came into use for the days when the Mass was followed by Vespers, for which the people stayed. It is now used in any Mass in which the *Gloria* is not said. The association of "*Ite, Missa est*" with the *Gloria* caused it to be omitted from requiem Masses. For these latter it became a general custom by the twelfth century to substitute "*Requiescant in*

Pace." The "*Deo Gratias*" merely means that the people have heard the announcement made by the deacon.

The Mass should logically end at this point, but here again we see the introduction of what were once private prayers said after Mass into the rite itself. The "*Placeat*" was a private ejaculation said by the priest as he took his leave of the altar by kissing it respectfully.

The *Blessing* began with the custom of the pope or bishop to bless the people on his way to the sacristy. Priests had begun to do this by the eleventh century. Our present form was fixed only in 1604.

The Last Gospel. The prologue of St. John's Gospel was an object of special devotion from the earliest times and increased in popularity during the Middle Ages, when an almost superstitious reverence was paid to it. Naturally it found its way into the Thanksgiving prayers said after Mass. At first, the Last Gospel was said on the way to the sacristy (bishops still must say it on the way to the throne after pontifical Mass); it did not become part of the Mass until 1570.

During the Middle Ages people had a great and at times almost a superstitious veneration for the practice of reading the prologue of the Gospel of St. John, and it appears that the custom of saying it after Mass was influenced by this veneration. The restored order for Holy Week eliminates the Last Gospel from the Masses said during that time—an indication that it will very likely disappear entirely from the contemplated Mass Ordo of the future. It is hard to see why it should not disappear and for the same reason that the practice of reading the gospels of commemorated Masses was discontinued: the Gospel of the day is the climax of the first part of the Mass—any other must be anti-climactic and therefore superfluous.

But as long as it remains part of the Mass rite, we are justified in seeing it as a daily reminder to us that its words have this day been fulfilled in our ears: "The Word became Flesh and dwelt amongst us"; the Mass continues and prolongs the Incarnation and its effects among men. All of us can echo the words of St. John: "And we saw his glory, glory as of the only-begotten of the Father—full of grace and truth."

The *Prayers after low Mass* were added by Leo XIII and St. Pius X. They may be omitted on certain days, which is an indication of their recent character. These prayers are almost the only instance (with the sermon) of the use of the vernacular in the Mass, if indeed they can be considered liturgical at all.

Thanksgiving After Mass

After celebrating Mass the priest is directed to recite appropriate prayers on his way to the sacristy and while taking off the vestments. These prayers consist of the Hymn of the Three Youths in the fiery furnace, a Canticle which summons all creation to join in praising God; Psalm 150, which bids the various members of the Church to praise and glorify Him; a brief litany with the Our Father and a series of appropriate versicles and responses; and, finally, three ancient collects. This is called the *Gratiarum Actio post Missam* and as a general practice goes back to the year 1000. Apparently it was once recited at the altar or in the sanctuary, at least in certain places.

The orations, which now number three, were at one time only two: the "*Deus qui tribus pueris,*" a prayer that was associated with the Canticle of the Three Youths, and the "*Actiones nostras,*" a prayer for God's blessing at the beginning of any work. The third prayer, which refers to St. Lawrence, is a much later addition and finds a place here because of the similarity seen between the circumstances of the sufferings of the three youths and the passion of St. Lawrence.

The theme of praise characteristic of the ancient idea of "thanksgiving," which includes blessing and magnifying God and proclaiming His excellence is expressed in this Canticle and this psalm; they thus continue the line of thought of the Mass itself, the *Sacrificium Laudis.* It is altogether natural and inevitable that there should be some such service of praise at the end of Mass, and certainly the *Benedicite* and Psalm 150 are well suited to this purpose. They also have the merit of not being too long and thus allow time for silent or private prayer. While there is now no evident precept enjoining the recitation of these prayers, they should not be omitted; they are the official "thanksgiving"; it is in the spirit of the Church to recite them, and they ensure some kind of prayer at this time. The devout recitation of this *gratiarum actio* and at least some of the prayers which follow them, is an excellent way of "making a thanksgiving," a practice which is so warmly recommended to priests and even enjoined upon them by law. For the ideal "thanksgiving" should cause us to be pervaded with the spirit of the Eucharist, which is a spirit of praise and sacrifice and makes us bring our lives into conformity with the mystery we have celebrated so that our whole life becomes itself a "thanksgiving"—"*In gratiarum actione semper maneamus*."

The Participation of the Faithful

One great fact stands out clearly in the minds of those who study the history and development of the liturgy of the Mass, and it is that the Mass was intended to be in every sense a *community* action. This becomes a conviction that is strengthened as one goes more deeply into the subject. From beginning to end the whole structure and content of the Mass proclaim that it is a service in which all are to join. Throughout it is a dialogue between priest and congregation; the faithful are constantly being addressed and constantly called upon to respond. The lessons are directed to them as are the chants, which are supposed to be sung by them. Even the Canon, which was once too exclusively regarded as a kind of private domain of the priest, clearly appears as a prayer intended to be declaimed aloud in the presence of the faithful, and it is still provided that they should give their assent to the sentiments expressed by saying "Amen" at the end. The priest is clearly the one who *leads* the assembly in prayer; he is not at the altar merely in *persona Christi* but also as the divinely appointed spokesman of the people, who expresses the sentiments and wishes that they have (or should have), and who guides them in a common action. He is not only a celebrant, but a *president*.

The growing realization of this great fact, or rather the *recapturing* of an idea that has been lost, has given great impetus to attempts at encouraging congregational participation. This is done not only by having the people sing their parts in the Mass, which is the ideal, but even by having them answer their part at a low Mass. This is surely to be encouraged whenever and wherever possible. Nor should it be regarded as a kind of concession; it could be demonstrated easily that the faithful have a right to answer their part at Mass. The only reason they do not do so more commonly today is that by the late Middle Ages the people no longer knew the responses; hence, they neither sang them at high Mass nor said them at low Mass (at least not generally, although the practice was kept up in some places). But the faithful did not thereby lose the *right* to answer. It is true that the server was directed to say the responses in the name of the faithful, but he was never intended to supplant them.

We do not mean to assert that everyone should be forced to answer the Mass prayers, but that those who wish to answer should not be deprived of the right to do so; we cannot *forbid* them to answer any more than we can forbid people to take an active part in the recitation of the rosary or any other prayer. At the very least the dialogue Mass is but one way of assisting at Mass; and one may follow any way of assisting at Mass. If the dialogue Mass had not fallen into disuse no one would look upon it as anything but normal and proper. (It is worthy of remark that all the other prayers said in the vernacular in Church—prayers after Mass, divine praises, litanies, rosaries, Our Fathers, Hail Marys—are always dialogues, answered by the congregation or recited together by priests and people, which indicates that the practice of answering prayers in Church services *is normal* and *natural.*) As it is now, the dialogue Mass is a method that has not only the approbation but the *explicit encouragement* of the Holy See. The only warning issued by the Pope in *Mediator Dei* about it is that we must not prefer it to the high Mass. With this there can be no quarrel: the ideal and the desirable is the high Mass; and if possible, the sung Mass should be a daily affair, the normal way of celebrating the Holy Sacrifice. But if that is not possible, the community aspect of the Mass should nevertheless be retained and people should be instructed in the idea that they are taking part in a common and corporate action when they go to Mass, and that it is not a private devotion. If they are instructed in this often enough and are encouraged to take their part, they will want to do it themselves, as the enthusiastic reception of the new Holy Week has strikingly demonstrated.

There are various methods of making the Mass a community celebration. The most obvious one is to have the faithful at least *answer* the prayers and respond to the greeting of the celebrant. During a low Mass, parts like the *Gloria* and *Credo* might be recited in English; and when the people have made some progress, the Introit, Gradual, Offertory, and Communion antiphons might be added to the list. They should have an experienced priest or layman to lead them.

The permission of the bishop should be asked because the law seems to demand it; besides, if he encourages it the practice has a better chance of succeeding.

The dialogue Mass can be taught to a congregation starting with the children; where there is a parochial school this should not be at all difficult. The children will thus learn from early youth that this is the normal and natural way to participate in the Mass.

Another way of having the congregation participate in the low Mass is to sing hymns during Mass. The hymns should bear some relation to the Mass or the liturgical season. There are many good hymns that can be sung, hymns that present the doctrine of the Church in an objective manner suited for congregational use. But these hymns should not be sung during those parts of the Mass which are to be said aloud; that is specifically forbidden. If the organ is played during Mass, it must be played softly during those parts which the celebrant says aloud.

We can easily see in the legislation with regard to the singing and the playing of the organ at Mass that the Church wishes to safeguard the reading of the texts. They take first place, and following them is regarded as the normal and natural way of assisting at Mass. They are indeed the Church's way of recalling and commemorating Christ and His redeeming work, and following them is abundantly indicated as the preferred way of joining with the Church in offering a particular Mass. They set the standard and express the norm. No matter what concessions be made to those who cannot or will not follow the texts, they remain the Church's own way of celebrating and "proclaiming the death of the Lord until He come again."

As the Holy Father has said:

> The Christian community is in duty bound to participate in the liturgical rites according to their station. . . .
>
> Strive earnestly, by methods and means which your prudence judges most effective . . . that the Christian people take such an active part in the liturgy that it becomes a truly sacred action of due worship to the eternal Lord in which the priest, chiefly responsible for the souls of his parish, and the ordinary faithful are united together. . . .
>
> Indeed it is very necessary that the faithful attend the sacred ceremonies, not *as if they were outsiders or mute onlookers*, but let them fully appreciate the beauty of the liturgy and take part in the sacred ceremonies, alternating their voices with the priest and choir, according to the prescribed norms.*

The case for the dialogue Mass has been greatly strengthened

* *Mediator Dei* 199, 192.

by the insistence upon *participation* in the new order for Holy Week. People are certain to ask why participation should be confined to one week of the year or why it should be *commanded* then while only *tolerated* at other times. It seems only logical, too, that we cannot expect people who are silent all during the year to become vocal and articulate for one week. Participation and the desire to participate must be the products of an atmosphere of community awareness and this atmosphere must be built up and maintained over a longer period. In any case, it is quite clear that participation is no longer looked upon as a fad or an eccentricity, if indeed it ever could be regarded as such.

CHAPTER 15

The Sacraments

The sacraments are signs that bear witness to the presence of Christ and His action among us. They are in the direct line of the redemptive Incarnation and make the Lord present in His person and in all His saving work. They show that Christ is acting in our midst as well as speaking to us and they are prolongations of the Incarnation and Redemption. In this sense Christ is Himself the Great Sacrament; through His Passion and cross He became an outward sign of inward grace, effecting what He signified.

The sacraments are also prophetic signs of the world to come. They point out the kingdom as well as introduce us to it. They bear witness to the salvation for all men that is in Christ and point to the new creation that will reach its term in the kingdom of God. Of that new creation they are at once the advance notice and the realization. The sacraments proclaim the King that is to come and at the same time call attention to His presence among us. They announce the final end of all things and point to the salvation that will be fully accomplished only then; yet they make that salvation enter into the here and now. By them and through them the Savior lays His hand upon us, and the blind see, the lame walk, the deaf hear, the dead rise again. "Power went forth from him and healed many" (Mark 3:10; Luke 6:19). "The events of our Savior's life are passed over into mysteries [sacraments]." *

The union that the sacraments bring about between Christ and His people is not merely a moral or a psychological one. It is a real union, a vital contact. We find Him there more than anywhere else. He *speaks* to us in His Word, through prayer and devout reading, through sermons and spiritual conferences, but He *gives* Himself to us in the sacraments. "I find thee in thy mysteries." † "You are dead and your life is hid with Christ in God" (Col. 3:2). "It is now no longer I that live, but Christ lives in me" (Gal. 2:20). It is no accident nor coincidence that the greater part of those texts of the New Testament which deal explicitly with the union between Christ and Christians are texts that speak of Baptism and the Eucharist.

Finally, the sacraments are corporate and community acts; they not only unite us to Christ but to His Body which is the Church. Baptism before all else joins us to the people of God, and establishes us in the covenanted relation to Him; the Eucharist renews and deepens the effect of Baptism and continues to build up the Body of Christ. Penance restores us to full membership in the flock of Christ. Social and communal acts as they are, they must be set in the framework of the community. The real meaning of St. Cyprian's "*Extra Ecclesiam nulla salus*" is precisely that salvation is mediated to us through the sacraments which are in the keeping of the Church and are a function of the assembly—the *Ecclesia*.

The saving work of Christ is carried on, then, through these sacred actions which prolong His Incarnation and make His redemption accessible to all men, and which are called sacraments. (*Sacramentum*, an oath taken by soldiers, came to mean

* St. Leo *Sermo*. 74, 2
† St. Gregory Nazianzen

"mystery," a sacred action by which the past is made present.) The great sacrament, crown and center of the others, is the Eucharist, which contains Christ Himself and in a special way. All the others are related to it and presuppose it. The liturgy is preoccupied with the rites and formulae by which the sacraments are brought to men and which set forth the meaning of each one. The sacraments must be seen as a whole; they are not separate, unrelated entities, but extensions of the priestly activity of Christ.

Christian Initiation: Baptism and Confirmation

Entrance into the Christian community is marked by an outward rite that is both a sign and a cause of the inward reality that one has been conformed to Christ. This entrance is called initiation and often is equated with Baptism, which is indeed the great sacrament of Christian initiation. In reality initiation into the Christian Church is not a single act but a series of acts or a process by which we are transferred from darkness to light, a process begun in Baptism, but brought to perfection in Confirmation and completed in the Eucharist.

Baptism is in the truest sense a new beginning: it is a rebirth, a new creation, in which our sins are washed away and we are incorporated into Christ; we truly "put on the new man who is created according to justice and true holiness"; we are signed with the seal that shows we belong to Christ; we become children of God and inheritors of the promises. The rite of Baptism must convey all this to us because it is a sacrament, a sign that points to and describes the change that has been made in the soul of the baptized. It does that by a most enlightening array of rites which themselves provide the great commentary on Baptism itself.

The aspect of new birth was brought out more clearly in Christian antiquity when the candidate for Baptism was plunged into the font and rose up out of the water, but now, in the Roman Rite at least, that aspect of the symbolism of Baptism is not so clearly shown. Yet, needless to say, the sacrament itself represents a new birth. Baptism is no mere outward sign; it presupposes and at the same time indicates that the person being baptized believes in Christ and has accepted the "good tidings," the gospel of salvation. Because it is the sign that the Christian believes, it is called the sacrament of Faith. Faith means the opening of the eyes of the mind to spiritual realities and thus brings enlightenment with it, which explains the great name by which this sacrament was known in the early centuries: *Illuminatio,* enlightenment. To be baptized was to be enlightened.

This faith comes only by hearing, so that Baptism demands some kind of preparation: a progressive instruction in the truths of faith, and a period of time during which the candidate is instructed in the meaning of the Christian life. At first this period was very short, at times non-existent, but by the second century at least a longer preparation called the *catechumenate* was everywhere observed in the Church. Those undergoing that preparation were called *catechumens,* "hearers"; a most important part of their instruction for Baptism was to *hear* the word of God in the Holy Scriptures. When they had reached a certain stage in their training, they were marked more immediately for Baptism and became *electi,* those chosen for the sacrament in the near future. This "election" usually took place at the beginning of Lent on the year they were to be baptized. During that Lent the *electi* now received instruction in the Apostles' Creed, which is a summary of the great Christian truths, and they were expected to know this Creed by heart.

The Our Father was regarded as the special and peculiar prayer of the Christian; it is not only a prayer but an instruction in the way to pray. As Easter drew near they were taught this prayer for the first time and committed it to memory. Even in our own day the candidates for Baptism (or their sponsors when the candidates are infants) are required to recite the Apostles' Creed and the Our Father before Baptism.

The last step in this preparation for Baptism was the exorcism or driving out of the evil spirit, a rite which was performed some days before Easter. In the early days of the Church and indeed well into modern times the Christians adopted a rather realistic attitude towards the presence of Satan in the world and the domain that he exercised over fallen and unredeemed man; they had a corresponding appreciation of the strength and extent of Christ's victory over the demon won by the cross. Hence, the insistence upon the exorcism, whereby Satan is driven out and the lordship of Christ proclaimed. This rite of exorcism is now part of the rite of Baptism itself. By it the devil is put to flight and the way prepared for Christ. Its meaning and significance are no less true and pertinent today because we moderns tend to regard it, and the uncompromising language in which it is expressed, as strange to our ears.

When the feast of Easter had arrived and the candidate presented himself for Baptism, he first solemnly renounced Satan and his works and pomps; then the candidate expressed his faith in Christ. Both these actions were in the form of answers to questions that were put to him: "Do you renounce Satan?"

"I do renounce him."

"Do you believe in Jesus Christ . . . ?"

"I do believe."

(The same procedure is followed today in conferring Baptism.)

Standing in the waters of the baptistery, the candidate first turned to the West, the region of darkness, to renounce Satan; then to the East, the abode of light, to profess his faith in Christ. Immediately before Baptism he was anointed with the oil of the catechumens, an anointing directed against Satan. After that he was finally plunged into the water three times in honor of the Holy Trinity whose names are invoked in the rite:

"I baptize thee in the name of the Father and of the Son and of the Holy Ghost." To baptize meant originally to dip, or better still to drench, a meaning clearly brought out by the ancient manner of baptizing. Nowadays in the Roman Rite we pour the water on the head, but Baptism is still by immersion in the Eastern rites, as well as in the Milanese Rite. Even in the Roman Ritual immersion is still provided for wherever it is the custom, "*ubi mos est.*"

Another anointing followed immediately, this time with Holy Chrism, intended to show that the newly baptized belonged to Christ, the Anointed One, and that they shared in His anointing. This same rite is observed in our own day and carries the same meaning with it.

The white cloth placed upon the newly-baptized in the modern baptismal service is all that remains of the robes once worn by neophytes for some time after their Baptism.

In the early centuries Confirmation immediately followed Baptism, after which the new Christian was admitted to the community of the faithful, there to take part in the Holy Sacrifice for the first time.

During the fourth and fifth century, the rite of Baptism was augmented by such additions as the sign of the cross made upon the forehead of the candidate, the laying on of hands during the exorcism, the *exsufflatio,* and the giving of salt. In the course of the centuries that followed, the ceremonies of Baptism were shortened and gathered into one rite. This abbreviated version appears in the Ritual of 1614. For children, the rite was shortened even more. Nevertheless, it retained all the elements of the ancient rite with certain changes.

During the later Middle Ages the custom grew up of giving a saint's name in Baptism.

Symbolism of Baptism. Baptism represents a cleansing from sin and at the same time a new birth brought about through association with the death of Christ and His Resurrection. The pouring of the water is a sign of cleansing; the fact that it covers the head of the baptized symbolizes the burial with Christ, a symbolism naturally much more evident when the whole man went down into the water. The words of St. Paul serve as the classic exposition of the relation between Baptism and the Death of Christ: "Do you not know that all we who have been baptized into Christ Jesus have been baptized in his death? For we were buried with him by means of Baptism into death; in order that, just as Christ has arisen from the dead through the glory of the Father, so we also may walk in newness of life" (Rom. 6:3–4).

The pouring of the water in the form of a cross shows that grace comes to us through the Passion of Christ, and the form "in the name of the Father and of the Son and of the Holy Ghost" shows that the person baptized is solemnly dedicated to the Holy Trinity and marked with the sign making him belong to the Three Persons. Baptism is an outward sign that the candidate is sealed by the spirit of God, made a child of God and set aside for the possession of eternal life. The anointing with the chrism of salvation and the clothing with the white garment represent the holiness that comes to us through this sacrament. The neophyte has become like Christ (*christos*—the Anointed One) and shares with him the dignity of the priesthood and kingship.

The decline of adult Baptism which came about with the gradual conversion of Northern Europe brought about changes in the structure of the baptismal font; it was no longer necessary that it be capable of accommodating grown-up persons. Apparently, too, the reluctance to plunge infants in northern lands into the cold waters helped to bring about the change from immersion to infusion.

The place of the sacrament of Baptism in the life of the Church is clearly seen in the rite of the blessing of the waters of Baptism—during the great Easter Vigil—which has been brought into greater prominence recently by being done in the sanctuary where it can be seen by all. Originally, of course, the blessing of the baptismal water took place with a view to its immediate use in the sacrament that was to follow that very night, a circumstance that gave the whole rite an immediacy and appropriateness that is not so apparent if no Baptism follows. Happily, in accordance with the wishes of the Holy See, the custom of baptizing at least one person at the Vigil is growing; certainly, there could be no better way of bringing home to all what Baptism really means to the person being baptized, to the Church at large, and to a particular congregation.

The water to be used in Baptism has not always been blessed beforehand, but the practice is nevertheless very ancient. Behind it is the scriptural idea of clean water and of freeing it from the power of the devil and calling God's blessing upon it to make it an instrument of spiritual cleansing, which it could not be in itself. Consequently, the most ancient forms of blessing the font comprise two elements: an exorcism and an *epiclesis*. The form now used is substantially that found in the Gelasian Sacramentary (seventh century), and it is probably older than that.

The rite begins with a prayer to God that He should be present in these mysteries and sacraments and should send forth the spirit of adoption to create anew the peoples which the font of Baptism will bear to God: the font is considered as the womb of the Church. A preface modelled on the ancient Eucharistic prayer and rich in doctrine follows. The Spirit of God brooded over the waters at the beginning of the world to fill them with sanctifying power; God wiped away the crimes of the world with the deluge, thereby showing that through water there would be an end made of sin and a beginning of holiness; now may He look upon the face of His Church and multiply new births in her. He gladdens His holy city with the tide of His rich graces and opens the fountain of Baptism for the renewal of the nations throughout the world; by the command of His majesty the Church may receive from the Holy Spirit the grace of the only-begotten Son. May that same Holy Spirit make fruitful this water prepared for the new birth of men, that a heavenly offspring conceived in holiness may emerge from the immaculate womb of this divine font, reborn to newness of life, and that grace may bring forth everyone into a like spiritual infancy. At God's bidding, therefore, may every unclean spirit depart; may this holy creature be free from every assault of the adversary; may it be a living fountain, a regenerating water, a purifying tide, that all who are washed in these saving waters may by the working of the Holy Spirit in them obtain the favor of perfect cleansing. We ask now that God will bless these waters and make them able to purify souls as well as cleanse bodies: may the stains of all sins be washed away, and our restored nature cleansed of foulness, so that every human being by entering this sacrament of regeneration may be born again into a new infancy of true innocence.

The singing of this truly magnificent preface, a real theology in prayer, is accompanied by a number of symbolic actions: touching the water with the hand, dividing the water, breathing upon it, signing it with the cross, and finally plunging the Paschal Candle into it three times. When it is over, the priest pours the oil of the catechumens into the font with the words: "May this font be sanctified and made fruitful by this oil of salvation to those who are born from it unto everlasting life." Then the chrism is poured in, while he says: "May the pouring in of this chrism of our Lord Jesus Christ and of the Holy Spirit the Paraclete be made in the name of the Holy Trinity." Last of all, he pours both oil and chrism into the water.

Confirmation, known also as the "Laying-on of Hands," "Chrismation" or "*Chrisma*," "*Consignatio*" or "*Signatio*," "*Consummatio*," "*Perfectio*," "*Signaculum*," was for a long time administered together with Baptism and even sometimes included with it under the general name of "Baptism." Nevertheless, it has always been a rite distinct from Baptism itself. In the early centuries it was administered immediately after Baptism by the bishop. The earliest rite of Confirmation consisted in the laying-on of hands, the anointing with chrism and a prayer calling down the Holy Spirit which closely resembles the prayer still used in the Roman Pontifical. It is mentioned by St. Ambrose but may be older than his time.* The laying-on of hands is, of course, recorded in the Acts of the Apostles, but the anointing with chrism is mentioned so early in connection with the rite that it too must go back to Apostolic times. It was this signing with chrism that gave Confirmation the name by which it was best known, "*Consignatio*" (signing) or "*Signaculum*" (seal).

In signing the forehead the declarative form was used for centuries: "The sign of Christ unto eternal life"; it still is in the Eastern rites: "The seal of the gift of the Holy Ghost. Amen." During the Middle Ages in the West the form became "I sign thee with the sign of the Cross . . ." The ancient rite concluded with the Kiss of Peace.

With a few changes this is substantially the same rite as that in the modern Pontifical: the stretching out of hands over those to be confirmed is the ancient imposition of hands; the Bishop at the same time says the venerable prayer calling down the seven-fold gift of the Spirit. Then he places his hand on those to be confirmed individually, signing them on the forehead with holy chrism, but the Kiss of Peace is no longer given, even though the greeting "*Pax Vobis*," which once accompanied it, still survives. Instead, the Bishop gives the person confirmed a slight blow on the cheek. This may be a survival of the Kiss of Peace, transformed into a slap during the Middle Ages, or it may be a symbolic gesture related to the mediaeval act of dubbing someone a knight, a kind of declaration of worthiness. Those who maintain that it is but the Kiss of Peace transformed have in their favor the fact that the bishop says "*Pax Vobis*" at the time he strikes the cheek. But it is not easy to be certain

* Ambrose, *De Mysteriis*, Chap. VII; *De Sacramentis*, Chap. II.

about such things. The usual explanation of the meaning of the gesture found in catechisms is a symbolic explanation which came long after the rite had developed into its present form and, like most such explanations, is of very little help in arriving at the original meaning and purpose. A blessing concludes the entire rite.

As it now stands in the Pontifical, the rite of Confirmation goes back to the eighth or ninth century, with some changes made in the later Middle Ages. The teaching of the Pontifical is extremely simple and clear: in Confirmation the Holy Spirit is bestowed. There is no attempt to go beyond that or to show why or in what manner. But the ancient practice of the Church, still observed in the East, of giving Confirmation immediately after Baptism, and the Greek name for the sacrament, "The Perfecting," indicate that this is the bestowing of the Spirit for the perfecting of the baptized Christian.

The ancient link between Confirmation and Baptism continues in the Eastern rites which permit priests to bestow the sacrament, but the insistence in the West upon allowing only the bishop to confirm led to a complete separation between the two and consequently to an obscuring in the popular mind of the relation of the one to the other. Naturally, the bishop could not be on hand (especially in a vast diocese) to confirm at once those who were baptized; they had to wait to be confirmed until he was able to get to the parish church, which might take some time. Consequently, Baptism was given independently of Confirmation more and more often, until it had become an accepted practice. The code of canon law still supposes that Confirmation will be given before First Communion, which shows that in the mind of the Church there should not be too great a delay between Baptism and Confirmation. Since 1946 the sacrament may be administered by priests under certain conditions.

After all have been confirmed, the choir sings the antiphon "*Confirma hoc Deus,*" followed by the versicles and an oration which ask that the graces of the sacrament may be granted to the confirmed in all their fullness. The whole rite concludes with a blessing expressed in a special form: "The Lord bless you out of Sion, that you may see the blessings of Jerusalem all the days of your life and may have eternal life."

In this rite the oil symbolizes the fullness of grace as well as strength, power, and spiritual health—preservation from corruption and divine enlightenment. The balsam imparts a sweet odor which makes us think of the words of St. Paul, "the good odor of Christ." The laying-on of hands signifies power from on high and the endowment with the spirit. The signing with the cross points to the source of all grace, the cross of Christ. By it the person confirmed is sealed with Christ's own mark, showing that he belongs to Christ; the mark is worn on the forehead to show that none should blush to proclaim that he belongs to Christ. "I sign thee with the sign of the Cross, and I confirm thee with the chrism of Salvation." Confirmation strengthens us and anoints us for battle with the enemy of our salvation.

Penance

Of all the sacraments, Penance is accompanied with the least ritual setting. The prayers and rites which unfold the meaning of the other sacraments are missing here. The words of the priest are hardly more than a declaration that the penitent is loosed from his sins, and there are no other prayers which clarify or develop what is said in the formula of absolution.

The administration of the sacrament of Penance has undergone great development in the course of centuries. Little used at first, because those who were baptized were supposed to have broken so completely with sin that a relapse was considered practically unheard of, the sacrament of Penance began to play a greater part in the lives of Christians when the number of converts grew and the primitive ardor began to cool. Those who were guilty of the greater sins were permitted after a long penance to be readmitted to Communion. The confession of sins was public, and when the penance was done the reconciliation was public. As the centuries went on, the season of Lent became the regular period for penance and Holy Thursday the day for reconciling the penitents. Reconciliation was made by laying hands upon the head of those absolved, and a formula or prayer was said which was in the declarative form, as it still is in the East.

During Lent there was a daily prayer said over the penitents which begged God to pardon and forgive. This prayer survives in the *oratio super populum* in the ferial Masses of Lent.

Between the fourth to the eleventh centuries, the discipline of penance was gradually mitigated; the penances were less severe; the confession itself became private, and the absolution was given at the time that the confession was made. All this was the inevitable concession to changing times and, particularly, to the influx of converts from the northern nations. The modern rite is thus considerably condensed, and as a result the essentially *judicial* character is not so easily perceived as it was in the days when the penitent presented himself before the bishop, was sentenced to perform a certain penance, performed it publicly and was publicly absolved.

During the centuries following the year 1000 the indicative forms, expressing a wish that God would pardon the sins of the penitent, formulae like the "*Misereatur*" and the "*Indulgentiam*," replaced the earlier prayer to God to deliver them from sin. In the later Middle Ages these in turn gave way to the declarative formula used today, which expresses directly the judicial or legal nature of the words of absolution.

In the modern administration of the sacrament some traces of the development it has gone through remain: confession is still public in the sense that normally it is made in church, although in secret; there is no longer an imposition of hands, perhaps because of the arrangement of the confessional; but the priest still raises his hand in absolution and the earlier forms

"*Indulgentiam*" and "*Misereatur*" remain, together with that which has supplanted them. The absolution begins with the expression of a wish, "*Dominus noster Jesus Christus te absolvat*," and we still absolve from excommunication and censure, reminiscent of the time when sins excluded people from the company of the faithful.

Holy Orders

The Priesthood of Christ is continued in His Church and given expression by the three orders, which have as their work to bring divine life to men and to nourish it in them by the Word and by the sacraments. These orders are received in the sacrament which most closely associates men to the priesthood of Christ.

The episcopate is the summit of Holy Orders and the fullness of the priesthood. The whole hierarchical organization presupposes that the pastoral office is confided to the bishop in each diocese and that he admits others to share in his office and responsibilities through the rite of Ordination to the priesthood and the Ordination to diaconate. Historically, the episcopate and, by association, the priesthood are more intimately concerned with the worship of the Church, the preaching of the word and the administration of the sacraments, while the diaconate was instituted to assist the bishop in the liturgy and in the charitable work of the Church. The other orders—those of subdeacons, acolytes, lectors—grew up either as a participation in some of the functions of the deacon (subdeacons) or as independent but subordinate to the priesthood and deacons (acolytes, readers, exorcists).

All three rites (episcopal consecration, Ordination to deaconship and priesthood) have this in common, that they consist essentially of the laying-on of hands and the great consecratory preface which sets forth the meaning of the ministry confided to those ordained or consecrated. Besides this laying-on of hands, there are a number of other lesser rites which act as a commentary upon those which are essential: the giving of the chalice and paten, the anointing of the head (for bishops) and of the hands (for priests), the giving of the book of the Gospel to deacons. These subordinate rites were added under Gallican influence in the tenth and subsequent centuries.

In the course of time some theologians, forgetting that these rites were later additions, tried to maintain that some of them were essential to the validity of the sacrament itself, but in 1947, by the constitution *Sacramentum ordinis*, Pius XII settled the question for all time, declaring that the imposition of hands and the accompanying preface were the essential rites; the others merely complete the ritual setting and serve to bring out the meaning of the essential rites.

The Consecration of a Bishop. The great traditional day for episcopal Consecration is Sunday, the Lord's Day and the day of His Resurrection. This was insisted upon in the early centuries; only in the eighth and ninth centuries were feasts of apostles allowed to become consecration days. Preferably, a bishop-elect was to be consecrated by the other bishops of the province, but in any case at least three bishops must consecrate him. The presence of three is to bring out the fact that this priest is being aggregated to the college of the bishops: it is not a matter of one individual conferring a sacrament upon another, but of a body admitting a person to its membership.

The core of the modern rite is the laying-on of hands by the consecrator and co-consecrators and the recitation of the preface which is in the traditional style of the great eucharistic prayer, with the usual introductory dialogue. This preface has been lengthened somewhat in the course of the centuries but is found substantially in the ancient Sacramentaries. The primitive rite of Consecration, as described in the *Apostolic Tradition* of Hippolytus, amounted to no more than that—the laying-on of hands and the prayer which indicated the office conferred by it. The ancient rite of the Church of Rome was of a like simplicity, except that the wording of the prayer was changed and the rite of placing the open gospel book with the pages downward upon the head of the ordinand was added, probably in the fourth century. Apparently, this latter rite was reserved originally to the one chosen to be Bishop of Rome.

When the Pontifical that had travelled north to the churches of the Frankish domains returned to Rome, it returned with a whole series of additional rites, and the modern rite of Consecration is an amalgamation of those rites originally used at Rome and those Gallican practices that had been added: the examination, the admonition, the anointing of the head, the formula "*Accipe Spiritum Sanctum*," and the conferring of episcopal insignia.

The newly consecrated bishop con-celebrates with the consecrator and receives Communion under two species; but originally and for many centuries he celebrated Mass alone. The present arrangement goes back to the thirteenth century.

The enthronement is part of the original rite; the new bishop was placed upon the *cathedra*, or seat of office, of the church over which he was to rule.

Priesthood. The Ordination to the Priesthood, even more than episcopal Consecration, has been profoundly altered from the earlier, more simple rite, which like the Ordination to the Priesthood in the Oriental Churches today, consisted only of the laying-on of hands and the usual prayer. The most ancient form of Ordination that we have, the *Apostolic Tradition* of Hippolytus, describes the laying-on of hands: done first by the bishop, then by all the priests (this action of the assisting clergy meant then what it means now; it is an expression of the solidarity among the priests themselves and with the bishop; they concur with him in this action) and the prayer which asks that God will send the spirit of His grace into the new priests to enable them to help and govern the people.

This rite was modified to a certain extent in the Church at

Rome during the period between the sixth and ninth centuries. The formulae of prayer developed into something closely resembling the present form, the consent of the faithful was formally asked, and the Litany of the Saints was added. Otherwise it remained very much as it had been from the earliest times.

Much of what strikes a modern witness of an Ordination—the admonition to the ordinands, the anointing of the hands, the vesting with the priestly vestments, the handing of the chalice and paten—were all added to the older simple rite in France and were admitted into the Roman Rite only in the thirteenth century when the Romano-Gallican Pontifical of Durandus of Mende became the official Pontifical of the Western Church. These additions can be clearly seen as an attempt to emphasize and bring out what is implicit in the ancient rite; they serve as a commentary on what must be regarded as the more important and essential rites. The consecrating preface asks that God give these men the dignity of the priesthood and renew in them the spirit of holiness. This is dramatized by vesting the newly ordained in priestly vestments for the first time and by anointing their hands, which is a symbol of the interior anointing by the spirit of God, and by giving the chalice and paten with the words: "receive the power to offer sacrifice to God . . ." a power they have in fact already received.

The chasuble folded upon the shoulders is usually explained by referring to the older form of chasuble which would need to be folded for the sake of convenience. This hardly seems to be correct. Why was it folded in back and not in front, where it would be more likely to get in the way? Rather, it would appear to have been done deliberately for symbolic reasons: The practice goes back to mediaeval times when men were not at all sure of the exact time in the rite a deacon became a priest. So the chasuble, the *vestis sacerdotalis*, was left folded until the last laying-on of hands, when it was believed that the power to forgive sins was given. That the priest was fully ordained then, there was no doubt. As a matter of fact, it is at this point in the rite that the chasuble is let down completely.

In the early centuries Sunday was the preferred day for Ordination to the Priesthood as it was for the Consecration of Bishops. Each one of the days set aside as official ordination days in the present Roman rite—the four Saturdays in the Ember Weeks, and the Saturday before Passion Sunday—has in fact superseded in this respect the Sunday which follows them: the Ordination was originally held in the early morning of the Sunday, but as the vigil service on those days was gradually pushed back into the morning of the Saturday, the Ordinations were pushed back likewise. This development has been so far forgotten that the law at present says that the bishop is to ordain on these Saturdays and may ordain on a Sunday only if he has a very good reason.

The Consecration of a Bishop gives a priest the full burden of the pastoral office. The Ordination of a Priest supposes all the way through that those ordained are set aside as the helpers and cooperators of the bishop in this pastoral office; furthermore, the words of the Ordination rite suppose that the bishop is ordaining his own priests for service in his diocese. Although men are ordained to the priesthood who are not going to be engaged directly in the pastoral office and who are often not diocesan priests at all, the words of the Pontifical have not been changed; they still take for granted that the man being ordained is called to exercise the pastoral office under the direction of the bishop. And the dominant theme of the rite of Holy Orders is that men receive the priestly dignity not for their own advantage and benefit, but as a stewardship and for the service of the Church. The grace conferred on them is the grace of holiness ("*innova in visceribus eorum spiritum sanctitatis*") which is stored up in them and from them is to pour out upon the Church. They are to build up the house of God by their preaching and example; they are to fulfill their ministry by being patterns to the flock ("*censuram vivendi suae conversationis exemplo insinuant*").

The third place in the ranks of the hierarchy is occupied by the deacons, who owe their origin to the need of providing someone to take care of the charitable works in the Church. Historically, they are in a special way the assistants of the bishop, not only in his discharge of the duty of charity, but in the celebration of the liturgy as well. In general, we may say that their function was to keep *order* in the house of God. To a large extent their duties have fallen to the priests in the Western rites, but deacons still play a great part in the life of the Church in the East, where men often remain deacons all their lives. In the West, deaconship is the necessary prelude to the priesthood. The rite as it stands takes for granted that those ordained will actively exercise the deacon's ministry although they have not done that for centuries.

The Ordination of a Deacon as described in the *Apostolic Tradition* resembled that of the priest and consisted of the imposition of hands with the prayer that accompanied it; it differed in this respect, that only the bishop laid hands upon the candidate for deaconship, "because the deacon is ordained only for the service of the bishop." * Like the priesthood the ordination to deaconship was also modified in the earlier Roman liturgy; the prayers were more developed and an ordination preface was provided. The laying-on of hands was moved from the place it originally had and inserted during the preface at the words "*Emitte quaesumus . . . Spiritum Sanctum.*" Later on in the Middle Ages this rite was further modified in the Pontifical of Durandus who introduced the custom of placing only one hand on the head of the deacon and of adding the formula "*Accipe Spiritum Sanctum ad Robur. . . .*"

The vesting of the deacon and the giving of the book with a formula parallelling that used in the ordination of priests,

* Chap. IX

"Receive the power to read the Gospel . . ." were also added in France. These modifications also passed into the Roman Rite when the Pontifical of Durandus was accepted at Rome in the late Middle Ages. The uncertainty about the precise matter and form of the diaconate was cleared up by Pius XII in 1947 when he declared that the general laying-on of hands before the Preface, together with the words "*Emitte quaesumus,*" rather than the later single laying-on of hands and the form "*Accipe Spiritum Sanctum ad robur,*" made up the matter and form.

Although subdiaconate has been counted as a major order in the West since the Middle Ages, it was originally a minor order as the very rite of Ordination to Subdeaconship in its present form shows. It follows the same pattern as the rite of Ordination to Minor Orders: there is no laying-on of hands and no consecrating preface. The giving of the book of the Epistles with the words "Receive the power to read the epistle . . ." a form modelled on that said to the deacon, and the vesting with the tunicle, all seem to have been part of a conscious attempt to put this order as far as possible in the class of a major order, assimilated to the diaconate.

The minor orders are usually explained as being developments of the diaconate, representing a sharing of the deacon's duties. That is true of subdeaconship (originally a minor order) and to a large extent of the acolythate, but it can hardly be true of the other minor orders—porter, lector, and exorcist—which had an origin independent of the deacon's office and function. They go back to the third century and during the first centuries all played an active part in the life of the Christian community. This was particularly true of the order of lector—which was held in the highest esteem (largely because of the extreme importance attached to hearing the word of God), and formed the usual avenue to advance in the Church. Acolytes, too, because of the many duties they performed relating to the worship of the Church, particularly that of carrying the Blessed Sacrament from the bishop's Mass to other churches as a mark of unity, had a high place in the ranks of the clergy.

Ordinations to the Minor Orders are first mentioned in the *Apostolic Tradition*—that for the order of lector. It is of the simplest kind, merely the giving of the book. This same simplicity, hardly more than a declaration that one is a reader, an acolyte or a subdeacon, marks the other early Ordination rites that have come down to us. Our modern Ordination, with its admonition, the giving of the instruments, and the blessing, grew up and developed particularly in France and from there passed over into the Roman Pontifical revised by Durandus.

Tonsure and the Entrance into the Clerical State. The rite of first tonsure which is the cutting of the hair and offering it to God stands at the head of the rite of Ordination—but it is not itself an Ordination; rather it is an independent ceremony. The practice of cutting the hair and offering it as a symbol of oneself and of one's dedication to God is a religious practice older than Christianity; it was adopted by the Church very early as a liturgical rite performed upon children. It is found as an accompaniment of entrance into the ecclesiastical state in the eighth century Sacramentary of Gellone. The ceremony described there is almost identical with that found in the modern Pontifical: the introduction, the cutting of the hair in the form of a cross, the final blessing. There is no vesting with the surplice, of course; the surplice did not exist at that time. Later on in the thirteenth century, when Durandus of Mende revised the Roman Pontifical for use in his diocese, he added the giving of the surplice, inspired in all likelihood by the words "*habitum religionis*" in the introductory prayer, which the surplice expressed in visible form.

Holy Communion Outside of Mass

During the first centuries, particularly during the time of persecution, the Christians were allowed to carry the Blessed Sacrament (under the form of bread only) to their homes where they kept it in a safe place and where they communicated during the week. The same practice was observed even later by those living in the rural districts who could not go to the church every day, and also by the early solitaries in the desert who lived apart from a community and were unable to get to church frequently.

The Eucharist was reserved for the sick to whom it was brought, first of all by the acolytes, then later on exclusively by deacons or priests. It was the administering of the sacrament to these sick people that gave rise to the rite of Communion outside of Mass. Those who were well received it during Mass; until relatively modern times Communion was almost never given outside of Mass except to the sick.

When Communion was brought to the sick it was usually under the species of bread, but there were times when the Precious Blood was carried alone and other times when Communion was given under both species. Once it had become the law that only the priest should receive Communion under both species, and that only at Mass, the practice of bringing Communion to the sick under both species at any time naturally stopped altogether.

The "*Pax huic domui,*" the sprinkling of the room with holy water and the *Asperges* recited by the priest were introduced before the ninth century. The *Confiteor* and the absolution survive from the custom of hearing the confession of the sick person before Communion; they are now recited whether or not he goes to confession at that time. The "*Ecce Agnus Dei*" and the "*Domine non sum dignus*" seem to have originated only in the fifteenth century in their present form. For those receiving Viaticum there is a special formula: "Receive, my brother [or sister], this food for your journey, the Body of our Lord Jesus Christ; that He may guard you from the wicked enemy and lead you into everlasting life. Amen." This formula is found for the first time in a Frankish Ritual of the twelfth century; various other forms were used for this during the

Middle Ages. The oration that follows, "O holy Lord" was in use by the ninth or tenth century; the blessing of the sick person with the Blessed Sacrament was introduced only in the seventeenth.

When Communion is given outside of Mass the recitation of the "*O Sacrum Convivium*"—the antiphon of the Office of the Blessed Sacrament with its versicle, response and collect—and the blessing of the priest closed the whole service. This was a late mediaeval addition. The entire rite was first officially set forth in the Ritual of 1614. In the antiphon, versicle and oration we find the doctrine of the Eucharist and the effects of Holy Communion most felicitously expressed: "O Sacred Banquet in which Christ is received, the memory of His Passion is recalled, the mind is filled with grace, and a pledge of future glory is thereby given us." The Eucharist is a sacrifice in which we share, that recalls and represents the whole redeeming work of Christ, lifts our minds to heavenly desires while we are still here on earth and is a foretasting of Heaven itself. Heaven is often represented in Christian antiquity and in the Scriptures under the figure of a banquet. Another aspect of Holy Communion that was much more prominent in the minds of the early Christians, that it is the bond of charity, is stressed in the prayer said during Easter time instead of the "*Deus qui nobis*": the "*Spiritum nobis domine*," which is taken from the Postcommunion of Easter: "Pour forth the spirit of thy love into our hearts, O Lord, that those whom thou hast nourished with these Easter mysteries may be of one mind in thy service, Through Christ our Lord."

Matrimony

This sacrament occupies a most special place in the Christian economy. It is not only the means which provides Christian men and women with the graces to help them to lead a holy life in the married state, but it is the great sign (sacrament) of the union of Christ and His Church, an ever-present reminder of God's great love for man, which He Himself willed to express under the singularly rich nuptial imagery of Holy Scripture. This is brought out beautifully in the brief address to the bride and groom in the new Ritual conceded by the Holy See to the Church in the United States in 1954.

The essence of this sacrament lies in the contract made between the bride and groom, but the Church has always attached a blessing to the contract itself and provided the service with a nuptial Mass since the sixth or seventh century. We know that only with the Council of Trent and with later legislation did it become necessary for this contract, which before that time had constituted in itself a valid marriage, to be celebrated in public, before the parish priest and two witnesses. The asking for and the giving of the consent, with the subsequent blessing by the priest, the blessing of the ring and of the newly-married pair, constitutes the modern wedding ceremony. During the Mass that should follow, the bride receives a special blessing.

It is most appropriate that this sacrament should be administered and received before the altar and should be followed by the Holy Sacrifice. For one thing, it is effected through the priestly power of Christ Himself, who acts here not by and through the ordained priest, but through the man and woman who administer and receive this sacrament. It is the one sacrament that can be administered only by the laity, and is a ministry exercised by them through the priesthood conferred on them in the sacraments of Baptism and Confirmation. Through this sacred contract they are to provide new members of the Mystical Body, who will gather around the altar and be joined to one another in Holy Communion. Over the children whom God may send them they will, to a certain extent, exercise the pastoral office. Furthermore, this contract is based upon sacrifice, and its success depends upon the degree to which, in submitting to the discipline of sacrifice demanded of married people, they become assimilated to the sacrifice of the cross, which is re-presented upon the altar.

The greater part of the usages and observances connected with the marriage rite, such as the joining of the hands, the marriage ring, the bridal-veil and wreath, are pre-Christian in origin. These customs were continued by the Christians but were given a Christian direction through the blessings associated with them. The couple joining hands were blessed by the priest, the ring received a special blessing, the veil was put on either by the priest or in his presence. This last mentioned rite has not survived in any form in our modern marriage ceremony, but the other two blessings remain and the prayers that conclude the marriage ceremony are to be found in the earliest Roman Ritual that we have.

The nuptial blessing, which is given to one who is a bride for the first time, has been altered since it first appeared in the ancient service books. It is in reality a treatise on the meaning of marriage, after the manner of the ancient prefaces used in the different rites of the Church. After an introductory part, it becomes a special blessing for the bride, and closes with the wish that they both may see their children's children to the third and fourth generation and reach a happy old age.

The final blessing appears to be of Gallican origin and is modelled upon the Jewish ritual blessings in the Old Testament: "May the God of Abraham and Isaac and Jacob bless you." It repeats the same wish which closed the nuptial blessing but adds the prayer that the bride and groom may attain to eternal life.

The Anointing of the Sick

The name "Extreme Unction," by which this sacrament is generally known, is explained in various ways: either as meaning the *last* of the three anointings which a person in danger of death receives, or as the anointing *in extremis*—at the hour of death. Certainly the second is the usual understanding of the term. An examination of the history of the sacrament shows that the name "Extreme Unction" goes back to the seventh or eighth century; before that it was known as "anointing of the sick," "holy oil of chrism," "mystic chrism," "holy oil." The earlier idea seems to have been that this sacrament was for the healing of the sick; only later was it so closely associated with the dying. The history of the sacrament is greatly complicated by the fact that in the earlier centuries there was a widespread custom of anointing the sick with oil blessed by the priest or bishop, whether the malady was grave or slight. Even laymen could do the anointing; all that was necessary was that the oil should be blessed. Nor is there any evidence that this anointing was ever given to those in danger of death; the main purpose seems to have been the healing of the body. Although spiritual healing was expected as an effect, it was secondary. This practice could hardly be the sacrament of Extreme Unction; it is more likely that it was a sacramental, yet it is not easy to be certain. The fact is that no other anointing is spoken of in all the documents of the first thousand years.

From the Carolingian period on both the doctrine and the practice of the sacrament became more ordered and systematized. The anointing of the sick was done only by priests and the spiritual effects received greater emphasis. For the first time this unction is related more to penance and is seen more as a sacrament of the dying than it had been hitherto. Theological thought became more clear on the nature and effects of the sacrament: the reasoning was that, since it was a sacrament, it must primarily have spiritual effects; it must be medicine for the soul rather than medicine for the body. The great effect of this sacrament must, then, be the wiping away of the remains of sin and the restoration to spiritual health. It gradually came to be regarded, to use St. Thomas' words, as the "anointing for glory" and therefore to be used only in the last sickness. This became substantially the doctrine of the Council of Trent, which was largely preoccupied with defending the very existence of the sacrament against the reformers.

The oil of the sick was originally blessed immediately before it was used, but it has been blessed on Holy Thursday at the end of the Canon of the Mass since at least the eleventh century. The oldest complete rite for the administration of Extreme Unction goes back to the eighth century; it was also the one which served as the model for all the various Rituals used during the Middle Ages and is the framework of our modern rite. The rite consisted of visiting the sickroom and sprinkling it with holy water, hearing the confession of the sick person, if that seemed necessary, reciting the seven penitential psalms, the litanies and orations, the profession of faith and the Our Father. Then the priest anointed the sick person and concluded with more prayers, gave him the kiss of peace and Holy Viaticum. It is altogether a much more elaborate rite than that we use today.

Well into the Middle Ages in the West, and even today in the Eastern rites, several priests anointed together, and the anointing was not confined to the five senses as it is today, but extended to other parts of the body as well and especially where the pain was greatest. (Was this last a survival of the time when the sacrament was looked upon primarily as a healing of the body?) These anointings were to be made in the form of a cross. It is a curious fact that in many places the rule was to repeat this anointing for seven successive days.

The greatest variety prevailed in the formula used for the anointings itself: it could be in the form of a prayer, in the form of a command or a wish, or a direct statement: "I anoint thee with oil. . . ." The form used at present is found for the first time in the tenth century, and it became general only in the sixteenth.

Of the many prayers recited either before or after the anointing to beg from God that the anointing would be profitable, only three remain today (the first two are from the ninth century, the third from the tenth). To those three, which ask for health of soul and body and make no reference whatever to death, the Ritual approved for use in the United States in 1954 adds another prayer which asks that if God should be pleased to call the person instead of restoring him to health, all his pains and sufferings may serve as a reparation for his sins.

The ancient custom was for Viaticum to follow Extreme Unction, but in later times this order was reversed. In several places throughout the Church, including the United States, the ancient order has been restored. This earlier and more traditional arrangement underlined the idea that Holy Communion, in the form of Viaticum, is the true sacrament of the dying, carrying with it, as it does, the *pignus futurae gloriae*.

The precise order of the effects of this sacrament is still disputed among theologians, but what these effects are is taught clearly enough. As with the other sacraments, the text of the Ritual and the symbolism of the sacred rites give us valuable insight into the working of this sacrament. The form used during the anointing itself ("By this anointing and his most indulgent mercy, may God forgive whatever you have sinned through . . .") is a prayer for forgiveness of sins and the wiping out of the remains of sin. The oil is a symbol of health and well-being; anointing with oil was the usual remedy against sickness in the time of Christ and for many years after His time. This anointing is made in the form of a cross, the source and the sign of eternal life and everlasting healing. Both words and actions bear witness to the spiritual healing that this sacrament brings with it. The prayers which follow the anointing are petitions for the healing of soul and body and, with the exception of the new prayer referred to earlier, take for granted that the person is going to get well. There is no reference whatever in the older prayers to death or dying. The close interrelation of the health of soul and body is constantly kept before our eyes in this sacrament, and to a very great extent it appears as an acting-out in advance of the resurrection of the body. Implicit in the healing is the idea of a strengthening of soul and body, since the two are so closely joined together that profit to the one brings profit to the other. This strengthening is of course most necessary when the Christian needs all his strength to resist effectively the power of the ancient enemy of man.

The same early Ritual referred to directions that the priest should see that the dying person has a crucifix by him, a prescription which is preserved in the modern Ritual. The sacred image of our Redeemer is in these circumstances a most powerful aid to the dying person, quickening and strengthening his faith and confidence in the merits of the sacred Passion and affording him strength and courage in his last moments.

In the new Ritual Holy Communion in the form of Viaticum regains its ancient position as the true last sacrament of the dying. This is in accord with the traditional practice regulated by the Council of Nicaea in 325. The special form used in giving Viaticum: "*Accipe, frater, viaticum . . .*" originally included a reference to the Precious Blood—"*corporis et sanguinis D.N.J.C.*" It is found for the first time in the twelfth century; our modern form is an adaptation of the longer mediaeval prayer which concluded with a reference to the Resurrection and the second coming: ". . . and may He raise thee up on the last day when He shall come to judge the living and the dead." Various other forms were used in the Middle Ages before the present one was officially adopted. We may be permitted to regret that the last clause quoted above did not remain in the final version.

CHAPTER 16

The Divine Office

"The eternal father has pre-destined us . . . unto the praise of the glory of his grace" (Eph. 1:5–6).

The Office is the prayer of the Church which she offers to God as a community through Christ and in union with Him. The eternal Word became flesh and dwelt among us so that He might reconcile the fallen human race with God and that He might restore perfect worship of God, a worship that was true and spiritual. This worship took the form of prayer and sacrifice.

The priestly prayer of Christ He willed to be continued by His Church, just as He willed His sacrifice on Calvary to be continued in an unbloody manner, and as He willed His grace to reach us through the sacraments. This prayer of Christ glorified God and was concerned with our salvation and our welfare, and so must any prayer be which continues His prayer.

Many places in the Gospels attest to the fact that Christ prayed in this way; the Epistle to the Hebrews and the seventeenth chapter of St. John's Gospel also tell us that His prayer was priestly. He taught His disciples to pray, and even commanded them to pray always. They were to pray with faith and confidence and especially (this gives a special character to New Testament prayer) in the name of Jesus; that is, by His merits and in union with Him by faith and charity, and as a member of His Body.

We can say, then, that Christ is the author of the Divine Office, not as it stands of course, but insofar as it is continual prayer in union with Jesus. The particular form that this prayer takes is determined by the Church. Christ gave His Church the fundamental law of prayer, and His apostles and their successors have the right to regulate it.

The Office has many names, and all of them are helpful to give us an idea of what it is and should be. It has been called *officium*—duty or service; *officium divinum*—divine duty or service, concerned with God and the things of God; *officium ecclesiasticum*—the official prayer of the Church which composed it; *officium canonicum*—said according to *rule; horae canonicae*—the hours said by rule; *cursus*—the prayer said in the course of the day; the divine praises; *psalterium*—from that which makes up the greatest part of it; and, finally, it is most commonly called the Breviary—meaning a compendium, an abridgement, many books fused into one (psalter, hymnary, antiphonary, lectionary, *etc.*).

It has been defined as "a determined form of public, social, vocal prayer which the Church has instituted to praise God and to voice our needs, which she has regulated, and which she performs at stated hours through the ministry of those deputed to discharge this obligation." The Office is, then, an hour prayer, a prayer that is public and common, a prayer that is vocal (yet, like all true prayer, mental as well), which has been confided to specially chosen men and women, but only in order that its recitation be assured, and not to exclude anyone from saying it who is so minded.

The excellence of the Divine Office should appear clearly

from what has been said thus far, the more so when we consider who is praying.

The Divine Office is liturgical prayer of the greatest and highest dignity; it is the prayer of Christ and the prayer of His Church, the loving and holy conversation of the beloved Spouse with her divine Bridegroom and with His heavenly Father and ours.

Part of the pre-eminence of the Office as a prayer comes from the fact that praise and adoration are its chief purpose. By contrast with other prayers that are man-centered (at least to a great extent), the Office is centered upon God and preoccupied with praise: "O Lord open my lips. And my mouth shall proclaim thy praise. . . ." "The Lord's name be praised, from henceforth now and forever."

The keynote of each day's Office is sounded by the words "*Venite Adoremus Dominum.*" Each hour is liberally sprinkled with frequent doxologies and invitations to bless God, all of which tend to remind us of the chief end of the Office, which is to praise and glorify God. Only the Mass is greater than the Office as a means of praising God; that is why the Office has been sometimes called the "*sacrificium laudis*" and we may apply to it the words of the Epistle to the Hebrews: "Through him, therefore, let us offer up a sacrifice of praise always to God, that is, the fruit of lips praising his name" (13:15).

The Office not only praises and glorifies God, it benefits us. The fruit of the Office is all those good things which come to the Church and to us through this prayer: spiritual and material blessings in abundance, particularly the grace of God, the pardon for our sins, the spirit of prayer, knowledge and instruction. This fruit comes to us according to the degree of the fervor with which we recite it. First of all, it is the prayer of Christ; He speaks with our lips and in our voice. "By assuming human nature, the divine Word introduced into this earthly exile a hymn which is sung in Heaven for all eternity. He unites to Himself the whole human race and with it sings this hymn to the praise of God." * St. Augustine expresses the idea beautifully in words quoted by the pope in the same encyclical: "God could not give a greater gift to men. . . . [Jesus] prays for us as our Priest, He prays in us as our Priest, He prays in us as our head; we pray to Him as our God. . . . We recognize in Him our voice and His voice in us. . . . Here created though not changed He assumes a created nature which is to be changed and makes us with Him one complete man, head and body." † In another part of the same encyclical the pope reminds us that "in every liturgical action Christ is present . . ." He is present in the prayer of praise and petition we direct to God, as it is written: "Where there are two or three gathered together in my name, there am I in the midst of them."

The Divine Office is the prayer of the Church, Christ's true bride and His Mystical Body diffused throughout the whole world, which through this Office "is persevering with one mind in prayer." Nor is she alone, for she is joined with the Church triumphant in heaven whose praise she echoes ("*Illi canentes jungimur, Almae Sionis aemuli*"), and with the Church suffering in Purgatory whose sorrows she commiserates. One author calls it "an exercise of the communion of saints." By and through this prayer the Church takes the place of those who neglect the duty of praising and loving God. The fact that this prayer is in reality said by the Church secures many blessings for its members, because the voice of the Bride sounds pleasantly in the ears of God. Even though the devotion of the priest may be lacking in intensity, the devotion of the Church whose prayer it is will secure God's blessing on the whole Church.

Because the Office is so fruitful for the Church at large and for those who recite it in particular, we are strongly urged by some authors to have intentions, both personal and for the

* *Mediator Dei.*
† *Enarrationes in Psalm.* 85.

Church, when reciting the Office. It does not often occur to us that here we have an excellent means of fulfilling the pastoral duty of praying for the flock committed to our care, and for the Church at large.

The History of the Divine Office

There is hardly a more difficult question in the whole field of liturgy, none so full of pitfalls for the unwary, than that of the origin and development of the Divine Office. One reason for this is the fragmentary information we have about its origins; and another is that at almost no time until the publication of the breviary of St. Pius V can we be sure that we understand what exactly is meant by the terms that are used in the documents. Closely related to this history of the Divine Office itself is the related problem of the origin and extent of the canonical obligation of the private recitation of the Office—a question that still awaits a historian.

The first traces of what were to become the canonical hours are found in the custom that Christians were to pray at certain hours of the day, attested by the *Didache*, by Tertullian, and others. The *Didache* speaks of saying the Our Father three times a day, but Tertullian is more explicit in referring not only to the custom of prayer at the third, sixth, and ninth hours, but also to the "regular prayers that are due at the beginning of day and night." * This statement exemplifies what we said above about the obscurity of the sources: Tertullian does not say whether these are public prayers or prayers said privately. However, on the basis of information from other sources—notably Origen's references in his sermons to morning and night prayers held in the churches, and Cyprian's remark that "our prayer is public and in common" (*De Oratione Dominica*) and his other admonition that we must pray in the morning and at sunset—we are justified in saying that this all points to the strong probability that the Christian Church took over *from*

* *De Oratione*, XXV.

the beginning the practice of the Synagogue and had daily morning and night prayers in common (whenever possible). That these prayers were in all likelihood modelled upon the synagogue prayers, which consisted of readings from the Scripture, psalms, and intercessory prayer, is an equally safe and valid conclusion. It is in these morning and night prayers, which later appear as Lauds and Vespers, that we find the origin and germ of the canonical hours. Side by side with these morning and night prayers, which appear to be of long standing at his time, Tertullian and other writers speak of prayers at the third, sixth, and ninth hours. These do not seem to be the same as the times of prayer mentioned in the Acts of the Apostles—indeed there is no clear indication that the Acts bears witness to a *custom* of prayers at the third, sixth, and ninth hours, as is so often asserted. Rather these times mentioned by Tertullian are spoken of as a recent custom. Where did they come from and why were these hours chosen, and finally, are they private or public prayers? The answer is that first of all these hours were the normal divisions of the Roman day and were therefore natural times for special prayer intended to sanctify the day; furthermore, they were associated by the Christians with the hours of our Savior's passion. Thus the *Apostolic Tradition* counsels prayer at the third hour, "for at this hour Christ was seen nailed to the tree"; at the sixth hour "when Christ had been hanged upon the wood, the daylight was divided and it became darkness"; and at the ninth hour, "for in that hour Christ was pierced in His side." * Other reasons are given but the chief reason seems to have been the one mentioned above, namely, that they corresponded to the hours of the Roman day. That these hours were private prayers is apparent from all the accompanying references to them, and from the absence of any reason to think that they were public. They were to become public prayers in time, however, as we shall see.

* Hippolytus, *Apostolic Tradition*, XXXVI, 2–6.

The *Apostolic Tradition* testifies to the custom of prayers held in the church at Rome, morning and evening, in the third century—community prayers at which the congregation is present and under the direction of the clergy. Joined to the morning prayers, or considered as a part of them, is a catechetical instruction by the priest taken from the Scriptures. Here we find the elements from which the later-developed Divine Office is made up: prayer and Scripture reading.

The evening prayer, which is connected with the *agape*, is described in greater detail. The prayer-service is made up of the blessing of the lamps—one of the names used for Vespers later on was *lucernarium* (lighting of the lamps)—and the singing of psalms. The clergy recite the *Alleluia* psalms and the people answer *Alleluia*. These are the Hallel psalms, some of which are still used in Sunday Vespers. The evening service that Hippolytus describes is not celebrated every day, but whenever there is a congregational supper, or *agape*.

Thus in the third century there were five set hours for prayer in the course of a Christian's day—two public hours, morning and evening; and three private hours, in the middle of the morning, at noon, and in the middle of the afternoon. These hours of prayer formed the nucleus of the later "Day-hours" of the Divine Office.

In the last part of the fourth century we find St. Ambrose urging that the people of Milan should as far as possible come to church each day in the morning and the evening. At the same period the *Apostolic Constitutions*, a work that is concerned with the church in Syria, admonishes the bishop to instruct the people to come to church in the morning and evening of every day, and commands that for morning prayer Psalm 62 with the appropriate beginning, "My God to thee I watch at break of day," should be recited, and for evening prayer Psalm 140, which contains the equally appropriate verse "The lifting-up of my hands shall be an evening sacrifice."

These texts from the fourth century show that persistence of the idea of a common and public prayer made by the Christian community at the traditional hours of morning and evening. The idea, it is important to note, is independent of monasticism or the monastic influence.

Until recent times it was confidently asserted by writers on the subject that Matins, the night-hour of the Office, was an outgrowth of the weekly all-night vigil supposedly held every Saturday in the pre-Nicene Church. There are still some who hold that theory today, but we cannot be as confident about it as we were in the past. The difficulty is that there is no conclusive evidence for the weekly all-night vigil and much evidence that argues against it. That there was a solemn vigil service at Easter, and possibly on a few other days as well, is well known, but the weekly vigil is improbable and unlikely. It has always seemed to this writer at any rate an unsatisfactory explanation for the origin of Matins. It seems more likely that it is to be traced to the custom, mentioned by Origen and earnestly recommended by him, of rising during the night to pray. Not everyone did this, of course, and there is no question of a public service, although no doubt if there were more than one person rising in the household to pray they prayed in common. But what Origen is referring to here is unquestionably private prayer. That this private prayer would be prayers in the spirit and the form of the prayers said in church (or in the assembly of the faithful) is extremely probable, but it was nevertheless private.

It can be seen from what we have said so far that the Divine Office—in the sense of prayers said at stated times—had its beginning very early in the Church, and that two of these "hours" are even more specifically "liturgical" in the sense that they were public and common prayers. These are the *matutinae laudes*, the morning praises, which became Lauds; and the *sacrificium vespertinum*, the evening "sacrifice of praise," that became Vespers. It is important to note this because it contradicts the mistaken notion that the Office is monastic in origin. Monasticism has indeed considerably influenced the development of the Office and contributed very much to the form it has taken, but the Office as such has always been the prayer of the whole Church.

The next stage in the development of the Office came with the rise of monasticism, which began with the ascetics and virgins in the third century. These were pious people who, while living in the world, led a life of greater perfection than the ordinary Christians about them, observing celibacy and gathering together for prayer not only at the regular times (morning and evening), but at the third, sixth, and ninth hours as well. They also appear to have met together for prayer during the night—not every night, but from time to time. But this was strictly their own affair, with nothing official about it, private prayer rather than public official prayer.

In the fourth century the Spanish pilgrim Etheria Sylvia describes the liturgical custom of the church of Jerusalem. She tells us that the ascetics and virgins gathered each day in the church of the Resurrection, not only for the regular morning and evening prayers, but also for prayers during the night and at the other hours of the day. During these hours, they sang psalms and hymns. She also records a new development: some of the clergy are present at these hours, delegated by the bishop to offer prayers at their conclusion. The private prayers have now become official and public, liturgical in the full sense. Thus the ascetics and virgins brought about the daily recitation of the full *cursus diei,* the canonical hours of the day and night. It is well to notice that the clergy were not expected to be all present at these hours; only some of them were required to be there, and even then only to say the concluding prayers. For a long time to come they would be required to take part only in Lauds and Vespers.

The monastic institution developed further in the fourth and fifth centuries; the ascetics and virgins gave up the practice of living in the world and fled to the desert where the monasteries grew up. Monasticism now involved living in community, and the cloister took its place in the Christian world. This new development in monasticism was to have considerable influence upon the Divine Office, bringing to it one of its chief enrichments. For the monks (and nuns) who cultivated the life of prayer in the desert made the singing of the psalms—the entire psalter—the great business of their lives, and found in this practice the great school of prayer. The psalms had been used before their time, of course, but it might be said that they had never been so appreciated.

If later on the psalter was to occupy so large a place in the prayer of the Church, it was because of the influence of the monks. Monasticism had begun to make its second great contribution to the formation of the Office: the preponderance of psalmody.

During the same centuries the basilicas were built in the cities, churches where the full worship of the Church could be carried out. To provide them with a community that would ensure the daily singing of the canonical hours, monasteries came in time to be built near the basilicas and the monks called in. This was particularly true of Rome and the Gallican churches. The full daily round of prayer was thus secured in the cathedrals and greater churches. But in the smaller churches only Lauds and Vespers were celebrated. The secular clergy confined themselves to these hours alone.

It is not easy to trace the history of the Office in the city churches from the fourth century when the monks abandoned the world for the monastery, and the sixth or seventh centuries when they began to come back to take over the singing of the Office in the cathedrals and great churches. From the scattered references that are made here and there, it appears that the clergy continued the practice of reciting the traditional morning and evening hours of Lauds and Vespers each day; they also on certain occasions observed the nocturnal vigils (Matins). These hours were altogether connected with the church; there was no question of a private recitation. Nor were all the clergy compelled to be at the vigil service—as near as we can see there was a policy of taking turns in some places, such as Gaul, or in other places of hiring substitutes. The clergy in general were not well disposed to the vigil (nocturnal) Offices, and do not seem to have felt themselves bound as a group to attend them. In the eastern part of the Empire, however, the Emperor Justinian commanded the clergy to be present at the vigils (night hours) as well as Lauds and Vespers under pain of expulsion from the ranks of the clergy.

The Bishops of the dioceses surrounding Rome were required in the early Middle Ages to promise at the time of their consecration that they would, together with their clergy, gather in their cathedrals each day at cockcrow to celebrate the Vigil (Matins and Lauds) and again in the evening for Vespers. At the same period we read of the different local councils of the Church in Gaul prescribing that the bishops were to assign clergy to provide the Office (Vigil, Lauds, Vespers) in the churches of the countryside, and later on of Bishops who arranged to have the Office celebrated in the different churches of their episcopal cities, not in all at once, but by a process of rotation. Another bishop provided that the Sunday Matins should be celebrated in all the churches, but the week-day Matins only in the cathedral with a different group of clergy each night providing the celebration. All these texts deal chiefly with the organization of the celebration of the "vigils"—that is, our modern Matins. There is no question here of Lauds or Vespers because these two hours, being ancient and well-established, had no need of being regulated, while the Vigils, being recent in France, needed organization.

In the course of the centuries from the fifth to the ninth, the daily chanting of the Office in the Roman basilicas and in many of the great churches outside of Rome passed over more and more to the monks. This was particularly true of the Benedictines who in time exercised great influence upon the

Roman Office itself. The secular clergy joined the monks only for Lauds and Vespers—and occasionally for Matins. They do not seem to have considered themselves bound to do this every day, at least when there were monks who could do this in their stead.

The Roman Office spread from Rome to Britain and Germany during the sixth, seventh, and eighth centuries, largely through the efforts of the Benedictine monks who went as missionaries to those regions. In the Frankish domains the Carolingian reform of the Gallican Rite resulted in a fusion of the Roman and Gallican Offices in which the Roman was mixed with Gallican elements. The result was the Office which remained substantially the same until the reform of St. Pius X.

The practice of having the canonical hours recited daily in the churches received further impetus from the development of the *vita communis* which some bishops fostered among their clergy as early as the fourth century. They lived together under a rule and recited the Office in common. From this *vita communis* developed the canonical life of the early Middle Ages and the later practice of celebrating the entire Office in the cathedrals and collegiate churches, by the chapter of canons. These canons were sometimes members of a religious order, the Canons Regular, but most often were secular priests. During the later Middle Ages the cathedrals might be served by any one of these groups, monks, Canons Regular, or Secular Canons.

With the return of the monks to the cities and the rise and spread of the canonical institute, the full round of the hours of the Office was held in the cathedrals and principal churches. In the smaller churches the canonical hours were no more than the two traditional hours of Lauds and Vespers, with Matins on Sundays and great feasts.

The only two hours of the Office that must be regarded as exclusively monastic in origin are Prime and Compline. Both of these in modified form existed in the Roman Office prior to the time of St. Benedict. Prime grew up in the monastery of

Bethlehem in the fifth century as a supplementary morning prayer—the latter part, a kind of chapter Office with special prayers begging God's blessing on the day's work, was developed into the present form by the Benedictines.

Compline was originally a special prayer—consisting mainly of Psalm 90—said in the dormitory before going to bed by St. Basil's monks in the fourth century. The practice later spread to the West. Both these hours received further organization by St. Benedict.

The Roman Office. It is difficult to be certain about all the details but it is clear that there was what we call the ancient Office of the Church at Rome existing in very simple form before the time of St. Benedict. Benedict modelled his Office upon this earlier form. The austere character of this ancient Office stands out in the Office for the last three days of Holy Week—with its absence of hymns, invitatory psalm or antiphon, *capitulum* at Lauds, Vespers, or the Little Hours. All these features were added by Benedict to the Office of his monks, then passed under their influence into the Office of the secular churches.

According to ancient tradition, St. Gregory the Great made many changes in the Roman Office, adding certain features from the Benedictine *cursus* and some of his own making as well. He suppressed the *Alleluia* and the *Te Deum* in the offices *de tempore* from Septuagesima to Easter and added antiphons and responsories from the Scriptures. It was he who placed the invitatory psalm at the beginning of the Office and who reduced the Sunday Matins to eighteen psalms. He also founded a *schola cantorum* to train singers for the Office.

Origin of the "Double" Office. At first there was an Office for each day called the ferial Office. During the fourth or fifth century it became the custom to add to this daily Office a special or proper Office for feasts, consisting of Matins, Lauds, and Vespers and made up of proper psalms, antiphons, lessons, and responsories. On the great feast days this Office was said side by side with the Office of the day, hence the name *duplex officium*, or double, which came to be the name describing the feast itself. This twofold Office was said in all the churches on the great feasts, but on saints' days was said only in the church or cemetery where the saint was buried. Later on in the eighth century it became the custom to celebrate these Offices of the saints in all the churches, not just in the churches which held the remains. With that change we have the formation of the sanctoral and its insertion into the canonical Office.

In the twelfth century we see the first attempts at shortening the Office and putting the whole complex service into one volume, whence the name Breviary; these were still choir-books, not portable offices. The principle was still retained that the Office was something to be recited publicly—those who were unable for one reason or another to be present at the public Office tried to supply privately for the public Office, but apparently there was no question, at least until portable Breviaries were common, of anyone being held to say the whole Office privately.

Before the Office was gathered into one volume, a whole library of books was needed for the lessons alone, a Legendary, a Passionary, a Homiliary, to say nothing of the Martyrology, the Antiphonary, the Responsiary, and other books for the rest of the Office. Obviously it would be a convenience to have all these in one book. Until that was done on a large scale, it is difficult to see how men could be expected to recite the Office privately when they were on a journey or absent from choir. It is often asserted that monks and canons and, later on, priests were held to say the Office privately, but it seems rather obvious that those documents that speak of the practice are referring to the recitation of the psalter, which many knew by heart and of which in any case there were copies available.

By the thirteenth century there were many divergencies in the manner of reciting the Office; even between the great basilicas of Rome there were great differences. The way to unity in this matter was prepared by the Franciscans, who adopted the Breviary of the Roman Court as their Office in the year 1260. This papal Office was derived from that said in the Lateran Basilica, near which the popes lived during the Middle Ages. The members of the papal court had taken to the custom of singing the Office apart from the canons of the Lateran Basilica in their own chapel. Nearly all authors assert that this was a shorter Office than that said in the Lateran, but it is not clear that it was actually shorter; rather, it was sung or recited more briskly than the Offices in the churches and monasteries.* Innocent III had gathered this Office of the papal court into one volume, a fact that gave it a considerable advantage over any other Office. This was the Office adopted by the Franciscans, who made it still more convenient by shortening and organizing the rubrics. Although the Franciscans adopted the Roman Breviary, they retained the Gallican psalter which they were used to, rather than the old *Itala* used in the *Breviarium Romanae Curiae*. It was this Office, put into one volume and made a Breviary by the members of the papal court, and then made more convenient by the Franciscans, that now spread through Europe, helping to bring about at one and the same time liturgical unity and the private recitation of the Office. The latter furnishes us with a good example of supply creating demand. The case is usually presented as the opposite, but it appears that there was no question of a really widespread private recitation until the means to do it were at hand.

By the fourteenth century the Roman Office, as adopted by the Franciscans and spread through Europe by their influence, was greatly changed from the old Roman Office, though the

* Cf. Van Dijk, "Liturgical Movements Past and Present," *Clergy Review* (September, 1956).

main outlines remained the same. The Gallican psalter was used instead of the old *Itala* version, the lessons from Scripture were greatly shortened, the *temporale* ran from the first Sunday of Advent to the last Sunday after Pentecost, the feasts of the saints were greatly multiplied and there was an abundance of octaves. The Matins of saints' days, made up of nine proper psalms and nine lessons, were shorter than the ferial Matins; as a result it was an advantage to have as many saints feasts as possible. Besides that, the seven penitential psalms and the gradual psalms, as well as the Office of the Dead, had to be recited on ferial days. No wonder that the saints' days with their shorter Office were preferred to the ferial Offices! The Little Office of the Blessed Virgin had to be said every day—the Carthusians still follow this practice—and the Marian antiphons were added after Compline.

The multiplication of saints' feasts and octaves resulted in a real invasion of the Temporal by the Sanctoral, and the whole Office suffered a resulting dislocation. The same limited number of psalms was repeated over and over and other parts of the psalter not read at all. Worse still the *lectio continuata* of the scriptures now gave place to the hagiographical lessons, often taken from accounts that were either apocryphal or of little or no value, certainly inferior to what they supplanted.

It is extremely significant that the first legislative texts on the Divine Office that we meet are concerned with the public recitation or celebration of the Office. It is truly a community prayer that they have in mind when they say that every cleric with a benefice must provide the Divine Office in the church attached to his benefice. So much is this true that the legal principle is expressed in the words "*beneficium datur propter officium*"—no Office, no benefice. The cleric was expected not only to pray in the name of the church, but in the church itself: *ecclesiam officiare*—to make the church a center of divine praise, to provide his church with the Office. If for some reason he could not be present at the Office in his church, he was to say it as best as he could; the idea was that he was supplying for the Office recited in common. The principle that the Office of itself should be common and public was maintained. Even when the concept of an obligation to supply for what had been missed gained currency, during the thirteenth century, there was no question of an independent obligation to recite the Office privately—it was always a question of supplying for the public recitation.

With the general breakdown of the old corporate concept of the Church and its public worship in the fifteenth century, there came a corresponding decrease in esteem for the public Office, so that the question came to be posed that would never have been asked in earlier centuries—whether the private recitation was more devotional than the public. The individualistic outlook was asserting itself—here as in other matters. By the late sixteenth and early seventeenth century the obligation was dealt with by the theologians as an obligation to say it in private—the public recitation had become the exception rather than the rule. As a consequence the Office has become in practice an individual affair—a duty to be done by individuals rather than the common praise of a specific community, as it once was. It is viewed as an "exercise of piety" on a par with meditation or the rosary, rather than as the *Opus Dei* rendered to God by a community.

By the sixteenth century the Office, because of its excessive length and many accretions, had become an almost intolerable burden, and it is no surprise to learn that it was not held in high esteem by many. It had become increasingly clear to thinking men as the Middle Ages came to an end that reform was imperative if the Office was to hold that place in the life of the Church that it had held in the past. Others longed to see it corrected and purged of its historical errors, and its Latinity purified.

The cry for reform and revision grew louder during the sixteenth century, and even before the Council of Trent had convened, the Spanish Cardinal Quinonez made a drastic revision of the Breviary, which was allowed by the popes for a while, but which received so much criticism that it was withdrawn. Quinonez' main principle was that the Office was to be recited in private by the great majority; so he suppressed all choral elements and made it more a reading than a prayer. It proved too great a departure from tradition, although there were many points about the experiment that were commendable.

The first official revision of the Breviary was made by the Council of Trent, and it is significant that the principle that the Office is essentially and ideally a community (choral) prayer, recited outside of choir only by necessity, was retained and reaffirmed. The calendar was somewhat lightened, and many of the mediaeval accretions trimmed off, but there was no radical change in the structure or length of the Office itself.

A most sweeping revision was projected by the great and learned Benedict XIV, but his death found it still in the project stage. Meanwhile, many of the French dioceses, impatient of reform from Rome, had adopted their own Breviaries, which were to have more than a little influence upon the next revision of the Office, that made by St. Pius X.

The Reform of St. Pius X. Unquestionably the most complete and thorough revision to date, the reform of Pius X greatly shortened the Office, rearranged the psalter and provided for its weekly recitation; restored the temporal and particularly the Sunday Office to its proper place; provided a complete Office for All Souls' Day and "second Lauds" for ferias. The guiding idea of St. Pius was to make the Office not a burden, but a source of spiritual nourishment for priests, as it should be. It is said that he contemplated even more thoroughgoing reforms, but he died before they could be carried out.

Pius XII has added the latest chapters to the history of the Breviary with the long-desired, amended and corrected version of the psalter in 1945 and the more recent changes in the rubrics, which aim at a more frequent recital of the psalter and a thorough-going simplification of the structure of the Office, as well as the elimination of distracting features. What is more significant is that we seem to have here only the first step in a revision that promises to give the Office that place in the liturgy and in the liturgical life which it has in theory and in fact, but which it has long ceased to have in practice.

The Various Hours of the Office

Content and Spirit. As the Office is now constructed it is an hour prayer and seems likely to remain so, at least in broad outline. This means that it is intended to be said at stated times during the day and that there is a link between the time of day and the words of the Office to be read at or about that time, and which renders it inappropriate for any other greatly different time and hour. The idea behind this arrangement is that the day, at least in general outline, is to be sanctified by prayer, and that prayers appropriate for certain hours are to be said at that time. It is certainly a great departure from the spirit and intention of the Church habitually to say Compline in the morning, for example, as the whole tone of this hour is the tone of a night prayer.

Matins. The longest and the richest of the hours of the Office is Matins with its nine psalms and its lessons, most often also nine in number, but sometimes three. It seems to have taken on its present form in the monasteries, where it became a night prayer rather than a morning prayer, as its name would seem to indicate; it developed from the prayers said once by all Christians during the night, and not from the Vigil as once was believed.

The basic form of Matins appears to be the ferial Matins, with its nine psalms and three lessons making up one nocturn, later expanded into three nocturns for doubles. It begins with

Psalm 94, an invitation to praise God, thus retaining one of the ancient ways of using the antiphon: as a responsory echoed after each verse. This antiphon serves a purpose analogous to the Introit of the Mass, setting the tone for the day's Office. On feast days the psalms are proper and related to the feast; they form with their antiphons a kind of meditation, or more precisely they are a contemplation of the ideas associated with the feast, a work that is continued in the lessons, responsories, and hymns. Matins is longest hour of the Office, and sets forth these ideas in the most complete and leisurely manner. On ordinary days the psalms are taken from the psalter, and are usually the longest or at least the most thought-packed psalms, maintaining the contemplative character of the hour. The antiphons are from the psalm itself and are made up of the dominant thought in the psalm. The lessons instruct and edify and continue to stir up affections and pious thoughts. The hymns on such days are either from the Proper, Common, or psalter. If from the psalter, they usually develop some thought related to the idea of night and prayer; they dwell on the thought of rising and watching, throwing off the darkness of night and of error, the torpor of sleep, and so on. Hymns for the season or feasts try to awaken the sentiments and affections that go with the occasion; that is, they consider the object of the feast or the season. The *Te Deum* concludes the whole Office and is a kind of summary and compendium of all that has gone before, a climax of prayer and praise.

Lauds. Lauds is the true morning prayer of the Church, as the various references to the dawning of the day in the daily hymns in the psalter show us. It is an hour that is devoted in a special way, as its name indicates, to praise: its full name in the past was "*Laudes matutinae,*" so-called because it was to be said at dawn when the morning star ("*matuta*") appeared. With Vespers it makes up the oldest part of the Office; these two hours were the first to become liturgical hours properly so-called.

The oldest parts of Lauds are the psalms, and the dominant theme of praise is indicated and assured by the fact that the last psalm is always one of the "*laudate*" psalms. Another characteristic is that the fourth of the five psalms is not a psalm at all but a canticle from the Old Testament. The general theme of praise is made more particular on feast days by the antiphons, which in one way or another set forth the tone for the feast. Those on Sundays or weekdays are taken from the psalter itself. The psalms are followed by the later additions: *capitulum*, hymn, Gospel Canticle and oration. The *capitulum* is a brief lesson which contains one of the dominant thoughts for the day taken from the Scriptures; on Sundays it is a doxology (song of praise) from the Apocalypse; on week days the appropriate "*Nox praecessit*" from the Epistle to the Romans. The hymn either contemplates the themes of the feast or season, or on ferial days describes the victory of light over darkness, the symbol of Christ's victory over Satan and sin, praying that we may conquer with Him. The apex and summit of Lauds is the *Benedictus*, chosen because it is a morning Canticle with its reference to Christ as the "*oriens ex alto*" and its allusion to the enlightenment which comes from Him. This canticle is fitted with an antiphon which is often taken from the Gospel of the day, and which highlights some thought proper to the season or the feast. The oration of Lauds is the oration of the day, linking the Office with the Mass to that extent at any rate.

Because Lauds was traditionally sung in the morning and preferably at dawn, the hour of our Lord's Resurrection, this hour has always been considered a commemoration of the Resurrection, and the first psalm is always one which alludes to the victory of Christ and of His Kingdom.

Prime. This hour is monastic in origin and more than any

other (except Compline) retains the imprint of monastic customs. It is a prayer said at the beginning of the day's work, a kind of morning offering, directed to God and asking His blessing. Prime is scarcely affected by the changes in the liturgical year, either seasonal or festal. Sometimes the psalms will fit the day of the week, as for example Psalm 117 on Sundays which is proper to the resurrection ("*Haec dies quem fecit Dominus*"); and Psalm 21 on Fridays, one of the few definitely Messianic psalms dealing with the Passion of our Lord. But other than these exceptions the main idea of Prime is that it is a morning offering directed to the day's work.

Actually, Prime is two offices in one: the first is an ancient prayer service with the psalms as the main element; the second a special service held in the chapter-house of the monastery marked by the reading of the Martyrology, prayers for the blessing of God on the day's work, and a reading of a chapter of the Rule of St. Benedict (which for seculars has become a reading from the Scriptures). That this second section was no part of the original Office is shown by the fact that it is omitted on the last three days of Holy Week, when the most ancient arrangement of the Office is retained. On feast days the proper antiphon and the reading of the *Lectio brevis* provide the few variants in Prime in accord with the season or feast.

Terce, Sext, and None. These hours grew out of the practice of praying during the day and their original nucleus is the Our Father or, in some instances, the psalms. For a long time after they became full-fledged liturgical hours, Terce, Sext and None closed with the *Pater Noster*, instead of the collect for the day as they do now. The only psalm recited at these hours for centuries was Psalm 118, until changes were introduced by St. Pius X.

The idea behind these hours was to sanctify the important hours of the day with prayer according to the Gospel precept, "Pray without ceasing." While the other, greater hours were preoccupied with contemplating and celebrating the feast or the season, the redemptive work of Christ and the mysteries of His life, Terce, Sext and None were intended to be hardly more than brief stops during the day to remember God and to think of Him. St. Benedict's idea was to keep them short and that idea influenced the arrangement of the non-monastic Office, too. This may explain the use of Psalm 118, as its general character made it suitable for everyday use. Terce, Sext and None were slow in becoming liturgical hours in the full sense; they retained a quasi-private character for a long time. Only later on were they equipped with the variable *capitulums* and brief responsories, which, together with the antiphon used for feasts, assimilate the hour to the main hours of the Office by providing at least for a partial commemoration of the feast or season. The assimilation is carried further by the use of the collect for the day instead of the *Pater Noster*.

The hymns, written in the ninth century, were admitted only in the thirteenth century and they now provide each one of the "Little Hours" with a kind of main thought peculiar to that time of day, no matter what the day of the year. Thus, Terce recalls the sending of the Holy Spirit; Sext the thought of the "noon-day devil" and our struggle against him; None the thought of death and the "*premium mortis sacrae.*"

These hours, of course, derive their names from the ancient Roman way of dividing the day: Terce, the third hour, from 9 to 12; Sext, the sixth hour, from 12 to 3; None, the ninth hour, from 3 to 6, and so on. We are not compelled to say them at these exact times, but we might to our profit refuse to lump them together. There should be some correspondence between the hour and the prayer, and to say them at the proper time should be an ideal for us, even if not always realizable.

Vespers. As Lauds is the true morning prayer, so Vespers is the true evening prayer of the Church. It gets its name from *Vesper*, the evening star, and has also been known as *lucerna-*

rium, the lighting of the lamps. The idea is that the Church gathers together, thanks God for the graces and blessings of the day and, therefore, gratefully *recalls* all that God has done to deserve our grateful recognition.

Vespers is dominated by the *Magnificat*, as Lauds is by the *Benedictus*, and in Mary's hymn we find our own thanksgiving expressed. The psalms chosen for Vespers, especially those used on Sunday, recall as far as possible the "mighty deeds" and acts of God; His deliverance of Israel in the Old Testament is a prophecy of the redemption in the New. "*Et ipse redimet Israel ex omnibus iniquitatibus ejus.*" These psalms present us with an objective contemplation of all that God has done; they are narrative and prophetic as well.

The *capitulum*, like that of Lauds, alludes to the feast or season, or on week days is a doxology from St. Paul extolling God for the consolation He has brought us: the redemption in Christ. On ferial days and on Sundays, the hymn deals with various aspects of the creation and makes petitions for our spiritual welfare based upon the creative act that is set forth in the first part; on feast days and in the seasons it is usually doctrinal and concerns some aspect of the feast or season. The *Magnificat* with its antiphon, less often taken from the Gospel than that of Lauds, and the oration closes the hour.

First Vespers goes back to the ancient idea that the new day began with the setting of the sun; thus, great feasts began the day before. If the feasts were important enough, they had Second Vespers as well, a prolongation of the feast. The change in the rubrics will do away with First Vespers on all except greater feasts and Sundays.

Compline. The last of the hours originated in the monasteries of the East as a prayer before retiring, when the monk put himself under God's protection by reciting Psalm 90, which is the nucleus of Compline. The first reference to it in secular churches shows that it was still a prayer said not in church, but in the sleeping quarters before going to bed; later it developed into its present form. Like Prime it retains a strong monastic imprint. Compline is distinguished for its frequent references to night and to sleep, which are seen as images of death; we therefore commend our souls to God, recalling His love for us that prompted our redemption. The hymn asks that God will watch over us and protect us, particularly from those sins associated with darkness. We ask for a quiet night and a peaceful end (when it shall come), and we are reminded to resist the devil who goes about seeking our downfall. We make confession of our sins and seek pardon for them.

Until St. Pius X's reform, the same psalms were said every day; all of them were especially appropriate as prayers to be said before going to sleep. Three of these now form the Compline for Sunday, while during the week as far as possible psalms have been selected which allude to sleep and to death. But the oration, which never changes, is a mosaic made up from the petitions of Psalm 90. The *Nunc Dimittis*, with its indirect reference to death (although that is not its main theme), was thought to be the ideal canticle for this hour.

The new revision calls for closing the Office with the appropriate Marian antiphon (which is said now only this once) and with nothing else.

Elements of the Office

The Psalms. The greatest part of the Office and a considerable part of the Mass is made up of the psalms, and we know that this has been true from earliest times. The Church has ever looked upon them as a most precious repository of prayer and doctrine, turning almost by instinct to them as the ideal expression in song of her deepest and most profound thoughts and sentiments. From the time that our Lord used them and St. Paul admonished the first Christians to speak their minds in psalms and hymns and spiritual canticles, down to our own day, when they form the staple of the Church's liturgy of praise, they have held an honored and unchallenged place. That is not to say that they have always been appreciated; in fact, they have suffered a decided eclipse in popular esteem. But during this present century with the liturgical revival, there has come a renewed interest in these hallowed forms of prayer, so much so that we can speak of a rediscovery of the psalms by Catholics that promises a more healthy and biblical spirituality, the inevitable result of a piety nourished by daily use of the very heart of Scripture, after the Gospel itself.

The abundant use of psalms in the liturgy, in the Mass, the Office and the Ritual, their great popularity whenever they were made accessible to the people and their inherent excellence, all point to the fact that the psalter is the book of devotion and public prayer above all others. Nothing is so well-calculated to develop and nourish the true liturgical spirit as the use of the psalms. For they are "the blessing of the people, the praise of God, the *plebis laudatio*, every one's applause, the universal discourse, the voice of the Church, the sung confession of the faith, authority's full devotion, the glad song of liberty, the cry of gladness, the redounding of joy," as St. Ambrose says. In the psalms the Church sings its rejoicing, its sorrows, its joys, its trials and sufferings. The psalms contain all the acts of true worship blended together: adoration, praise, thanksgiving. As St. Athanasius said:

> It happens that there is in the psalms a wonderful power to stir up in the hearts of all zeal for virtue. Even though all Scripture, the Old and New Testaments alike, divinely inspired as it is, be useful for teaching, as it is written . . . but the book of Psalms is, as it were, a paradise of all the other books of Scripture, containing fruit, setting it forth in song and showing its own, together with that of the others, while singing the psalms.*

It must be admitted that many do not take naturally to the psalms; they must be educated to them. Here, as elsewhere, the

* Letter to Marcellinus on interpreting the psalms.

liturgy provides the best pedagogy; making use of the psalms is the only way to grow into them. Demonstration and exemplification, insistence upon their richness and value is all very good and necessary, but *use* is the best teacher, and *intelligent* use of the psalms will be more instructive than hours of lectures. In any case, the liturgy is never preoccupied primarily with our wishes, our likes, or even our needs. The psalms happen to be the best way of expressing the praise of God; they are best suited to telling us what God is and what He has done; they are *in themselves* objectively best fitted for the task. The Church has sensed this from the beginning; so she uses them—it is as simple as that. The liturgy is not supposed to adapt itself to us, but we are supposed to adapt ourselves to the liturgy. This should not be a very difficult task, since the liturgy, being objective, has something to offer to everyone.

The psalms are more than prayers; they are hymns which were written to be sung to the accompaniment of the psalter, a stringed instrument resembling the harp. It would be well for us to remember that, because half of the beauty and power of the psalms lies in the singing of them and is lost when they are only recited, especially when they are recited silently! The psalms were intended to be used in the temple and the synagogue to glorify God. They are not private religious poems, but in concept, range and expression are essentially liturgical; their true theatre is common worship. The peculiar characteristic of the psalms is parallelism: an idea expressed in one verse is repeated or developed or added to in the next; the ideas are thus driven home and kept before us by the soundest of all pedagogical principles, namely, repetition. These ideas are, furthermore, always expressed in the most concrete language; the Hebrew mind did not take kindly to abstractions. Herein lies one of the great reasons for their universal appeal: they speak the language of everyman.

That the first Christians should have continued to use the psalms even after they ceased to take part in Jewish worship, should not surprise us if we remember that they were nearly all Jews and as such were deeply attached to the psalms. Christ Himself evidently was like all Jews in that respect; we find Him using the psalms in some of the great moments of His life and with a spontaneity which suggests His thorough familiarity with them. As time went on, however, the Christians found a new and more compelling reason for employing the psalms than the fact that they had been used by the Jews and even by our Lord Himself. They saw the psalms as prophecies of Christ and His work, and consequently not any longer as the songs of Israel, but as the inspired hymns of the new Israel, the Church. Had not Christ Himself said that "all things must be fulfilled that were written . . . in the psalms concerning me"? For the Christians, then, the psalms became their own property. Far from regarding them as Hebrew literature, they felt that these ancient songs had only now attained their full meaning and development; they took them over as if they had been written, not by David, but by Christ Himself.

What we might call the Christian interpretation of the psalter is, then, traditional in the Church. It may be traced back to the second century, when the first beginnings of commentaries on the psalter appear at the time of St. Augustine, who, of all the Fathers, developed a Christian interpretation in all its implications. The same interpretation is behind the psalms in the liturgy and becomes most apparent on the feasts of the ecclesiastical year, when certain psalms become quite obviously descriptions of the activity of Christ—for example, on Christmas, Ascension, Epiphany.

That the psalms were used not only in the public services, which is what we would expect, but that they were regarded as the Christians' most beloved prayers in private life as well, is abundantly evident, and the implications of this fact should be profoundly instructive for us.

St. Paul is apparently speaking of more than a strictly liturgical use of the psalms when he says ". . . be filled with the

Spirit, speaking to one another in psalms and hymns and spiritual songs, singing and making melody in your hearts to the Lord" (Eph. 5:19). Or again, "Let the word of Christ dwell in you abundantly: in all wisdom teach and admonish one another in psalms, hymns and spiritual songs, singing in your hearts to God by his grace" (Col. 3:16). And St. James recommends singing a psalm as a way of expressing joy and equanimity. Later on, in sermons to the people, preachers like St. Basil and St. Augustine bear witness to the familiarity with the psalms enjoyed by even very unlearned people, people without formal education. St. Basil in particular assigns a rôle in the spiritual education of Christians to the psalms that would be impossible unless his hearers were thoroughly familiar with them.

It must be said that, until the nineteenth century, the psalms entered far more into the lives of the people, clergy and laity, than they do today. St. Augustine's "*Psalterium meum gaudium meum*" could be echoed by many thousands of Christian hearts in all the centuries, and the educational power of the psalms must have been well-nigh incalculable.

Principle of Interpretation. The key to understanding the psalter, then, is to remember that we do not recite the psalms as individuals; it is the Church which recites them and we join in not as isolated individuals but as members of the Church sharing in common praise and prayer. The "I" of the psalms is not, as we might think, the individual worshipper, but Christ speaking in His own person or speaking in the members of His Body. The psalms are not personal religious hymns like many modern compositions, but the songs of a corporate body. Originally some of them were private hymns, but they have been gathered into a hymnbook for the use of all Israel and as the expression of its sentiments; they become the prayer of a Person, but that Person is Christ—Head and Members.

First of all, the Psalms are to be understood in their literal sense, but transposed into a Christian key, as someone very happily expressed it. We must remember that the Old Testament is fulfilled in Christ and the same is true of the psalms. Much in the psalms points to Christ, directly in the messianic psalms, indirectly in all of them. The references to David, to Jerusalem, to Sion, to the deliverance from Egypt are all to be taken literally; but seen in the light of the Incarnation, they become *for us* references to Christ, to the Church, to the redemption. Nor is this an accommodation in the rather disparaging sense in which the word is sometimes used; rather we see now the full meaning of these symbols in a way that the ancient Jews could not have seen it; we see them now as reaching their full meaning and development. So the Church uses psalms like "*Lauda Jerusalem*" on the feast of the dedication of churches, and the Psalm "*In Exitu*" on the feast of the Resurrection. We are, then, reciting the psalms in their literal sense, but we see much more in them than was originally intended.

Of course, there are many places in the psalms where there is no history of God's mighty deeds in the past, no references to Jerusalem, nor to the manna in the desert and the like. Nevertheless, they are filled with prayers and sentiments which we can easily make our own; they express the way we feel and they do it much better than we could hope to do. Page after page is strewn with praise, thanksgiving, petition, sorrow for sin, cries to God in every and all circumstances of life. Here we have one reason why the psalms have made such a universal appeal: they are everyman's prayer and everyone feels at home with them.

Many of the psalms are messianic: they deal directly or indirectly with Christ and are to be applied to Him not merely in a typical sense, but in a literal sense. Christ Himself said that all things were to be fulfilled that were written about Him in the psalms, and the Church has always interpreted certain psalms as fully messianic. The classical example is Psalm 109, used by our Lord Himself to show His divinity and by St. Peter and St. Paul to the same end; but there is also Psalm 2, which speaks of the eternal generation of the Son; and Psalm 44, with its reference to the anointing of Christ; and Psalm 21, describing in detail the Passion of our Lord.

Other psalms are of the indirect type: they are applied to Christ even though they are not obviously messianic like those mentioned above. For example, in Psalm 8:3 we have, "Out of the mouths of children and infants at the breast thou hast perfected praise," which our Lord applied to Himself; and in Psalm 117:22, "The stone rejected by the builders has become the cornerstone," which is also applied to Christ. St. Peter uses Psalm 15:8–10, "Thou shalt not leave my soul in the grave nor let Thy holy one see corruption," as a demonstration of the Resurrection.

Besides these general and particular interpretations of the psalms, there are the many adaptations to the different feasts of the Church year. We can say that the psalms are often accommodated, given a new sense from that which they had originally. It is not a matter of a fuller meaning, but of applying the psalms in a way that the literal sense does not provide for. The Church has always done this. The principle is that the psalms in one way or another admirably express the spirit of the feast. Those used on the feasts of the Blessed Virgin are an excellent example of this broad accommodation: those used at Matins refer to the tabernacle of the Most High and of His dwelling place, yet they are applied to our Lady. Psalm 44 is a nuptial chant which is applied to our Lady and not to the original bride spoken of in the psalm. Psalm 86 refers to Jerusalem, the holy city of God; yet is also accommodated to our Lady.

On feast days of the saints who are confessors the Psalm "*Beatus Vir*" is referred to them. While not written about the saints it is nevertheless a perfect description of them; indeed, it is a better description of them than of the "just man" of the Old Law, since they exemplify the keeping of the perfect law which is the Gospel.

That the Church has always used the psalms in her worship

is, of course, known to everyone, but the implications of that fact are not always fully grasped. Psalmody was contemporaneous with the beginning of the Church, as the Acts of the Apostles shows, and its use spread outside Palestine and outside the ranks of Jewish converts; this indicates that there was a general agreement among Christians that the psalms were suitable or at least adaptable to Christian worship. They must have sensed that the psalms belonged to the Christian community, that there was something intrinsically suitable about them, which implies that the psalter is always and at all times the ideal Christian prayer book (and hymnbook).

Furthermore, the fact that psalmody was so naturally and even spontaneously used for liturgical worship argues that there must have been some kind of agreement at least on the broad general lines of its interpretation. It was to be read in the light of Christ, and Christ was to be found not in one psalm or another, but in the whole psalter. Another indication of agreement is found in the fact that when proper psalms came to be selected there was a remarkable unanimity throughout the Church about the psalms to be selected for the commemoration and celebration of the events in our Lord's life, as well as of His death and Resurrection. The tendency to select the same psalms is most remarkable and cannot be explained otherwise than by admitting that the Church everywhere instinctively recognized their appropriateness, and that she gave them a markedly Christian interpretation.

There is another point implicit in the Church's use of the psalms for worship, and it is this: by using them in her worship she asserts her right to understand them in a Christian sense and to give them an interpretation that is her own (not in an arbitrary way, but as the result of a deeper insight). These hymns composed by the Hebrews for the honor and glory of Jahweh are now clothed by the Church with a special Christian meaning and reflect *for us* the glory of Christ and the honor of His name. It is but another way of saying that the psalms are capable of bearing new meanings in the light of Christian faith.

The psalter is, then, a prayer book for common and corporate worship. The "I" that recurs so often is not the individual "I" denoting the particular person reciting the words. It refers most often to Christ or to the Church, and though it may be applied to the individual–and it often can be–it is not applied to him in isolation, but to him as a member of the Church. Otherwise many of the sentences in the psalms would be unreal upon our lips. We cannot say "But I have walked in innocence," for example, nor say large parts of Psalm 118 as our own words; these assertions can be made only by Christ, or about Him. They express His sentiments and His frame of mind, which as they stand do not correspond with the truth as far as "I" am concerned. They express what Christ as the perfect adorer of His Father felt and thought, but they are true of me only insofar as I am united with Him and conformed to His likeness. And by saying them in the proper spirit I can arouse the like sentiments in my own soul. In the same way the penitential psalms express an intensity of sorrow and compunction of which most men are not capable, but on the lips of Christ they become perfect expressions of ideal repentance. The historical psalms, in turn, become rather records of the history of the Church than accounts of the triumphs and trials of the old Israel.

Even the imprecatory psalms can, and indeed must be understood in a Christian sense: not as the expression of desire for vengeance and bodily harm to human enemies, but as prayers for the triumph of God and Christ over the enemies of God and His Church, or as referring to the Passion of Christ. Their general theme is well expressed in the words of one of the psalms, "Let God arise and let his enemies be scattered." Furthermore, they must be understood as prophetic of the triumph of God's justice, which they describe in concrete language.

Thus the *whole* psalter will be seen as full of Christ and His

Church. This is the way that the Church has understood it from the beginning and it is the only way that the psalter can truly become the great expression of the Church's worship.

The Distribution of Psalms in the Office. The ancient principle regarding the distribution of the psalms was that the entire psalter should be recited in the course of a week. The foundation of that principle is not so easy to discover unless it was intended to make the reading of the psalms less burdensome (some saints were accustomed to say the whole psalter each day!) and still secure frequent recitation. This, of course, applied only to the Offices of Sundays and ferial days, of which there were many in the first thousand years. For feast days of our Lord, our Lady and the saints there were proper psalms to be said. Consequently, as time went on and more saints were added to the calendar, the earlier principle was less and less observed; the same psalms were said over and over. St. Pius X removed this difficulty by ordering that the psalms of the occurring day should be recited even on feast days, except doubles of the first and second class and some proper feasts. This set the psalter free again. Pius XII has carried this rule even further: the psalms of the occurring day are now recited for the "Little Hours" on all except first class feasts. Besides that, St. Pius ordered a new distribution of the psalter for the week. As it is now, Psalm 94 is recited every day as the invitatory, and of the other psalms some are chosen with an eye to their fitness for certain hours and the remainder distributed in numerical order.

Those psalms which are appropriate as morning prayers or which express the idea of praise are selected for use at Lauds. Those used at Compline are appropriate for night prayers or because they express confidence in God. Psalm 118 is in a class by itself; it is a long meditation on the law of God and on doing His will. It was, therefore, said daily until 1912, and is now assigned for the "Little Hours" on Sundays and first class feasts. Similarly, Psalm 117, which is a Paschal Psalm, was considered appropriate for Sundays.

The Psalms from 21–25 were originally part of Sunday Matins but were taken out of the latter by St. Pius V and spread through the week—not, however, in numerical order, because Psalm 21, the voice of Christ in His Passion, was thought to be more fitting for Friday, and Psalm 22, "*Dominus Pascit me*" is a Eucharistic Psalm, appropriate for Thursday. The other three psalms were distributed in numerical order and later each divided into three parts.

This arrangement left us 93 psalms—1 to 108 and 109 to the end. Those of the first group are morning psalms and are distributed through Matins of Sunday and the weekdays and through the "Little Hours" of weekdays in their numerical order. The other group is made up of evening or Vesper psalms. Psalms 109 to 113 are assigned to Sunday Vespers, while the remaining psalms, not otherwise used, are assigned to Vespers on the other days.

By dividing the longer psalms into sections, all are reduced to about the same length, which relieves the tedium that long psalms would cause.

Some modern liturgists have suggested a re-distribution of the psalter over two weeks as is the Milanese custom. This arrangement would bring about a still greater shortening of the Office and provide even greater variety, but there is no real indication that the ancient traditions of the Roman Church in this regard will be abandoned, although it is, of course, always possible that a change of this kind may be made.

Canticles. The Canticles are similar in composition and in many respects in content to the psalms, but they come from other books of the Scriptures. The classic example of a canticle is that of Moses, sung after the passage over the Red Sea, a song especially beloved by the Jews and used in their synagogue worship as epitomizing God's mighty deeds in their behalf.

All the canticles, because of their character as songs of praise, are well suited for divine worship, and we find that the Christians borrowed the custom of singing them from the synagogue worship. From the fifth century it has been the practice of the Roman Church to use one of the Old Testament canticles as the fourth of the five psalms at Lauds. The present arrangement, by which the canticles used for First Lauds on the different days of the week are all short and preoccupied with praise, while those used for Second Lauds are all rather long, was established by St. Pius X. This arrangement excepts Sunday, when the canticle used at First Lauds is much longer than that used at Second Lauds. Those now found in Second Lauds were all originally used in First Lauds before the time of Pius X.

What has been said about the psalms applies also to the canticles. They are to be conceived as the canticles of the new Israel, as they once were of the old. This applies particularly to the Canticle of Moses, "*Cantemus Domino*," which upon our lips becomes a song of praise to God for the blessing of the redemption.

On Sundays we invite all creation to bless God, that is, to give praise to Him together with the youths in the fiery furnace. On Monday we join with David in praising God; we thank Him with Tobias on Tuesday; and we rejoice with Judith over her victory on Wednesday. And at the same time we express our joy over our own deliverance from our spiritual enemy. Thursday, the traditional day on which we recall the blessing of the Holy Eucharist, we read the Canticle of Jeremias with its reference to the refreshment which comes from "wheat and wine and oil" and to filling the soul of the priest with spiritual fatness. On Friday, when we commemorate our redemption, the canticle is about "the hidden God, the God of Israel, the *Savior*"; and finally, Saturday's canticle from Ecclesiasticus is in the tradition of those Old Testament hymns which extol God's mighty deeds and, by proclaiming what God has done, praise and glorify His name. The last part, replete with allusions to the people of God, to Jerusalem His dwelling place, to Sion the place of His glory, makes it easy to transfer it into a prayer for the Church and its welfare.

Many will regret that the finest and best of all the Old Testament canticles, the first Canticle of Moses, a glad song of deliverance and triumph (redemption), is used only infrequently during the year, on Thursday, at Second Lauds.

Antiphons. The Book of Psalms could be used in the Office without antiphons but they unquestionably enhance it. They serve the psalms as a frame serves a picture; they set them off and impart a flavor and a quality to their liturgical recitation. The Office would be poor indeed without them. It is interesting to note that Cardinal Quignonez, who suppressed them altogether in the first edition of his famous and controversial *Breviarium Sanctae Crucis,* restored them in the second edition.

The original purpose of the antiphon was twofold: it served as a musical introduction to show how the psalm was to be sung, and as a statement of the theme or main idea of the psalm itself. This second purpose is still the function of the antiphons in the psalter for the week, and in many of the Offices from the Proper and the Common. In that way it often furnishes us with the key to the interpretation of the psalm, and the same psalm can be given a variety of emphasis just by the antiphon that is used with it. Classic examples of this are the way Psalm 129, the "*De Profundis,*" is presented in the Office of the Dead, where the antiphon "*Si iniquitatis observaveris Domine, Domine quis sustinebit*" accents an aspect of the psalm that is altogether solemn and even awe-inspiring; and in the Office of Christmas when the antiphon "*Apud Dominum misericordia, et copiosa apud eum redemptio*" transforms the psalm into a joyous Canticle of redemption.

We may say, then, that the antiphon makes the psalter

come to life and sets it off. When the antiphons are not taken from the psalter, as often happens on feast days, they create and sustain the atmosphere proper to the feast or season. Taken all together, they give fullness, variety and beauty to the Office and contribute their own invaluable part to making it truly the contemplative prayer that it is. The Book of Common Prayer, admirable though it is in many ways, gives us an idea of how dull the Office would be without antiphons. An antiphon is one of the elements that transforms the Office from a Scripture-reading into a prayer.

Antiphons as such are very ancient. They certainly were known in the fourth century and may even be older than that. The manner of using them has changed, however. There are indications that the oldest way was to sing them before the psalm and during it as well, after every verse or every two verses, as the invitatory psalm is sung in the daily Office today. But to double the antiphons as we do today became the favorite practice by the fifth or sixth century.

By far the greatest number of antiphons are taken from the psalms, and unquestionably the psalter is their oldest source. These psalmodic antiphons are made up of a brief sentence taken from the beginning of the psalm or from one of its most striking verses; thus they seize our attention from the beginning. Sometimes these phrases reproduce the chosen verse as it is in the psalm; at other times it is retouched a little, worded in a slightly different way. Often, especially in the longer antiphons, they are mosaics made up of pieces taken from various verses.

These psalmodic antiphons are found, first of all, in the psalter for the week and besides that in the Matins of Easter, Christmas, Epiphany, the *Triduum Sacrum*, and in the Commons of the Saints and our Lady. On these feast days they are either chosen (with admirable discrimination) or made up from those verses of the psalm that have a special relation to the feast. Psalmodic antiphons are also found at Lauds and Vespers in certain feasts but that is most exceptional. We must include the *Alleluia* antiphon among them because this joyful cry is found in some of the psalms.

The extreme literary and melodic simplicity of so many of these antiphons from the psalms is certainly indicative of their great antiquity (they are supposed to go back to the fifth or sixth centuries).

What we said about the antiphons in general and the part they play in opening up the psalm is of course especially applicable to the antiphons from the psalter. There are many others which are not taken from the psalms but from other books of the Bible, and even from non-scriptural sources. These antiphons naturally do not interpret the psalm but rather create the atmosphere of the feast or season. They may be connected together, as the psalms of Vespers often are, and in that way build up a picture of the event or the saint commemorated. Thus they furnish us with the object to be contemplated. On All Saints Day, for example, the antiphons unfold for us the great scene depicted in the Apocalypse of St. John: "*Vidi turbam magnam quam dinumerari nemo poterat ex omnibus gentibus stantes ante thronum*," and we hear the Canticle of the redeemed: "*Redemisti nos Domine in sanguine tuo*." These antiphons, taken from other books of the Bible, furnish us with an excellent example of the contemplative approach to the mystery of salvation so much loved by the Church; they introduce us into the heart of the mystery commemorated and help us to live it.

There is a special class of antiphons used with the *Benedictus* and the *Magnificat* called Gospel antiphons. On week days they are taken from the Canticle itself and in an extraordinary way point it up, giving us a new and different insight into the Canticle each day. On Sundays and on certain feasts this is taken from the Gospel of the day; here again it often selects with nice discrimination the most striking verses from the Gospel and by thus concentrating upon them gives us new understanding of the Gospel texts. Attached to the *Benedictus*, the canticle of praise, and the *Magnificat*, the canticle of thanksgiving, they give the motive for the special praise and thanksgiving that is suited to a particular Sunday or a particular feast. We even find at times (though this should not be pushed too far!) that the melody which accompanies the antiphon tries to interpret the sense of the words. These antiphons from the Gospel contribute to the solemnity with which the Canticles of the *Benedictus* and *Magnificat* are invested.

Some antiphons are not taken from Scripture but from the "Acts" of the saints—usually martyrs—whose feast is commemorated. Many of these are marked with a strong mystical flavor; this is particularly true of those for the feast of St. Agnes; with the responsories they make this Office one of the most beautiful in the Breviary. Those of St. Laurence also deserve to be mentioned. Unfortunately, most of these "historical antiphons" are drawn from "Acts" that are apocryphal; this is one of the reasons, together with the idea that antiphons from non-scriptural sources should not be used, which prompted the editors of the Neo-Gallican Breviaries to cut them out ruthlessly. Insofar as they reflect the sentiments that a martyr or a virgin should have, and insofar as they are like those of St. Agnes, that is, poetic and noble in the expression of their sentiments, it would seem that they should not be sacrified to the rigid canons of historicity. But those that merely recount the marvelous, without any historical foundation at all, hardly seem to deserve a place in the Offices of the Church, and very likely they will be dropped from them in a future revision.

There are many other antiphons which do not fit into any of the above named categories; we might call them independent antiphons. They may be inspired by Scripture but they are not drawn from it, and they cannot be classed as historical antiphons either. Their number is not inconsiderable when we look over the Office of the entire year.

Prominent among this class of antiphons are those used for the *Magnificat* on the days of Advent between the seventeenth of December and the twenty-third, called because of the first word the "O" antiphons. These marvelous compositions are well-known to those who live the prayer of the Church and are deeply loved by all. They contain, as one author has put it so well, the very marrow of Advent, and it is hard to imagine Advent without them. While not taken *directly* from Scripture they nevertheless form a series of pieces woven from the themes and the ideas which make up the *substance* of Scripture; besides, many of the phrases used in composing them are taken directly from the Bible.

Everyone knows how they are made up: Christ is invoked by some title taken from the Old Testament and this is in turn used as the basis for an earnest plea that He should come and work in us to fulfill the promise latent in that title. What is not always appreciated is the unusually refined liturgical sense shown in selecting these titles, in the skillful arrangement of the Scripture texts, and in the composition of the whole prayer. Between the title given to the Son of God and the object of each request there is a perfect harmoniousness that is certainly striking. The very melody of these antiphons puts them in a class apart; without ever intruding itself, it still succeeds in conveying in the term *veni* all the vehemence of the Church's desire for her Savior and Spouse and all her longing for her redemption. Everyone knows that they are sung (or recited) in full before and after the *Magnificat,* and that they are used from the seventeenth to the twenty-third of December. What is not so well known is that they were originally intended to accompany the *Benedictus* rather than the *Magnificat,* which should not surprise us if we reflect that the Canticle of Zachary is in general much more closely related to them, and that one at least (the *O Oriens*) approaches directly to one of the verses of the *Benedictus*.

Several times during the year, and that on the greatest feasts, the antiphon of the *Magnificat* is a *Hodie* antiphon—one of those priceless compositions which so dramatically recalls the events which the feast celebrates and which conveys a sense of actuality. We feel we are not so much commemorating what is past as celebrating what is being re-enacted. They belong to a type of religious ode that is much more common in the Eastern rites and it is most probable that we owe them to the Greek and Syrian popes of the seventh and eighth centuries. They are not the only borrowings from the East that have enriched the Roman Office; there are a good number of others during the year, for example, those of the feast of the Birth of the Blessed Virgin, "*Nativitas tua*," the well-known and greatly loved "*Sub Tuum*," the matchless antiphons of Vespers on the Octave Day of Christmas, "*O Admirabile Commercium*." They retain the strongly laudative and contemplative flavor of the Oriental liturgies, particularly those used on feasts of our Lady who is so beautifully and tirelessly praised in these rites.

Marian Antiphons. To call these antiphons is in reality a misnomer; they are rather hymns or odes in honor of the Blessed Virgin. They owe their present place in the Breviary to the Franciscans who added them in the thirteenth century. It is interesting, in the light of the new decree which prescribes that they are to be said or sung only after Compline in the future, to find that this was the rule when they were first introduced; it was St. Pius V who first ordered that they were to be said after the other hours. As we might suppose, the Marian antiphons were actually composed long before they found their way into the Roman Breviary. They were all originally antiphons used at different hours in various places in the Church for certain feasts.

The "*Alma Redemptoris Mater*," sung during Advent and Christmastide, is the most "theological" of these antiphons. Made up of different passages from the Fathers, it amounts to a little treatise on Mariology; Mary's part in our redemption is its theme. Originally it was an antiphon for Sext on the feast of the Assumption. "*Ave Regina Coelorum*" was originally an antiphon for None on the same feast; hence the references to the

Queen of the Heavens and of the Angels, as well as the title "Glorious Virgin." It is a farewell to our Lady as she mounts to Heaven. It was composed somewhere between the tenth and the twelfth centuries. "*Regina Coeli Laetare*" was originally a rhyming antiphon used with the *Magnificat* during the octave of Easter; it appears about the twelfth century. It is a greeting to our Lady but even more a proclamation of the Resurrection. The favorite of them all is the "*Salve Regina*" which enjoyed immense popularity during the Middle Ages. St. Bernard was credited with having added the conclusion "*O Clemens, O Pia*" but it has been found in a manuscript earlier than his time. Who the composer of the whole antiphon was, no one knows for certain, but it was probably written by Hermanus Contractus (eleventh century). This hymn is filled with the ardent, tender, personal piety towards the Blessed Virgin which characterized the Middle Ages. It was first used as a processional hymn. In modern times it has received new emphasis by being placed at the head of the prayers after Mass, where it must be said that in English at least it suffers in part from a too-literal translation which gives it in places a rather remote and artificial sound.

The Responsories. The greatest single cause of the variety and the beauty of the Office is unquestionably the responsory, which provides the dramatic element as well. With the lessons the responsories form the oldest part of the Office, because the psalms were first sung in the Christian assembly responsorially, that is, the cantor sang a verse and the people sang the refrains. The custom, like so many other usages in our liturgy, was borrowed from the synagogue worship of the Jews. The rule among the Jews and the Christians was that a chant should follow the lesson as an echo of it, at least to the extent that it reflected the mood. There is, then, a relation, at times direct and intimate, between the lesson and the responsory, so that strictly speaking the responsory does not nor cannot stand alone. This singing of a chant of some kind was a natural provision against the too-great monotony that reading alone would produce; but it is also possible that—at least as it developed—the responsory was influenced by the same impulse that created the chorus in Greek drama, and that the idea was to provide a kind of acted-out commentary on what had been read, reflecting the sentiments and sensations of the hearers, as the chorus reflected those of the spectators. The responsory, like the chorus, relates, instructs, prays, rejoices, weeps, and laments, according to what is contained in the lesson (Holy Week, Advent, Office of the Dead). Thus it is a kind of echo, or answer in song, to the lesson. The ideal, therefore, would be a complete union between the lesson and the responsory, so that the chant would directly echo what is in the lesson, but that is hardly possible very often. Rather what we have is the idea of the feast or season acted out in song, or the vivid representation of some theme that runs through the whole book that is being read. An example of this are the responsories that go with the Book of Job. They are taken from other and later parts of the Book and act as a kind of theme-chant or background music for the reading of the Book. They are thus most often related to the Book as a whole, or to the feast as a whole, rather than to the individual lesson.

The responsory as a result has great variety and many purposes. It arouses our attention, stimulates prayer and the prayerful frame of mind, illustrates the lesson or the feast, expresses the various meanings of the feast or season, stirs up compunction and contrition, helps us to participate more actively in the event we are celebrating; it deepens our insight into the meaning of the season or the feast. The responsory belongs to the poetic part of the Breviary; all kinds of poetry are represented in it: narrative, didactic, epic, lyric. Many of them are intensely dramatic; in them, as in the Introits, we hear the voice of Christ, of our Lady, of the Saints, or of the prophets of old. A superb example of such a responsory and one of the finest in the whole group is the "*Aspiciens a longe*" for the first Sunday of Advent.

The ultimate purpose of the responsory is to enable us to enter more deeply into the Scriptures, to penetrate to the heart of the message that they contain. The texts are often so arranged that they lead into one another, and the repetition helps to drive the idea home. It is meditation in the ancient sense of the word. The general effect is to present the ideas from the inside, giving the whole responsory that tone and flavor which we associate with contemplation. We do not so much contemplate the idea as *live* it, and thus enter more completely into the spirit of the feast or season. The responsory awakens and sustains the atmosphere proper to the time. It is the Church's meditation upon the lesson, or upon the themes contained in the feast or the season of the year.

By the responsories the Scriptures are opened up to us and their true meaning is seen. The former thus play one of their greatest roles, which is to interpret the Scriptures, to present the great themes which unite them and to show the continuity between the Old and the New Testaments. Indeed, some of the responsories, notably those of Corpus Christi, are made up by a happy juxtaposition of texts from the Old and New Testaments, forming one responsory. Those taken from the Old Testament serve as a guide: they select the significant passages, or at least the most arresting, and help to point up the whole direction of the Old Testament as leading us to Christ. They enshrine much of the noblest thoughts and prayers of the Old Testament and thus act also as a school of prayer and a repository of good thoughts and holy affections. By means of the responsory we make our own the prayers of the great and holy men who lived before Christ and pointed the way to Him. Those taken from the New Testament afford us an insight into the teaching of the Gospel and of the apostles; they help us to savor the great and nourishing ideas that the New Testament contains, and they point the way to a piety based solidly upon the Gospel.

The responsories are, then, a most valuable and necessary part of the Office; like the antiphons, only more so, they transform what would be merely reading of the Scriptures into prayer. They impart unction and devotion to the Office and consequently arouse the spirit of prayer in those who recite it.

Responsories taken from the Psalms. These responsories form a rather large group in the Office, particularly in the season after Epiphany. They may either be direct quotations from the psalter, using as a rule the most significant passages from the psalms and serving as a kind of compendium or condensation; or they may be a cento made up of phrases from the psalter, so that while they come from the psalter indirectly they are not to be found as such anywhere in the Scriptures themselves. Psalmodic responsories are the original responsories; as a group in the Office they form the most ancient nucleus of the *Responsoriale Romanum* and apparently were once much more numerous than they are today, when they are confined almost exclusively to the *Pars Hiemalis.* They are a continual source of delight to the observant reader, giving an insight into the psalms that makes one feel as though he were reading them for the first time.

Responsories taken from other books of the Bible. These run through the year and are usually taken from the book that is being read at the time. They usually seize upon some dominant theme and thus illustrate and comment upon the book itself. They serve as a kind of recapitulation, or as a key that unlocks the general meaning of the book that is being read. Very often they are made up of certain exclamatory passages that condense a whole situation into a few words. These responsories may be taken from books other than those that are being read but they will, nevertheless, be appropriate to the season itself.

Worthy of special mention among these scriptural responsories are those of Holy Week: superb compositions often drawn from the Gospel, which they sometimes quote directly and at other times paraphrase or rearrange, for example, "*In monte Oliveti.*" In them the contemplative character of the responsory is seen at its best; they are filled with unction and communicate to us, as almost nothing else can, the spirit and the tone of the Word of God.

Non-Scriptural Responsories. The number of these is not very great, nor is their quality as high as those taken from the Scriptures. Some are taken from the "acts" of the martyrs. The value of these lies more in the way they express the thoughts of the saint rather than in the history they narrate. Others are compositions by different authors; some of these latter, like the "*Regnum mundi et omne ornatum*" of the Common of Holy Women, are very fine, others are not especially distinguished. Like the antiphons of this type, a certain number have a strong mystical flavor. The non-scriptural responsories entered into the Office about the seventh or eighth century.

Brief Responsories. They were introduced into the "Little Hours" of Terce, Sext, and None in the fifth century, and into Prime and Compline in the ninth. To this day those of the latter two hours never change except for one verse at Prime which varies according to the feast or season. Those used for the other "Little Hours" change with the Office. On feast days they serve to awaken devotion by presenting different aspects of the feast; on ordinary Sundays they are taken from Psalm 118 read in the "Little Hours"; on week days they are drawn from other sources, inspired by some word or phrase in the *capitulum;* on ferial days in Advent, Lent, and Passiontide they recall some of the themes of these seasons.

The *Responsoria breva* are in keeping with the original purpose and character of the "Little Hours"; they provide a brief but effective way to lift up our hearts to God at certain times during the day.

Scripture Lessons. The reading of the Scriptures has always been part of Christian worship as it was with Jewish worship and for about the same reason. They were read not primarily as a collection of edifying thoughts nor even primarily for their spiritual content, but as the history of salvation, as the account of God's dealing with men and as His word addressed to the children of men. Both the Old and New Testaments are linked together and the strand that unites them is God's mysterious purpose which runs through them, giving them order and coherence and culminating in the Revelation of His Son. Since this Word of God was directed to the people of Israel, it had to be read in the full assembly in order that they might recall together as a people what God had done and what He had promised. The Scriptures are, then, addressed to the Church and it is in the surroundings of the assembly that they take on their full meaning. What is more, the Church is *entrusted* with the Scriptures; only the Church can truly give them to us.

The reading of the Scriptures in the Office is a meditative, prayerful reading in which the spiritual sense of the Word of God is shown to us. The Lamb opens the Book; Christ is the key to the Scriptures and their spiritual sense is ultimately a direction towards Him. "Read the prophets without Christ in them—what is more tasteless or more flat? Find Christ in them, then they will not only taste well, they will make you drink." *

The reading of the Scriptures in the Christian assembly derived from the Jewish synagogue practice. It was a *lectio continuata*: the entire Scripture was read straight through. With the passing of time the principle was that as the psalter was read every week the entire Scripture should be read through every year, but in a different order. When it was introduced into Matins (before the sixth century) the reading was arranged so that those parts would be read that were appropriate for the different seasons and feasts of the year. The lessons were longer at first, but were shortened during the Middle Ages. The Scripture readings of the liturgy remind us that Christian

* St. Augustine.

worship is first of all objective: it is the proclamation of something that has happened, an event in the past which we in some wonderful way have in the present. What happened is that God entered into history, and it is this fact that the Scriptures announce and comment upon. It is God speaking to us; our worship is above all else the proclamation of what He has done, and to proclaim is of necessity to praise.

The order of the Scripture reading is, as we have said, not arbitrary, but accommodated to the liturgical year. In Advent we see that because Isaias is the evangelist among the prophets and so minutely describes the King that is to come, and because he expresses so well the ardent longing of humanity for a Redeemer, the Book of Isaias is read. St. Paul had such marvelous insight into the divinity of Christ and the meaning of the Incarnation that we can find no one better to listen to during the Christmas and Epiphany season. During Septuagesima and in Lent (which seems at one time to have marked the beginning of the Church year) we turn to the Old Testament and to those books which deal with the fall of man and the beginning of God's merciful dealing with men, and which treat of the great patriarchs, types and figures of the Redeemer, introducing us to the new Covenant which is prayerfully recalled, commemorated, and represented at Easter. In Passiontide our reading is from Jeremias who is the prophet of the Passion. At Easter we return to the New Testament and read those books which expound and unfold for us the new and eternal Covenant—the kingdom of God and His Christ—the Acts of the Apostles, the Epistles and especially the Apocalypse. During the season after Pentecost the Church reads those Old Testament writings which present the kingdom of Christ under the types of the Old Testament kingdom and theocracy. We see it from without in the Books of Kings—the kingdom strengthened and spread—and with Samuel, David and Solomon, all figures of Christ. In times of decadence God sends His prophets Elias and Eliseus as the forerunners of His Son.

The inner nature of the kingdom is dealt with in great detail in the Sapiential Books. Christ is perfect Wisdom, foreshadowed and described in these books which someone has beautifully described as the "Beatitudes in advance." Next come the concrete figures of Job, Tobias, Judith and Esther, giving instruction and inspiration in the form of history. The heroic struggle for the cause of God and His Kingdom is described in the Books of Machabees. With the prophets we turn in the last weeks of the declining year to the eschatological concept of the kingdom, contemplating the passage from the city of God on earth to the heavenly city and the eternal kingdom of God.

Thus, each year we are given an opportunity to read the essential parts of Scripture and to be penetrated by its spirit. We follow the unfolding of God's design and penetrate into the heart of revelation, seeing it all as an ordered and harmonious whole. We would see this even better if we could read more of the Scriptures and especially of the Gospels. A restoration of longer Scripture lessons is earnestly to be desired. The Benedictine custom of reading the entire Gospel pericope for each day would be a welcome addition to the Breviary. If the historical and patristic lessons were cut down and the Scripture lessons lengthened somewhat, a better balance would be attained.

Patristic Lessons. The custom of commenting on the Scripture that has been read in the liturgy goes back to Jewish times and was continued by the Christians. During the Mass, the Fathers were accustomed to give sermons either on the Gospel or upon the other lessons that were read. Later on, when Matins had been established for some time, it became customary to add those sermons and homilies of the Fathers which had some bearing on the Scripture that had been read. The idea was to provide a kind of meditation upon the sacred text that would stir up devotion (dedication of the spirit to God).

Because it was felt that the Fathers more than anyone else had grasped most perfectly the sense and meaning of the Scriptures, what they had to say about the Word of God was regarded with the greatest reverence. Besides that, in the Fathers we find Christian teaching at its best and richest, ranging over the whole field of doctrine and relating it to life.

The Patristic lessons of the Office form a real treasury of Christian thought and when they are at their best the Fathers have much to say to us. Perhaps the best passages from their writings have not always been chosen, but even granting this there is a great residue of noble and uplifting thoughts to be found in the passages from SS. Leo, Augustine, Ambrose, Gregory, Jerome and John Chrysostom, to mention only those who recur most frequently; there are as well many beautiful ideas from illustrious writers who appear less frequently, like St. Cyprian. The sermons of St. Leo, which occur at the great seasons of the Church year, are particularly rewarding and instructive for the insight they give us into the meaning of the feast or season. Chrysostom's sermons are full of real unction and the spirit of the Gospel. St. Augustine's are exceedingly lively and stimulating, and are especially good on his favorite topic: the Mystical Body of Christ.

Perhaps future revisions will give us more and better selections from the Fathers (and Doctors) and provide us with greater variety.

The Lives of the Saints. The early Christians when they met at the tombs of the martyrs read their "*Acta*" (accounts of martyrdom) in order to draw inspiration and courage from their example. When Matins took form this ancient custom was continued by reading the life of the saint whose feast was being celebrated. This reading was known as the Second Nocturn. Unfortunately, much that is legendary and apocryphal found its way into these accounts which became proverbially inaccurate; they were so preoccupied with edification that they overlooked historical accuracy. This is not true of the lessons dealing with saints canonized since the sixteenth century. Much revision of this part of the Office is needed, as everyone admits, but it is not an easy task.

Nevertheless, we can still profit much by what we read. The great majority of these accounts are calls to the heart; they edify and uplift us, furnish us with inspiration and encouragement. They remind us of the saint and of his virtues, and by so doing put us to shame. Any saint was and is a living commentary on the Gospel. They were models of prayer, of charity, and of all virtues; they present Christian life in the concrete.

We could wish for more details perhaps, for a more living presentation of the man, and in the more recent lessons we could ask for greater simplicity and less art, but we still have fine spiritual reading here. These lessons imbue us with the spirit of the saint and make us more conscious of him. We live with him on his feast day!

Hymns. With the responsories the hymns go to make up the affective and lyrical element of the Divine Office, and thus contribute to giving it variety and richness. As the very name indicates (*hymnein* means to sing in Greek), they are in reality songs—poems set to music; the text and the melody are regulated by the laws of prosody and rhythm. They are, then, intended to be sung; like the psalms they cannot be fully appreciated unless heard in their musical setting. Yet even when only recited the poetic rhythm and their doctrinal content makes them a source of joy and edification.

The singing of hymns is as old as the Church itself, as the reference to them in St. Paul's Epistles and the fragments found both in his writings and in the Apocalypse testify. These early hymns were not the metrical hymns that we associate with the Word, but a kind of Christian psalm after the manner of the Canticles of the Old Testament; they are therefore called "*psalmi idiotici,*" private psalms, in contradistinction to the inspired psalms. The term used to describe them is comprehensive enough to embrace anything that was sung and thus would include such diverse productions as the *Benedictus* of Zachary and the *Gloria in Excelsis* which is more related to the short doxologies that fill the Scriptures. We have no way of knowing for certain when these hymns were introduced into Christian worship, but we do know that their misuse by the Gnostics caused them to be used more cautiously by orthodox Christians, and even prompted one Council (Laodicaea) to forbid the singing of any "private psalm" in Church.

The beginning of Christian hymnody properly so-called came in the fourth century both in the East and West. At first, these hymns were composed according to the laws of classical prosody, the verse based upon the quantity of the syllables. The great difficulty about this form was that hymns written according to these laws would never be popular; they were too difficult for people to learn. St. Ambrose must be counted as the father of Christian Latin hymnody, for he composed hymns in which the verse was built upon the number of syllables and the tonic accent of the words. This new and simplified way of composing hymns meant that henceforward they could belong to the people and be used in Church to express the truths of religion, instead of being a kind of luxury for musical aesthetes. St. Ambrose made abundant use of his new invention and enriched the public worship of the Church with many marvelous compositions. Furthermore, he was imitated by many other writers in the course of time who wrote so well in the Ambrosian metre that it became a real problem for scholars later on to distinguish the authentic compositions of Ambrose from those written by others. All these "Ambrosian" hymns have this in common: they are profoundly doctrinal and altogether objective, admirably suited for the conveying of Christian truths. Some of the hymns actually composed by Ambrose are in our modern Breviary, and are among the finest we have: "*Aeterne Rerum Conditor*" at Lauds on Sunday, the glorious "*Splendor Paterni*

Gloriae" for Lauds on Monday, "*Consors Paterni Luminis*" for Matins on Tuesday. Many others in the Ambrosian style, but not written by him, are nevertheless excellent examples of their kind, like the "*Te Lucis*" at Compline.

During the next few centuries others continued to add to the literature of Christian hymnody: Prudentius, who is represented by a good number of our best hymns; Venantius Fortunatus, to whom we owe the incomparable "*Pange Lingua*" of Passion time and the impressive "*Vexilla Regis*"; Sedulius, who wrote the lovely "*A solis ortus cardine*" used at Christmas time, and St. Gregory the Great, who probably wrote "*Lucis Creator Optime.*"

The mediaeval period produced many fine hymn writers of whom St. Thomas Aquinas is perhaps the best known. Taken all together, they were not in the same class with the writers of the centuries that preceded them and it is a fact that with the close of the Middle Ages hymn-writing began to decline. The accent is on personal devotion rather than on doctrine; the "*Stabat Mater*" is worlds apart from "*O Gloriosa Virginum.*" The older hymns, even when they were not composed for liturgical services, have a liturgical character about them; they speak as the Church would speak. The more modern hymns are the voice of individuals—subjective rather than objective.

In any case, the hymns written for the Breviary in modern times are far inferior to those of the patristic and mediaeval period. Certainly they lack the simplicity and naturalness which distinguish the earlier works, largely because their authors aim at writing in the classical vocabulary ("*Te Joseph celebrent*" is an example). However, the hymns written for the feasts of our Lord keep close to the tradition that Christian hymns should be doctrinal rather than moral in tone.

Although most of the Breviary hymns were written in the patristic period and in the early Middle Ages (St. Benedict had introduced them into the monastic Office in his day), they were not admitted to the Roman Office until the twelfth century. That is one reason why they still do not appear in the Offices of the *Triduum Sacrum,* of Easter, and of the Dead. These are the oldest Offices we have, and the Church has been traditionally conservative about admitting new elements into them.

"*Cantare amantis est*"; "Sung prayer is doubly prayer." The hymns express doctrine in song and nourish both the mind and the affections, causing us to admire, wonder, adore and imitate what we contemplate in the hymns. Poetry in general is intended to express the inner nature of something, to get at what is essential and universal about the object. A poet sees what other people see but he sees it in a new light; he sees it more clearly and feels more intensely about it. That is one reason why we can say that poetry expresses the real truth about things, truths only half expressed in prose. Christian poetry and Christian hymns must, then, be the expression on a higher level of truths that we believe. We see these truths in a new light when they are presented to us in song and in hymns.

The hymns of the Breviary draw their themes from the feast or the season or the particular hour of the day. Those that are written for feasts of our Lord usually recount in poetic form some incident in the history of salvation and then base petitions upon the event; those for the feasts of our Lady and the saints describe their virtues or address them directly, and ask their help or intercession; or they may ask God for favors through the intercession of the saints. The hymns that draw their themes from the hours of the day usually make an analogy between the material and physical circumstances—light, darkness, day, night—and the spiritual grace or form that they ask for. In general, the purpose of the hymn is to raise our minds and hearts to God and to spiritual things, to edify us, to awaken and maintain in us religious sentiments and emotions.

The quality of the hymns of the Breviary is necessarily uneven. There are many splendid hymns but there are also hymns which are little better than ordinary. We can say, however, that in the main they are remarkably faithful to the tradition of what hymns used in Christian worship should be: they have that doctrinal temper, that emphasis upon God, that solemn joy which befits the service of God, and they are free from that mere subjective emotion which disfigures so many later Christian hymns.

The text of the hymnary was revised under Urban VIII in the seventeenth century by a commission of Jesuits whose aim it was to correct the Latinity of the hymns. Unfortunately, they succeeded only in spoiling the hymns and in robbing them of most of their charm and simplicity. The attempt to clothe these ancient Christian hymns in the classical vocabulary in vogue with the Humanists was not at all a happy one, and it may be that in the promised revision of the Office the original unspoiled version will be restored.

The Athanasian Creed, which in the future will be recited only on Trinity Sunday, is more an exposition or a catechesis than it is a profession of faith. Nor has it any connection with St. Athanasius, having been composed long after his time. No one knows for certain who the author is. The precise doctrine on the Incarnate Word indicates that it comes from the time of the great Christological debates or soon after them (fifth century). It is a true masterpiece, distinguished both for the lucidity and beauty of its doctrinal exposition and the artistry with which its ideas are expressed. It was introduced into the Office in the ninth century.

The Gospel Canticles. The daily prayer of the Church draws upon the Gospel for three of the canticles which, each in its own way, set forth the theme of the Incarnation and the Redemption. We might say that they are the Gospel in song. A canticle is traditionally a song of praise and thanksgiving to God for some great benefit; the gospel Canticles are, in addition, a comment on the whole range of Sacred Scripture. Each of these three great Canticles will have its special attraction for different persons, but the *Benedictus* can claim a greater and more developed range of ideas than either of the other two; it is pre-eminently a theologian's work. It has been well said that the *Magnificat* is royal, while the *Benedictus* is sacerdotal—the priestly Canticle of the Incarnation, "the last prophecy of the Old Testament; the first of the New."

The Benedictus. Its most frequent use is at Lauds. It has been sung or recited there perhaps since the fifth century; the words "to enlighten them that sit in darkness" may have inspired its selection, but the words "day-star from on high" make it especially appropriate for an hour that (ideally) is said in the early morning. The reference to "directing our steps in the way of peace" no doubt influenced its choice for use in the prayers to be said before going on a journey; and "to enlighten them that sit in darkness and in the shadow of death" explains its use at funerals. Because it is in a very true sense the Canticle of the Incarnation, it is most appropriate for Advent and Christmas time although it is never out of place at any time of the year. How it enlightens and instructs us! What morning freshness it always retains!

The Benedictus is indeed a Gospel canticle, not only because it is taken from the Gospel, but because it gathers up the whole meaning of the Gospel even in its first lines: "Blessed be the Lord God of Israel, because he has visited and redeemed his people." For this is the Gospel—the glad-tidings: salvation is brought to us by God in Christ. The rest of the Canticle is but a development of this one great idea; it is a messianic Canticle packed with allusions to the Old Testament and saturated with the loftiest spirit of the latter. At the same time it looks to the New Covenant and the blessings of the messianic order that has already begun to dawn.

The *Benedictus* is divided rather naturally into two parts. In the first part, Zachary gives thanks to God for the coming of the salvation brought by the Messiah, and speaks of the rôle his son, the forerunner, is to play in that work. In the first eight verses he greets the mighty salvation that God has raised up in the House of David. This is what the prophets have foretold: salvation from the hands of our enemies and deliverance from the hands of those who hate us. God has delivered Israel in the past from her enemies and now He delivers her from the greatest enemies of all and frees her from the bondage of Satan and sin. It is a wider deliverance and a more abundant redemption. It is a salvation that reached to the depths of the human soul and fashioned a new race of men. Now is fulfilled the oath made to Abraham that he should form an elect and chosen people whose purpose would be to serve God in holiness and righteousness all the days of their lives. "That without fear, delivered from the hands of our enemies, we might serve him in holiness and justice before him all the days of our life."

There is the Redemption, the messianic salvation conceived and expressed in the most concrete imagery possible; this is the work of the Redeemer inspired by God's mercy and loving kindness towards us. We are delivered from our enemies and enjoy the peace of Christ—a peace that permits us to live out our lives in His presence and in that dedicated service that the Redemption makes possible and at the same time fruitful.

Zachary then addresses the new-born child, the son God has granted him in his old age, hails him as the prophet of the Most High and indicates what his mission will be. John will announce the coming of the Messiah; he will prepare the way before him in the hearts and minds of men. He will give knowledge of salvation to his people by showing men that it consists in the remission of their sins, which will be attained by the contrite of heart and those whose minds are converted to God. The messianic kingdom is to be a spiritual kingdom and the remission of sins the fruit of God's mercy which He has shown by visiting us: "The day spring from on high—to enlighten them that sit in darkness and the shadow of death—and to direct our feet in the way of peace." In the last verses Zachary returns to the theme of the benefits of the Gospel and insists particularly on the two greatest of all that it brings—light and peace.

When the Church sings this glad and tranquil hymn, she adopts the words of Zachary and makes them her own. They become for her and for us the renewed affirmation of faith in Christ and the description of His redeeming work. Each new day is a day of salvation; during the course of each day God visits us and redeems us; each day Christ, the Daystar and the Sun of Justice, shines upon us in the holy mysteries and visits us in all the events of our lives. He enlightens us and directs our steps into the way of peace, enabling us to serve Him in holiness and justice. As each day is a new day of salvation, a new space of time for the working out of our redemption, so the Canticle of Zachary becomes each day a new song upon new lips, a fresh approach to the Mystery of "Christ in us, your hope of glory."

When Lauds is solemnly sung the altar is incensed during the *Benedictus* and the people stand. The chant is more solemn than that of the psalms. There is a special antiphon to accompany it, often taken from the Gospel of the day. All this serves to highlight the Canticle and to emphasize its dignity, making it the culmination of the morning Office.

The Magnificat. This is a very ancient part of the Office, going back at least to the fifth century. The Canticle of the Blessed Virgin, because it is so filled with the idea of thanksgiving, has long been associated (since the time of St. Benedict in the sixth century) with Vespers, the hour of the Office which traditionally recalls at the end of the day God's many gifts to men and gives thanks for them. Modelled on the Canticle of Anna in the Book of Kings, it is nonetheless an original synthesis of the whole Old Testament, a rich mosaic of its great themes, expressing the joy of the lowly and meek whom our Lady represents and typifies at the fulfillment of God's promise to Israel (His people, the Church) by the Incarnation and the redemption. Originally sung by Mary, the Daughter of Sion, it becomes each day the Canticle of the Church which Mary typified and of each Christian soul who rejoices that "He who is mighty has done great things to me."

Nunc Dimittis. The Canticle of Simon was introduced into the Office with the addition of Compline (fifth or sixth century), and has always been deeply loved by the Church. The shortest of the Gospel canticles, it is, nevertheless, in many ways the most developed of the three. It looks upon the Incarnation as already achieved (while the others look forward to it), and contemplates its *universal* meaning. Christ is the salvation of all men, the light that enlightens the Gentiles, as well as the glory of His people Israel. Already Simeon sees the full development of the messianic hope. It is singularly appropriate at the close of the day when the darkness of night, symbol of death and the prince of darkness, has set in. Only the light of Christ can dissipate the darkness by conquering Satan and death at the same time.

The Te Deum. The long morning prayer of the Church closes with a magnificent canticle redolent of the piety of the ancient Church, rich in scriptural allusions, moving in its majestic progress from praise of the Trinity to praise of Christ the Redeemer, then to earnest petition for God's help and protection, and closing with the expression of supreme confidence and trust. Even when recited it is awesome, but when joined to the superb melody which accompanies it, its effect is overwhelming. It is a chant for great occasions, the hymn of thanksgiving for great and signal manifestations of God's merciful providence and the inevitable climax of great events in the Church's life. Through many centuries this glorious triumphal song of the Church in Heaven and on earth has echoed through the vaults and arches of stately cathedrals and venerable abbey churches, climaxing the Consecration of bishops, the blessing of abbots, and the anointing of kings.

The name that is given to it in the Breviary, *Hymnus Ambrosianus*, is misleading on two accounts. For one thing, its connection with St. Ambrose is most doubtful; certainly the legend about St. Ambrose and St. Augustine composing it spontaneously at the Baptism of the newly converted Augustine is pure fabrication; for another it is not a single hymn at all but a composite affair made up of three distinct parts which were amalgamated together from pre-existing hymns. Some parts of it appear to go back to the third century, but the final definite edition is credited to a fifth-century bishop, Nicetas of Remesiana. Much of the confusion and the discussion regarding authorship springs precisely from its composite character which becomes quite apparent under even the most superficial analysis.

The first part, comprising the first to the thirteenth verses, is classed as a Trinitarian hymn, although the Trinity is mentioned only in the last three verses:

> *Patrem immensae majestatis*
> *Venerandum tuum verum et unicum filium*
> *Sanctum quoque paraclitum spiritum.*

The second part, which seems to be a separate hymn in itself, runs from the fourteenth to the twentieth verse—"*Tu Rex Gloriae Christe*" down to "*Aeterna fac cum sanctis tuis in gloria numerari*"—and is directed to Christ. The last part is a series of invocations drawn from the psalms. The melody adapts itself to this division, changing at the fourteenth and twenty-first verses.

Upon close analysis the full beauty of the *Te Deum* is revealed to a degree which does not appear in the ordinary recitation. Like so many other prayers and rites of the liturgy, we have long taken it for granted, unaware that we are passing treasures hidden in a field.

In the first part we seem to be admitted into an impressive service of praise which reaches from Heaven to earth and back again. The whole earth, all created things, join in a chorus of praise led by the angels. Heaven opens before us and we hear the unceasing cry which the prophet Isaias heard before the throne of God. The cherubim and seraphim, Heaven and all the powers therein are singing with one voice, "Holy, Holy, Holy Lord God of Hosts, Heaven and earth are full of the majesty of Thy glory." The saints take up the cry, and each group in its place adds to the joyful hymn first, the glorious company of the apostles, then the praiseworthy ranks of the prophets, and the white-robed army of the martyrs. The Holy Church of Christ, His Bride redeemed by His precious Blood, unites on earth with the liturgy of Heaven to acknowledge the Lord and to praise "the Father of Infinite Majesty, Thy adorable, true and only Son, the Holy Ghost the Comforter."

The language of this first part is altogether sublime, steeped in scriptural associations, and conceived in the spirit of the psalms. We notice the use of the *Te* as the form of address in this part by contrast with the use of *Tu* in the second part. The references to the saints betray the extreme antiquity of this section. No confessors or virgins are mentioned, only the martyrs, thus taking us back to the time when the veneration of the saints was confined to those who had shed their blood for Christ. These martyrs are clad in white, which was their original color, rather than the red which has become associated with them. The "prophets" do not appear to be the Old Testament prophets, but rather those enigmatic figures who flourished in the very early Church, gifted with the charisma of prophecy, and who supplemented the work of the apostles. The fact that they are named after the apostles seems to confirm this theory.

If we examine the second part, we will notice not only the obvious fact that it is a Christological hymn extolling the redeeming work of Christ, but that it follows in a general way the Apostles' Creed. All the titles and the honors of Christ are enumerated in majestic sequence: He is the King of glory, the Everlasting Son of the Father, the Risen Lord, the Savior, the

Judge that is to come. The Christ who is portrayed here for us is the *Kyrios Pantocrator* so well beloved in the piety of the ancient Church, whose image in majesty adorned the apses of the ancient basilicas. The accent is upon His triumph; His redeeming work is presented as His great victory over death, a victory in which we share. There is ineffable tenderness in the allusion to the Incarnation, whereby He did not abhor the Virgin's womb. Notice the way the doctrine of redemption is presented: "When Thou didst take man upon Thee to deliver him." The redemption is not separated from the Incarnation which it presupposes and completes. This redemption was brought about by overcoming the sting of death and thus opening the Kingdom of Heaven to all believers. Here is the full glory of the resurrection from the dead, which opens the gates that were closed to us and transplants us into the Kingdom of God where Christ is now actually sitting at the right hand of God "whence He shall come to judge the living and the dead."

Mindful of what Christ has done—of the plentiful redemption that is ours—we beg a share in it by reminding Christ that we are bought at a great price, His precious Blood. This part closes with a prayer for the eternal and everlasting effects of redemption: that we may thereby be numbered forever among the saints and that we, the "People of God," "Thy People," may be saved; and that we, "Thy Inheritance," may be ever blessed; that as the Good Shepherd, He may guide us and rule us and lift us up for ever and ever.

The last part of the *Te Deum* is a series of short prayers, mainly petitions based upon the psalms (some parts are direct quotations), following no logical pattern yet sufficiently inclusive in range. "Deign this day, O Lord, to keep us without sin." "Have mercy on us, O Lord, have mercy on us." "Let Thy mercy be upon us because we have hoped in Thee." The whole extraordinary hymn ends with a grand cry of hope and confidence: "In Thee O Lord I have hoped; let me never be confounded."

Preces. The decree of April, 1955, modifying the rubrics of the Breviary abolished altogether the *Preces*, or litany prayers, once said at Prime and Compline and greatly reduced the number of times that the remaining *Preces* (at Lauds and Vespers) were to be said. This was in every way a happy solution of the problem; the recitation of *Preces* so often had become burdensome, yet many would regret to see them go altogether, because those said at Lauds and Vespers supplied for the lack of directly intercessory prayer in the Office. In the present arrangement only those *Preces* are retained, and by confining their recitation to Fridays and Wednesdays in Lent the decree avoids the possibility of their becoming a burden.

The idea of intercessory prayer is very ancient in the Church, going back in fact to apostolic times; St. Paul exhorts Timothy to give a large place to it in the Christian assembly (1 Tim. 2:12), and as we saw earlier in this book, this type of prayer occurred twice in the Mass: once in litany form, then after the Gospel in collect form. It appears in the Office during the sixth century. The use of psalm verses for responses instead of the "*Domine Miserere*" which was more usual in the Roman Rite seems to have been borrowed from Gaul. The *Preces* early acquired and have largely retained a strong penitential note. St. Pius X altered them somewhat and added the prayer for the pope and the bishop.

The Litany of the Saints. The Church knows no more solemn and impressive prayer of supplication than that Litany which for centuries has been called the Litany of the Saints. On all the great occasions in her life when God's help is most earnestly sought she turns to these noble forms to express her need and to implore divine aid and assistance. At the ordination of priests, the consecration of bishops, the blessing of abbots, the dedication of churches, on Holy Saturday, during the Rogation days, and twice during those special days of prayer for peace that are known as the "Forty Hours," these noble phrases well up from the very heart of the Church, are sung as by one man, deepening our awareness of the Body of Christ and intensifying our hope and certainty that the prayers of the Bride must be heard by the Bridegroom.

In spite of the fact that the saints occupy such a prominent place in the Litany, their invocation is in reality a much later addition to the original nucleus of the prayer, namely, the petitions which follow the list of saints. Because these petitions are addressed to God and because they more perfectly correspond to the very meaning of the word itself, we must say that the ancient nucleus is still the most important, as it is certainly the most developed part of the Litany.

The word litany itself comes from the Greek and means "prayer," but carries with it the special connotation of supplication, a humble but insistent prayer for definite intentions arranged in a series. As it developed it took the form of petitions announced by the leader and answered by the people. Indeed this form of prayer was known in a special way as the "prayer of the faithful." Litanies are very ancient in the Church, and there is warrant in the Epistles of SS. Peter and Paul for tracing them back to Apostolic times. They were extremely popular, answering as they did the natural and universal desire to make intercession. As might be expected, they were in time introduced into the Mass, where they were recited by the deacon. These supplications were prayers for the welfare of the Church, its rulers, and for its members, particularly those in distress or affliction. To each petition, spoken by the deacon, the congregation answered "*Kyrie Eleison*" or "*Domine Miserere.*" With the passing of time this litany dropped out of the Masses of the Roman Rite, although it was retained in the Gallican Rite and is still used in Milan on certain days. Our

Litany is one of these ancient formularies with the invocation of the saints added.

The prayer begins with the *Kyrie* and all three invocations are directed to the Son whose ancient title was "*Kyrios*," and not to the Three Persons of the Trinity as the usual explanation has it. Those that follow are specifically directed to the Persons of the Trinity individually and together. Then comes the invocation to our Lady and the saints. The list of saints developed until the Middle Ages when it stopped, as we can see by the fact that no modern saints are invoked. The arrangement is traditional but not altogether so. Mary is invoked by her most glorious titles, then the angels mentioned in Scripture, followed by St. John the Baptist and St. Joseph (this is very likely the most recent addition). The patriarchs and prophets are called upon as a group, then the apostles, martyrs (mostly those honored in the Church of Rome). The next list is mixed: there are two popes, three doctors of the Western Church but none of the East, and two bishops who were highly honored in the Middle Ages, St. Martin and St. Nicholas. All bishops and doctors are next invoked as a group. After them come the great monastic lawgivers, followed by a general invocation of holy priests and deacons, monks and hermits.

The list of women saints is the most undeveloped of all, containing no saints later than the age of the martyrs, and strangely enough omits Perpetua and Felicitas, whom we would expect to find here because they are always associated with the others in this list.

With the invocation "*Omnes Sancti et Sanctae Dei*" the first part of the prayer ends. From this point on the Litany is specifically addressed to our Lord. It is a noble series of entreaties for the spiritual and temporal welfare of the Church at large and the individual members in particular. We ask these blessings through the power of the great events in our redemption which give us a sure and certain hope that we will obtain them. The series begins with the versicle "Be Thou propitious" and its response "Spare us O Lord." Then follow the petitions for deliverance, or "deprecations." The grouping of these phrases is designed to bring together the related evils from which we pray to be delivered. First from all evil, then from foes spiritual within and without, from all sin, from God's wrath (the result of sin), from a sudden and unprovided death (from a death that finds us unprepared).

The Christian soul is a battlefield where evil passions, instigated by the devil, contend for mastery. From the heart proceed evil desires, hatred, wrath, ill will, the sins against God and neighbor and self which lead to the "second death." We see this simple and uncomplicated spiritual psychology of the time in which it was written reflected in the deprecations which deal with this situation: "From the snares of the devil, from wrath and hatred and all ill will, from the spirit of uncleanness, deliver us O Lord."

Spiritual disasters are always to be feared above all others, but while realizing that bodily disasters are the inevitable consequence of sin, the Church has always given place in her prayer to petitions against the many scourges that have so often devastated cities and even whole nations. "From lightning and tempest, from the scourge of earthquake, from disease, famine, and war, deliver us O Lord." We know that these things will come, yet by our prayers and by God's grace they may be lessened and their full fury not unleashed upon us. Lastly, we pray against the greatest evil that can come to body and soul: "From eternal death, deliver us O Lord."

The next ten petitions are "obsecrations" whereby we plead Christ's life and death and redeeming work as our title to hope for deliverance. They are an admirable summary of all that He has done to accomplish our redemption: the holiest mysteries of His most holy life, a detailed commentary in brief, incisive phrases on the text "Blessed is the Lord God of Israel who has visited and redeemed his people." "By the mystery of thy Holy Incarnation, by thy Coming, by thy Birth, thy Baptism and thy

Holy Fast, by thy Cross and Passion, by thy Death and Burial, by thy Holy Resurrection and admirable Ascension, by the coming of thy Comforting Spirit; in the Day of Judgment, deliver us O Lord."

The fourth part of the Litany is the most richly developed: the petitions look to the most thorough building up of the Body of Christ, "*aedificatio Corporis Christi,*" in the lives of individual members and throughout the whole Church, by bringing us all to true penance, raising our minds to heavenly desires, strengthening us, and keeping us in His holy service. We pray for the Church, that the Eternal Shepherd should govern and keep it, preserve it; for the pope and the clergy, that they should be kept in the full practice of the whole Christian life; for the peace and unity of all the holy people of God; for the return of those who have left the Church; for the spread of the light of the Gospel to all men. The prayer "for Christian kings and princes" sounds strangely out of date with the decline of the institution of the monarchy.

Among all these petitions there is only one for any material benefit, and it is a short and simple request: "That thou shouldst deign to give and to preserve the products of the earth, we beseech thee to hear us."

For special occasions such as ordinations and consecrations there are three petitions for God's blessing upon the person or church to be "blessed, consecrated, and sanctified." This part of the Litany closes with the solemn appeal to the Redeemer: "Son of God, we beseech thee to hear us, Lamb of God who takes away the sins of the world, have mercy on us."

The last part of the Litany is perhaps the latest addition; there is a psalm, versicles, and a series of orations, some Roman and some Gallican, which stress the idea of pardon for sin but also ask God's blessing on all the various members of the Church, upon the living and the dead.

The litanies have been associated very much with processions in the past; they are a form of prayer which lends itself to use in processions and they are still used in Rome when people go in procession to the stational churches during Lent. The laws prescribe their singing during the Rogation procession, but if there is no procession the litanies are recited kneeling.

The Litany of the Saints is unlike other sacred rites which once were held in honor and now have fallen into disuse. We have preserved this treasure but we could give it greater prominence and revitalize it, making it truly what it is—the "Prayer of the Faithful."

The Office of the Dead

The liturgy provides for a votive Office for funerals made up of Vespers, Matins and Lauds. It is one of the oldest in the Breviary, going back certainly to the seventh century and perhaps even beyond that. Like the Offices of the last three days of Holy Week, it preserves all the elements of the ancient Roman Office. Yet it was not originally recited or sung upon the day of burial; only in the eleventh century do we find it as part of the funeral service. During the entire Middle Ages and even into modern times it was also a votive Office said on certain days in addition to the Office of the day.

In contrast to the other Offices used by the Church, the psalmody of this Office is spoken in the name of the departed soul, expressing the frame of mind in which this soul finds itself: the sorrows of death and the perils of hell have surrounded it; its exile is prolonged; in its distress it turns to God and cries out to Him. It is truly remarkable how well the psalms and antiphons of this Office fit their purpose of reflecting the mood and state of mind of the departed soul. The lessons, taken from the Book of Job, have a like appropriateness. The responsories are mostly ecclesiastical compositions inspired by Scripture and are strikingly impressive for the most part. Though the full Ritual provides for it, this Office is rarely said now except for priests and religious. It deserves to be better known.

For funerals, one Nocturn of Matins, Lauds and Vespers are recited; since the time of St. Pius X, a full Office including the "Little Hours" is said on November second. With the changes made in 1955, Vespers of the Dead is transferred from November first to the afternoon of November second, a most satisfactory arrangement.

The Priest and the Divine Office

To derive the greatest profit from the Office there is a certain way in which we should approach it, and this might be expressed in the word "surrender": we must in fact yield ourselves to its influence and to the influence of grace. We must not approach it only as an *obligation;* if we do, we shall be condemned never to understand it and shall find it alien and burdensome all the days of our lives.

To view the Breviary exclusively as an obligation can and does lead to many undesirable practices. We have to "get it in," as we say, and we find ourselves impelled to say it at the strangest times and places, cramming it in whenever and wherever we can, in crowded busses and subways, in public places, even on the street, in places where conversation is going on or where there are many distractions. There may be times when this is necessary, but we are speaking now of an habitual attitude and one that is undesirable. It sometimes leads to saying the Office at Mass when we should be participating and giving an example to the people on how to assist at Mass. Especially during the past three decades, more and more efforts have been made to draw the people into taking an active part in the Mass; would it not be a good thing to set the tone by taking an active part ourselves? The general effect of too legalistic an approach to the Office is that we tend to consider it as "my" Office rather than "the" Office, as a personal obligation and often as a burden, rather than as the prayer of the Church which has been committed to our loving care. All this is understandable, but is it either inevitable or desirable?

We know that the Office is an obligation, but this in itself is a barren and arid conception of it which never takes us any further along the road of understanding. Rather we should try to see *why* it has become an obligation, what it is about the Office itself that warrants making it an obligation in the first place. This is but another way of saying that we must appreciate the Office itself and for its own sake. Such an appreciation does not come all at once nor can it be obtained merely by reading a book on the subject, though that might help and never does any harm. We really come to appreciate the Office only by constant use; we must grow in understanding with time and practice; we must grow into the outlook and frame of mind that the Office forms in us. At the same time we must bring something to the recitation of the Office, a certain alertness and responsiveness to what it contains; let us call it a spirit or a set of attitudes or convictions.

The first of these is that the Office is a *prayer* and a prayer of praise. That means, first of all, that we much approach it as a prayer, as we would approach any other prayer: "Before prayer prepare thyself. . . ." "*Agnoscite quod agitis,*" in a recollected spirit, aware that we are talking to God, and as far as possible in surroundings and under conditions that remove distractions. When we remember that the Office is a prayer we will say it more slowly, trying to pay attention to what we say, instead of plunging into it with only the idea of getting it said as fast as we can. We do not treat our other prayers that way, prayers that are nowhere near as important as this! A little pause here and there to look ahead or to look back will be of great help. Nor does that mean taking all day to say it; but merely bringing to it the care and attention we consider quite normal and natural for meditation or the rosary or the way of the cross. Particularly we must be ready to pay more attention to the psalms: first of all by studying them outside the time of prayer, then by using them as prayers at other times. The psalter makes an excellent meditation book. Or we may use a commentary which will sum up the meaning of each psalm. It is a good practice to write these summaries in the Breviary itself or keep them on a separate sheet of paper.

The Office is predominantly a prayer of praise. That means we must get into the frame of mind which makes us at home with that type of prayer; it is contemplative, objective, and to a great extent we are unfamiliar with prayer of that sort. We must make the effort to enter into its spirit. We will not find ideas set forth as they are in a spiritual treatise; nevertheless, the Office treats of the great themes of prayer and the Christian life: God, the divine plan for the salvation of the nations, the riches of Christ and of His Church, the glories of Mary and the splendors of the saints. We will find that this prayer is at once a school and a discipline.

Not only is the Office a prayer, but it is a *community* prayer. The ideal form of the Church's prayer must be prayer in common, which becomes obvious when we consider what the Church is. It is, then, more than an anomaly that the Church's prayer should be said privately all the time. Private recitation was intended as a substitute for public recitation when it was not possible for an individual priest or religious to take his place in the public Office. Until the Reformation and long afterward in many places (in France until the Revolution, for example), and even to this day in monastic choirs and cathedral chapters, the Office was sung publicly as a matter of course. Although this practice is now so largely neglected, it still remains true that just as each community in the Church (parish, religious community, seminary) must give expression to its corporateness by offering Sacrifice, so it must engage in corporate prayer, at least at certain times. When this duty is neglected, the Church—as a community in any given place—is silent when it should be singing the praises of God.

This is not to be interpreted as a plea for the revival of the entire Office in choir; the point is that public recitation is the ideal setting for the Office and that we should be glad of an opportunity to join in this public recitation. There is little danger really that the public recitation will be revived on a great scale, at least not as the Office is set up at present; the danger rather lies in our forgetting that it is essentially a public and common prayer. We are made more aware of this latter fact when we join in the common recitation.

This duty of common prayer which belongs to the whole Church and all its members has in practice fallen on priests and religious who thus continue Christ's prayer in the Church. By their voices the Church pays her debt of prayer to God. It is not merely a personal debt which we discharge, according to our own wishes, at our own time, still less according to our own whims, but a sacred task committed to our care, a task to which we must devote our best efforts, our hearts, wills, minds, the best time of our days and of our lives.

The Office is not only a prayer and a public common prayer, but it is an hour prayer, arranged in such a way that the whole day is sanctified by it; no day nor any part of the day is left without its prayer. "Day by day we bless thee"; "Seven times a day did I praise thee." By the Office, as we have seen, the day is made holy, consecrated and offered to God. Apt dispositions are expressed for each time of the day: night, morning, noon, evening. The Office should pervade our day with the spirit of prayer. The logical conclusion is that these hours should be said sometime near the time indicated. The Office is an hour prayer, not a chore to be discharged whenever we have an opportunity. To leave it *habitually* to the end of the day, or to say it all in the morning "to get it out of the way" is to condemn ourselves to utter failure ever to understand its purpose or meaning. To say, "*Te lucis ante terminum—Noctem quietam et finem perfectam*" in the morning—what is this but "praying with the lips"? Where is there any correspondence with reality? Cramming the "Little Hours" all together, beginning over and over again all at once something that was intended to be spread out through the day does not make sense. Besides, it is most difficult to say so much at once without losing one's devotion quite completely. Needless to say, the Office was never intended to be said in this way.

Even granted that the pressure of parish work may demand that at times we must say the Office when we can, we should not make this a general rule. It does not seem likely, for example, that one is always so busy that he cannot reserve a few minutes before going to rest in the evening to say Compline. Certainly, if a choice has to be made, it is preferable to make Compline our night prayers, rather than to substitute private night prayers for the Compline which we have already said earlier in the day or even in the morning! In any case, no matter how busy we may be, we are expected to sanctify the entire day with prayer. We emphasize the obligation of saying the Office each day, and that is proper, but we often forget that there is also a secondary obligation to say it, as far as possible, at certain hours, an obligation which deserves to be emphasized more than it is. If anyone fights shy of calling it a secondary obligation, let us say that it is certainly in the spirit of the law to do our best to say the Office at or near the proper times.

The following schedule might be followed by those who are obliged to say the Office (it has been tried and found practical even by men who are reasonably busy, and in any case it is only a suggestion): begin the day with Lauds and Prime (Lauds before Mass and Prime after), say Terce before noon, Sext and None around noon or in the early afternoon, Vespers in the late afternoon or early evening, Compline just before going to bed. Matins can be anticipated any time after one o'clock, or, if one wishes, said very early in the morning. Ideally, Matins is a prayer said at night; in practice it is best to anticipate it. By anticipating before Vespers and Compline there is no inverting of the hours involved, as some assert, for the Offices involved are not the same day's Office, and there is no law saying that you must finish one day's obligation before beginning another. In any case, Vermeersch says that it is laudable to keep Compline for night prayers, even though one anticipates before it.* Besides, any good reason permits one to invert the hours.

Another aid to saying the Office well and making it a pleasure and joy is to say some of the hours in the church, the great hours of Matins, Lauds, and Vespers in particular, thus giving them a little more solemnity. All the hours of the Office are not equal in dignity and importance and any little practice that will give the greater ones more prominence merits our attention and consideration.

The Divine Office reveals itself upon closer inspection as the matchless prayer for everyone. It goes back, at least in its oldest parts (Lauds and Vespers), to a time when people knew what was being said and could take part in it. It was really their prayer, the prayer of the Church considered as the *Ecclesia*, the assembly of the redeemed. It will always remain the favorite prayer of the Church not to be superseded by any other in her affections; nothing else can ever replace it.

As long ago as 1945 the Holy See sent out a special letter directing that those in charge of seminaries were to devote special care to imbuing candidates for the priesthood with the right attitudes towards the Office. They are to see it not as an obligation, but as a prayer, to acquire a love for it. To that end everyone on the seminary faculty was entreated to devote himself to explaining the Breviary and arousing enthusiasm for it.

Perhaps the day is not too far off when this will be carried to its logical conclusion and the two most venerable hours of the Office, Lauds and Vespers, will be used as the normal morning and night prayers of the seminary. When Christians meet together to pray, they need never seek elsewhere for an ideal prayer, because one is provided for them in the Office, the

* *Theologia Moralis,* Vol. III, pp. 43–44.

The Triumph of the Cross
(Mosaic in the Apse of the
Church of Sant Appolinare in Classe, Ravenna)

prayer of the Church. It is a heritage which we earnestly hope will be restored to us much more generally in our lifetime.

The Laity and a Vernacular Office

In our day there are many signs that some efforts will be made to have at least some parts of the Office used by the laity. The pope has encouraged the revival of Sunday Vespers and has urged people to become familiar with the prayers used at Vespers. One of the effects of the latest revision of the rubrics, whether intended directly or not, has been to make it easier for people who have no specialized training to find their way about in the Office. Certainly the latter is less confusing than it once was. But it is safe to say that as long as the Office remains in Latin, it will never become "popular" in any sense of the word. For here again it is a question of participation: the faithful should ideally sing or recite the Office, and there is no inducement for people who do not know Latin to sing or recite Latin prayers. That a vernacular Office would be an immense advantage all around is amply and abundantly testified by the Sisters who have begun to use the short Breviary in English for the choral recitation of the Office.

The old maxim, "who sings prays twice," implies that some one understands the language that he sings. "*Psaliter sapienter*" is the ideal St. Benedict set before his monks: not only that they sing the psalms but that they know what they are singing. We might carry the matter even further and say that the clergy, priests and religious, would reap enormous benefit by having at least the option of reciting the Office in their own tongue. Even if we granted that a man knows Latin very well, the fact remains that he does not think in Latin. This means that even when he understands here and now what he is reading, it does not pass over into his mind. It registers only incompletely; he is not familiar with it. How else can we explain the fact that it is possible for us to read from a book every day for hours and for years and yet retain so little of it as part of the ordinary background of our thoughts? The verses of the psalms which should occur to us with the greatest of ease and readiness do not come to our minds at all. If we were to read them in English we should be saturated with them, as we are not when we read them in Latin nor ever will be.

There is one fact true about Latin today that was not true in the sixteenth century, and it is that Latin is a dead language. It is used much less than it once was outside the Church and, for good or ill, no longer is learned by the great majority of educated men. As a result it is much more foreign and strange to us than it was to our predecessors of even one hundred years ago. That is the situation, whether we like it or not; and it will not improve but grow worse. Meanwhile, we must face the question: is it more important to preserve the tradition that the Church's prayers must be in Latin or to open the door to the attainment and the preservation of a truly biblical and patristic culture—to make the Breviary what it should be in the life of individual priests and the whole Church? Always this is a matter to be decided ultimately by authority, but in all such things authority shows itself open to respectful representations from those most interested.

CHAPTER 17

The Greater Sacramentals

To understand the sacramentals aright we must see them as pertaining to or related to the sacraments. Many of the sacramentals provide the setting for the sacraments and all of them touch upon the sacramental world itself—hence the name. They should not be conceived as divorced from the sacraments, existing somehow by themselves; they are sacramental of and pertaining to that consecrated order that results from the sacraments. Through the sacramentals the Church brings all created things into the orbit of God's blessing, in reality touches everything with the grace of the redemption, making so many material things and persons instruments and channels of the grace of God. Many of them, at least of the greater sacramentals, are drawn within the orbit of the Mass, the rites which dedicate them to God; the blessings (Preface) even bear a likeness to the great prayer of the Mass itself and are expressed in Eucharistic language. Nor should that surprise us, because the one great blessing that is poured out upon the world, from which all lesser blessings derive their meaning and power, is the blessing of the cross, and that blessing is stored up in the Holy Sacrifice of the Mass. Only by signing with His sign, the sign of the cross, can we bless and consecrate anything, that is, pervade it with the spirit of Christ or Christianize it. The whole world of blessings is a kind of process by which all things are assimilated to Christ.

But the term "sacramental" is not confined only to blessings and those things that are blessed; it embraces also all those rites which are not themselves sacraments in the strict sense, but which provide the setting for the sacraments, and which express in one way or another the fuller meaning of these sacraments. The prayers, lessons, and chants of the Mass, the Divine Office, the liturgical year with its changing texts and chants, all these are sacramentals: they do in their own way what the sacraments do. They are signs, outward indications of what is going on within. They are altogether in accord with the body, spirit, and nature of man, and with the Incarnation wherein the divine was manifested in visible form; they embody in words and deeds the whole world of the spirit. Their purpose is to convey divine realities to men, to enlighten our faith and quicken it, to excite devotion and create the supernatural atmosphere in which we must live.

From what has been said it should be plain that the term sacramental has a wide application; we may apply it to any one of the multitudinous rites instituted by the Church which are calculated to lead men to God and which aim at the spiritual and even material profit of the faithful.

Among these rites some are more important and exert greater influence than others. We call them the great sacramentals: the dedication of churches, the consecration of virgins, the blessing of abbots, the blessing and distribution of ashes, palms and candles, the consecration of bells, the solemn profession of religious. Some of these are more solemn than others; the consecration of virgins for example, revived during our own time in this country, is perhaps the longest and most elaborate rite in the Pontifical, longer even than the dedication of churches, itself a sufficiently lengthy and elaborate rite. Indeed it is interesting to note and more than a little surprising that many of these rites are more detailed and in a sense more solemn than almost any one of the sacraments. In their present form, most of them originated in the early Middle Ages and some have elements borrowed freely from the more florid and detailed Gallican Rite.

During the course of the Church year there are two or three great sacramentals which enter in a special way into the lives of the priests and people: the blessing of candles and the procession on Candlemas Day, the blessing and distribution of ashes, and the blessing and procession of palms on Palm Sunday.

As far as the first is concerned, it would perhaps be better to say that it should enter in a special way into the lives of priests and people. Actually it does not nowadays and has fallen into disuse in many places. That is a pity because it is one of the most impressive rites that we have, rich in a natural symbolism that has been "baptized" and made the vehicle of most solid instruction. On Candlemas Day the Church goes forth with Holy Simeon as he meets the Bridegroom and holds in his hands the "Light that enlightens the Gentiles." With him she sings the joyful *Nunc Dimittis*. The candles are blessed with a view to the procession that follows; if there is no procession, the candles should not be blessed publicly. Begun as a kind of penitential procession, the Candlemas solemnity developed into its present form some time between the ninth and the thirteenth centuries. That which is most characteristic of the present-day procession, the singing of the *Nunc Dimittis* with its antiphon interspersed between the verses, was added during the twelfth century. The other antiphons sung during the procession were borrowed from the Greek Church.

The blessing and distribution of ashes originated in the ancient Roman penitential rites. When a man became a penitent he was sprinkled with ashes, dressed in sackcloth, and forced to remain apart from the community until his penance was finished. By the Middle Ages, this was at first recommended for all Christians on Ash Wednesday and later prescribed. The thought of death now attached to the rite is a later development; primarily it is penitential and remains largely so today.

The procession of the palms began very early at Jerusalem where there arose a natural desire to re-enact the scenes from the last days of our Savior's life in the very place where they had happened. This procession was rather connected with the idea of the messianic dignity of Christ and for that reason played an apologetic as well as a devotional and historical role. The Spanish pilgrim Etheria informs us that at Jerusalem in the fourth century the bishop and the people went to the Mount of Olives and there held a kind of service during which the Gospel describing our Lord's entrance into Jerusalem was read. Then they went in procession to Jerusalem, carrying palm and olive branches and singing "Blessed is he who comes in the name of the Lord."

No one knows for certain when this practice passed over from the East, but it is found in the West in the seventh century in its main outlines, to be fully developed by the tenth and given its present form during the Middle Ages.

The present rite amounts to a separate commemoration of Christ as the Redeemer and the Messias, and has throughout the character of a great triumph, in striking contrast to the sorrowful Mass of the Sunday itself. During the Middle Ages it was the custom in many places to gather together in one church for the blessing and distribution of the palms, then to go in procession to another church, which represented Jerusalem, for the Sunday Mass. The restored rite recommends reviving the practice of blessing palms in one place and going in procession to another.

The Rites of Burial. The rites of Christian burial, exclusive of the Mass and Office, and the absolution over the body and the prayers at the grave are sacred rites or sacramentals in which the Church signs the body to burial and commends the soul to God's mercy.

When the Mass is finished the priest, vested in cope, conducts a short service for the dead consisting of the responsory *Libera me Domine*, a brief litany with the *Pater Noster*, the incensing of the corpse, sprinkling with holy water, and a final prayer. This is known as the absolution, but does not of course mean absolution from sins, but rather that the Church asks remission of the payment of the debt due to sin.

This rite is not ancient, but arose in the tenth century, apparently in the Frankish domains. The introductory prayer originally came from the ancient *commendatio animae*. The most striking feature of this "Little Office of the Dead" is the responsory *Libera* which goes back to the ninth century. In mood and content it represents a later phase in the development of the liturgy of the dead with its emphasis on the terror of death and judgment, in decided contrast to the note of hope and joy which pervades the texts of the Missal, particularly the lessons and the orations. It is, as it is intended to be, solemn and awe-inspiring. The short series of verses and responses beginning with the *Kyrie* and the *Pater* are a familiar feature of liturgical prayer. During the silent recitation of the *Pater* the celebrant sprinkles the coffin and incenses it. The incensation is older, going back to the twelfth century; the sprinkling is a fourteenth century rite. The oration *Deus cui proprium* is Gallican in origin and construction.

While the body is being carried from the church, a joyful antiphon, in decided contrast to the responsory spoken of before, the beautiful *In Paradisum*, is sung by the choir. It is filled with the spirit of the primitive Church at its best, and marked with that note of rejoicing hope that accompanied the concept of death in the early centuries, as reflected in the inscriptions in the catacombs and in the Canon of the Mass. We note the references to the angels who are conceived as carrying souls to Heaven, a rôle frequently assigned to them in Christian antiquity. The antiphon was originally shorter; the last part, *Chorus Angelorum*, was added from another source, as the change in the music indicates.

At the grave the note of "rejoicing in hope" is maintained by the glorious antiphon taken from St. John's Gospel: "I am the Resurrection and the Life," and the Canticle of Zachary which is singularly appropriate for the occasion by its whole tenor, but particularly by the verse that no doubt inspired its selection for this service: "To enlighten those that sit in darkness and the shadow of death, to direct our steps in the way of peace."

Then follows the usual short litany of prayers with the Our Father, the prayer that accompanies the Christian all through life from the baptismal font to the tomb, and the touching oration: "That as true faith joined him with the company of the faithful on earth so Thy mercy may make him now the companion of the angels in Heaven."

The whole service ends with the words that echo so often through the liturgy of the dead: "Eternal rest grant unto him, and let perpetual light shine upon him."

The Consecration of the Holy Oils. The poetry which underlies so many of the Church's rites receives its fullest expression in the blessing of the oils on Holy Thursday, when something of the splendor and richness that we associate with the Eastern rites invades the restrained Roman liturgy and focuses attention upon that mysterious substance which God uses to be the consecrated instrument of unmeasurable grace. The oils that stand in the *ambries* of Catholic churches throughout the diocese during the year, ready to spread abroad the good odor of Christ, have their hour of glory and triumph when they are escorted to the sanctuary by a cortege of vested priests, solemnly prayed over with some of the most remarkable prayers, and greeted with reverent and majestic salutations. There is an ancient legend that at the time of Christ's birth a fountain of oil sprang up on the site of the Church of St. Mary-across-the-Tiber; every Holy Thursday a fountain of oil is set to flow in every cathedral church, a fountain which brings health and strength and vigor—all the graces of the Redemption—to the people of the diocese during the year. And lest we forget that, or look upon the oils too lightly, the Church in the rites and prayers of blessing unfolds for us the significance of the oils and their effect upon the people of God.

While the blessing of the oils is an ancient custom in the Church, we cannot prove that it goes back to apostolic times; it is mentioned very early, particularly in the oldest liturgical documents that we possess. For a time it took place on different days, but was finally fixed on Holy Thursday, the last time Mass would be offered before the great baptismal night between Holy Saturday and Easter Sunday, when the oils would be needed in abundance. Originally, there was a special Mass for the blessing of the oils and this "chrismal Mass" had a strong baptismal flavor. The new rite for Holy Week revives this chrismal Mass.

The solemnity that surrounds the blessing of the oils carries us back, whether we are aware of it or not, to the primitive Church, when the bishop was on all occasions attended by concelebrating priests. On one day of the year a modern bishop is accompanied with the splendor and circumstance of the bishops of the past. The twelve priests, seven deacons, and seven subdeacons, all vested in white according to their order, assist him in the performance of the rite "as witnesses and co-operators in the ministry of the chrism." For many centuries they entered more actively into the rite, saying the words along with the prelate, a real con-celebration of the blessing.

The blessing of the oil of the sick is first in order and simplest in form. The prayers are short, yet expressive of the purpose of the oil: "a spiritual anointing for the strengthening of the Temple of the living God, that the Holy Spirit might dwell therein," and "for the nourishment of mind and body and the protection thereof."

But it is for the holy chrism that the Church reserves its most impressive treatment. It is brought in to the accompaniment of the noble hymn "*O Redemptor*," is mixed with balm and consecrated in the most solemn way possible by the singing of a Preface reminiscent of and paralleling the great Eucharistic prayer itself.

The theology and the doctrine of the "*O Redemptor*" merit the closest attention. At the very outset of the rite it awakens the consciousness of the Church to the meaning of the chrism. Addressed to Christ, it hails Him as the Redeemer who brings redemption to His people by anointing them with His Spirit, which the anointing of the chrism conveys and represents.

This oil which we bring is the fruit of the olive tree which promises the peace of Christ. The mitred bishop consecrates it, but may Christ consecrate it the more, making it a "living sign" and a protection from the demon that the whole human race might be renewed by the anointing of this chrism, that our "wounded glory" might be healed and restored to us. May the holy unction of this chrism bring the gifts of the Spirit with it. May the Redeemer grant light and keep death away from those anointed by this chrism.

Chrism is made by mingling olive oil and balm, which perfumes the oil and symbolizes the presence of the Spirit who will make this oil the "Chrism of Salvation." Eastern rites are more prodigal in this respect, mixing large quantities of precious spices with the oil and "filling the whole house with the perfume thereof." The balm thus recalls the good odor of Christ which is poured upon the Christian soul, making it agreeable, pleasing, and holy in God's sight. The outward anointing, says the Pontifical, is the symbol of inward unction, reminiscent of Him who was "anointed with the oil of gladness," Christ our Lord, whose very name means "the anointed one."

After this mixture is made, the exorcism follows by which the Holy Spirit takes possession of the chrism and prepares it for His purpose, to be the instrument and vehicle of His grace.

Then the bishop sings the solemn Preface of consecration, which, true to its type, reaches back in to the Old Testament for the symbols foreshadowing the holy chrism and relates them to the New and Eternal Covenant inaugurated by Christ.

The heart of the preface is reached with the words which ask that God should sanctify by His blessing this creature of oil, pour into it the power and virtue of the Holy Spirit through the grace of Christ from whom the chrism takes its name. This theme of sanctifying the chrism continues:

To all who shall be made new in the heavenly font of Baptism, be this oil a sure pledge of health and restored life, that the corruption of their first birth being absorbed by the infusion of this holy anointing, they may become a holy temple, perfumed with the fragrance of innocence and of a holy life. According to what thou hast appointed in this mystery, bestow upon them the dignity of Kings, Priests, and Prophets, by vesting them in the robes of incorruption. May this oil be to them that are born again of water and the Holy Ghost, a Chrism of Salvation making them partakers of life everlasting and co-heirs of heavenly glory.

By this remarkable and truly extraordinary prayer, the chrism becomes in a certain way the dwelling of the Spirit, who abides in it and by it makes us prophets, priests, and kings, "a holy race, a chosen people, a royal priesthood," sharers in the life of Christ (the *anointed* above all others), clad in the shining robes of His immortality, and partakers of His resurrection from the dead. The heavenly glory which transfigures Him and makes Him beautiful above the sons of men becomes ours. Chrism makes us like to Christ, partakers of His glory, which opens before those who are marked with His sign, the anointed of His Spirit.

Like all the rites of the Church, this preface is directed and oriented to the final consummation of all things, the day of the Lord and of His coming in might, power and glory.

Now the bishop and the priests advance and genuflect before

the newly consecrated chrism, saluting it with the threefold greeting, "Hail, holy chrism," a procedure which becomes natural and normal in the light of the doctrine on the nature of the chrism which is unfolded in the preface. The Holy Spirit dwells in this oil and His holy unction pours forth from it. It is indeed holy and worthy of grateful reverence.

The Oil of Catechumens is the last to be blessed by a ceremony analogous to but longer than the blessing of the Oil of the Sick. It is intended, as the prayer of blessing shows, to prepare those about to be baptized for the gift of the Holy Spirit granted to them in Baptism. In reality, the unction with this oil is conceived as an anointing for conflict, as athletes were anointed in the past. Those who are baptized engage themselves in a never-ending war with the demon and this sacramental of the Church helps to condition them for the conflict. The oil is then greeted "Hail, Holy Oil," but it would seem that there is much more reason for thus honoring the chrism, which is *consecrated* rather than blessed.

The procession forms again and the second half of the "*O Redemptor*" is chanted as the holy oils are brought back to the sacristy where they are distributed to the priests who spread their consecrated influence through the episcopal city and the diocese.

The Prayers for the Dying. They are called in the Ritual the *Commendatio Animae* and go back in their present form to the Gelasian Sacramentary, but some of the individual parts must be much older. There are a number of these prayers, but the most prominent are the litany for the dying, the psalms and the reading of the Passion according to St. John.

The Litany of the Saints is one of the oldest elements of this *commendatio* and contains the names of those saints who for one reason or another are especially invoked at this solemn hour. After this follows the "Depart O Christian soul" found in the eighth century Gelasian Sacramentary, a prayer of very great beauty, especially the words "today may thy resting-place be in peace, and thy dwelling in Mount Sion." The prayers which follow this are in the form of exorcisms, directed against the demon and his assaults, which are greatest at this time. These are not all equally old and some of them entered the Ritual only in 1614. The most striking are the series "Deliver O Lord" which are very likely the oldest part of the entire rite, dating from early Christian times, as their strong biblical flavor and their allusions to incidents pictured in the catacombs indicates. We ask God to deliver this soul as he delivered Daniel from the lion's den, Noah from the deluge, Moses from the hands of the Egyptians, and so forth. Last of all is the only non-biblical reference, to the deliverance of St. Thecla who was regarded in early times as the special patron of the dying. To these invocations are added three prayers which have the character of absolutions from sins, and (since 1913) the prayers to the Blessed Virgin and St. Joseph. This concludes the first part of the *commendatio*. The second part is complementary to the first: it may be used but it is not required; Psalms 117 and 118 are appropriate because of the confidence and trust in God which they show; the reading from the Passion of St. John reminds the dying person that his death is a sacrifice to God, an offering that is identified with that of Christ and a sharing in the Passion of Our Lord.

The Blessing of Holy Water. Holy water is one of the most important, as it has a good claim to be regarded as the oldest, of the sacramentals. An element so universally used and prized as water was certain to receive the special blessing of the Church at a very early time and to be thus drawn into the influence of the redemption. It is one of the most natural symbols that we have, denoting cleanliness, purity and life; it is admirably suited for that reason to be the symbol of supernatural cleansing and eternal life. As such it figures prominently in the Gospel of St. John and later in the Apocalypse.

In the courtyards at the entrance of the earliest churches stood the fountains or large basins of water intended to serve for ritual purification. It seems fairly certain that our modern holy water fonts at the doors of our churches are derived from this custom, which in turn had pagan antecedents. Water blessed by the priest with the sign of the cross was sometimes used as a protection against evil spirits, or drunk as a means of obtaining health in sickness. But our modern holy water seems to be derived indirectly from the custom of using baptismal water, which was believed to have special power and efficacy, as a protection and a defense and a means of calling God's blessing upon house, fields, and persons. From that to the blessing of water independently of the baptismal water, which would nevertheless have the same power and efficacy, was a rather easy step to make.

Holy water as we understand it, water specially blessed to be an instrument of blessing and a sign of God's favor, is referred to for the first time in the Gelasian Sacramentary, where the form for blessing it corresponds very closely to that now used in the Ritual. This blessing indicates that the chief purpose of holy water is to sprinkle it in the homes of the faithful as a protection against evils to soul and body. Other related prayers in the same Sacramentary indicate that a special blessing of the homes of the people was customary at the time and it was evidently done with prayers and the sprinkling of the water.

CHAPTER *18*

Extra-Liturgical Devotions

Inevitably the question must arise: what attitude are we to take towards the many devotional practices that are not a part of the liturgy in any way but which have nevertheless been highly recommended by the Church? The first and simplest answer is to say that there is only one attitude any one priest or layman can take: these devotions are to be respected and honored to the extent that one finds them helpful or as far as laws oblige us to practice any of them. Considered purely as devotional practices, they have the blessing of the Church and they can be of great benefit to those who use them. Naturally, we are speaking here of such practices as the rosary, the Way of the Cross, litanies, novenas, and all the many ways of arousing piety and devotion that a modern Catholic has at his disposal. These practices should be encouraged by priests and given the support of example. They represent in general a type of piety which flourishes side-by-side with the piety nourished and stimulated by the liturgy. They are not in any way rivals of the liturgy, still less are they substitutes for it, except among those who for one legitimate reason or another cannot draw upon the liturgy for their devotional life; and even then devotions can be substitutes only to a certain extent. All must take part in the Mass and receive the sacraments and nothing can take their place. Priests and religious are expected to lead a more liturgical life than others; they are not supposed merely to recite their Office in a formal manner, or only to celebrate Mass correctly, but they are supposed to be imbued with the spirit of the texts they are reading. It would be wrong, for example, to rush through Mass and the Office in order to have more time to say the rosary or to make the Way of the Cross. Liturgical prayer is in itself more important than these other things. It is a question here of a hierarchy of values. Wherever there is a conflict—supposing that there is and, of course, there need not be—there should be no question about what comes first.

During the first centuries there were no devotions such as we know today. Everyone took an active external part in the worship of the Church and that was his devotion and the source of his piety and his spirituality. He listened to the lessons read from Scripture, sang the psalms, answered the prayers, received the sacraments. For him it was truly a living worship and had a great part in forming his outlook and attitudes. The great truths on which all this worship was based were grasped and held firmly, realized as it were, by the faithful. Liturgical worship created the atmosphere in which they lived—an atmosphere of community, of solidarity; an awareness of belonging to a Body, the Body of Christ; a strong conviction of deliverance, salvation and redemption; of Christ as Mediator and High Priest and of their own access to God through Him; of God as their Father and Christ as their Brother; of the need of struggle against the demon, but also of the victory already gained over him; of the need to carry the cross, but also of the certainty of the resurrection. As a result of all this, inutterable joy and the peace that surpasses all understanding filled their hearts and overflowed into their lives, making joy the dominant temper of the Christian and the Christian Church. The piety bred by this one great devotion was a communal piety, a Christo- and theocentric piety, a joyful and joyous piety.

As time went on and men ceased to understand the liturgy and take part in it, they turned to new practices of devotion and were formed now by the piety which was engendered and nourished by these new devotions. It is a fact that these devotions did not grow up in the Church until men no longer understood the liturgy nor took part in it; it is also true that many of these devotions were unknown in the East where the liturgy was understood for a longer time by the people. This new devotional piety was essentially individualistic. True enough, it was Christocentric, but in an altogether different way from the piety of the patristic period. The new devotional piety was largely pre-occupied with a psychological analysis rather than a dogmatic presentation of the person and work of Christ. It had, again, a scriptural framework, but was not *based* upon the Scriptures as was the older and earlier spirituality. Devotional piety was more man-centered, concerned with salvation it is true, but with the salvation of the *individual* soul made more conscious of sin and guilt. The awareness of belonging to a body and a living organism receded more and more into the background; the emphasis was laid on the working out of individual perfection; the primacy was given in practice to those spiritual disciplines which furthered individual advance in holiness.

It is important to insist that all of this was perfectly orthodox; yet the spiritual world in which these men moved was somehow altogether different from that of their forefathers in the faith. This was particularly true of the ordinary layman who lacked the theological training which would have enabled him to keep matters in a proper perspective, and who was cut off by ignorance of Latin from *any* contact with the liturgy. For the layman, the many devotions that arose were substitutes for the liturgy, and these devotions had an altogether different subject matter from that of the liturgy. They concentrated on arousing feelings rather than on contemplating truth, on edification rather than on instruction. These devotions were not drawn directly from the Scriptures and were only remotely biblical; thus the solid nourishment which only the Scriptures can give was denied to the layman. If the concept of the Mystical Body became obscured for their spiritual leaders and rulers, how completely must it have been obliterated for them! The great dogmatic truths were believed, but hardly realized, and the means whereby the faithful are nourished were taken away from them. What we know of mediaeval preaching, particularly in the later Middle Ages, shows us that very little dogma and doctrinal instruction were given. The sermons were moral and aimed at edification. So it was that for hundreds of years a new spirituality, altogether independent of the liturgy, grew up in the Church, a spirituality which at its best was capable of forming deeply spiritual and immensely pious *individuals,* but which at the same time could and did lead to a great and general lessening of awareness of the great traditions of Christian spirituality and of the sound dogmatic and scriptural principles upon which it was built. And for many, far too many, it resulted in a greatly unbalanced religious outlook, with a much too great insistence upon the merely negative and accidental rather than upon the positive and essential.

The picture is further complicated, and real analysis rendered more difficult, by the fact that none of these practices which grew up and which have continued into our own time are bad in themselves. It was the way they were used and the fact that they became substitutes for the liturgy, that caused them to have the effects they had. Rightly used, infused with the proper spirit and subordinated to the worship of the Church, they can even now be made to produce great fruit. The solution is certainly not to do away with them, even if we could. Still more confusion and misunderstanding arise because the proper distinctions are not made. People speak of "popular devotions" as though they were all of equal value and dignity. In that way an equal importance is assigned alike to the many intensely subjective novenas which flourish in such abundance and to the Litany of the Sacred Heart, which is profoundly doctrinal and scriptural, altogether objective, and an excellent example of a real community prayer.

Lovers of the liturgy are often accused of minimizing popular devotions, and it is true that some may appear to do so. However, it is not always a case of minimizing non-liturgical devotions so much as it is a case of protesting against the more common tendency to minimize the liturgy. How often, for example, do we find that the liturgy is kept to a minimum and some parts of it omitted altogether, while devotions are insisted upon at the expense of the traditional practices of the Church! How often Mass is celebrated with an absolute minimum of liturgical observance, while Benediction is made as solemn as possible! To do this is to emphasize the secondary at the expense of the primary. That we should be able to recognize this reversal of values and should protest against it, is not this in accord with the mind of the Church? The Holy Father in his encyclical *Mediator Dei* asked for the return of Vespers to parish churches; yet in most places Benediction and the rosary are said instead. Can we be satisfied with this situation, and must we not ask why Benediction should be substituted for Vespers?

Again, the liturgical-minded are accused of scant regard for popular devotions when in reality what they are objecting to is the way these devotions are *presented*. It is one thing to find fault with making the Way of the Cross, and another thing altogether to criticize some of the methods which are employed. The Way of the Cross is more a spiritual exercise than a ritual act, it is true, but if it is made in public, we must remember that devotions for a community and devotions for an individual are not to be presented in the same way; what might satisfy the needs or stir up the devotion of an individual simply will not reach a congregation. Not to take account of so fundamental a fact results in using the forms and prayers which came naturally to those who composed them but which sound strained and unnatural in public, where they were not primarily intended to be used. Very often too they are not the objective setting forth of the great events upon which our faith feeds, but the wholly subjective psychological reflections of an individual, more often than not almost entirely divorced from dogma and Scripture. We might, then, in these circumstances borrow the method of the liturgy and present an objective consideration of the Passion of our Savior drawn from the Scriptures, the sermons of the Fathers and the teaching of the Church, allowing the individual worshiper to make the application himself. So many of our devotions seem to be in a great hurry to draw a lesson or to edify. We must have more confidence in the truths themselves to edify and to arouse contrition, compunction and all other good thoughts. What is said here of the Way of the Cross may be said also of all devotions that are used in public: novenas, hymns, holy hours. We must make the adjustments that public services demand if these devotions are to be really suitable for public use.

In the same connection, we must say that another reason for the apparent lack of enthusiasm for certain practices is the *language* in which some of these prayers and devotions are expressed. Those whose habitual nourishment is derived from the strong bread of the Scriptures and the objective, theocentric prayer of the liturgy are understandably ill at ease with some of the formulae that are found in certain types of hymns and prayers. They find them unbearably sentimental and emotional, often impoverished doctrinally, rootless and lifeless, inferior compositions in every way. It argues no lack of piety to find such poor material unsatisfactory and unsatisfying. The blame lies not with those who cannot respond to these things but with those who compose and promote them.

Let us remember too that these extra-liturgical practices of piety are rarely *prescribed*. They are *recommended*, and there is no restriction put upon our choice in these matters. That in itself should be sufficient indication of the emphasis which should be put upon them. With regard to the use of devotions, then, we should insist upon liberty of spirit. Better to practice a few and do them well than to get lost in a multiplicity of "devotions." Above all, the worship of the Church should not be in any way subordinated to them, nor should we substitute them for the liturgy, nor encourage these practices at the expense of the liturgy.

The recent restoration of the Holy Week rite with its manifest aim of encouraging popular participation and the express declaration in the decree establishing these rites, that they cannot be equalled in their salutary effects by *any* devotions that may have been created to supply for their loss, lends much support to the idea that the liturgy itself is itself the *true* popular devotion. We have so long grown accustomed to the notion that there is necessarily a conflict between those rites that the Church creates to express her devotion and those practices which the people presumably prefer, that we do not see that there is a fundamental misconception behind it—namely, that in some way the Church is one thing and the people another. In reality the two are, of course, the same and from that follows the conclusion that the liturgy is the true popular devotion: whatever non-liturgical practices people may be drawn to, the worship of the Church is itself enough to satisfy them. That this is true is shown by the fact that when they are given an opportunity to participate and when the liturgy is made attractive to them, they respond wholeheartedly. The reason is that the liturgy is not just a way of worshipping God; it is *the* way, "primary and indispensable"; while not excluding other ways, it alone can claim that authority and authenticity which make it in every sense the worship of the Church.

The Angelus. The commemoration three times a day of the mystery of the Incarnation is an excellent example of a popular devotion which has been influenced by the liturgy. The Angelus is pervaded with the objective and dogmatic and biblical spirit that marks the official worship of the Church. It grew up in the late Middle Ages (thirteenth century), and at first was said only in the evening in connection with the practice of the curfew. During the fourteenth century the morning Angelus was added and the midday Angelus only in the fifteenth. The Hail Mary seems to be the oldest part; then the versicles and responses with the oration were added. Particularly worthy of note is the *participation* involved in this devotion and the noble collect which was originally (and still is) an Advent Postcommunion, a prayer that in a short space ranges over the entire redemptive activity of Christ. "Pour forth, we bessech thee O Lord, *thy grace into our hearts,* that we to whom the *Incarnation of thy Son was made known by the message of an angel,* may *by his Passion and Cross* be brought *to the glory of the Resurrection.*"

The Way of the Cross or the Stations. The original idea behind the Stations was to provide a miniature pilgrimage to the Holy Land for those who were prevented from actually going there. In this way the benefits of visiting the scenes of our Lord's life and meditating upon them, particularly upon the Passion and death of Christ, were secured for all. This was the idea, but the growth and development of the idea until its present form was reached is much more complicated.

We find the first Way of the Cross with halting places or Stations (not as yet fourteen in number) in Jerusalem in the early Middle Ages. Introduced into Europe during the fifteenth century, the devotion did not take its present form until some time later; even as late as the eighteenth century there were less than fourteen stations in some places and the incidents commemorated differed considerably from the present series.

The general use of the Way of the Cross in churches began only in the eighteenth century and the popularity of the practice was largely caused by the indulgences attached. The devotion was spread by the Franciscans and notably by St. Leonard of Port Maurice. It was richly indulgenced by the popes and Clement XII definitely set the number of stations at fourteen in 1731.

The indulgence is gained by passing from one station to another in a church where they are validly erected, and by meditating on the sacred Passion. It is not necessary to say any vocal prayers, nor to advert to the subject of each station. Meditation on the Passion is enough. The indulgence is attached to the wooden crosses which mark the stations, not to the pictures or images, which are not even required. These "stations" should not be too large or conspicuous.

The Rosary. The greatest of all the popular devotions is without question the rosary, which occupies so large a place in modern Catholic life. The essence of this devotion lies in meditation upon the great events in the life of the Blessed Virgin—the mysteries as they are called. As such, this devotion goes back to the fourteenth century; but as a recitation of a series of prayers with the use of a string of beads to keep count, it is much older than that, going back in all probability to the eleventh century. The root of the whole devotion is the recitation of the 150 psalms, a practice enjoined upon monks at certain times, chiefly for the relief of the souls of deceased brethren. Later on, the practice spread to the lay brothers and to the lay members of orders of Knighthood who could not recite the psalter in whole or in part; so they were allowed to say the Our Father instead. That is one reason why the rosary was known as the *Pater Noster* during the Middle Ages; the beads were used to count the Our Fathers. When the Hail Mary came into general use during the twelfth century, Hail Marys took the place of the Our Father. The Hail Mary was conceived as a salutation or an acclamation rather than as a prayer, and it was the custom then as now to repeat acclamations and salutations to great personages; the more often they were repeated the greater the honor shown. The practice was also influenced by the custom of reciting the psalms in groups of fifty as a practice of devotion by religious and learned persons; the unlearned and busy people wished to imitate this practice as far as they could; so they said fifty Hail Marys instead. This led to calling the rosary "Our Lady's Psalter." The final development was the introduction in the fifteenth century of the meditation on the mysteries by a Carthusian, Dominic of Prussia; the recitation of the Hail Marys was to form a kind of accompaniment to meditating on the mysteries.

The rosary thus became in time a real Godsend to those who were unable to participate in the Office or to recite the psalter, and who were shut out of the contemplation of the mysteries of our Lord's life afforded by the liturgical year. The rosary has, therefore, played a great role in keeping alive the spirit of prayer and devotion and has rightly received so much and so great praise from the sovereign pontiffs in recent decades. It has not been confined to the simple and unlearned by any means and has taken up a large place in the devotional life of everyone; it is the one devotion which is imposed on priests by law. It is profoundly doctrinal and evangelical in its content and therefore recommends itself to everyone; but because it essentially consists of personal meditation upon the mysteries, and is characterized by the repetition of certain forms over and over, it lends itself more readily to private than public recitation. And it is no disparagement of the rosary to say that, while it is infinitely preferable to say it during Mass rather than to say no prayers at all, it is better to follow the words of the Missal, which are the Church's own "devotions at Mass."

Exposition of the Blessed Sacrament. The practice of exposing the Blessed Sacrament in the monstrance for the adoration and veneration of the people is comparatively late in the

Church, developing as it did in the fourteenth century. Two chief causes contributed to the rise and spread of this practice: the increase in devotion to the Blessed Sacrament which the institution of the Feast of Corpus Christi brought to the Church, and the widespread desire in the Middle Ages to see the Host, an action which was believed to be the source of many graces and blessings. The same period witnessed the related development of the monstrance itself, a sacred vessel patterned upon the earlier reliquaries of the saints, and which made it possible to look directly upon the Host. At first, this monstrance had the form of a tower or the front of a church; in the Baroque period the sun-ray type came into vogue. At the present time both forms are used.

Benediction of the Blessed Sacrament. During the Middle Ages it became the custom to bless people with a sacred object of one kind or another at the end of a ceremony—with the relic of a saint after it had been exposed for veneration, for example, or with the holy oils after extreme unction. It was very natural that this custom should be extended to blessing the people with the reliquary containing the Blessed Sacrament at the close of exposition. The modern ceremony seems to have developed from that practice because the first clear record that we have of anything like it is from the fourteenth century, after the practice of exposition had been in vogue for some time. Exposition itself was limited to the feast of Corpus Christi and its octave; to this day the Carthusians, who preserve many mediaeval customs intact, have Benediction only at that time. In the fourteenth century the practice of exposition and Benediction had been extended to the other Thursdays of the year, which were observed as weekly commemorations of the Blessed Eucharist. At that stage of its development Benediction consisted only of singing the hymn "*Tantum Ergo*" and of blessing the people with the monstrance during the singing of the doxology "*Genitori Genitoque.*" That concluded the ceremony.

As it is today Benediction is a kind of Little Office of the

Blessed Sacrament, with hymns that are a species of antiphon with a versicle and response and a concluding oration. These last parts after the "*Tantum Ergo*" appear to have been added during the sixteenth century. The oration is, of course, the collect for the Feast of Corpus Christi. Whether the service is strictly speaking liturgical has been a debated question; it would seem that it can be called liturgical only in the sense that it is a sacramental, having no independant existence of its own in the sense that the Office has. Rather, it is a devotional practice related to the elevation in the Mass, a flowering of devotion to the Eucharist itself. It partakes of the nature of the related and the accidental, rather than of the substance of Eucharistic devotion, which must always, to be genuine, be primarily a devotion to the Sacrifice and to the sacrificial banquet.

To say this is in no way to detract from the practice itself, but merely to assert a truth which may easily become obscured.

Conclusion

"Whatever pertains to the external worship of the Church has assuredly its importance; however, the most pressing duty of Christians is to live the liturgical life and increase and cherish its supernatural spirit." * These words of the sovereign pontiff in his *Mediator Dei* find a fitting place at the close of this book, in which we have tried at least in part to survey a vast subject. Of necessity we have had to dwell upon details which when seen out of context might lead one to forget the great principle stated so clearly by the Pope. Once we have grasped that principle clearly, we see everything in its proper perspective and what could be only a complicated set of rules, a bewildering ceremonial, or a mere art-form, becomes what it is intended to be, a way of life and the working out of the mystery of salvation. Living the liturgical life and increasing and cherishing its supernatural spirit means living by and in the worship of the Church. First of all, it means "living"—not just playing

* Mediator Dei, No. 197.

at it nor going through the motions. It means that by participating in the Church's worship we are giving ourselves up to its influence entirely. It means living the Mass, the first and greatest of the liturgical acts, the center and core of the liturgy, by yielding ourselves up to its influence, by sharing in the offering the Church makes of herself, by immolating our selfishness, our lower nature, our pride, vanity and sensuality. "Upon this altar let pride be immolated. Let wrath be smothered upon it, let the passions be beaten down upon it." *

It means, if we are sincere, much charity, patience, understanding and tolerance on our part. It means entering into its spirit of community, joining with others in mind and heart and, if possible, in voice and action. It means praying together whenever we can. It means living according to the rhythm of the Church year, the Christian week, and the Christian day—entering into the spirit of the season, of the feasts, of the day and even of the hour. It means taking advantage of all that the Church puts at our disposal in the liturgy. We should be educated, nourished, formed and instructed by it and turn to it for light, strength, wisdom and power. It must be the mainspring of our actions and the source of our spiritual life. Once again let it be said that it is not a parade or a show or a spectacle; it is a work to be done and a life to be lived—a life that involves the whole man, his outward senses as well as his intelligence and will.

Nor does living the liturgical life mean abandoning any of the other practices recommended and indeed insisted upon by the Church: reading of solid spiritual works, mental prayer, retreats, the study of doctrine, the private reading of the Scriptures. On the contrary, living the liturgical life leads to valuing these practices more, not less. Indeed they can only help us "to grow in virtue and to strengthen us in sanctity so as to enable us to derive from the sacred liturgy more efficacious

* Roman Pontifical, "Consecration of an altar."

and abundant benefits. . . . By nourishing our spiritual life they prepare us to take part in sacred public actions with greater fruit and they lessen the danger of liturgical piety becoming an empty ritualism." *

* *Mediator Dei.*

APPENDIX A.

The purpose of this appendix is to provide the reader with some of the significant texts that have either a bearing on the history of the liturgy, or that will serve as examples of their kind. These examples are reprinted here for the convenience of the student.

THE FIRST APOLOGY OF ST. JUSTIN MARTYR *

The Eucharist

65. After thus baptizing the one who has believed and given his assent, we escort him to the place where are assembled those whom we call the brethren, to offer up sincere prayers in common for ourselves, for the baptized person, and for all other persons wherever they may be, in order that, since we have found the truth, we may be deemed fit through our actions to be esteemed as good citizens and observers of the law, and thus attain eternal salvation. At the conclusion of the prayers we greet one another with a kiss. Then, bread and a chalice containing wine mixed with water are presented to the one presiding over the brethren. He takes them and offers praise and glory to the Father of all, through the name of the son and of the Holy Spirit, and he recites lengthy prayers of thanksgiving to God in the name of those to whom he granted such favors. At the end of these prayers and thanksgiving, all present express their approval by saying "Amen." This Hebrew word, "Amen," means "So be it." And when he who presides has celebrated the Eucharist, they whom we call deacons permit each one present to partake of the Eucharistic bread, and wine and water; and they carry it also to the absentees.

* *St. Justin Martyr*, trans. & ed. by Rev. Thomas B. Falls, Vol. VI, *Fathers of the Church* (New York, 1948), 99 ff.

The Real Presence

66. We call this food the Eucharist, of which only he can partake who has acknowledged the truth of our teachings, who has been cleansed by baptism for the remission of his sins and for his regeneration, and who regulates his life upon the principles laid down by Christ. Not as ordinary bread or as ordinary drink do we partake of them, but just as, through the word of God, our Savior Jesus Christ became Incarnate and took upon Himself flesh and blood for our salvation, so, we have been taught, the food which has been made the Eucharist by the prayer of His word, and which nourishes our flesh and blood by assimilation, is both the flesh and blood of that Jesus who was made flesh. The Apostles in their memoirs, which are called Gospels, have handed down what Jesus ordered them to do; that He took bread and, after giving thanks, said: "Do this in remembrance of Me; this is My body." In like manner, He took also the chalice, gave thanks, and said: "This is My blood"; and to them only did He give it. The evil demons, in imitation of this, ordered the same thing to be performed in the Mithraic mysteries. For as you know or may easily learn, bread and a cup of water, together with certain incantations, are used in their mystic initiation rites.

The Sunday Service

67. On the day which is called Sunday we have a common assembly of all who live in the cities or outlying districts, and the memoirs of the Apostles or the writings of the Prophets are read, as long as there is time. Then when the reader has finished, the president of the assembly verbally admonishes and invites all to imitate such examples of virtue. Then we all stand up together and offer up prayers, and, as we said before, after we finish our prayers, bread and wine and water are presented. He who presides likewise offers up prayers and thanksgivings, to the best of his ability, and the people express their approval by saying "Amen." The Eucharistic elements are distributed and consumed by those present, and to those who are absent they are sent through the deacons. The wealthy, if they wish, contribute whatever they desire, and the collection is placed in the custody of the president.

THE DIDACHE *

The Agape-Eucharist:

9. Regarding the Eucharist. Give thanks as follows: First, concerning the cup:

* *The Didache, or the Teaching of the Twelve Apostles,* trans. by James A. Kleist, S.J., Vol. VI, *Ancient Christian Writers* (Westminster, Md.: The Newman Press, 1948), 20–21.

"We give Thee thanks, Our Father, for the Holy Vine of David Thy servant, which Thou hast made known to us through Jesus, Thy Servant."

"To Thee be the glory for evermore."

Next, concerning the broken bread:

"We give Thee thanks, Our Father, for the life and knowledge which Thou hast made known to us through Jesus, Thy Servant."

"To Thee be the glory for evermore."

"As this broken bread was scattered over the hills and then, when gathered, became one mass, so may Thy Church be gathered from the ends of the earth into Thy Kingdom."

"For Thine is the glory and the power through Jesus Christ for evermore."

Let no one eat and drink of your Eucharist but those baptized in the name of the Lord; to this, too, the saying of the Lord is applicable: *Do not give to dogs what is sacred.*

10. After you have taken your fill of food, give thanks as follows:

"We give Thee thanks, O Holy Father, for Thy holy name which Thou hast enshrined in our hearts, and for the knowledge and faith and immortality which Thou hast made known to us through Jesus, Thy Servant."

"To Thee be the glory for evermore."

"Thou, Lord Almighty, *hast created all things* for the sake of Thy name and hast given food and drink for men to enjoy, that they may give thanks to Thee; but to us Thou hast vouchsafed spiritual food and drink and eternal life through Jesus, Thy Servant."

"Above all, we give Thee thanks because Thou art mighty."

"To Thee be the glory for evermore."

"Remember, O Lord, Thy Church: deliver her from all evil, perfect her in Thy love, and *from the four winds assemble* her, the sanctified, in Thy kingdom which Thou hast prepared for her."

"For Thine is the power and the glory for evermore."

"May Grace come, and this world pass away!" "*Hossana to the God of David!*" "If anyone is holy, let him advance; if anyone is not, let him be converted. *Marana tha!*" "Amen."

THE LITURGY OF ST. HIPPOLYTUS *

Preface

The Lord be with you. And the people shall say: And with thy spirit. Lift up your hearts. We have them with the Lord. Let us give thanks unto the Lord. It is meet and right. And forthwith he shall continue thus:

Eucharistic Prayer or Canon

We render thanks unto thee, O God, through Thy Beloved Child Jesus Christ, Whom in the last times Thou didst send to us (to be) a Saviour and Redeemer and the Messenger of Thy counsel; Who is Thy Word inseparable, through Whom Thou madest all things and in Whom Thou wast well pleased; Whom Thou didst send from heaven into the Virgin's womb and Who conceived within her was made flesh and demonstrated to be Thy Son being born of the Holy Spirit and a Virgin; Who fulfilling Thy will and preparing for Thee a holy people stretched forth His hands for suffering that He might release from suffering them who have believed in Thee; Who when He was betrayed to voluntary suffering that He might abolish death and rend the bond of the devil and tread down hell and enlighten the righteous and establish the ordinance and demonstrate the resurrection:

Words of Institution

Taking bread and making eucharist (*i.e.*, giving thanks) to Thee said: Take eat: this is my Body which is broken for you. Likewise also the cup, saying: This is my Blood which is shed for you. When ye do this, ye do my "anamnesis."

The Anamnesis

Doing therefore the "anamnesis" of His death and resurrection we offer to Thee the bread and the cup making eucharist to Thee because Thou has bidden us to stand before Thee and minister as priests to Thee.

The Epiclesis

And we pray Thee that Thou wouldest send Thy Holy Spirit upon the oblation of Thy holy Church and that Thou wouldest grant to all Thy Saints who partake to be united to Thee that they may be fulfilled with the Holy Spirit for the confirmation of their faith in truth, that we may praise and glorify Thee through Thy Beloved Child Jesus Christ through whom glory and honour be unto Thee with the Holy Spirit in Thy holy Church now and for ever and world without end. Amen.

* *Apostolic Tradition of St. Hippolytus of Rome*, ed. by Dom Gregory Dix (New York: The Macmillan Company, 1938), pp. 45, 58.

The Alexandrine Rite

THE LITURGY OF SERAPION *

Preface and Sanctus

It is meet and right to praise, to hymn, to glorify Thee the uncreated Father of the only-begotten Jesus Christ. We praise Thee, O uncreated God, who art unsearchable, ineffable, incomprehensible by any created substance. We praise Thee who art known of Thy Son, the only-begotten, who through Him art spoken of and interpreted and made known to created nature. We praise Thee who knowest the Son and revealest to the saints the glories that are about Him: who art known of Thy begotten Word, and art brought to the sight and interpreted to the understanding of the saints. We praise Thee, O unseen Father, provider of immortality. Thou art the Fount of life, the Fount of light, the Fount of all grace and all truth, O lover of men, O lover of the poor, who reconcilest Thyself to all, and drawest all to Thyself through the advent of Thy beloved Son. We beseech Thee make us living men. Give us a Spirit of light, that "we may know Thee the True [God] and Him whom Thou didst send, (even) Jesus Christ." Give us Holy Spirit, that we may be able to tell forth and to enunciate Thy unspeakable mysteries. May the Lord Jesus speak in us and Holy Spirit, and hymn Thee through us. For Thou art "far above all rule and authority and power and dominion, and every name that is named, not only in this world, but also in that which is to come." Beside Thee stand thousand thousands and myriad myriads of angels, archangels, thrones, dominions, principalities, powers: by Thee stand the two most honourable six winged seraphim, with two wings covering the face, and with two the feet and with two flying and crying holy, with whom receive also our cry of 'holy' as we say: Holy, holy, holy, Lord of Sabaoth, full is the heaven and the earth of Thy glory.

Epiclesis of God's Power

Full is the heaven, full also is the earth of Thy excellent glory.

* Quoted in Msgr. Louis M. O. Duchesne, *Christian Worship: Its Origin and Evolution,* trans. by M. L. McClure (New York: The Macmillan Company, 1904), p. 76 f.

Lord of hosts (powers) fill also this sacrifice with Thy power and Thy participation: for to Thee have we offered this living sacrifice, this bloodless oblation. To Thee we have offered this bread, the likeness of the Body of the Only-begotten.

Words of Institution

This bread is the likeness of the Holy Body, because the Lord Jesus Christ in the night in which He was betrayed took bread and broke and gave to his disciples saying, "Take ye and eat, this is My Body, which is being broken for you for remission of sins." Wherefore we also, making the likeness of the death, have offered the bread, and beseech Thee through this sacrifice, be reconciled to all of us and be merciful, O God of truth; and as this bread had been scattered on the top of the mountains and, gathered together, came to be one, so also gather Thy holy Church out of every nation and every country and every city and village and house and make one living Catholic Church. We have offered also the cup, the likeness of the Blood, because the Lord Jesus Christ, taking a cup after supper, said to His own disciples, "Take ye, drink, this is the new covenant, which is My Blood, which is being shed for you for remission of sins." Wherefore we also offered the cup, presenting a likeness of the blood.

Epiclesis of Divine Word

O God of Truth, let Thy Holy Word come upon this bread, that the bread may become Body of the Word, and upon this cup, that the cup may become Blood of the Truth; and make all who communicate to receive a medicine of life for the healing of every sickness and for the strengthening of all advancement and virtue, not for condemnation, O God of Truth, and not for censure and reproach. For we have invoked Thee, the uncreated, through the Only-begotten in Holy Spirit. . . .

Memento of the Dead

(After the recitation of the names): Sanctify these souls; for Thou knowest all. Sanctify all laid to rest in the Lord. And number them with all Thy holy powers and give them a place and mansion in Thy kingdom.

Memento of the Living

Receive also the thanksgiving of the people, and bless those who have offered the offerings and the thanksgivings, and grant health and soundness and cheerfulness and all advancement of soul and body to this whole people through the only-begotten Jesus Christ in the Holy Spirit; as it was and is and shall be to generations and to all the ages of ages. Amen.

The Antiochene Rite

JERUSALEM: "ST. JAMES" *

The love of the Lord and Father, the grace of the Lord and Son and the communion and gift of the Holy Spirit be with us all.
And with thy spirit.
Let us lift up our mind and our hearts.
We lift them up unto the Lord.
Let us give thanks unto the Lord.
It is meet and right.

It is in truth meet and right, fitting and due, to praise Thee, to hymn Thee, to bless Thee, to worship Thee, to glorify Thee, to give thanks to Thee, Who art the Creator of all things visible and invisible; the Treasure of eternal good things, the Fountain of Life and immortality, the God and Master of all things; Whom Heaven and the Heaven of Heavens hymn, and all the Powers of them; the sun, the moon, and the whole choir of stars; the earth, the sea, and all that in them is; Jerusalem the heavenly assembly, the church of the first-born written in heaven; the spirits of just men and of prophets; the souls of martyrs and apostles; Angels, Archangels, Thrones, Dominations, Principalities, Authorities and the terrible Powers, the many-eyed Cherubim and the six-winged Seraphim, who with twain of their wings go cover their faces, with twain they cover their feet, and with twain flying they cry the one to the other with unresting mouths and unsilenced doxologies, the triumphal hymn to the Majesty of Thy glory; with clear voice singing, shouting, praising, crying aloud and saying—

Holy, Holy, Holy, Lord God of Hosts,
Heaven and earth are full of Thy glory,
Hosanna in the Highest.
Blessed is He that cometh in the Name of the Lord.
Hosanna in the Highest.

Holy art Thou, King of the Ages, and Lord and Giver of all holiness; Holy also Thine Only-Begotten Son, our Lord Jesus

* Arthur Linton, *Twenty-Five Consecration Prayers* (New York: The Macmillan Company, 1944), pp. 39–44.

Christ through Whom Thou didst make all things; Holy also Thy Spirit, the All-Holy, Who searcheth all things, even the deep Things of Thee, Who art God. Holy art Thou, Ruler of all, Omnipotent, Good, Terrible, Merciful, of fellow-feeling especially toward Thy creature; Thou Who didst make man from the earth after Thine image and likeness, and didst bestow upon him the delight of Paradise, and when he transgressed Thy command and fell away, Thou didst not disregard him nor forsake him, O Good One, but didst discipline him as a merciful Father, didst call him by the Law, didst educate him by the Prophets; and finally didst send forth into the world Thine Only-Begotten Son Our Lord, Jesus Christ, in order that by His coming He might renew and restore Thine image. Who having descended from heaven and having been made flesh of the Holy Ghost and Mary the Virgin, and Mother of God, lived in fellowship with men, and accomplished all things for the salvation of our race. And when He was about to endure His voluntary and life-giving death on the Cross, the Sinless for us sinners, in the night in which He was betrayed or rather surrendered Himself, for the life and salvation of the world, taking bread in His holy and spotless and pure and immortal hands, and looking up to heaven, and showing it to Thee, the God and Father, He gave thanks and hallowed and brake and gave to His holy disciples and Apostles saying (The Deacons: For the remission of sins and eternal life): TAKE, EAT: THIS IS MY BODY, WHICH IS BROKEN FOR YOU AND GIVEN FOR THE REMISSION OF SINS. (Amen.) Likewise also after supper, having taken the cup and mixed it with wine and water and having looked up to Heaven and showed it to Thee, the God and Father, He gave thanks and hallowed and blessed and filled with the Holy Ghost and gave to His holy and blessed disciples, saying: DRINK YE ALL OF IT: THIS IS MY BLOOD OF THE NEW TESTAMENT, WHICH FOR YOU AND FOR MANY IS SHED AND GIVEN FOR THE REMISSION OF SINS. (Amen.) DO THIS FOR MY MEMORIAL. FOR AS OFTEN AS YE EAT THIS BREAD AND DRINK THIS CUP YE PROCLAIM THE DEATH OF THE SON OF MAN AND CONFESS HIS RESURRECTION, TILL HE COME. (The Deacons: We believe and confess. The People: We proclaim Thy death, O Lord, and confess Thy resurrection.)

Therefore we also, who are sinners, remembering His lifegiving passion, His saving cross, His death, His tomb, and resurrection from the dead on the third day, His ascension into Heaven and the session on the right hand of Thee, the God and Father, and His glorious and terrible second coming when He shall come with glory to judge the quick and the dead, when He shall render to every man according to his works; offer to Thee this terrible and unbloody sacrifice, beseeching Thee that Thou wouldest not deal with us after our sins, nor reward us according to our iniquities, but according to Thy gentleness and unspeakable love towards man, passing by and blotting out the handwriting that is against us Thy supplicants, wouldest grant us Thy heavenly and eternal gifts, which eye hath not seen nor ear heard neither hath entered into the heart of man, the things which Thou, O God, hast prepared for them that love Thee. And do not, O Lord and Lover of Men, because of me and my sins, set at nought the people. For Thy people and Thy church entreat Thee. Have mercy upon us, O God, the Ruler of all. Have mercy upon us, O God, our Saviour. Have mercy upon us O God according to Thy pity, and send down upon us, and upon these gifts lying before Thee, Thy Spirit, the All-Holy, the Lord, and Life-giver, the sharer of the Throne with Thee, the God and Father, and Thy Only-Begotten Son; the sharer of the Kingdom, co-essential and co-eternal, Who spake in the Law and the Prophets and in Thy New Testament; Who descended in the form of a dove upon Our Lord Jesus Christ in the river Jordan and rested upon Him, Who descended upon Thy Holy Apostles in the likeness of fiery tongues in the upper room of the holy and glorious Sion on the day of the holy Pentecost. Send down the same Spirit, the All-Holy, O Master, upon us and upon these holy gifts lying before Thee; that He may come upon them with His holy and good and glorious presence, and may hallow and make this bread to be the Holy Body of Christ (Amen), and this cup the precious Blood of Christ (Amen), that they may be to all those who partake of them for the remission of sins and for eternal life, for the sanctification of soul and of bodies, for the bringing forth of good works, for the confirmation of Thy Holy Catholic and Apostolic Church, which Thou hast founded upon the rock of faith, in order that the gates of Hell may not prevail against it, freeing it from all heresy and scandals that work wickedness, guarding it even to the consummation of the age.

(Here follow the Intercessions.)

Through the grace and mercies and compassion of Thy Only-Begotten Son, with Whom Thou art to be blessed and glorified, together with Thy All-Holy and good and lifegiving Spirit, now and always and to the ages of the ages. Amen.

Gallican Mass

MISSALE RICHENOVENSE *

The Lord be with you.
And with thy spirit.
Lift up your hearts.
We lift them up unto the Lord.
Let us give thanks unto the Lord.
It is meet and right.

It is meet and right that we should give thanks unto Thee, O Lord God, through Jesus Christ Thy Son, Who, although He was Eternal God, yet deigned to become man for our salvation. O wholly singular and manifold mystery of our Saviour! For one and the same, both Highest God and perfect man, the great High Priest and most hallowed Sacrifice, in His divine power created all things, in His human condition gave freedom to men; in the power of His Sacrifice He cleansed our pollutions, in the right of His Priesthood He made amends for our offences.

O wholly singular mystery of redemption! In which the Lord healed those ancient wounds by a new remedy; and the privileges of our Salvation annulled the sentence against the first man. The one, impelled by the goad of desire, the other transfixed by the nails of obedience; the one without restraint stretched out his hand to the tree, the other in patience fitted His hands to the cross; the one satiated his appetites allured by pleasure, the other was afflicted by the torture of unmerited pain. Rightly, therefore, did the punishment of the innocent become the acquittal of the debtor, for debts are lawfully forgiven to the guilty which He, Who had no debt, has paid for them. Which matchless mystery, not only men upon earth, but even the Angels in heaven, do venerate. To Whom, rightly, do all Angels and Archangels unceasingly render praise, and say—

Holy, Holy, Holy, Lord God of Hosts.
Heaven and earth are full of Thy glory,
Hosanna in the Highest.

* Linton, *op. cit.*, pp. 114–115.

Blessed is He that cometh in the Name of the Lord.
Hosanna in the Highest.

Truly Holy, truly Blessed, is our Lord Jesus Christ, Thy Son, Who came from heaven, that He might live in fellowship with men; was made man that He might dwell in us, and became a Victim that He might make us Priests.

Who, on the day before He suffered for our salvation, and that of all men, took bread, and lifted up His eyes to heaven, to Thee, God, His Almighty Father, and giving thanks to Thee, He blessed and broke, and gave to His disciples, saying to them: TAKE, AND EAT YE ALL OF THIS: FOR THIS IS MY BODY. In like manner after they had supped, taking the cup, He raised His eyes to Thee, God, His Almighty Father, also giving thanks to Thee, and blessed, and gave to His disciples, saying to them: TAKE, AND DRINK YE ALL OF IT: FOR THIS IS THE CUP OF MY BLOOD, OF THE NEW AND ETERNAL TESTAMENT, A MYSTERY OF FAITH, WHICH FOR YOU AND FOR MANY SHALL BE SHED FOR THE REMISSION OF SINS. Commanding also and saying to them: AS OFTEN AS YE SHALL DO THESE THINGS, YE SHALL DO THEM FOR A MEMORIAL OF ME, YE SHALL PROCLAIM MY DEATH AND ANNOUNCE MY RESURRECTION, YE SHALL HOPE FOR MY ADVENT TILL I SHALL COME AGAIN TO YOU FROM THE HEAVENS.

We beseech the glory of our Lord and our Eternal God, praying that Thou wouldest bless this Sacrifice with Thy benediction, and besprinkle it with the dew of Thy Holy Spirit, that to all who receive, it may be a valid Eucharist; through Jesus Christ Thy Son, Lord and God, and our Preserver: to Whom, with Thee, O Lord, and the Holy Spirit, is the everlasting kingdom and the unending Godhead, world without end. Amen.

THE CANON OF THE ROMAN MASS

P. Dominus vobiscum.	P. The Lord be with you.
R. Et cum spiritu tuo.	R. And with thy spirit. (And with you also.)
P. Sursum corda.	P. Lift up your hearts.
R. Habemus ad Dominum.	R. We have lifted them even unto the Lord.
P. Gratias agamus Domino Deo nostro.	P. Let us give thanks to the Lord our God. (Let us offer the Thanksgiving.)
R. Dignum et justum est.	R. It is proper and right to do so.
Vere dignum et justum est, aequum et salutare, nos tibi semper et ubique gratias agere: Domine sancte, Pater omnipotens aeterne Deus: per Christum Dominum nostrum. Per quem majestatem tuam laudant Angeli, adorant Dominationes, tremunt Potestates. Caeli caelorumque Virtutes ac beata Seraphim socia exsultatione concelebrant. Cum quibus et nostras voces ut admitti jubeas, deprecamur, supplici confessione dicentes:	It is truly proper and right, it is our duty and our salvation, to give thanks to you always and everywhere, O Lord, Holy Father, Almighty and everlasting God, through Christ our Lord, through him the Angels praise your majesty, the Dominations adore it, the Powers stand in awe before it, the Heavens and the heavenly armies, with the blessed Seraphim celebrate it, joined together in the same joyous exultation. We beg you to let us join our voices to theirs proclaiming in humble praise:
Sanctus, sanctus, sanctus Dominus Deus Sabaoth. Pleni sunt	Holy, holy, holy is the Lord of the heavenly hosts. The heavens

caeli et terra gloria tua. Hosanna in excelsis. Benedictus qui venit in nomine Domini. Hosanna in excelsis.

and the earth are full of your glory. [Your glory fills heaven and earth.] Hosanna in the highest heaven. Blessed is he who comes in the name of the Lord. Hosanna in the highest heaven.

Te igitur, clementissime Pater, per Jesum Christum, Filium tuum, Dominum nostrum, supplices rogamus, ac petimus, uti accepta habeas et benedicas, haec dona, haec munera, haec sancta sacrificia illibata. *In primis, quae tibi offerimus pro Ecclesia tua sancta catholica: quam pacificare, custodire, adunare, et regere digneris toto orbe terrarum: una cum famulo tuo Papa nostro N., et Antistite nostro N., et omnibus orthodoxis, atque catholicae et apostolicae fidei cultoribus.*

We therefore humbly ask and beseech you, most kind and gracious Father, through Jesus Christ your Son our Lord, to receive and to bless these gifts, these presents, these holy and untouched sacrificial offerings. We offer them first of all for your Holy Catholic Church—Deign to keep it in peace, to protect it, to gather it together and to govern it throughout the whole world; and for your Servant our Pope Pius and our Bishop N., and for all those who, faithful to true doctrine, have the care of the Catholic and Apostolic Faith.

Memento, Domine, famulorum famularumque tuarum N. et N. et omnium circumstantium, quorum tibi fides cognita est et nota devotio, pro quibus tibi offerimus: vel qui tibi offerunt hoc sacrificium laudis, pro se suisque omnibus: pro redemptione animarum suarum, pro spe salutis et incolumitatis suae: tibique reddunt vota sua aeterno Deo, vivo et vero. Communicantes, et memoriam venerantes, in primis gloriosae semper Virginis Mariae, Genitricis Dei et Domini nostri Jesu Christi: sed et beatorum Apostolorum ac Martyrum tuorum Petri et Pauli, Andreae, Jacobi,

Be mindful O Lord of your servants and handmaids and of all those who are assembled here together, whose faith and attachment [to your service] are known to you, for whom we offer or who offer to you this sacrifice of praise for themselves and for those who belong to them, to obtain the redemption of their souls and in hope of their salvation and security. They pay their tribute of sacrifice to you, the living and true God, united in fellowship with and venerating the memory, first of all, of the glorious ever Virgin Mary, Mother of our God and Lord, Jesus Christ,

Joannis, Thomae, Jacobi, Philippi, Bartholomaei, Matthaei, Simonis et Thaddaei: Lini, Cleti, Clementis, Xysti, Cornelii, Cypriani, Laurentii, Chrysogoni, Joannis et Pauli, Cosmae et Damiani: et omnium Sanctorum tuorum; quorum meritis precibusque concedas, ut in omnibus protectionis tuae muniamur auxilio. Per eundem Christum, Dominum nostrum. Amen.

and of the blessed Apostles and Martyrs: Peter and Paul, Andrew, James, John, Thomas, James, Philip, Bartholomew, Matthew, Simon and Jude, Linus, Cletus, Clement, Sixtus, Cornelius, Cyprian, Lawrence, Chrysogosus, John and Paul, Cosmos and Damian and of all your saints. By their merits and their prayers grant us that we may in all things [in every way] be defended by the help of your protection. Through the same Christ our Lord.

Hanc igitur oblationem servitutis nostrae, sed et cunctae familiae tuae, quaesumus, Domine, ut placatus accipias: diesque nostros in tua pace disponas, atque ab aeterna damnatione nos eripi, et in electorum tuorum jubeas grege numerari. Per Christum Dominum nostrum. Amen.

This offering, then, which we your servants [the clergy], and also your whole family, present to you, be pleased to accept, and order all the days of our life in your peace, and command that we be delivered from eternal damnation and numbered in the flock of Your chosen sheep. Through Christ our Lord. Amen.

Quam oblationem tu, Deus, in omnibus, quaesumus, benedictam, adscriptam, ratam, rationabilem, acceptabilemque facere digneris: ut nobis Corpus, et Sanguis fiat dilectissimi Filii tui, Domini nostri Jesu Christi.

Be pleased, O God, to bless this same offering in every respect, to accept it and approve it fully and completely, making it spiritual and well pleasing to you, that it may thus become for us the Body and Blood of your well-beloved Son, our Lord Jesus Christ.

Qui pridie quam pateretur, accepit panem in sanctas ac venerabiles manus suas, et elevatis oculis in caelum ad te Deum, Patrem suum omnipotentem, tibi gratias agens, benedixit, fregit, deditque discipulis suis, dicens: Accipite, et man-

Who on the eve of his passion [on the day before he suffered death] took bread into his holy and adorable [worshipful] hands, and lifting up his eyes toward heaven, unto you, O God, his almighty Father, giving thanks to you, he blessed

ducate ex hoc omnes. Hoc est enim Corpus meum.

the bread, broke it and gave it to his disciples saying: "Take, all of you, and eat of this, for this is my body."

Simili modo postquam coenatum est, accipiens et hunc praeclarum Calicem in sanctas ac venerabiles manus suas, item tibi gratias agens, benedixit, deditque discipulis suis, dicens: Accipite, et bibite ex eo omnes. Hic est enim Calix Sanguinis mei, novi et aeterni testamenti: mysterium fidei: qui pro vobis et pro multis effundetur in remissionem peccatorum. Haec quotiescumque feceritis, in mei memoriam facietis.

In the same fashion, after the supper was over, taking this precious chalice into his holy and adorable [worshipful] hands and again giving thanks to you, he blessed it and gave it to his disciples saying: "Take, all of you, and drink of this, for this is the Chalice of my blood, the blood of the New and Eternal Covenant, the Mystery of Faith, which shall be poured out for you and for many unto the remission of sins. Each time you do this you will do it for a re-presentation of me [for my memorial]."

Unde et memores, Domine, nos servi tui, sed et plebs tua sancta, ejusdem Christi Filii tui, Domini nostri, tam beatae passionis, necnon et ab inferis resurrectionis, sed et in caelos gloriosae ascensionis: offerimus praeclarae majestati tuae de tuis donis ac datis, hostiam puram, hostiam sanctam, hostiam immaculatam, Panem sanctum vitae aeternae, et Calicem salutis perpetuae.

That is why, O Lord, we your servants, and all your holy people as well, recalling the most blessed Passion of this same Christ your Son our Lord, likewise his Resurrection from the grave, and his glorious Ascension into heaven, offer to your excellent majesty from your own gifts and presents a victim that is pure, a victim that is holy, a victim that is without spot [unblemished], the holy bread of eternal life and the chalice of never-ending salvation.

Supra quae propitio ac sereno vultu respicere digneris: et accepta habere, sicuti accepta habere dignatus es munera pueri tui justi Abel, et sacrificium Patriarchae nostri Abrahae: et

Upon these offerings deign to look with favorable and gracious countenance and receive them as you were pleased to accept the gifts of your servant Abel the Just, the sacrifice of Abra-

quod tibi obtulit summus sacerdos tuus Melchisedech, sanctum sacrificium, immaculatam hostiam.

Supplices te rogamus, omnipotens Deus: jube haec perferri per manus sancti Angeli tui in sublime altare tuum, in conspectu divinae majestatis tuae: ut quotquot ex hac altaris participatione sacrosanctum Filii tui Corpus, et Sanguinem sumpserimus, omni benedictione caelesti et gratia repleamur. Per eundem Christum Dominum nostrum. Amen.

Memento etiam, Domine, famulorum famularumque tuarum N. et N., qui nos praecesserunt cum signo fidei, et dormiunt in somno pacis. Ipsis, Domine, et omnibus in Christo quiescentibus, locum refrigerii, lucis, et pacis, ut indulgeas, deprecamur. Per eundem Christum, Dominum nostrum. Amen.

Nobis quoque peccatoribus famulis tuis, de multitudine miserationum tuarum sperantibus, partem aliquam et societatem donare digneris, cum tuis sanctis Apostolis et Martyribus: cum Joanne, Stephano, Matthia, Barnaba, Ignatio, Alexandro, Marcellino, Petro, Felicitate, Perpetua, Agatha, Lucia, Agnete, Caecilia, Anastasia, et omnibus Sanctis tuis: intra quorum nos consortium non aestimator meriti, sed veniae, quaesumus, largitor admitte. Per Christum Dominum nostrum.

ham the Father of our race and the sacrifice Melchisedech your high-priest offered you—a holy sacrifice and a spotless victim.

We beseech You Almighty God to command that these offerings be carried by the hands of Your holy angel to Your altar on high, in the presence of Your divine majesty. And when we receive in communion from this altar the infinitely holy Body and Blood of Your Son may we all be filled with every heavenly grace and blessing. Through Christ Our Lord.

Be mindful also O Lord of Your servants and handmaids who have gone before us, marked with the sign of faith, and who sleep the sleep of peace. To these O Lord and to all who rest in Christ, grant we beseech You, a place of happiness, light and peace. Through Christ our Lord.

To us also Your servants, sinful as we are, who put our trust in Your countless acts of mercy, deign to grant some share and fellowship with Your holy apostles and martyrs, with John and Stephen, Matthias, Barnabas, Ignatius, Alexander, Marcellinus, Peter, Felicitas, Perpetua, Agatha, Lucy, Agnes, Cecilia, Anastasia, and all Your saints, into whose company we pray You admit us, not weighing our merits, but freely granting us forgiveness. Through Christ our Lord.

Per quem haec omnia, Domine, semper bona creas, sanctificas, vivificas, benedicis et praestas nobis.

Through Him You never cease to create all these good things [to make all things good] and You make them holy, You give life to them and You bless them and bestow them upon us.

Per ipsum, et cum ipso, et in ipso est tibi Deo Patri omnipotenti in unitate Spiritus Sancti omnis honor et gloria. Per omnia saecula saeculorum. Amen.

By Him, with Him, and in Him You receive, O God the Father Almighty, in the unity of the Holy Spirit, all honor and glory for ever and ever. Amen.

INTROITS

Ascension

Act. Apos. 1, 2. Viri Galilaei, quid admiramini aspicientes in caelum? alleluia: quemadmodum vidistis eum ascendentem in caelum, ita veniet, alleluia, alleluia, alleluia. *ps.* 46, 2. Omnes gentes, plaudite manibus: jubilate Deo in voce exsultationis. V. Gloria Patri.

Pentecost

Sap. 1, 7. Spiritus Domini replevit orbem terrarum, alleluia: et hoc quod continet omnia, scientiam habet vocis, alleluia, alleluia, alleluia. *Ps.* 67, 2. Exsurgat Deus, et dissipentur inimici ejus: et fugiant, qui oderunt eum, a facie ejus. V. Gloria Patri.

Wednesday of Pentecost

Ps. 67, 8, 9. Deus, dum egredereris coram populo tuo, iter faciens eis, habitans in illis, alleluia: terra mota est, caeli distillaverunt, alleluia, alleluia. *Ps.* 67, 2. Exsurgat Deus, et dissipentur inimici ejus: et fugiant, qui oderunt eum, a facie ejus. V. Gloria Patri.

Corpus Christi

Ps. 80, 17. Cibavit eos ex adipe frumenti, alleluia; et de petra, melle saturavit eos, alleluia, alleluia, alleluia. *Ps.* 80, 2. Exsultate Deo adjutori nostro; jubilate Deo Jacob. V. Gloria Patri.

Immaculate Conception of the Blessed Virgin Mary

Isai. 61, 10. Gaudens gaudebo in Domino, et exsultabit anima mea in Deo meo: quia induit me vestimentis salutis: et indumento justitiae circumdedit me, quasi sponsam ornatam monilibus suis. *Ps.* 29, 2. Exaltabo te, Domine, quoniam suscepisti me: nec delectasti inimicos meos super me. V. Gloria Patri.

St. John Damascene

Ps. 72, 24. Tenuisti manum dexteram meam: et in voluntate tua deduxisti me, et cum gloria suscepisti me. *Ps.* 72, 1. Quam bonus Israel Deus his, qui recto sunt corde! V. Gloria Patri.

Holy Thursday

Gal. 6, 14. Nos autem gloriari oportet in cruce Domini nostri Jesu Christi in quo est salus, vita, et resurrectio nostra: per quem salvati, et liberati sumus. *Ps.* 66. Deus misereatur nostri, et benedicat nobis: illuminet vultum suum super nos, et misereatur nostri.

Nativity of St. John the Baptist

Isai. 49, 1, 2. De ventre matris meae vocavit me Dominus nomine meo: et posuit os meum ut gladium acutum: sub tegumento manus suae protexit me, et posuit me quasi sagittam electam. *Ps.* 91, 2. Bonum est confiteri Domino: et psallere nomini tuo, Altissime. V. Gloria Patri.

SS. Peter and Paul

Acts 12, 11. Nunc scio vere, quia misit Dominus Angelum suum: et eripuit me de manu Herodis, et de omni exspectatione plebis Judaeorum. *Ps.* 138, 1–2. Domine, probasti me, et cognovisti me: tu cognovisti sessionem meam, et resurrectionem meam. V. Gloria Patri.

First Sunday of Advent

Ps. 24, 1–3. Ad te levavi animam meam: Deus meus, in te confido, non erubescam: neque irrideant me inimici mei: etenim universi, qui te exspectant, non confundentur. *Ps.* 24, 4. Vias tuas, Domine, demonstra mihi: et semitas tuas edoce me. V. *Gloria Patri.*

Second Sunday of Advent

Isai. 30, 30. Populus Sion, ecce Dominus veniet ad salvandas gentes: et auditam faciet Dominus gloriam vocis suae in laetitia cordis vestri. *Ps.* 79, 2. Qui regis Israel, intende: qui deducis, velut ovem, Joseph. V. Gloria Patri.

Second Mass of Christmas

Isai. 9, 2, 6. Lux fulgebit hodie super nos: quia natus est nobis Dominus: et vocabitur Admirabilis, Deus, Princeps pacis, Pater futuri saeculi: cujus regni non erit finis. *Ps.* 92, 1. Dominus regnavit, decorem indutus est: indutus est Dominus fortitudinem, et praecinxit se. V. Gloria Patri.

Mass of St. Stephen

Ps. 118, 23, 86, 23. Sederunt principes, et adversum me loquebantur: et iniqui persecuti sunt me: adjuva me, Domine, Deus meus, quia servus tuus exercebatur in tuis justificationibus. *Ps. 118, 1.* Beati immaculati in via, qui ambulant in lege Domini. V. Gloria Patri.

St. Thomas a Becket

Gaudeamus omnes in Domino, diem festum celebrantes sub honore beati Thomae Martyris: de cujus passione gaudent Angeli, et collaudant Filium Dei. *Ps. 32, 1.* Exsultate, justi in Domino: rectos decet collaudatio. V. Gloria Patri.

Epiphany

Mal. 3, 1. Ecce, advenit Dominator Dominus: et regnum in manu ejus, et potestas, et imperium. *Ps. 71, 1.* Deus, judicium tuum regi da: et justitiam tuam Filio regis. V. Gloria Patri.

Common of a Confessor Bishop

Eccli. 45, 30. Statuit ei Dominus testamentum pacis, et principem fecit eum: ut sit illi sacerdotii dignitas in aeternum. *Ps. 131, 1.* Memento, Domine, David: et omnis mansuetudinis ejus. V. Gloria Patri.

Common of a Confessor not a Bishop

Ps. 91, 13–14. Justus ut palma florebit: sicut cedrus Libani multiplicabitur: plantatus in domo Domini: in atriis domus Dei nostri. *Ps. 91, 13–14.* Bonum est confiteri Domino: et psallere nomini tuo, Altissime. V. Gloria Patri.

Precious Blood

Isai. 55, 1. Sitientes, venite ad aquas, dicit Dominus: et qui non habetis pretium, venite, et bibite cum laetitia. *Ps. 77, 1.* Attendite, popule meus, legem meam: inclinate aurem vestram in verba oris mei. V. Gloria Patri.

Seven Sorrows of the Blessed Virgin Mary

Joann. 19, 25. Stabant juxta crucem Jesu mater ejus, et soror matris ejus Maria Cleophae, et Salome, et Maria Magdalene. *Joann. 19, 26–27.* Mulier, ecce filius tuus: dixit Jesus; ad discipulum autem: Ecce mater tua. V. Gloria Patri.

St. Margaret Mary

Cant. 2, 3. Sub umbra illius, quem desideraveram, sedi; et fructus ejus dulcis gutturi meo. *Ps. 83, 2–3.* Quam dilecta tabernacula tua,

Domine virtutum! concupiscit et deficit anima mea in atria Domini. V. Gloria Patri.

Christ the King

Apoc. 5, 12; 1, 6. Dignus est Agnus, qui occisus est, accipere virtutem, et divinitatem, et sapientiam, et fortitudinem, et honorem. Ipsi gloria et imperium in saecula saeculorum. *Ps. 71, 1.* Deus, judicium tuum Regi da: et justitiam tuam Filio Regis. V. Gloria Patri.

COLLECTS

Against the Persecution of the Church

Ecclesiae tuae, quaesumus, Domine, preces placatus admitte: ut, destructis adversitatibus et erroribus universis, secura tibi serviat libertate. Per Dominum.

For the Intercession of the Saints

A cunctis nos, quaesumus, Domine, mentis et corporis defende periculis: et, intercedente beata et gloriosa semper Virgine Dei Genitrice Maria, cum beato Joseph, beatis Apostolis tuis Petro et Paulo, atque beato N. . . ., et omnibus Sanctis, salutem nobis tribue benignus et pacem; ut destructis adversitatibus et erroribus universis, Ecclesia tua secura tibi serviat libertate. Per eundem Dominum.

Of the Blessed Virgin

Concede nos famulos tuos, quaesumus, Domine Deus, perpetua mentis et corporis sanitate gaudere: et, gloriosa beatae Mariae semper Virginis intercessione, a praesenti liberari tristitia, et aeterna perfrui laetitia. Per Dominum.

Vigil of Apostles

Da, quaesumus, omnipotens Deus, ut beati N. Apostoli tui, quam praevenimus, veneranda solemnitas, et devotionem nobis augeat, et salutem. Per Dominum.

For a Bishop Martyr

Infirmitatem nostram respice, omnipotens Deus; et, quia pondus propriae actionis gravat, beati N. Martyris tui atque Pontificis intercessio gloriosa nos protegat. Per Dominum.

Also for a Bishop Martyr

Deus, qui nos beati N. Martyris tui atque Pontificis annua solemnitate laetificas, concede propitius; ut, cujus natalitia colimus, de ejusdem etiam protectione gaudeamus. Per Dominum.

Common of Abbots

Intercessio nos, quaesumus, Domine, beati N. Abbatis commendet; ut, quod nostris meritis non valemus, ejus patrocinio assequamur. Per Dominum.

Dedication of Churches

Deus, qui nobis per singulos annos hujus sancti templi tui consecrationis reparas diem, et sacris semper mysteriis repraesentas incolumes: exaudi preces populi tui, et praesta; ut, quisquis hoc templum beneficia petiturus ingreditur, cuncta se impetrasse laetetur. Per Dominum.

Second Sunday of Advent

Excita, Domine, corda nostra ad praeparandas Unigeniti tui vias: ut per ejus adventum, purificatis tibi mentibus servire mereamur: Qui tecum.

Vigil of Christmas

Deus, qui nos redemptionis nostrae annua exspectatione laetificas: praesta; ut Unigenitum tuum, quem Redemptorem laeti suscipimus, venientem quoque judicem securi videamus, Dominum nostrum Jesum Christum Filium tuum: Qui tecum.

First Sunday in Lent

Deus, qui Ecclesiam tuam annua quadragesimali observatione purificas: praesta familiae tuae: ut, quod a te obtinere abstinendo nititur, hoc bonis operibus exsequatur. Per Dominum.

First Monday in Lent

Converte nos, Deus, salutaris noster: et, ut nobis jejunium quadragesimale proficiat, mentes nostras caelestibus instrue disciplinis. Per Dominum.

First Tuesday in Lent

Respice, Domine, familiam tuam, et praesta: ut apud te mens nostra tuo desiderio fulgeat, quae se carnis maceratione castigat. Per Dominum.

Seven Sorrows of the Blessed Virgin Mary

Deus, in cujus passione, secundum Simeonis prophetiam, dulcissimam animam gloriosae Virginis et Matris Mariae doloris gladius pertransivit: Concede propitius; ut, qui transfixionem ejus et passionem venerando recolimus, gloriosis meritis et precibus omnium Sanctorum cruci fideliter astantium intercedentibus, passionis tuae effectum felicem consequamur: Qui vivis.

Palm Sunday

Omnipotens sempiterne Deus, qui humano generi ad imitandum humilitatis exemplum, Salvatorem nostrum carnem sumere, et crucem subire fecisti: concede propitius; ut et patientiae ipsius habere documenta, et resurrectionis consortia mereamur. Per eundem Dominum.

Third Sunday after Easter

Deus, qui errantibus, ut in viam possint redire justitiae, veritatis tuae lumen ostendis; da cunctis qui christiana professione censentur, et illa respuere, quae huic inimica sunt nomini; et ea quae sunt apta, sectari. Per Dominum.

Fourth Sunday after Easter

Deus, qui fidelium mentes unius efficis voluntatis, da populis tuis id amare quod praecipis, id desiderare quod promittis: ut inter mundanas varietates ibi nostra fixa sint corda, ubi vera sunt gaudia. Per Dominum.

Fifth Sunday after Easter

Deus, a quo bona cuncta procedunt, largire supplicibus tuis: ut cogitemus, te inspirante, quae recta sunt; et, te gubernante, eadem faciamus. Per Dominum.

Ascension

Concede, quaesumus, omnipotens Deus: ut, qui hodierna die Unigenitum tuum Redemptorem nostrum ad caelos ascendisse credimus, ipsi quoque mente in caelestibus habitemus. Per eundem Dominum.

Pentecost

Deus, qui hodierna die corda fidelium Sancti Spiritus illustratione docuisti: da nobis in eodem Spiritu recta sapere; et de ejus semper consolatione gaudere. Per Dominum . . . in unitate ejusdem.

Pentecost Tuesday

Adsit nobis, quaesumus, Domine, virtus Spiritus Sancti: quae et corda nostra clementer expurget, et ab omnibus tueatur adversis. Per Dominum . . . in unitate ejusdem.

Pentecost Wednesday

Mentes nostras, quaesumus, Domine, Paraclitus, qui a te procedit, illuminet: et inducat in omnem, sicut tuus promisit Filius, veritatem: Qui tecum . . . in unitate ejusdem.

Corpus Christi

Deus, qui nobis sub Sacramento mirabili passionis tuae memoriam reliquisti: tribue, quaesumus, ita nos Corporis et Sanguinis tui sacra mysteria venerari; ut redemptionis tuae fructum in nobis jugiter sentiamus: Qui vivis.

Second Sunday after Pentecost

Sancti nominis tui, Domine, timorem pariter et amorem fac nos habere perpetuum: quia numquam tua gubernatione destituis, quos in soliditate tuae dilectionis instituis. Per Dominum.

Third Sunday after Pentecost

Protector in te sperantium, Deus, sine quo nihil est validum, nihil sanctum: multiplica super nos misericordiam tuam, ut, te rectore, te duce, sic transeamus per bona temporalia, ut non amittamus aeterna. Per Dominum.

Thirteenth Sunday after Pentecost

Omnipotens sempiterne Deus, da nobis fidei, spei, et caritatis augmentum: et, ut mereamur assequi quod promittis, fac nos amare quod praecipis. Per Dominum.

Seventeenth Sunday after Pentecost

Da, quaesumus, Domine, populo tuo diabolica vitare contagia: et te solum Deum pura mente sectari. Per Dominum.

St. Titus

Deus, qui beatum Titum Confessorem tuum atque Pontificem, apostolicis virtutibus decorasti: ejus meritis et intercessione concede; ut juste et pie viventes in hoc saeculo, ad caelestem patriam pervenire mereamur. Per Dominum.

St. John the Baptist

Deus, qui praesentem diem honorabilem nobis in beati Joannis nativitate fecisti: da populis tuis spiritualium gratiam gaudiorum; et omnium fidelium mentes dirige in viam salutis aeternae. Per Dominum.

St. Gorgonius

Sanctus tuus, Domine, Gorgonius sua nos intercessione laetificet: et pia faciat solemnitate gaudere. Per Dominum.

St. Jane Frances de Chantal

Omnipotens et misericors Deus, qui beatam Joannam Franciscam tuo amore succensam, admirabili spiritus fortitudine per omnes vitae semitas in via perfectionis donasti, quique per illam illustrare

Ecclesiam tuam nova prole voluisti: ejus meritis et precibus concede; ut, qui infirmitatis nostrae conscii de tua virtute confidimus, caelestis gratiae auxilio, cuncta nobis adversantia vincamus. Per Dominum.

First Mass of Christmas

Deus, qui hanc sacratissimam noctem veri luminis fecisti illustratione clarescere: da, quaesumus; ut, cujus lucis mysteria in terra cognovimus, ejus quoque gaudiis in caelo perfruamur. Qui tecum.

Second Mass of Christmas

Da nobis, quaesumus, omnipotens Deus: ut, qui nova incarnati Verbi tui luce perfundimur; hoc in nostro resplendeat opere, quod per fidem fulget in mente. Per eundem Dominum.

Baptism of Our Lord

Deus, cujus Unigenitus in substantia nostrae carnis apparuit: praesta, quaesumus, ut per eum, quem similem nobis foris agnovimus, intus reformari mereamur: Qui tecum.

GRADUALS

First Sunday of Advent

Ps. 24, 3, 4. Universi, qui te exspectant, non confundentur, Domine. V. Vias tuas, Domine, notas fac mihi: et semitas tuas edoce me. Alleluia, alleluia: *Ps.* 84, 8. V. Ostende nobis, Domine, misericordiam tuam: et salutare tuum da nobis. Alleluia.

Second Sunday of Advent

Ps. 49, 2–3, 5. Ex Sion species decoris ejus: Deus manifeste veniet. V. Congregate illi sanctos ejus, qui ordinaverunt testamentum ejus super sacrificia. Alleluia, alleluia: *Ps.* 121, 1. V. Laetatus sum in his, quae dicta sunt mihi: in domum Domini ibimus. Alleluia.

Christmas: Midnight Mass

Ps. 109, 3, 1. Tecum principium in die virtutis tuae: in splendoribus sanctorum, ex utero ante luciferum genui te. V. Dixit Dominus Domino meo: Sede a dextris meis: donec ponam inimicos tuos, scabellum pedum tuorum. Alleluia, alleluia: *Ps.* 2, 7. V. Dominus dixit ad me: Filius meus es tu, ego hodie genui te. Alleluia.

Immaculate Conception of the Blessed Virgin Mary

Judith 13, 23. Benedicta es tu, Virgo Maria, a Domino Deo excelso, prae omnibus mulieribus super terram. V. Tu gloria Jerusalem, tu laetitia Israel, tu honorificentia populi nostri. Alleluia, alleluia: *Song of Sol.* 4, 7. V. Tota pulchra es, Maria: et macula originalis non est in te. Alleluia.

Nativity of St. John the Baptist

Priusquam te formarem in utero, novi te: et antequam exires de ventre, sanctificavi te. V. Misit Dominus manum suam, et tetigit os meum, et dixit mihi. Alleluia, alleluia: V. Tu, puer, propheta Altissimi vocaberis: praeibis ante Dominum parare vias ejus. Alleluia.

TRACTS

Passion Sunday

Ps. 128, 1–4. Saepe expugnaverunt me a juventute mea. V. Dicat nunc Israel: saepe expugnaverunt me a juventute mea. V. Etenim non potuerunt mihi: supra dorsum meum fabricaverunt peccatores. V. Prolongaverunt iniquitates suas: Dominus justus concidit cervices peccatorum.

Palm Sunday

Ps. 21, 2–9, 18, 19, 22, 24, 32. Deus, Deus meus, respice in me: quare me dereliquisti? V. Longe a salute mea verba delictorum meorum. V. Deus meus, clamabo per diem, nec exaudies: in nocte, et non ad insipientiam mihi. V. Tu autem in sancto habitas, laus Israel. V. In te speraverunt patres nostri: speraverunt, et liberasti eos. V. Ad te clamaverunt, et salvi facti sunt: in te speraverunt, et non sunt confusi. V. Ego autem sum vermis, et non homo: opprobrium hominum, et abjectio plebis. V. Omnes qui videbant me, aspernabantur me: locuti sunt labiis, et moverunt caput. V. Speravit in Domino, eripiat eum: salvum faciat eum, quoniam vult eum. V. Ipsi vero consideraverunt, et conspexerunt me: diviserunt sibi vestimenta mea, et super vestem meam miserunt sortem. V. Libera me de ore leonis: et a cornibus unicornium humilitatem meam. V. Qui timetis Dominum, laudate eum: universum semen Jacob, magnificate eum. V. Annuntiabitur Domino generatio ventura: et annuntiabunt caeli justitiam ejus. V. Populo, qui nascetur, quem fecit Dominus.

Votive Mass of the Most Blessed Sacrament

Mal. 1, 11. Ab ortu solis usque ad occasum, magnum est nomen meum in gentibus. V. Et in omni loco sacrificatur, et offertur nomini meo oblatio munda: quia magnum est nomen meum in gentibus. V. Venite, comedite panem meum: et bibite vinum, quod miscui vobis.

OFFERTORY ANTIPHONS

Corpus Christi

Lev. 21, 6. Sacerdotes Domini incensum et panes offerunt Deo: et ideo sancti erunt Deo suo, et non polluent nomen ejus, alleluia.

Seventh Sunday after Pentecost

Dan. 3, 40. Sicut in holocaustis arietum et taurorum, et sicut in millibus agnorum pinguium: sic fiat sacrificium nostrum in conspectu tuo hodie, ut placeat tibi, quia non est confusio confidentibus in te, Domine.

St. Gabriel Possenti

Ps. 115, 16–17. Domine, quia ego servus tuus, et filius ancillae tuae: dirupisti vincula mea, tibi sacrificabo hostiam laudis.

Exaltation of the Holy Cross

Protege, Domine, plebem tuam per signum sanctae Crucis, ab omnibus insidiis inimicorum omnium: ut tibi gratam exhibeamus servitutem, et acceptabile fiat sacrificium nostrum. Alleluia.

St. Margaret Mary

Zach. 9, 17. Quid bonum ejus est, et quid pulchrum ejus, nisi frumentum electorum, et vinum germinans virgines?

Requiem Mass

Domine Jesu Christe, Rex gloriae, libera animas omnium fidelium defunctorum de poenis inferni et de profundo lacu: libera eas de ore leonis, ne absorbeat eas tartarus, ne cadant in obscurum: sed signifer sanctus Michael repraesentet eas in lucem sanctam: Quam olim Abrahae promisisti, et semini ejus. V. Hostias et preces tibi, Domine, laudis offerimus; tu suscipe pro animabus illis, quarum hodie memoriam facimus: fac eas, Domine, de morte transire ad vitam: Quam olim Abrahae promisisti, et semini ejus.

Common of the Blessed Virgin Mary

Luke I, 28. Ave Maria, gratia plena: Dominus tecum: benedicta tu in mulieribus, et benedictus fructus ventris tui.

Dedication of Churches

I Par. 29, 17, 18. Domine Deus, in simplicitate cordis mei laetus obtuli universa; et populum tuum, qui repertus est, vidi cum ingenti gaudio: Deus Israel, custodi hanc voluntatem, alleluia.

Epiphany

Ps. 71, 10, 11. Reges Tharsis et insulae munera offerent: reges Arabum et Saba dona adducent: et adorabunt eum omnes reges terrae: omnes gentes servient ei.

Fourth Sunday after Easter

Ps. 65, 1, 2, 16. Jubilate Deo, universa terra: psalmum dicite nomini ejus: venite, et audite, et narrabo vobis, omnes qui timetis Deum, quanta fecit Dominus animae meae, alleluia.

Holy Thursday

Ps. 117, 16, 17. Dextera Domini fecit virtutem, dextera Domini exaltavit me: non moriar, sed vivam, et narrabo opera Domini.

Pentecost

Ps. 67, 29, 30. Confirma hoc, Deus, quod operatus es in nobis: a templo tuo, quod est in Jerusalem, tibi offerent reges munera, alleluia.

SECRET PRAYERS

The Blessed Virgin, on Saturdays

Tua, Domine, propitiatione, et beatae Mariae semper Virginis intercessione, ad perpetuam atque praesentem haec oblatio nobis proficiat prosperitatem et pacem. Per Dominum.

Circumcision

Muneribus nostris, quaesumus, Domine, precibusque susceptis: et caelestibus nos munda mysteriis, et clementer exaudi. Per Dominum.

First Sunday of Advent

Haec sacra nos, Domine, potenti virtute mundatos, ad suum faciant puriores venire principium. Per Dominum.

Third Sunday of Advent

Devotionis nostrae tibi, quaesumus, Domine, hostia jugiter immoletur: quae et sacri peragat instituta mysterii, et salutare tuum in nobis mirabiliter operetur. Per Dominum.

Fourth Sunday of Advent

Sacrificiis praesentibus quaesumus, Domine, placatus intende: ut et devotioni nostrae proficiant, et saluti. Per Dominum.

First Mass of Christmas

Accepta tibi sit, Domine, quaesumus, hodiernae festivitatis oblatio: ut, tua gratia largiente, per haec sacrosancta commercia, in illius inveniamur forma, in quo tecum est nostra substantia. Qui tecum.

Second Mass of Christmas

Munera nostra, quaesumus, Domine, Nativitatis hodiernae mysteriis apta proveniant, et pacem nobis semper infundant: ut, sicut homo genitus idem refulsit et Deus, sic nobis haec terrena substantia conferat quod divinum est. Per eundem Dominum.

Third Mass of Christmas

Oblata, Domine, munera, nova Unigeniti tui Nativitate sanctifica: nosque a peccatorum nostrorum maculis emunda. Per eundem Dominum.

St. Stephen

Suscipe, Domine, munera pro tuorum commemoratione Sanctorum: ut, sicut illos passio gloriosos effecit; ita nos devotio reddat innocuos. Per Dominum.

Epiphany

Ecclesiae tuae, quaesumus, Domine, dona propitius intuere: quibus non jam aurum, thus, et myrrha profertur; sed quod eisdem muneribus declaratur, immolatur, et sumitur Jesus Christus Filius tuus Dominus noster. Qui tecum.

Fifth Sunday after Pentecost

Propitiare, Domine, supplicationibus nostris: et has oblationes famulorum famularumque tuarum benignus assume; ut, quod singuli obtulerunt ad honorem nominis tui, cunctis proficiat ad salutem. Per Dominum.

Ninth Sunday after Pentecost

Concede nobis, quaesumus, Domine, haec digne frequentare mysteria: quia, quoties hujus hostiae commemoratio celebratur, opus nostrae redemptionis exercetur. Per Dominum.

St. Paul of the Cross

Coelestem nobis, Domine, praebeant mysteria haec passionis et mortis tuae fervorem: quo sanctus Paulus, ea offerendo, corpus suum hostiam viventem, sanctam, tibique placentem exhibuit: Qui vivis.

St. John the Baptist

Tua, Domine, muneribus altaria cumulamus: illius nativitatem honore debito celebrantes, qui Salvatorem mundi et cecinit adfuturum, et adesse monstravit, Dominum nostrum Jesum Christum Filium tuum: Qui tecum.

Precious Blood

Per haec divina mysteria ad novi quaesumus, testamenti mediatorem Jesum accedamus: et super altaria tua, Domine virtutum, aspersionem sanguinis melius loquentem, quam Abel, innovemus. Per eundem Dominum.

St. Ignatius Loyola

Adsint, Domine Deus, oblationibus nostris sancti Ignatii benigna suffragia: ut sacrosancta mysteria, in quibus omnis sanctitatis fontem constituisti, nos quoque in veritate sanctificent. Per Dominum.

First Sunday after Epiphany

Oblatum tibi, Domine, sacrificium vivificet nos semper, et muniat. Per Dominum.

Second Sunday after Epiphany

Oblata, Domine, munera sanctifica: nosque a peccatorum nostrorum maculis emunda. Per Dominum.

Third Sunday after Epiphany

Haec hostia, Domine, quaesumus, emundet nostra delicta: et ad sacrificium celebrandum, subditorum tibi corpora mentesque sanctificet. Per Dominum.

Fifth Sunday after Epiphany

Hostias tibi, Domine, placationis offerimus: ut et delicta nostra miseratus absolvas, et nutantia corda tu dirigas. Per Dominum.

Second Sunday after Easter

Benedictionem nobis, Domine, conferat salutarem sacra semper oblatio: ut, quod agit mysterio, virtute perficiat. Per Dominum.

Fourth Sunday after Easter

Deus, qui nos per hujus sacrificii veneranda commercia, unius summae divinitatis participes effecisti: praesta, quaesumus: ut, sicut tuam cognoscimus veritatem, sic eam dignis moribus assequamur. Per Dominum.

Ascension

Suscipe, Domine, munera, quae pro Filii tui gloriosa Ascensione deferimus: et concede propitius; ut a praesentibus periculis liberemur, et ad vitam perveniamus aeternam. Per eundem Dominum.

Sunday after Ascension

Sacrificia nos, Domine, immaculata purificent: et mentibus nostris supernae gratiae dent vigorem. Per Dominum.

Pentecost

Munera, quaesumus, Domine, oblata sanctifica: et corda nostra Sancti Spiritus illustratione emunda. Per Dominum . . . in unitate ejusdem.

Pentecost Monday

Propitius, Domine, quaesumus, haec dona sanctifica: et hostiae spiritalis oblatione suscepta, nosmetipsos tibi perfice munus aeternum. Per Dominum.

Corpus Christi

Ecclesiae tuae, quaesumus, Domine, unitatis et pacis propitius dona concede: quae sub oblatis muneribus mystice designantur. Per Dominum.

PREFACES

Nativity

Vere dignum et justum est, aequum et salutare, nos tibi semper et ubique gratias agere: Domine sancte, Pater omnipotens, aeterne Deus: Quia per incarnati Verbi mysterium, nova mentis nostrae oculis lux tuae claritatis infulsit: ut dum visibiliter Deum cognoscimus, per hunc in invisibilium amorem rapiamur. Et ideo cum Angelis et Archangelis, cum Thronis et Dominationibus, cumque omni militia caelestis exercitus, hymnum gloriae tuae canimus, sine fine dicentes:

Epiphany

Vere Dignum et justum est, aequum et salutare, nos tibi semper et ubique gratias agere: Domine sancte, Pater omnipotens, aeterne Deus: Quia, cum Unigenitus tuus in substantia nostrae mortalitatis apparuit, nova nos immortalitatis suae luce reparavit. Et ideo cum Angelis et Archangelis, cum Thronis et Dominationibus, cumque omni militia caelestis exercitus, hymnum gloriae tuae canimus, sine fine dicentes:

Lent

Vere dignum et justum est, aequum et salutare, nos tibi semper et ubique gratias agere: Domine sancte, Pater omnipotens, aeterne Deus: Qui corporali jejunio vitia comprimis, mentem elevas, virtutem largiris, et praemia: per Christum Dominum nostrum. Per quem majestatem tuam laudant Angeli, adorant Dominationes, tremunt Potestates. Caeli caelorumque Virtutes ac beata Seraphim socia exsultatione concelebrant. Cum quibus et nostras voces ut admitti jubeas, deprecamur, supplici confessione dicentes:

Holy Cross

Vere dignum et justum est, aequum et salutare; nos tibi semper et ubique gratias agere: Domine sancte, Pater omnipotens, aeterne Deus: Qui salutem humani generis in ligno Crucis constituisti: ut unde mors oriebatur, inde vita resurgeret: et qui in ligno vincebat, in ligno quoque vinceretur: per Christum Dominum nostrum. Per quem majestatem tuam laudant Angeli, adorant Dominationes, tremunt Potestates. Caeli caelorumque Virtutes ac beata Seraphim socia exsultatione concelebrant. Cum quibus et nostras voces ut admitti jubeas, deprecamur, supplici confessione dicentes:

Easter

Vere dignum et justum est, aequum et salutare: Te quidem, Domine, omni tempore, sed in hac potissimum die (in hoc potissimum) gloriosius praedicare, cum Pascha nostrum immolatus est Christus. Ipse enim verus est Agnus, qui abstulit peccata mundi. Qui mortem nostram moriendo destruxit, et vitam resurgendo reparavit. Et ideo cum Angelis et Archangelis, cum Thronis et Dominationibus, cumque omni militia caelestis exercitus, hymnum gloriae tuae canimus, sine fine dicentes:

Ascension

Vere dignum et justum est, aequum et salutare, nos tibi semper et ubique gratias agere: Domine sancte, Pater omnipotens, aeterne Deus: per Christum Dominum nostrum. Qui post resurrectionem suam omnibus discipulis suis manifestus apparuit, et ipsis cernentibus est elevatus in caelum, ut nos divinitatis suae tribueret esse participes. Et ideo cum Angelis et Archangelis, cum Thronis et Dominationibus, cumque omni militia caelestis exercitus, hymnum gloriae tuae canimus, sine fine dicentes:

Pentecost

Vere dignum et justum est, aequum et salutare, nos tibi semper et ubique gratias agere: Domine sancte Pater, omnipotens aeterne Deus: per Christum Dominum nostrum.
Qui ascendens super omnes caelos, sedensque ad dexteram tuam, promissum Spiritum Sanctum (hodierna die) in filios adoptionis effudit. Quapropter profusis gaudiis, totus in orbe terrarum mundus exsultat. Sed et supernae Virtutes, atque angelicae Potestates, hymnum gloriae tuae concinunt, sine fine dicentes:

Trinity

Vere dignum et justum est, aequum et salutare, nos tibi semper et ubique gratias agere: Domine sancte, Pater omnipotens, aeterne Deus: Qui cum unigenito Filio tuo, et Spiritu Sancto, unus es Deus, unus es Dominus: non in unius singularitate personae, sed in unius Trinitate substantiae. Quod enim de tua gloria, revelante te, credimus, hoc de Filio tuo, hoc de Spiritu Sancto, sine differentia discretionis sentimus. Ut in confessione verae sempiternaeque Deitatis, et in personis proprietas, et in essentia unitas, et in majestate adoretur aequalitas. Quam laudant Angeli atque Archangeli, Cherubim quoque ac Seraphim: qui non cessant clamare quotidie, una voce dicentes:

Blessed Virgin

Vere dignum et justum est, aequum et salutare, nos tibi semper et ubique gratias agere: Domine sancte, Pater omnipotens, aeterne Deus: Et te in . . . beatae Mariae semper Virginis collaudare, benedicere et praedicare. Quae et Unigenitum tuum sancti Spiritus obumbratione concepit: et virginitatis gloria permanente, lumen aeternum mundo effudit, Jesum Christum Dominum nostrum. Per quem majestatem tuam laudant Angeli, adorant Dominationes, tremunt Potestates. Caeli, caelorumque Virtutes ac beata Seraphim, socia exsultatione concelebrant. Cum quibus et nostras voces, ut admitti jubeas, deprecamur, supplici confessione dicentes:

St. Joseph

Vere dignum et justum est, aequum et salutare, nos tibi semper et ubique gratias agere: Domine sancte, Pater omnipotens, aeterne Deus: Et te in Festivitate beati Joseph debitis magnificare praeconiis, benedicere et praedicare. Qui et vir justus, a te Deiparae Virgini Sponsus est datus: et fidelis servus ac prudens, super Familiam tuam est constitutus: ut Unigenitum tuum, Sancti Spiritus obumbratione conceptum, paterna vice custodiret, Jesum Christum Dominum nostrum. Per quem majestatem tuam laudant Angeli, adorant Dominationes, tremunt Potestates. Caeli caelorumque Virtutes ac beata Seraphim socia exsultatione concelebrant. Cum quibus et nostras voces, ut admitti jubeas, deprecamur, supplici confessione dicentes:

Apostles

Vere dignum et justum est, aequum et salutare, te, Domine, suppliciter exorare, ut gregem tuum pastor aeterne non deseras: sed per beatos Apostolos tuos, continua protectione custodias: Ut iisdem rectoribus gubernetur, quos operis tui vicarios eidem contulisti praeesse pastores. Et ideo cum Angelis et Archangelis, cum Thronis et Dominationibus, cumque omni militia caelestis exercitus, hymnum gloriae tuae canimus, sine fine dicentes:

Requiem

Vere dignum et justum est, aequum et salutare, nos tibi semper et ubique gratias agere: Domine sancte, Pater omnipotens, aeterne Deus: per Christum Dominum nostrum. In quo nobis spes beatae resurrectionis effulsit, ut quos contristat certa moriendi conditio, eosdem consoletur futurae immortalitatis promissio. Tuis enim fidelibus, Domine, vita mutatur, non tollitur, et dissoluta terrestris hujus incolatus domo, aeterna in caelis habitatio comparatur. Et ideo cum Angelis et Archangelis, cum Thronis et Dominationibus, cumque omni militia caelestis exercitus, hymnum gloriae tuae canimus, sine fine dicentes:

Sacred Heart

Vere dignum et justum est, aequum et salutare, nos tibi semper et ubique gratias agere: Domine sancte, Pater omnipotens, aeterne Deus; qui Unigenitum tuum in cruce pendentem lancea militis transfigi voluisti, ut apertum Cor, divinae largitatis sacrarium, torrentes nobis funderet miserationis et gratiae, et quod amore nostri flagrare nunquam destitit, piis esset requies et poenitentibus pateret salutis refugium. Et ideo cum Angelis et Archangelis, cum Thronis et Dominationibus, cumque omni militia caelestis exercitus, hymnum gloriae tuae canimus, sine fine dicentes:

Christ the King

Vere dignum et justum est, aequum et salutare, nos tibi semper et ubique gratias agere: Domine sancte, Pater omnipotens, aeterne Deus: Qui unigenitum Filium tuum Dominum nostrum Jesum Christum, Sacerdotem aeternum et universorum Regem, oleo exsultationis unxisti: ut seipsum in ara crucis, hostiam immaculatam et pacificam offerens, redemptionis humanae sacramenta perageret, et suo subjectis imperio omnibus creaturis, aeternum et universale regnum, immensae tuae traderet majestati: regnum veritatis et vitae; regnum sanctitatis et gratiae; regnum justitiae, amoris et pacis. Et ideo cum Angelis et Archangelis, cum Thronis et Dominationibus, cumque omni militia caelestis exercitus, hymnum gloriae tuae canimus, sine fine dicentes:

COMMUNION ANTIPHONS

Second Sunday after Easter

John 10, 14. Ego sum pastor bonus alleluja: et cognosco oves meas, et cognoscunt me meae.

Second Sunday after Epiphany

John 2, 7–11. Dicit Dominus: implete hydrias aqua, et ferte architriclino. Cum gustasset architriclinus aquam vinum factam, dicit sponso: Servasti bonum vinum usque adhuc. Hoc signum fecit Jesus primum coram discipulis suis.

Septuagesima

Ps. 30, 17–18. Illumina faciem tuam super servum tuum, et salvum me fac in tua misericordia: Domine, non confundar, quoniam invocavi te.

Quinquagesima

Ps. 77, 29–30. Manducaverunt, et saturati sunt nimis, et desiderium eorum attulit eis Dominus: non sunt fraudati a desiderio suo.

First Sunday in Lent

Ps. 90, 4–5. Scapulis suis obumbrabit tibi Dominus, et sub pennis ejus sperabis: scuto circumdabit te veritas ejus.

Wednesday, the Fourth Week in Lent

John 9, 11. Lutum fecit ex sputo Dominus, et linivit oculos meos: et abii, et lavi, et vidi, et credidi Deo.

Friday, the Fourth Week in Lent

John 11, 33, 35, 43, 44. Videns Dominus flentes sorores Lazari ad monumentum, lacrimatus est coram Judaeis, et exclamavit: Lazare, veni foras: et prodiit ligatis manibus et pedibus, qui fuerat quatriduanus mortuus.

Passion Sunday

I Cor. 11, 24–25. Hoc corpus, quod pro vobis tradetur: hic calix novi testamenti est in meo sanguine, dicit Dominus: Hoc facite, quotiescunque sumitis, in meam commemorationem.

Easter

I Cor. 5, 7–8. Pascha nostrum immolatus est Christus, alleluia: itaque epulemur in azymis sinceritatis, et veritatis, alleluia, alleluia, alleluia.

St. Thomas the Apostle

John 20, 27. Mitte manum tuam, et cognosce loca clavorum, alleluia: et noli esse incredulus, sed fidelis, alleluia, alleluia.

Pentecost

Acts 2, 2, 4. Factus est repente de caelo sonus, tanquam advenientis spiritus vehementis, ubi erant sedentes, alleluia: et repleti sunt omnes Spiritu Sancto, loquentes magnalia Dei, alleluia, alleluia.

Corpus Christi

I Cor. 11, 26–27. Quotiescunque manducabitis panem hunc, et calicem bibetis, mortem Domini annuntiabitis, donec veniat: itaque quicunque manducaverit panem, vel biberit calicem Domini indigne: reus erit corporis et sanguinis Domini, alleluia.

Holy Mary, on Saturday

Beata viscera Mariae Virginis, quae portaverunt aeterni Patris Filium.

Fourth Sunday in Advent

Isai. 7, 14. Ecce, virgo concipiet, et pariet filium: et vocabitur nomen ejus Emmanuel.

Second Sunday in Advent

Bar. 5, 5; 4, 36. Jerusalem surge, et sta in excelso, et vide jucunditatem, quae veniet tibi a Deo tuo.

Third Sunday in Advent

Isai. 35, 4. Dicite: pusillanimes, confortamini, et nolite timere: ecce Deus noster veniet, et salvabit nos.

Second Mass of Christmas

Zach. 9, 9. Exsulta, filia Sion, lauda, filia Jerusalem: ecce, Rex tuus venit sanctus, et salvator mundi.

Third Mass of Christmas

Ps. 97, 3. Viderunt omnes fines terrae salutare Dei nostri.

Sacred Heart

John 19, 34. Unus militum lancea latus ejus aperuit, et continuo exivit sanguis et aqua.

Eighth Sunday after Pentecost

Ps. 33, 9. Gustate et videte, quoniam suavis est Dominus: beatus vir, qui sperat in eo.

Ninth Sunday after Pentecost

John 6, 57. Qui manducat meam carnem, et bibit meum sanguinem, in me manet, et ego in eo, dicit Dominus.

Twelfth Sunday after Pentecost

Ps. 103, 13–15. De fructu operum tuorum, Domine, satiabitur terra: ut educas panem de terra, et vinum laetificet cor hominis: ut exhilaret faciem in oleo, et panis cor hominis confirmet.

St. John the Baptist

Luke 1, 76. Tu, puer, propheta Altissimi vocaberis: praeibis enim ante faciem Domini parare vias ejus.

Requiem

Lux aeterna luceat eis, Domine: Cum sanctis tuis in aeternum: quia pius es. Requiem aeternam dona eis, Domine: et lux perpetua luceat eis: Cum Sanctis tuis in aeternum: quia pius es.

St. Stephen

Acts 7, 56–60. Video caelos apertos, et Jesum stantem a dextris virtutis Dei: Domine Jesu, accipe spiritum meum, et ne statuas illis hoc peccatum.

POSTCOMMUNIONS

Ember Saturday in September

Perficiant in nobis, Domine, quaesumus, tua sacramenta quod continent: ut, quae nunc specie gerimus, rerum veritate capiamus. Per Dominum.

Eighteenth Sunday after Pentecost

Gratias tibi referimus, Domine, sacro munere vegetati: tuam misericordiam deprecantes; ut dignos nos ejus participatione perficias. Per Dominum.

Nineteenth Sunday after Pentecost

Tua nos, Domine, medicinalis operatio, et a nostris perversitatibus clementer expediat, et tuis semper faciat inhaerere mandatis. Per Dominum.

St. Paul of the Cross

Sumpsimus, Domine, divinum sacramentum immensae caritatis tuae memoriale perpetuum: tribue, quaesumus; ut, sancti Pauli meritis et imitatione, aquam de fontibus tuis hauriamus in vitam aeternam salientem, et tuam sacratissimam passionem cordibus nostris impressam moribus et vita teneamus: Qui vivis.

St. Catherine of Siena

Aeternitatem nobis, Domine, conferat, qua pasti sumus, mensa caelestis: quae beatae Catharinae Virginis vitam etiam aluit temporalem. Per Dominum.

Precious Blood

Ad sacram, Domine, mensam admissi, hausimus aquas in gaudio de fontibus Salvatoris: sanguis ejus fiat nobis, quaesumus, fons aquae in vitam aeternam salientis: Qui tecum.

St. Ignatius Loyola

Laudis hostia, Domine, quam pro sancto Ignatio gratias agentes obtulimus: ad perpetuam nos majestatis tuae laudationem, ejus intercessione, perducat. Per Dominum.

Dedication of Churches

Deus, qui de vivis et electis lapidibus aeternum majestati tuae praeparas habitaculum: auxiliare populo tuo supplicanti; ut, quod Ecclesiae tuae corporalibus proficit spatiis, spiritualibus amplificetur augmentis. Per Dominum.

Second Sunday of Advent

Repleti cibo spiritualis alimoniae, supplices te, Domine, deprecamur: ut hujus participatione mysterii, doceas nos terrena despicere et amare caelestia. Per Dominum.

Ember Wednesday in Advent

Salutaris tui, Domine, munere satiati, supplices deprecamur: ut, cujus laetamur gustu, renovemur effectu. Per Dominum.

Fourth Sunday of Advent

Sumptis muneribus, quaesumus, Domine: ut cum frequentatione mysterii, crescat nostrae salutis effectus. Per Dominum.

First Mass of Christmas

Da nobis, quaesumus, Domine Deus noster: ut, qui Nativitatem Domini nostri Jesu Christi mysteriis nos frequentare gaudemus; dignis conversationibus ad ejus mereamur pervenire consortium. Qui tecum.

Second Mass of Christmas

Hujus nos, Domine, sacramenti semper novitas natalis instauret: cujus nativitas singularis humanam repulit vetustatem. Per eundem Dominum.

Third Mass of Christmas

Praesta, quaesumus, omnipotens Deus: ut natus hodie Salvator mundi, sicut divinae nobis generationis est auctor: ita et immortalitatis sit ipse largitor. Qui tecum.

Sixth Sunday after Epiphany

Caelestibus, Domine, pasti deliciis: quaesumus: ut semper eadem, per quae veraciter vivimus, appetamus. Per Dominum.

Septuagesima Sunday

Fideles tui, Deus, per tua dona firmentur: ut eadem et percipiendo requirant, et quaerendo sine fine percipiant. Per Dominum.

Easter Vigil

Spiritum nobis, Domine, tuae caritatis infunde: ut, quos sacramentis Paschalibus satiasti, tua facias pietate concordes. Per Dominum . . . in unitate ejusdem.

Ascension

Praesta nobis, quaesumus, omnipotens et misericors Deus: ut, quae visibilibus mysteriis sumenda percepimus, invisibili consequamur effectu. Per Dominum.

Pentecost

Sancti Spiritus, Domine, corda nostra mundet infusio: et sui roris intima aspersione foecundet. Per Dominum . . . in unitate ejusdem.

Corpus Christi

Fac nos, quaesumus, Domine, divinitatis tuae sempiterna fruitione repleri: quam pretiosi Corporis et Sanguinis tui temporalis perceptio praefigurat: Qui vivis.

Seventh Sunday after Pentecost

Tua nos, Domine, medicinalis operatio, et a nostris perversitatibus clementer expediat et ad ea quae sunt recta, perducat. Per Dominum.

Eighth Sunday after Pentecost

Sit nobis, Domine, reparatio mentis et corporis caeleste mysterium: ut, cujus exsequimur cultum, sentiamus effectum. Per Dominum.

Ninth Sunday after Pentecost

Tui nobis, quaesumus, Domine, communio sacramenti, et purificationem conferat, et tribuat unitatem. Per Dominum.

Twelfth Sunday after Pentecost

Vivificet nos, quaesumus, Domine, hujus participatio sancta mysterii: et pariter nobis expiationem tribuat, et munimen. Per Dominum.

ANTIPHONS

After Compline—Advent to Candlemas

Alma Redemptoris Mater,
quae pervia caeli
Porta manes, et stella maris,
succurre cadenti,
Surgere qui curat, populo:
tu quae genuisti,
Natura mirante,
tuum sanctum Genitorem,
Virgo prius ac posterius,
Gabrielis ab ore
Sumens illud Ave,
peccatorum miserere.

Monday at Matins, First Nocturn

Dominus de caelo prospexit super filios hominum.

Qui operatur justitiam, requiescet in monte sancto tuo, Domine.

Monday at Matins, Second Nocturn

Diligam te, Domine, virtus mea.

Monday at Matins, Third Nocturn

Exaudiat te Dominus in die tribulationis.

Domine, in virtute tua laetabitur rex.

Monday, at Lauds I

Jubilate Deo in voce exsultationis.

Intende voci orationis meae, Rex meus et Deus meus.

Laudate Dominum, omnes gentes.

Monday, at Prime

Innocens manibus et mundo corde ascendet in montem Domini.

Second Sunday of Advent, at Vespers

At Magnif. Tu es qui venturus es, an alium exspectamus:

Dicite Joanni quae vidistis: Ad lumen redeunt caeci, mortui resurgunt, pauperes evangelizantur, alleluja.

Christmas, at First Vespers

1 Rex pacificus magnificatus est, cujus vultum desiderat universa terra.

5 Levate capita vestra: ecce appropinquat redemptio vestra.

Christmas, at Second Vespers

1 Tecum principium in die virtutis tuae; in splendoribus

sanctorum, ex utero ante luciferum genui te.

2 Redemptionem misit Dominus populo suo: mandavit in aeternum testamentum suum.

3 Exortum est in tenebris lumen rectis corde: misericors, et miserator, et justus Dominus.

4 Apud Dominum misericordia, et copiosa apud eum redemptio.

At Magnif. Hodie Christus natus est: hodie Salvator apparuit: hodie in terra canunt Angeli, laetantur Archangeli: hodie exsultant justi, dicentes: Gloria in excelsis Deo, alleluja.

First Sunday of Advent, at Lauds

1 In illa die stillabunt montes dulcedinem, et colles fluent lac et mel, alleluja.

2 Jucundare, filia Sion, et exsulta satis, filia Jerusalem, alleluja.

3 Ecce Dominus veniet, et omnes Sancti ejus cum eo: et erit in die illa lux magna, alleluja.

4 Omnes sitientes, venite ad aquas: quaerite Dominum, dum inveniri potest, alleluja.

5 Ecce veniet propheta magnus, et ipse renovabit Jerusalem, alleluja.

Feast of the Circumcision, at Vespers

1 O admirabile commercium: Creator generis humani, animatum corpus sumens, de Virgine nasci dignatus est: et procedens homo sine semine, largitus est nobis suam Deitatem.

2 Quando natus es ineffabiliter ex Virgine, tunc impletae sunt Scripturae: sicut pluvia in vellus descendisti, ut salvum faceres genus humanum: te laudamus, Deus noster.

3 Rubum quem viderat Moyses incombustum, conservatam agnovimus tuam laudabilem virginitatem: Dei Genitrix, intercede pro nobis.

4 Germinavit radix Jesse, orta est stella ex Jacob: Virgo peperit Salvatorem: te laudamus, Deus noster.

5 Ecce Maria genuit nobis Salvatorem, quem Joannes videns exclamavit, dicens: Ecce Agnus Dei, ecce qui tollit peccata mundi, alleluja.

Feast of the Circumcision, at Second Vespers

At Magnif. Magnum hereditatis mysterium: templum Dei factus est uterus nescientis virum: non est pollutus es ea carnem assumens: omnes gentes venient, dicentes: Gloria tibi, Domine.

Feast of the Epiphany, at Lauds

At Bened. Hodie caelesti Sponso juncta est Ecclesia, quoniam in Jordane lavit Christus ejus crimina: currunt cum muneribus Magi ad regales nuptias, et ex aqua facto vino laetantur convivae, alleluja.

Feast of the Epiphany, at Second Vespers

At Magnif. Tribus miraculis ornatum diem sanctum colimus: hodie stella Magos duxit ad praesepium: hodie vinum ex aqua factum est ad nuptias: hodie in Jordane a Joanne Christus baptizari voluit, ut salvaret nos, alleluja.

Feast of St. Lucy, at First Verspers

1 Orante sancta Lucia, apparuit ei beata Agatha, et consolabatur ancillam Christi.
2 Lucia virgo, quid a me petis quod ipsa poteris praestare continuo matri tuae?
3 Per te, Lucia virgo, civitas Syracusana decorabitur a Domino Jesu Christo.

Feast of St. Agnes, Second Nocturn

Mel et lac ex ejus ore suscepi, et sanguis ejus ornavit genas meas.

Feast of St. Agnes, at Lauds

3 Anulo suo subarrhavit me Dominus meus Jesus Christus, et tamquam sponsam decoravit me corona.

Feast of St. Agatha, at First Vespers

At Magnif. Stans beata Agatha in medio carceris, expansis manibus orabat ad Dominum: Domine Jesu Christe, magister bone, gratias tibi ago, qui me fecisti vincere tormenta carnificum; jube me, Domine, ad tuam immarcescibilem gloriam feliciter pervenire.

Common of Several Martyrs, First Nocturn

Tamquam aurum in fornace probavit electos Dominus: et quasi holocausta accepit eos in aeternum.

Common of Several Martyrs, Second Nocturn

Sancti, qui sperant in Domino, habebunt fortitudinem, assument pennas ut aquilae, volabunt, et non deficient.

Common of Several Martyrs, at Second Vespers

1 Isti sunt Sancti, qui pro testamento Dei sua corpora tradiderunt, et in sanguine Agni laverunt stolas suas.
2 Sancti per fidem vicerunt regna, operati sunt justitiam, adepti sunt repromissiones.
3 Sanctorum velut aquilae juventus renovabitur: florebunt sicut lilium in civitate Domini.
4 Absterget Deus omnem lacrimam ab oculis Sanctorum: et jam non erit amplius neque luctus, neque clamor, sed nec ullus dolor: quoniam priora transierunt.
5 In caelestibus regnis Sanctorum habitatio est, et in aeternum requies eorum.

Common of Confessor not a Pontiff, at First Vespers

At Magnif. Similabo eum viro sapienti, qui aedificavit domum suam supra petram.

HYMNS

Ambrosian Hymn, Ordinary at Matins

Te Deum laudamus: te Dominum confitemur.
Te aeternum Patrem omnis terra veneratur.
Tibi omnes Angeli, tibi Caeli, et universae Potestates:
Tibi Cherubim et Seraphim incessabili voce proclamant:
Sanctus, Sanctus, Sanctus Dominus, Deus Sabaoth.
Pleni sunt caeli et terra majestatis gloriae tuae.
Te gloriosus Apostolorum chorus,
Te Prophetarum laudabilis numerus,
Te Martyrum candidatus laudat exercitus.
Te per orbem terrarum sancta confitetur Ecclesia,
Patrem immensae majestatis;
Venerandum tuum verum et unicum Filium;
Sanctum quoque Paraclitum Spiritum.
Tu Rex gloriae, Christe.
Tu Patris sempiternus es Filius.
Tu, ad liberandum suscepturus hominem, non horruisti Virginis uterum.
Tu, devicto mortis aculeo, aperuisti credentibus regna caelorum.
Tu ad dexteram Dei sedes, in gloria Patris.
Judex crederis esse venturus.
Te ergo quaesumus, tuis famulis subveni, quos pretioso sanguine redemisti.
Aeterna fac cum Sanctis tuis in gloria numerari.
Salvum fac populum tuum, Domine, et benedic hereditati tuae.
Et rege eos, et extolle illos usque in aeternum.
Per singulos dies benedicimus te;
Et laudamus nomen tuum in saeculum, et in saeculum saeculi.
Dignare, Domine, die isto sine peccato nos custodire.
Miserere nostri, Domine, miserere nostri.
Fiat misericordia tua, Domine, super nos, quemadmodum speravimus in te.
In te, Domine, speravi: non confundar in aeternum.

Sunday at Matins

Primo die, quo Trinitas

Beata mundum condidit,
Vel quo resurgens Conditor
Nos, morte victa, liberat:

Pulsis procul torporibus,
Surgamus omnes ocius,
Et nocte quaeramus Deum,
Propheta sicut praecipit:

Nostras preces ut audiat,
Suamque dextram porrigat,
Et expiatos sordibus
Reddat polorum sedibus:

Ut, quique sacratissimo
Hujus diei tempore
Horis quietis psallimus,
Donis beatis muneret.

Jam nunc, Paterna claritas,
Te postulamus affatim:
Absint faces libidinis,
Et omnis actus noxius.

Ne foeda sit, vel lubrica
Compago nostri corporis,
Ob cujus ignes ignibus
Avernus urat acrius.

Mundi Redemptor, quaesumus,
Tu probra nostra diluas;
Nobisque largus commoda
Vitae perennis conferas.

Praesta, Pater piissime,
Patrique compar Unice,
Cum Spiritu Paraclito
Regnans per omne saeculum.
Amen.

Sunday, at Lauds I

Aeterne rerum Conditor,
Noctem diemque qui regis,
Et temporum das tempora,
Ut alleves fastidium.

Nocturna lux viantibus
A nocte noctem segregans,
Praeco diei jam sonat,
Jubarque solis evocat.

Hoc excitatus Lucifer
Solvit polum caligine:
Hoc omnis erronum cohors
Viam nocendi deserit.

Hoc nauta vires colligit,
Pontique mitescunt freta:
Hoc, ipsa petra Ecclesia,
Canente, culpam diluit.

Surgamus ergo strenue:
Gallus jacentes excitat,
Et somnolentos increpat,
Gallus negantes arguit.

Gallo canente, spes redit,
Aegris salus refunditur,
Mucro latronis conditur,
Lapsis fides revertitur.

Jesu, labantes respice,
Et nos videndo corrige:
Si respicis, labes cadunt,
Fletuque culpa solvitur.

Tu, lux, refulge sensibus,
Mentisque somnum discute:
Te nostra vox primum sonet,
Et vota solvamus tibi.

Deo Patri sit gloria,
Ejusque soli Filio,
Cum Spiritu Paraclito,
Nunc et per omne saeculum.
Amen.

Monday, at Lauds I

Splendor Paternae gloriae,
De luce lucem proferens,
Lux lucis, et fons luminis,
Diem dies illuminans:

Verusque sol illabere,
Micans nitore perpeti:
Jubarque Sancti Spiritus
Infunde nostris sensibus.

Votis vocemus et Patrem,
Patrem potentis gratiae,
Patrem perennis gloriae:
Culpam releget lubricam.

Confirmet actus strenuos:
Dentes retundat invidi:
Casus secundet asperos:
Agenda recte dirigat.

Mentem gubernet et regat:
Sit pura nobis castitas:
Fides calore ferveat,
Fraudis venena nesciat.

Christusque nobis sit cibus,
Potusque noster sit fides:
Laeti bibamus sobriam
Profusionem Spiritus.

Laetus dies hic transeat:
Pudor sit ut diluculum:
Fides velut meridies:
Crepusculum mens nesciat.

Aurora lucem provehit,
Cum luce nobis prodeat
In Patre totus Filius,
Et totus in Verbo Pater.

Deo Patri sit gloria,
Ejusque soli Filio,
Cum Spiritu Paraclito,
Nunc et per omne saeculum.
Amen.

Advent, at Vespers

Creator alme siderum,
Aeterna lux credentium,
Jesu, Redemptor omnium,
Intende votis supplicum.

Qui daemonis ne fraudibus
Periret orbis, impetu
Amoris actus, languidi
Mundi medela factus es.

Commune qui mundi nefas
Ut expiares, ad Crucem
E Virginis sacrario
Intacta prodis victima.

Cujus potestas gloriae,
Nomenque cum primum sonat,
Et caelites et inferi
Tremente curvantur genu.

Te deprecamur ultimae
Magnum diei Judicem,
Armis supernae gratiae
Defende nos ab hostibus.

Virtus, honor, laus, gloria
Deo Patri cum Filio,
Sancto simul Paraclito,
In saeculorum saecula.
Amen.

Christmas, at Vespers

Jesu, Redemptor omnium,
Quem lucis ante originem
Patrem Paternae gloriae
Pater supremus edidit.

Tu lumen, et splendor Patris,
Tu spes perennis omnium,
Intende quas fundunt preces
Tui per orbem servuli.

Memento, rerum Conditor,
Nostri quod olim corporis,
Sacrata ab alvo Virginis
Nascendo, formam sumpseris.

Testator hoc praesens dies,
Currens per anni circulum,
Quod solus e sinu Patris
Mundi salus adveneris.

Hunc astra, tellus, aequora,
Hunc omne, quod caelo subest,
Salutis auctorem novae
Novo salutat cantico.

Et nos, beata quos sacri
Rigavit unda sanguinis,
Natalis ob diem tui
Hymni tributum solvimus.

Jesu, tibi sit gloria,
Qui natus es de Virgine,
Cum Patre, et almo Spiritu,
In sempiterna saecula.
Amen.

Feast of Holy Innocents, at Vespers

Salvete, flores Martyrum,
Quos lucis ipso in limine
Christi insecutor sustulit,
Ceu turbo nascentes rosas.

Vos prima Christi victima,
Grex immolatorum tener,
Aram sub ipsam simplices
Palma et coronis luditis.

Jesu, tibi sit gloria,
Qui natus es de Virgine,
Cum Patre, et almo Spiritu,
In sempiterna saecula.
Amen.

Christmas, at Lauds

A solis ortus cardine
Ad usque terrae limitem,
Christum canamus Principem,
Natum Maria Virgine.

Beatus auctor saeculi
Servile corpus induit:
Ut carne carnem liberans,
Ne perderet quos condidit.

Castae Parentis viscera
Caelestis intrat gratia:
Venter Puellae bajulat
Secreta, quae non noverat.

Domus pudici pectoris
Templum repente fit Dei:
Intacta nesciens virum,
Concepit alvo Filium.

Enititur puerpera,
Quem Gabriel praedixerat,
Quem ventre Matris gestiens,
Baptista clausum senserat.

Foeno jacere pertulit:
Praesepe non abhorruit:
Et lacte modico pastus est,
Per quem nec ales esurit.

Gaudet chorus caelestium,
Et Angeli canunt Deo;
Palamque fit pastoribus
Pastor, Creator omnium.

Jesu, tibi sit gloria,
Qui natus es de Virgine,
Cum Patre, et almo Spiritu,
In sempiterna saecula.
Amen.

Feast of Holy Name, at Vespers

Jesu, dulcis memoria,
Dans vera cordis gaudia:
Sed super mel et omnia,
Ejus dulcis praesentia.

Nil canitur suavius,
Nil auditur jucundius,
Nil cogitatur dulcius,
Quam Jesus Dei Filius.

Jesu, spes poenitentibus,
Quam pius es petentibus!
Quam bonus te quaerentibus!
Sed quid invenientibus?

Nec lingua valet dicere,
Nec littera exprimere:
Expertus potest credere,
Quid sit Jesum diligere.

Sis, Jesu, nostrum gaudium,
Qui es futurus praemium:
Sit nostra in te gloria,
Per cuncta semper saecula.
Amen.

Feast of the Epiphany, at Vespers

Crudelis Herodes Deum
Regem venire quid times?
Non eripit mortalia,
Qui regna dat caelestia.

Ibant Magi, quam viderant,
Stellam sequentes praeviam:
Lumen requirunt lumine:
Deum fatentur munere.

Lavacra puri gurgitis
Caelestis Agnus attigit:
Peccata, quae non detulit,
Nos abluendo sustulit.

Novum genus potentiae:
Aquae rubescunt hydriae,
Vinumque jussa fundere,
Mutavit unda originem.

Jesu, tibi sit gloria,
Qui apparuisti gentibus,
Cum Patre, et almo Spiritu,
In sempiterna saecula.
Amen.

RESPONSORIES

First Sunday of Advent, First Nocturn

R. Aspiciens a longe, ecce video Dei potentiam venientem, et nebulam totam terram tegentem. Ite obviam ei, et dicite: Nuntia nobis, si tu es ipse, Qui regnaturus es in populo Israel. V. Quique terrigenae, et filii hominum, simul in unum dives et pauper. Ite obviam ei, et dicite. V. Qui regis Israel, intende, qui deducis velut ovem Joseph. Nuntia nobis, si tu es ipse. V. Tollite portas, principes, vestras, et elevamini, portae aeternales, et introibit Rex gloriae. Qui regnaturus es in populo Israel. V. Gloria Patri, et Filio, et Spiritui Sancto. R. Aspiciens a longe, *usque ad* V. Quique terrigenae.

First Sunday of Advent, First Nocturn

R. Aspiciebam in visu noctis, et ecce in nubibus caeli Filius hominis veniebat: et datum est ei regnum, et honor: Et omnis populus, tribus, et linguae servient ei. V. Potestas ejus, potestas aeterna, quae non auferetur: et regnum ejus, quod non corrumpetur. —Et.

First Sunday of Advent, Second Nocturn

R. Salvatorem exspectamus Dominum Jesum Christum, Qui reformabit corpus humilitatis nostrae configuratum corpori claritatis suae. V. Sobrie, et juste, et pie vivamus in hoc saeculo, exspectantes beatam spem, et adventum gloriae magni Dei. —Qui.

First Sunday of Advent, Second Nocturn

R. Obsecro, Domine, mitte quem missurus es: vide afflictionem populi tui: Sicut locutus es, veni, Et libera nos. V. Qui regis Israel, intende, qui deducis velut ovem Joseph, qui sedes super Cherubim. —Sicut. Gloria Patri. Et.

First Sunday of Advent, Third Nocturn:

R. Ecce virgo concipiet, et pariet filium, dicit Dominus: Et vocabitur nomen ejus Admirabilis, Deus, Fortis. V. Super solium David, et super regnum ejus sedebit in aeternum. —Et.

First Sunday of Advent, Third Nocturn

R. Ecce dies veniunt, dicit Dominus, et suscitabo David germen justum: et regnabit rex, et sapiens erit, et faciet judicium et justitiam in terra: Et hoc est nomen quod vocabunt eum: Dominus justus noster. V. In diebus illis salvabitur Juda, et Israel habitabit confidenter. —Et hoc. Gloria. Dominus.

First Nocturn of Christmas

R. Hodie nobis caelorum Rex de Virgine nasci dignatus est, ut hominem perditum ad caelestia regna revocaret: Gaudet exercitus Angelorum: quia salue aeterna humano generi apparuit. V. Gloria in excelsis Deo, et in terra pax hominibus bonae voluntatis. —Gaudet. Gloria Patri.

Feast of St. John, Apostle and Evangelist, Second Nocturn

R. Qui vicerit, faciam illum columnam in templo meo, dicit Dominus: Et scribam super eum nomen meum, et nomen civitatis novae Jerusalem. V. Vincenti dabo edere de ligno vitae, quod est in paradiso Dei mei. —Et.

Feast of St. John, Apostle and Evangelist, Third Nocturn

R. Iste est Joannes, qui supra pectus Domini in coena recubuit: Beatus Apostolus, cui revelata sunt secreta caelestia. V. Fluenta Evangelii de ipso sacro Dominici pectoris fonte potavit. —Beatus. Gloria Patri. Beatus.

Feast of the Holy Innocents, Third Nocturn

R. Vidi sub altare Dei animas interfectorum propter verbum Dei quod habebant, et clara voce dicebant: Vindica, Domine, sanguinem Sanctorum tuorum, qui effusus est. V. Sub throno Dei omnes Sancti clamant. —Vindica.

Septuagesima Sunday, First Nocturn

R. In principio creavit Deus caelum et terram, et fecit in ea hominem, ad imaginem et similitudinem suam. V. Formavit igitur Deus hominem de limo terrae, et inspiravit in faciem ejus spiraculum vitae. —Ad imaginem.

R. In principio creavit Deus caelum et terram, et Spiritus Dei ferebatur super aquas: Et vidit Deus cuncta quae fecerat, et erant valde vona. V. Igitur perfecti sunt caeli et terra, et omnes ornatus eorum. —Et.

R. Formavit Dominus hominem de limo terrae, Et inspiravit in faciem ejus spiraculum vitae, et factus est homo in animam viventem. V. In principio fecit Deus caelum et terram, et plasmavit in ea hominem. —Et. Gloria Patri. Et.

Septuagesima Sunday, Third Nocturn

R. Ecce Adam quasi unus ex nobis factus est, sciens bonum et malum; Videte, ne forte sumat de ligno vitae, et vivat in aeternum. V. Fecit quoque Dominus Deus Adae tunicam pelliceam, et induit eum, et dixit. —Videte.

Monday in Week of Septuagesima at Nocturn

R. Dum deambularet Dominus in paradiso ad auram post meridiem, clamavit, et dixit: Adam, ubi es? Audivi, Domine, vocem tuam, Et abscondi me. V. Vocem tuam audivi in paradiso, et timui, eo quod nudus essem. —Et.

Feast of St. Agnes, First Nocturn

R. Dexteram meam et collum meum cinxit lapidibus pretiosis, tradidit auribus meis inaestimabiles margaritas, Et circumdedit me vernantibus atque coruscantibus gemmis. V. Posuit signum in faciem meam, ut nullum praeter eum amatorem admittam. —Et.

Feast of St. Agnes, First Nocturn

R. Amo Christum, in cujus thalamum introibo, cujus mater virgo est, cujus Pater feminam nescit, cujus mihi organa modulatis vocibus cantant: Quem cum amavero, casta sum; cum tetigero, munda sum; cum accepero, virgo sum. V. Anulo fidei suae subarrhavit me, et immensis monilibus ornavit me. —Quem. Gloria Patri. Quem.

Feast of St. Agnes, Second Nocturn

R. Induit me Dominus vestimento salutis, et indumento laetitiae circumdedit me: Et tamquam sponsam decoravit me corona. V. Tradidit auribus meis inaestimabiles margaritas, circumdedit me vernantibus atque coruscantibus gemmis. —Et.

Feast of St. Agnes, Third Nocturn

R. Ipsi sum desponsata, cui Angeli serviunt, cujus pulchritudinem sol et luna mirantur: Ipsi soli servo fidem, ipsi me tota devotione committo. V. Dexteram meam et collum meum cinxit lapidibus pretiosis, tradidit auribus meis inaestimabiles margaritas. —Ipsi soli.

R. Omnipotens, adorande, colende, tremende, benedico te, Quia per Filium tuum unigenitum evasi minas hominum impiorum, et spurcitias diaboli impolluto calle transivi. V. Te confiteor labiis, te corde, te totis visceribus concupisco. —Quia. Gloria Patri. Quia.

Common of Apostles, Second Nocturn

R. Vidi conjunctos viros, habentes splendidas vestes, et Angelus Domini locutus est ad me, dicens: Isti sunt viri sancti facti amici Dei. V. Vidi Angelum Dei fortem, volantem per medium caelum, voce magna clamantem et dicentem. —Isti.

Common of Apostles, Second Nocturn

R. Isti sunt triumphatores et amici Dei, qui contemnentes jussa principum, meruerunt praemia aeterna: Modo coronantur, et accipiunt palmam. V. Isti sunt, qui venerunt ex magna tribulatione, et laverunt stolas suas in sanguine Agni. —Modo. Gloria Patri. Modo.

Common of One Martyr, First Nocturn

R. Justus germinabit sicut lilium: Et florebit in aeternum ante Dominum. V. Plantatus in domo Domini, in atriis domus Dei nostri. —Et.

Common of One Martyr, Third Nocturn

R. Corona aurea super capur ejus, Expressa signo sanctitatis, gloria honoris, et opus fortitudinis. V. Quoniam praevenisti eum in benedictionibus dulcedinis, posuisti in capite ejus coronam de lapide pretioso. —Expressa.

Common of several Martyrs, First Nocturn

R. Absterget Deus omnem lacrimam ab oculis Sanctorum: et jam non erit amplius neque luctus, neque clamor, sed nec ullus dolor: Quoniam priora transierunt. V. Non esurient, neque sitient amplius, neque cadet super illos sol, neque ullus aestus. —Quoniam priora.

R. Viri sancti gloriosum sanguinem funderunt pro Domino, amaverunt Christum in vita sua, imitati sunt eum in morte sua: Et ideo coronas triumphales meruerunt. V. Unus spiritus, et una fides erat in eis. —Et.

Common of Several Martyrs, Second Nocturn

R. Sancti tui, Domine, mirabile consecuti sunt iter, servientes praeceptis tuis, ut invenirentur illaesi in aquis validis: Terra apparuit arida, et in Mari Rubro via sine impedimento. V. Quoniam percussit petram, et fluxerunt aquae, et torrentes inundaverunt. —Terra apparuit.

Common of Several Martyrs, Second Nocturn

R. Tamquam aurum in fornace probavit electos Dominus, et quasi holocausti hostiam accepit illos; et in tempore erit respectus illorum: Quoniam donum et pax est electis Dei. V. Qui confidunt in illum, intelligent veritatem: et fideles in dilectione acquiescent illi. —Quoniam. Gloria Patri. Quoniam.

Common of Confessor Pontiff, Third Nocturn

R. Sint lumbi vestri praecincti, et lucernae ardentes in manibus vestris: Et vos similes hominibus exspectantibus dominum suum, quando revertatur a nuptiis. V. Vigilate ergo, quia nescitis qua hora Dominus vester venturus sit. —Et. Gloria Patri. Et.

Common of Virgins, Third Nocturn

R. Haec est virgo sapiens, quam Dominus vigilantem invenit, quae acceptis lampadibus sumpsit secum oleum: Et veniente Domino, introivit cum eo ad nuptias. V. Media nocte clamor factus est: Ecce sponsus venit, exite obviam ei. —Et.

R. Media nocte clamor factus est: Ecce sponsus venit, exite obviam ei. V. Prudentes virgines, aptate vestras lampades.—Ecce. Gloria Patri. Ecce.

APPENDIX B.

The following points, omitted in the text, should be made about the season of Passiontide and the pre-Lenten period:

The pre-Lenten Period

Since the sixth century a pre-Lenten time of three weeks beginning with Septuagesima Sunday has been observed at Rome, and under Roman influence the practice spread through the West in succeeding centuries. It is not certain that the Roman practice was borrowed from the Eastern Church; its gradual development seems to argue against this. Quinquagesima was the oldest and Septuagesima the last to be added.

This three-week period is in reality an anticipation of Lent itself and has a strong penitential flavor expressed in the purple vestments and the absence of the *Alleluia*. The texts of the first two Sundays are rather sombre and of almost unrelieved seriousness; while those of the third Sunday, though brightened by the allusion to the Resurrection and the healing of the blind man (a figure of Baptism), announce nevertheless the coming Passion of the Son of God. It is thought that the pressure of the Lombard invasions of the sixth century is reflected in the chants of these Masses and in the prayers, but the stational church and the proximity of Lent undoubtedly have affected the lessons of these days. The Book of Genesis is read at Matins during these three weeks and this circumstance has led some to advance the theory that the pre-Lenten period was originally the beginning of the liturgical year; but it seems rather that Genesis was originally read in Lent as part of the instruction of the catechumens and then later on anticipated here.

Passiontide

The veiling of the crucifix and other sacred images in Passiontide has been explained in various ways, but the most satisfactory seems to be that it is a survival of the custom of drawing a curtain across the sanctuary all during Lent. This in turn was inspired by the custom of excluding the penitents from the Church itself until Holy Thursday. Today, of course, the practice is a sign of mourning appropriate to this particular season.

GENERAL BIBLIOGRAPHY

Aigrain, R., *Liturgia: Encyclopédie populaire des connaissances liturgiques*, Paris, 1930.

Ancient Christian Writers, ed. by J. Quasten and J. C. Plumpe, Westminster (Md.), in progress since 1946.

Baumstark, A., *Liturgie comparée*, Paris, 1953.

Baur, B., *The Light of the World*, St. Louis, 1952.

Beauduin, L., *Liturgy, the Life of the Church*, Collegeville (Minn.), 1926.

Bishop, E., *Liturgica Historica: Papers on the Liturgy and Religious Life of the Western Church*, Oxford, 1918.

Bona, G., *Rerum liturgicarum libri II*, Paris, 1676.

Bopp, L., *Liturgical Education*, Milwaukee, 1937.

Bouyer, L., *Liturgical Piety*, Notre Dame (Ind.), 1955.

Braun, J., *Liturgisches Handlexikon*, Regensburg, 1924.

Cabrol, F., *Liturgical Prayer: Its History and Spirit*, Westminster (Md.), 1950.

———, *The Prayer of the Early Christians*, New York, 1930.

Callewaert, C., *Caeremoniale in missa privata et solemni aliisque frequentioribus functionibus liturgicis servandum*, Bruges, 1934.

———, *Liturgicae institutiones, Tract I*, Bruges, 1933; *Tract II*, Bruges, 1931.

Catholic Dictionary, ed. by Donald Attwater, New York, 1949.

Clarke, W. K. L., *Liturgy and Worship*, London, 1932.

Dictionary of Christian Antiquities, London, 1908.

Dictionnaire d'archéologie chrétienne et de liturgie, ed. by F. Cabrol and H. Leclercq, Paris, 1903.

Dix, G., *The Shape of the Liturgy*, London, 1945.

Duchesne, L., *Christian Worship, Its Origin and Evolution*, New York, 1903.

Eisenhofer, L., *Grundriss der katholischen Liturgik*, Freiburg, 1926.

———, *Handbuch der katholischen Liturgik*, Freiburg, 1932.

Eisenhofer, L., and J. Lechner, *Grundriss der liturgik des Römischen Ritus*, Freiburg, 1950.
Ellard, G., *Christian Life and Worship*, Milwaukee, 1933.
Fortescue, A., *The Ceremonies of the Roman Rite Described*, Westminster (Md.), 1949.
Guardini, R., *The Church and the Catholic*, New York, 1935.
———, *Sacred Signs*, New York, 1931.
———, *The Spirit of the Liturgy*, New York, 1935.
Guéranger, P., *The Liturgical Year*, Westminster (Md.), 1950.
Hebert, A., *Liturgy and Society*, London, 1935.
Howell, C., *Of Sacraments and Sacrifice*, Collegeville (Minn.), 1954.
Introduction to Theology, ed. by A. M. Henry, Chicago, in progress since 1955.
Jungmann, J., *Der Gottesdienst der Kirche*, Innsbruck, 1956.
———, *Die Stellung Christi im Liturgischen Gebet*, Muenster, 1925.
———, *Liturgical Worship*, New York, 1941.
Klauser, T., *The Western Liturgy and Its History*, Chicago, 1952.
Koenker, E., *The Liturgical Renaissance in the Roman Catholic Church*, Chicago, 1954.
Lefebvre, G., *Catholic Liturgy: Its Fundamental Principles*, St. Louis, 1937.
Lives of the Saints, ed. by H. Thurston and D. Attwater, New York, 1956.
Michel, V., *The Liturgy of the Church*, New York, 1937.
Molien, L., *La prière de l'église*, Paris, 1924.
Mueller, T., *Family Life in Christ*, Collegeville (Minn.), 1941.
Oppenheim, P., *Notiones liturgiae fundamentalis*, Turin, 1941.
———, *Principes Theologiae liturgicae*, Turin, 1946.
Paquier, R., *Traite de liturgique*, Paris, 1954.
Parsch, P., *Le petit guide dans l'année liturgique*, Mulhouse, 1955.
———, *The Church's Year of Grace*, Collegeville (Minn.), 1953.
Righietti, M., *Manuale di storia liturgica* (4 vols.), Milan, 1946–54.
Rossi, G. de, *La Roma sotteranea cristiana*, Rome, 1864–1877.
Rousseau, O., *The Progress of the Liturgy*, Westminster (Md.), 1951.
Ryan, M., *Speaking of How to Pray*, New York, 1950.
Schuster, I., *The Sacramentary* (5 vols.), New York, 1925–1931.
Srawley, J., *Early History of the Liturgy*, New York, 1947.
Stapper, R., *Catholic Liturgics*, New York, 1935.
Steuart, B., *Development of Christian Worship*, London, 1953.
Thalhofer, V., *Handbuch der Katholischen Liturgik*, Freiburg, 1912.

Trethowan, I., *Christ in the Liturgy*, New York, 1952.
Underhill, E., *Worship*, New York, 1937.
Van der Stappen, F., *Caeremoniale*, Mechlin, 1933–35.
Von Hildebrand, D., *Liturgy and Personality*, New York, 1943.
Wuest, J., *Matters Liturgical*, New York, 1931.
Young, K., *The Drama of the Medieval Church*, Oxford, 1933.

TOPICAL BIBLIOGRAPHIES

Altar

Bliley, N., *Altars According to the New Code of Canon Law*, Washington, 1927.
Braun, J., *Der christliche altar in seiner geschichtlichen entwicklung*, Munich, 1924.
———, *Die christliche altargeraat in seiner geschichtlichen entwicklung*, Munich, 1932.
————, *Die liturgische gewandung im Orient und Okzident*, Freiburg, 1907.
Webb, G., *Liturgical Altar*, London, 1933.

Ceremonies

Ahearne, P., *Pontifical Ceremonies*, London, 1942.
Fortescue, A., *The Ceremonies of the Roman Rite Described*, Westminster (Md.), 1949.
Nabuco, J., *Pontificalis Romani expositio juridico practica* (4 vols.), Vozes, 1945.
Perkins, Mary, *At Your Ease in the Catholic Church*, New York, 1950.
O'Connell, J., *The Celebration of Mass* (3 vols.), Milwaukee, 1940–41.
O'Connell, L., *Book of Ceremonies*, Milwaukee, 1943.
Stehle, A., *Manual of Episcopal Ceremonies*, Latrobe (Pa.), 1916.

Sullivan, J., *The Externals of the Catholic Church*, New York, 1951.
Wuest, J., *Matters Liturgical*, New York, 1925.

The Church

Adam, K., *Christ Our Brother*, New York, 1931.
Congar, Y., *Lay People in the Church*, Westminster (Md.), 1957.
De la Taille, M., *Mystery of Faith* (2 vols.), New York, 1941.
De Lubac, H., *The Splendor of the Church*, New York, 1956.
Hasseveldt, R., *The Church: A Divine Mystery*, Chicago, 1954.
Herbert, A., *Liturgy and Society*, London, 1937.
Journet, C., *The Church of the Word Incarnate*, New York, 1954.
Jungmann, J., *Mass of the Roman Rite* (2 vols.), Chicago, 1955.
Mascall, E., *Christ, the Christian and the Church*, New York, 1946.
———, *Corpus Christi*, New York, 1953.
Mersch, E., *The Whole Christ*, Milwaukee, 1938.
Michel, V., *The Liturgy of the Church*, New York, 1937.
Spicq, C., *L'épitre aux Hébreux* (2 vols.), Paris, 1953.
Thornton, L. S., *Common Life in the Body of Christ*, London, 1954.
Walsh, E. A., *The Priesthood in the Writings of the French School*, Washington, 1945.

Devotional

Adam, K., *Spirit of Catholicism*, New York, 1936.
———, *Christ Our Brother*, New York, 1931.
Barsotti, D., *Vie mystique et mystère liturgique*, Paris, 1954.
Bouyer, L., *Liturgical Piety*, Notre Dame (Ind.), 1955.
Chautard, J. B., *Soul of the Apostolate*, Gethsemani (Ky), 1941.
Clerissac, H., *The Mystery of the Church*, New York, 1937.
Hild, J., *Dimanche et vie Paschale*, Paris, 1949.
Marmion, C., *Christ the Life of the Soul*, St. Louis, 1923.
———, *Christ in His Mysteries*, St. Louis, 1919.
———, *Christ the Ideal of the Monk*, St. Louis, 1926.
Plus, R., *In Christ Jesus*, Westminster (Md.), 1948.
Stolz, A., *Doctrine of Spiritual Perfection*, St. Louis, 1938.
Thorold, A., *The Mass and Prayer*, London, 1945.
Tyciak, J., *Life in Christ*, New York, 1937.
Zundel, M., *The Splendour of the Liturgy*, New York, 1939.

Divine Office

Bacquez, L., *L'Office divin et la vie de l'église*, Paris, 1925.
———, *The Divine Office*, London, 1885.
Baeumer, S., *Geschichte des Breviers*, Freiburg, 1895.
Batiffol, P., *History of the Roman Breviary*, London, 1912.

Baudot, J., *The Breviary: Its History and Contents*, St. Louis, 1929.
Boylan, P., *The Psalms* (2 vols.), Dublin, 1920–1924.
Britt, M., *The Hymns of the Breviary and Missal*, revised edit., New York, 1924.
Bugnini, A., *The Simplification of the Rubrics*, Collegeville (Minn.), 1955.
Cagin, P., *Te Deum ou Illatio?*, Solesmes, 1906.
Callewaert, C., *De breviarii Romani liturgia (Liturgicae Institutiones, II)*, Bruges, 1931.
———, *La réforme du Bréviaire*, Bruges, 1912.
Connelly, J., *Hymns of the Roman Liturgy*, Westminster, (Md.), 1957.
Daniel, H., *Thesaurus hymnologicus*, Halle-Leipzig, 1841–1856.
De Candole, *Christian Use of the Psalms*, London, 1955.
De Puniet, P., *Le Psautier liturgique* (2 vols.), Paris, 1935.
Dugmore, C., *The Influence of Synagogue on The Divine Office*, London, 1944.
Eaton, R., *Sing Ye to the Lord* (2 vols.), St. Louis, 1947.
Graf, E., *The Church's Daily Prayer*, London, 1938.
Hoornaert, G., *Le Bréviaire*, Paris, 1932.
Hoornaert, R., *The Breviary for the Laity*, Collegeville (Minn.), 1936.
Hugueny, E., *Le Psautier du bréviaire*, Paris, 1932.
Julian, J., *A Dictionary of Hymnology*, London, 1907.
Martindale, C., *Toward Loving the Psalms*, New York, 1941.
Miller, A., *Die Psalmen*, Klosterneuburg, 1933.
Parsch, P., *The Breviary Explained*, St. Louis, 1952.
Quigley, E., *The Divine Office*, Dublin, 1930.
The Roman Breviary (4 vols.), New York, 1936–37.
Watkin, E. I., *The Praise of Glory*, New York, 1943.
Willi, C., *Le Bréviaire expliqué* (2 vols.), Paris, 1922.
Wilmot, C., *Priest's Prayer Book*, London, 1949.
Wolter, M., *Psallite sapienter*, Freiburg, 1903.

Liturgical Arts

Anson, P. F., *Churches: Their Plan and Furnishing*, Milwaukee, 1948.
Collins, J., *The Church Edifice and Its Appointments*, Westminster (Md.), 1946.
Fortune, P., *Notes on Art for Catholics*, Paterson (N.J.), 1944.
Knapp, J., *Christian Symbols*, Milwaukee, 1935.
Marucchi, O., *Manual of Christian Archaeology*, Paterson (N.J.), 1935.
O'Connell, J., *Church Building and Furnishing*, Notre Dame (Ind.), 1956.

Reinhold, H. A., *Speaking of Liturgical Architecture*, Notre Dame (Ind.), 1952.
Roulin, E., *Modern Church Architecture*, St. Louis, 1947.
Webber, F., *Church Symbolism*, Cleveland, 1938.
Winzen, D., *Symbols of Christ*, New York, 1955.

Liturgical Books

Kirsch, J. P., *Die stationskirchen des missale Romanum, Ecclesia orans XIX*, Freiburg, 1926.
Martindale, C. C., *The Mind of the Missal*, New York, 1929.
———, *The Prayers of the Missal*. Vol. I, *The Sunday Collects*, New York, 1937.
———, *The Words of the Missal*, New York, 1932.
De Puniet, J., *The Roman Pontifical: A History and Commentary*, New York, 1932.
Schuster, I., *The Sacramentary* (5 vols.), New York, 1925–31.
Vagaggini, G., *The Riches of the Missal*, St. Louis, 1949.

Liturgical Education

Bopp, L., *Liturgical Education*, Milwaukee, 1937.
Bussard, P., and Kirch, F., *Meaning o fthe Mass*, New York, 1942.
Confraternity of Christian Doctrine, *The Holy Sacrifice of the Mass*, Paterson (N.J.), 1941.
Rutledge, D., *Catechism Through the Liturgy*, London, 1949.

Liturgical Language

Korolevskij, C., *Liturgie en langue vivante*, Paris, 1955.
Murphy, J. L., *The Mass and Liturgical Reform*, Milwaukee, 1956.
Schmidt, H., *Liturgie et langue vulgaire*, Rome, 1950.

Liturgical Seasons and Feasts

Baur, B., *The Light of the World*, St. Louis, 1952.
Botte, B., *Les origines de la Noel et de l'Epiphanie*, Louvain, 1932.
Bouyer, C., *The Paschal Mystery*, Chicago, 1950.
Cabrol, F., *The Year's Liturgy*, London, 1940.
Callewaert, C., *La durée et le caractère du Careme ancien dans l'Eglise latine*, Bruges, 1920.
Guéranger, P., *The Liturgical Year* (15 vols.), Westminster (Md.), 1948.
Haering, O., *Living with the Church*, New York, 1930.
Henry, P., *The Liturgical Year*, Milwaukee, 1940.
Hild, J., *Dimanche et vie Chrétienne*, Paris, 1949.
Kellner, K., *Heortology: A History of the Christian Festivals from Their Origin to the Present Day*, London, 1908.
Lawrence, E., *The Week with Christ*, South Bend (Ind.), 1950.

McGarry, W., *He Cometh*, New York, 1941.
MacArthur, J. S., *The Evolution of the Christian Year*, London, 1953.
Marmion, C., *Christ in His Mysteries*, St. Louis, 1923.
Messenger, E., *The Apostolate of the Sunday Mass* (4 vols.), Westminster (Md.), 1950.
Mueller, T., *Our Children's Year of Grace*, St. Louis, 1943.
Oldmeadow, E., *Layman's Christian Year*, London, 1939.
Parsch, P., *Das Jahr des Heiles* (3 vols.), Vienna, 1933–34.
———, *The Church's Year of Grace*, Collegeville (Minn.), 1953.
Pepler, C., *Lent*, St. Louis, 1944.
Reuter, F., *In Season*, New York, 1934.
Rickaby, J., *The Ecclesiastical Year*, New York, 1927.
Schlarman, J., *Catechetical Sermon Aids*, St. Louis, 1942.
Thurston, H., *Lent and Holy Week*, New York, 1904.
Wesseling, T., *Cleansing of the Temple*, New York, 1945.

Liturgical Music

Aigrain, R., *Religious Music*, London, 1931.
Hugle, G., *Catechism of Gregorian Chant*, New York, 1928.
Hume, P., *Catholic Church Music*, New York, 1956.
Johner, D., *New School of Gregorian Chant*, Collegeville (Minn.), 1940.
The People's Hymnal, Cincinnati, 1955.
Pierik, M., *Song of the Church*, New York, 1947.
———, *Spirit of Gregorian Chant*, Boston, 1939.
Pius X Hymnal, Boston, 1954.
Selner, J., *Chant at the Altar*, Baltimore, 1933.
Sunol, G., *Textbook of Gregorian Chant*, New York, 1925.
Thuis, S., *Gregorian Chant, Barometer of Religious Fervor*, St. Meinrad's (Ind.), 1952.
Wagner, P., *Geschicte der Messe*, Leipzig, 1913.
Ward, J., *Gregorian Chant*, Washington (D.C.), 1930.

Liturgies and Rites

Attwater, D., *The Catholic Eastern Churches*, Milwaukee, 1935.
Bishop, W., *The Mozarabic and Ambrosian Rites*, London, 1924.
Fortescue, A., *The Byzantine Rite in Italy, Sicily, Syria, and Egypt*, London, 1923.
———, *The Lesser Eastern Churches*, London, 1913.
———, *The Orthodox Eastern Churches*, London, 1929.
———, *The Uniate Eastern Churches*, New York, 1923.
King, A., *Notes on the Catholic Liturgies*, New York, 1931.
———, *The Rites of Eastern Christendom*, London, 1950.

Martène, E., *De Antiquis ecclesiae ritibus* (4 vols.), Antwerp, 1736–38.
Salaville, S., *Eastern Liturgies*, London, 1938.

The Mass

Batiffol, P., *Lecons sur la Messe*, Paris, 1927.
Biskupek, A., *Our Sacrifice*, Milwaukee, 1940.
Boeser, F., *The Mass-Liturgy*, Milwaukee, 1932.
Bonniwell, W., *Interpreting the Sunday Mass*, New York, 1949.
Bott, B., *Le Canon de la Messe Romaine*, Louvain, 1935.
———, *L'Ordinaire de la Messe*, Paris, 1953.
Busch, W., *The Mass Drama*, Collegeville (Minn.), 1930.
Bussard, P., and F. Kirsch, *The Meaning of the Mass*, New York, 1942.
Cabrol, F., *The Mass of the Western Rites*, St. Louis, 1934.
———, *The Mass—Its Doctrine and History*, New York, 1931.
Casel, O., *Das christliche kultmysterium*, Regensburg, 1932.
Cecilia, Sr. M., *Companion to the Missal*, Milwaukee, 1954.
Croegaert, A., *Les Rites et prières du Saint Sacrifice de la Messe*, Bruges, 1948.
D'Arcy, M., *The Mass and Redemption*, New York, 1927.
De Puniet, J., *The Mass, Its Origin and History*, New York, 1931.
De la Taille, M., *The Mystery of Faith* (2 vols.), New York, 1940.
Ellard, G., *The Mass of the Future*, Milwaukee, 1948.
———, *Men at Work and Worship*, New York, 1940.
Fortescue, A., *The Mass: A Study of the Roman Liturgy*, New York, 1937.
Frere, W., *The Roman Gospel-Lectionary*, London, 1934.
Gassner, J., *The Canon of the Mass*, St. Louis, 1949.
Graf, E., *The Priest at the Altar*, New York, 1926.
Grimaud, C., *My Mass*, New York, 1928.
Husslein, J., *The Mass of the Apostles*, New York, 1929.
Jungmann, J., *Das eucharistische hochgebet*, Wurzburg, 1954.
———, *The Mass of the Roman Rite* (2 vols.), New York, 1951.
Kramp, J., *Eucharistia: Essays on Eucharistic Liturgy*, St. Paul (Minn.), 1926.
———, *The Liturgical Sacrifice of the New Law*, St. Louis, 1928.
Lebbe, B., *The Mass*, Westminster (Md.), 1949.
LeBrun, P., *Explication de la Messe*, Paris, 1949.
LeDuc, C., and J. Baudot, *Liturgy of the Roman Missal*, New York, 1924.
Martindale, C., *Mind of the Missal*, New York, 1929.
———, *Words of the Missal*, London, 1932.

Michel, V., *My Sacrifice and Yours*, Collegeville (Minn.), 1926.
Norman, J., *Handbook to the Christian Liturgy*, London, 1944.
Parsch, P., *The Liturgy of the Mass*, St. Louis, 1937.
————, *Study the Mass*, Collegeville (Minn.), 1953.
Rohault de Fleury, C., *La Messe: Etudes archéologiques sur les monuments* (8 vols.), Paris, 1883–89.
Vandeur, E., *The Holy Sacrifice of the Mass*, New York, 1937.
Vonier, A., *Key to the Doctrine of the Eucharist*, Westminster (Md.), 1956.
Williamson, H., *The Great Prayer*, New York, 1956.

The Mystical Body

Adam, K., *Christ Our Brother*, New York, 1931.
Anger, J., *Doctrine du corps mystique de Jésus Christ, d'après les principes de la théologie de St. Thomas*, Paris, 1933.
Benson, R., *Christ in the Church*, New York, 1941.
De Lubac, H., *Corpus mysticum*, Paris, 1941.
Grimaud, C., *One Only Christ*, New York, 1939.
Mersch, E., *The Whole Christ*, Milwaukee, 1938.
Noppel, C., *Shepherd of Souls*, St. Louis, 1939.
Pius XII, Encyclical *Mystici Corporis*, 1943.
Sheen, F., *Mystical Body of Christ*, New York, 1935.
Vann, G., *Of His Fullness*, New York, 1939.

Sacramentals

Gasquet, A., *The Sacramentals and Some Catholic Practices*, St. Paul (Minn.), 1928.
Lambing, A., *Sacramentals*, New York, 1903.
Thurston, H., *The Stations of the Cross*, London, 1906.

Sacraments

Coppens, J., *L'imposition des mains et les rites connexes dans le Nouveau Testament et dans l'église ancienne*, Paris, 1925.
Daniélou, J., *The Bible and the Liturgy*, Notre Dame (Ind.), 1956.
Ellard, G., *Ordination Anointings in the Western Church before 1000 A.D.*, (Cambridge, Mass.), 1933.
Gihr, N., *Die heiligen sakramente der katholischen kirche* (2 vols.), Freiburg, 1902–03.
Guardini, R., *Sacred Signs*, St. Louis, 1955.
Kelly, B., *Sacraments of Daily Life*, New York, 1943.
Laros, M., *Confirmation in the Modern World*, New York, 1938.
Roguet, A., *Christ Acts through the Sacraments*, Collegeville (Minn.), 1954.

Tixeront, J., *Holy Orders and Ordination*, St. Louis, 1928.
Villien, A., *History and Liturgy of the Sacraments*, New York, 1932.

Sacred Places

Davis, J., *Origin and Development of Early Christian Church Architecture*, London, 1952.
Diehl, C., *Manuel d'art byzantin*, Paris, 1925.
Fletcher, B., A *History of Architecture*, New York, 1928.
Lowrie, W., *Christian Art and Archeology*, New York, 1901.
Marucchi, H., *Manual of Christian Archeology*, Paterson (N.J.), 1935.
Morey, C., *Christian Art*, New York, 1935.
O'Connell, J., *The Building and Furnishing of Churches*, Notre Dame (Ind.), 1956.
Roulin, A., *Modern Church Architecture*, St. Louis, 1947.
Van Treeck, C. and A. Crofts, *Symbols in the Church*, Milwaukee, 1936.
Webber, F., *Church Symbolism*, Cleveland, 1927.

Texts

Assemani, J., *Codex liturgicus ecclesiae universalis* (13 vols.), Rome, 1749–66.
Brightman, F., *Liturgies Eastern and Western*, Vol. I, *Eastern Liturgies*, Oxford, 1896.
Connolly, R., *The So-Called Egyptian Church Order and Derived Documents*, Cambridge, 1916.
Collectio Rituum, Milwaukee, 1954.
Daniel, H., *Codex liturgicus ecclesiae universae in epitomen redactus* (4 vols.), Leipzig, 1853.
Easton, B., *The Apostolic Tradition of Hippolytus*, London, 1934.
Feltoe, C., *Sacramentarium Leonianum*, Cambridge, 1896.
Férotin, M., *Le Liber mozarabicus sacramentorum et les manuscrits mozarabes*, Paris, 1912.
————, *Le Liber Ordinum en usage dans l'église wisigothique et mozarabe d'Espagne du cinquième au onzième siècle*, Paris, 1904.
Goar, J., *Euchologion sive Rituale Graecorum*, Paris, 1647; 2nd rev. ed., Venice, 1730.
Greenwell, W., *The Pontifical of Egbert, Archbishop of York*, Durham, 1853.
Maclean, A., *The Ancient Church Orders*, Cambridge, 1932.
Missale Ambrosianum, Milan, 1946.
Mohlberg, K., *Das Fraenkische Sakramentarium Gelasianum in alemannischer Ueberlieferung*, Munich, 1918.
————, *Missale Gothicum*, Augsburg, 1929.

Muratori, L., *Liturgia Romana vetus* (2 vols.), Venice, 1748.
Neale-Littledale, *The Liturgies of SS. Mark, James, Clement, Chrysostom and Basil and the Church of Malabar*, London, 1869.
Quasten, J., *Monumenta eucharistica et liturgica vetustissima*, Bonn, 1935-36.
Renaudot, E., *Liturgiarum orientalium collectio*, Frankfurt, 1847.
Swainson, C., *The Greek Liturgies Chiefly from Original Authorities*, Cambridge, 1884.
Wilson, H., *The Gelasian Sacramentary*, Oxford, 1894.
Wordsworth, J., *Bishop Serapion's Prayer-Book*, London, 1899.

Vestments

Braun, J., *Die Liturgischen paramente in gegenwart und vergangenheit*, Freiburg, 1924.
Norris, H., *Church Vestments—Their Origin and Development*, London, 1949.
Roulin, E., *Vestments and Vesture*, Westminster (Md.), 1950.

Periodicals

Altar and Home, Conception (Mo.), 1922—
Ambrosius, Milan, 1925—
Antike und Christentum, Munich, 1929—
L'Art de l'Eglise, Bruges, 1932—
L'Art Sacré, Paris, 1937—
Bibel und Liturgie, Klosterneuburg, 1926—
Bulletin of the Liturgical Week, Conception (Mo.), 1940—
Jahrbuch fuer Liturgiewissenschaft, Munich, 1921—
Liturgical Arts, New York, 1931—
Living Parish, St. Louis, 1939-1953 (suspended publication)
Maison Dieu, Paris, 1945—
Paroisse et Liturgie, 1918—
Questions Liturgiques et paroissales, Louvain, 1910—
Revue Bénédictine, Maredsous, 1884—
Worship (formerly *Orate Fratres*), Collegeville (Minn.), 1926—

Index

B

D

E

L

N

O

A NOTE ON THE TYPE

IN WHICH THIS BOOK WAS SET

This book has been set in Electra, a type face created in 1935 by W. A. Dwiggins, the well-known Boston artist. This type falls within the "modern" family of type styles, but was drawn to avoid the extreme contrast between "thick and thin" elements that marks most "modern" type faces. The design is not based upon any traditional model, and is not an attempt to revive or to reconstruct any historic type. Since its birth, Electra has met with success because of its easy-to-read quality. This book was composed and printed by the York Composition Company, Inc., of York and bound by Moore and Company of Baltimore. The design and typography of this book are by Howard N. King.